A Legal Handbook for the Helping Professional

SECOND EDITION

Edited by
Max R. Uhlemann & David Turner

THE LAW FOUNDATION
OF BRITISH COLUMBIA

THE SEDGEWICK SOCIETY FOR CONSUMER AND PUBLIC EDUCATION
VICTORIA, BRITISH COLUMBIA, CANADA

Printed in Canada.

Canadian Cataloguing-in-Publication Data

A legal handbook for helping professionals

ISBN 1-55058-118-X

1. Law--Canada. 2. Domestic relations--Canada. 3. Children--Legal status, laws, etc.--Canada. 4. Mental health laws--Canada. I. Uhlemann, Max R. (Max Reinhold), 1944 - II. Turner, David, 1944 - III. Sedgewick Society for Consumer and Public Education. IV. Law Foundation of British Columbia.

KE448.L43 1998   349.71   C97-910847-0
KF389.L43 1998

This handbook has been prepared to provide helping professionals with legal information about federal and provincial law. It is not intended to be a substitute for legal advice for helping professionals or their clients. Opinions expressed are strictly those of the authors of the chapters.

Brief Table of Contents

DETAILED TABLE OF CONTENTS

Part II Skills for Action

Part III Conclusion

In Memory

Professor Terry J. Wuester taught at the University of Victoria Faculty of Law from its inception in 1975 until his retirement in 1996. He died of a brain tumour in July, 1996, just weeks after receiving the national William Paul McClure Kennedy Award, presented annually to one law professor for excellence in teaching. Professor Wuester had taught a wide variety of subjects from 1967 - 1996, and in 1995 had been awarded the University of Victoria Alumni Award for excellence in teaching. He was also a five-time recipient of the University of Victoria law students' Master Teacher Award, which was retired with him and re-named the "Terry J. Wuester Master Teacher Award." In recognition of his uncompromising pursuit of excellence, his family, colleagues, and former students have endowed a graduation award at the University of Victoria Faculty of Law to be awarded annually to the graduate achieving the highest cumulative standing.

Editors

Max R. Uhlemann (Ph.D., R. Psych.) is Professor in the Department of Psychological Foundations at the University of Victoria, Victoria, British Columbia. His academic interests include the education of counsellors and psychologists and research in stress management, cognitive factors in the therapeutic change process, and ethical decision-making in professional practice. His professional practice interests include stress management, post-traumatic stress, and loss. He is a Registered Psychologist in British Columbia and a member of the Canadian Psychological Association and the Canadian Guidance and Counselling Association.

David Turner (LLB., Dip. S.W., R. S. W.) is Associate Professor in the School of Social Work at the University of Victoria, Victoria, British Columbia. He teaches law and legal skills for social work and child and youth care work students. His major interests are in children's rights, advocacy, and conflict resolution techniques as they apply to professional practice. He is a Registered Social Worker and has developed several community, crime prevention, and cross cultural programs. He has been Mayor of Victoria, Chair of the Police Board, and a School Board Trustee.

Contributors

Kathy Absolon, M.S.W.
Program Coordinator
B'saanibamaadsiwin Nation Mental
   Health Program
Parry Sound, Ontario

Peter Carver, LL.B., LL.M.
Member, Immigration and Refugee Board
Government of Canada
Vancouver, British Columbia

Gerrit W. Clements, B.A., LL.B.
Special Health Law Consultant
Ministry of Health and Ministry Responsible for Seniors
British Columbia
and
Adjunct Professor (Health Law)
University of Victoria
Victoria, British Columbia

Lorrainne Dixon, LL.B.
Director, Information and Privacy
Office of the Information and
   Privacy Commissioner for British Columbia
Victoria, British Columbia

Glen Gallins, B.A., LL.B., M.S., LL.M.
The Law Centre
Victoria, British Columbia

Lesley Giles, LL.B.
Former Administrative Crown, Youth Court
Ministry of Attorney General
Victoria, British Columbia

Nicholas Lang, B.A., LL.B.
Crown Counsel
Ministry of Attorney General
Victoria, British Columbia

Alan Markwart, B.A., B.Ed., M.A.
Director
Youth Justice Section
Ministry for Children and Families
Victoria, British Columbia

Yvonne Martin, Ph.D.
Professor
Department of Communications and
   Social Foundations
University of Victoria
Victoria, British Columbia

Dulcie McCallum, LL.B.
Ombudsman for the Province
   of British Columbia
Legislative Assembly
Victoria, British Columbia

John MacDonald, B.A., LL.B., M.S.W.
Professor Emeritus
School of Social Work
University of British Columbia
Vancouver, British Columbia

M. Jerry McHale, B.A., M.S.W., LL.B.
Director
Dispute Resolution Office
Ministry of Attorney General
Victoria, British Columbia

James R. P. Ogloff, B.A., M.A., J.D., Ph.D.
Associate Professor and Associate Chair
Department of Psychology
Simon Fraser University
Burnaby, British Columbia
and
Adjunct Professor
Faculty of Law
University of British Columbia
Vancouver, British Columbia

Natalie H. Polvi, B.A., M.A.
Psychologist
Regional Psychiatric Centre (Prairies)
Correctional Service of Canada
and
Doctoral Candidate in Law and Psychology
Department of Psychology
Simon Fraser University
Burnaby, British Columbia

Jo-Anne Sargent
Department of Psychological
  Foundations in Education
University of Victoria
Victoria, British Columbia

Bill Trott, B.A., LL.B.
Portfolio Officer
Office of the Information and
  Privacy Commissioner for British Columbia
Victoria, British Columbia

Terry J. Wuester, B.A., M.A., J.D., LL.M.
Professor Emeritus
Faculty of Law
University of Victoria
Victoria, British Columbia

Terry Wuester Milne, B.A., J.D.
Judicial Clerk to the
  Honourable Henry W. Saad
Michigan Court of Appeals
Southfield, Michigan

Acknowledgements

We want to express our appreciation to The Law Foundation of British Columbia for the grant that supported the development of the first edition of this manuscript. The second edition has been possible through the proceeds obtained from the sale of the first edition. The project could not have been completed without this support.

We also want to thank Jo-Anne Sargent and Marny Stevenson for their editorial suggestions and proofreading. Finally, we want to express our appreciation to Bette Cameron, Debra Nikula, Melissa Ozard, and Edward Ross for their work in preparing revisions of the manuscript and the final copy used for printing.

Preface

Helping professionals function in a wide range of roles when providing assistance to individuals, groups, and the community. They act as providers of psychological, social, physical and educational services, as developers of social programs and social policy, as advocates for disadvantaged individuals and groups, and as advocates of change at the community and individual levels. This range of roles requires that they have an increasing knowledge of the law and an awareness of the legal implications of their actions. Without a solid knowledge of the law, the rights of consumers might be in jeopardy, and the legal and ethical liability of helping professionals increases. From our experience in teaching and field practice, however, we have found that it is often difficult for helping professionals to have easy access to clear and concise legal information to provide direction in their practice.

The purpose of this handbook is to provide helping professionals, including psychologists, counsellors, social workers, child and youth care workers, teachers, nurses, and physicians with much of the legal information that is relevant to their practice. To achieve this purpose, the editors identified a group of contributors who are expert in their fields of practice and who have a particular interest in communicating legal information to service providers.

The handbook is composed of seventeen chapters that are divided into three sections. Thirteen chapters are presented under the heading of Legal Knowledge. Each of the chapters in this section summarizes key legal information in a specific area of law. The heading of Skills for Action includes three chapters that provide information for skill development and action by helping professionals. Under the last heading of Conclusion, the reader is presented with an examination of future issues to be encountered in the areas of law presented in the handbook. At the end of each of the first 16 chapters, a section is included which provides answers to questions frequently asked by helping professionals. A resource list of additional reading material is included at the end of each chapter for those interested in reading further on their own. The first chapter presents an overview of the general legal system we believe a helping professional needs to know in order to function effectively in daily practice. The second chapter is on the *Charter* and human rights, and presents concepts which are the legal foundation for our system of law. The following 11 chapters cover areas of the law specific to areas of practice by helping professionals. Chapters 3, 4, and 5 cover various aspects of child welfare, while chapters 6 and 7 address civil and criminal aspects of family law. Chapter 8 examines youth criminal justice, and chapters 9 and 10 cover aspects of practice in mental health and working with the physically and mentally disabled, respectively. Chapter 11 examines the law relevant to public education, chapter 12 reviews the law relevant to access and privacy of written information, and chapter 13 examines the law regarding legal liability. Chapters 14, 15, and 16 present information to assist helping professionals in serving as an advocate for clients, resolving conflicts between parties, and presenting legal evidence in the role of an expert witness, respectively. Finally, chapter 17 presents a brief exploration of emerging issues in law for helping professionals.

This handbook is not intended to be a series of legal treatises. It is intended to be a resource presenting legal information and issues on which helping professionals might reflect. As everyone knows who has dealt with law and the court system, legal rules are neither absolute nor static, and opinions can vary greatly about interpretation and application. It is important to remember that the law is forever changing as the Canadian social context evolves.

In summary, it should be stated that each chapter represents the views of the contributors of each chapter, and is drawn from their wealth of experience in those areas. The content of this handbook is not to be considered as legal advice. Also, this information is not intended as the basis for offering legal advice to clients. A lawyer should be consulted for legal advice.

PART I

Legal Knowledge

Chapter 1

CORE LEGAL KNOWLEDGE FOR THE HELPING PROFESSIONAL

David Turner and Max R. Uhlemann

INTRODUCTION

The purpose of this chapter is to familiarize helping professionals with the general legal knowledge necessary for competent practice. In the course of their work, professionals may encounter a variety of legal problems. Clients with marital problems may be considering separation or divorce. Some clients may be violent or suicidal, and children who are clients may display symptoms of physical or sexual abuse. Administrators in human services may have to deal with substandard performance by an employee, or complaints or formal appeals about a worker's decision. All of these situations can have serious legal, professional, and personal implications for helping professionals and their clients.

In the following chapter, key aspects of legal knowledge will be identified and briefly discussed, together with answers to common questions. Examples will highlight the importance of understanding the legal system and process. Some useful additional resources will also be suggested. The law is stated as of March 1, 1997.

Material on the law relating to specific areas (such as family issues or mental health law) will be covered in later chapters. The following topics of general legal knowledge are the subject of this chapter:

a) the nature of law;

b) the function of law in society;

c) characteristics of the legal system;

d) sources of law;

e) the dispute resolution process;

f) procedural fairness;

g) confidentiality and privilege; and

h) the relevance of specific legal knowledge.

THE NATURE OF LAW

Law is a system of rules that orders society, defining a code of behaviour and establishing a framework of social institutions within which certain freedoms may be exercised. Law is the crystallized expression of Canadian public and social policy which, in turn, reflects the values of members of society. The elected officials in government who create laws are responding to their perception of public demands. These demands may reflect the values and interests of the majority in society (the consensual model of lawmaking), or the values of the powerful minority (the conflictual model), or they can reflect the interests of the group able to exert the most influence on a particular situation (the competitive model). The reader's philosophical perspective will suggest the preferred model.

For the most part, the consensual/majority view seems most appropriate in trying to explain the source of the myriad of laws enacted in federal or provincial statutes or municipal by-laws. However, when looking at contentious legal issues on which public opinion is often polarized, the authors prefer the competing interest model (competitive) combined with the notion of the entrenchment of powerful interests (conflictual). This view argues that laws respond to the interests of groups most able to exert pressure on the political process, with powerful sectors having a clear advantage. As Canadian society becomes more diverse, this modified competitive model best seems to describe current conflicts and legal outcomes. Examples that illustrate this model in action include the recent political upheaval over cross-cultural issues (the "distinct society" clause for Quebec, or the refugee legislation and policy), Native land claim litigation, the abortion controversy, and the debate over Free Trade.

What are the implications of this analysis for the helping professional? An awareness of these models in operation, coupled with information on the law-making process, is most useful to the helping professional who is interested in legislative reform. The analysis shows how lobbying can be an effective strategy for change. An excellent example of this process was the women's lobby, which in 1982 persuaded the federal government to include formal provision for male and female rights within the *Charter of Rights and Freedoms*[1] (section 28). Women in the helping professions, law, and politics were the backbone of this effective lobbying effort and understood how to influence law makers. Today, helping professionals are working with victims groups in lobbying for legislation to improve the rights to compensation and emotional support for sexually abused children and adults, or with AIDS coalitions for faster approval of new drugs, or with poverty groups to oppose regressive changes to unemployment insurance regulations.

In order to practice effectively and to bring about legal change, helping professionals need to understand how law functions, the characteristics of the legal system and their implications, the sources of law, and types of legal processes used to resolve disputes.

THE FUNCTION OF LAW IN SOCIETY

I. Three Major Functions of Law

A. Regulatory

A basic principle of our legal system is that a person may do anything that is not expressly prohibited by law. A complex set of laws, however, does control the behaviour of individuals and organizations. The most obvious example is the *Criminal Code,*[2] which sets out standards of behaviour and provides penalties for deviation.

B. Empowering and Obligating

The law also gives powers and obligations to individuals and organizations to exercise their rights and/or to provide for others. For example, individuals may use their common law rights to sue someone who has injured them, or use the powers of the *Employment Standards Act*[3] to improve their working conditions. Governments pass laws to give priority to their policy and to the funding of programs and services. The British Columbia Government, in passing the *Child, Youth and Family Advocacy Act*[4] affirmed its commitment to child-centred child welfare practice, declared its priority to the rights of children in care, and established the Child Advocate as an Office of the Legislature. Sometimes the law gives special powers to agencies, such as the Office of the Ombudsman, or to individuals, such as police officers. These are empowering functions of law. Sometimes special obligations (duties) may be imposed. In British Columbia the duty of providing income assistance to eligible persons is given to the Ministry of Human Resources under the *British Columbia Benefits (Income Assistance) Act.*[5]

C. Dispute Resolving and Enforcing

The law provides dispute resolution mechanisms and processes (courts, tribunals), that administer remedies enforced by a legally mandated system (police, corrections). Having a system in place for resolving disputes discourages people from settling conflicts by themselves in unlawful ways.

Understanding these functions is very important for the helping professional, especially in dealing with specific agencies and appreciating the mandates given to their workers. In British Columbia, for instance, a statutory authority such as the Ministry of Human Resources carries within its enabling legislation (*British Columbia Benefits (Income Assistance) Act*) all three functions - (a) regulatory (enforcing eligibility criteria for income assistance); (b) empowering and obligating (empowering their workers with limited discretion and obligations to disperse public monies under certain conditions to eligible individuals); and (c) dispute-resolving (providing the welfare appeal tribunal system). Workers administering the *Benefits Act* need to clearly distinguish for themselves and their clients which of their functions are discretionary powers and which are obligatory duties.

What distinguishes the law from other rules such as norms of behaviour, etiquette, or customs? The law carries with it governmental authority that has the legal power to enforce its rules. Norms, customs, and traditions carry social sanctions only. The following section provides a brief description of our system of law and the legal process.

CHARACTERISTICS OF THE LEGAL SYSTEM

The legal system is a system that is adversarial, hierarchical, dynamic, and remedial. These components are examined in detail below.

A. The System

The legal system is a combination of units functioning together for a purpose, which is to bring an ordered structure to society. Professionals can usefully apply a systems perspective to the various components of the legal system: law-making, application of laws, adjudication, and enforcement. These components are very much inter-related. In the justice field, for instance, the increased input of more police officers at the crime detection (application) level increases the amount of detected crime that has to be processed by the rest of the system (courts and corrections). All aspects of the system have to be taken into account.

B. The Adversarial System

Our adversarial system of law pits one party against the other. It is based on the premise that "legal truth" and justice will emerge when both sides in a dispute have an equal opportunity to present their cases and to challenge the other side's evidence and credibility. This adversarial feature is often disquieting to helping professionals who are accustomed to less competitive methods of resolving conflicts.

In fact, lawyers do have a duty to try to resolve their client's disputes by agreement before resorting to litigation (court action). However, when a case does reach the courtroom, the full impact of the adversarial system is evident. The roles of opposing lawyers in court are often difficult to accept when the professional's own credibility is being attacked. But it must be remembered that lawyers are ethically bound to act as partisan advocates and to do their utmost within the law for their clients according to the canons of legal ethics[6]. Nevertheless, as officers of the court, lawyers are prevented from engaging in improper, misleading, or fraudulent behaviour, or other "conduct unbecoming."

Professionals who have observed the court system sometimes perceive a discrepancy between legal outcomes and moral justification. This discrepancy is often difficult to accept. But the acquittal of a young offender on a so-called "legal technicality", for example, should not be viewed as a system shortcoming. As lawyers will explain, guilt must be proved according to the law and the legal process, and these are the only criteria for conviction. This kind of strict adherence to the law protects our freedom and prevents abuse.

C. The Court Hierarchy

The court system is hierarchical, comprising three or four levels within each province and two levels federally. Figure 1[7] below illustrates this.

It is useful for helping professionals to understand the functions and powers of the various courts in their provinces, such as Criminal, Small Claims, Family, and Supreme (called Queen's Bench in some provinces). Each level and division has specialized jurisdictions. For instance, in British Columbia most criminal actions are commenced at the Provincial Court (Criminal Division), but full trials of more serious crimes generally take place in Supreme Court. Most family matters can be handled by the Family Court Division of the Provincial Court or the Supreme Court. However, only the Supreme Court can hear divorce petitions and family property disputes. Young offenders and child welfare actions take place in the Family Division in Youth Courts and Family Courts respectively.

This hierarchy of courts also has another function. It provides an ascending ladder for appeals from lower court decisions. It is also the source of the principle of precedence. This means that judges must follow the law as it was decided in previous similar cases, and lower courts must follow the decisions of higher courts unless it is patently unreasonable to do so.

D. A Dynamic System

The principle of precedence ensures that a kind of consistency and stability will remain within our governing body of laws. The law is always changing, however, as new legislative enactments are incorporated and new interpretations in daily decisions are handed down by our courts. In this sense, it is dynamic. Decisions are also affected by such things as the physical structure of courts, the degree of procedural formality, and place of the court in the hierarchy. The court's progressive or traditional stance is determined by the participants, primarily the judge. Judges are appointed provincially to the Provincial Court level or federally to other court levels on the recommendation of judicial councils. The values applied by judges do have a role in shaping law; however, these values are predominantly those of white privileged males. A Law Society report in British Columbia[8] has criticized the legal profession for its discrimination against women. The report calls for increased representation of women in the courtroom and on the judicial selection committees. In 1993 in British Columbia, only 3 of 22 judges of the Court of Appeal, 10 of 98 of the Supreme Court, and 16 of 123 of the Provincial Court were women.

The ideologies of judges and the powerful in society are viewed by critics of the legal system as one reason why inequities in power and privilege are perpetuated. With predominantly conservative judges interpreting the laws made by predominantly conservative government politicians, so the argument goes, the tendency of the legal system to support the status quo is to be expected. Even though most Canadians believe that laws such as the *Criminal Code* are viewed as the consensual expression of social policy, upon closer examination the criminalization of certain behaviours but not others may be found, together with the imposition of serious penalties and selectivity in enforcement. Certain drugs are prohibited with serious penalties, yet corporations continue to put addictive and deadly substances into cigarettes that can cause death. In addition, corporations pollute the environment, often with minimal prosecution. Welfare fraud seems to merit

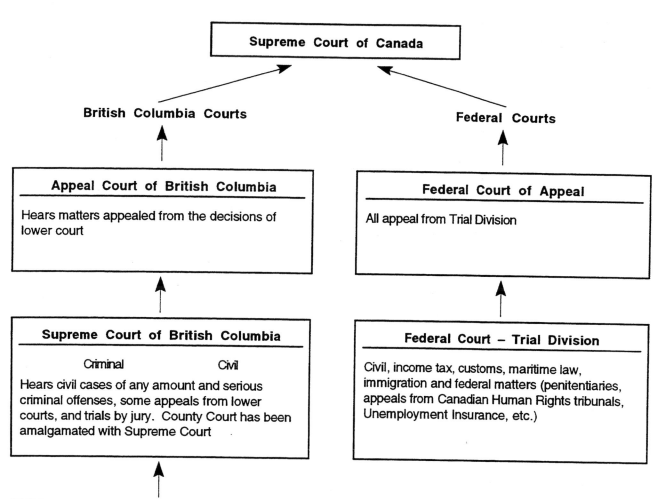

Supreme Court of Canada

British Columbia Courts

Federal Courts

Appeal Court of British Columbia

Hears matters appealed from the decisions of lower court

Federal Court of Appeal

All appeal from Trial Division

Supreme Court of British Columbia

Criminal   Civil

Hears civil cases of any amount and serious criminal offenses, some appeals from lower courts, and trials by jury. County Court has been amalgamated with Supreme Court

Federal Court – Trial Division

Civil, income tax, customs, maritime law, immigration and federal matters (penitentiaries, appeals from Canadian Human Rights tribunals, Unemployment Insurance, etc.)

Provincial Court

Criminal   Civil

Criminal Division	Family Division	Small Claims Division
Most of BC's criminal matters	Youth Court (Young Offenders)

Family Court (Custody, Maintenance, Separation and Child Protection | Minor civil disputes up to $10,000 |

Figure 1. The Court System for British Columbia

inordinate criminal attention compared with tax evasion or the underground economy. Family law reflects white, male, mainstream values to the disadvantage of women, First Nations, and cultural minorities. Evidence of this exists in seemingly token child maintenance payments for single parent women, or the still greatly disproportionate numbers of aboriginal children and youth in care or correctional institutions. The law and legal system reflects the values and interests of powerful sectors.

As feminists point out, "Law is not a free-floating entity, it is grounded in patriarchy, as well as class and ethnic divisions."[9] It operates as if it incorporated truth, but only from certain standpoints. Much of female and minority experience is denied. Gall,[10] a Canadian legal commentator, offers the following statement in his brief treatment of critical legal theory: "That the *Charter (of Rights and Freedoms)* has been used in the courts most effectively by the rich and powerful, including large corporations which can afford high-priced lawyers. Some would even argue that the real purpose of the *Charter* is to placate minorities and the disadvantaged without really assisting them." However, he states further that "most lawyers and scholars are unconvinced by the views of critical theorists. Many regard critical theorists as extremists and reject their view of law and the legal system." It is this conformist view of law that is problematic for many progressive helping professionals. The power, self-righteousness, and exclusiveness of legal thought, tradition, and the legal profession needs to be challenged.

These are important criticisms and lead to calls for a complete democratic overhaul of the system. As we shall see in the next chapter on the *Charter* and Human Rights, common law or judge-made case law is a significant source of legal development in Canada, and our judges need to better reflect overall values and experience. Most legal change, however, derives from the actions of legislators, not the courts.

E. A Remedial System

Finally, the legal system is remedial. It provides remedies (a legal recourse or solution) to correct a violation or settle a conflict. The law provides a framework for behaviour that is honoured by most people most of the time. By setting out rules in advance, which most people obey, conflicts are avoided and problems can be resolved without the need to resort to courts. A simple example would be cases dealing with the division of family assets. Because the *Family Relations Act*[11] in British Columbia sets out basic rules for dividing assets, most divorcing couples can resolve their property problems in terms of those existing rules. It is only when the meaning of those rules is obscured or a client is obstinate that a case comes to court.

The courts themselves are primarily reactive, and only rarely preventive. Some of the few preventive remedies available to the courts include injunctions or restraining orders (preventing further action by one party), peace bonds (requiring the keeping of the peace and other conditions to prevent violations such as injury to a spouse), and sentencing powers over offences of conspiracy to commit crimes that have not yet occurred. (Since conspiracy is itself a crime, this is not truly preventive.) The helping professional should be aware that courts are limited in the remedies they can grant.

SOURCES OF LAW

A. Case Law

Canada's legal system is based on the English "common law" system, which relies on case law. In case law, judges' decisions are recorded in law reports and used to determine the principles upon which future cases are decided. All the provinces except Quebec use this system. Quebec's civil law system derives from France's Napoleonic Code and French Customary Law.[12] Working with case law requires professional training and may involve complicated research in law libraries.

B. Statute Law

Statute law differs from case law in that it is based on written law created by our governments (federal, provincial, and municipal) within their sphere of jurisdiction through a formal process of law making. Formal procedures for law making vary with the type of government.

Courts do not make statute law. Judges only interpret laws or declare certain laws invalid. It should be recognised that some key legislation is neither debated in parliament nor court-initiated. Regulations can be passed by directives (known as Orders in Council) of the federal or provincial cabinets. For instance, the *British Columbia Benefits (Income Assistance) Act* includes regulations that establish income assistance rates. These regulations, published as an addendum to statutes, have the force of law.

Regulations should be distinguished from policies, which are the government's instructions to its administrators about how to interpret and apply particular statutes and regulations. Policies are usually consolidated in administrative manuals, but have no official legal status. However, it is important to understand that regulations must fit within and be authorized by statute, and policy must be compatible with the regulations and statute. Unless both the regulations and policy fall within the parameters of the statute, they risk being declared *ultra vires* (going beyond the power of) and thus being invalidated by the courts.

An example taken from British Columbia's welfare legislation illustrates how regulations can be challenged if they are incompatible with the law or its intent. Welfare advocates have often argued that regulations that unduly restrict the eligibility criteria for income assistance violate the intent and purpose of the former parent legislation, the *Guaranteed Available Income for Need (GAIN)* (now the *Benefits Act*), which defines income assistance as "aid that is necessary for the purpose of relieving poverty, neglect or suffering" (section 1). Others argue that this provision is merely descriptive of a type of assistance and does not define intent and purpose. For a question of interpretation such as this, the courts would be the final arbiter. In October 1996, the British Columbia Supreme Court invalidated the province's 90-day residency requirement for income assistance eligibility, passed by cabinet in 1995 under the *GAIN Act*, stating it went beyond the powers of the cabinet and was inconsistent with the purpose of the *GAIN Act*. The Government responded within a few days by proclaiming the *Benefits Act*, which contained the same residency provision. This has since been removed by the Provincial Government in amending the regulations in 1997.

C. Jurisdiction: Federal and Provincial Powers

As we have seen, statutes, regulations, and policies must be internally consistent. But they must also be enacted by the appropriate jurisdictional sphere of government. Figure 2[13] below illustrates how legislation derives its legitimate authority under our legal system.

Canada's constitution (especially sections 91 and 92 of the *British North America Act*, now called the *Constitution Act* (1867) distributes powers to the provincial and federal levels of government to pass laws in different areas. For example, criminal laws in the *Criminal Code* can only be altered by the federal government, although the provincial government can enact legislation defining less serious offences. Civil law and the administration of justice are provincial responsibilities.

The Constitution, which includes the *Charter of Rights and Freedoms*, is the supreme law and the template for all legislation and policy. Laws must comply, unless explicitly exempted, or they risk being challenged and invalidated as <u>unconstitutional</u> (see Chapter 2).

Jurisdictional issues can often provide the grounds for challenging controversial legislation. In 1978, for example, the *Heroin Treatment Act*[14] enacted by the British Columbia legislature under its health program, was challenged in court. Counsel for a detained heroin user argued that enforced confinement for the treatment of heroin users was tantamount to the use of penal powers normally reserved for the federal government alone. The program was alleged to be *ultra vires* or beyond the power of the provincial government to implement. (It was subsequently disbanded before the higher courts could make a final determination.)

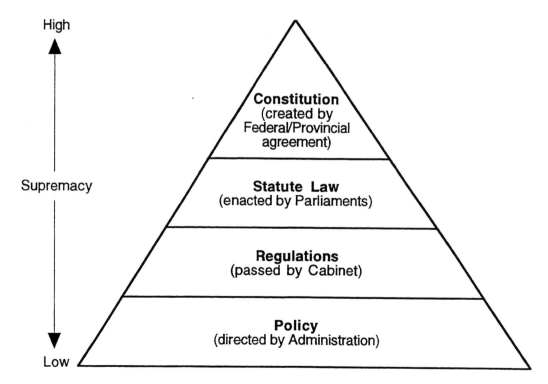

Figure 2. The Hierarchical Pyramid of Government Powers

More recently in British Columbia, a provincial health order was issued for the detention of an HIV-positive prostitute. This order could be similarly challenged, because again, it may be intruding in areas of federal power by applying criminal sanctions to behaviour that does not violate a federal criminal statute.

D. Proclamation

Legislation on the statute book does not become effective until proclaimed by the Lieutenant Governor (provincial), or Governor General (federal) as each government directs. British Columbia's welfare law looks quite progressive when one reads in the *Guaranteed Available Income for Need Act (GAIN) Act* (now the *Benefits Act*) that welfare rates are going to be indexed to the consumer cost of living (section 8), and that appeals against denials of social services can be directed to a tribunal (section 25, (3) and (4)). It should be noted that any service involving a cash payment or grant, such as in provision of daycare or employment training, is now under policy being interpreted as "income assistance" and is covered by the appeal provisions of the *Benefits (Appeals) Act*. (The helping professional has to read the fine print to note that these subsections have not been proclaimed since they were adopted in 1976, and therefore are not law.)

THE DISPUTE RESOLUTION PROCESS

Understanding the stages of the formal legal process can help professionals to prepare their clients emotionally for what may be perceived as a cumbersome, drawn out, or intimidating procedure. In court hearings, two types of law are operating simultaneously. <u>Substantive law</u> is the law of the substance of the legal action normally contained in a statute, unless, for example, the hearing is dealing with a tort, which is a civil wrong found in common law. Torts are compiled by legal authorities from case law in Britain and Canada over several centuries and consolidated in legal textbooks. <u>Procedural law</u> is that which governs the process of the hearing and is often a combination of processes developed at common law and rules contained in the relevant statute. Criminal hearings are based on processes in the *Criminal Code*, the *Canada Evidence Act*,[15] and at common law. In civil cases procedure is based on rules of court such as Small Claims Rules or Supreme Court Rules, and on common law processes.

What follows is a brief description of Civil and Criminal process. It should be noted that the procedures outlined below are sometimes shortened and simplified in civil cases heard by provincial small claims courts that adjudicate claims involving smaller amounts of money (under $10,000 in British Columbia).

I. The Civil Legal Process

A civil action is a legal process that allows individuals (including corporations) to sue others for damages for civil wrongs known as torts. Torts are described in detail in Chapter 13. The following stages are the key components of the civil legal process. Certain other civil actions such as child welfare or family law applications have equivalent stages, although the outcomes may be court orders other than damages. For details see Chapters 3 and 6.

A. Negotiation For Settlement

Parties in a dispute usually consult lawyers prior to initiating legal action, and the lawyer normally attempts to negotiate a settlement of the dispute with the other party. If both sides have a lawyer, then the lawyers negotiate on their clients' behalf. Many legal problems are resolved in this fashion. If negotiation fails, a neutral third party may be called in to mediate or arbitrate a dispute; this is becoming an increasingly popular method to attempt resolution without court intervention. For details of the mediation process, see Chapter 15. Usually legal action would only be commenced if negotiation or mediation fails.

B. Application To Court

Legal process is started by an application to a court or to a tribunal, which is usually less formal than court. The nature of this civil process varies depending upon the specific remedies or sanctions sought. However, in a typical application to Supreme Court, a lawyer will draw up a writ of summons, which is formally issued out of the court registry and delivered to ("served on") the opposing party (the "defendant"). The writ of summons sets out the claim of the party initiating the action (the "plaintiff") and requires a response (an "Answer" or an "Appearance") within a specified time period. The defendant's response indicates whether or not the plaintiff's claim will be contested. If the defendant fails to respond, the plaintiff may ask the court to award a "default judgment," an immediate order awarding the money or other remedy demanded in the writ of summons.

Many other claims or complaints are handled by internal review within government ministries and by specialized tribunals or boards that have been established by legislation to hear particular kinds of disputes. Reviews or tribunals are often the forums used for resolving landlord and tenant disputes, for example, or for determining immigration status or human rights issues. While such administrative review procedures are not obliged to follow the strict rules of evidence and procedure expected of the courts, they are required to apply certain standards of procedural fairness, which is discussed in more detail below.

C. The Pleadings

When a defendant files a response to the initial writ of summons, a further exchange of documents takes place. The plaintiff's lawyer files a "Statement of Claim" and the defendant's lawyer files a "Statement of Defence" (and "Counterclaim" if there is one). These documents identify in more detail the remedy sought and the issues in dispute. Many cases are settled at this point, once each party has had the chance to weigh the other's position.

D. Examination for Discovery

A preliminary session known as an examination for discovery typically takes place. Its purpose is to help define the issues. Each lawyer has the opportunity to question the opposing party under oath in an informal setting. Questions and answers are officially recorded and may later be entered as evidence at trial. Each party is accompanied by his/her own lawyer, who may object to inappropriate questions and thereby prevent a damaging answer. "Discovery" also applies to documents and "physical evidence" (relevant things that may need to be examined).

Each side is entitled to apply for the right to preview or examine evidence of this kind before trial. Before trial, parties may also apply to have medical examinations take place if, for instance, physical injuries are at issue. Once again, settlement is a strong possibility as further information emerges.

E. Hearings or Trials

Hearings before boards or tribunals are, by their very nature, intended to be financially and procedurally accessible to the public. Often the complainant will represent her/himself and there are rarely any court costs to be paid. Many administrative review processes are complicated, however, and clients often require legal advice and representation in order to successfully advance their claims. Procedures for case presentation may be set out in the relevant legislation but these procedures usually vary from one tribunal process to another.

Because court and legal costs are high, lawyers will seek to settle most civil cases out of court, with the result that very few disputes actually go to trial. In a typical supreme court civil action, a trial begins with the lawyer for each side addressing opening remarks to the judge and/or jury. The plaintiff's lawyer must then "prove the claim" on a "balance of probabilities" by calling and examining witnesses and presenting any other supporting evidence. The defendant's lawyer is then permitted to cross-examine the plaintiff's witnesses before calling further witnesses who testify in support of the defendant's case. The plaintiff's lawyer may then cross-examine these witnesses. Both sides then address the judge and/or jury. In a jury trial the judge instructs the jury on the law and sums up the evidence for them. The jury must then come to a conclusion based on the facts.

F. Judgment

In an administrative review or tribunal hearing, the adjudicators may grant whatever remedies are available under their empowering legislation. For example, a foreign refugee may be granted permission to remain in Canada, an unemployment insurance recipient may be awarded back-dated benefits, or a landlord may be entitled to terminate a tenancy.

In a civil case, courts can order the losing side to pay "damages" (financial compensation) and all or some of the court costs incurred. Other types of remedies may also be granted, such as orders for "specific performance" requiring something to be done, injunctions restricting some forms of behaviour, or declarations granting certain rights to the winning party.

G. Enforcement

Further court action may be required to enforce an original civil court order. The successful party may have to obtain an enforcement order to collect the money owed from the losing party, who is now a "debtor" for that sum. Orders can be obtained to force the seizure or sale of the debtor's property. The provincial Sheriff's office, or a privatized equivalent in some parts of British Columbia, acts as bailiff in such cases. Another common collection method involves serving a garnishment order on the debtor's bank or employer, requiring any money on deposit or wages owed to be paid to the successful party.

II. The Criminal Legal Process

In many ways, the stages of the criminal legal process parallel the civil process. The intention of the civil process, however, is to settle disputes between private individuals or individuals and government agencies. The criminal law process, on the other hand, is designed to protect the public from undesirable and dangerous behaviour, although it employs very strict rules of evidence to ensure that an accused person is only convicted if there is evidence "beyond a reasonable doubt." Criminal law provides a variety of sanctions ranging from fines to imprisonment to enforce the rules laid out in the federal *Criminal Code* and other statutes. Criminal law is the jurisdiction of the federal government. However, there are also many regulatory or "quasi-criminal" offences (i.e. *Motor Vehicle Act* violations) that involve procedures similar to those followed in the prosecution of criminal offences. These are within provincial jurisdiction. Understanding the stages in the criminal process is also crucial for the helping professional. The following are the key steps.

A. Complaint and Police Investigation

Police are called upon to investigate reported incidents of crime and to recommend what charges should be made. The police officer, upon finding a violation of criminal or provincial law, will swear or solemnly affirm an information (a legal document initiating a criminal complaint) before a justice of the peace. This action may also be taken by any citizen and commences criminal proceedings.

A criminal charge may proceed in several ways and may not always require an accused person to be arrested and brought to the police station. If the accused has been arrested and detained in custody, the issue of custody, bail, or other form of release order will be determined at the first court appearance. In any case, the charging document will command the accused to attend court (Provincial Court in British Columbia) on a specified day to answer the charge.

B. The Decision to Prosecute

Crown Counsel (the prosecutor) decides whether or not to proceed with prosecution. Under certain circumstances a citizen can launch a private prosecution with the permission of Crown or the Attorney General. In most provinces, Crown decides upon the charges (in Alberta and Ontario, the police make this decision). The Crown's prerogative to prosecute or not is not reviewable and can only be changed by intervention of the Attorney General of the province. Again, leaders should note that the administration of justice is a provincial responsibility.

C. The Right to Counsel

At any stage in criminal proceedings the accused has the right to consult legal counsel. Police officers must advise all persons who have been detained of their right not only to a lawyer, but the right to contact Legal Aid if they do not have the financial resources to retain their own counsel.

The Legal Services Society of British Columbia has established a special service whereby a person who has been detained can telephone from anywhere in the province to obtain advice. Counsel might persuade the Crown to withdraw or reduce charges. Diversion, an alternative to the formal court process, is also a possibility for people accused of minor offences, and operates at Crown discretion. Diversion allows an accused person who has committed a minor offence to make reparations to the victim or perform community work service. In return, the Crown does not proceed with criminal charges (see Chapters 7 and 8).

D. The Court Appearance

Steps are taken for the accused to appear in court by arrest, summons, or notice to appear. An accused is always entitled to ask for an adjournment in order to obtain legal representation. The charge is read out and the accused may plead guilty or not guilty at that time. A guilty plea means that the accused is usually sentenced right away unless the court is adjourned for further information, such as a pre-sentence report prepared by a probation officer. When a guilty plea is entered, the Crown will present the "facts" as they appear on the police record. Defence Counsel, or the accused if unrepresented, then has an opportunity to explain the circumstances and present information that could influence the type and severity of the sentence to be passed.

Criminal prosecutions proceed by way of summary conviction process (for less serious offences punishable by a maximum of six months imprisonment, a $2,000 fine, or both), or by indictment (for more serious offences with greater penalties). Most indictable offences, and all of those punishable by imprisonment for five years or more, give the accused a choice of trial method: by judge alone, or by judge and jury.

When someone pleads not guilty a trial date is set, usually scheduled for a time several months away. In serious cases, a "preliminary hearing" before a provincial court judge must first be held before the case can proceed to trial in the higher court. At the preliminary hearing the Crown prosecutor must provide enough evidence to prove that there is at least a *prima facie* or apparent case against the accused.

E. Judicial Interim Release (Bail) or Custodial Remand

Should a trial or court appearance be adjourned, the court must decide whether the accused will be released on bail (the legal term is judicial interim release) or remanded in custody (detained in jail). The *Criminal Code* establishes criteria for this decision, which is discussed in detail in Chapter 7.

F. Conviction or Acquittal

A guilty plea or a finding of guilt after a trial by judge alone, or judge and jury, is followed by sentencing. An acquittal results in the immediate release (discharge) of the accused, whereas a conviction results in a criminal record.

G. Sentencing

A convicted offender will serve a prison sentence, if any, within either the provincial or federal corrections system, depending on the length of the prison term. Prison sentences of two years or more are served in a federal penitentiary. Often a judge will place the offender on probation for a time and require that the offender follow the direction of the probation officer in obtaining treatment, for example, for alcohol addiction or other relevant problems. If a judge imposes a fine that an offender fails to pay, that fine will be enforced using the kinds of civil enforcement measures outlined above (in paragraph G of the section on Civil Legal Process), unless the judge specifies a jail term in default of payment.

An appeal against a conviction and/or sentence must be filed within 30 days. The Appeal Court can extend this filing time under extenuating circumstances in criminal matters. This power does not extend to civil matters.

PROCEDURAL FAIRNESS

Many helping professionals, especially those with statutory powers such as teachers who discipline students, psychiatrists who commit patients to mental hospitals, or financial assistance workers who grant or deny monetary benefits, must ensure that both the substance of their decision and the process by which these decisions are made are legal and fair. Known also as the rules of natural justice, the concept of administrative fairness means that all courts, tribunals, and administrators must follow fair procedures in making their decisions.

The British Columbia Ombudsman's Code of Administrative Justice[16] provides useful guidelines for fairness. There are three main elements of fairness in the decision-making process:

a) an adequate opportunity to be heard;

b) an unbiased decision-maker; and

c) reasons for the decision.

The first element involves an adequate opportunity for the person affected by the decision to be heard. The particular mechanism by which this can be accomplished will vary depending on the circumstances. It may include one, some, or all of the following procedures:

a) notice of the proposed action;

b) notice of the criteria to be applied;

c) an opportunity to make representations;

d) an opportunity to present evidence;

e) an opportunity to call witnesses;

f) disclosure of adverse evidence;

g) oral hearing (public or private);

h) representation by counsel; or

i) a record of the proceedings.

If other appropriate procedures are needed, (e.g. the provision of an interpreter), they should be used. The degree of formality required will generally relate to the seriousness of the consequences of the decision for the individual concerned and his/her ability to use the available procedures. The more dire the consequences of an adverse decision the greater the need for the opportunity to be heard and the greater the need for full formality in the hearing process.

The second element of fairness requires that the decision-maker is unbiased and demonstrates qualities of good faith and an open mind. These qualities are essential for maintaining the integrity and credibility of public administration. Even the most upright person could not be sure that her/his decision was untainted if he/she had an interest in its outcome. Neither could anyone else who was aware of that interest.

The third element of fairness in the decision-making process requires that reasons for the decision are made explicit. The need for procedural fairness continues after a decision is made. If a decision is adverse, it would be expected that reasons be given. However, a favourable decision may also warrant the giving of reasons if it exemplifies a new policy or an important principle. Giving reasons enhances public understanding of public administration and provides an opportunity for rational scrutiny of public policy. At the same time, this procedure negates the arrogance implied by a failure to give reasons and promotes the legitimacy of administrative power.

The context of each decision will determine what kind of notice, process, evidence, and reasons are appropriate to meet the test of fairness. The above guidelines do not mean that "a mini-court hearing" has to take place before every decision is made. However, it is generally accurate to say that the greater the impact a decision will have (loss of liberty or livelihood, for instance), the higher the standard of procedural fairness imposed. Decisions that fail to incorporate the required level of procedural fairness run the risk of being set aside by the courts or other administrative bodies.

Some examples illustrate the importance of these principles of fairness in decision-making. In the first example, a social worker employed by the government apprehended a child under child protection legislation and then, shortly afterwards, returned the child home. The worker, however, failed to arrange an initial court review of the action within one week as required by law and failed to provide the parents with notice of their entitlement to a court hearing. The Ombudsman determined that the worker had violated the parents' right to administrative fairness, even though formal notification of a hearing was not required under British Columbia's legislation of the time. It is now specifically required under the more recent *Child, Family and Community Service Act*.[17]

The second example involved a 12-year-old child brought to a detention centre in handcuffs by the sheriff. The handcuffs were being used only for convenience since the child was not a high runaway risk. The use of handcuffs was determined by the Ombudsman to be inappropriate and the sheriff's department was ordered to make a conscious determination of risk in each situation before using handcuffs.

Administrative and judicial decisions must not, of course, violate the law or be improper in any other way. Section 22(1) of the *Ombudsman Act*[18] of British Columbia lists the grounds on which the

Ombudsman may take action to remedy any such violations or abuse. Should such errors exist in the decision, they may form the basis for a judicial review by the Supreme Court. This section of the *Ombudsman Act* reads as follows:

Where, after completing an investigation, the Ombudsman believes that

a) a decision, recommendation, act or omission that was the subject matter of the investigation was:

   i) contrary to law;

   ii) unjust, oppressive or improperly discriminatory;

   iii) made, done or omitted pursuant to a statutory provision or other rule of law or practice that is unjust, oppressive or improperly discriminatory;

   iv) based in whole or in part on a mistake of law or fact or on irrelevant grounds or consideration;

   v) related to the application of arbitrary, unreasonable or unfair procedures; or

   iv) otherwise wrong;

b) in doing or omitting an act or in making or acting on a decision or recommendation, an authority

   i) did so for an improper purpose;

   ii) failed to give adequate and appropriate reasons in relation to the nature of the matter; or

   iii) was negligent or acted improperly; or

c) there was unreasonable delay in dealing with the subject matter of the investigation,

the Ombudsman shall report his (sic) opinion and the reasons for it to the authority and may make the recommendation he considers appropriate.

The above guidelines should provide a useful template for fair decision-making by the helping professional or administrator. Helping professionals should be aware of the application of these principles to decision-makers, including themselves.

One of the most important aspects of a helping professional relationship is the ability to communicate clearly and candidly with the client, in an atmosphere of trust and confidence. The following section deals with two concepts that are basic to that atmosphere.

CONFIDENTIALITY AND PRIVILEGE[19]

A. Definitions

The concepts of confidentiality and privilege are sometimes confused. Under the principle of confidentiality, a helping professional is ethically and legally bound not to disclose any information about a client unless the client has consented or the professional is lawfully compelled (e.g., by subpoena or court order) to release the information. Privilege, on the other hand, refers to a relationship in which one individual cannot be compelled, even in court, to disclose information about another, and may do so only with the consent of the other party. Most helping professionals are not in a privileged relationship with their clients.

B. Basis for Confidentiality

Aspects of confidentiality for helping professionals can be found in three areas - in professional codes of ethics, in common law (case law), and in statute.

Ethical obligations include professional codes of ethics such as the *Canadian Code of Ethics for Psychologists*,[20] which states that psychologists have a responsibility to protect and promote the client's rights of privacy, self-determination, and autonomy, and to develop and follow procedures for confidentiality consistent with these rights.[21]

Similarly, the *Canadian Code of Ethics for Social Workers*[22] states:

A social worker shall protect the confidentiality of all information acquired from the client or others regarding the client and the client's family during the professional relationship unless

a) the client authorizes in writing the release of specified information,

b) the information is released under the authority of a statute or an order of a court of relevant jurisdiction, or

c) otherwise authorized under this Code.

In common law in Canada, cases have recognised the legal duty of confidentiality owed by physicians to their patients.[23] This can be extended to other helping professionals and is supported by the ethical codes mentioned above.

Where statute law is concerned, the major relevant legislation in British Columbia is the *Freedom of Information and Protection of Privacy Act*,[24] which took effect in 1992. This statute and its regulations address the creation, maintenance, disclosure, correction, and protection of records that are in the custody or under the control of provincial and municipal public bodies (e.g., ministries of the provincial government, hospitals and universities, and self-governing professions); common law principles no longer apply to such records. The legislation provides that anyone is entitled to make a request, in writing, for access to these records. It also sets out numerous factors that must be considered in determining the appropriate response to a request, including whether an applicant is seeking access to his or her own information or someone else's, and whether the subject of a record has consented to its disclosure to a third party.

Public bodies have developed detailed "Freedom of Information" procedures which their employees, including helping professionals, are required to follow, and many have hired information and privacy specialists to coordinate the process. The legislation provides that applicants may be charged reasonable fees for the costs of reproducing records other than their own personal information, but permits public bodies to waive such fees on a discretionary basis.

When helping professionals are not employed by public bodies, the *Freedom of Information and Protection of Privacy Act* does not apply. Instead, the records maintained by helping professionals in private practice are subject to the common law principles summarized in *McInerney v. MacDonald*,[25] a 1992 decision of the Supreme Court of Canada.

This was a case in which a patient, Mrs. Margaret MacDonald, sought access to all of the information in her medical file, which was in the possession of Dr. Elizabeth McInerney. Dr. McInerney willingly provided copies of the documents that she had created, but refused to provide Mrs. MacDonald with copies of reports from other physicians on the grounds that the reports were the physicians' property and it would be unethical to release them without their consent.

Mrs. MacDonald sought and obtained an order from the New Brunswick Court of Queen's Bench requiring Dr. McInerney to provide copies of the records she had withheld. This order was twice appealed and twice upheld. The following were among the reasons cited by the Supreme Court of Canada for upholding the order:

a) Physicians are in a fiduciary relationship with their patients, for whom they hold sensitive information in trust.

b) Physicians own the records that they compile, but the patients own the information contained in the records.

c) Physicians are under a duty to make proper disclosure of recorded information to their patients.

d) A patient's right of access is not absolute; a physician may deny access to all or part of a medical record if there is "a significant likelihood of a substantial adverse effect on the physical, mental or emotional health of the patient or harm to a third party...."[26] If a physician denies access to medical records, the patient may apply to the courts for a remedy. The onus will then be on the physician to justify non-disclosure.

Although *McInerney v. MacDonald* refers only to physicians and their patients, the same principles apply, by analogy, to other health-care professionals and their clients. Therefore, even in the absence of information and privacy legislation, most individuals are entitled to examine and copy the information contained in their health-care records. Helping professionals in private practice are entitled to recover from their clients the costs of reproducing the records.

C. Exceptions to the Principle of Confidentiality

During the intake interview or first meeting, it is very important for a helping professional to explain that sensitive information concerning the client may be recorded in some fashion or merely retained in the professional's memory, as appropriate to the needs of the client and as required by law or policy, and to advise the client of the professional's duty of confidentiality.

However, it is equally important to explain the limits of the duty of confidentiality. The client should be advised that the professional must comply with the terms of a valid court order, subpoena, or search warrant requiring the disclosure of client information. The client should also be informed that certain legislation requires the disclosure of client information. For helping professionals, the following are the most important statutory reporting obligations:

a) The *Child, Family and Community Service Act*[27] requires anyone who has reason to believe that a child "has been, or is likely to be, physically harmed, sexually abused or sexually exploited by a parent or another person, or [otherwise] needs protection...."[28] to report the matter promptly to the Ministry for Children and Families. The only exceptions to this duty apply to information obtained by a lawyer in the course of the solicitor-client relationship and information prohibited from disclosure under other legislation. Failure to report as required constitutes an offence.

b) Under the *Health Act Communicable Disease Regulation,*[29] anyone who knows or suspects that a person may be suffering from, or has died from, a communicable disease listed in the *Regulation* must report the matter to a Medical Health Officer without delay.

c) Under the *Motor Vehicle Act,*[30] registered psychologists, optometrists, and physicians are required to report to the Superintendent of Motor Vehicles the name, address and medical condition of any patient over the age of 16 who, in the opinion of the professional making the report, "has a medical condition that makes it dangerous to the patient or to the public for the patient to drive a motor vehicle...."[31] and who continues to do so after being warned of the danger.

Certain other legislation requires helping professionals to make information available upon demand. In particular:

a) Under the *Insurance (Motor Vehicle) Act,*[32] the Insurance Corporation of British Columbia has the authority to demand the production of reports concerning persons injured in motor vehicle accidents in British Columbia from physicians, chiropractors, dentists, physiotherapists, and hospital employees.

b) Under the *Workers Compensation Act,*[33] the Workers' Compensation Board has "the like powers as the Supreme Court to compel the attendance of witnesses and examine them under oath, and to compel the production and inspection of books, papers, documents and things...."[34]

If a helping professional is uncertain about the applicability of an obligation to report or the validity of a demand for disclosure, specific legal advice should be obtained.

D. Duty to Warn or Protect

There is another difficult category of cases in which information may have to be disclosed without client consent (see Chapter 13). These are cases giving rise to the duty to warn or protect (see Chapter 13), which was first recognized in an American decision, *Tarasoff v. Regents of U.C.*[35]

In *Tarasoff*, a client uttered death threats against his former fiancee during a counselling session at the University of California. The psychologist had good reason to believe that the client, if not hospitalized, would follow through on his threats. The psychologist notified campus police, who picked up the client and questioned him, but subsequently released him on the basis that he appeared rational. The psychologist's superior concurred with campus police that further action was not warranted. Two months later, the client murdered his former fiancee, just as he had threatened to do.

In finding for the victim's parents in their suit against the University, the court held that, in such situations, "the psychotherapist can take one or more of various steps, depending on the nature of the case, including warning the intended victim or others likely to apprise the victim of the danger, notifying the police, or taking whatever steps are reasonably necessary under the circumstances...."[36] Thus the phrase "the duty to warn," often used as a short-hand reference to *Tarasoff*, is a misnomer; the actual duty, when a credible threat is made against an identifiable victim, is broader.

Although *Tarasoff*, an American decision, is not binding in Canada, it has been cited with approval in several Canadian judgments. Most notably, in *Wenden v. Trikha*[37] a voluntary patient eloped from the psychiatric ward of the Royal Alexandra Hospital in Edmonton, located his car keys, drove recklessly across the city, and struck another car. The second driver eventually lost custody of her children due to the severely disabling injuries she sustained in the accident. In the ensuing litigation against the patient, the treating psychiatrist, and the hospital, the court held that a psychiatrist who was aware that a patient represented a serious danger to others would be under a duty to take reasonable steps to protect them. (In the facts of this particular case, however, the court found that there was no way to foresee that the patient would pose such a threat, and, therefore, that the psychiatrist had not breached any such duty.)

As discussed earlier, helping professionals who are employed by public bodies in British Columbia are subject to the provisions of the *Freedom of Information and Protection of Privacy Act*. Thus any intended release, pursuant to the duty to warn or protect, of information that is in the custody or under the control of a public body must also meet the requirements of this legislation and follow established procedures (see Chapter 12). Helping professionals in private practice should seek specific legal advice when faced with a situation that may trigger the duty to warn or protect.

E. Complying with a Subpoena or Notice of Motion

As mentioned previously, evidence must be provided if required by a court of law. As an officer of the court, any lawyer can issue a subpoena and thereby compel a helping professional to appear in court, disclose records, and testify about a particular client. The subpoena will indicate where and when the professional is required to appear, but will have no legal effect before that date and time.

A subpoena does not have to be personally served to be valid. Service may be effected by regular mail or fax unless the party issuing the subpoena proposes to institute contempt proceedings for non-compliance. In those circumstances, personal service must be proven. A conviction for contempt of court can attract a fine, a term of imprisonment, or both.

If a lawyer wants access to client records but does not require the testimony of the helping professional, or, if the records are not subject to simple disclosure by subpoena (e.g., counselling records of sexual assault victims -- see Chapter 7), the lawyer may instead proceed by way of notice of motion. The professional and, typically, the client will receive written notice that an application is to be made in court, on a particular date and at a specified time, for an order granting access to the records in question. Both the client and the professional are entitled, at their discretion, to appear at the hearing and argue that access should be limited or denied. If the application is granted, the resulting court order will likely specify that the helping professional must make photocopies of the records, certify them as being true copies, and provide them to the lawyer who obtained the order. In addition, that lawyer and opposing counsel will probably be given the right to inspect the original records to ensure that the copies are complete.

Helping professionals who receive a subpoena or a notice of motion should discuss it promptly with legal counsel to determine the appropriate response. It is never appropriate to remove information from a file in anticipation of, or on receipt of, a subpoena or notice of motion. Such conduct could attract contempt or disciplinary proceedings or both.

E. Privilege

Statutory privilege for professionals is quite common in the United States, but Canadian law does not recognize many instances of privileged professional communication. In Canada, for example, there is no privilege between health-care providers and their clients, or between clergy and their parishioners. Apart from the well-known privilege between lawyers and their clients, privilege is available only for some very specialized undertakings.

For example, section 3 of British Columbia's *Family Relations Act*[38] creates a privilege for family court counsellors in the performance of their duties. Similarly, section 10(4) of the *Divorce Act*,[39] which is federal legislation, creates a privilege for an experienced marriage counsellor, guidance counsellor, or "in special circumstances, some other suitable person"[40] nominated by the court to assist separated spouses in attempting to reconcile.

F. Common Law Basis of Privilege

Canadian courts have recognized that there are circumstances in which the scope of privilege should be expanded. For example, evidence of communications between counsel in an attempt to settle litigation is not admissible in court. The rationale is simply that it is in the public interest to see disputes settled as efficiently as possible and without resort to the courts. Any information exchanged in this context should, therefore, be privileged.

From time to time, the courts have applied this rule in family disputes, disallowing evidence of discussions or negotiations between the parties when these negotiations were conducted by a therapist, a mediator, a physician, a priest, or even a friend. There is, however, no guarantee that a court will recognize this privilege in any particular case.

A presiding judge always has the discretion to allow a witness to refuse to disclose confidential information under certain circumstances. Often, a helping professional will not be compelled to disclose confidential information unless it is both relevant and necessary in the interests of justice. In short, a judge may refuse to hear evidence of confidential communications between clients and professionals when, in the opinion of the judge, the importance of maintaining confidentiality outweighs the usefulness of the information in the proceeding.

A number of cases have referred to four fundamental conditions for the creation and enforcement of a privilege.[41] Josefowitz[42] describes these as consisting of the following:

a) The communications must originate in the confidence that they will not be disclosed.

b) This element of confidentiality must be essential to the full and satisfactory maintenance of the relationship between the parties.

c) The relationship must be fostered because the community desires it.

d) Injury inflicted on the relationship as a result of disclosure or communication must be greater than the benefit from proper disposal of litigation.

THE RELEVANCE OF SPECIFIC LEGAL KNOWLEDGE

Each helping professional should understand the laws relating to her/his own specific professional role and mandate and the legal basis for the key rights pertaining to particular client groups. Detailed information on particular fields of practice will be found in later chapters.

As will be seen from Chapter 13, the task is to reduce the vulnerability of professionals to legal action or intervention from offices such as social service inspectors or the Ombudsman. Inspectors monitor whether social workers and financial assistance workers are following Ministry procedures while the Ombudsman monitors administrative fairness in provincial government ministries, Crown corporations and, more recently, in hospitals, schools, and municipalities. As Canadian society becomes more "rights conscious," the actions of helping professionals are becoming more subject to legal scrutiny. Professional liability claims and disciplinary action often arise through ignorance of professional legal and ethical obligations.

For example, a child care worker in a hospital was disciplined for failing to follow his ethical obligation to notify the supervisor when his own medical condition might have been interfering with patient safety. The worker should have been aware of the duties inherent in his job description and the resulting legal implications of his actions.

The law directly connected to an area of practice is crucial, yet it is often unknown to helping professionals. It goes without saying that every professional employed by an agency must be aware of agency policy and procedures. Conversely, an introduction to the specific statutes pertaining to a professional's mandate should also be an integral part of employee orientation, particularly since boards and employers can be held accountable for the discriminatory actions of employees, even if these actions are unknown or not condoned.[43]

The following are examples of specific legal knowledge essential for professionals: teachers should be aware of the *School Act* and *Regulations*;[44] youth workers and probation officers require a working knowledge of the *Young Offenders Act*[45] (both federal and provincial) and the *Criminal Code*; child care specialists in British Columbia need to know about provisions for daycare in regulations[46] and the *Child, Family and Community Service Act*; social workers in mental hospitals must be familiar with the *Mental Health Act*[47] and the *Power of Attorney Act*[48] and the *Infants Act*;[49] and family and relationship counsellors must understand the *Family Relations Act, Divorce Act*,[50] and *Family Maintenance Enforcement Act*.[51]

Similarly, the specific rights and remedies of special client groups are important. A social worker involved with victims of crime needs to know about possible criminal and civil remedies. The worker should be aware that the *Criminal Injuries Compensation Act*,[52] which is administered through the Workers' Compensation Board, can provide victims of crime with financial compensation. Knowing where to obtain a remedy can be as important as knowing it exists. The lawyer who advises the agency can provide invaluable consultation in this area.

STRATEGIES FOR DEALING WITH LAWYERS AND THE ADVERSARIAL SYSTEM

As we have seen, the unique adversarial nature of the legal system may lead to potential role conflicts or value dilemmas for the helping professional. Here are some strategies that may be helpful for dealing with, or avoiding, these conflicts.

A. Work in Partnership with Lawyers

Much has been written about the competing perceptions between lawyers and helping professionals (especially lawyers and social workers) and the negative stereotypes each has of the other professions.[53] Many lawyers perceive the courtroom as their "ballpark" where they retain control and play by their rules. Lawyers focus on the individual and his/her partisan rights. This can often conflict with the more holistic perception of the helping professional, especially one who represents a statutory authority such as a child welfare agency. Such lawyers may see themselves as the last bastion of protection for the client from the leviathan of an all powerful government.

Other research, however, has identified more productive ground for collaboration.[54] Strategies for promoting collaboration include joint training by shared curriculum in law schools, social work schools, departments of education, medicine and counselling, and by discussions of the respective roles. Pre-court case conferencing, working groups in court settings who meet to discuss concerns, and interprofessional public forums can all assist in improving relationships and enhancing working partnerships for the benefit of clients.

B. Enhance Own Legal Competence

The legal arena is the working environment of lawyers. Professional credibility of helping professionals will be promoted by their demonstration of competence in the areas of legal knowledge, protocols, and skills whenever they are involved in the legal system. An opposing lawyer may take a less adversarial approach to questioning a helping professional witness who displays such competence. In negotiations or advocacy on behalf of clients, the helping professional's knowledge of potential legal outcomes is useful information for developing a bargaining strategy.

C. Promote Client Choice in Use of the System

It is well known how courts can re-victimize victims, humiliate complainants, and shelter some offenders from responsibility. Legal representation in court, though necessary, can sometimes be disempowering for the client by limiting his/her participation. When possible, clients need to be able to make informed choices about engaging with the legal system. This means identifying the realistic advantages and disadvantages of engagement with the system. With those who have no choice, such as compellable witnesses and alleged offenders, the impact of stress and publicity through giving testimony needs to be minimized as much as possible. Helping professionals might act as support persons for disempowered clients as they give instructions to lawyers, for witnesses in testifying and debriefing courtroom experiences, and for promoting alternatives such as diversion from court.

D. Explore both Law and Professional Practice with a Critical Lens

Without a critical analysis, helping professionals may become unwitting pawns or apologists in an unjust system. Courts are essentially arenas of power plays. Mechanisms to equalize power and access to resources need to be developed. One example is the support that is being given to some groups of victims who were abused during their residential school or orphanage experience, and who are now testifying against or suing the perpetrators. Connecting victims with each other is often seen as necessary to boost their readiness to give evidence, although the law may not welcome this if it contaminates that evidence. More class actions could also be empowering, but are often a threat to governments. For instance, in 1996 the provincial government of Alberta began a legal challenge of a class action launched by "mentally retarded" persons for coerced sterilization in Alberta in the 1950's. The outcome of this has yet to be decided.

It is also important for helping professionals to develop their own beliefs and definitions of "justice," "equality," and "fairness." They must realize and accept that the law and morality (justice) do not necessarily coincide in the legal arena, and they should strive to point this out to politicians, the courts and the general public.

E. Be Involved Politically in Reforming the Legal System

Finally, change in the legal system will come about only through political action. A critical analysis will identify areas for reform, but only public pressure will effectively bring about change. Helping professionals, with their egalitarian values, are encouraged to seek political office as a means of ensuring that laws, bylaws, and policies truly reflect principles of social justice. The skills of critical analysis, effective communication, and dispute resolution that helping professionals bring to a cause can have a significant, positive impact in the political arena.[55] Other ways of producing positive change include actively supporting political candidates or causes at various levels of government, and becoming involved in the governance of professional associations and unions who act for them. In the community, helping professionals should be centrally involved in organizing and supporting groups and coalitions in challenging repressive laws and practices.

An understanding of the legal process will help professionals positively influence legislative reform, whether it is by appearing before public hearings or committees, in the drafting of legislative proposals, or by lobbying groups of politicians. But most importantly, helping professionals must be able to detect when clients need legal advice, and use their knowledge of the system to direct clients to appropriate legal resources.

COMMON QUESTIONS

1. How can helping professionals know when they or their clients should obtain legal advice?

The boundary for helping professionals between advising or counselling on issues that have legal implications, and providing legal information is often unclear. Professionals are brokers of resources and should bring legal resources to the attention of clients. Specific legal advice, however, must remain the duty of lawyers. Lawyers alone have the authority to give legal advice.

Nonetheless, assisting a client to obtain legal advice is a crucial skill for the helping professional. Because an apparently minor problem may turn out to have significant legal ramifications, it is important to direct clients to legal consultation at the first hint of potential legal problems. For example, if clients are involved in disputes that can have an impact on their marital or parental status, financial situation (eg. a dispute over property), or rights, freedoms, or livelihood (e.g., a threat of criminal conviction, civil liability, or dismissal from employment), then legal advice should be sought.

Legal aid centres and lawyer referral services (in the Yellow Pages of telephone directories) can provide consultation for clients who cannot afford a lawyer or who need help choosing one. Clients should be encouraged to find a lawyer with whom they are comfortable. Helping professionals should find their own lawyers for private consultation or ensure their agencies retain a lawyer to provide necessary advice on professional practice issues. Timely legal advice can prevent future problems. Before embarking on any action that might have a major impact, consult a lawyer.

The terms by which lawyers govern themselves prevent lawyers from holding themselves out as specialists in any given area. However, lawyers do develop individual preferred areas of practice. The experiences of friends, colleagues, and clients of different lawyers can be a good guide for referral. Clients can also call the Lawyer Referral Service, and after explaining the nature of the legal service required, will be given the name of one lawyer who practises in the area of the client's concern. The client will be able to meet with the lawyer and will be charged $10 for the first half hour of consultation.

2. How much do lawyers cost and how are they paid?

Typically, lawyers charge an hourly rate. The particular rate of any given lawyer will be a function of several variables, the most important of which is years of experience. Rates vary considerably. Legal services can be secured for an hourly fee of less than $100 per hour to more than

$200, with many lawyers charging between $100 and $150 per hour. A lawyer charging an hourly fee will typically require a "retainer" upon first being hired. The retainer will be held in trust to the credit of the client for future legal services to be rendered. Often lawyers will bill on an interim basis: that is, accounts will be rendered (billed) periodically as the time invested in the file by the lawyer mounts. Such accounts will often be payable within 30 days of billing. Most lawyers will require that these accounts be kept current as a condition for continuing to act. At times, arrangements can be made to defer payment or make payment over time, or to pay for legal services out of proceeds, such as a division of family property or award of damages, which may be the outcome of the proceedings. Occasionally, in such actions as personal injury, lawyers will make a contingency agreement with the client. This means that payment is conditional on a successful result and reflects an agreed-upon proportion of the award.

The Legal Aid program available through the Legal Services Society makes lawyers' services available to some individuals who are unable to afford them. The program is not available universally and qualification for the program is tied to the means of the applicant. Further information respecting Legal Aid can be secured by calling the Legal Services Society as listed in the Yellow Pages of the telephone directory. Typically, the arrangement made between the Legal Services Society and the client is that the society will pay for the cost of the lawyer's services. If however, as a result of the litigation, sufficient funds become available, the client may be required to pay for some or all of the lawyer's fee.

3. <u>How might criminal and civil liabilities overlap in the conduct of professional practice?</u>

Helping professionals are accountable for their behaviour, both criminally and civilly. These actions are not mutually exclusive. For example, a physician who sexually assaults a child patient may be prosecuted by the Crown, sued by the patient's family for assault and battery, and disciplined by the governing body (College of Physicians and Surgeons) for engaging in unprofessional conduct. At the same time, there may be a child abuse investigation by a child welfare agency, although this may not directly affect the physician. Because the burden of proof is different in civil and criminal actions, a criminal acquittal is not a bar to a successful civil action. In other words, if the physician were acquitted on the assault charge (not proved "beyond a reasonable doubt"), he/she might still be found liable for civil damages because the assault was proved "on a balance of probabilities."

Similarly, clients may have separate actions. When the notorious serial child killer Clifford Olson was prosecuted for murder, the families of his victims sued him and his estate for a share of the $100,000 paid to his wife by the RCMP as an inducement to reveal the graves of the victims.

4. <u>What common misunderstandings in law can cause problems for professionals?</u>

Sometimes professionals make decisions based on a confusion about where to direct clients to go for legal information or help. For example, in a welfare appeal heard by one of the authors, the complainant reported that her financial assistance worker had instructed her to obtain from her estranged spouse a property settlement at Family Court; the settlement was a precondition for her eligibility for income assistance. In British Columbia, property claims can only be dealt with at Supreme Court, usually with legal assistance. This advice created undue delay and hardship, and resulted in the Ministry of Social Services (now Human Resources) being directed to pay for legal fees. Needless to say, the worker's credibility was questioned.

With the confusing duplication of federal and provincial programs in similar areas (for instance, unemployment insurance is federal, income assistance is provincial, and parole can be federal or provincial), it is easy for clients who need government services to be misdirected. Another example of a common misconception is that human rights law is uniform throughout Canada. This is not so. Some fundamental differences exist among federal human rights law and various provincial statutes. Protection varies and is not all encompassing. For instance, a client who is unable to obtain accommodation for economic or family reasons may not be entitled to any remedy or protection under human rights law. The scope and limits of the law need to be understood by the helping professional.

The law is often complicated and difficult to discover without the benefit of legal advice. How many professionals realize that when clients consider marital separation, legal implications about property entitlement can flow from this decision? As professionals become more vulnerable to negligence actions by clients, they must take steps to avoid liability by increasing their legal knowledge and ensuring that their practices are legally sound.

5. <u>What information can be shared about clients during case conferences?</u>[56]

Since case conferences are normally held only for consultation purposes to determine the best method of serving the needs of the client, any non-identifying information can be shared. This principle applies to individuals in the same agency as well as to other helping professionals who are trying to provide for the client's needs. Still, non-identification may be difficult in smaller centres. In such circumstances, inform the client of proposed case conferences and document that the client had been advised and did not object. Without such authorization, case conferences, particularly with police representatives, are extremely questionable from a confidentiality point of view.

6. <u>What should a helping professional do if a client reveals a crime committed in the past or planned for the future?</u>[57]

Unlike United States law, Canadian law does not require any reporting of criminal activity or suspicion of criminal activity, including planned crimes. The *Criminal Code of Canada* is silent on these issues. This is not to be confused, of course, with assisting a client to hide illegal activities, such as, at a client's request, destroying parts of records that might provide evidence of illegal conduct. Moreover, illegal activities may be ethically and legally reported to the police[58] if the best interests of society or the safety of one of its members demand it.

Before reporting, it is important to determine whether or not the client is likely speaking the truth. Some individuals fantasize or want to impress others with stories of crimes they have committed in the past. If the helping professional does believe that the client likely committed such a crime, a number of factors should be considered: how serious was the crime, how long ago was it allegedly committed, and is there any reasonable possibility that the client may commit a similar crime? In most circumstances, legal and ethical advice should be obtained. If police demand information, they should not be given access without a search warrant. However, many, although by no means all, professionals consider it acceptable to confirm that a particular person is their client so that the police may have sufficient information to obtain a search warrant from a justice of the peace.

7. How should professionals respond to telephone inquiries or requests for information about a client?[59]

Professionals should always be extremely cautious about disclosing confidential information over the telephone. One should know for certain to whom one is speaking and ensure that no information is released until the purpose is known and until the express consent of the client to release the information has been obtained.

8. What are the obligations of a helping professional if a spouse or family member wants to know the whereabouts of the client?[60]

This information should not be disclosed unless the client has consented. This obligation may be overridden by the director under the *Child, Family and Community Service Act*[61] if necessary for the safety of a child, such as when a child has gone missing.

9. What should a helping professional do if a client comes to a counselling session under the influence of alcohol or drugs and intends to drive after leaving the office?[62]

It is legally and ethically acceptable to caution the client not to drive and to call the police if the client still insists on driving. The professional should only call the police if he or she is concerned about the safety of the client or others.

10. How should a helping professional manage records in her/his custody?[63]

Helping professionals, among others, need to keep adequate records of their professional involvement with their clients for two main reasons. First, good record keeping is in the best interests of the client. No one can remember for any length of time all of the vital information that clients disclose. Also, if more than one professional is involved in the case, or the case needs to be transferred to another professional, then there should be an adequate record available of treatment or counselling to date. A second important reason for record keeping is to preserve evidence about the details of the professional relationship in case the client should take future legal action against the professional or the agency.

Regardless of one's particular profession, all helping professionals are advised to follow certain basic guidelines for record keeping. These guidelines include the following:

a) Records should be legible.

b) An entry in a record should be made "contemporaneous with the event" (i.e., at the same time or as soon as possible thereafter). Working notes should be incorporated into the permanent record as soon as possible.

c) The resulting record will then be in proper chronological order, which will enhance its apparent reliability.

d) The record should be made by the professional who is in direct contact with the client or, if it is made by someone else on the professional's behalf, both should sign the record.

e) Abbreviations should be avoided if at all possible. Any abbreviations that cannot be avoided should be in common usage, either by an entire profession or within a particular organization, and a list of their meanings should be readily available.

f) If a correction is necessary, the original wrong entry should not be completely obliterated. Rather, it should be struck out but left legible, and a clear link should be made to the subsequent correction.

g) All information included in the record should be relevant and factual. "Editorializing" (i.e., subjective commentary) is not appropriate. This is perhaps the most common ground rule, but it is also the one most often breached.

Other useful sources for guidelines on record keeping include the Privacy Code for Private Physicians' Offices in British Columbia[64] (Appendix A). and the Health Professions Model Bylaws.[65] These documents require that record keeping be accurate, up to date, and legible.

11. <u>What are the implications of improper record keeping?[66]</u>

A helping professional who includes inappropriate statements in a record, or makes untoward comments to a third party concerning a client, may be faced with a defamation suit. Helping professionals should take particular care not to indulge in subjective commentary in their records. A client who subsequently reads such a record may perceive the comments as defamatory.

A statement is defamatory if it is false, derogatory, and made without proper justification. It must address the subject's character and tend to lower his or her reputation in the eyes of others. In defending a lawsuit based in defamation, a helping professional may find it difficult or impossible to prove that the statement was true. A more common defence, therefore, is that of "qualified privilege." This defence is available if there was a duty (which normally exists for helping professionals) to record matters arising out of the professional relationship. However, for the defence of "qualified privilege" to succeed, there must also have been good faith on the part of the professional. This defence is not available if the client can prove that the professional was motivated by malice.

It is not a good defence to claim that the statement was originally made by someone else. Mere repetition of a defamatory statement amounts to republication, which is also actionable.

CONCLUSION

The importance of acquiring appropriate legal knowledge, general and specific, cannot be overstated. The helping professional must be able to detect when clients' rights are being violated and know where to direct their clients for help. It is now commonplace to find in professional codes of ethics a duty to act as an advocate for the rights of the client. For example, the *Canadian Association of Social Workers Code of Ethics*[67] states: "The social worker will respect the intrinsic worth of clients and act to ensure through reasonable advocacy and other intervention activities that dignity, individuality and rights of persons are safeguarded." Helping professionals also have ethical responsibilities to bring about constructive change in their profession, workplace, and in society as a whole. Understanding how these arenas are structured through law and the legal system is a basic step in pursuing that responsibility. Such ethical obligations demand that helping professionals have sound legal knowledge and can function competently in the legal arena.

RESOURCES

J. Blackwell, *The Courtwatcher's Manual* (Vancouver: Legal Services Society of B.C., 1985).

R. Carson & L. Olivo, eds., *Introduction to Law in Canada* (North York: Captus Press, 1996).

P. Fitzgerald & K. McShane, *Looking at Law, Canada's Legal System* (Ottawa: Bybooks, 1982).

G. Gall, *The Canadian Legal System*, 4th ed. (Calgary: Carswell, 1995).

E. J. Vayda & M. T. Satterfield, *Law for Social Workers: A Canadian Guide*, 3rd ed. (Toronto: Carswell, 1997).

R. W. Yates & R. A. Yates, *Canada's Legal Environment: Its History, Institutions and Principles,* (Scarborough: Prentice-Hall Canada, 1993).

INDEX TO LAW REPORTS AND JOURNALS

The following is a list of abbreviations found in the Notes section of each chapter. These abbreviations refer to the major Canadian law reports, journals and court designations. Reports and journals can be found in your local university law library. Ask your librarian for assistance in locating them.

B.C.L.R.	British Columbia Law Reports
B.C. Reg.	British Columbia Regulations
C.C.C.	Canadian Criminal Cases
C.L.L.C.	Canadian Labour Law Cases
Can.J.Fam.L.	Canadian Journal of Family Law
C.H.R.R.	Canadian Human Rights Reporter
C.N.L.R.	Canadian Native Law Reporter
C.R.	Criminal Reports
D.L.R.	Dominion Law Reports
McGill L.J.	McGill Law Journal
O.R.	Ontario Reports
R.F.L.	Reports of Family Law
R.S.B.C.	Revised Statues of British Columbia
R.S.C.	Revised Statutes of Canada
S.A.	Statutes of Alberta
S.B.C.	Statutes of British Columbia
S.C.R.	Canada Supreme Court Reports

S.C.C.	Supreme Court of Canada
S.C.C.D.	Supreme Court of Canada Digest
S.M.	Statutes of Manitoba
S.N.	Statutes of Newfoundland
S.N.B.	Statutes of New Brunswick
S.N.S.	Statutes of Nova Scotia
S.O.	Statutes of Ontario
S.P.E.I.	Statutes of Prince Edward Island
S.Q.	Statutes of Quebec
S.Y.T.	Statutes of the Yukon Territory
W.W.R.	Western Weekly Reports

END NOTES

1. *Charter of Rights and Freedoms*, Part I of the *Constitution Act*, 1982, being Schedule B of the Canada Act 1982 (U.K.), 1982, c. 11. section 28. "C" means Chapter and indicates the location of the statute within the Parliamentary session. For a good illustration of the strategy of lobbying for women's rights, see P. Kome, "Anatomy of a Lobby," (January 1983) 98 Saturday Night.
2. *Criminal Code of Canada*, 1985, R.S.C. c. C-46.
3. *Employment Standards Act*, 1996, R.S.B.C. c.113.
4. *Child, Youth and Family Advocacy Act*,, R.S.B.C. 1996, c.47.
5. *British Columbia Benefits Act*, R.S.B.C. 1996, (*Appeals*), c.25 (*Child Care*), c.26 (*Income Assistance*), c.27 (*Youth Works*), c.28, replacing the *Guaranteed Available Income for Need Act*, R.S.B.C. 1979, c.158.
6. *Canons of Legal Ethics*, ruling 1.3.(5) in The Law Society of B.C., Professional Conduct Handbook, (1921)
7. Chart adapted from B.C. Legal System. (Vancouver: Legal Services Society of B.C. and Law Courts Public Education Program, 1980).
8. Hughes Commission on Gender Equality in the Legal Profession, (Vancouver: The Law Society of B.C., 1993.)
9. C. Smart, *Feminism and the Power of Law* (London, U.K.: Routledge, 1989), p.88.
10. G.L. Gall, *The Canadian Legal System*, (Toronto: Carswell, 1990), pp.15-17.
11. *Family Relations Act*, R.S.B.C. 1996, c.128, Part 3.
12. R. Lesperance, "Quebec Law Based on Roman Civil Law" (February 1991) 15 Legal Perspectives 3:12.
13. This chart has been adapted from an unknown source.
14. *Heroin Treatment Act*, R.S.B.C. 1979 c. 166. In the case dealing with this issue, *Schneider v. The Queen*, (1982) 139 D.L.R. 3rd 417, it was held that the *Act* was *intra vires* (within the power) of provincial legislation since it was related to health. The program was abandoned before higher courts could rule on this issue.
15. *Canada Evidence Act*, R.S.C. 1985, c.C-5.
16. Annual Report of the Ombudsman to the Legislative Assembly of British Columbia, (Victoria, B.C.: Queen's Printer, 1982) at 3-13.
17. *Child, Family and Community Service Act*, R.S.B.C.1996, c.46 (proclaimed February 1996) section 31. See Chapter 3.
18. *Ombudsman Act*, R.S.B.C. 1996, c.340.
19. This section was written by G.W. Clements, Special Health Law Consultant, Ministry of Health and Ministry Responsible for Seniors (British Columbia), and L. J. Soloway, Legal Services Branch, Ministry of the Attorney General (British Columbia).
20. *Canadian Code of Ethics for Psychologists*, (Ottawa, Canadian Psychological Association, 1991.)
21. N. Josefowitz, "Confidentiality," in D. Evans, *The Law, Standards of Practice, and Ethics in the Practice of Psychology*, (Toronto: Edmond Montgomery Publications, 1997), p. 112.
22. *Social Work Code of Ethics*, (Ottawa, Canadian Association of Social Workers, 1994.)

23. For such recognition by the courts see *Re: Inquiry into the Confidentiality of Health Records in Ontario* (1979), 98 D.L.R. (3rd) 704 (Ont. C.A.), *Solicitor General of Canada v. The Royal Commission of Inquiry into the Confidentiality of Health Records in Ontario* [1981] 2 S.C.R. 494 and *R. v. Dyment* (1988), 66 C.R. (3d) 348 (S.C. C.).

24. *Freedom of Information and Protection of Privacy Act*, R.S.B.C. 1996, c. 165.

25. *McInerney v. MacDonald*, (1992), 2 S.C.R. 138.

26. *Ibid.*, at 158.

27. *Child, Family and Community Service Act*, R.S.B.C. 1996, c. 46.

28. *Ibid.*, s. 14.

29. *Health Act Communicable Disease Regulation*, B.C. Reg. 4/83.

30. *Motor Vehicle Act*, R.S.B.C. 1996, c. 318.

31. *Ibid.*, s. 230.

32. *Insurance (Motor Vehicle) Act*, R.S.B.C. 1996, c. 231.

33. *Workers Compensation Act*, R.S.B.C. 1996, c. 492.

34. *Ibid.*, s. 87.

35. *Tarasoff v. Regents of U.C.* (1974), 118 Cal. Reptr. 129, aff'd (1976), 131 Cal. Reptr. 14 (S.C.Cal.).

36. *Ibid.*, p.

37. *Wenden v. Trikha* (1991), 116 Alta.R. (2d) 81 (C.A.).

38. *Family Relations Act*, R.S.B.C. 1996, c. 128.

39. *Divorce Act*, R.S.C. 1985, c. 3 (2nd Supp.).

40. *Ibid.*, s. 10(2).

41. The so-called "Wigmore" conditions, discussed by the Supreme Court of Canada in *Slavutych v. Baker* (1975), 4 W.W.R. 620.

42. N. Josefowitz, "Confidentiality," in D. Evans, *The Law, Standards of Practice, and Ethics in the Practice of Psychology*, (Toronto: Edmond Montgomery Publications, 1997), p.129.

43. *Robichaud v. The Queen* (1987), 8 C.H.R.R. D/4326 (S.C.C.).

44. *School Act*, R.S.B.C. 1996, c.412. See Chapter 11.

45. *Young Offenders Act*, R.S.C. 1985, c. Y-1; *Young Offenders (British Columbia) Act*, R.S.B.C. 1996, c. 494.

46. Schedule E of the *British Columbia Benefits Act Regulations*. See note 5.

47. *Mental Health Act*, R.S.B.C. 1996, c.288.

48. *Power of Attorney Act*, R.S.B.C. 1996, c.370.

49. *Infants Act*, R.S.B.C. 1996. c.223. Most important is section 17 (was section 16 until April 1, 1996) which allows children under 19 to consent to treatment where the health treatment provider has explained the nature and consequences and reasonable foreseeable benefits and risks and is satisfied the child understands, and has concluded the health care is in the child's best interests.

50. *Divorce Act*, R.S.C. 1985, c.3.

51. *Family Maintenance Enforcement Act*, R.S.B.C. 1996, c.127.

52. *Criminal Injuries Compensation Act.* R.S.B.C. 1996, c.85.

53. See A. Smith, "The Social Worker in the Legal Aid Setting: a Study of Interprofessional Relationships," Social Service Review, June 1970, 44:2.

54. See Marie Weil, "Research in Issues in Collaboration between Social Workers and Lawyers." Social Service Review, September 1982 56:3.

55. D. Turner, "Social Work Skills in the Political Sphere: a Case Study of Community Empowerment, Advocacy and Conflict Resolution," Unpublished paper presented to Social Workers World Conference, Colombo, Sri Lanka, (1994, School of Social Work, Victoria, Canada). See also J. G. Cameron and P. Kerans, "Social and Political Action," in S. A. Yelaja (ed), *An Introduction to Social Work Practice in Canada*, (Scarborough: Prentice-Hall, Canada, 1985) pp.111-144.

56. This question and answer was written by G. W. Clements, Special Health Law Consultant, Ministry of Health and Ministry Responsible for Seniors (British Columbia), and L. J. Soloway, Legal Services Branch, Ministry of the Attorney General (British Columbia).

57. *Ibid.*

58. See COACH Guidelines to Promote the Confidentiality and Security of Automated Health Related Information, (Edmonton, Canadian Organization to Promote the Confidentiality and Security of Automated Health Related

Information, 1989).

59. *Supra*, at 56.

60. *Ibid.*

61. *Child, Family and Community Service Act*, R. S.B.C., 1996, c.46, section 75.

62. *Supra*, at 56.

63. *Ibid.*

64. Privacy Code for Private Physicians' Offices in British Columbia, (1997), *British Columbia Medical Journal*, 39(12), 646-649.

65. *Guidelines for developing bylaws under the Health Professions Act.* Ministry of Health and Ministry Responsible for Seniors (Legislation and Professional Regulation Division: Victoria, British Columbia, September, 1996).

66. *Supra*, at 56.

67. *Supra, note 22*, section 5.1.

Chapter 2

THE CHARTER AND HUMAN RIGHTS

David Turner and Max Uhlemann

INTRODUCTION

All citizens or residents of Canada enjoy some basic human rights that the helping professional must acknowledge and respect in offering effective assistance. The helping professional, who is often both counsellor to the client and the broker of public or private social services, requires an understanding of the overall principles of fairness and the law of human rights. This is necessary to ensure that practice and programs conform to basic standards of equality and fair treatment.

The first chapter of this handbook described how the law is dynamic and is constantly being updated. The evolution of case law on human rights is accelerating as more people become empowered to seek legal remedies. As any lawyer will point out, a right is not a right unless it is legally enforceable. The statutory authority (location in law) for various rights, their scope and limitations, and in particular the mechanisms available to remedy alleged violations are crucial pieces of information for the helping professional.

In Canada, human rights are contained primarily in two types of legislation: the *Charter of Rights and Freedoms*,[1] and both federal and provincial *Human Rights Acts*.[2] The founding document of the *United Nations Convention on Human Rights*[3] is also an important standard by which to judge the human rights record in Canada. We will begin with a definition of human rights, then look at the key provisions, remedies, and limitations of each type of legislation. The law is stated as of April 1, 1997.

DEFINITION OF HUMAN RIGHTS

Broadly speaking, a human right is the freedom to do something without undue interference, or the entitlement to a service or process without unreasonable discrimination. Freedom of speech or association, for example, permits people to participate in a peaceful demonstration against poverty. The right to consult legal counsel illustrates an entitlement to a service. Many clients will seek help from professionals in securing a range of rights and entitlements such as housing, employment opportunities, or access to public facilities.

Many members of the public, in their efforts to de-emphasize rights and liberties, might argue that these should be limited by responsibilities and duties. This is a philosophical premise only. It will be remembered from the first chapter that everyone is legally free to do anything that is not prohibited by law. The responsibility and duty that lie with all citizens is to act within the law and to allow another's right or freedom to be exercised.

INTRODUCTION TO THE *CHARTER OF RIGHTS AND FREEDOMS*

A. Provisions

Our Constitution is the primary source of legal authority in Canada. Section 52(1) of the *Constitution Act*[4] states:

> The Constitution of Canada is the supreme law of Canada, and any law that is inconsistent with the provisions of the Constitution is, to the extent of the inconsistency, of no force or effect.

The *Charter of Rights and Freedoms* (hereafter referred to as the *Charter*) forms an important part of the Constitution, comprising Part 1, sections 1 through 34. Among other things, the *Charter* proclaims fundamental freedoms, democratic rights, mobility rights, equality rights, language rights, and aboriginal rights. The *Charter* may be viewed as a key part of the Canadian social contract, revealing much about the ideals of Canadian society. The need for the protection of rights and freedoms against the power of government or of a police state is well demonstrated by several dark examples in Canadian history, such as the internment of the Japanese Canadians during the Second World War,[5] or the suspension of civil rights in Quebec in 1970 during the F.L.Q crisis.

The following list illustrates some of the rights and freedoms that are contained in sections 2 through 15 of the *Charter*:

a) freedom of conscience and religion;

b) freedom of thought and belief;

c) freedom of opinion and expression;

d) freedom of the press and other media of communication;

e) freedom of peaceful assembly and association;

f) the right to vote and be elected;

g) the right to enter, remain in and leave Canada;

h) the right to move to and work in any province;

i) the right to life, liberty and security of the person;

j) the right to be secure against unreasonable search and seizure;

k) the right not to be arbitrarily detained or imprisoned;

l) the right on detention to retain and instruct counsel;

m) the right to be presumed innocent until proven guilty according to law in a fair and public hearing by an independent and impartial tribunal;

n) the right not to be subjected to any cruel and unusual treatment or punishment; and

o) the right to equal protection and benefit of the law without discrimination.

The above list provides a template for the laws, policies, or administrative decisions of all levels of government (federal, provincial, regional, and municipal) or government agencies (for example, police, school boards, hospital boards) in Canada. The last provision mentioned on equality (section 15) protects broadly against discrimination in laws or actions of any level of government and adds, for the purposes of greater specificity only, the grounds of "race, national or ethnic origin, colour, religion, sex, age or mental or physical disability." This general protection should be contrasted with the specific grounds of prohibited discrimination in the Canadian and the provincial *Human Rights Acts* to be discussed later. Other key provisions include the right to use both official languages in dealings with the federal parliament and government, minority language educational rights, and gender equality as well as multicultural and aboriginal rights.

B. Remedies

A remedy is a legal action that is intended to correct a violation of a person's legal rights and freedoms. The *Charter* provides a general method to respond to any alleged violation of these rights and freedoms by government or its agents. Section 24(1) of the *Charter* allows anyone whose rights or freedoms have been infringed upon or denied to apply to a court for an appropriate and just remedy in the circumstances. The court may declare invalid a governmental law that violates the *Charter*. For example, the seven year minimum sentence of imprisonment for importing a narcotic under the *Narcotic Control Act*[6] (now the *Controlled Drugs and Substances Act*) was determined by the court to be unconstitutional because it would be grossly disproportionate in minor cases.[7] The minimum sentence provision was invalidated.

The *Charter* is frequently used as a defence in a criminal trial. Evidence obtained in a way that violates rights or freedoms will not be admitted in court if it could "bring the administration of justice into disrepute" (section 24(2)). The exclusion of such evidence, however, is not automatic and in each case the court must assess the impact of admission or exclusion on the reputation of the justice system.

The *Charter* provisions can have a direct impact on particular helping professionals, especially those who work in the disciplines with strong social control components such as corrections, mental health, income assistance, and child welfare. For instance, the *Charter* has been used successfully to invalidate indeterminate prison sentences for "dangerous offenders" as violating the provision against cruel and unusual punishment.[8] Similarly, the automatic and indeterminate detention of a person found not guilty by reason of insanity was found to violate the *Charter* protections against arbitrary detention and the principles of fundamental justice[9] (see the concept of natural justice in Chapter 1). It is expected that section 7, which protects the "right to life, liberty and security of the person and the right not to be deprived thereof except in accordance with the principles of fundamental justice," will be used to challenge the validity of the processes for mental health committals (see Chapter 9) and for child protection removals (see Chapter 3).

If a court finds a law violates the *Charter*, the court can strike it down in whole or in part immediately as did the Supreme Court of Canada in invalidating the therapeutic abortion procedures in the *Criminal Code*[10] because they violated the rights in section 7.[11] However, in invalidating the automatic indeterminate detention of persons found not guilty because of insanity, the Supreme Court of Canada took a pragmatic approach and, instead of releasing immediately all patients so detained, gave mental institutions a period of six months to implement a new system and to reassess these patients.[12]

Because the *Charter* is supreme and entrenched in our Constitution, the rights contained in it supersede those rights and protections in the federal or provincial human rights acts. Therefore, as will be discussed later, the *Charter* can be used to remedy deficiencies in human rights protections in other statutes.

C. Limitations

The *Charter* contains a number of important self-limiting provisions. The first is that these rights and freedoms are not absolute. The opening section of the *Charter* states:

1. The Canadian Charter of Rights and Freedoms guarantees the rights and freedoms set out in it subject only to such reasonable limits prescribed by law as can be demonstrably justified in a free and democratic society.

This section gives authority to the judiciary to decide how the *Charter* should be applied in context. For example, the *Charter* will not provide a shield for libel or slander under the banner of freedom of expression. In a narrow decision,[13] the Supreme Court of Canada did agree that the anti-hate provision (section 319.2) of the *Criminal Code* violated freedom of expression as identified in section 2 of the *Charter*. However, the court decided it was justified to protect minority groups from hate campaigns, a reasonable limit under section 1 upon this freedom. Similarly, it has been used to uphold several other *Criminal Code* provisions including the prohibition on communications in public for the purpose of prostitution,[14] and the limitation of the freedom of the press contained in the provisions that permit a ban on the publication of the identity of the complainant in a prosecution for sexual assault.[15]

On the other hand, section 1 of the *Charter* has not saved legislation in Alberta that was intended to put a blanket on the publication of details of divorce and separation cases,[16] nor to narrowly restrict advertising by dentists.[17] Helping professionals will realize that, in many situations relevant to their practice where court cases arise, the competing parties may each depend on *Charter* arguments of rights in their submissions to the court. The court has to decide between these conflicting rights, often considering section 1 in determining which should have priority in a free and democratic society. A recent example involves social workers in a Winnipeg child welfare agency trying to coerce into treatment a pregnant woman who was sniffing glue and solvents and had attempted suicide and self-mutilation, in order to protect the health and welfare of her unborn child. Two of her three children in care were born suffering the effects of her addiction. A judge in the Manitoba Court of Queen's Bench supported her committal to treatment but the decision was overruled unanimously by the judges of the Manitoba Court of Appeal in September 1996, who refused to recognize the rights of a foetus as a person, relying on previous Supreme Court of Canada decisions. The Court of Appeal decision stated: "If the unborn child is to be recognized as having rights, those rights can only be protected by infringing the mother's." The Supreme Court of Canada recently supported the Court of Appeal and ruled in favour of the mother. The Supreme Court found that forcing a woman into treatment against her will is a serious infringement of her rights and that elected officials are "in a much better position to weigh the competing interests and arrive at a solution that is principled and minimally intrusive to pregnant women."[18]

How this conflict of rights is resolved often depends on the value system of the judge. A recent majority decision at the Supreme Court of Canada[19] to allow defendants to access the private counselling records (including health and student records) of victims of sexual assault affirms the priority given to the rights of accused assaulters over the rights of sexual assault victims, providing defendants can establish that the records are likely to have relevance to their defense. The need for the trial judge to determine whether the confidential information sought is likely to be relevant was again asserted in a case of civil discovery, but access to psychiatric records was also reaffirmed.[20] Traditional legal scholars would view this decision as the justices correctly asserting the rights of individual liberty over rights to privacy. Others with a more feminist or structural viewpoint would argue it asserts the rights of powerful males over disempowered females,[21] revictimizes them and undermines the importance of confidentiality in the counselling relationship.

An interesting case[22] on judicial values and perceptions has recently come before the Supreme Court of Canada in September, 1997. In 1994, a Nova Scotia Youth Court Judge acquitted an Afro-Canadian youth of assaulting a police officer, citing pervasive problems of racism and strained relationships between police and such youth in Nova Scotia. On appeal, this decision was overturned on the grounds that the judge's remarks supported a finding of reasonable apprehension of bias against the police and in favour of the accused on the basis of race. This judge is the first and only black woman to be appointed to the bench in Nova Scotia. In a majority decision, the Supreme Court found the judge's comments improper but did not amount to a reasonable apprehension of bias. The youth's acquittal stands. The case raises, but does not answer definitively, the question as to how far judges can take into account their own experience or structural issues such as racism and the socio-political context in reaching their decisions. The Court accepted that the "requirement for neutrality does not require judges to discount the very life experience that may so well qualify them to preside over disputes."

The *Charter* identifies some limits on a person's mobility rights, such as a reasonable residency requirement in a jurisdiction (city, province, or country) before becoming entitled to certain public social services. Section 1 means that additional reasonable limits such as passport controls or deportation powers can apply. Allowance is expressly made for programs to ameliorate social or economic disadvantages in high unemployment areas. Similarly, the equality right does not preclude affirmative action programs. Section 15(2) clearly states that the equality provisions cannot be used to invalidate any law, program, or activity designed to better the conditions of disadvantaged individuals or groups. Thus an affirmative action program for women or ethnic minorities, or a special rehabilitation program for young offenders, would probably be supported under the *Charter* as long as it could be demonstrated that the program was fairly applied and administered and was designed to meet the objectives mentioned above.

The second limitation is found in section 32, which states that the *Charter* applies to federal and provincial legislatures and governments. This has been interpreted to mean that the *Charter* does not apply to private matters nor the private sector when there is no element of governmental action involved. However, the governmental action requirement may be found to exist if one of the parties relies on a statute that offends the *Charter*. Any statute, including the *British Columbia Human Rights Code*, can be declared deficient if it does not meet *Charter* standards. For example, a Victoria complainant took legal action against the British Columbia government, alleging its *Human Rights Code* was substandard because it did not protect against family status discrimination in its housing section. The Code has subsequently been amended.

The fact that the *Charter* does not apply to relations between private individuals but only between governments and individuals, raises a question about whether private agencies operating in the public realm are covered by the provisions of the *Charter*. As the field of social services becomes increasingly privatized, it is unclear whether the protection of the *Charter* will actually be applicable for many clients. The courts have found that the *Charter* did not apply to two universities and a hospital[23] because they did not form part of government. But in a contrasting case both the provincial legislation that established and controlled a community college as an agency of the Crown and a collective labour agreement were regarded as "law" (governmental involvement) for the purpose of applying the *Charter*.[24] It would seem logical that government contracts and funding to the private sector would be covered.

Corporations in Canada, however, have invoked the *Charter* to consolidate their legal status as persons and protect their business rights. For instance, business advertising has been protected by the Supreme Court of Canada as a fundamental freedom of expression,[25] and has been used to strike down federal laws restricting tobacco advertising. Retail corporations have used section 7 of the *Charter* to fight Sunday closing laws. The resources of corporations can give easier financial access to the courts than most individuals.

The third limitation is regarded by many as the *Charter*'s greatest weakness. Section 33 gives both the federal and provincial governments the power to pass laws that opt out of the provisions of the *Charter*. This legislative override allows legislation to be expressly exempt from the freedoms, legal rights, and equality protections. This exemption can last for a renewable term up to five years so that there will be opportunity for it to be addressed during a government's re-election bid.

Examples of the section 33 exemption can already be found in the Quebec sign legislation[26] and in a Saskatchewan act[27] ending a government employees strike in 1986. Supporters of the concept of override argue that the concept of supremacy of an elected parliament is consistent with democratic values. Critics state that only an independent judiciary should allow exemptions to the fundamental principles of the *Charter* and only those that can "be demonstrably justified in a free and democratic society."

Finally, not every successful *Charter* challenge has the desired outcome.[28] The British Columbia Government, when faced with a *Charter* decision which overruled its different rates for welfare recipients based on age, reduced all its benefits to the same level.[29] As Trakman indicates, "Few have the economic and personal resources to mount a *Charter* challenge. Few, beyond the corporate wealthy and politically agile, have the stomach for the arduous battle up the judicial ladder to the Supreme Court of Canada."[30] Helping professionals should be aware that, in view of the above limitations, not all equality or rights violations will find a remedy under the *Charter*.

THE ROLE OF JUDGES

Constitutions proclaim general principles and use general language out of necessity. Courts apply these principles to the context. For instance, the Supreme Court of Canada has decided that the right, on arrest or detention, "to retain and instruct counsel without delay and to be informed of that right" in section 11(b) of the *Charter* includes an additional obligation for the police.[31] When the arrested person is unable to obtain counsel on his or her own resources, the police must give information as to where legal advice can be obtained under legal aid. There is often a great deal of latitude in interpreting the possible meaning of wording. What, for example, is the meaning of "fundamental justice" in section 7 of the *Charter*? When is a search or seizure "unreasonable" in contravention of section 8? This is the type of question that must be answered when the Constitution is invoked in particular cases. Just as the common law has developed over time through the interpretation of individual cases, the actual meaning of our Constitution is becoming known through the cumulative experience of specific court judgments.

Interpretation and application of the *Charter* is a very challenging task. Even the final court of appeal, the Supreme Court of Canada, is frequently divided on the reasons for judgment when cases are brought to it following extensive argument and analysis in the courts below. Judicial division is not a feature peculiar to constitutional cases. There are also differences in the interpretation of statutes, regulations, wills, and contracts. However, in constitutional cases, court judgments often amount to important declarations of public policy. Controversial social issues are now debated and sometimes settled in court, while long-standing legislation is sometimes nullified there.

RELEVANT CHARTER CASES[32]

Rapid and numerous changes from litigation makes keeping abreast of *Charter* decisions difficult. The following is a brief summary of decisions particularly relevant to the practice of many helping professionals.

The rights and freedoms in the *Charter* continue to impact criminal law and procedure. For instance, courts across Canada are trying to define what is "unreasonable delay" in coming to trial (the Supreme Court of Canada in *R. v. Askov*[33] ruled a 6 to 8 month delay from committal to trial was unreasonable and stayed charges), and whether such delay always prejudices the accused and therefore should automatically result in the staying of charges.

In 1991, the Supreme Court of Canada struck down the "rape-shield law" in section 276 *Criminal Code of Canada*, which limited the questioning of sexual assault victims about their sexual history. The Court decided the provision violated the accused's rights to a fair trial in accordance with the principles of fundamental justice in section 7 of the *Charter*.[34] A narrower limitation was introduced by Parliament in 1992, which gives discretion to judges to consider whether the question is "relevant."

Again on the topic of fair trials, the issue of the appropriate composition of juries has risen. A First Nations defendant's request to ask jurors whether they were prejudiced ("if their ability to judge the evidence without bias or prejudice would be affected if the person charged is native and the complainant non-native") was denied by the British Columbia Supreme Court and Court of Appeal because of the additional burden such challenges would place on the court system. The defence must first show potential racial bias. The Court of Appeal stated that while there is widespread bias in society against Aboriginal people, it is not such that it would affect jurors.[35]

In another *Charter* issue that also relates to the family violence information contained in Chapter 7, the Supreme Court of Canada in 1992 ruled that while the prohibition in section 163 of the *Criminal Code of Canada* against the distribution of hard-core pornographic videos, magazines and paraphernalia did violate the freedom of expression protected in section 2 (b) of the *Charter*, it was justified by section 1 since its legislative purpose was the avoidance of harm to society, especially to women and children.[36] The Women's Legal Education Fund (LEAF)[37] also argued that the regulation of pornography can be constitutionally justified, using a "harms-based" equality approach, which focusses on the harm done by and through pornography against women and children. The Court found that the social interests of equality outweighed the accused's right to free expression, after evidence was shown of the harmful effects of pornography. It is now illegal to sell or rent pornographic material that depicts sexual relations jointly with violence, cruelty, or degradation.

Search and seizure issues often reach the Supreme Court, thus determining whether the inclusion of evidence obtained in violation of *Charter* rights in section 8 will bring the administration of justice into disrepute, in accordance with section 24(2). For example, police approached a house on an anonymous tip, and smelled marijuana plants when the door was opened. A warrant was sought and the occupants were arrested for possession for purposes of trafficking. The Court ruled the warrant was invalid because of the "search" (going to the door) but agreed that admission of the drug evidence would not bring administration of justice into disrepute.[38] Conversely, the police's forcible seizing of samples of hair and saliva from a 17-year- old charged with murder, after the youth's lawyer had left, did violate sections 8 and 24(2), although obtaining DNA from the mucous of a disposable nose tissue did not.[39]

For unionized workers, which includes most helping professionals who work for provincial or federal governments, a significant Supreme Court of Canada decision is *Lavigne v. Ontario Public Service Employees Union*.[40] The Court decided that a union's compulsory dues deduction and union financial support for the New Democratic Party, the pro-choice, and peace movements, did not violate the *Charter*'s right to freedom of association. The Court also stated that, even if the right was violated, the right of the union to deduct and contribute to causes of its choice would be justified by section 1 of the *Charter*.

The "equal protection and benefit of law" provision in section 15 of the *Charter* continues to be defined, though not always in an "equal" fashion. The interpretation of the legal concept of equality appears to be evolving in the case law. The *Charter* prohibits discrimination (section 15) based on the following specific grounds: race, national or ethnic origin, colour, religion, sex, age, mental and physical disability. But the question arises of how far protection should be extended to analogous (similar) grounds, such as sexual orientation being subsumed under the ground of sex.[41] Black and Smith[42] found that the interpretations of section 15 differed among the justices at the Supreme Court of Canada, depending upon how narrowly section 15 was limited to the enumerated and analogous grounds, and depending upon the application of section 1. The scope of the notion of equality relates in part to the values of the judge. For example, a provincial court judge in Ontario[43] recently accepted native spirituality as grounds for acquittal of a young aboriginal adult charged with manslaughter, in the belief that the young man was defending himself against an evil spirit. This has been called a legal precedent that will affect the notion of equal treatment of aboriginals in the justice system.

On gender issues the Supreme Court in 1993 ruled that the rights of male prisoners to privacy and life, liberty, and security are not violated by body-frisking or cell searches by female guards, even though male guards are prevented by policy from doing this with female inmates. The Court said prison inmates cannot expect much privacy, and that female guards are not as intrusive for men as male guards are for women.[44]

Section 15(2) allows for laws, programs, or activities that have as their objective the amelioration of conditions of disadvantaged individuals or groups, including those disadvantaged because of race, national, or ethnic origin, colour, religion, sex, age, or mental or physical disability. In 1994, the Supreme Court[45] decided that businesswomen cannot deduct child care expenses from their income tax (in the same manner that business people, still predominantly men, can deduct lunches as an expense). The Court identified the appellant as a wealthy entrepreneurial lawyer and not part of a disadvantaged group under section 15(2) of the *Charter*. This selective protection may be too narrow an interpretation of the intention of the drafters of the *Charter*. It is interesting to note that in 1989, the Supreme Court had decided that a white, Oxford-educated, male, United States citizen was a member of a disadvantaged group, namely non-citizens, and was illegally discriminated against on the grounds of national origin by the British Columbia Law Society.[46]

In 1997, Ontario's Court of Appeal[47] found that the government did not discriminate when it handed over huge profits from a native-run casino solely to status Indian bands and not also to Metis and other non-status bands. The aim of the casino was to benefit one disadvantaged group at the exclusion of another as allowed by section 15(2).

Differential treatment in citizenship provisions between children born abroad of Canadian mothers, who were required to undergo a security check and oath, and those of Canadian fathers, who were not required to undergo the same procedures, was determined to violate section 15 and was therefore invalidated.[48] In *Thibaudeau v. Canada (Minister of Revenue)*,[49] the Supreme Court ruled 5-2 (split on gender lines) that child support payments to recipients, mainly women, are taxable and are tax deductible to payers, mainly men, on grounds that the scheme gives more money to children overall. It had been argued that this tax law placed an unfair burden on low-income women. Although the Court found against Mme. Thibaudeau, a Quebec single parent social worker, the Federal Government in response closed the legal loophole in subsequent 1996 budget provisions[50] and in guidelines for judges in setting child support amounts in divorce actions.

The Supreme Court recently decided on the issue of segregating children with disabilities within the school system. It held that the segregation of a girl with cerebral palsy in a wheelchair into a special class was not a violation of section 15, arguing that the issue must be viewed from the position of the child and not the parents, and that segregation can be both protective and violative depending on the person and the nature of the disability.[51] Then the Supreme Court also ruled that the British

Columbia government's refusal to provide sign language interpreters for deaf people receiving medical services violated section 15.[52]

One area that supports the editors' earlier contention that, in many instances, judges interpret the law based on their personal value system, is that of recognition of equal rights for persons of same sex sexual orientation. In 1993, the Supreme Court in *Mossop v. Secretary of State for Canada*[53] ruled that "family status" in the *Canadian Human Rights Act* protections did not include homosexual relationships. There was no section 15 argument made. In June 1994, Ontario's proposed amendments to protect homosexual status and family benefits were defeated in the Legislature. In May 1995, the Supreme Court of Canada delivered two key rulings which support traditional views of the family. In *Egan and Nesbit v. The Queen*,[54] it agreed 5-4 that the federal government is justified in denying spousal pensions to homosexual couples if it supports traditional heterosexual marriage, even though it was also decided that the *Charter* prohibits discrimination against homosexuals. In a third case, the Court ruled it was discriminatory to deny insurance benefits to common law (heterosexual) couples, a type of relationship that has long been deemed acceptable. So the Court left it to politicians to update policies as they think fit. Federally, the furthest Parliament has gone in bringing about change was to add sexual orientation to the list of prohibited grounds for discrimination under the *Canadian Human Rights Act* in 1996 in response to a section 15 *Charter* challenge,[55] after which the Treasury Board agreed to abide by the decision of a Canadian Human Rights Tribunal (see below) to provide medical and dental benefits to partners of gay and lesbian employees. In a recent arbitration case[56] in British Columbia, the province was ordered to grant 12 weeks parental leave to the lesbian partner of a woman who had given birth. The definition of "spouse" under the *Family Relations Act of British Columbia* was recently amended[57] to include same sex partners for the purposes of child and spousal support.

The framework for the application of section 15 is too comprehensive to present in detail here. Briefly, the Supreme Court[58] identified the test as determining:

a)   whether there was denial of equality or equal protection and benefit,

b)   if denial, was it with discrimination and unfair (not affirmative action), and

c)   was this a reasonable limit under section 1 of the *Charter*.

Interest groups who have a special point of view on a particular case may apply, with or without the support of the litigant, for special standing as an "intervenor." In May 1991, in what appears to be the first time section 15 has been deemed to cover low-income people, the Federated Anti-Poverty Groups of British Columbia was allowed standing in court to represent poor women on welfare who were obliged to assign their maintenance rights against spouses over to the provincial government for recovery. This power was removed from the then *Guaranteed Available Income for Need Act* (now *British Columbia Benefits (Income Assistance) Act*),[59] and is now optional for the welfare recipient.

Thus *Charter* decisions reveal both specific and general principles. These are not always straightforward but are viewed in the context of section 1. How judges apply this context is crucial but not always predictable. One thing that is clear is that the *Charter* has raised the importance of the judiciary and their ideologies in the context of our legislative system.

OTHER HUMAN RIGHTS LEGISLATION

In addition to the *Charter*, human rights are referred to in a variety of other statutes and codes ranging from international protocols to federal and provincial legislation.

I. The *United Nations Declaration of Human Rights*[60]

The *United Nations Declaration of Human Rights* is a founding document of human rights principles for a group of signatory countries, including Canada. Its major limitation, however, is that it is not a "law" and is not legally enforceable. Article 25 states: "Everyone has the right to a standard of living adequate for the health and well-being of himself [sic] and his family . . .," but this principle remains only an ideal. Across Canada, rates for income assistance continue to be substantially less than accepted poverty levels.[61] This probable violation of Article 25 could conceivably be the subject of a complaint to an international human rights court. However, assuming a court could define the concept of "adequacy" here, enforcement of any finding and court order could be done only through diplomatic channels.

One important Canadian example of this process is helpful. Sandra Lovelace of the Tobique Indian Reserve in New Brunswick complained to the United Nations Human Rights Committee at The Hague when Canada's highest courts upheld a provision in the pre-Charter Indian Act that allowed men and women to be treated unequally. The Committee decided that the *Indian Act* violated the Equal Protection Article 7 of the *Declaration* and unfairly discriminated against the applicant. International pressures forced Canada to amend its *Indian Act* after much controversy and delay. Thus, although the *U.N. Declaration* does not have the force of law, its principles can often be heard expressed in the courts as persuasive moral arguments.

A *Convention on the Rights of the Child*[62] has been approved by the United Nations General Assembly. It is questionable whether the federal and provincial laws that deal with Canadian children and the resources provided by our governments really do uphold the principles in that *Convention*.[63] For example, Article 27.1. reads: "States Parties recognize the right of every child to a standard of living adequate for the child's physical, mental, spiritual, moral and social development." Article 27.3 continues: "States Parties, in accordance with national conditions and within their means, shall take appropriate measures to assist parents and others responsible for the child to implement this right and shall in the case of need provide material assistance and support programmes, particularly with regard to nutrition, clothing and housing." The facts are that in British Columbia family income assistance levels fall well below accepted poverty lines[64] and many families with children are unable to find adequate housing.[65] The federal anti-discrimination act prohibits discrimination on grounds of family status, (British Columbia has recently added this ground to its *Human Rights Code*), but many provincial statutes that cover housing (other than federal projects) in Canada do not take this principle into account. The reader should note that a more detailed description of child and youth rights is contained in Chapter 14.

Until there is the political will to incorporate these principles into both federal and provincial legislation and provide effective enforcement mechanisms, these United Nations principles will remain simply ideals. Nevertheless, helping professionals should be aware of the potential for these international principles to be used as moral arguments in negotiating with governments and other agencies for more appropriate resources.

II. Federal and Provincial Human Rights Acts

In contrast to the *Charter*, which applies only to activities between governments and private individuals, federal and provincial human rights acts also regulate behaviour of individuals, such as employers and landlords. The federal and provincial governments each have legislation that prohibits discrimination by the government or by individuals on specific grounds within particular spheres of jurisdiction. The following material describes the important distinctions between federal and provincial acts in their spheres of operation, prohibited discrimination grounds, limitations, and complaint and resolution mechanisms.

A. *Canadian Human Rights Act*[66]

1. Provisions

The *Canadian Human Rights Act* is the federal statute that provides protection against discrimination in the services provided by all federal government departments, crown agencies, and corporations. These may be external services to the public at large or internal services or procedures for federal employees. Helping professionals, in particular, may be involved with the following federal departments: the Ministries of Health and Welfare (pensions), Employment and Immigration (immigrant, refugee, and employment insurance issues), Indian and Northern Affairs, Canada Mortgage and Housing, Solicitor-General of Canada (R.C.M.P., penitentiary, and parole issues), National Defence, and Veterans Affairs. Private institutions under federal regulation such as banks, airlines, and railway companies are also covered by this legislation.

Eleven types of discrimination are prohibited under this statute:

discrimination based on race, national or ethnic origin, colour, religion, age, sex, (including pregnancy and childbearing), sexual orientation, marital status, family status, a criminal conviction for an offence that has been pardoned, and physical and mental disability (including dependence on alcohol or drugs). (section 3 (1))

No one can use these reasons to discriminate in dealings under federal jurisdiction in the areas of employment, the provision of goods and services, and the purchasing or renting of accommodation. Harassment on these grounds, including sexual harassment, is also prohibited. For example, women cannot be refused credit at a bank because of their marital status. Federal housing projects cannot refuse to accept persons because of their religion, and the R.C.M.P. cannot refuse to hire people because of their ethnic origin. However, in the case of employment, discrimination is permitted if based upon a *bona fide* occupational requirement.

In the denial of services, facilities, or accommodation, there must be "a *bona fide* justification for that denial or justification" (section 14(g)). One illustration of this occurred in the immigration case of *Anvari v. Employment and Canada*.[67] An Iranian person with a spinal condition was refused landed immigrant status on the grounds that his health problems would cause excessive demands on health services. The Federal Court ruled that these health services were customarily available to the general public and this immigration ruling amounted to discrimination on the prohibited ground of refusing to provide a service based on a disability. There was no evidence of any excessive demands to constitute a *bona fide* justification. In another case, a cook was fired from his job with a Canadian Pacific Rail gang when it was discovered he was HIV positive.[68] A tribunal found that his condition did not detract from any *bona fide* occupational requirement, and therefore found discrimination based on disability. Any tribunal or court will consider the total context in determining whether the facts justify discrimination. Helping professionals or advocates should assist complainants to take action whenever job requirements or justification appear to be an excuse for unreasonable discrimination.

A tribunal has the power to stop a government agency from applying a discriminatory law. Several women were denied employment insurance benefits because they worked for companies that were largely owned by their husbands. A tribunal found the provision to be discriminatory on the ground of sex and ordered the women to be paid the benefits, plus a thousand dollars each for their self-respect. Although the Government appealed, neither the Federal Court of Appeal nor the Supreme Court of Canada would agree to interfere with the tribunal decision.[69]

2. Limitations

Several important grounds of potential discrimination are not protected by the *Canadian Human Rights Act*. An unemployed person may be refused housing since neither occupational nor economic status is a prohibited ground. Similarly, federal government employers might be able to discriminate on grounds of political affiliation (when it is not part of a job requirement) since this is also not prohibited.

One form of "positive discrimination" is not limited by the *Act*. Special programmes, often developed by helping professionals to assist disadvantaged groups, are protected under this *Act* as they are under the *Charter*.

3. Remedies

Complaints can be directed to the Canadian Human Rights Commission, which has offices in Ottawa and most provincial capitals. In British Columbia the phone number is listed in the Federal Government section entitled Human Rights Commission in the Blue Pages of the phone book.

The Commission has the following powers:

a) to investigate, enter, and search premises with a warrant from a judge of the Federal Court;

b) to inspect documents;

c) to appoint a conciliator to settle the complaint; or

d) to establish a Human Rights Tribunal.

A Human Rights Tribunal hearing must follow the procedural fairness and due process requirements outlined in Chapter 1. If the complaint is substantiated, the tribunal may order the discriminator to end the practice, adopt special measures to prevent discrimination reoccurring, such as establishing programmes to correct unfairness or producing a plan to correct discriminatory practices, and to compensate the victim (for lost wages, for instance) and/or provide the opportunities that were being denied. The tribunal may also order payment of up to $5,000 to the victim if the discrimination was willful or reckless, or if the victim has suffered with respect to feelings or self-respect as a result of the practice. Appeals can be made to a Review Tribunal or to the Federal Court.

B. The *Human Rights Code of British Columbia*[70]

1. Provisions

The *Human Rights Code of British Columbia* (changed from *Human Rights Act* in 1995) prohibits specific discrimination in areas of provincial jurisdiction, and resembles the federal act in many ways. The relevant areas of provincial jurisdiction are accommodation, service or facility "customarily available to the public," purchase of property, renting or leasing of premises, and employment (including employment advertisements). The grounds for prohibited discrimination are similar to the federal act with some important exceptions.

2. Limitations

Because the grounds for prohibited discrimination vary slightly with each area, each section will be examined individually. Race, colour, ancestry, place of origin, religion, marital and family status, physical or mental disability, and sex (gender) and sexual orientation are the standard prohibited grounds in all the areas. It is interesting to note that sexual orientation protection now exists in all provincial human rights legislation except in Alberta, Prince Edward Island, Newfoundland and North West Territories.

In the areas of accommodation, service, or facility customarily available to the public (section 8), the grounds of discrimination on the basis of age, political belief, and economic status are conspicuously absent. Thus, under this *Act*, one could not complain about a restaurant that banned high school children at lunch times (and did not use the indirect method of imposing a minimal charge). Since that time, the limited-age protection of between 45-64 in the *Act* (intended to protect the middle-aged job applicant) has been invalidated on the grounds that it was too narrow and violated the equality provisions of the *Charter*.[71] As a result, the definition of "age" in the *Act* was amended in 1992 to mean 19 years and over and less than 65. This still violates the *Charter* in that other ages are not covered, or are absent altogether from section 8 (discrimination in public facilities). Consequently, the British Columbia Human Rights Commission has stated it will investigate all age-related discrimination complaints.

The interpretation of the phrase "accommodation, service or facility customarily available to the public" is important. For example, not until 1993[72] was it clear that a university education was such a service and was, therefore, not restricted to a privileged class, namely university students, which would have prevented the *Human Rights Code* from applying to universities.

The same gaps in protection apply to the purchase of property or the rental of housing or apartments (sections 9 and 10). In accommodation cases, landlords are allowed to discriminate against tenants if the potential tenants are to share sleeping, bathroom, or cooking facilities with the landlord. An amendment in 1992 allowed apartment buildings to accept only residents over 55 years of age, thus discriminating on the basis of age and family status, where every rental unit is reserved for this age group.[73]

In the area of employment (section 13), the grounds of age, political belief, and conviction for an unrelated criminal or summary charge are added to the standard prohibitions. The exemption of occupational requirement (described in the *Canadian Human Rights Act*) also applies here. For instance, obesity has been deemed a disability which was found not to interfere with the requirements of a warehouse job.[74]

Job requirements themselves can be discriminatory. A British Columbia Ferries condition that a captain had to be able-bodied was overturned when it was shown that a paraplegic applicant possessed the necessary skills for the position. Discrimination may not be found, however, if the requirement is necessary and applies to an occupational group as a whole. Thus a court decided that the religious rights of a school custodian who was a Seventh Day Adventist were not violated when he was required, contrary to his religious beliefs, to work some Friday night shifts, as were all custodians in the school district.[75] However, when an Alberta dairy failed to accommodate the religious beliefs of an employee "up to the point of undue hardship" to the company, the court determined there was religious discrimination.[76] The employer must make every effort to accommodate diversity in its workforce. In June 1994, this principle of reasonable accommodation was affirmed by the Supreme Court of Canada. The Court ruled that employers must make reasonable accommodation for minority workers; in this case the school board should reimburse three Jewish teachers for lost pay when taking time off to celebrate the religious holiday of Yom Kippur.[77]

In addition to determining fair requirements for jobs, employers need to develop mechanisms to review how relevant a criminal record may be to a specific position. Many social service agencies are requiring criminal record checks before hiring. Helping professionals themselves may be subject to discrimination when applying for jobs working with vulnerable clients. One example involved a graduate from the University of Victoria School of Social Work who was denied a child welfare position by the provincial ministry because of a past criminal record. A tribunal awarded compensation when relevancy was successfully disputed because it found that the Public Service Commission did not have a fair way to determine the issue of relevancy.[78]

The 1984 enactment of the British Columbia *Human Rights Act* (now *Code*) altered the original concept of prohibiting all unreasonable discrimination, which had been the hallmark of the previous *Human Rights Code*. Consequently, gaps have emerged, such as a lack of protection for economic status, lifestyle, and language. Only progressive tribunal interpretations, which, for example, have extended the definition of sex to include pregnancy and sexual harassment protection, can adequately cover new situations.

A recent report entitled *Human Rights for the Next Millennium*[79] has just been released by the Human Rights Commission of British Columbia. The report contains several recommendations for amendments to the *Human Rights Code*. These recommendations include amending the definition of age in the *Code* to "19 years or more" so that people over 65 (which was the previous upper limit) are protected from discrimination. This definition of age applies to prohibit discrimination in accommodation, services, and facilities. It should be noted that, despite public requests to the contrary, this recommendation does not cover persons under 19. However, the Commission did recommend that all provincial legislation affecting those under 19 should be examined in the light of the *United Nations Convention on the Rights of the Child*.[80] Age and family status are recommended for inclusion as prohibited grounds for discrimination in the purchase of property, although an exemption is allowed for seniors-designated (55 and over) residential buildings, as currently exists for rental properties. In the report the Commission indicates it will conduct the necessary research to determine if mandatory retirement adversely affects women and to what extent further changes to the *Code* may be necessary.

Other important recommendations include amending the *Code* to prohibit discrimination on the basis of gender identity, and on the basis of pregnancy for life or employee insurance, retirement, and pension plans. The Commission also recommended amendments to protect poor people generally and suggested that the appropriate wording is protection from discrimination based on "social condition," which has been judicially interpreted to include people in receipt of income assistance, as well as single women and single mothers. If this recommendation is not implemented, the Commission recommends protection from discrimination based on "lawful source of income." This means for instance that a landlord could not discriminate against a tenant just because the person is on employment insurance. Another suggested amendment prohibits any request by employers for information from a job applicant about a prohibited ground of discrimination, unless needed for a special program or needed for legitimate purposes once the person has been hired. Individuals who refuse, have refused, or will refuse to contravene the *Code* are protected from retaliation by such persons as employers.

Most provincial legislation includes a major exemption to anti-discrimination provisions. A charitable, philanthropic, educational, or religious organization, not operated for profit, can grant preference to an identifiable group of persons and therefore discriminate on a prohibited ground if its primary purpose is to promote the welfare of such a group.[81] The organization's actions, however, must be consistent with its goals. For example, The Yukon Order of Pioneers was ordered not to discriminate against women on the ground that males were not the only pioneers. However, this ruling was reversed in 1996 by the decision of the Supreme Court of Canada,[82] which split along gender lines. Likewise, if an organization offers a public service, then the prohibitions apply. A Legion hall in Alberta that banned a Sikh wearing a turban at a private banquet was found to have discriminated on religious grounds under Alberta's *Individual Rights Protection Act*. Since membership rules were not enforced and the hall had been rented out, a tribunal determined that the function amounted to a public service.[83]

3. Remedies

Complaints to the British Columbia Human Rights Commission can be filed up to only one year after the alleged discriminatory incident unless there are exceptional extenuating circumstances. Third party complaints by persons not directly affected are allowed, though the Commission may refuse to deal with it unless it is satisfied that the person alleged to have been discriminated against consents, or that proceeding is in the interest of the group on behalf of which the complaint is made. The complaint process and tribunal powers are similar to the federal mechanisms. The investigator may try to resolve the issue through mediation before resorting to a hearing. Provincial offices can be accessed by toll-free lines; the phone number is available in the Blue Pages of the phone book under the heading of "Human Rights Commission" in the Provincial Government section. In British Columbia $2,000 is the maximum amount of damages payable to a victim for injury to feelings, dignity and self-respect, in addition to possible compensation for direct losses (such as wages). The alleged discriminator can be directed to undergo remedial training, such as attending a course on "sexual harassment prevention" for managers.

COMMON QUESTIONS

1. <u>To which jurisdiction should one turn to determine whether a human rights violation has occurred?</u>

The different jurisdictions described above can be confusing. The Ombudsman or Human Rights Complaint office can provide direction. In summary, the *Charter*, which applies to the government at all jurisdictional levels covering legislation and government dealings with individuals or groups, focuses on rights and freedoms violations. The federal and provincial *Human Rights Acts* cover allegations of discrimination in the specific areas of public services, housing, and employment, and thus may involve private individuals as well as government officials. The federal act applies only to federal government agencies or services. All other services in the areas listed above fall under the provincial human rights acts.

2. <u>Does legislation protect pay and employment equity?</u>

Only partly. Provincial acts prohibit unequal wages for the same work. The notion of work of equal value is mentioned in the *Canadian Human Rights Act* and in Ontario's recent pay equity laws. Section 11 of the federal *Act* states that it is discriminatory to establish or maintain differences in wages between male and female employees who are working in the same establishment and who are performing work of equal value, unless discrimination is based on a reasonable factor (except gender). This applies to the federal sector within the same workplace. The Canadian Human Rights Commission has proposed that active implementation of pay equity be mandated during contract bargaining. Ontario's legislation requires that a variety of public and private sector employers establish plans to gradually implement pay equity within specific time frames. In other provinces, some public service employers such as school boards have established individual plans. But only wholesale provincial and federal laws that mandate pay equity will ever reduce the wide gap between male and female wages. (The 1989 Employment Equity Report[84] shows that among federal employers, women earned a percentage of male wages ranging from a low of 55.9% in the banking sector to a high of 79.8% in the communications sector. Statistics Canada in 1995 confirmed an average of 70%, which had slipped 2% over the previous two years.)

The federal *Employment Equity Act*[85] (1986, revised 1995) is intended to ensure that key groups long under-represented in the workplace get a fair opportunity at jobs and promotions. These groups are women, visible minorities, persons with disabilities, and aboriginal peoples, and the *Act* applies to the Federal public service, Crown corporations, and federally-regulated private sector employers with 100 or more employees. Each employer must prepare an annual report, available to the public, examining the four groups, identifying and removing barriers, and establishing goals to improve their representation.

The *Act* has resulted in an increase in the hiring of women in federal public service to 47.4%, which is similar to the availability rate. However, this number is skewed by traditionally female dominated clerical jobs, as indicated in the Annual Report of the Canadian Human Rights Commission (1995).[86] Visible minority representation has also improved in certain sectors, but except for banking, not at the managerial level. Persons with disabilities made only questionable gains, falling short of their availability within the Canadian workforce, and not achieving much more representation than in 1987. Aboriginal people similarly lacked significant progress, adding up to only one third of availability, with high resignation rates, and predominance in manual and clerical operations and in Indian Affairs. With visible minorities, persons with disabilities, and aboriginal people, increased self-identification may actually inflate gains.

3. <u>What remedies are available for rights violations?</u>

Remedies are either court-based or complaint-based. Court remedies include the following:

a) an application to the Supreme Court of the province (or Federal Court for that jurisdiction) for violation of *Charter* rights under section 24; a *Charter* violation may constitute a defence or invalidate evidence in a criminal case, as discussed earlier;

b) subsequent appeals;

c) an application for a writ of *habeas corpus* (for violations of liberty);

d) an application for judicial review for alleged unfair process;

e) a civil action in tort for damages (see Chapter 13); and

f) an initiation of the criminal process (see Chapter 1) by reporting the allegation to the police or pursuing a private prosecution for an alleged crime.

Complaint-based remedies may be internal or external. Internal procedures include the following:

a) complaints to administration and supervisors;

b) internal investigative procedures, such as those of the Corrections Inspectorate Branch or the Director of Family and Child Service; or

c) internal appeal routes, such as police complaints or unemployment insurance and income assistance appeals.

External procedures include the following:

a) complaints to outside investigative bodies such as the Ombudsman, the Human Rights Council of British Columbia, the Federal Privacy Commissioner, or to the appropriate Member of Parliament. Some Legislatures have Standing Committees on Human Rights where public briefs can be discussed; and

b) professionals who violate rights may also be subjected to disciplinary (internal) or ethical (external) consequences. Complaints should be referred to the Boards of Registration of the profession concerned.

The various complaint mechanisms may have different outcomes. Only courts or quasi-judicial bodies such as welfare appeal or human rights tribunals can make orders that are legally enforceable. Others, notably the Ombudsman, can make recommendations only. A lawyer is a useful source of advice to determine the most appropriate avenue for complaint.

4. <u>What are the common misconceptions in rights issues?</u>

Commonly assumed rights may not be rights in law. A right must impose a corresponding duty to allow or enforce that right. For example, the public may assume that every child has the right to an appropriate education. Yet providing an individualized education program for special needs children is not necessarily a school board's legal obligation or duty. Rights to services remain at the discretion of the governmental authority.

Because the law is dynamic, interpretation of human rights can change. Courts and tribunals may apply them to new situations that are not always anticipated. During the House of Commons debates on the *Charter* in 1981 prior to its enactment, the then Prime Minister, the Right Honourable P.E. Trudeau stated,[87] "the *Charter* does not say whether abortions will be easier or more difficult to practice in the future. The *Charter* is absolutely neutral on this matter." But eight years later, the Supreme Court of Canada[88] struck down the abortion procedure in the *Criminal Code* as violating the right to security for women and breaching the principles of fundamental justice in section 7 of the *Charter*. Furthermore, not all rights are permanent. Aboriginal fishing and hunting rights, for example, can be extinguished by sale or treaty, although the Supreme Court of Canada has ruled that they continue to exist until legally terminated.[89]

Rights are not absolute. The *Charter's* section 1 on reasonable limits allows for flexible application, but *Charter* human rights and fairness principles are being increasingly used as a standard for professional practice.

Helping professionals are in a unique position to observe social service agency's policies and practices, and attempt to ensure that they accord with these principles. Unfortunately, many professionals are often afraid to complain for fear of repercussion by their employer. The *Human Rights Acts* and some statute-mandated complaint mechanisms such as the Ombudsman contain clauses that protect against reprisals. Some legislation also allows third party complaints with the victim's consent. Making a complaint in the name of a union or professional association is one further way of providing some anonymity and protection.

It should be recognized that other legislation pertinent to professional practice may address specific rights and remedies. For instance, the *Young Offenders Act*[90] (see Chapter 8) provides young persons charged with crimes with the right to the least interference with their freedom consistent with the protection of society. The chapters on child protection, adoptions, mental health, the physically and mentally disabled, and on family violence and the criminal process also mention some specific rights.

5. <u>What other resources are available to assist victims of human rights violations?</u>

Victims can often feel disempowered, their self-esteem damaged. Knowledge of rights and processes need to be coupled with support and advocacy skills to assist clients to pursue a complaint. Victims of violations require information, advocacy, emotional support, and financial assistance in pursuing their complaints. The first three functions are often provided by volunteer groups, such as human rights coalitions, civil liberties associations, agencies for the disabled, the poor, or visible minorities, or advocacy centres often found in politicians' community offices or in law centres. For example, the Canadian Arab Federation supported the complaint to the Ontario Human Rights Commission of a 10-year-old girl sent home from school for wearing a pro-Palestinian T-shirt.[91] These groups can usually be located through a community services information line or through the Yellow Pages of the phone book. Government agencies may also provide support services through their human rights branch or ombudsman offices (in the Blue Pages).

Legal advice may be essential for many victims. Each province is responsible for setting its own legal aid criteria. In British Columbia a special budget category (known as a tariff) was established to fund complaints under the *Human Rights Code*. But because of financial priorities, legal aid for human rights complainants in the province has been restricted to the provision of a lawyer only when the Human Rights Commission investigator has determined that there should be an Inquiry or Tribunal hearing. This means that many complainants will not get legal advocacy or assistance in formulating their complaint and presenting evidence to the investigator, which is a serious flaw in the process.

Federally, the Court Challenges Program[92] provides some financial assistance to disadvantaged groups pursuing *Charter* cases mainly in areas of federal jurisdiction, but also more recently in some provincial cases. An Equality Rights Panel and a Language Rights panel of appointed members decide which equality or linguistic rights cases meet the funding criteria.

CONCLUSION

This chapter has briefly outlined the major components in human rights legislation, along with their key provisions and limitations. This information, together with the answers to some common questions, should assist the helping professional to monitor his or her practice and social programs, both to avoid violations of human rights and fairness principles, and to promote a more respectful and egalitarian society.

In the views of activist helping professionals, the *Charter* and *Human Rights Acts* have failed to live up to their promised purpose of equal protection for all. The mixed package of results on human rights coverage confirms the view that law remains an instrument of oppression for the wealthy and privileged, is sexist, and homophobic. Others are more optimistic about what social progress law can achieve, given time.

Nevertheless, despite limitations, the *Charter* and human rights legislation are developing an increasingly important profile, establishing a standard of conduct for government legislation and activities. This new focus on human rights will have a strong impact on current and future professional practice.

RESOURCES

The Canadian Human Rights Reporter (C.H.R.R.) reports legal judgments on human rights from Canadian courts and tribunals.

T. Berger, *Fragile Freedoms, Human Rights and Dissent in Canada* (Toronto: Clarke, Irwin, 1982).

Equality and the Charter: Ten Years of Feminist Advocacy before the Supreme Court of Canada, Women's Legal Education and Action Fund, (LEAF), (Toronto: Edmond Montgomery Publications, 1996).

D. Gibson, *The Law of the Charter: Equality Rights* (Toronto: Carswell, 1990).

E. Kallen, *Ethnicity and Human Rights in Canada* (Toronto: Gage, 1982).

B. Landau, ed., *Children's Rights in the Practice of Family Law* (Toronto: Carswell, 1988).

F. S. Seidle, ed., *Equity and Community: The Charter, Interest Advocacy and Representation* (Montreal: The Institute for Research on Public Policy, Renouf Publishing, 1993).

D. Turner, *Holding Governments Accountable for Children's Rights: The Canadian Experience* (Victoria: The Society for Consumer and Public Education, University of Victoria School of Social Work, 1990).

END NOTES

1. *Canadian Charter of Rights and Freedoms*, Part I of the *Constitution Act*, 1982, which is Schedule B of the *Canada Act* 1982 (U.K.), 1982, c. 11.
2. The federal statute is the *Canadian Human Rights Act*, R.S.C. 1985, c.H-6. and each province has its own statute for provincial jurisdiction. In British Columbia, it is the *Human Rights Code*, R.S.B.C. 1996, c.210.
3. *Universal Declaration of Human Rights*, 1948, U.N. Doc. A/811. Subsequent addenda focusing on particular aspects of rights are also important to consider, such as the *Declaration of the Rights of the Mentally Retarded* (1971), the *Covenant on Economic, Social and Cultural Rights* (1966) and the *Convention on the Rights of the Child* (1989).
4. *Constitution Act*, 1982, formerly the *Canada Act* 1982 (U.K.), 1982, c. 11.
5. See K. Adachi, *The Enemy that Never Was: A History of the Japanese Canadians*. (Toronto: McClelland and Stewart, with the Multiculturalism Program, Secretary of State for Canada, Supply and Services, Ottawa, 1991).
6. *Narcotic Control Act* R.S.C. 1985, c. N-1: *Controlled Drugs and Substances Act*, 1996, S.C. c. 19.
7. *Smith v. The Queen* (1987), 1 S.C.R. 1045 interpreting the *Narcotic Control Act*, R.S.C. 1985, c.N-1.
8. *Steele v. Mountain Institution* 25 S.C.R. 1385.
9. *Swain v. The Queen* (1991), 1 S.C.R. 993.
10. *Criminal Code*, R.S.C. 1985, c.C-46.
11. *Morgentaler, Scholing and Scott* (1989), 44 D.L.R. (4th) 390 (S.C.C.).

12. *Supra*, note 9.

13. *Taylor v. Canadian Human Rights Commission* (1990), 3 S.C.R 892; *R. v. Keegstra* (1990), 3 S.C.R 697.

14. Reference re sections 193 and 195.1(1)(c) of the *Criminal Code* (1990), [1990] 1 S.C.R. 1123.

15. *Canadian Newspapers Co. v. Canada (Attorney General)*, (1988), 2 S.C.R. 122.

16. *Edmonton Journal v. Alberta (Attorney General)* (1989), 2 S.C.R. 1326.

17. *Rocket v. Royal College of Dental Surgeons of Ontario* (1990), 2 S.C.R. 232.

18. *Winnipeg Child and Family Services (Northwest Area) v.G. (D.F.)* (1997) 3 S.C.R. 925 The quote is attributed to Madame Justice Beverly McLachlin for the majority.

19. *R. v. Bishop O'Connor* (1996) 4 S.C.R. 411. The Federal Government has announced they intend to introduce legislation to more clearly define the issue of relevance that the courts must use as a criterion.

20. *M(A) v. Ryan* (1997) S.C.C.D. 260 30.72 30.

21. See K. Bushby, "Supreme Court decisions on the use of personal records in sex assault cases: What it means for women." (Toronto: Leaf Lines (1996) Spring 4, Vol. 7 No. 1).

22. *R. D. S. v. The Queen*, heard by Supreme Court of Canada, September 26th, 1997, reported in Canadian Press, Times Colonist, September 27, 1997, p. A10.

23. *McKinney v. Board of Governors, University of Guelph* (1990) 3 S.C.R 229; *Stoffman v. Vancouver General Hospital* (1990) 3 S.C.R.483.

24. *Douglas College v. Douglas/Kwantlen Faculty Association* (1990) 3 S.C.R. 570.

25. *Irwin Toy Ltd v. Quebec* (A.G) (1987); *Rothman,* For details see T. Clarke, *Silent Coup: Confronting the Big Business Takeover of Canada,* (Ottawa: Centre for Policy Alternatives, Lorimer and Co., 1997), pp.108-112.

26. *An Act to amend the Charter of the French Language,* S.Q. 1988 c. 54, section 10.

27. *Government of Saskatchewan v. Employees Union Dispute Settlement Act* (1986) S.S.C. 111, preamble and s. 9(2). The preamble states "whereas as section 33 of the Canadian Charter of Rights and Freedoms exists for the purposes of permitting publicly accountable legislators to finally determine essential economic and social policy . . ."

28. See A. Petter, "Legitimising Sexual Inequality: Three Early Charter Cases" (1989) 34 McGill L.J. 358.

29. *Sylvano v. British Columbia* (1987), 16 B.C.L.R. (2d) 113 (S.C.).

30. L.E.Trakman, *Reasoning with the Charter* (Toronto: Butterworths, 1991) p.13.

31. *R. v. Brydges* (1990) 53 C.C.C. 3.

32. This section was developed with the valuable assistance of Dr. Mary Ann Murphy, at the School of Social Work, University College of the Okanagan, Kelowna, British Columbia.

33. *R. v. Askov* (1990) S.C.C. 1199.

34. *Seaboyer v. The Queen; Gayme v. The Queen* (1991) 2 S.C.R. 577.

35. *R. v. Williams*, reported in Victoria Times-Colonist, October 9, 1996.

36. *R. v. Butler* (1991) 1 S.C.R. 452.

37. See *Equality and the Charter: Ten Years of Feminist Advocacy before the Supreme Court of Canada.* Women's Legal Education and Action Fund, (LEAF), (Toronto: Edmond Montgomery Publications, 1996).

38. *R. v. Evans* (1996) 1 S.C.R. 8.

39. *R. v. Stillman* (1997) S.C.C.D. 260.30.44.

40. *Lavigne v. Ontario Public Services Employees Union* (1991) 2 S.C.R. 211.

41. In *Haig v. Canada* (1992) 10 C.C.R. (2nd) 287, the court ruled that the *Canadian Human Rights Act* violated the equality section of the *Charter* by omitting sexual orientation as a prohibited ground for discrimination.

42. For a discussion of the concept of equality and its interpretation, see W. Black and L. Smith, "The Equality Rights," in W. Tarnopolsky and E. Mendes, eds, *The Canadian Charter of Rights and Freedoms* (3rd Edition), (Toronto: Carswell 1997).

43. *R. v. Jacko*, Provincial Court, Gore Bay, Ontario, reported in Canadian Press, Victoria Times Colonist, May 30th 1997.

44. *Conway v. Solicitor General of Canada* (1993) 2 S.C.R. 872.

45. *Symes v. Canada* (1993) 4 S.C.R. 695.

46. *Andrews v. Law Society of British Columbia* (1989) 1 S.C.R. 143.

47. Reported in The Canadian Press, Victoria Times Colonist, June 7th 1997.

48. *Benner v. Canada Secretary of State* (1997) S.C.C.D 170 42.20.

49. *Thibaudeau v. Canada (Minister of National Revenue)* (1995) 2 SCR 627.

50. New tax rules and support guidelines were implemented as Bill C41, given Royal Assent in February 1997. The new tax rules apply only to orders made on or after May 1st 1997.

51. *Eaton v. Brant County Board of Education* (1997) S.C.C.D. 170 42.

52. *Warren and Eldridge v. Province of British Columbia*, reported in Canadian Press, Victoria Times Colonist October 10th, 1997.

53. *Mossop v. Secretary of State for Canada* (1993), 1 S.C.R. 554. For more information in this area, see J.Yogis, R. Duplak, and J.R.Trainor, *Sexual Orientation and the Law: An Assessment of the Law Affecting Lesbian and Gay Persons,* (Toronto: Edmond Montgomerey Publications, 1996).

54. *Egan and Nesbit v. The Queen in right of Canada et al* (1995), 2 S.C.R. 513.

55. *Haig v. Canada* (1992), 10 CCR (2nd) 287.

56. *Gold v. Province of British Columbia*, reported in Victoria Times Colonist, July 16th, 1997.

57. *Family Relations Amendment Act*, Bill 31, July 1997, reported in Victoria Times Colonist, July 16th, 1997.

58. This test and several other principles were enunciated in *R. v. Turpin* (1989) 1 S.C.R. 1296 and *Andrews*, supra, note 46.

59. *British Columbia Benefits (Income Assistance) Act*, R.S.B.C. c. 27, 1996 proclaimed spring 1997, section 15.

60. *Universal Declaration of Human Rights*, Resolution 217A(III), December 1948. This has been supplemented by further covenants on economic, social, cultural, and political rights.

61. National Council on Welfare, *Poverty Profile 1995* (Ottawa: Supply and Services, Spring 1997).

62. United Nations Resolution. *Declaration on the Rights of the Child*. U.N. General Assembly, December 1989.

63. See D. Turner, *Holding Governments Accountable for Children's Rights: The Canadian Experience*. (Victoria: The Sedgewick Society for Consumer and Public Education, School of Social Work, University of Victoria, 1990).

64. See M. Goldberg, *Regaining Dignity: An Examination of Subsistence Costs and Adequacy of Income Assistance Rates in B.C.* (Vancouver: Social Planning and Research Council), 1989.

65. Vancouver Island Human Rights Coalition, *Children's Rights to Adequate Housing*. (Victoria: unpublished, 1987).

66. *Canadian Human Rights Act*, S.C. 1976-77 (2d Sess.), c. 33.

67. *Anvari v. Employment and Immigration, Canada* (1989), 10 C.H.R.R. D/5816 (Canadian Human Rights Tribunal).

68. *Fontaine v. Canadian Pacific Ltd.* (1990), 11 C.H.R.R. D/288 (Canadian Human Rights Tribunal).

69. Human Rights and the Canadian Human Rights Commission: *Equality . . . We all have a Hand in it*, Booklet by the Commission (1996, Ministry of Supplies and Services, Ottawa), p. 16.

70. *Human Rights Code of British Columbia*. (1996) R.S.B.C. c. 210.

71. *Sniders v. Nova Scotia (Attorney General)* (1988), 10 C.H.R.R. D/5785 (N.S.S.C.A.D.).

72. *University of British Columbia v. Berg* (1993), 2 S.C.R. 353.

73. *Human Rights Code*, R.S.B.C. 1996, c. 210, section 8.

74. *Hamlyn v. Cominco Ltd.* (1990), 11 C.H.R.R. D/333 (B.C.H.R.C.). Diabetes and hepatitis have also been accepted as disabilities in *Hutchison v. British Columbia* (1990), 12 C.H.R.R. D/241 (B.C.C.H.R.) and in *Trudeau v. Chung* (1991), 16 C.H.R.R. D/25 (B.C.C.H.R.) respectively.

75. *Renaud v. Board of School Trustees* (S.D. 23 Central Okanagan), (1989), 11 C.H.R.R. D/62 (B.C.C.A.).

76. *Alberta (H.R.C.) v. Central Alberta Dairy Pool* (1990), 2 S.C.R. 489.

77. *Syndicat de L'Enseignment de Champlain v. Commission Scolaire Regionale de Chambly* (1994) 2 S.C.R. 525.

78. *Iwanchuk v. Her Majesty the Queen in Right of B.C.* as Represented by Ministry of Human Resources (1987) B.C.H.R.C. 76 (B.C. Human Rights Council Decisions).

79. *Human Rights for the Next Millenium: Recommended BC Human Rights Code Amendments for British Columbians by British Columbians*, (Victoria: British Columbia Human Rights Commission, January, 1998)

80. *United Nations Convention on the Rights of the Child.*, Resolution of the United Nations General Assembly, December, 1989.

81. *Human Rights Code*, R.S.B.C. 1996, c. 210, section 24.

82. *Gould v. Yukon Order of Pioneers* (1996), 4 S.C.C. 571.

83. *Singh v. Royal Canadian Legion, Branch 255* (1990), 11 C.H.R.R. D/357 (Alta. Board of Inq.).

84. *Equity Report, Employment and Immigration Canada*. (Ottawa: Ministry of Supply and Services, 1989).

85. *Employment Equity Act*, S.C.1995, c.44.

86. Annual Report (1995) Canadian Human Rights Commission, Ministry of Supply and Services, Ottawa, Canada 1996.

87. Debates of the House of Commons, 1981, 675.
88. *Supra*, note 11.
89. *R. v. Sparrow* (1990), 1 S.C.R. 1075.
90. *Young Offenders Act*, R.S.C. 1985. c.Y-1.
91. Reported by Canadian Press, Victoria Times Colonist, July 1990.
92. Court Challenges Program, Winnipeg, Manitoba.

Chapter 3

CHILD PROTECTION AND THE LEGAL PROCESS

David Turner and Max R. Uhlemann

INTRODUCTION

Child abuse has continued to confront the public as a serious social problem in Canada. While helping professionals have long been involved in this controversial area, they have often been criticized for either failing to act on allegations or for reacting too precipitously. The dilemma of how to respond to suspected child abuse and neglect situations affects all helping professionals, not just child welfare workers. For example, helping professionals such as physicians can be prosecuted for failure to report their abuse suspicions to the appropriate child protection authorities as the law demands.

This chapter outlines the essential knowledge of law, the legal system, and legal issues in child welfare. Helping professionals can use this information to prepare their clients to face what can be an intimidating investigation and court process. In addition, this knowledge will help professionals avoid becoming unwittingly vulnerable at law.

We begin with a brief discussion of some current issues in child welfare, then move on to questions of common concern to all helping professionals. Practical implications will be illustrated by child welfare examples. The discussion will take a western Canadian perspective, focusing primarily on British Columbia. The law is stated as of April 1, 1997.

CURRENT ISSUES

Callahan[1] identifies three differing perspectives on child welfare in Canada: residual, institutional, and radical.

a) According to the residual perspective, the state intervenes to limit parents' powers and responsibilities only as a last resort when children's lives are threatened or the level of care is well below community standards.

b) The institutional view sees the child welfare process and services as part of the normal social services offered by a caring society. All children should have basic opportunities for full development, with those in special need having a right to additional services.

c) The radical perspective is a conflictual view of law (as described in Chapter 1), arguing that the child welfare system is designed to control families and children, usually the poor, "who might otherwise embarrass those in power or seriously threaten the status quo in Canadian society."[2]

These positions reflect the competing value systems that can clash in the arena of child welfare, a clash that is particularly evident in the tenuous balance between state intervention and family integrity. The relevant legislation of each province incorporates aspects of these values.

British Columbia's *Child, Family and Community Service Act*[3] (hereafter referred to as *CFCSA)* with its limits on services to children, seems to take a residual point of view combined with a more institutional approach in defining the rights of children. However, it confines those rights only to children in the care of the Ministry for Children and Families (the director of Child, Family, and Community Services, to be legally correct). Its child-centered focus, together with an advocacy service in complementary legislation to support child rights, could be described as more radical, at least in principle. The *Act* in practice remains residual perhaps for fiscal and resource reasons rather than lack of political will. In Canada as a whole, child and parental rights have been generally downplayed.[4] The radical view could describe the issues from the *Mount Cashel Inquiry*[5] in Newfoundland, where complaints against the religious order of sexual abuse of boys were ignored. But it is the political context that leads public support to swing between extremes of for and against parent or adult rights, and for and against social worker intervention. In the late 1980s and early 1990s, across North America there developed a backlash against what has been perceived as an overly interventionist approach that has ignored the rights of unjustly accused parents.[6] The notorious *Cleveland Inquiry*[7] in northern England, where numerous children were taken into local authority care on the basis of dubious medical evidence, was fueled by the same concerns. However, recent child deaths such as that of Matthew Vaudreuil in British Columbia have resulted in a stinging critique of the lack of intervention by social service and medical personnel, resulting in the high profile *Gove Inquiry*[8] and recommendations for substantial legislative (hence modifications to an *Act* are already being developed) and child welfare system reform.

The challenge for the legal system and the child welfare process in particular is to balance these competing interests. Helping professionals must be knowledgeable about legal aspects of child welfare and of rights if they are to play an effective part in a service delivery that respects that balance.

Another continuing debate has developed around the model of the child protection process itself, where several different models currently exist. In some Scandinavian countries, an informal panel of community representatives and child experts meets to determine the child's needs. However, in Canada, the child welfare system of adjudication is court-based and legalistic, lacking direct community involvement (apart from the judge, although the new *Act* in British Columbia allows for community involvement in planning and delivery of services), and remaining lukewarm on child rights issues. Some jurisdictions are piloting alternate dispute- resolution models[9] that focus on mediating the issues between parents and child or between the ministry and families. These processes have nevertheless been criticized for failing to take into account the legal rights of the parties, though the type of model of mediation used can determine whether this happens or not.

Ideally perhaps, Canada should develop a hybrid model that mandates services for all children, balances the rights of all interested groups, and provides a community connection for the child welfare court. Canada's evolution into an increasingly diverse society culturally makes community involvement in the system very important in determining community standards. British Columbia's previous child protection legislation did allow for community representatives to sit as advisors to the judge, although this mechanism was rarely used.

A final issue involves the provision of both preventive and support services to families and children. Across Canada, the delivery of these services remains at the discretion of the child welfare authority. Parents and children can only request, not demand, assistance. In British Columbia, the ministry often contracts out services such as group homes, child care workers, and homemakers to the voluntary and private sector, a situation that raises potential problems of accountability for standards. Though the ministry is accountable to the Ombudsman, Child Advocate, and courts for the actions of its contractors, contracting out services can make monitoring more difficult. Both governments and community agencies need to promote the establishment of even more effective child welfare services that will support a fairly well-developed court process, and ensure that the service system is fully funded and accountable.[10]

ESSENTIAL KNOWLEDGE OF LAW AND PROCESS

Helping professionals should be familiar with the following aspects of child welfare law and process:

a) the basic information on law and the legal system, especially the civil nature of child welfare;

b) the social context of child welfare;

c) the jurisdictional responsibility for child welfare;

d) the guiding principles;

e) what constitutes abuse or neglect;

f) the obligations to report suspicions of need for protection;

g) the stages in the legal process; and

h) the rights and duties of the persons involved.

A discussion of these subjects follows.

I. Basic Legal Knowledge

It is assumed that the helping professional is now familiar with the information contained in Chapter 1. In particular, understanding the court system, how to read a statute, regulations and policy, and being clear about the civil nature of child welfare is important. Child welfare cases are handled by means of a civil (as opposed to a criminal) law process. Nevertheless, an action to protect the child does not preclude other legal actions such as criminal prosecution, a civil suit (in tort), or disciplinary consequences (see Chapters 7 and 13). The civil character of this process has several implications for clients and for helping professionals.

First, in British Columbia, a civil action to protect a child is pursued by the director of Child, Family and Community Service within the Ministry for Children and the Family. In some provinces, a private agency (such as Metro Toronto Children's Aid Society) acts on behalf of a child. Parents or guardians may contest this application for a court order, but the all-important child is not, in law, a direct party to the action. Under the *CFCSA*, the child can now be made a party to the action by order of the court.

Second, the civil standard of proof, a determination "on the balance of probabilities" that the child is in need of protection, is the standard applied by the court. In a criminal trial the standard of proof is the more onerous "beyond a reasonable doubt." Thus it is possible for a parent to be acquitted of a criminal charge of assaulting the child while, at the same time, a child welfare court finds that the assault took place and the child requires protection. It should also be noted that in child welfare court criminal sanctions cannot be placed on the abuser. A judge may only impose conditions upon parents as a prerequisite for returning the child to their care. Nevertheless, some commentators believe that the involvement of a state agency and the grave consequences that can result from a child welfare hearing give it "quasi-criminal" qualities. Judges' decisions, however, have confirmed its civil nature. Section 66 of the *CFCSA* states that a hearing is civil in nature, that it may be as informal as a judge may allow, and that it must be held at a different time or place than criminal matters.

Third, the child welfare court is a more informal setting, usually located as a branch of the Provincial (first level) Court. In most provinces, the child welfare courts are public, yet child confidentiality is closely guarded. Rules of evidence are not nearly as strict as in criminal courts, although a contested child welfare hearing can still be an intense, adversarial process. Learning how to give credible evidence (see Chapter 16) is a crucial skill for child welfare workers and any other professionals who deal with families and children in this arena.

II. The Social Context of Child Welfare

Child welfare laws are designed to protect children from harm. The State as represented by an agency is empowered to intervene to protect children who are at risk or where minimal standards for acceptable parenting or care have been allegedly violated. This interventionist legislation is clearly social control, so this power is utilized by the State under strict conditions of process that are intended to protect the rights of the child and of relevant adults. Drastic action such as removal of the child is always reviewed by the courts.

The volume of complaints requiring attention across Canada is steadily increasing. In the year ending August 1994, the then Ministry of Social Services in British Columbia received 27,400 complaints citing neglect most frequently, followed by physical and sexual abuse. About 25% of children are considered to be at risk, 40% are determined to require no service and others are referred for assistance or subject to further monitoring. More than 7000 children are in care, with approximately 5500 admitted annually. In the United States a study[11] by the Department of Health and Human Services stated that from 1986 to 1993, the number of abused and neglected children doubled from 1.4 million to 2.8 million. Children from families with an annual income under $15,000 US were 22 times more likely to experience maltreatment than those from families averaging $30,000 US.

The debate continues as to why this increase is happening. Frequent themes include structural issues of society, such as the increasing poverty of many families with children, the disempowerment of families, limited access to supportive resources, the emotional stress on the contemporary family, the shift from a child-focussed community, and the publicity that selected high profile cases of neglect and abuse receive in the media, with the resultant increased reporting of suspicions.

Child welfare is a pressured system, with its performance and budgets under surveillance by politicians, the public, and media. Its focus is often reactive to political priorities and sensitivities. Yet, because demands require a large child welfare bureaucracy, the system may not shift as fast as some of the public would wish. This volatile context means that helping professionals such as social workers and others who commit themselves to this important function must be able to work effectively within a highly scrutinized legal and political environment.

III. The Importance of Jurisdiction

Child welfare is a provincial responsibility. This means that laws and processes can vary between provinces that have slightly different definitions of abuse and different legal steps, timeliness, and possible court process outcomes. There are also commonalities, which will be identified in the coming discussion. The child welfare process in British Columbia is established by a provincial statute entitled the *CFCSA*.[12]

Jurisdiction is an important issue in native child welfare. Natives on reserves are under federal jurisdiction and the federal government funds most of their services, yet the provinces are responsible for all child welfare services. This confusing overlap has resulted in a crucial gap in services. This gap is starting to be bridged, however, now that many native bands are entering into agreements with the provinces to take over their own child welfare programs (see Chapter 4).

IV. Guiding Principles

Most child welfare statutes contain a statement of basic philosophy. Themes include supporting family autonomy and integrity (as in Ontario's and Manitoba's child welfare legislation), least disruptive alternative (Alberta and Ontario), continuity and stability for the child (Manitoba, Quebec, and British Columbia), prevention and family support (Quebec, Manitoba, Alberta, New Brunswick, and Ontario), and special provisions for First Nations aboriginal children (British Columbia and Ontario).[13]

In British Columbia, the *CFCSA* sets out the guiding principles explicitly in section 2. The Gove Commission reaffirmed that "the safety and well being of children are the paramount considerations," and the statute was amended to reflect this.[14] Other principles include that:

a) children are entitled to protection;

b) a family is the preferred environment for the care and upbringing of children and responsibility for protection rests primarily with the parents;

c) support services should be provided to family if it can provide a safe and nurturing environment with available support services;

d) the child's views should be taken into account;

e) kinship ties and a child's attachment to the extended family should be taken into account;

f) the cultural identity of aboriginal children should be preserved; and

g) decisions relating to children should be made and implemented in timely fashion.

So, while these principles are subservient to the ultimate importance of the child's safety and well-being, there is nonetheless considerable deference paid to the importance of the family and to the potentially constructive role of the family in the child's life. Many provinces have moved toward legislation premised on the principle that where it is safe, or can be made safe to do so, the child should be maintained in an intact family unit. Such statutes typically recommend voluntary services, such as childcare or home support, to try to enhance the family as a safe environment for the child.

Service delivery principles contained in section 3 include that families and children be informed of decisions and encouraged to participate, that services should be sensitive to the needs and cultural, racial, and religious heritage of recipients, that the community should be involved in planning and delivery of services, and aboriginal people should be involved in services to aboriginal children and families. Principles of integration "wherever possible and appropriate with services provided by other ministries and community agencies" and "involvement of the community in the planning and delivery of services, including preventive and support services to families and children," have now been incorporated in recent legal amendments.[15]

V. Definition of Neglect and Abuse

As we shall see, the Ministry can voluntarily provide services to children voluntarily to prevent neglect and abuse. However, a key stage in the child welfare process begins when a child is found to be in need of protection as legally defined. The definition in law is crucial. Consult the *Act* for the accurate wording. Section 13(1) and (2) of the *CFCSA* gives an expanded definition of when a child is "in need of protection" to include when a child has been or is likely to be physically harmed, sexually abused, or exploited by the child's parent, or by another person if the child's parent is unwilling or unable to protect the child. Also included is when a child has been or is likely to be physically harmed because of neglect by the parent or emotionally harmed by the parent's conduct. Section 13(2) defines that a child is emotionally harmed if he/she demonstrates severe anxiety, depression, withdrawal, or self-destructive or aggressive behaviour, and a causal connection with the parent's conduct can be established. Other circumstances include when a child is deprived of necessary health care, or the child's development is likely to be seriously impaired by a treatable condition where parents refuse to provide or consent to treatment. Again, where there is no adequate provision for the child's care, if the parent is unable or unwilling to care for the child, if the parent is dead or the child has been abandoned, then a child is in need of protection. This also involves when a parent is unable or unwilling to resume care after the end of a care agreement with the ministry or another person. Similarly, when a child is absent from home in circumstances that endanger the child's safety or well-being, the child is also in need of protection.

A "child" in British Columbia is defined as anyone under 19 (18 in Alberta and most other provinces). Courts and social workers have been struggling to assess what factors endanger safety or well-being, particularly in the last category of "absence from home." Many teens live on the streets in most Canadian cities. Is homelessness or prostitution alone enough to constitute endangerment? Obviously, it depends on the context and on the value judgments of the workers. According to Cruickshank,[16] these fairly broad definitions do not limit state intervention sufficiently. The definition of emotional harm may be too wide, making it difficult to link the child's disturbance to parental conduct. Others see it as too limiting. Alberta has an even more elaborate definition. Its *Child Welfare Act* defines "emotional injury" as "impairment of mental or emotional functioning evidenced by a mental or behaviourial disorder." The *Act* requires that there are reasonable and probable grounds to believe emotional injury can result from (among other things) rejection, deprivation, exposure to domestic violence, inappropriate criticism or threats, or from the mental or emotional condition of the guardian, or chronic alcohol or drug abuse of anyone living in the same residence as the child.[17]

The professional in contact with a family will need to identify and record any such evidence in the event that it may be required by a court. Legal issues cannot be separated from practice. In his child welfare practice the first author found that a hand-held tape recorder was very useful for documenting any observations immediately after an interview. Those professionals centrally involved in this field need to have access to practical information and strategies that take into account the legal arena.[18]

The definition of "child" in British Columbia has been interpreted by the courts to include a foetus and has extended the notion of "in need of protection" to include anticipatory neglect.[19] The British Columbia Supreme Court supported the actions of a social worker who apprehended (removed) a baby born addicted to his mother's Methadone habit, even before the mother had an opportunity to care for the child herself. However, in 1988, the court ruled against an attempt by the Superintendent (now director) to apprehend an unborn foetus whose mother was risking her child's safety by refusing a caesarian section. The Superintendent's powers were determined to be restricted to living children.[20] The rights of the unborn have long been debated but rarely used to infringe upon the mother's freedom (see Chapter 2).

VI. The Obligation to Report Suspicions of Need for Protection

According to section 14 of *CFCSA*, it is the legal duty of all persons to report immediately to the responsible agency (director) situations in which they have reason to believe that a child needs protection or has been, or is likely to be, physically harmed, sexually abused, or sexually exploited by a parent or other person. This is arguably a lesser test than reasonable grounds to believe, and so puts a serious obligation upon all persons. Helping professionals need especially to be aware of this obligation. Many professionals, especially in medicine and the church, are unaware that this legal obligation to report overrides any duty of confidentiality and protection of privilege, except that between a lawyer and a client. In British Columbia, both failure to report and the making of a false report knowingly constitutes an offence (punishable by a fine of up to $10,000 and/or up to six months in prison).

The obligation is discharged by reporting the situation directly to the appropriate authority. In British Columbia, this authority is the director of Child and Family Services or designate, whose delegates are social workers in the Ministry for Children and Families. It is not sufficient, for instance, for the admitting physician of an emergency ward to mention a child's suspicious injuries to the hospital's social worker.

Child abuse crisis phone lines (in British Columbia known as the Helpline: Zenith 1234) are common across Canada and provide fast connection to the appropriate authority. These lines are open evenings and weekends, when children are often most at risk.

Many people fear reporting because they believe that their suspicions may be unfounded, their complaint will become public knowledge, or a report will put the child at further risk. People reporting are protected from civil action unless they knowingly reported false information. It is the policy of child welfare investigators to keep complainants' identities confidential unless the investigator is obliged to divulge. A complainant's identity might have to be revealed, for example, when she/he is a crucial witness to the allegation and is subpoenaed to give evidence in a contested child welfare (or criminal) trial.

An interesting example occurred in Victoria, British Columbia, where the court upheld this basic principle of anonymity. A couple against whom a complaint had not been substantiated tried to have the British Columbia Supreme Court order disclosure of the complainant's identity so that they could launch a civil suit for false or malicious reporting.[21] The court denied their application.

While this chapter focuses on the child protection process, it is important to identify the several ways children in British Columbia can be brought into the care and protection of the director of Child and Family Services. There are three main routes:

a) voluntarily, upon private agreement with parents or guardians;

b) automatically upon the death of both parents or guardians under legislation (in British Columbia, the *Family Relations Act*);[22] or

c) under the removal provisions in the child welfare statute.

A brief description of these three mechanisms follows.

A. Private Agreements

Parents or guardians often seek the temporary assistance of the child welfare authority in caring for their children. This might arise when a parent is incapacitated for a short time, perhaps upon admission to a hospital, or when special care is required for a needy child. In British Columbia, the director has the discretion (the power but not the obligation) to provide short term, time-limited care, with the parents' consent. Section 6 speaks to these written voluntary care agreements, indicating parents may give to the director or delegate "as much of the parent's authority as guardian of the child's person as is required to give effect to the agreement." Parents usually retain their legal powers over the child's education, religion, discipline, and medical treatment, and can terminate the agreement at any time. The director must take into account the child's views where possible, explain the effect of the agreement to the child, and consider whether there is a less disruptive way of assisting the parents to look after the child, such as providing services in the home,[23] and whether the agreement is in the child's best interests. The agreement must include a description of the plan of care, including where the child will be placed, a promise by the director to keep the parents informed and involved in decisions affecting the child, and a promise by the parents to maintain contact with the child. Initial agreements cannot exceed three months for children under five, and six months for others. They may be renewed for a further nine months only for children under five, fifteen months for children under twelve and 21 months if over twelve.

Should a parent refuse or be unable to resume custody at the end of the agreement, unless the agreement is extended, the child is regarded as needing protection (after a grace period of 30 days in British Columbia) under protection provision in section 13(1).

The director may also make agreements with parents of a child with special needs, or with persons who have established a relationship or have a cultural or traditional responsibility toward the child. This recognizes such persons as grandparents, extended family, aboriginal elders, and formal and informal foster parents. Section 9 allows for agreements of up to six months to be made with youths who need assistance (residential, educational, and other services) and who cannot be re-established in their family or have no parent or other person willing to care for them. The services to be provided and the goals to be met by the youth must be identified. These agreements expire on the youth's 19th birthday but can be extended to the age of 24 if the youth received such services earlier and are intended to assist with an educational, vocational-training, or rehabilitative program.

B. Death of Parents

When parents or guardians die suddenly without naming a guardian in a will, a provision in British Columbia's *Family Relations Act* provides that their children automatically come into care. This is done to ensure that there is no hiatus in care for or guardianship of a child. Parents, of course, should be encouraged to prepare a will naming a guardian so that their wishes for the child's future will be known and respected. Although a will is not an ironclad guarantee, it will be respected unless the child care authorities have other concerns about the child's welfare.

C. The Child Protection Process

The third way of bringing children into care is under court order through the process defined by provincial statute. This process has several stages with which helping professionals should be familiar. Most provincial legislation has some similar components. The process in British Columbia will be described next in more detail.

VII. The Stages in the Legal Process

This section will describe the stages in the formal legal process of child protection. Before this, however, a comment on preventative measures employed by governments is necessary.

All child welfare legislation contains some preventative provisions to ameliorate the conditions that might increase the risk to children and families. In British Columbia, income assistance, child care, homemaker, respite care, and family support services may be provided at the discretion of the ministry under the *British Columbia Benefits (Income Assistance) Act*, formerly the *Guaranteed Available Income for Need Act, and Regulations*.[24] The ministry, under section 93 *CFCSA*, also provides grants to communities to assist agencies in providing some preventative assistance to families and children, youth support services, and family dispute resolution services. They may enter into agreements with aboriginal bands and communities for the provision of child welfare and preventative services (see Chapter 4). The legislation also allows special services such as counseling, in-home support, parenting programs, and support for children who witness family violence to be provided to specific families under written agreements.[25] This allows service without removal of the child where safety can be assured.

In British Columbia, there are seven stages in the protection process for bringing a child into care. These stages are illustrated below in Figure 1. Their legal implications are listed below and each stage is then discussed.

    Stage 1: Report
    Stage 2: Investigation
    Stage 3: Decision to remove
    Stage 4: Presentation hearing
    Stage 5: Protection hearing
    Stage 6: Court decision and order
    Stage 7: Implementation and review

A. Stage 1: Report

A "report" is a complaint received by the ministry that a child is believed to be in need of protection. It will be recalled that all persons, whether they be relatives, neighbors, or professionals, are under an obligation to report whenever they believe that a child is in need of protection. These reports are received by social workers on duty at a local Ministry for Children and Families, in the district where the child is presumed to reside. The information is usually obtained over the phone, with the worker noting the specifics on an intake sheet/computer. The complainant's statement may turn out to be pivotal evidence in a court decision. This information is used to determine the initial urgency and veracity of the report. Professionals who report need to give details that are as full and accurate as possible, to enable the worker to make an informed decision, especially concerning any immediate risk to the child's safety. A parent's request for assistance with a child may also be viewed as a report.

It is interesting to note that, unlike emergency calls to the police, these telephone complaints are not usually audio-recorded. This could cause concern when a call comes in from a confused or distressed person or a young child.

B. Stage 2: Investigation

Section 16 of the *CFCSA* requires the director to assess the information from a report, and the director may then offer support services to the child and family, or refer them to a community agency,

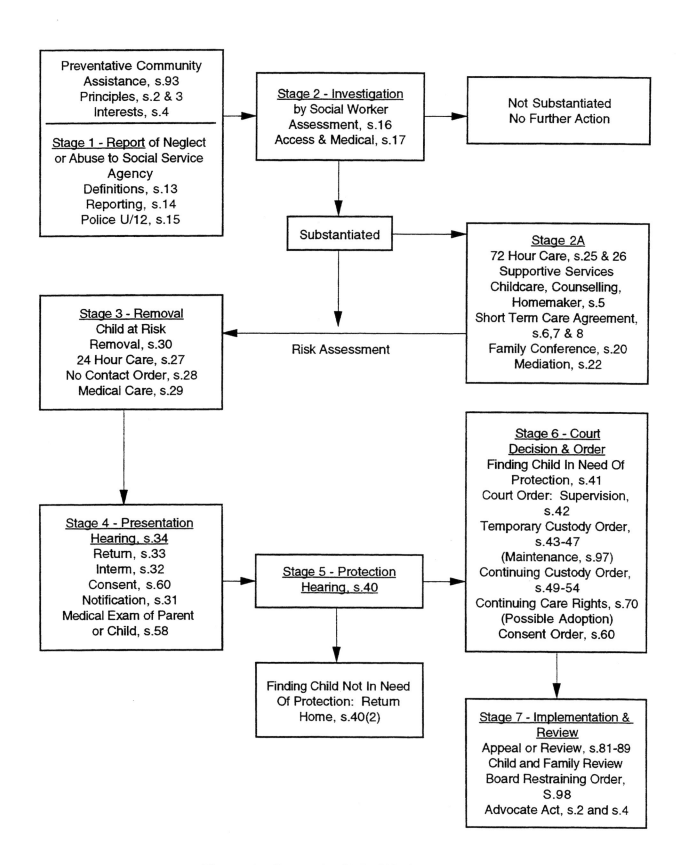

Figure 1. Stages in Child Welfare Process

or investigate the need for protection. Although the discretion as to whether to launch a formal investigation is limited by the principle that the health and safety of the child is the paramount consideration, some critics are arguing that there should be a mandatory obligation to investigate all complaints except those blatantly frivolous or malicious.

Consistent with its guiding principles, the *CFCSA* sets out a continuum of possible responses to child abuse or neglect. The continuum moves from less intrusive family support and assistance provisions through to increasingly more intrusive interventions up to and including removal of a child. Those working with the *Act* now have alternatives steps available to them in circumstances where formerly they would only have been able to apprehend or remove the child. For example, social workers frequently receive complaints about unattended young children. Sometimes there are extenuating circumstances, as when child care arrangements did not work (in one case the babysitter fell asleep, allowing the infant to wander). The ministry has the power to care for children in the child's own home. Section 25 gives a director[26] the opportunity to care temporarily for a child or to place a homemaker on the premises for up to 72 hours where that child is found without adequate supervision. If the family resumes care of the child within 72 hours no further steps are necessary. If the family does not resume care then the director may proceed to formally remove the child[27] and thus initiate the court process. The director can also take charge of lost or runaway children for up to 72 hours under section 26 of the *Act*, without triggering the formal court process that accompanies legal removal. This can allow return the of child to the parents or repatriation to another jurisdiction. The court can in some circumstances authorize required health care for a child without the necessity for the child to be removed into the director's care.

An investigation involves the initial collection of evidence through a search of records and interviews with the child and other key persons. Its purpose is to determine whether the alleged abuse or neglect has in fact occurred, and whether the child's safety risk is sufficient to warrant immediate removal of the child or the alleged abuser. If the allegation is one of sexual or physical abuse, policy in the Interministry Child Abuse Handbook[28] establishes protocols directing the social worker to contact the police about an appropriate investigative procedure. Although this might be initially confusing and intimidating for the inexperienced professional and other participants, criminal law enforcement authorities need to be involved at this stage to avoid the contamination of evidence, especially in potential criminal proceedings. Independent yet coordinated investigations by the social worker and police will then likely take place.

The director is obliged to make reasonable efforts to report the result of the investigation to the parent and complainant, and also to the child if she/he is capable of understanding the information. This does not apply if it would cause physical and emotional harm to any person or endanger the child's safety or if a criminal investigation is contemplated.

Assessment of the circumstances will dictate the specific process. The social worker will normally begin the investigation by checking personal and other agency records for past "founded" allegations. Then every effort will be made to see the child separately from the alleged abuser in sexual or physical abuse allegations and to arrange an immediate medical examination as necessary. Under section 7, the director or social worker as delegate has the power to seek a court order to enter premises by force if necessary and to authorize a medical examination, if access to a child is denied. The court can order disclosure of a child's location and warrants can be obtained in person, by telephone or other means (fax, electronic mail). A police officer who has reasonable grounds to believe that the "child's health or safety is in immediate danger"[29] may without a warrant enter premises, a vehicle, or a vessel, take charge of the child, and take the child to a director or his/her delegate for up to 24 hours for investigation. Throughout the province, the ministry has social workers on duty or accessible after regular office hours. A director has similar powers of entry as discussed below under removal.

While the *CFCSA* identifies circumstances that constitute when children are in need of protection, these may not always be explicit. The Interministry Child Abuse Handbook and various authors[30] have identified possible indicators of the need for protection, but it would be precipitous for the professional to conclude that any single factor indicates abuse or neglect. For instance, all parents when confronted by the authority of a worker to remove the child will normally display anxiety and fear, which might be interpreted as hostility or cover-up. Investigation must be done carefully, using medical and other expert help. A worker assumes a serious responsibility when accumulating the evidence necessary to convince a court that a child is in need of protection. The end goal, however, is that the child's safety should not be compromised. On the basis of a reasonable belief of risk, the worker may decide to remove the child and continue the investigation.

School principals and teachers often have difficulty balancing their roles as substitute parents against their participation with an investigative team. Most school boards have developed protocols for interviewing children in school. The social worker and police usually have authority to see the child alone without a school staff member present.

The *CFCSA* has incorporated several innovative ways to resolve disputes over the need for protection or the child's plan of care without having to resort to litigation, or as a support to the court Chart process. Mechanisms in the *Act* facilitate the use of family and community resources. Section 20[31] creates the "family conference" but is not yet in force. This is a process that is intended to provide parents, relatives, and others with a forum to help create a "plan of care" to protect the child. In other jurisdictions the family conference has been used with great success and has been particularly effective as a tool to reduce state involvement by enlisting extended family as a resource to help care for children. This provision is consistent with the principle expressed at section 2(e) of the *Act* that kinship ties and a child's attachment to the extended family should be preserved if possible.

Where possible, issues relating to the care of children should be resolved collaboratively. In section 22 the *Act* provides that the director and any persons who are unable to resolve an issue relating to a child may agree to mediation or other alternative dispute resolution mechanisms as a means of reaching an agreement.[32] These processes may avoid the need for removal of the child. Alternately, where court has been invoked, the court may adjourn a proceeding and suspend the running of time-frames for a period of up to three months to allow mediation or a family conference to proceed. Except in limited circumstances, a person must not disclose or be compelled to disclose information obtained in mediation or a family conference.[33]

C. Stage 3: Decision to Remove Child

Section 30 authorizes the director to remove a child without a court order when there are reasonable grounds to believe the child needs protection, when the child's health and safety is in immediate danger, or when no other less disruptive measure that is available is adequate to protect the child.

"Removal" is a legal term for when a social worker, believing a child is in need of protection, decides to employ the formal legal procedure of removing a child from the custody of the parents or guardian. This decision is one of a range of several options, which include taking no further action, providing supportive or remedial services, or arranging for voluntary monitoring. The worker is responsible for making the decision with consultation from a supervisor whenever possible. However, only a social worker with statutory powers conferred by the director as his/her delegate in a "Letter of Authority" can remove a child. Other social workers may receive the report, but without this authority, they can neither investigate nor remove. The director must "promptly make all reasonable effort to notify" each parent of the removal and where practicable in writing and with a statement of reasons.

Temporary protections include having the police arrest suspects for an alleged crime against a child, or imposing no-contact terms in bail provisions (see Chapter 7). The director may also apply to a court for a protective intervention order if there are reasonable grounds to believe that contact between a child and another person would cause the child to need protection. This can include a prohibition on contact, interference, and residing at or entering premises where the child resides, including at that person's own premises.

Certain interventions can stop short of removal. Unattended, lost, or runaway children may be taken to a place of safety for up to 72 hours until the parent or person responsible resumes custody. This procedure does not amount to removal and does not trigger the court process unless the parent fails to reassume custody and removal becomes warranted.

As mentioned, neither parents nor children have the legal right to alternative services such as homemaker assistance or a child care worker. These services remain at the agency's discretion and are not appealable beyond the administrative level in British Columbia.[34] Professionals need to be able to advise parents of avenues of appeal if they feel that alternative services have been unreasonably withheld. These avenues include the Child, Youth and Family Advocate and the Ombudsman Offices. Information written especially for parents can be useful here.[35] The following example illustrates the possible, though limited, remedies for parents.

A single mother contacted the first author to explain that she had requested help with homemaking and budgeting from the (then) Ministry of Social Services. Instead of granting her request, a social worker had directed her to receive counseling for parenting from a child- and youth-care worker trained, as the mother described it, in a confrontative and exotic model of therapy. She had voiced her objections but had been told to cooperate if she did not want to lose her son. The author directed her to a lawyer, who informed the ministry that her client would not cooperate. Moreover, the lawyer challenged the worker to remove the boy and stated they would be waiting on the courthouse steps, ready to contest. Needless to say, the ministry got the message, changed workers, and provided appropriate service. Also, because the worker in this case appeared to be making an unreasonable use of authority, an ethical complaint was filed with the Association of Social Workers (see Chapter 13). Fortunately, this kind of thing rarely happens. Most workers take great pains to offer supportive services without court intervention where appropriate. Often it is the parents' refusal or inability to utilize services that compels removal.

Removal triggers the formal court process. Sections 33 and 34 state that the director must, within 7 days, attend Family Court for a presentation hearing or present a written report if the child has already been returned to the parent. In the meantime, a child can remain in the interim care of the director who may consent to the child's participation in routine school, social, or recreational activities. If the director consents to health care for the child, the director must if practicable notify the parent who had custody at the time of removal.

An attempt must be made, if practicable, to inform those involved of the date, time, and place of the presentation hearing, which is the next step in the process. This means informing each parent, the child if over 12, the Public Trustee if the parent is under 19, and the appropriate aboriginal organization if the child is aboriginal.

D. Stage 4: Presentation Hearing

At the presentation hearing, the director presents to the court a written report of the circumstances of the removal, information about less disruptive measures considered by the director before removal, and an interim plan of care for the child. If the child is aboriginal, the plan must include the steps taken to preserve the child's aboriginal identity. The court has the jurisdiction to make orders returning the child, either with or without supervision, or retaining the child in the custody of the director. When such an interim order is made, the court must set "the earliest possible date" for a hearing to determine if the child needs protection, and the date for "commencing" this protection hearing must not be more than 45 days after the conclusion of the presentation hearing.[36] If the child was returned home, the director can again remove the child whenever it is believed that the interim order will not protect her/him.

The written report is reviewed by a judge to determine whether the social worker as the director's delegate had reasonable grounds to believe the child was in need of protection. In contested removals, sometimes this mini-hearing can evolve into a "preliminary trial" that examines the worker's grounds for his or her belief, a practice which was not intended by the *Act*. An amendment to the *CFCSA*[37] states that a presentation hearing is a summary hearing and must be concluded as soon as possible. The court is mainly concerned about where the child will reside pending a full hearing.

Even if the child has already been returned to the home, and the director intends to withdraw, the director must present to the court a written report about the reasons for both removing and returning the child. There is some legal debate about whether a hearing rather than submission of a report should be obligatory in all circumstances. It does ensure that all due process of law is followed and is especially important to parents who want a court review of the initial removal. In this presentation hearing, the court can approve the director's actions and grant a temporary (interim) custody order pending a full protection hearing, or return the child to the parent or guardian, with or without agency supervision. A protection hearing would determine whether in fact the child is in need of protection. An example occurring prior to the *CFCSA* will illustrate this distinction between the presentation hearing and the protection hearing.

A teenage girl told a school counselor that her father was beating her badly and showed serious bruises. A social worker was called, the girl repeated the same story, and the worker decided to remove the girl for her protection pending further investigation. Following protocols, the police were involved and, under investigation by detectives, the girl admitted she had concocted the allegation to get out of the home, as her older sister had done. At the presentation hearing, the court upheld the action to remove. The court's ruling was based on the worker's belief that there were reasonable grounds to suspect abuse, even though the belief proved, in fact, to be mistaken. Subsequently, the child was returned home, without further need for a protection hearing. A protection hearing would have been dismissed based on the new facts that she was not actually in need of protection. Therefore, the presentation hearing assesses whether or not the director has reasonable grounds to believe the child is in need of protection, and the full protection hearing looks at the actual facts. Furthermore, if circumstances arise after the removal which amount to grounds for protection, the court may consider them too.

The helping professional may need to assist the parents in recognizing the importance of prompt legal representation to protect their rights and to avoid future delays. For many parents, this right to a lawyer may not be a practical possibility unless they qualify for legal aid. The child also might require a separate counsel if his/her interests conflict with both parents and the ministry.

E. Stage 5: Protection Hearing

The protection hearing is a civil inquiry or hearing to determine whether a child is in fact in need of protection. The social worker has two key responsibilities here. First, the worker must officially serve formal notice of the hearing on all persons who fit the definition of "parent" under the *Act*, on the child if over 12, and on an Indian band representative if the child is registered or is entitled to be registered. This last provision is intended to alert the band so that it can mobilize resources to assist the child in his/her own community, or have the child go into an aboriginal home. It is debatable whether this strategy has actually reduced (especially in the western provinces) the disproportionately large number of aboriginal children coming into care and ending up in non-aboriginal homes. Helping professionals should be aware that culturally selective perceptions may crucially affect the outcome of child welfare decisions.[38] This "notice" is served personally or, with the court's permission, in substituted form (e.g., a newspaper notice).

Secondly, the worker is responsible for marshaling the evidence that is presented to the court by the counsel on behalf of the director. This evidence will be challenged if the issue is contested. Therefore, case preparation is the focus for the worker, who must pay meticulous attention to format as well as substance. The social worker and other professionals may become central witnesses whose testimony and credibility are crucial. Of course, experience with the process will enhance competence in testifying.

A significant innovation occurs at the commencement of the protection hearing. In registries where the docket is crowded, the "commencement" consists of parties being identified, counsel going on the record, certain preliminary documents being filed, and a future date for a full hearing being booked. Rule 2 of the *Provincial Court(CFCSA) Rules*, which came into force on June 3, 1996, provides that where a consent order is not made or where the matter is not otherwise dealt with at the commencement of the protection hearing, there will be a mandatory referral to a judicial case conference. At that case conference, the judge may mediate or otherwise facilitate the resolution of any issues in dispute. In addition to other powers available to the judge at the case conference she/he may, with the consent of the parties, direct a mini-hearing. As a matter of practice these case conferences will typically occur within 30 days and each case conference will last for approximately 1 and 1/2 hours. Experience in other jurisdictions with the case conference in the child protection setting suggests that it can be a fair and effective settlement tool.[39]

The hearing begins with counsel for the director outlining why the child is believed to be in need of protection. If the issue is consented to by the parents, detailed evidence is not usually required, although the judge will want to be sure that parents understand the implications of agreeing to an order. A full hearing of the case, including cross examination, will take place if the matter is contested. The child protection worker will need to collaborate with the director's counsel in assembling and presenting the evidence and witnesses. For example, an application can be made to the court for an order for a medical, psychiatric, or other examination of the child or parent if it will assist in determining the need for protection or the type of court order. As the presence of lawyers in child welfare matters becomes increasingly common, the procedures tend to become more legalistic and issues more frequently challenged.

In British Columbia, the Family Court is public and open. However, the publication of the names and identifying particulars of the child is prohibited unless "disclosure is necessary to ensure the safety or well-being of a child,"[40] such as tracing a missing child. Records have to be kept confidential.

The courtroom is normally small and intimate, which draws attention to the demeanours of the social worker and witnesses alike. Operating in close proximity to potentially hostile parents and adversarial counsel demands exceptional skills from the worker.

The staffing of Family Court is similar to other Provincial Courts, with a judge, opposing counsel, perhaps a Family Advocate for the child, a court clerk, who often serves as a court reporter, and a sheriff to maintain order. Family Court is a court of record, which means all testimony and evidence is recorded and decisions can be documented in published law reports. Transcripts are available for workers and counsel to review the evidence.

F. Stage 6: Court Decision and Order

If a court finds that the child is not in need of protection, the director must return the child to the parent apparently entitled to custody. Once a finding is made that the child is in need of protection within the meaning of the *Act*, the judge has several choices after considering the plan of care presented by the director and after hearing any further evidence.

The judge can return the child home under the supervision of the director. This is done when, in the court's opinion, there is no immediate risk to the child. Supervision provides an opportunity for support and monitoring of the parents' care of the child, and lasts for a maximum period of six months. Conditions recommended in the plan of care (services for parents in the home, day care, or respite care) and the right of the director to visit the child can be specified.[41]

The judge can order the child into the temporary custody of another person under the director's supervision. This is often a relative or friend of the child's family. It is important to note that temporary custody is under the ministry's supervision, and is reviewable at the end of the order.

The judge can order the child to remain in temporary custody of the director for a specified period. Parental rights of consent to health care, education, and religious upbringing, along with guardianship, are transferred to the director for that temporary period of up to three months for children under five, six months for children aged five to twelve, and twelve months for children over twelve. Extensions are allowed if "the circumstances that led to the child being removed are likely to improve within a reasonable time," but maximum periods are 12 months, 18 months, and 24 months for the respective age groups.[42] The court, in an effort to keep parents involved, may agree to their exercising some of these rights unless failure to adequately exercise those rights were the grounds for the initial removal. Parents pay maintenance, albeit sometimes a nominal sum, to the ministry, and may possibly have reasonable access to the child. The child is placed in a child care resource, such as a receiving home, group home, or foster home and a social worker acts as legal parent on behalf of the director.

Finally, the judge may order the child be placed in the continuing custody of the director. Because the permanent extinction of parents' rights is such a drastic step, courts do not normally make a continuing order right away. A temporary custody order is often used first to give the parents an opportunity to try to change their child care skills and behaviours. Section 41(2) states that the court must not make a continuing order unless the identity and location of the parents has not been found after a diligent search nor is likely to be, unless no parent is able or willing to resume custody, or the nature and extent of the harm suffered (or likely to be) is "such that it would never be in the child's best interests to be returned to the parent." In these circumstances the court must make a continuing order. An application for continuing custody can also be made within the last 30 days of the temporary order if these conditions apply. Notice must be given as previously discussed at least ten days prior to a hearing.

The court has the discretion to make a continuing order "if there is no significant likelihood that the circumstances that led to the child's removal will improve within a reasonable time or the parent will be able to meet the child's needs."[43] The court has to consider the past conduct of the parent, the plan of care, and the child's best interests. Past parental conduct was defined in the *Family and Child Service Act*, which preceded the *CFCSA*. It included such factors as a parent's emotional and mental condition; use of drugs or alcohol, and their effect on the child's care; abuse or neglect of any child in the family; the child's feelings towards and emotional ties with the parents; and efforts made by parents to adjust their circumstances for the child to return home, including any continuing contact with the child while in care, the extent of maintenance paid, and other relevant factors. These are not specified in the *CFCSA* but presumably are still indicators of past parental conduct. It is in this area particularly that professionals in health, psychiatric, social work, and child care fields might be expected to give valuable testimony. Prior to making an order, the court will also want to know the worker's plan for the child's future, but the court does not continue monitoring beyond this hearing.

Section 71 says that a director must consider the child's best interests when deciding where to place a child. Priority is to be given to placing the child with a relative or in a location where the child can maintain contact with relatives and friends, in the same family as the child's brothers and sisters, and where the child can continue in the same school. The priority for aboriginal children is to be placed with their extended family or within their aboriginal cultural community or, if safety is an issue, with another aboriginal family.

Helping professionals need to understand fully the status of a child who is the subject of a care order. Unlike the position under a private agreement or unless otherwise explicitly indicated, the social worker has full legal rights over the child, including his/her schooling, religion, discipline, and medical treatment. Although parents' wishes would be considered under a temporary order, they are not normally taken into account under a continuing order. The social worker takes on the position of the parent, acting on the director's behalf. Under a continuing order, the director becomes the sole guardian, and can place the child for and consent to adoption, although under the *Adoption Act*[44] a child over 12 years old must consent to being adopted (see Chapter 5). The Public Trustee becomes the sole guardian of the child's estate (property and money). The custody status does not affect inheritance or property rights. Continuing orders terminate at the age of 19, upon adoption, marriage, or cancellation by the court.

These orders can be made by consent without hearing evidence, under section 60 of the *Act*. The consent must be in writing and before making the order the court must satisfy itself that each person consenting has been advised to consult independent legal advice, understands the nature of the consent, and is consenting voluntarily. It is an important feature of this provision that such orders are made without the court finding that the child needs protection, and without any express or implied admission as to the accuracy of any grounds alleged by the director for removing the child. This provision is presumably premised on the rationale that if the order is sufficient to protect the child, and the director would not agree to it otherwise, then there is no need to find the child in need of protection or to secure an admission from a parent.

The court can also order that a child or parent undergo medical, psychiatric, or other examination to assist in determining whether the child needs protection or which order it should make. The director, through the court, can access relevant records and information in the control of a public body as defined under the *Freedom of Information and Protection of Privacy Act*[45] (see Chapter 12). However, the director must also disclose to the parent in a timely manner the orders sought, the reasons for, and the intended evidence (including a summary of the evidence of each witness).

G. Stage 7: Implementation and Review

Custody orders given to the director or other persons can be enforced by a peace (police) officer, and preventing enforcement amounts to an offence. It is also an offence punishable by a $10,000 fine, six months imprisonment, or both, to violate a protective intervention or restraining order. Under a supervision order, the director has the power to remove a child for a parent's failure to comply, such as refusal to allow visits or access. Removal again triggers a hearing within seven days to determine whether removal was in accordance with the supervision order.

Where circumstances have changed significantly since a supervision, access, or temporary custody order was made, any party can apply to vary (change or amend) the order. The court will consider whether the change is in the child's best interests. A continuing order can also be set aside through an application to the provincial court (Family Division). If it can be shown that the original circumstances for the order have changed significantly, then the matter may proceed to a full hearing.

An appeal is available to the Supreme Court within 30 days, and then with leave (permission) to the Court of Appeal of the province. The *Act* under section 83 has established a Child and Family Review Board of up to 15 members to review any breach of the rights given to children in care under section 70 (see below), or other matters referred by the Minister. In the summer of 1996, the role of the board was questioned politically when it had not received any referrals to examine the recent deaths of children in care. A Commissioner for Children to examine such situations was appointed in September 1996 to work with the Board, and in 1997 was given legislative authority[46] to investigate children's deaths and critical injuries. The Commission can set standards of children's services and internal review mechanisms, such as ensuring they are geographically accessible and responsive to individual needs. Requests for review of complaints can be made by the child, parents, or any representative and the Child, Youth, and Family Advocate. A child or other person who requests a review is protected from reprisals, intimidation, and discrimination.[47] Unlike the Ombudsman and Child Advocate, which are both Offices of the Provincial Legislature, the Chair of the Review Board reports directly to the Minister and Cabinet, where it may have more limited public impact. It is anticipated that the Review Board and Commission for Children may be combined in the near future.

VIII. The Rights and Duties of the Persons Involved

Apart from the procedures already mentioned, parents also have the right to a lawyer and the right to fairness at all stages of the investigation and decision-making process. In British Columbia, for example, a worker returned a child home shortly after removal after realizing a mistake had been made. The Ombudsman admonished the worker for failing to tell the parents about the legal requirement of a report to the court within seven days. The report to court had never been made and the parents were thus denied the opportunity in court to protest their child's removal. Similarly, parents have a right to be notified of the outcome of an investigation, especially when their child might have been interviewed without their knowledge.[48]

In British Columbia, while the child is not automatically a party to a child welfare action, they do have some of a party's rights, such as notice of a court hearing if over 12 years old. However, legal representation for the child is entirely discretionary. The director's purpose is to represent the safety, welfare and best interests of the child, but the action taken and plans developed may be in direct conflict with the child's legal interests and wishes. For instance, the child may wish to reside with a relative of whom the director does not approve. One of the problems is that provincial government funding for independent family and child (legal)advocates has been drastically reduced. A Provincial Justice Reform Committee has recommended more funding for legal advocates when a judge decides it is appropriate.[49] Often the court will recommend an advocate for the child in cases where information or evidence will not otherwise likely emerge. In Saskatchewan's proposed amendment to its child welfare legislation, the court will have power to order legal representation for the child when the allegation involves physical or emotional harm or sexual exploitation by, or with the knowledge of, parents. But until independent counsel becomes mandatory for children, professionals need to emphasize their own advocacy role.

Children in care have explicit rights listed under section 70 of the *CFCSA*. The philosophy and limitations of the concept and implementation of children's rights is explored in Chapter 14. This list includes three categories of rights: (1) relating to the standard and quality of care; (2) relating to appropriate involvement in and understanding of the process in the making of decisions about them;

and, (3) relating to assistance in exercising their rights. Highlights of the first category include the right to be fed, clothed, and nurtured according to community standards, the right to reasonable privacy and to be free from corporal punishment, to receive medical and dental care when required, to social and recreational activities, to guidance to maintain their cultural heritage, and to religious instruction of their choice. The notion of community standards is what the social worker reviewed by the court is always striving to apply, but this can allow for variation across the province and the nation. Section 104 allows the government through regulation to establish pilot projects where community tribunals act in the place of courts.

The second category of rights for children in care includes to be informed about their rights and procedures under this *Act*, about their plans of care, and about the standard of behaviour expected by their care givers. The right to be consulted and to express their views in significant decisions affecting them is particularly important given the director's powers over children in care. There is also the crucial right to an interpreter if language or disability is a barrier to consulting with them.

The third category allows such children to private discussions with family members, a lawyer, the Child, Youth and Family Advocate, the Ombudsman, or an M.L.A or M.P., and particularly to assistance in contacting the Advocate. It should be noted here that under section 83 of the *CFCSA*, the Child and Family Review Board is responsible for reviewing complaints of any breach of these rights.

Many of the powers and functions of the Child, Youth and Family Advocate involve systemic advocacy. However, there are some key case functions including investigation and review of individual cases of children, youth, and families undergoing the process and not simply in care. This includes reviewing cases where no complaint is made, and assisting children, youth, and families to participate in case conferences, administrative reviews, and mediations about the provision of designated services. The Advocate may not act as legal counsel.[50] The right to have counsel provided to children is not explicit.

COMMON QUESTIONS

1. <u>What if child abuse happens and there are no witnesses?</u>

Over recent years, the criminal trial process has already encountered the difficulties of corroborating child testimony, and is developing effective strategies to protect children who have to appear in court. The civil nature of child welfare hearings with its lesser burden of proof, allows for a doctrine known as *res ipsa loquitor*, which is common in negligence cases. Translated it means "the matter speaks for itself," and it allows the circumstances to be taken into account in assessing causation. For instance, when there are no witnesses to a child abuse allegation but, in the mind of a reasonable person, the bruising and other circumstances are consistent with non-accidental injury, then the court can presume the injuries were intentional. Moreover, the court recognizes the difficulty for children giving testimony. A child may be too young to testify or the experience may be too traumatic. The child may be excluded and the court can accept hearsay evidence that it considers reliable. The court may also admit as evidence any oral or written statement considered relevant, such as a criminal or civil transcript. It may look beyond the child to see if there is another credible source of information.

2. What can professionals do if they or their client are dissatisfied with services?

There are several legal, administrative, political, ethical, and disciplinary routes to consider. Civil suits in trespass or negligence are becoming more common in Canada. Recently, an adult who was once a foster child in Victoria sued the ministry and the worker as well as the foster parent who had sexually abused her while in care. The foster parent was found liable (he had also been convicted criminally), but evidence of the ministry's and the worker's negligence in failing to monitor the home was not substantiated.[51] Legal advice is necessary to launch such an action. Foster parents recently sued successfully the ministry when a foster child sexually abused their daughter. Civil action is also beginning to be launched against churches and governments who ran residential schools where many aboriginal children were physically and sexually abused.

It should be noted that section 101 of the *CFCSA* protects persons operating under the *Act* from personal liability, as long as "done or omitted in good faith." This of course does not preclude action for behaviour which is grossly negligent, criminal, or malicious (see Chapter 13). This protection does cover instances when a worker is honestly mistaken in her/his belief. Thus, when a child welfare worker believed honestly but mistakenly that a child needed protection, the Superintendent (at that time) was found not to be liable in a negligence action[52] (see Chapter 13).

Obviously, if a crime is suspected, the police should be contacted. Professionals should be prepared to hold the system and each other accountable for the manner in which our vulnerable children are served. However, a recently publicized criminal charge[53] against an Ontario Children's Aid social worker for alleged criminal negligence causing death in the starvation of a five-week-old infant while at a Toronto women's shelter with his mother, has probably heightened the anxiety of helping professionals in child welfare in making decisions about children in governmental or agency care.

Comments have been made about the limits on administrative appeals. The Ministry has its own investigative section. If an external review is more appropriate, then a complaint to the Deputy Ombudsman for Children in British Columbia, the Child Advocate in both British Columbia and Alberta, the Office of Child and Family Advocacy in Ontario, the Youth Protection Committees in Quebec, and their equivalents in other provinces should be explored.[54]

On the political level, legislatures often have standing committees on children's services that hold public hearings. The *Provincial Court Act*[55] in British Columbia provides that Family Courts are to be advised and monitored by Family Court Committees of elected and appointed citizens. These are possible avenues for complaint, especially when services are substandard.

Standards for care resources are not enshrined in law, but exist in licensing regulations or policy in most provinces. Concerns should be addressed to the relevant board or administration.

Complaints against individual workers who may have violated a code of ethics should be referred to the appropriate professional association. For instance, the Board of Registration for Social

Workers can discipline its members, although registration is voluntary except in the provinces of New Brunswick and Prince Edward Island. In addition, the professional association can often take a public stance when an employee cannot. It may operate at a political level by lobbying or advocating for a public inquiry.

3. How confidential is information about children and families under the *Child, Family and Community Service Act*?

Under section 7 of the *Act*, information obtained shall not be disclosed under section 75 except in very limited circumstances, including information about a child under 12 to persons who have those children in their legal care. A director may disclose when it is necessary to ensure the safety or well-being of a child (such as when a young child in care has gone missing), when required as part of evidence in a child welfare hearing, when necessary for a family conference or mediation, to a child's care givers about children in their care, and when it is to the director's own legal counsel. Access to information by persons with the right of access must be refused if it is an unreasonable invasion of a third party's personal privacy, or might reasonably reveal the identity of a complainant who has not agreed to disclosure. Access to information may be denied by the director if it might result in physical or emotional harm to a person or jeopardize a criminal investigation.

4. What reforms are needed?

Many of the limitations in British Columbia's former child welfare statute have been addressed in the *CFCSA*. It remains to be seen how these provisions will work in practice. Social workers in child welfare in the ministry now require Bachelor of Social Work degrees and enhanced training in operating under the new *Act*. However, with increased legal rights of children and parties coupled with tighter time lines and greater political scrutiny, the social workers now have even more administrative work to be completed in a short time.

Child rights to legal advocacy should be guaranteed. A better system of accountability that families can use has been developed with the Advocate and Child and Family Review Board. Again, rights to services should be guaranteed, especially by placing an obligation on government to provide preventative assistance, both financial and social. As the community panel report[56] leading to child welfare reform stated, poverty is a crucial factor among the reasons why many families cannot care adequately for their children. While safety is a paramount consideration, the *Act* should explicitly identify removal of children as a very last resort. As British Columbia's Deputy Ombudsman for Children has reported,[57] standards of care require more backing in law and need to be wider than for children in the director's care. However, there can never be a substitute for community support and resources, which is where helping professionals must play an important role in assisting their communities. Judges need training in child development and consultation with community panels. As always, a continuing shortage of appropriate resources for children plagues the system.

Finally, helping professionals can assist in promoting legal reforms and changes in political priorities, but legal reforms will not remedy the situation. Helping professionals need to empower parents, families, and communities to support their children in their own homes.[58]

5. What protection is there for elderly person abuse or neglect?

As mentioned earlier, a child is defined as under the age of 19 in British Columbia (18 elsewhere in Canada). Some provinces, such as Newfoundland, New Brunswick, Nova Scotia, and Prince Edward Island,[59] have enacted legislation that provides "a legal framework for health and social service personnel to intervene in family settings where elder abuse or neglect is believed to be occurring."[60] This resembles child protection legislation, though only two of the four provinces have chosen to include mandatory rather than voluntary reporting provisions.[61]

With an estimated 100,000 elderly Canadians likely to have recently experienced serious abuse (financial, physical, psychological, or neglect) in their own homes,[62] the urgent need for protective systems is becoming apparent. Until such legislation is enacted in British Columbia, existing protections remain in the *Criminal Code*[63] (see Chapter 7), or at civil law (see Chapter 13), or under mental health laws (see Chapter 9).

6. What rights do foster parents have once a child is in care?

Unlike some other provinces such as Alberta, which give foster parents some rights after a qualifying period of continuous care of the child, foster parents in British Columbia have no such rights legally. Foster parents, unless granted custody or guardianship under the *Family Relations Act*,[64] do not fit the definition of "parent" under section 1 of the *CFCSA*, which specifically excludes a care giver or the director. Foster parents are not parties to the proceedings nor specifically entitled to notice, although the court may decide to serve them if considered appropriate. Foster parents groups are lobbying for rights to challenge the arbitrary removal of children from their homes by the director or social worker. At this point, only Ontario gives them an opportunity for review before removal of the child.[65]

Again the director, through the social worker, has the legal control over the child in care, including religious, educational, disciplinary matters, and medical treatment. The foster parent has daily care and control. In British Columbia, policy prohibits physical discipline or restraint of children in care by foster parents or social workers. The *Act*, as mentioned above, prohibits corporal punishment. Exceeding these bounds could make the foster parent liable in criminal law or civil law, or administratively by investigation from the director, the Advocate, or the Review Board.

CONCLUSION

This chapter has provided an overview of the philosophy and issues in child welfare, basic aspects of the law and legal process, and the rights and duties of the participants. Some suggestions for reform have also been mentioned. This information, coupled with the ability to obtain helpful and accurate legal advice, should prepare helping professionals for the challenge of protecting abused and neglected children. It is incumbent on us all to ensure that our colleagues and other participants in the legal system are responding appropriately to this difficult social problem.

RESOURCES

N. Bala, J. Hornick and R. Vogl, *Canadian Child Welfare Law* (Toronto: Thompson Educational, 1990).

N. Falconer, *Preparing for Practice: The Fundamentals of Child Protection* (Toronto: The Children's Aid Society of Metropolitan Toronto, 1983).

B. Friesen, *Social Worker Empowerment in Child Protection Court* (Springfield, Ill: Charles Thomas, 1990).

E. Vayda & M. Satterfield, *Law for Social Workers: A Canadian Guide*, 3rd ed. (Toronto: Carswell, 1997) (especially Chapters 13 and 14).

B. Wharf & K. Levitt, eds., *The Challenge of Child Welfare*, (Vancouver: University of British Columbia Press, 1985).

B. Wharf, ed., *Rethinking Child Welfare in Canada*, (Toronto: McLelland and Stewart, 1993).

J. Wilson & M. Tomlinson, *Children and the Law*, 2d ed. (Toronto: Butterworths, 1986).

END NOTES

1. M. Callahan, "Public Apathy and Government Parsimony: A Review of Child Welfare in Canada", in K. Levitt & B. Wharf, eds, *The Challenge of Child Welfare* (Vancouver: University of British Columbia Press, 1985) 2 at 2-6.
2. *Ibid* at 4.
3. *Child, Family and Community Service Act*, R.S.B.C. 1996, c.46.
4. D.A.R. Thompson, "Why Hasn't The Charter Mattered In Child Protection?" (1989) 8 Can. J. Fam. L. 133.
5. See M. Harris, *Unholy Orders: Tragedy at Mount Cashel*, (Markham, Ontario: Viking, 1990).
6. See D. Hechler, *The Battle and the Backlash* (Lexington, Mass.: Lexington Books, 1988).
7. *Report of Inquiry into Child Abuse in Cleveland, England* (1987) (London: H.M.S.O., 1988).
8. *Report of the Gove Inquiry into Child Protection*,(1995) Ministry of Social Services, Victoria, British Columbia.
9. J. Wildgoose, "Alternate Dispute Resolution of Child Protection Cases," (1987) 6 Can. J. Fam. L. 61.
10. D. Turner, *Holding Governments Accountable for Children's Rights; the Canadian Experience* (monograph, Victoria: School of Social Work, Sedgewick Society for Consumer and Public Education, 1990).
11. National Incident Study of Child Abuse and Neglect, U.S. Health and Human Services Department, reported in Victoria Times Colonist, Victoria, British Columbia, September, 19th 1996.
12. *Child, Family and Community Service Act, supra,* note 3.
13. This list is taken from D. Barnhorst and B. Walter, "Child Protection Legislation in Canada," in N. Bala, J.P Hornick and R. Vogel, eds, *Canadian Child Welfare Law: Children, Families and the State,* (Toronto: Thompson Educational Publishing Inc. 1991) pp. 18-20.
14. *Child, Family and Community Service Amendment Act,*1995 S.B.C.c.19. Incorporated in *Child, Family and Community Service Act, supra,* note 3, s.2.
15. *Child, Family and Community Service Amendment Act*, 1997, Bill 24, section 2(d) and 2(e).
16. D. Cruickshank, "The Berger Commission Report on the Protection of Children: The Impact on Prevention of Child Abuse and Neglect," in *The Challenge of Child Welfare, supra,* note 1 at 182.
17. *Child Welfare Act*, S.A. 1984, c-8.1, s. 1(2) and (3).

18. N. Falconer, *Preparing for Practice: The Fundamentals of Child Protection*, (Toronto: The Children's Aid Society of Metropolitan Toronto, 1983).

19. *Superintendent of Family and Child Service v. M.(B.) and O.(D.)* (1982), 37 B.C.L.R. 32, 28 R.F.L. (2d) 278 (S.C.).

20. *Re "Baby R"* (1988), 30 B.C.L.R.(2d) 237 (S.C.).

21. *Re Infant* (1981), 32 B.C.L.R. 20 (S.C.).

22. *Family Relations Act*, R.S.B.C. 1979, c. 121, section 29.

23. *Child, Family and Community Service Act*, *supra*, note 3, section 6(3)(a) and (b), and 6(4)(a) and (b).

24. S.B.C 1996., c. 6. New *B.C. Benefits Act* regulations were released in February 1997.

25. *Child, Family and Community Service Act*, *supra*, note 3, section 5.

26. A director of Child, Family and Community Service is designated by the Minister for Children and Families under section 91 of the *Act*. A director, who has extensive powers and duties under the legislation, acts through social workers who are delegated in varying degrees of statutory authority under section 91.

27. Under the *Family, Child Service Act*, a child taken into the care or custody of the Superintendent was "apprehended": under the *Child, Family and Community Service Act* a child taken into the care of the director is "removed". See sections 1 and 30.

28. *Interministry Child Abuse Handbook: An Integrated Approach to Child Abuse and Neglect*, (Victoria: Crown Publications, 1982). The Ministry is revising procedures for the new *Child, Family and Community Service Act*.

29. *Child, Family and Community Service Act*, *supra*, note 3, section 27.

30. J. McLaren & R. Brown, "Childhood Problems Associated with Abuse and Neglect," in (1989) 37(3) Canada's Mental Health Journal. See also, L. Walker, *Handbook on Sexual Abuse of Children*. (New York: Springer, 1988).

31. Not yet in force.

32. Regulations made under the *Child, Family and Community Service Act* require the director to establish a "Roster of Mediators." Mediators, at arms-length from both the Ministry and the family, will be retained on contract from private practice through the Ministry of Attorney General.

33. *Child, Family and Community Service Act*, section 24.

34. See Turner, *supra*, note 10 for a detailed analysis.

35. M. Martin, B. McRae & L. Reid, *The Child Protection Law: What Every Parent Should Know*, (Vancouver: Public Legal Education Society,1986).

36. *Child, Family and Community Service Act*, *supra*, note 3, section 37.

37. *Child, Family and Community Service Amendment Act*, 1997, Bill 24, section 33.3.

38. P. Johnston, *Native Children and the Child Welfare System*, (Toronto: Lorimer, 1983) See also, R. Dumont, "Culturally Selective Perceptions in Child Welfare Decisions", in 1988 56(4) The Social Worker (Ottawa) (1988).

39. An article detailing the mechanics of the Rule 2 case conference appeared in the September 1996 issue of The Advocate.

40. *Child, Family and Community Service Act*, *supra*, note 3, Part 5, section 75.

41. *Child, Family and Community Service Amendment Act*, 1997, Bill 24, section 29(1).

42. *Child, Family and Community Service Act*, note 3, section 44.

43. *Ibid*, section 49(5).

44. *Adoption Act*, R.S.B.C. 1996, c.5, section 8(1)(a).

45. *Freedom of Information and Protection of Privacy Act*, R.S.B.C 1996, c.165.

46. *Children's Commission Act*, Bill 23, 1997. Sections 3, 4 and 5 deal with guiding principles, jurisdiction and powers of investigation respectively.

47. *Child, Family and Community Service Amendment Act*, 1997, Bill 24, section 101.1.

48. Excellent examples of the Ombudsman in British Columbia reviewing fairness of an investigation and apprehension are documented in *British Columbia Annual Report of Ombudsman to the Legislature Assembly* at 107 and 113 (1989).

49. British Columbia, *Access to Justice: Report of the Justice Reform Committee* (Victoria, British Columbia: Crown Publications, 1988), Recommendation 34.

50. *Child, Youth and Family Advocacy Act*, R.S.B.C. 1996, c.47, c.28 sections 4 and 5.

51. *M.(M.) v. K.(K.)* (1987), 35 D.L.R. (4th) 222, 11 B.C.L.R. (2d) 90 (S.C.).

52. *Gareau v. British Columbia (Family and Child Services)* (1986), 5 B.C.L.R. (2d) 352 (S.C.).

53. Reported in Canadian Press, Victoria Times Colonist, August 9, 1997, p. A7.

54. See Turner, *supra*, note 10 at 24-34.

55. *Provincial Court Act*, R.S.B.C., 1996, c.379.

56. *Making Changes: A Place to Start*, (Victoria: Ministry of Social Services, 1994).

57. Report of the Ombudsman, *Public Services to Children, Youth and Their Families in British Columbia: The Need for Integration*, (Public Report No. 22) (Victoria, B.C.: Crown Publications, 1990) Recommendations 5-10 at 91-95

58. R. Hegar & J. Hunzeker, "Moving Toward Empowerment-Based Practice in Public Child Welfare," (1988) 33(6) Social Work Journal 419.

59. *Neglected Adults Welfare Act*, S.N. 1973. no. 81. *Family Services Act*, S.N.B. 1980, c.C-21 (now c.F-2-2). *Adult Protection Act*, S.N.S. 1985, c.2. *Adult Protection Act*, S.P.E.I. 1988 c.6.

60. Gordon & S. Tomita, "The Reporting of Elder Abuse and Neglect: Mandatory or Voluntary ?" in (1990) 38(4) Canada's Mental Health Journal 1.

61. *Idem* p. 4.

62. E. Podnieks, K. Pillemer, J.P. Nicholson, T. Shillington, & A. Frizzel, *National Survey on Abuse of the Elderly in Canada*, (Toronto: Ryerson Polytechnic Institute, 1990).

63. *Criminal Code of Canada*, R.S.C. 1985 c. C-46 as amended.

64. *Family Relations Act*, R.S.B.C. 1996 c.128.

65. See N. Bala et al, *Canadian Child Welfare Law*, *supra* note 13, Resources at 104-107.

Chapter 4

ABORIGINAL SELF-DETERMINATION
AND CHILD PROTECTION LAW

Kathy Absolon and John A. Macdonald

INTRODUCTION

Over a decade ago, in 1983, a well-publicized parliamentary committee report (referred to as the Penner Report)[1] on Indian self-government noted that the proportion of First Nations [2] children in the protective care of provincial child welfare authorities was more than five times the national average. The Report noted that only 20 percent of Indian children graduated from secondary schools in Canada compared to a national rate of 75 percent. Native people were significantly over-represented in the inmate populations of provincial prisons and federal penitentiaries and in offences committed by young persons. Moreover, Indian people experienced higher than national average rates of violent death and death by suicide, with the latter most pronounced among Indian people in the age range of 15 to 24 years. These statistics reveal both wide-spread human tragedy and unfulfilled human potential, which should be of concern to helping professionals throughout Canada. The situation documented in the Penner Report in 1983 remains unchanged, and this chapter highlights the events and changes that have occurred in Aboriginal child welfare law and system. The law is stated as of February 1, 1997.

In 1992 in British Columbia a community panel looking at First Nations child welfare issues[3] again confirmed this tragic history and current state. In 1996 a new child welfare act was implemented in British Columbia (*Child, Family and Community Service Act*).[4] For details see Chapter 3. The child welfare laws as they relate to First Nations people are the focus of this chapter. This field of law has been chosen because child welfare practices have been central to the oppression of First Nations communities. Child removal and family breakdown among native peoples is often a precursor to a range of serious adjustment problems experienced later in life. These can include a drift through multiple foster care settings, where contact with parents and siblings may be limited or non-existent and continuity with Aboriginal values and traditions disrupted. Adoptions into non-native homes creates further disruption and confusion in children's sense of their own aboriginal identity. The consequences of such disruptions in family, home, and community can be alienation, and anti-social and self-destructive behaviours. These responses are evident especially among many native youth, and particularly in urban settings. Further, these unresolved traumas result in generations of youth seriously challenged in school, work and future family relationships.

Child protection law is also instrumental in raising the fear and insistence, often expressed by First Nations leaders during the past 20 years, that the child removal (apprehension) and foster home placement policies of provincial child protection authorities have posed a serious threat to the survival of First Nations bands and cultures. The reader will be aware that we are living through a challenging period in relations between Aboriginal peoples and governments in Canada, both federal and provincial. Increasingly, First Nations are action orientated and are demanding new constitutional, political, and economic arrangements geared toward ensuring a foundation for self-determination within the Canadian federation. Included in the range of areas over which First Nations people are working toward self-governing powers is the field of child protection and family law.

This chapter begins by acquainting the reader with the constitutional environment within which Canadian child protection laws[5] affecting First Nations must be examined. It then moves to a short historical review of child protection policies for First Nations people in the Province of British Columbia, with major emphasis on the wide-spread separation of Aboriginal children from their families that occurred following the extension of the province's child protection legislation to Indian reserves in 1955. The chapter then reviews selected legal initiatives taken by federal and provincial governments and native organizations during the past two decades in an effort to develop child protection policies that are designed both to protect native children and preserve their ties with their own cultural, family, and community environments. More specifically, the chapter examines provisions in the *Child, Family and Community Service Act* of 1996 in British Columbia. We then explore the challenge of urban native child welfare, connecting prospects for future progress to the wider struggle of First Nations peoples for self-determination within Canada. Finally, the authors answer a series of questions commonly asked by helping professionals, especially those who work with child wefare legislation and who endeavour to serve the interests of native Indian families and children in crisis.

FIRST NATIONS AND THE CANADIAN LEGAL SYSTEM

A. Definition of the First Nations Peoples of Canada

Defining First Nations peoples can open a Pandora's Box, in that such definitions of people often become exclusionary for one purpose or another. Defining one's identity and roles within a particular Nation really ought to be left to the Nations themselves. The imposition of external definitions on Aboriginal people by colonial governments has resulted in divisions among the people, which have only benefitted those seeking power over the land, its original inhabitants, and its resources. Native peoples are the descendants of the Aboriginal people who occupied most of Canada prior to its colonization by European governments during the 16th, 17th, and 18th centuries. Depending on whether they possess registered status under the *Indian Act*[6] of Canada, First Nations peoples may be categorized as status Indians or non-status Indians. In addition, the *Constitution Act*,[7] 1982, recognizes Inuit and Metis as aboriginal peoples. The Inuit are the descendants of the original inhabitants of Canada's far north. The Metis are the descendants of marriages between 17th and 18th century European fur traders and Indian women. The marriages between Indian men and white women are not identified because of the inherent sexual discrimination of the *Indian Act*, which granted Indian status to white women upon marriage to an Indian man, while Metis became the category under which Indian women were identified upon marriage to a white man.

B. Status Versus Non-Status Indians

The distinction in Canadian law between classifying First Nations peoples as either status or non-status Indians is significant in the way it relates to the division of legislative responsibility between the federal and provincial levels of government.

To begin with, it should be noted that the *Constitution Act,*[8] 1867 (originally entitled the *British North America Act*), assigns exclusive legislative authority to the federal government for "Indians and lands reserved for Indians." Pursuant to this power the federal parliament since confederation has enacted a series of *Indian Acts*, which deal with Indian reserve lands and the governance of Indians who reside on reserves. Important sections of these *Indian Acts* have defined the word "Indian" for the purpose of delineating federal legislative and financial responsibility. Persons who are officially registered as Indians under the current *Indian Act* are referred to as status Indians. Persons of Indian descent who are not registered under the *Indian Act* are referred to as non-status Indians.

Non-status Indians include the descendants of native people who were not enumerated when the original lists of registered Indians were compiled shortly after confederation. They also include the descendants of persons whose Indian status was lost as a result of the operational provisions of the *Indian Acts*. Some of these provisions included, among many others, attending post-secondary education, being able to attain employment off reserve lands, or having one's own land base. For many years, this category also included Indian women who lost registered status through marriage to non-Indians. Paradoxically, non-Indian women could claim Indian status through marriage to status Indian men. As a result of amendments to the *Indian Act* enacted in 1985, registered status has now been restored to surviving Indian women and their children who had earlier been deprived of Indian status.[9]

The distinction between status and non-status Indians has significant implications for the roles of the federal and provincial governments. Status Indians are potentially entitled to reside on Indian reserves and to receive federal health and educational benefits. If they are members of a registered Indian band, they are also entitled to share in the distribution of funds resulting from the sale or lease of resources on Indian lands. The federal government also assumes the full cost of social assistance provided to status Indian people on reserves. Treaty agreements have ensured to a degree that in exchange for government use of lands and resources, the federal government would in return ensure the overall well-being and care of the first peoples who occupied those lands and territories. However, the government assumes no special legislative or financial responsibility for non-status Indians or Metis. Historically, Metis were recognized as having some special status, but for the purposes of legislation and legislatively mandated programs, non-status Indians and Metis are dealt with in the same manner as other residents of Canada. This is currently changing as Metis organizations become more mobilized in lobbying for recognition of their rights.

C. Federal and Provincial Jurisdiction

Although the Constitution of Canada makes no specific reference to child protection as a subject of legislation, judicial decisions have consistently held that child protection falls within the field of provincial legislative jurisdiction.[10] Accordingly, each province has a child protection statute that defines circumstances where designated persons may intervene to protect children who have been abused or neglected or are at serious risk of abuse or neglect. It should also be noted that provincial child protection statutes apply to status Indian peoples residing both on and off Indian reserves, notwithstanding the fact that the federal government has been given the constitutional power to legislate for "Indians and lands reserved for Indians."[11] This requires an explanation.

To begin with, it should be noted that the federal parliament, under its paternalistic powers to legislate for Indian peoples, could enact child protection legislation applicable to registered Indians on or off reserves. This could be done either in separate Indian child welfare legislation or as an amendment to the *Indian Act*. Instead, the federal government has chosen to refrain from exercising its potential legislative power in this area by accepting provincial legislative authority in the child welfare field. The statutory authority for deferring to provincial legislatures in child protection matters is contained in section 88 of the *Indian Act*, which reads as follows:

Subject to the terms of any treaty and any other Act of the Parliament of Canada, all laws of general application from time to time in force in any province are applicable to and in respect of Indians in the province, except to the extent that such laws are inconsistent with this *Act* or any other, rule, regulation, or by-law thereunder, and except to the extent that such laws make provision for any matter for which provision is made by or under the *Act*.

This section has been interpreted to mean that registered Indian people are subject to all laws in force in a province as long as the laws are not inconsistent with the *Indian Act* or a treaty with Indians, and as long as the laws apply generally to all persons and do not purport to legislate specifically with respect to Indians or in a manner designed to alter or affect Indian status.[12] A clear indication that the federal government accepts this interpretation of the law in regard to child welfare is seen in a policy directive issued by the Department of Indian and Northern Affairs in 1982, which reads, in part, as follows:

Section 91(24) of the *British North America Act* empowers Canada to enact legislation in respect of Indians and Indian lands. Canada has not exercised this discretionary power in respect of legislation to govern the protection and care of Indian children and, accordingly section 88 of the *Indian Act* makes Indian people residing on reserves subject to provincial child welfare laws unless and to the extent that such laws conflict with the *Indian Act* and Treaties.[13]

By way of illustration it should be noted that the Supreme Court of Canada has upheld the validity of British Columbia adoption legislation, permitting the adoption of a registered Indian child by non-Indian adoptive parents. The same decision, however, also makes it clear that the operation of such legislation can in no way impair the continuing registered Indian status of the adopted child.[14] However, as a result of the legislative panel review in British Columbia in 1992,[15] the province has placed a moratorium on the adoption of Aboriginal children into non-Aboriginal homes. The treaty-making process in British Columbia will also impact provincial child welfare policy and its application to First Nations.

Judicial decisions have also confirmed that provincial child protection legislation extends to Indians residing on reserves.[16] A very significant British Columbia case has reiterated the application to status Indians of provincial child protection law by rejecting a submission that such a ruling would infringe an Aboriginal right of native Indians on reserves to exercise full responsibility for the care and upbringing of Aboriginal children. In rejecting this submission, Judge Gordon of the British Columbia Provincial Court at Kamloops stated that such recognition would undermine the authority of a single constituted government to exercise powers needed to protect all children in the province, including aboriginal children.[17]

Although the federal government has chosen to defer to provincial legislative jurisdiction in the field of native Indian child protection, it has assumed significant financial responsibility for protective services to native Indian children. In the case of non-status Indians and Metis the federal government under the *Canada Health and Social Transfer*[18] (formerly the *Canada Assistance Plan*) pays one-half of the costs of professional and child maintenance services arising under provincial child protection legislation. In the case of status Indian children residing either on or off reserves, the federal government assumes the full cost of provincial child protection services and maintenance for children in care. As will be explained later, the federal government also pays the full cost of child welfare programs now being delivered by native Indians on some reserves in several Canadian provinces.

THE EXTENSION OF PROVINCIAL CHILD PROTECTION SERVICES TO INDIANS ON RESERVES IN BRITISH COLUMBIA

Prior to the arrival of the Europeans in British Columbia in the late 18th century, the Aboriginal peoples lived communally in small tribal groups sustained by common languages, and shared social and religious values, and the natural resources of the lands, sea, and rivers. Although they had no written laws, codes of conduct were expressed in customs that applied to marriage, child rearing, religious ceremonies, and the management of family crises. Children were cherished both for themselves and for their future contribution to the well-being of the tribe or tribal band. Special emphasis was placed on the child's extended family of cousins, aunts, uncles, and grand parents, who were expected to provide support and, if necessary, substitute care when the parents were unable or unwilling to fulfill this role. Tribal elders were utilized as mediators and advisors in resolving family disputes. Consensual decision-making was generally practiced. Thus, when children were orphaned through the death of their parents, custom law required that they be adopted by members of their tribe, preferably by extended family members, who then would assume ongoing responsibility for their care and training in life skills. In these circumstances the removal of Indian children from their tribal culture and familiar geographical surroundings would have been clearly inconsistent with Indian custom law.[19]

Indian customary practices of child rearing and child care were generally accepted by colonial authorities prior to the establishment of the system of Indian reserves in the mid-19th century. After that time federal Indian agents and Christian missionaries increasingly assumed responsibility for the physical, educational, and spiritual well-being of Indian children. Although the extended family continued to be a major resource for placement of orphaned and neglected children, federal authorities also utilized residential schools operated by church personnel for the physical care, socialization, and education of Indian children. A total of sixteen residential schools were established in British Columbia commencing in the 1880s, reaching their full development in the 1920s before a gradual phasing out occurred following the 2nd World War that lasted well into the 1970s.[20] Children placed in these schools were usually separated from their parents for ten or more months each year, while often being subjected to punitive regimes that prohibited the use of native languages and denigrated native cultures. Prolonged separation from parents and native cultural traditions has contributed to problems the people of residential schools experienced later in rearing their own children. The impact continues on further generations. Several authors have identified this concerted State action as institutionalized racism based upon a racist colonial ideology.[21] Racism, when manifested at institutional levels, becomes the very policies and practices that control and ultimately exterminate one's cultural identity. It stems from the perceived belief of the superiority of one race (European Canadians) over another (First Nations), and that the first then has the perceived right to dominate. Domination by European Canadians has been exercised, legislated, and institutionalized. This domination is evidenced in the consequent omission of positive Aboriginal values and cultural identity in mainstream perceptions, and has resulted in oppressive (and to some, genocidal) practices and policies.

Although recent accounts of life in residential schools have confirmed many acts of adult cruelty and sexual abuse toward Indian children,[22] the decision to close the schools was based on emerging federal and provincial policies aimed at promoting integration and assimilation of native people within the institutions of mainstream society. The period after 1950 saw the beginning of accelerated migration of Indian people from reserves to urban centres of the province. Also since 1950, large numbers of Indian children were integrated into regular public school programs. In addition, provincial social assistance benefits were made available to First Nations people who had established themselves for at least a year off the reserve, and by 1955 the British Columbia Department of Social Welfare had assumed child protection responsibilities for Indians, both on and off reserves. These policies also reflected practices and token gestures to assimilate and rid Canada of any trace of distinctness of First Nations peoples. Notably, however, services to Indians on reserves did not include preventive family counselling services. Moreover, foster home placements were not developed on reserves except in a few instances. From the First Nations perspective, therefore, the extension of provincial child protection legislation and services to Indian reserves meant a steady and frightening escalation of child removals (apprehensions), followed by placement of Indian children in off-reserve Caucasian foster homes. Several authors[23] have identified these practices as reflecting institutional racism.

In 1955 a report[24] issued by the Indian Advisory Committee to the British Columbia Government noted that native children comprised only 19 of the 3,433 children then in the care of the provincial superintendent of child welfare. By 1960 the number of Indian children in care had reached 849 and four years later it had climbed to 1,446. The numbers admitted to care continued to escalate, reaching 2,324 by 1968, or 38 percent of all children in provincial care.[25] Moreover, these statistics did not take into account native children who were adopted out. High rates of Indian admissions to care continued into the 1970s and by 1972 it was estimated that 10.4 percent of all registered Indian children in the province were residing in various forms of child protective care outside of their families. This amounted to about ten times the rate for non-Indian children.[26]

The British Columbian experience with respect to native child protection intervention was paralleled elsewhere in Canada, especially in the prairie provinces. Thus, in 1977 it was estimated that there were 15,500 native children in child welfare placements in Canada, amounting to 20 percent of all children in care in the country, including 60 percent of the children in care in Manitoba, 51.5 percent in Saskatchewan, 44 percent in Alberta, and 39 percent in British Columbia.[27] Similar findings were reported by Patrick Johnston in 1983 in his landmark critique of native Indian child welfare policies in Canada.[28]

An Aboriginal Peoples Survey[29] in British Columbia in 1991 identified 32.29 % of children in care as Aboriginal, so there has not been a great reduction over the last 15 years. The decade of the 1980s witnessed considerable soul-searching by child welfare specialists in an effort to identify those shortcomings in child protection laws and practices that may have contributed to the massive influx of native children into the care of provincial child welfare authorities. This self-examination, together with concerns forced by native leaders, led to major revisions in the child protection laws of several provinces. It also resulted in the development of several native-administered child welfare and child protection programs. A discussion of some significant examples of recent reforms and innovations follows.

REFORMS IN CHILD PROTECTION LEGISLATION AND ADMINISTRATION DURING THE 1980s and 1990s

The decade of the 1980s was a period during which the provinces of Alberta, Manitoba, and Ontario enacted major revisions to their child welfare statutes. This was also a decade when the federal government and several provincial governments entered into special agreements with Indian organizations for Indian administration of child protection and child welfare programs on a number of reserves in New Brunswick, Ontario, Manitoba, Alberta, and British Columbia. The legislative reforms undertaken in Ontario were significant, because they reflected a serious attempt to incorporate special sections within general legislation regarding provincial child protection designed to respond to the cultural values of native families. The native administered programs on reserves also utilized native culture and values in developing a range of preventive and remedial measures, which engaged the services of both paid staff and concerned members of Indian communities.

I. The Ontario *Child and Family Services Act*[30] of 1984

The Ontario legislation, in the first author's opinion, has been foremost in Canada in responding creatively to the needs of native children in situations of neglect, abuse, or family crisis. The Chiefs of Ontario agreed to accept this new act as an alternative measure to the existing system, but also saw it as an interim measure until either federal child welfare legislation was enacted or until full self-government was realized, when Aboriginal laws would then preside.[31]

The *Act* commences with a comprehensive declaration of guiding principles emphasizing that all services to Indian children and families should be provided "in a manner that recognizes their culture, heritage and traditions, and the concept of the extended family."[32] The principles also affirm that Indian people, including non-status Indians, "should be entitled to provide, wherever possible, their own child and family services."[33] Some key sections are identified here.

The declaration of principles also emphasizes that, where possible, child welfare services should be provided on the basis of mutual consent and should be designed to support the autonomy and integrity of the family unit (section 1(b)). In addition, the principles endorse child protective interventions that involve the least restrictive and disruptive measures to help a child and family (section 1(c)).

The foregoing principles are consistently reflected in the operational sections of the Ontario statute. Important sections of the *Act* are devoted to facilitating client access to voluntary social services, including the provision of temporary foster care by agreement (Part II). The grounds for protective intervention are set forth without moralistic overtones and in lucid language describing a range of circumstances where the health or safety of children would clearly be in jeopardy or at substantial risk (section 37(2)). The intrusiveness and trauma of involuntary protective intervention is potentially reduced by a section that permits a judge to consider a child protection case, on application of a children's aid society, without prior apprehension of the child (section 40(1)). Where an apprehension is deemed necessary, the *Act* requires that the social worker obtain a judicial warrant to apprehend a child, except in a situation where delay would pose a significant danger to the health or safety of the child (section 40(1) and (6)).

The Ontario *Act* also contains provisions designed to ensure that Indian parents and children are not without emotional support from their own people during child protection hearings in Family Court. Thus, a representative of the child's band or native community (in the case of non-status Indians) is entitled to participate at any stage of the protection hearing or during a subsequent judicial review of dispositions (sections 39 and 60).

The Ontario statute also incorporates Indian custom law in the provisions dealing with placement of Indian children who have been found by a judge to be in need of protection. Protection orders must give first priority to supervision of children in their own home. Where it is considered essential to place children outside their home, preference must be given to a placement that permits children to reside with a member of their extended family, a member of their band or native community, or with another Indian family (sections 53 and 57). Indian custom law is also incorporated in section 195 of the *Act*, which authorizes a provincially licensed children's aid society to grant a subsidy to a person caring for an Indian child according to the custom of the children's band or native community.

Several of the foregoing policy features of the Ontario legislation are illustrated by a 1987 case where a judge of the Ontario Provincial Family Court was required to interpret the *Act* with respect to the foster care placement of three Indian siblings.[34] The judge in this case concluded that he was obligated to order placement of the children in a native Indian foster home located on the same reserve where their mother was residing. The judge also used a supervision order rather than an order granting custody to the Crown or a children's aid society. The effect of this decision was to implement at the judicial level a legislative policy geared to ensuring that placement preference be given to a native foster family setting where ongoing contact with the children's biological parent and cultural community could be facilitated.

The Ontario *Child and Family Services Act* also contains special provisions to facilitate delivery of services by an Indian child and family service authority (Part X). Thus, section 194 authorizes the Ontario Minister of Community and Social Services to contract with a designated Indian child welfare agency, with band approval, for provision of services to members of an Indian band or native community. This section also empowers the Minister to designate an Indian child and family service authority as a children's aid society for the province, with full statutory powers of protective intervention and service provision. Timpson reports that in April 1990 there were three native-run children's aid societies providing some or all aspects of child and family services to members of Indian bands in northern Ontario.[35] Section 194 of the legislation may also be applied to non-status Indians and Metis when they reside in a designated native community, although no such communities had been designated by 1990.[36]

Subsequent initiatives that occurred as a result of the new *Child and Family Service Act* (1984) involved Aboriginal organizations entering into Provincial agreements, which became designated Children Aid Societies under section 15(2) of the *Act*.[37] Aboriginal groups both on- and off-reserve sought to establish both mandated and non-mandated services under the *Act*. Examples include the Tikinagan Child and Family Services in Sioux Lookout, Payukotayno Family Services in Moosonee, Weechi-it-te-whin Child and Family Services in Fort Frances area, and the Urban Native Child and Family Services in Toronto. The current legislation provides for the designation of delegated authority, and some Aboriginal organizations are in the process of working out protection mandates, while others remain non-mandated with services such as treatment, prevention, and family and child support.

Since the newly elected Harris government of 1996, movements in actualizing the delivery of services by a First Nations child and family service have become impaired. Aboriginal child and family service organizations that were on the horizon of having protection mandates are now thrown back into struggles of battling for rights and funding and are being received by an unsupportive government. Other organizations that were in developmental phases with non-mandated services are in crisis states, because the provincial government is calling those services redundant alongside of mainstream child and family service agencies. Funding allocations are being cut, and stringent measures are being applied without consideration to existing legislation. Developmental initiatives are in crisis as they struggle to deliver some services with grossly inadequate funding. The provincial agenda seems to be to rid the province of excessive bureaucracy. Autonomous Aboriginal child and family centres are being interpreted as a duplication of service, which has become the justification for not sponsoring or supporting further developments. The current political will is stalled, and Aboriginal organizations and Chiefs are fighting hard to protect what progress has been made to date. Nonetheless, Aboriginal organizations and leadership do know that their solutions rest in the existing *Act's* commitment to the delivery of child welfare services by Aboriginal run organizations. The goal continues to be self-determination through control of mandates, services, and programs.

II. The British Columbia *Child, Family and Community Service Act* of 1996

Many of the reforms of Ontario legislation in 1984 have been echoed in the new *Child, Family and Community Service Act* (hereafter referred to as the CFCSA) in British Columbia proclaimed in 1996. The position of First Nations people in British Columbia, like the position of the Chiefs in Ontario, is that they would accept this piece of legislation as an interim measure towards self-government and the eventual transfer of full authority to First Nations. In many cases First Nations child and family services will be administering non-mandated services themselves with some sort of agreement that combines federal funding with provincial legislation and First Nation organizational structures. Still, in many other cases, existing mainstream child welfare authorities will continue to administer the *Act* in its application to Aboriginal families and their children. The provisions of the *Act* are perceived and interpreted as temporary, pending future changes to be suggested by the Aboriginal peoples of British Columbia. This transitory nature is reflected in the following statement of the Aboriginal Community Panel: "Interim measures requiring a Non-Aboriginal legal sanction cannot be interpreted as consent by our Nations and communities to the extension of provincial legislative jurisdiction into Aboriginal family life."[38]

Presented below is a summary of the provisions of the *Act* and comments that deal directly with Aboriginal children. This summary and comments are taken directly from a report prepared by Mitchell, Absolon, and Armitage.[39] Following this material the first author (an Aboriginal woman) of the current chapter presents her perspective on the impact of these provisions on Aboriginal people.

Part I Introductory Provisions
Section 2
Guiding Principles

(2)   *This Act is to be administered and interpreted in accordance with the following principles:*
- *(e)   kinship ties and a child's attachment to the extended family should be preserved if possible*
- *(f)   the cultural identity of Aboriginal children should be preserved*

For the first time in the history of British Columbia child welfare legislation, the new CFCSA acknowledges that cultural identity is important to an Aboriginal child's well being. Further, the Act encourages the preservation of Aboriginal cultural identity, including an acknowledgment of the extended family system. Considering that most government policies relating to Aboriginal people have been based on assimilation strategies, this section can be considered a breakthrough in the Ministry's (for Children and the Family) traditional practice of projecting dominant society values and standards onto Aboriginal people.

<u>Comment:</u>

This is an important section as it also encourages non-Aboriginal service providers to re-examine definitions of family and identity that are solely based on dominant society standards. As a guiding principle, the direction to acknowledge and maintain Aboriginal identity and kinship ties can be applied to each section throughout the Act and therefore makes this provision all the more significant.

The principle of recognizing the cultural identity of Aboriginal children is challenging to non-Aboriginal child welfare service providers who have traditionally viewed individual rights as paramount over collective/community rights. The practice of removing Aboriginal children from their families and communities has occurred without regard to the culture shock or deprivation, experienced by both the child being removed and the families and communities left behind.

The value of this guiding principle cannot be overstated. It will hopefully end the removal of Aboriginal children from their cultural surroundings, while still upholding the principle of protecting all children from harm. The past practice of placing 2Aboriginal children in middle-class, white families gives children the message that it is their entire Aboriginal community that is "harmful" and that no one in their extended family or community is "capable" of providing care for them. The condition of widespread poverty amongst Aboriginal peoples contrasts with the foster parents' situations as Ministry foster parent criteria usually restrict placements to those homes reflecting status quo standards: middle-

class, white, heterosexual, married, and able-bodied. By placing children in the care of an extended family member, other community member, or at the very least, maintaining kinship ties throughout the apprehension period, the child receives the message that his or her culture is worthy and respected.

Section 3
Service delivery principles

- • (b) *Aboriginal people should be involved in the planning and delivery of services to Aboriginal families and their children,*
- • (c) *services should be planned and provided in ways that are sensitive to the needs and the cultural, racial and religious heritage of those receiving the services,*
- ☐ (d) *the community should be involved, if possible and appropriate, in the planning and delivery of services to families and children.*

The Aboriginal Community Panel called for the full transfer of authority for Aboriginal child welfare to Aboriginal communities. However, the province concluded that it did not have the constitutional authority to legislate in this way. Instead of a more radical approach that would enable Aboriginal communities to regain full authority over their child welfare decisions, the Act allows for the transfer of authority to Aboriginal child welfare organizations. The first step in transferring this authority is to include Aboriginal people in the planning and delivery of services to their families, communities and Nations.

Comment:

With the acknowledgment that Aboriginal people have an identity separate from the dominant society, this section further acknowledges the essential role that Aboriginal families, communities, culture and traditions play in the lives of Aboriginal children. The Act states that they 'should be involved' which suggests that there is some room for variations in practice in this section. Since the primary child welfare service provided to Aboriginal people has traditionally been the apprehension of their children, this section should result in child welfare authorities including Aboriginal community members in their decisions. Ideally, this section of the Act will lead child welfare authorities to consult with, and follow the instruction of, Aboriginal people involved in the child's life. This would include extended family members and community members concerned with the children of their Nation.

If Aboriginal cultural identity is to be preserved, then it must be seen as valuable. This section of the Act directs the Ministry and those administering the CFCSA, to "decolonize" their minds and accept that the Aboriginal world view is not only important to a child's well being, it is essential.

Section 4
Best interests of child

(2) *If the child is an Aboriginal child, the importance of preserving the child's cultural identity must be considered in determining the child's best interests.*

The addition of this subsection is an important element in beginning to shift the views of non-Aboriginal individuals who make decisions about the lives of Aboriginal children and families. Traditionally, best interests ideology has been based on mainstream, dominant societal standards. These standards reflect white, middle class values and norms and have proven to be inappropriate and, in most cases, extremely harmful to Aboriginal people. Traditional Aboriginal views of child care and child rearing are different than those of traditional European based views; different, not better or worse.

Comment:

Interpretation of the best interests test when pertaining to Aboriginal children has been difficult as child welfare authorities come from the dominant society and have had difficulty in understanding the importance of considering race and culture as factors in determining the best interests of a child. The domination of non-Aboriginal people in child welfare authority positions, such as social workers, judges, lawyers, supervisors, etc., combined with the structural reality of racism that permeates every mainstream institution in Canadian society, have resulted in not only a misinterpretation of the best interest of Aboriginal children, but also a lack of understanding of the challenges faced by Aboriginal peoples as a whole.

The situation of under representation of Aboriginal peoples amongst the administration and staff of the Ministry contributes to this misinterpretation of best interest tests. Joy MacPhail (then the Minister of Social Services) did point out in a June 29th, 1995 interview that more Aboriginal people are now administering the Act through delegation of authority agreements with the province. However, many Aboriginal people live in urban settings, and with so few Aboriginal people working within the Ministry, the best interests tests are often administered by individuals unfamiliar with authentic Aboriginal world views. As a result, the Ministry will find it necessary to engage Aboriginal people to educate their child protection staff as to how they can uphold the principle of preserving an Aboriginal child's cultural identity when determining the best interest of that child.

Part II - Support Services And Agreements
Section 8
Agreements with child's kin and others

(1)   The director may make a written agreement with a person who
- *(a)   has established a relationship with a child or has a cultural or traditional responsibility toward a child.*

In general, support services to Aboriginal peoples living on reserves, or living off the reserve for less than a year, have traditionally been available on an irregular basis. Support services include day care, counselling, in-home support, respite care, parenting programs, and services to support children who witness family violence (Bill 46:8).

Section 8 (1)(a), provides the opportunity for Aboriginal people who have a cultural or traditional relationship with an Aboriginal child to make an agreement with the director to contribute to the child's care. This could take the form of financial support for the participation of an Elders council in a child welfare plan of care including travel expenses.

Comment:

This would acknowledge the widespread poverty that exists throughout the Aboriginal community. It will be interesting to see how this manifests itself in practice. Again we look at the lack of presence of Aboriginal people in positions of child welfare authority where decision making power lies. The possibility of using these provisions becomes more feasible where Aboriginal communities are able to determine how the resources will be allocated.

Division 2 - Cooperative Planning and Dispute Resolution
Section 20 *(not yet proclaimed)*
Family Conference

(1)   The purpose of a family conference is to enable and assist the family to develop a plan of care that will
- *(d)   take into account the child's culture and community.*

The Report of the non-Aboriginal community panel, <u>Making Changes: A Place to Start</u> [40] *recommended family conferences as a means to bring together significant people in the child's family to develop a plan that would ensure the best interest of the child. The subsection stipulates that the child's culture and community must, among other things, be taken into account at this family conference. In an interview with Jeremy Berland, Acting Director of Family and Children's Services at the Ministry on July 4, 1995, he stated that the family conference coordinators will be separate from Ministry social workers positions and will be located in offices separate from other social service providers employed by the Ministry. This separation will allow family conference coordinators to be viewed as less threatening than, say, a child protection worker.*

In the same interview, Mr. Berland also agreed that Aboriginal family conference coordinators would be the most appropriate people to work with Aboriginal families, as there may be less likelihood of cultural misunderstandings and intimidation than between Aboriginal clients and non-Aboriginal service providers.

Comment:

The non-Aboriginal service provider may not necessarily be consciously racist, but until the Ministry and the social work education field have undertaken extensive anti-racist training, the results of internalized dominance or unchecked racist assumptions are real, and harm to Aboriginal peoples results.

Provision 4 - Child Protection Hearings and Orders
Section 34
Duty to attend and inform others of presentation hearing

(3) The director must, if practicable, inform the following of the time, date and place of the hearing,

- *(d)   the applicable Aboriginal organization prescribed in the regulations for the purpose of this section, if the child is an Aboriginal child.*

Section 35
Presentation hearings and orders

(1) At the presentation hearing the director must present to the court the following:

- *(c)   an interim plan of care for the child that includes, in the case of an Aboriginal child, the steps to be taken to preserve the child's Aboriginal identity.*

Section 38
Notice of protection hearing

(1) At least 10 days before the date set for a protection hearing, notice of the time, date and place of the hearing must be served as follows:

- *(c)   If the child is registered or entitled to be registered as a member of an Indian band, on a designated representative of the band.*
- *(d)   if the child is not registered or not entitled to be registered as a member of an Indian band but is an Aboriginal child, on a designated representative of an Aboriginal community that has been identified by*
  - *(i)   the child, if 12 years of age or over, or*
  - *(ii)   the parent who at the time of the child's removal was apparently entitled to custody, if the child is under 12 years of age*

Section 39
Parties to proceedings

(1) If the following persons appear at the commencement of the protection hearing, they are entitled to be parties at the hearing:

- *(c)   if the child is an Aboriginal child, a representative of an Indian band of Aboriginal community served with notice of the hearing.*

These sections of the Act are similar to, but much more comprehensive than, the provisions of the Family and Child Service Act, the predecessor of the new Act. Informing Aboriginal community members of child protection actions involving members of their Nations is an essential element to restructuring power in relations between the Ministry and Aboriginal communities. The inclusion of this section is also important to direct the actions of child protection authorities.

<u>*Comment:*</u>

Many Aboriginal people reside off reserve for a variety of reasons, and the assumption made by many non-Aboriginal child welfare authorities is that ties to the family's Nation are then unimportant. In reality, poverty, unemployment, and lack of housing on reserves are some of the main reasons that Aboriginal people are forced to leave their home communities. As well, many Aboriginal people have been displaced from their Nation's communities for generations due to the enfranchisement initiatives by the federal government, which removed Aboriginal status, and therefore, their rights and benefits as Aboriginal people. Lack of opportunity for education, training, and employment also figure the myriad of reasons that Aboriginal peoples migrate to the cities. This by no means should be construed to mean that Aboriginal peoples do not have a vested interest in the lives of their community members. Therefore, Aboriginal communities must be involved in and continue to be informed about decisions relating to all children from their Nations and communities, who are taken into the care of the Ministry. This provides the Aboriginal community the opportunity to support the families and document their needs for further research and action.

Division 5 - Continuing Custody Hearings and Orders
Section 49
Continuing custody hearings and orders

(2)   *At least 10 days before the date set for hearing the application, notice of the time, date and place of the continuing custody hearing must be served as follows: (c) if the child is registered or entitled to be registered as a member of an Indian band, on a designated representative of the band,*

- (d)   *if the child is not registered or not entitled to be registered as member of an Indian band but is an Aboriginal child, on a designated representative of an Aboriginal community that has been identified*

Division 6 - Related Orders
Section 60
Consent orders

(1)   *With the written consent of the following, the court may, at any time after the presentation hearing, make any custody or supervision order that is provided for in the Part, including a continuing custody order:*

- (e)   *if the child is an Aboriginal child, the person who is or would have been entitled under section 38 (1) (c) or (d) to notice of any protection hearing concerning the child.*

Many Aboriginal communities are in Northern and remote areas of British Columbia. Often these communities are isolated and have few local resources such as legal aid, libraries, or other means through which information about the legal system can be accessed. The Canadian judicial system has been frequently cited as being biased against First Nations peoples, and statistics about the numbers of Aboriginal people in prison populations support this bias. The judicial system is largely considered inappropriate when applied to Aboriginal peoples, and child welfare hearings and orders are no exception. Northern communities experience "travelling court days" where a judge and legal counsel fly into remote communities and conduct court. These realities must be considered when one attempts to understand the relationship that Aboriginal peoples have with the imposed Canadian judicial system.

Comment:

The cited section of the new Act states that Aboriginal communities or organizations must be informed at least 10 days before a hearing for a continuing custody order is held. This may be appropriate for people who do not have to travel from remote areas to attend court sessions, but may be problematic for those living in isolated communities. Poverty also means that a person may not be able to afford to attend these hearings. The importance of informing the Aboriginal community representatives is only the beginning. Unless Aboriginal communities are provided with financial and other support to attend and address the child protection hearings, this section will have limited impact.

Part 4 - Children In Care
Section 71
Out-of-home living arrangements

(3)   If the child is an Aboriginal child, the director must give priority to placing the child as follows:
  - *(a)   with the child's extended family or within the child's Aboriginal cultural community*
  - *(b)   with another Aboriginal family, if the child cannot be safely placed under paragraph (a)*
  - *(c)   in accordance with subsection (2), if the child cannot be safely placed under paragraph (a) or (b) of this subsection. [Subsection (2) governs the placement of non-Aboriginal children]*

Granted there are times when biological parents are unable or unwilling to care for their children. These situations have always occurred in Aboriginal communities whether through the death, grieving or illness of parents. Traditionally, situations where parents were unable or unwilling to care for their children were dealt with by extended family and community members taking over parental duties. Section 71 directs the Ministry to look for its placements in a similar manner.

The overwhelming message given to the Aboriginal community panel during the legislation review community consultation sessions was that Aboriginal people demanded "an end to the legalized abduction of their children" from their families and communities.

Comment:

Aboriginal people have always been the most appropriate people to care for their children. By keeping Aboriginal children in the Aboriginal community, identity issues, which have caused so much pain and confusion, can be avoided. The source of these identity problems has been "white privilege".

The phenomenon of "white privilege" is largely unacknowledged by the dominant society, and therefore the extent to which this privilege puts others at a disadvantage is unexamined. Peggy McIntosh[41] writes about how white people remain quite oblivious to the privilege that their skin

102

colour affords. "Whites are taught to think of their lives as morally neutral, normative, and average, and also ideal, so that when we work to benefit others, this is seen as work by which we allow 'them' to be more like 'us.' The assumption held by well meaning white foster and adoptive parents, is that they are offering a "better" life to Aboriginal children. This unexamined assumption creates a phenomenon of "internalized dominance," which is described by Barbara Findlay[42] as "the incorporation of the fact of social privilege into the thought patterns, the behaviour patterns, and the expectations of people in the dominant place."

Unexamined white privilege and internalized dominance have both been extremely harmful to Aboriginal children, families, communities and Nations because they do not question why Aboriginal people are poor, why Aboriginal people have the highest suicide rates in the country, why Aboriginal people are dispossessed in their homelands, and why Aboriginal children make up 30% of the children-in-care of the Ministry. One way for social workers and other helping professionals to be allies to the thrust towards Aboriginal self-determination is to support initiatives that keep Aboriginal children in their homes and communities and to ensure the allocation of necessary resources to Aboriginal child welfare initiatives.

Section 71 of the CFCSA provides a directive to those implementing the Act to consider Aboriginal homes for children in need of care. This is a very positive move towards maintaining children's ties with their communities and cultures. Placing Aboriginal children in Aboriginal homes also gives the Aboriginal communities the message that they are valued as child care providers. This contrasts sharply with previous actions by child welfare authorities. The inclusion of this section in the new Act promises to curb the conscious or unconscious assimilation practices of the dominant culture and institutions of Canadian society.

Part 7 - Administration
Section 90
Minister's authority to make agreements

For the purposes of this Act, the minister may make an agreement with any of the following:
- *(a)   an Indian band or a legal entity representing an Aboriginal community,*
- *(b)   the government of Canada, the government of a province of Canada or the government of a jurisdiction outside Canada, or an official or agency of any of those governments*

Section 93
Other powers and duties of directors

(1)   A director may
- *(f)   make agreements, including but not limited to agreements*
     (iii)   with an Indian band or a legal entity representing an Aboriginal community for the provisions of services, and
     (iv) with the government of Canada, the government of a province of Canada or the government of a jurisdiction outside Canada, or an official or agency of any of those governments, to promote the purposes of this Act, and

- (g)	*promote and encourage the participation of the community in the planning, development and delivery of services*

Perhaps most importantly, sections 90-93 provide an opportunity for Aboriginal self-government. Through agreements with the federal governments and B.C. First Nations regarding the authority to provide child and family services, this aspect of Aboriginal self-government can be developed. Section 93 provides for a broad range of possibilities in terms of how First Nations child welfare agencies may be established and allows for the delegation of authority and services to Aboriginal agencies or communities. It also provides the opportunity for the Minister to negotiate with the federal governments on behalf of First Nations in B.C., or for negotiations to take place between the First Nations of B.C., the federal and provincial governments. The agreements between various First Nations and provincial and the federal governments can all be quite different from one another.

<u>Comment:</u>

This approach differs from the traditional one of attempting to create a "generic" way of dealing with very diverse First Nations. The ability of the Ministry to recognize that all First Nations peoples and communities are not the same is a valuable acknowledgment of the range of 'readiness' with respect to transferring control of child welfare to Aboriginal communities and agencies.

Part 8 - Miscellaneous Provisions
Section 103
Power to make regulations

(2)	*Without limiting subsection (1), the Lieutenant Governor in Council may make regulations as follows:*
- (e)	*prescribing Aboriginal organizations for the purposes of section 34 (notice of presentation hearing)*
- (f)	*designating, by name or position, those representatives of Indian bands and Aboriginal communities who are entitled to notice under Part 3 and to be parties under sections 38 or 50*
- (g)	*respecting the standards for foster homes and residential services*

Callahan and Wharf[13] describe regulations as "a bridge between the Act and the very specific policies established by Ministries . . . and provide some elaboration as to how an Act is to be implemented." The power to make regulations as outlined in this section has potential to be both beneficial or limiting to Aboriginal communities.

<u>Comment:</u>

In the past, the long-standing practice of viewing Aboriginal people as less capable than whites prevented the inclusion of Aboriginal perspectives while creating and authorizing regulations that affect Aboriginal people's lives. However, the potential for including Aboriginal perspectives within regulation development is now increased by the presence of an Aboriginal services team within the Ministry. This small but influential team may be employed in the development of regulations, or in the very least, have the opportunity to examine drafts of such regulations. The Ministry must remain committed to seeking Aboriginal perspectives in the development of any and all policies and regulations that affect the lives of Aboriginal peoples. Above all, they must learn to follow First Nations directions and allocate the resources necessary to carry out this commitment.

In the opinion of the first author of the current chapter, the inclusion of these provisions within the *Child, Family and Community Service Act* reflects a constructive beginning of a concrete recognition by the Ministry for Children and Families (formerly Social Services) of issues of accountability to the Aboriginal peoples of British Columbia. The inclusion of guiding principles that instruct child welfare authorities to consider the culture, identity, and extended family of Aboriginal children is positive. If the *Act* is adhered to, Aboriginal children will be removed from their families and communities with less frequency. In implementing these provisions, the Ministry must then recognize the issues of unresolved community trauma. It must increase avenues of community support and funding with a goal of facilitating First Nations' capacity to respond to the treatment, prevention needs, and issues of their own community members. Aboriginal culture and identity should be taken into consideration when considering the interest of Aboriginal children. Increased consultations should also be occurring between Aboriginal families and communities on decisions affecting their children. Avenues for future agreements for Aboriginal communities to partially control and administer child and family services have been created.

The provisions raise two critical issues. They are a positive a step, and are simply that - a step in legislatively recognizing both the distinctness of Aboriginal children, families, and communities, and the need for government accountability in responding to these issues. The limitations are still present, and at the end of the day, the provincial and federal governments still exercise ultimate authority and control. As witnessed in the Ontario experience, First Nations are left with limited power. With an unsupportive and unsympathetic government, the *Act* can still be interpreted and manipulated to meet the needs of the dominant government agenda. The caution remains and the interim measures must be regarded as just that: temporary.

Secondly, the issues of fiscal responsibility still exist, as more responsibility is delegated to, and is dependent upon, First Nations' capacity to respond. Resources must now accompany authority. Without adequate developmental resources, First Nations' capacity to respond independently to the needs of their children and families will be seriously impeded. The dangers of not having adequate supports and treatments within communities exists, and could result in many more child tragedies. For the *Act*'s intentions to be realised, the Ministry must provide financial support to Aboriginal child welfare initiatives and take direction from Aboriginal people.

III. Two Models of Native Indian Administered Child Welfare Services in British Columbia

The Province of British Columbia cannot claim to have developed innovative child protection legislation with respect to native peoples. Indeed, the earlier *Family and Child Service Act* made no reference to First Nations in its short and very general statement of principle.[44] The only mention of Indian people was found in section 12 of the *Act,* which required that the band social development officer or band manager be notified of a child protection hearing dealing with a registered Indian child who is a band member. It would be incorrect, however, to state that provincial and federal authorities in British Columbia have been unresponsive to the urgent needs of native families and children in the child welfare field, even if political pressure by native groups and others has undoubtedly had a major influence. Indeed, a child welfare program administered by the 400 member Spallumcheen Indian Band at Enderby has been in operation since 1981, and is unique in Canada in affording this band almost complete autonomy of decision making in child protection matters. A second program, operated by the Nuu Chah Nulth Tribal Council under delegated provincial authority, has since 1987 been providing child welfare services to families on reserves on the west coast of Vancouver Island, where over 6,000 status Indians reside. Since the legal parameters of each program[45] differ, it is useful to identify the salient features of each.

A. The Spallumcheen Band Program

The Spallumcheen child welfare program has been operating for a number of years under the authority of a band by-law passed in 1980, which asserts exclusive band jurisdiction over any custody proceeding involving an unmarried band member under the age of 21 years.[46] Although the constitutionality of the by-law is doubtful, the Minister of Indian Affairs chose not to exercise his power of veto, and the federal government has entered into agreements for funding the band's child welfare services since the spring of 1981. Moreover, provincial child welfare authorities have adhered to a 1980 memorandum of understanding entered into between the band and former British Columbia Minister of Human Resources, Grace McCarthy, whereby the provincial government agreed to respect the band's authority in child welfare matters.

For purposes of child protection, the by-law authorizes the Chief and members of the Band Council to apprehend and bring a band child before a meeting of the council in specified circumstances where the child is believed to be in need of protection. After considering the circumstances, including the wishes of the child (whenever the latter is old enough to appreciate his/her situation), the Chief and Council are authorized to reach a decision on future placement in the order of preference set forth in the by-law. This commences with a parent (followed sequentially by a member of the child's extended family living on the reserve), a member of the extended family living off the reserve, an Indian person living on a reserve, an Indian person living off the reserve, and, as a last resort, with a non-Indian person living off the reserve. However, in making placement decisions the Chief and Band Council are required to give paramount consideration to the child's best interests. Placement decisions are reviewable by a general band meeting at the request of any band member, including the child's parent.

It will be noted that this by-law differs from conventional child protection statutes in assigning apprehending, fact finding, and disposition powers to the same persons, namely the Chief and members of the Band Council. Moreover, decisions are made not in the context of a formal judicial hearing but rather by discussion and vote at a Band Council meeting. An obvious danger exists that important decisions could be made without due process safeguards. According to the staff members involved in the Spallumcheen program, this potential danger has not materialized, partly because of the careful and consensual decision making within the Band Council, and also because parents almost always have supported placement decisions of the Chief and Council. Regardless, concerns remain about the potential for arbitrary or vindictive actions by band decision makers, which would be greatly alleviated if provision were made for fact-finding and placement decisions by a body independent of the persons assigned apprehending powers. How feasible such a process would be in small communities is still a question.

There is no doubt, however, that the Spallumcheen by-law, supported by continuity of federal funding for child welfare services, has ensured both band self-determination in child welfare matters and development of child care resources designed to ensure that the band children in jeopardy or at risk will have their needs met within a native Indian cultural and family environment. Indeed, one of the tangible benefits resulting from this program is that resources developed by the band over the past decade have made it possible for all children requiring out-of-home care to be placed in familiar Indian surroundings. The child welfare program is also carefully integrated with the cultural, health, and educational services provided by the Spallumcheen Band, and retains the resources of the social service industry within the community.

B. The Nuu Chah Nulth Tribal Council Program

This program is legally structured by means of separate bilateral agreements between the Tribal Council and representatives of the federal and provincial levels of government. An agreement with the Superintendent (now director) of Family and Child Services in British Columbia, concluded in November, 1985, authorizes the Tribal Council to assume child protection powers as delegated by the director within the boundaries of fourteen Indian reserves. Service delegation also extends to children of band members in the care of the director. A parallel agreement with the Department of Indian and Northern Affairs signed in February, 1987, provides federal funding for a range of child welfare services on the reserves.[47] The funding includes monies for staff training and preventive community services.

The autonomy of the Tribal Council is potentially limited by two clauses in the agreement with the director. Clause 2 provides that tribal council staff who are assigned delegated statutory power remain subject to the direction of the director in discharging the child protection mandate of the *Child, Family and Community Service Act* (formerly *Family and Child Service Act*). This clause makes it clear that protective services are to be provided within the parameters of the provincial child protection statute. This includes recourse to the Provincial Court (Family Division) when child removals occur. It is also evident from Clause 2 that the director is afforded the power to exercise supervision over this program. This power is reinforced by Clause 7, which authorizes the director to terminate the delegation of statutory child protection functions at any time.

In spite of the potential within the legal language of the agreement for control of this program by provincial child welfare authorities, the experience over the past few years has been one of genuine support by provincial staff for Indian administration of this program. A senior specialist with the provincial government has played an active consultative role in establishment of the program. The School of Social Work at the University of Victoria also has assisted in training native Indian child protection workers employed by the Nuu Chah Nulth Tribal Council. Also of significance has been the utilization by each participating band of child welfare committees composed of paid staff and volunteers to assist in review of protection cases and counseling of families. The Tribal Council also calls upon an elders' advisory committee for guidance in program and policy development. In these ways the administrators of the program have minimized their involvement with the formalities of the provincial child protection legislation.

Indian-administered child welfare programs with legal parameters similar to the Nuu Chah Nulth program, are currently serving status Indians on most reserves in Manitoba and several reserves in New Brunswick and Alberta.

THE CHALLENGE OF URBAN INDIAN CHILD WELFARE

This section will raise the issues of developing urban Indian child welfare programs. Several proposals will be discussed to address these issues and the section concludes with a call for authentic on-going consultation with First Nations peoples.

Although one must be encouraged by the development of Indian administered programs in several provinces, it is also important to recognize the limitations of these programs and the challenges that could arise with such limited power. A key shortcoming lies in the fact that federal program funding applies only to services provided to status Indian families and children who reside on reserves. As indicated earlier, the past few decades have witnessed an accelerated migration of Canadian Indians from reserves to urban centres of population. In 1989 approximately 47 percent of status Indians in British Columbia were residing off reserves.[48] If the mainly urban population of non-status Indian and Metis is added to this number, it is evident that the majority of persons of native descent now reside in the cities and towns of the province. Although British Columbia has the highest percentage of Indians in Canada living off reserves, a similar trend toward urban migration is evident in other provinces as well, especially in other provinces of Western Canada.

Another shortcoming lies in the fact that because child welfare lies in provincial legislation, First Nations people can become vulnerable to changes in the agenda of the provincial government. Without fully instituting Aboriginal child welfare law in the hands of Aboriginal Nations, the ultimate control and power is still in the hands of the government, which has used this power oppressively.

The need for policy makers to give careful attention to urban Indian child welfare issues is also confirmed by the fact that in British Columbia in 1989 native children without registered Indian status comprised 60 percent of all children of native descent in government care. This is a significant increase compared to a figure of 42 percent ten years earlier.[49] As a consequence there is an obvious need for programs, mandated in legislation, that are responsive to the child welfare needs of native families in the city regardless of whether or not they possess registered Indian status. And in 1996, the number of Aboriginal children in the care of the Ministry for Children and Families was one third of its total figure. It is also important to note that most of these Aboriginal children in care live off reserve and have little access to culturally relevant services or service providers. That is, they receive service from existing child and family agencies.

Vancouver, however, is quickly becoming the exception with the development of an urban Aboriginal child and family organization. In March of 1990, the Ministry undertook a significant policy initiative in establishing a special native family and child service unit located in Vancouver's downtown eastside. This unit is staffed mainly by native Indian personnel who serve over 100 status and non-status Indian children in the care of the Ministry. The staff members also provide preventive family counselling services, although they do not assume responsibility for child removals, court presentations, or the initial investigation of child protection complaints.

It should be noted, however, that this Vancouver-based native child welfare unit is structured as an integral part of the provincial government's child welfare bureaucracy. In the opinion of the second author, the Ministry could have pursued two alternative policy options with potential to engage much wider participation by native social service personnel and native volunteers in the city. The then Minister could have utilized his authority under section 3(4) of the existing *Family and Child Service Act* to delegate to a native Indian child and family service organization some or all of the Ministry's statutory responsibilities for child protection of native children in the city. Alternatively, the Minister could have arranged for amendments to child welfare legislation, similar to the legislation now in force in Ontario, to establish and license native family and children's societies to discharge a comprehensive child welfare mandate covering native families and children in Vancouver and other major urban centres of the province.

Persons seeking policy innovations in urban Indian child welfare legislation should give serious consideration to two proposals first put forward by the British Columbia Royal Commission on Family and Children's Law[50] in the mid 1970s. In relation both to native and non-native families, the Commission was concerned to reduce or avoid the trauma caused to parents and children by formal proceedings in Family Court. As an alternative to such proceedings, the Commission recommended legislation to mandate a "child care conference" forum[51] for the mediation of problems associated with child care in cases which did not require urgent measures to protect a child. The Commission suggested that a mediating conference could be initiated by consensus between a parent and the child welfare authorities or upon referral by a judge. This proposal, although not adopted in legislation, was strongly supported by native Indians.

A second proposal, which was adopted in 1974 amendments to British Columbia's child protection legislation, entailed establishment of child protection panels composed of two lay volunteers and a Family Court judge, when requested by a child, parent, the Superintendent of Child Welfare or the presiding judge.[52] This system was designed to reduce social class and ethnic biases and to draw upon the wisdom and cultural insights of carefully screened and trained lay persons. Twenty native Indians were recruited to serve on panels in a special unified Family Court project, which operated for about three years in the lower mainland municipalities of Surrey and Richmond. The panel system was used in only about a dozen cases before being discontinued in 1976. The enabling legislation was repealed when the Social Credit government enacted the *Family and Child Service Act* in 1980.

The foregoing proposals were deemed innovative and progressive by helping professionals fifteen years ago. They are deserving of renewed consideration at the present time, when Aboriginal child welfare problems continue to be critical concerns of First Nations and non-First Nations across Canada.

Authentic consultations must continue with the Aboriginal peoples of British Columbia. The process of having separate consultations with First Nations through the community panel review,[53] mentioned near the beginning of this chapter, was a start, ending with legislation that established some windows to further developments. What this separate process achieved was the opportunity to highlight the needs and issues by giving voice to the Aboriginal people of British Columbia. It also exposed, once again, the disproportionate numbers of Aboriginal children in care of the Ministry and the conditions under which this care occurs. The long overdue, yet essential action of consulting with First Nations peoples, has proven to be helpful in creating child welfare legislation that reflects some of the needs of Aboriginal peoples. The Aboriginal-specific sections of this new *Act* have been necessary for a very long time. Administration and implementation of the new *Act* will require an effort to educate Ministry social workers about the colonial and cultural history of the First Nations in Canada and British Columbia. Increased awareness and training regarding the distinct nature of needs and issues of First Nations would be followed by a consistent and authentic implementation process by Ministry practitioners.

COMMON QUESTIONS

It is useful to identify some of the problems experienced by First Nations families that render them powerless and vulnerable to child protection interventions. It is also important to identify the racist ideology inherent in specific features of provincial child protection laws that have exacerbated the problems of First Nations families and children. In addition, it is necessary to determine the linkages between reform of child protection laws and contemporary demands by native leaders for major constitutional reforms. These subjects will be addressed by answering a series of questions that could be posed by helping professionals.

1. <u>What kinds of problems do the First Nations families experience that lead to child protection interventions</u>?

As previously mentioned, child welfare law, when applied to First Nations families without accurate knowledge about First Nations culture and oppressive government agendas, becomes not a part of a solution, but part of a problem. Families must then deal with ignorance, racist attitudes and practices, and perceptions of superiority of the dominant Euro-Canadian culture. Laws without conscience, laws without choice and without respect for the family languages, traditions, and practices have in fact created the symptoms and problems many First Nations parents face today. The problems that First Nations families experience cannot be examined without first acknowledging their roots. Apart from the First Nations' history of racial oppression, cultural genocide, and other problems, the problems of native parents are somewhat similar to those of non-Indian families where parenting behaviours raise concerns for the safety or well-being of children. The differences, however, do lie in the consequences of poverty, powerlessness, and having no control over one's life. Often the symptoms to such conditions include alcohol abuse resulting in frequent absences from home, family violence, or neglect of the basic physical needs of children. The differences also may include severe parental health problems that may limit the capacity to nurture and respond to the everyday physical, social, and psychological needs of children.

What distinguishes many native families from non-native families is their chronic experiences of psychological trauma and chronic levels of stress associated with symptoms of racial oppression: high levels of unemployment, poor housing, poverty-level incomes, and discrimination. Stress is also caused by the conflict felt by many native Indians in reconciling traditional Indian values with those of the surrounding society. In addition, Indian children, more than other Canadian children, are much more likely to be raised in single-parent families where the mother often assumes a heavy burden of child rearing in an environment of poverty and social isolation. These women are often unsupported by fathers and are left to deal with or fend off child welfare authorities on their own. There are few services and supports to aid women parenting children alone, and society's racism and sexism makes coping all that more challenging. A survey of Indian families in 1981 found that over 20 percent were single parent families and 80 percent of these were headed by women.[54] This was about double the rate for non-Indian families. The same study also revealed that the percentage of native single parent families was significantly higher in urbanized areas. For example, nearly 35 percent of all native families in Winnipeg were single parent families and 92 percent of these families were headed by women.

2. <u>Why have provincial child protection laws in the past been inadequate in dealing effectively and positively with the problems of First Nations families?</u>

Traditional child protection statutes, which prevailed in most Canadian provinces from about 1900 until the early 1980s, were mainly designed to facilitate the removal of children from family surroundings and did so by making allegations of neglect or abuse. This was achieved by vaguely worded statutory mandates, which authorized social workers to apprehend children who were believed to be in moral or physical danger according to dominant societal values. Thus, in British Columbia, a child prior to 1968 could be apprehended where her/his home "by reason of neglect . . . was an unfit place for the child" or where he/she had "no parent capable of exercising proper parental control."[55] In 1951 there were only 29 Aboriginal children in care. Most of the children were still in residential schools. By 1964 the number of children in care had climbed to 1466 while residential schools were being closed. Significantly, most child protection statutes in Canada failed to emphasize or mandate provision of services to improve family functioning and avoid the necessity of child apprehensions. Native families, especially those experiencing above-average social stress, were therefore highly vulnerable to interventions leading to the removal of their children. Additionally, non-native social workers were not trained to assess, intervene, and work with cultures different from their own or to recognize community and family strengths. Schools of Social Work had neither authentic Aboriginal curriculum nor accurate accounts of the history of colonial oppression and racism against First Nations families. Hence, non-native social workers were basically ignorant about the conditions and issues that were impacting negatively and tragically on First Nations children and their families.

Native parents whose children were apprehended also experienced confusion and bewilderment when they were participants in child protection hearings conducted by non-Indian judges of the provincial family courts. They felt alienated both by the legalistic language of the proceedings and the formal atmosphere of the court[56] and often were not properly informed of their rights. The violent intervention of removal to residential school and the negative impact of the residential school experience on those parents' lives was rarely acknowledged by the courts.

Prior to the early 1980s child protection statutes assigned no priority to dispositions that would enable a judge to order that a neglected Indian child be cared for within a native family milieu. Typically, native children admitted to care were placed in non-native foster care settings, often at a considerable distance from parents, relatives, and friends. This type of placement exposed children to cultural discontinuity while at the same time preventing or impeding family visitations.[57] The problem was especially pronounced in western Canada in the case of native children placed for adoption. For example, in Manitoba in 1981, 45 percent of Indian adoptees were placed in out-of-province adoption homes, a majority located in the United States, and only one with Indian adoptive parents.[58] These practices led to vigorous protests by native people, with the result that Manitoba amended its child welfare legislation in 1985 to impose restrictions on out-of-province adoption placements of both native and non-native children. These restrictions include a requirement that the provincial cabinet approve all proposals for adoption placement of Manitoba children outside of Canada.[59]

A final factor of special concern to native people was the fact that the child protection programs mandated by legislation were administered and delivered predominantly by non-native personnel. This only perpetuated racist policies and practices and left the abuse inflicted upon First Nations people unquestioned. Communication with native families in crisis was non-existent, and interventions occurred without consideration or consultation with First Nations families or leaders. The lack of respect for the Aboriginal community and consequent intrusions into native families made it more difficult, if next to impossible, to recruit native people to serve as resource persons for children admitted to care. Working with and for the oppressor was the last place an Aboriginal person would be found because of the perception of betrayal to one's own community. Trust was eroded and was replaced with suspicion and fear of child welfare authorities.

3. <u>Is there a need for First Nations to control and administer their own child protection programs</u>?

For many of the reasons already mentioned, the answer to this question is yes. Native-administered programs could eliminate or reduce the problems of mistrust between non-Indian professional social workers and native clientele. Such programs could also enhance the development of support systems designed to reach out to families at risk. Native-administered programs could also introduce decision making structures and procedures for neglected or abused children that are congruent with traditional custom law and evolving native values. Two of the native-administered child welfare programs currently in operation in British Columbia are discussed earlier in this chapter. Child protection should be part of self-administered community social and economic programs within the larger process of the move towards First Nations self- government.

4. <u>What is the relationship between recent demands for Indian self-government and child protection law</u>?

The issue of self-government has been a major priority of Indian organizations for the past twenty years. Self-government has assumed importance at a time when Indian leaders are seeking political powers that would enable native people to have control over their lives and their futures. At the present time, apart from special federal legislation mandating local government for the Sechelt Indian Band in British Columbia and the Cree and Nascapi Bands in northern Quebec, self-governing authority for Aboriginal peoples is confined to the limited band by-law powers provided for in section 81 of the *Indian Act* and applicable only to Indians who reside on reserves. These powers include authority for Indian Bands to enact by-laws dealing with such subjects as health measures, traffic regulation, preservation of order on a reserve, and the allotment of certificates of possession for housing. The powers do not include authority to enact by-laws dealing with child protection or education. Moreover, all by-laws passed by Indian Bands are subject to veto by the federal Minister of Indian Affairs (section 82 (2)).

In 1983 a special Parliamentary Committee chaired by Keith Penner issued a report calling for a constitutional amendment that would entrench a right to self-government for Indian First Nations in Canada.[60] The report also recommended that self-governing powers encompass social and cultural development, including family and child welfare law. This recommendation was subsequently debated and discussed at three First Ministers' Conferences held between 1984 and 1987. The proposal failed when agreement could not be achieved on the specifics of self-governing powers.

Native self-government, however, continues to be highly relevant to child protection legislation because it could lead to the enactment of child protection laws for Native people that reflect contemporary native values in such salient areas as grounds for protective intervention, procedures for judicial decision making, protective dispositions, and the administration and delivery of child welfare programs. This legislation could contribute also to reducing and eventually eliminating the colonial legacy of dependency that has oppressed the native people of this country since confederation.

5. <u>What is the relationship between the resolution of current Indian land claims and Indian child welfare?</u>

In the final analysis, native land claims represent a just demand by the native peoples of this country for a more equitable distribution of the resources of Canada. They also represent a strongly felt need to share with other Canadians in the management of land, fishery, forestry, mineral, and water resources. Many First Nations perceive reserve lands as being mismanaged by the federal Department of Indian and Northern Affairs and provincial ministries responsible for public lands off reserves. The successful resolution of the land question through the courts and political negotiations could in time provide Aboriginal peoples with the economic base needed to finance native controlled social programs, including child welfare and child protection services. In the absence of a viable, self-sustaining economic base, child welfare services, no matter how culturally sensitive or progressive, are unlikely to resolve the chronic dependency and poverty that contributes to the break-down of many native Indian families in this country. Successful resolution of land claims is closely linked with Indian self-government in achieving the objective of self-determination.

CONCLUSION

Earlier in this chapter, the view was expressed that child welfare services to First Nations children and their families are closely linked to the broader political and constitutional events now shaping the future for both native and non-native peoples of Canada. It is reasonable to anticipate that the next quarter century will witness constitutional changes that will create self-governing structures for First Nations in Canada in fields of activity essential to strengthening and preserving their identity, pride, and security as first citizens of this country. The field of family and child welfare law is likely to be included in the legislative powers conferred on native units of government. One can also anticipate that constitutional reforms will create an Aboriginal order of government in which the artificial and divisive distinctions between status and non-status Indian people are brought to an end. Child welfare is one process among many in which First Nations are engaging with government structures to regain control and autonomy over their children, families, and communities.

To their great credit, many helping professionals have already contributed to the goal of First Nations self-determination in the child welfare field by helping to design and implement legislation and programs that create opportunities to reflect First Nations values and facilitate a progressive expansion of First Nations autonomy. Child welfare reforms can and must contribute to the major societal changes required to ensure a better life for the aboriginal peoples of Canada in the years ahead. The many contemporary problems that First Nations families experience, however, are not going to be resolved by progressive child welfare legislation alone.

The challenge next lies in implementation and follow up support in the form of training, resources and funding to First Nations tribal groups and organizations, as they begin to develop and administer the *Child, Family and Community Service Act* to their own people. Philosophical questions remain, such as the appropriateness of the *Act* in its entirety, its application to First Nations by First Nations, and the readiness of First Nations to address their own trauma issues. Perhaps one day First Nations political organizations will explore and draft their own legislation that parallels the provincial legislation. This could begin to lay the foundation for full authority and control of child welfare by First Nations themselves. With the treaty making process evolving and First Nations negotiating transfer of authority of child welfare under treaty agreements, one must wonder what kind of legal and political opportunities are evolving.

RESOURCES

D. Durst, J. McDonald & C. Rich, Aboriginal Government of Child Welfare Services: Hobson's Choice? In J. Hudson & B. Galaway, eds., *Child Welfare in Canada: Research and Policy Implications* (Toronto: Thompson Educational Publishing, 1995).

P. Johnson, *Native Children and the Child Welfare System* (Ottawa: Canadian Council on Social Development, 1983).

Liberating our Children, Liberating our Nations, Report of the Aboriginal Panel on Child Welfare, (Victoria: Ministry of Social Services, 1992).

B. MacKenzie & P. Hudson, Native Children, Child Welfare, and the Colonization of Native People. In K.L. Levitt & B. Wharf, eds., *The Challenge of Child Welfare* (Vancouver: University of British Columbia Press, 1985).

M. Sinclair, D. Phillips & N. Bala, Aboriginal Child Welfare in Canada. In N. Bala, J. P. Hornick, & R. Vogl, eds., *Canadian Child Welfare Law: Children, Families, and the State* (Toronto: Thompson Educational, 1990).

J. B. Timpson, Indian and Native Special Status in Ontario's Child Welfare Legislation: An Overview of the Social, Legal, and Political Context (1990) 7 *Social Work Review* 49.

B. Wharf, *Toward First Nation Control of Child Welfare: A Review of Emerging Developments in B.C.* (Victoria: University of Victoria, 1987) (unpublished).

S. Imai, K. Logan & G. Stien, *Aboriginal Law Handbook* (Scarborough, Ontario: Carswell Thompson Professional Publishing, 1993).

END NOTES

1. *Report of the Special Committee on Indian Self-Government in Canada* (Ottawa: Queen's Printer, 1983) (Chair: K. Penner). This report is usually referred to as the "Penner Report."
2. The terms First Nations, Aboriginal, Native and Indian are used interchangeably and are meant to include status and non-status Aboriginal peoples as well as Inuit and Metis peoples.
3. *Liberating our Children, Liberating our Nations*: Report of the Aboriginal Committee, Community Panel, Family and Child Services Legislation Review in British Columbia, (Victoria: K.J. Lee and Associates Ltd, 1992).
4. *Child, Family and Community Service Act*, R.S.B.C. 1996 c.46.
5. The reader will note the term Indian in reference to First Nations peoples. This term, because it omits any reference to people, has contributed to the dehumanization of Aboriginal people in its usage and policy applications.
6. *Indian Act*, R.S.C. 1985, c.I-5, sections 5-17.
7. *Constitution Act*, 1982, section 35(1), being Schedule B of the *Canada Act* 1982 (U.K.), 1982, c.11.
8. *Constitution Act*, 1867 (U.K.), 30 & 31 Vict., c.3, section 91(24).
9. For a thorough discussion of the *Indian Act's* definitions of persons entitled to registered Indian status, as well as the effects of the 1985 amendments, see J.S. Frideres, *Native People in Canada: Contemporary Conflicts*, 3d ed. (Scarborough, Ont.: Prentice Hall, 1988) c.2.
10. Reference Re *Adoption Act* (1938), [1938] S.C.R. 398.
11. *Constitution Act, supra,* note 8, section 91(24).
12. *Kruger v. R.* (1977), [1978] 1 S.C.R. 104, [1977] 4 W.W.R. 300.
13. Indian and Inuit Affairs, *Child Welfare Policy* (Program Circular) (Ottawa: Queen's Printer, May 1, 1982).
14. *Natural Parents Association v. British Columbia (Superintendent of Child Welfare)* (1976), [1976] 2 S.C.R. 751, [1976] 1 W.W.R. 699.
15. *Supra*, note 3.
16. *Manitoba (Director of Child Welfare) v. B.* (1979), [1979] 6 W.W.R. 229, [1981] 4 C.N.L.R. 62 (Man. Prov. Ct).
17. Re *Family and Child Service Act of British Columbia and An Application Relating to the Child Joseph Ignace* (6 June 1990), Kamloops (B.C. Prov. Ct) [unreported], Gordon J.
18. *Canada Health and Social Transfer*, Part V. *Budget Implementation Act* 1995, c.17 sections 13-56.
19. C. Lewis, *Indian Families of the Northwest Coast: The Impact of Change* (Chicago: University of Chicago Press, 1970) c.2. See also, E. Hill, *The Impact of the Dominant Culture's Values on the Native Indian Family* (major paper for the degree of Master of Social Work, School of Social Work, University of British Columbia, 1982) [unpublished]. Note especially Chapter 1, "The Native Families Evolution from Identities Based on Tribal Membership to the Legal Identification Imposed by the Dominant Culture."
20. P. Tennant, *Aboriginal Peoples and Politics* (Vancouver: University of British Columbia Press, 1990) c.6.
21. See J. Mitchell, K. Absolon, A. Armitage, *The Development of the Child, Family and Community Service Act: An Aboriginal Perspective.* (Victoria, School of Social Work, University of Victoria, 1996) pp. 8-11.
22. C. Haig-Brown, *Resistance and Renewal: Surviving the Indian Residential School* (Vancouver: Tillicum Library, 1988). See especially Chapter 3, "School Life."
23. K. Absolon & E. Herbert (1997). "Community action as a practice of freedom: A First Nations perspective." In B. Wharf & M. McClague (eds.) *Community Organizing: Canadian Experiences.* (Toronto: Oxford Press, 1996).
    A. Armitage (1993). "Family and Child Welfare in First Nations Communities." In B. Wharf (ed.) *Rethinking Child Welfare in Canada.* (Toronto: McClelland & Stewart Inc., 1993).
    M. Battiste (1995). "Introduction." In M. Battiste & J. Barman (1995). *First Nations Education in Canada: The Circle Unfolds.* (Vancouver: UBC Press, 1995).
    E. Herbert (1995). An Overview and Analysis of First Nations Child and Family Services in B.C. Prepared for

the Gove Inquiry into Child Protection (1995).

J. Timpson (1993). *Status Indians, Child Welfare Policy and the Canadian State: Historical Context and Contemporary Considerations for First Nations Controlled Service.* (Ottawa: Royal Commission on Aboriginal Peoples, 1993).

24. *Report of the B.C. Indian Advisory Council,* (Victoria: British Columbia Government, 1955).

25. For a fuller discussion of the development of this extension of child protection services to Indians on reserves in B.C., see J.A. MacDonald, "The Spallumcheen Indian Band By-Law and its Potential Impact on Native Indian Child Welfare Policy in British Columbia" (1983) 4 Can. J. Fam. L. 75.

26. B.C. Royal Commission on Family and Children's Law, *The Social and Economic Conditions of Indian Families in British Columbia* by W.T. Stanbury (Vancouver: B.C. Royal Commission on Family and Children's Law, 1974).

27. H.P. Hepworth, *Foster Care and Adoption in Canada* (Ottawa: Canadian Council on Social Development, 1980) c.8.

28. P. Johnston, *Native Children and the Child Welfare System* (Toronto: Lorimer, 1983).

29. Statistics Canada, *Aboriginal Peoples Survey: Untangling the Social Safety Net for Aboriginal People,* Background paper 6., (Ottawa, 1991).

30. *Child and Family Services Act,* S.O. 1984, c.55.

31. J. B.Timpson "Indian and Native Special Status in Ontario's Child Welfare Legislation: An Overview of the Social, Legal and Political Context," (1990) 7 Canadian Social Work Review no.1 pp.49-68.

32. *Supra,* note 30, section 1(f).

33. *Idem,* section 1.

34. *Re Catholic Children's Aid Society of Metropolitan Toronto and M.* (1986), [1987] 3 C.N.L.R. 39 (Ont. Prov. Ct).

35. Timpson, *supra,* note 31.

36. N. Bala et al., eds, *Canadian Child Welfare Law: Children, Families, and the State* (Toronto: Thompson Educational, 1990) c.8.

37. Timpson, note 31.

38. *Liberating our Children, Liberating our Nations,* Report of the Aboriginal Panel on Child Welfare, (Victoria, 1992), *supra,* note 3, p.64.

39. This section and comments are published with the kind permission of J. Mitchell, K. Absolon and A. Armitage, see note 21, pages 38-47.

40. *Making Changes: A Place to Start,* Report of the Community Panel, Family and Child Services, Legislation Review in B.C (Victoria, Ministry of Social Services, K.J.Lee and Associates, 1992).

41. P. McIntosh, *White Privilege: Unpacking the Invisible Knapsack,* (1989) July, Peace and Freedom, 10.

42. B. Findlay, *With All of Who We Are: A Discussion of Oppression and Dominance,* (Vancouver: Lazara Press, 1991), p.5.

43. M. Callahan and B. Wharf, *Demystifying the Policy Process: A Case Study of the Development of Child Welfare Legislation in B.C.,* (Victoria, Sedgewick Society, School of Social Work, 1982) p.30.

44. *Family and Child Service Act,* S.B.C. 1980, c.11.

45. Currently, there are many other First Nation bands with plans to take over some aspect of child and family services and each are at varying stages of transfer. One current example would be the Kowizhan Child & Family Services in Duncan, B.C., which operates under a delegated provincial authority agreement.

46. Spallumcheen Indian Band, *By-Law for the Care of Our Indian Children* No.3 (1980).

47. J.K. Nutley, *The Squamish Indian Band Family and Child Services Program: A Study of the Evolution of a Band-based Program,* (major paper for the degree of Master of Social Work, School of Social Work, University of British Columbia, 1989) [unpublished].

48. Department of Indian and Northern Affairs, *Indian Register Population by Sex and Residence, 1989* (Ottawa: Department of Indian and Northern Affairs, 1990).

49. R.S. Ratner, *Child Welfare Services for Urban Native Indians,* (Vancouver: United Native Nations, May, 1990). The statistical appendices record the fact that native children comprised about one-third of the children in the care of the B.C. Ministry of Social Services and Housing in 1989. These statistics also reveal that the number of status Indian children in care fell from 1686 to 854 between 1979 and 1989. During the same period the number of native children in care without registered Indian status increased from 1198 to 1290.

50. B.C., Royal Commission on Family and Children's Law, *The Protection of Children (Child Care)* (Report No.5, Part V) (Vancouver: Royal Commission on Family and Children's Law, 1975).

51. *Idem*, at 18-22.

52. *Protection of Children Amendment Act*, S.B.C. 1974, c.69, section 2.

53. See Aboriginal Panel, *supra*, note 3.

54. Department of the Secretary of State, *Native Women: A Statistical Overview* (Ottawa: Supply and Services, 1985).

55. *Protection of Children Act*, R.S.B.C. 1948, c.47. section 7(k).

56. K. Amacher & K. Mair, *Apprehensions of Native Children in Vancouver: An Exploratory Study*, (School of Social Work, University of British Columbia, 1979) [unpublished].

57. American social research has demonstrated that regular parental visitation with children in care is the best predictor of family re-unification. See D. Fanshell & E. Shinn, *Children in Foster Care: A Longitudinal Investigation*, (New York: Columbia University Press, 1978) c.4.

58. B. McKenzie & P. Hudson, "Native Children, Child Welfare, and the Colonization of Native People" in K.L. Levitt & B. Wharf, eds, *The Challenge of Child Welfare*, (Vancouver: University of British Columbia Press, 1985) 125 at 126.

59. *Child and Family Services Act*, S.M. 1985, c.8, section 64.

60. *Report of the Special Committee on Indian Self-Government in Canada*, *supra*, note 1 at 141.

Chapter 5

ADOPTIONS

Glenn Gallins

INTRODUCTION

This chapter will introduce counsellors, psychologists, social workers, youth care workers and people working in the medical field to some basic information about adoption laws and procedures in British Columbia, Canada. The material addresses the concerns of people thinking about adopting a child, those who may be giving up a child for adoption, and those who may themselves be the subject of an adoption.

In Canada, the law and legal procedures governing adoptions fall under the jurisdiction of the provinces. In British Columbia the main sources for the law and practice governing adoptions are the *Adoption Act*[1] and *Regulations*.[2] The *Adoption Act*[3] was significantly amended in November 1996 and new regulations came into force. In addition the policies of the director of Family and Child Service and decisions of the Supreme Court of British Columbia effect the way in which adoptions are implemented. The law is stated as of November 1, 1996.

TERMINOLOGY

In this chapter the word <u>director</u> refers to the director of Family and Child Service. <u>Ministry</u> refers to the Ministry for Children and Families. The word <u>Court</u> refers to the Supreme Court of British Columbia.

THE EFFECT OF AN ADOPTION ORDER

Basically, an adoption is a permanent transfer of the relationship of parent and child from the birth (i.e., biological) parents to the persons who adopt the child.[4] Not only will the child have new parents, but by becoming a full member of a new family, the child may also gain new brothers, sisters, grandparents, aunts, and uncles. In addition to obtaining new relatives, the adopted child will ordinarily take on the surname of the adoptive parents. As part of a new family, the adopted child will have the same rights of inheritance as her/his new brothers and sisters.

When an adoption order is granted, the adoptive parents incur the duty to support and maintain the adopted child. They obtain custody and guardianship. Ordinarily, adoptive parents hope to eliminate any ties that the child might have to his/her natural parents. They want to create a new permanent relationship with the child. To help achieve this objective, the *Adoption Act* states that "(a) the child becomes the child of the adoptive parent, (b) the adoptive parent becomes the parent of the child, and, (c) the birth parents cease to have any parental rights or obligations with respect to the child."[5] This objective has been reinforced by the Court in a case called

Re: Chappelle.[6] In this case, the Court expressed the view that it is in the public interest that there should be complete confidence in the permanent nature of an adoption order. To allow orders to be set aside would cause great uncertainty. In this case, the Court considered many arguments for setting aside an adoption order, including the fact that the adopting parents, natural parents, the adopted person, and the director all consented to having it set aside. Nevertheless, the Court refused to set aside the order for fear of setting a dangerous precedent.

Although the objective of the *Adoption Act* is to have the adopted child cease to be a child of her/his birth parents, there are limitations to this objective. One limitation relates to the rules against incest and the rules that prohibit marriage between people who are related. For example, the rules that prohibit the marriage of a girl to her natural father continue to apply even if the girl has been adopted.[7] A second limitation relates to aboriginal rights. A child who would have acquired aboriginal rights from a birth parent will continue to be entitled to those rights after an adoption takes place.[8] Similarly, a child who had a vested right in property before an adoption order is made will continue to have that right.[9]

ELIGIBILITY TO ADOPT A CHILD

There are three fundamental rules pertaining to who is eligible to adopt a child in British Columbia. First, a child may be adopted by one <u>adult</u> or two <u>adults</u> jointly. Since the wording in the current *Adoption Act* no longer requires the adoptive parents to be a husband and wife, same sex couples are now eligible to adopt a child. Second, the prospective adoptive parents must be residents of British Columbia.[10] To be a resident a person must have a permanent abode in British Columbia, to which that person intends to return whenever the person leaves the Province. In addition the person must have resided continuously in the province for six months prior to receiving a child for placement.[11] The third requirement is that the prospective adoptive parents must be able to demonstrate that it will be in the best interests of the child that they be allowed to adopt the child. In determining what is in the best interests of the child the *Act* states that all relevant facts must be considered, including the following:

a) the child's safety;

b) the child's physical and emotional needs and level of development;

c) the importance of continuity in the child's care;

d) the importance to the child's development of having a positive relationship with a parent and a secure place as a member of a family;

e) the quality of the relationship the child has with a birth parent or other individual and the effect of maintaining that relationship;

f) the child's cultural, racial, linguistic and religious heritage;

g) the child's views; and

h) the effect on the child if there is a delay in making a decision.[12]

Bearing in mind that adoption decisions must be made in accordance with the above rules, what are the eligibility requirements to adopt a child? In British Columbia, eligibility for placement of a child in the home of a prospective adoptive parent is largely determined by the source of the child. Children may be available from three sources. They may be available directly from the birth parent(s), they may be the children from a spouse's former relationship, they may be children put up for adoption by the director or by an agency.

A. Children Available from a Birth Parent

If a child is to be placed for adoption directly by a birth parent, the director must prepare a pre-placement assessment of the prospective adoptive parents. A copy of that report must be given to the birth parent before the child is placed in the home of the prospective adoptive parents.[13] The report must include information about the following: whether there is or was drug or alcohol use by the prospective adoptive parents that would affect their ability to care for the child; whether the prospective adoptive parents have physical or mental problems or criminal records; whether the adoptive parents are capable of understanding the child's cultural, racial, linguistic, and religious heritage; the developmental, social, and behavioural progress of any other children of the prospective adoptive parent; and several other factors relevant to the best interests of the child.[14]

In addition, before a child can be placed in the home of a prospective adoptive parent, consent must be obtained from the child if he/she is 12 years or older, from the birth mother, the father, and any person appointed as the child's guardian. The *Adoption Act* provides for situations in which consents cannot be reasonably obtained.[15] There are no additional formal eligibility requirements before a child can be placed in the home of a prospective adoptive parent. Thus, the suitability for placement in the home of a prospective adoptive parent is essentially determined by the birth parents.

Although the birth parents can decide whether to place the child in the prospective adoptive parent's home, before an adoption order will be granted the director must prepare a post-placement report for the Court. In that report the director must either recommend that the adoption should or should not be made, or advise the Court that there is insufficient information to make a recommendation.[16] As a practical matter a negative report from the director will greatly increase the difficulty of obtaining an Adoption Order by the prospective adoptive parents.

B. Children from a Spouse's Prior Relationship

In British Columbia, if the child's legal guardian marries, he/she determines the suitability of the new spouse who may wish to adopt the child. In many cases, the guardian will have to obtain the consent of the other birth parent. However, the law does not require the director to determine suitability of the adoptive parent, or conduct a home study at any stage of the proceedings unless the Court directs such a study to be made.[17]

C. Children from the Director or an Adoption Agency

The *Adoption Act* provides that a child can be placed for adoption by the director or by an adoption agency. At the time this chapter was written there were no such agencies in operation in British Columbia. However, the *Act* states that an adoption agency must be licensed in accordance with the regulations.[18] Under the *Society Act*,[19] a society is a corporate entity that carries out its objectives without having the making of a profit as its goal.

The *Adoption Act* permits a birth parent to voluntarily transfer care and custody of a child to the director or an adoption agency.[20] The director may also obtain continuing care and custody of a child who is found in need of protection under the *Child, Family and Community Service Act.*[21]

Once a child is in the care and custody of the director or an adoption agency and the birth parent has consented to an adoption (or the Provincial Court of British Columbia has given continuing care of the child to the director under the *Child, Family and Community Service Act*), the director or adoption agency can transfer care and custody of the child to a prospective adoptive parent.[22]

Currently, a person must meet only two qualifications to apply for a child. A prospective adoptive parent must be 19 years of age or older, and must be a resident of British Columbia. Before a child will be placed in the home of a prospective adoptive parent a preplacement homestudy will be conducted. Thereafter, the director must make a decision about whether it would be in the best interests of the child for the child to be placed with a prospective adoptive parent.

Formerly, the director's guidelines[23] required a couple to be legally married, not have more than one child of their own, and be unable to give birth to another child before they were eligible to receive a healthy child. These guidelines are no longer applied.

Children with special needs may be available for adoption. A special needs child is one who may have or may develop a physical, emotional, mental, or behavioural problem. Some special needs children have been classified as such because they are older or because they comprise a family of several children who should be adopted together. Again, applicants for special needs children must undergo a pre-placement homestudy and be approved by the director. The best-interests-of-the-child test is paramount. Naturally, applicants for a special needs child must demonstrate that they have the qualities and skills necessary to deal with the type of child requested. Where aboriginal children are concerned, discussion usually takes place with a band representative if birth parents wish to preserve aboriginal identity.

HOW TO FIND A CHILD TO ADOPT

There are several sources from which children may be adopted. These include the director, private sources, and children from another province or country. Each source will be examined below.

A. The Director

Until 1995-96, the number of director and private placement adoptions in British Columbia, excluding international adoptions, was similar. In that governmental year, the director had 128 provincial adoptions and 71 international adoptions compared to 173 and 307 respectively that were private placements.[24] The director becomes responsible for placing children for adoption in several ways. First, the director, through staff of the Ministry, works with parents who are expecting a child and who indicate they wish to voluntarily give up their child for adoption. Secondly, the director may place for adoption children who are taken involuntarily from their parents because they are in need of protection. The Provincial Court of British Columbia deals with these children after they are taken by the director. Over a period of time efforts may be made to return them to their parents, if that is in the child's best interests. However, if the children are committed to the continuing custody of the director, they may become available for adoption.[25]

Family Relations Act "wards" are the third source of children available from the director. Under section 29 of the *Family Relations Act*, if a child has no guardians (usually because the legal guardian or guardians have died) the director acquires guardianship and the child may be placed for adoption, provided the child, if 12 years or over, consents.[26]

B. Private Adoptions

A second source of children is friends, acquaintances, and relatives. Essentially, if a person knows of a child that the natural parents may wish to put up for adoption, arrangements for adoption can be made privately. Regarding private adoptions, MacDonald has observed that:

Adoption practitioners have long been aware of the hazards of placement through intermediaries. In the absence of careful pre-placement selection and preparation of adoptive parents, there is a grave possibility that a child may be placed in the home of parents ill-prepared or unsuitable for adoptive parenthood. In addition, there is the danger of undue pressure being exerted on unwed expectant mothers (a time of high personal vulnerability) by persons motivated by the expectation of financial gain. One result of this is a much greater likelihood of subsequent efforts by the natural parent to revoke the adoption consent. Finally, in the absence of specialized medical services prior to placement, there is a substantial risk that potential adoptive parents will receive a child with a physical or mental impairment.[27]

Ontario prohibits direct placements except through the director of Child Welfare or licensed charitable agencies, which must notify the director in advance of intended placements for adoption. "Moreover, no person may receive a child for adoption without the director's approval."[28] As noted above, the director's approval is not required in British Columbia before a child is placed in the home of a prospective adoptive parent. All that is required to address the first issue identified by MacDonald is that a homestudy be prepared and given to the birth parent. To address the issue of a prospective adoptive parent receiving a child with physical or mental impairment, the director is required to prepare a report detailing the health and social history both of the birth parents and the child.[29]

C. Children from Another Province or Another Country

If a person wishes to be considered for placement of a child from another province or country, arrangements may be made through the Ministry to be registered with the National Adoption Desk in Ottawa. At the time this chapter was written, the National Adoption desk had arrangements with 12 countries to expedite adoptions. Most children, however, were coming from China and Haiti. If a child from another country is being sought, usually the prospective adoptive parents select one country to be the source of the child. It is expected that the prospective adoptive parents would develop an appreciation of the culture and language of the child.

Alternatively, a person may discover privately that a child is available in another province or country. Most children being brought into British Columbia privately are from Russia and Central America.

What rules apply to children being brought from another country to be adopted in Canada? On April 1, 1997, the *Convention on Protection of Children and Cooperation in Respect of Intercountry Adoption* (which is often referred to as "*Hague Convention on Intercountry Adoptions*")[30] was ratified by Canada. The *Adoption Act* states that the provisions of that convention have the force of law in British Columbia.[31] The Convention sets out the basic rules that apply to an intercountry adoption. These rules require the authorities in the child's country of origin to:

a) establish that the child is adoptable;

b) determine that an intercountry adoption is in the best interests of the child (after considering whether a placement within the country of origin is possible);

c) counsel the child's family about the legal effects of a consent to adoption;

d) obtain in writing the necessary consents and ensure that such consents are freely given, and are not induced by a payment of any kind;

e) ensure that the consent of the mother, where required by the country of origin, is obtained only after the birth of the child;

f) ensure that the child, having regard to the child's age and maturity, is counselled about the effects of adoption, and considers the child's wishes and opinions; and

g) obtains where required, in writing, the child's consent to adoption, and ensure that such consent is not induced by payment or compensation of any kind.[32]

In addition, the convention requires that the director must ensure that:

a) the prospective adoptive parents are eligible and suited to adopt the child;

b) the prospective adoptive parents have been counselled as may be necessary; and

c) the parents have determined that the child is or will be authorized to enter and reside permanently in Canada.[33]

Once the child is in the home of the prospective adoptive parents, the usual steps must be followed to obtain an Adoption Order (see below: What legal steps must be taken to adopt a child?).

The following question often arises: If a child from another country is adopted by a Canadian citizen, is the child automatically a Canadian citizen? The answer is no. After the child has been "landed" under the *Immigration Act*[34] and an adoption order has been obtained, an application must be made to obtain Canadian citizenship for the child.

CONSENTING PARTIES TO AN ADOPTION

An Adoption Order cannot be granted unless the consent of the parties required under the *Adoption Act* is obtained or dispensed with by an Order of the Court. The requirements pertaining to the child and birth parents are as follows:

A. The Child

The *Adoption Act* requires the director or adoption agency to provide counselling to the child about the effects of an adoption order and to advise all children over the age of 12 that they have the right to consent (or refuse consent) to the adoption.[35] Moreover, a child has the right to revoke consent to an adoption any time before an adoption order is made by the Court.[36]

A significant innovation in the *Adoption Act* pertains to children between the ages of 7 and 12. Although the consent of these children is not required, a person authorized by the director must meet with the child and prepare a report that includes the views of the child with respect to the proposed adoption and any proposed change in the child's name.[37] This report must be furnished to the Court, and considered by a judge when deciding whether an adoption order should be granted.[38]

B. Birth Parents

Unless the Court dispenses with the need for consent, the consent of both birth parents to a proposed adoption is required. Even if a birth parent is under 19 years of age, that parent can give a legally valid consent.[39] When a person gives consent, that consent must be an informed consent. The person giving consent must understand that adoption may terminate that person's legal rights to the child. In British Columbia the person must receive advice from a lawyer or a social worker to ensure that the consent is informed. The birth parent must, in turn, swear in an Affidavit that the effect of the consent to adoption was fully explained, that the consent was signed freely and voluntarily, and that the circumstances under which consent could be revoked were fully explained.[40]

It is important to note, however, that not all birth fathers are considered birth parents under the *Adoption Act*. Under the former *Adoption Act*, a provision was introduced to restrict the definition of a parent so as to avoid the need to obtain the consent of a birth father where that person had virtually no involvement with the child after conception. This was particularly useful in situations in which the birth mother subsequently married a person other than the birth father, and the birth mother wished to have her husband adopt her child. By eliminating the need for the consent of the birth father by statutorily denying him to be a parent, the former *Adoption Act* helped avoid the need to reinvolve the birth mother with the birth father, and also avoided the need to apply to the Court to dispense with the need for the birth father's consent where such consent was refused. Under the former *Act* the consent of the birth father was not needed unless:

a) he acknowledged paternity of the child by having signed the registration of live birth;

b) he is or was the guardian of the child or joint guardian of the child with the mother;

c) he had acknowledged paternity and had custody or access rights by Court order or agreement; or

d) he had acknowledged paternity and had, pursuant to a Court order or otherwise, supported, maintained, or cared for the child.[41]

If none of these criteria applied, then the birth father was not a parent within the meaning of the former *Adoption Act*. So, for example, if a child was born as a result of a casual sexual encounter and the father never had custody, access, or guardianship, or never supported the child nor signed the registration of live birth, that father was not a parent within the meaning of the *Adoption Act*. By eliminating such a father from the definition of parent, the birth mother alone was in a position to make binding decisions about the adoption of a child.

The current *Adoption Act* has considerably increased the rights of the birth father. First, section 13 has expanded the definition of a parent. Two additional criteria have been added. A birth father is now considered a parent for the purpose of requiring his consent to an adoption if:

a) he has acknowledged paternity and is named by the birth mother as the child's father; or

b) he is acknowledged by the birth mother as the father and is registered on the Birth Father's Registry as the child's father.[42]

The Birth Father's Registry was created by the current *Act*.[43] To register, a birth father must complete, sign, and date an application, and provide proof of identity. The birth mother does not need to acknowledge the birth father's claim to paternity by signing the application.[44]

The second way in which the current *Adoption Act* has increased the birth father's rights is to require notice of the proposed placement of a child be given to him if his name is on the Birth Father's Registry (unless the Court grants an order dispensing with such notice).[45] Having received this notice, a birth father may wish to take steps to gain custody of the child or access to the child.

C. The Director

If the director is the child's guardian under the *Family Relations Act* or under a permanent order made under the *Child, Family, and Community Service Act* (or its predecessor, the *Family and Child*

Service Act),[46] only the director's consent is required. In other words, the birth parents' consent is not required.[47]

DISPENSING WITH THE NEED TO OBTAIN CONSENT OF A BIRTH PARENT

If there is concern about whether a birth parent will consent to an adoption, the first question to be asked is whether that person's consent is required (see the above definition of "parent"). If the person is not a parent under the *Adoption Act*, then the consent to the adoption will not be required.

Assuming the person is a parent within the definition of the *Adoption Act*, then the test set out in section 17 of the *Act* must be met. The Court can dispense with consent if it is satisfied that it is in the best interests of the child to do so or that the person whose consent is to be dispensed with:

a) is not capable of giving an informed consent;

b) has abandoned or deserted the child;

c) has not made reasonable efforts to meet their parental obligations;

d) is not capable of caring for the child; or

e) there are other circumstances justifying the dispensing of consent.[48]

Under the former *Adoption Act* many cases were considered that dealt with the issue of whether consent should be dispensed with. The grounds for dispensing with consent were similar to those found in the current *Act*. A case that demonstrates some of the potential difficulties in obtaining an order dispensing with consent was a case called *Re: British Columbia Birth Registration #77-09-101612*.[49] This case involved an adoption by a step-parent. In this case, the birth parents separated in 1978 when the child was one year old. From 1979 on, the birth father had no further contact with the child, because the mother made it clear she would not allow any interference, and she discouraged access. The birth father paid maintenance until late 1981 when the mother stated she no longer wished to have maintenance paid. In 1982 the birth parents divorced. In 1985 the birth mother remarried. In 1989 the birth mother and her new husband applied to the Court to dispense with the consent of the birth father to an adoption of the child. The Court held that despite a ten-year separation, the birth father remained concerned about the child, and had not abandoned or deserted the child. As well, he had not neglected to pay for support, since the mother had indicated she did not want it. The Court then considered whether there were other circumstances justifying dispensing with the consent of the birth father. The Court stated that the welfare of the child must be considered in relation to the fitness of the parent. The absence of a relationship between child and birth parent should not be considered an important reason to dispense with consent if the birth parent has a sincere parental interest and a desire to establish a beneficial relationship with the child.

Another case, called *Re: British Columbia Birth Registration #72-09-024034*,[50] demonstrates a different outcome. In this case, the birth father and mother were divorced in 1981, and in 1983 the birth father was denied access. His applications for access thereafter were also denied. Since 1984, the birth father refused to pay maintenance. In this case, the Court found that the birth father's primary interest was not in the child but rather in winning a battle against his former wife. In addition, the Court found that the birth father had a duty to contribute to the maintenance of the child and failed to do so. On this basis, the Court decided that it was appropriate to dispense with the consent of the birth father to the adoption.

REVOCATION OF CONSENT TO AN ADOPTION

A child who is being adopted can revoke consent at any time before an adoption order takes place.[51] This effectively gives a mentally fit child 12 years of age a veto over whether an adoption order will be made. This is because section 32 of the *Act* requires that consent be obtained from children who are 12 years of age before an adoption order is granted, and section 17 only allows a Court to dispense with consent if the child was not capable of giving an informed consent.

The ability of birth parents to revoke consent is considerably different. The current *Adoption Act* permits a birth mother to consent to an adoption on the 11th day after the child's birth.[52] A birth father can consent any time after the birth of a child. Under the former *Adoption Act*, if a consent were given voluntarily, it could not be revoked unless the Court was satisfied that the revocation would be in the best interests of the child. In other words, once voluntary consent was given, the interests of the birth parents became secondary to the interests of the child.

Depending on the circumstances, the current *Adoption Act* may provide a greater opportunity for a birth mother to withdraw her consent. Section 19 of the *Act* allows a birth mother to revoke her consent in writing to the director or adoption agency within 30 days of the child's birth, or any time before the director actually places a child in the home of a prospective adoptive parent.[53] In these circumstances, the child is to be returned as soon as possible. Revocation is not normally subject to legal appeal. However, a limitation on a birth mother's right to revoke her consent is readily apparent upon close reading of the *Act*. If a birth mother consents to an adoption more than 30 days after the birth of her child she will not have any time to reconsider and revoke her consent if the child is immediately placed in the home of a prospective adoptive parent by the director.

A valid consent is fundamental to obtaining an adoption order, and a consent to adoption has to be given voluntarily. The Court may be prepared to set aside a consent without applying the best interest of the child test, if a consent to adoption was not signed voluntarily. Similarly, a consent to adoption has to be a fully-informed consent. If a consent was signed because the effect of an adoption order was misrepresented, again, the best interest test may not apply, and the birth parents may be allowed to revoke their consent to the adoption.

Another circumstance that could affect the ability of a birth mother to voluntarily consent to an adoption would be payment for her child. For example, a birth mother in difficult financial circumstances might be under sufficient financial duress to part with her child involuntarily if the financial incentive was strong enough. And yet, as the birth mother, she must not only carry the physical burden of bearing the child, but also the psychological burden of giving up the child for adoption. Should she be compensated for carrying these burdens? On the other hand, there is currently a critical shortage of healthy babies available for adoption. With such an imbalance in supply and demand, unconscionable amounts of money could be demanded by a birth mother for the surrender of her child. The law in British Columbia has dealt with these competing interests. Section 84 of the *Adoption Act* says that no person shall offer or accept payment or reward of any kind to provide a child for adoption.

STEPS AND TIME INVOLVED IN AN ADOPTION

A person who wants to adopt a child usually wants to know how long the process will take. Unfortunately, there is no easy way to predict how long it will take. However, it is useful to respond by saying that the adoption will take as much time as is necessary to complete each required step. So, what legal steps must be completed to adopt a child? The requirements differ slightly depending on whether the child is being placed for adoption by the birth parents or the director. However, here is a list of the steps that generally apply, together with the section number of the *Adoption Act* that mandates the step.

Step 1. If a child is being placed for adoption directly by a birth parent, the prospective adoptive parents must notify the director before receiving the child (see section 8).

Step 2. Before a child is directly placed or placed by the director, someone appointed by the director must do the following:

a) provide information to the birth parent about adoptions and the alternatives to adoption (see sections 6 and 8);

b) obtain information about the medical and social history of the child's biological family (see sections 6 and 8);

c) give the prospective adoptive parents information about the medical and social history of the child's biological family (see sections 6 and 8). Note that if the birth parents and the prospective adoptive parents are not known to each other, the director must provide the information and at the same time ensure that the parties' identities do not become known to one another (see section 42);

d) prepare a preplacement assessment of the prospective adoptive parents (see section 8);

e) if the child is to be placed directly by the birth parent, give a copy of the preplacement assessment to the birth parent (see section 8); or if the child is to be placed by the director but the birth parent wishes to select the child's prospective adoptive parents, the director must conduct a pre-placement assessment of the prospective adoptive parents and give the result to the birth parents (see section 60);

f) make sure the child, if sufficiently mature, has been counselled about the effect of an adoption. If the child is over the age of 12 it is important to make sure he/she has been informed of the right to consent (or refuse consent) to the adoption (see sections 6 and 8).

Step 3.   If the child is to be directly placed by the birth mother, the prospective adoptive parents must make reasonable efforts to give notice of the proposed adoption to the birth father in two circumstances, *viz.*, 1) if he is registered in the Birth Father's Registry; or 2) if he is named as the birth father by the birth mother but his consent is not required to the adoption because he is deemed not to be a parent by section 13 of the *Act* (see sections 9 and 13).

Step 4.   If the child is to be directly placed by the birth mother, the prospective adoptive parents must make reasonable efforts to give notice of the proposed adoption to the birth father if he is registered in the Birth Father's Registry, or if he is named as the birth father by the birth mother. However, his consent is not required to the adoption if he is not deemed to be a parent according to the definition in section 8 of the *Act* (see sections 9 and 13).

If the director or an adoption agency is placing the child for adoption, each party must comply with the notice requirements to the birth father in the situations described above (see sections 6 and 13). Alternatively, if it is in the best interests of the child or the circumstances justify it, an application can be made to the Court to dispense with the notice to the birth father (see section 12).

Step 5.   If the child is an aboriginal child, the director must make reasonable efforts to discuss the placement with a band or representative of a band unless the child is 12 years or older and objects, or the birth parents placing the child for adoption object (see section 7).[54]

Step 6.   The child can now be placed in the home of the prospective adoptive parents.

Step 7.   Within 14 days of receiving a child in their home for the purpose of adoption, the prospective adoptive parents must notify the director that they have received the child (see section 12).

Step 8.   The prospective adoptive parents and a relative of the child may (but do not have to) enter an openness agreement. The purpose of the openness agreement is to facilitate communication or maintain relationships between the prospective adoptive parents and a relative of the child, any other person who has established a relationship with the child, or the prospective adoptive parents of a sibling of the child (see section 59).

Step 9.   A document may be prepared transferring care and custody of the child to the prospective adoptive parents (see sections 25 and 26).

Step 10.   Unless the Court dispenses with this requirement, the child should reside in the home of the prospective adoptive parents for 6 months (see section 33 and 35).

Step 11.   A copy of the child's Birth Registration should be obtained from the director of Vital Statistics.

Step 12. A post-placement report must be prepared by the director (see section 33).

Step 13. At least 30 days notice of a date set for the Court hearing of an application for an adoption order must be given to the director (if the child was placed directly) and to any person with access rights to the child by a Court order or an agreement enforcement under the *Family Relations Act* (see section 31).

Step 14. An application to the Court for an adoption order should be prepared. In some circumstances the application may take the form of an application in writing without the need for lawyers or other persons to actually be in Court. However, if a Court hearing is necessary, the Court may order the hearing to be conducted in private (see section 41). In deciding whether to grant an adoption order the paramount issue is whether it is in the child's best interests to be adopted by the prospective adoptive parents (see sections 3 and 35).

Step 15. After an adoption order is made, the director must make reasonable efforts to notify the birth parents (see section 39).

And that's all there is to it!

ALTERNATIVES TO AN ADOPTION ORDER

While an adoption order may provide psychological comfort by making a child legally the child of the adoptive parents, there may be reasons to avoid obtaining an adoption order. One reason, which particularly applies in step-parent adoptions, is to avoid having any dealings with the child's other birth parent. In most cases, the consent of the other birth parent to the adoption will be required. Obtaining that consent may reawaken a birth parent's interest in the child. Sometimes, the fear of reawakening such interest and involvement is sufficient to discourage adoption proceedings.

In addition, one must consider the birth parents' rights of access to the child. Even if an adoption order is signed, there are some cases which indicate that a birth parent could apply for access to the child if it was in the best interests of the child. So, it is possible that the objective of the persons who wish to adopt a child and exclude prior parental involvement may fail. If an adoption order will not preclude the continued involvement of a birth parent with the child, the motive for obtaining an adoption order may no longer exist for some people.

Loss of benefits obtained from the Ministry may be another reason to avoid obtaining an adoption order. For example, if the child to be adopted is in the home of a relative and the relative is receiving payments from the Ministry to support the child, those payments may cease if the child is adopted by the relative. However, there is a way of gaining some of the benefits of an adoption order without obtaining the order itself.

An adoption order gives a right to custody and guardianship, a right to change names, and a right to inherit upon the death of the adoptive parents if they do not provide for the child in a will. In a step-parent situation, custody and guardianship of a child can be obtained by a written custody agreement between the parent who has custody of the child and the person wishing to have custody.

For example, if a parent has custody of her children, she could enter into a joint custody agreement with her new spouse. Alternatively, an application can be brought before the Court for an order for custody of a child. Custody agreements and custody orders are not nearly as binding and final as an adoption order. Nevertheless, such agreements or orders may suffice for the step-parent who wants a legal right to the child.

A change of name can be obtained through an application to the Division of Vital Statistics. Consent of the birth parent will not be required if the birth parent's name does not appear on the birth registration. If it does appear on the birth registration, then the birth parent's consent would be required. Sometimes it may be difficult to obtain the birth parent's consent to a change of name. However, the *Name Act*[55] does provide a procedure for dispensing with this consent.

Finally, anyone who is concerned about the child having inheritance rights merely needs to have a will prepared leaving assets to the child.

ACCESS ORDERS

Once consent has been given and an adoption order has been made, it is very difficult to set aside the adoption order to reinstate the birth parent as a legal parent. Some birth parents have therefore tried to maintain their relationship with their child by obtaining an order for access. An order for access gives people the right to have the child visit them. Prior to 1984, the Courts held that access by a birth parent to an adopted child was inconsistent with an adoption order and was in conflict with the concept that, when an adoption order was granted, a child ceased to be the child of its birth parent.

However, in a 1984 decision called *Re: A Male Child Alberta Birth Registration #83-09-023440*,[56] the Supreme Court of British Columbia pronounced a different rule. Essentially, the Court applied the best-interests-of-the-child test. The Court noted that decisions by Courts in other jurisdictions appeared to indicate that access may be granted only in exceptional circumstances. However, on closer examination of those decisions, the Court found that the true test being applied was what is in the best interests of the child. This concept was embodied in section 30 of the current *Adoption Act*. It states that an access order or agreement terminates when an adoption order is made unless the Court finds that it is in the best interests of the child not to terminate the order or agreement.

DISCLOSURE OF INFORMATION

The adoption issue that has had the highest profile in recent years is easy to define. Should the law protect the birth parents' right to remain anonymous, or should adopted people have the right to know who their birth parents are? Until 1988 the law prohibited disclosure of birth parents unless the disclosure was essential for the health and well-being of the adopted person.

The law was set out in section 15 of the former *Adoption Act*. Section 15 said that "all adoption orders and documents filed in the Court in connection with adoptions are not open for inspection by any persons except:

a) a person authorized in writing by the Attorney General of British Columbia; or

b) a person authorized by the Court."[57]

The Court considered this issue in a case reported in 1981 called *Kelly v. director of Child Welfare*.[58] In that case, a man named Kelly who had been adopted attempted to get an order from the Court to allow him to have access to his adoption file so that he could learn the identity of his birth parents. The Court held that no order could be granted unless "good cause" was shown, as required by the *Adoption Act*. The term "good cause" was not defined in the *Act*. The Court heard evidence from Mr. Kelly regarding his emotional problems and possible medical concerns. However, the Court did not find the evidence sufficient in the Kelly case to order disclosure. A similar provision is found in section 43 of the current *Act*. It only allows a Court file to be searched at the request of the director or by order of the Court. Thus, if the current *Act* went no further we still would not know what issues would have to be presented to the Court to obtain an order for disclosure. However, section 61 of the current *Act* now gives specific authorization for the director to disclose information that is necessary for the safety, health, or well-being of a child, or for the purpose of allowing a child to receive a benefit. Presumably a Court could at the very least grant an order on the same basis to disclose material in a Court file that pertained to these issues.

However, the goal of many children who have been adopted is to discover more than just information about their health, safety, and property rights. They want to know who their birth parents are. A major advance in facilitating disclosure of information about birth parents occurred in 1988 when the Adoption Reunion Registry came into being in British Columbia. The Registry allowed the birth parents of persons adopted in British Columbia to register with the Reunion Registry. Adopted persons could also register. The information required from the adopted person included name, address, telephone number, date of birth, place of adoption, and name of adoptive parents. The birth parents provided their current name, address, telephone number, the names of the mother and father at the time of the child's birth, the date of birth of the mother and father, the name of the child at birth, the child's date and place of birth, and the place of adoption. When an application was submitted to the Division of Vital Statistics, the information was cross-referenced, and a search undertaken for a corresponding registration for the birth parent or adopted child. If a match was made the information was revealed to both parties.

When the current *Adoption Act* came into force it incorporated a revolutionary change. Under the former *Adoption Act* a birth parent or adopted person did not have to worry about disclosure unless they consented to it by registering with the Adoption Reunion Registry. Now the onus is on the birth parent or adopted person over the age of 18 years to take a positive step to remain anonymous. They must file a disclosure veto or non contact declaration with the Director of Vital Statistics to prohibit the Director from revealing their identity.[59]

Perhaps even more significant is that adoptions that occur under the provisions of the current *Act* will not provide for the anonymity of the birth parents or adopted person at all. Rather, a birth parent or adopted person will be able to file only a non-contact declaration with the Director of Vital Statistics.[60] Under section 63 of the current *Act*, the Director of Vital Statistics must give an adopted person over the age of 19 a copy of the adopted person's original birth registration and adoption order unless a disclosure veto was filed, or a non contact declaration was filed. If a non contact declaration was filed, only the adopted person could still receive a copy of the birth registration and adoption order if the adopted person signs an undertaking. In that undertaking the adopted person must agree not to contact or have another person contact the person who filed the non contact declaration, and must not use the information obtained to intimidate or harass the person who filed the declaration.[61]

Once an adopted person obtains a birth registration and adoption order, the adopted child may apply to the director of family and child services for help in locating birth parents, siblings of the adopted child, and siblings of the birth parent, if the birth parent has died. The director can use the records of any public body as defined in the *Freedom of Information and Protection of Privacy Act*[62] to help locate a person.

Under section 64 of the current *Act*, the Director of Vital Statistics must give the birth parents of an adopted person over the age of 19 who apply a copy of the adopted person's original birth registration, the birth registration that was substituted after the adoption, and the adoption order unless a disclosure veto or a non contact declaration was filed by the adopted person. However, before giving the birth parents the requested documents, the Director of Vital Statistics must delete identifying information about the adoptive parents.

To assist in uniting relatives of an adopted child, the current *Act* has also created a new registry. If an adopted person over the age of 19 years and an adult relative of the adopted person both register, the director of family and child services must notify them and disclose the identifying information provided by each other.[63]

COMMON QUESTIONS

1. Can an adult be adopted by another adult?

Section 44 of the *Adoption Act* allows an adult or two adults jointly to adopt another adult under certain conditions. These include the following:

   a) the person to be adopted must, while still a child, have lived with the adopting parent as a member of the family and must have been maintained by the adoptive parent until he/she became self-supporting, or became an adult;

   b) the person being adopted must consent to the adoption; or

   c) the Court considers the reason for the adoption to be acceptable.

The former *Adoption Act* required the spouse (if any) of the person being adopted and the spouse (if any) of the adopting parent to consent to the adoption. The consent of these persons is no longer necessary.[64]

2. When will the court dispense with notice to the birth father?

The authority of the Court to dispense with the notice to the birth father is less clearly defined than the authority dealing with the dispensing of consent. The Court can dispense with notice if it finds that it is in the best interests of the child to do so, or that the circumstances justify dispensing with the notice.[65] Since these provisions were newly proclaimed at the time this chapter was written, there have been no cases decided by the Court to indicate under what circumstances the Court would consider justifying the dispensing of notice.

3. How much will an adoption cost?

As noted above, section 84 of the *Adoption Act* prohibits anyone from receiving a payment or reward for procuring a child for adoption. However, a birth mother can receive from a prospective adoptive parent reasonable expenses allowed under the regulations. The regulations allow expenses for accommodation, medical services, transportation, counselling, and gifts.[66] In addition, significant fees are associated with an adoption. For example, at the time this chapter was written a pre-placement homestudy cost $1500. Approval of a placement based on the homestudy cost $250. A post-placement report cost $750.[67] An application to the Court for an adoption order cost $250. This amount does not include the legal fees payable to a lawyer for the preparation of the documentation needed to apply to the Court for an adoption order.[68]

4. Can adoptive parents receive any financial subsidy?

Some persons may be inhibited from adopting because of the cost of raising a child. In particular, foster parents may be reluctant to adopt a foster child if they will lose their fostering allowance.

In British Columbia, financial assistance is now available for certain children (called "designated children") to assist persons to adopt them. To be a designated child, the child must be under 19 years. The child must be in continuing care of the director under the *Child, Family and Community Service Act*, or *Adoption Act*, or be under the guardianship of the director under the *Family Relations Act*. Finally, the child must have special service needs because of one or more of the following:

    a) a physical or mental disability or emotional disturbance or a high risk of developing such a disability or disturbance;

    b) a special placement need because of the child's age or the desire to place siblings together;

    c) the child's emotional attachment to the prospective adoptive parents; or

    d) the child's cultural background that requires a culturally compatible placement.[69]

An adoptive parent of a designated child, who meets the financial needs test set out in the regulations, may receive maintenance payments not to exceed the basic amount for foster care. As well, assistance may be provided with medical, educational, housing, transportation of the child, and homemaker, respite, and other services for the adoptive parent.[70]

5. <u>Can an adoption order be set aside by the court?</u>

After an adoption order is made there is a 30-day appeal period during which a party who is dissatisfied could appeal to the Court of Appeal. After the 30-day appeal period expires an application to the Court can only be made to set aside an adoption order on the grounds that it was the result of fraud. Even then the Court will only set aside the adoption order if it is in the best interests of the child to do so.[71]

6. <u>Are helping professionals who facilitate adoptions regulated?</u>

All adoptions in British Columbia must now proceed through the Ministry for Children and Families, or through a licensed adoption agency. Professionals wishing to be facilitators of adoptions, including international adoptions, must be affiliated with the Ministry or licensed adoption agencies under the Adoption Agency Regulations. The current list of such agencies in British Columbia is presented at the close of this chapter.

CONCLUSION

This chapter has addressed both the current issues relating to adoption and questions that are frequently asked by persons wishing to adopt a child. However, as in all areas of the law, the law relating to adoptions is not static. The *Adoption Act* and regulations came into force on November 4, 1996. They will undoubtedly be the subject of amendment, litigation, and judicial interpretation, which will affect the accuracy of the information contained in this chapter.

ADOPTION AGENCY LICENSES

The following agencies have been awarded a license to operate an adoption agency as stipulated by the Adoption Act (1995) and the Adoption Agency Regulations as of January 1998.

LDS Social Services of Canada
British Columbia Agency
10122-140th Street, Surrey, BC V3T 4M9
Ph: (604) 585-7735

The Adoption Centre (Kelowna Community Resources)
255 Lawrence Avenue, Kelowna, BC V1Y 6L2
Ph: (604) 763-8008

Prince George Regional Community Care Society
1552 S. Lyon Street, 2nd Floor, Prince George, BC V2N 1T2
Ph: (604) 960-2273

Hope Services
304-2975 Gladwin Road, Abbotsford, BC V2T 5T4
Ph: (604) 850-1002

Choices Adoption and Counselling Services
4351 Cedar Hill Road, Victoria, BC V8N 5L8
Ph: (250) 477-4497

Family Services of Greater Vancouver
#205 - 1600 West 6th Avenue, Vancouver, BC V8P 1R3
Ph: (604) 736-7613

Sunrise Adoption Centre
IBM Tower at Pacific Centre
#1500 - 701 W. Georgia Street, Vancouver, BC V7Y 1E9
Ph: (604) 984-2488 Toll Free: 1-888-984-2488

RESOURCES

C. Bagley, "Adoption and Mental Health: Studies of Adolescents and Adults,"c. 21 at 254;
    A. Westhues and J.S.Cohen, "Intercountry Adoption in Canada : Predictors of Well-Being," c.22
    at 266;   C. Bagley and P. Gabor, "Adoptions : Themes, Policy Implications and Research
    Agenda," in J.Hudson and B.Galaway,eds., *Child Welfare in Canada: Research and Policy
    Implications*,(Toronto:Thompson Educational Publishing, 1995).

H. M. G. Braker, G. R. Holland & L. Reynolds. "Adoption; Materials prepared for Continuing Legal
    Education," (Vancouver: Continuing Legal Education Society of British Columbia, 1997).

Citizenship and Immigration Canada, *International Adoption and the Immigration Process.* (Ottawa:
    Citizenship and Immigration Canada, 1994).

Indian and Inuit Affairs Program (Canada), *Adoption and the Indian Child,* (Ottawa: Indian and
    Northern Affairs Canada, 1993).

H. L. Katarynych, "Adoption," in N. Bala, J. P. Hornick, and R. Vogl, eds., *Canadian Child Welfare
    Law: Children, Families and the State*, (Toronto: Thompson Educational Publishing, 1991) ,
    c.7 at 133.

*Report to the Minister of Social Services of the Panel to Review Adoption Legislation in British
    Columbia,* (Victoria, B.C.: Queen's Printer, 1994).

P. Sachdev, ed. *Adoption: Current Issues and Trends* (Toronto: Butterworths, 1984) especially J. A
    MacDonald, "Canadian Adoption Legislation: An Overview," c. 4 at 51.

E. J. Vayda & M. T. Satterfield, *Law for Social Workers, A Canadian Guide*,(Toronto:Carswell, 1997) especially "Adoption," c.15 at 189.

More information can be obtained from the following sources:

The Ministry for Children and Families
Adoption Division
716 Courtenay Street, Victoria, BC, V8W 1C2
250 387-3660

Adoptive Parents Association of British Columbia
205-15463 104 Avenue, Surrey, BC, V3R 1N9
604 588-7300

Special Needs Adoptive Parents
1150- 409 Granville Street, Vancouver, BC, V6T 1TZ
604 687-3113

END NOTES

1. *Adoption Act*, R.S.B.C. 1996 c. 5.
2. In November 1996 three Regulations came into force dealing with adoptions. These Regulations were *BC Regulation 291/96, 292/96* and *293/96*.
3. The former Adoption Act was cited as *Adoption Act*, R.S.B.C. 1979, c. 4.
4. *Adoption Act, supra*, note 1, section 37.
5. *Ibid.*
6. *Re Chappelle* (1977), 4 B.C.L.R. 374 (S.C.).
7. *Adoption Act, supra*, note 1, section 37.
8. *Ibid.*
9. *Ibid.*
10. *Ibid* section 5. Section 3 of the former *Adoption Act* provided that an adult person or an adult husband and wife together could apply to adopt a child. No case was ever decided under that *Act* to determine whether the words "husband and wife" could refer to a same sex couple. However, in a case called *Re: Female Infant Child British Columbia Birth Registration #77-09-004366*, the Court held that a couple who were not married to each other could not adopt a child. Assuming a couple of the same gender could not legally be married, it appeared that a same sex couple would have had a difficult hurdle to cross if they had attempted to adopt a child. An interesting result of allowing adoptions by same sex couples is this: until now there existed no statutory provision for obtaining maintenance for a child raised by a same sex couple upon the dissolution of the relationship. Now if a same sex couple adopts a child the custodial parent will be able to pursue a maintenance claim for the child if the relationship terminates. The Legal Services Society of British Columbia considered this such an important right that, as of the time this chapter was written, it was prepared to grant legal aid to financially eligible same sex couples for the purpose of obtaining an adoption. Legal aid for that purpose was denied to heterosexual couples because they could obtain a maintenance order upon the break up of their relationship either pursuant to the *Family Relations Act*, or if they were married, the *Divorce Act*.
11. *B.C. Regulation 291/96* section 2.
12. *Ibid* section 3.
13. *Ibid* section 8. This is a significant change from the situation under the previous *Adoption Act*. Under that *Act* no pre-screening took place. While a homestudy was required, the child was already in the home of the prospective adoptive parents while the study was underway.

14. *B.C. Regulation, supra*, note 11, section 7.

15. *Adoption Act, supra*, note 1, sections 9 and 13.

16. *Ibid* section 33.

17. *Ibid* section 34.

18. *Ibid* section 1.

19. *Society Act*, R.S.B.C. 1996, c. 433.

20. *Ibid* section 23.

21. *Child, Family, and Community Service Act*, R.S.B.C. 1996 c. 46 section 50.

22. *Adoption Act, supra*, note 1, section 25.

23. Unpublished policy statements obtained from Ministry personnel.

24. *Research, Evaluation and Statistics*, (Ministry for Children and Families), 1996. Victoria. Figures include Landed Immigrant Data System Statistics (Ministry of Government Services, Victoria) which involve a projected number for 1996.

25. *Child, Family, and Community Service Act, supra*, note 21, section 50.

26. *Family Relation Act*, R.S.B.C. 1996, c.128 section 29.

27. J.A MacDonald, "Canadian Adoption Legislation: An Overview" in P. Sachdev, ed. *Adoption: Current Issues and Trends* (Toronto: Butterworths, 1984) c. 4 at 51.

28. *Ibid* at 52.

29. *BC Regulation 291/96*, section 4.

30. 32 *International Legal Materials* 1134.

31. *Adoption Act*, supra, note 1 section 51.

32. *Convention on Protection of Children and Cooperation in Respect of Intercountry Adoption, supra*, note 29, article 4.

33. *Ibid* article 5.

34. *Immigration Act*, R.S.C. 1985, I-2.

35. *Ibid*, section 6.

36. *Ibid*, section 20.

37. *Ibid*, section 30.

38. *Ibid*, section 32.

39. *Ibid*, section 15.

40. *Ibid*, section 16 and *BC Regulation 291/96*, section 9 and Form 2.

41. *Adoption Act*, supra note 3, section 8.

42. *Adoption Act*, supra, note 1, section 13.

43. *Ibid*, section 10.

44. *BC Regulation 291/96*, section 13.

45. *Ibid*, sections 6 and 9.

46. *Family and Child Service Act*, S.B.C. 1980, c. 11.

47. *Adoption Act*, supra, note 1, section 13.

48. *Adoption Act*, supra, note 1, section 17.

49. *Re British Columbia Birth Registration #77-09-010612* (1989), Rossland 320513 (B.C.S.C.) [unreported].

50. *Re British Columbia Birth Registration #72-09-024034* (1990), Vancouver 555/89 (B.C.S.C.) [unreported].

51. *Ibid*, section 12.

52. *Ibid*, section 14.

53. *Ibid*, section 18.

54. For a list of bands and their representatives, see Schedule 1 of *British Columbia Regulation 291/96*.

55. *Name Act*, R.S.B.C. 1996, c. 328.

56. *Re A Male Child Alberta Birth Registration #83-09-023440* (1984), Kelowna 9/84 (B.C.S.C.) [unreported].

57. *Adoption Act, supra*, note 3, section 15.

58. *Kelly v. Director of Child Welfare* (1980), 23 B.C.L.R. 299 (S.C.).

59. *Adoption Act, supra*, note 1, section 65.

60. *Ibid*, section 66.

61. *Ibid*, section 66.

62. *Ibid*, sections 70 and 71.

63. *Ibid*, section 69.

64. *Adoption Act* R.S.B.C. 1979, c.4 section 3.

65. *Adoption Act*, supra, note 1, section 11.

66. *Ibid*, section 84. At the time this chapter was written no regulation had been adopted prescribing the type and amount of expenses a birth parent could receive. However, in a case decided under the former *Act*, the Court declared medical, counselling, legal, and travel expenses to be expenses for which the birth mother may be compensation. In *The Matter of the Adoption Act and A Female Infant* the birth mother wanted travel, legal, and medical costs to be paid by the prospective adoptive parents before she would consent to the adoption. The prospective adoptive parents were concerned about violating section 15 of the former *Adoption Act,* which prohibited paying a person money to procure a child. The prospective adoptive parents applied to the Court to determine whether those payments were appropriate. The Court agreed that such payments were appropriate. *BC Regulation 291/96*, section 17 requires prospective adoptive parents to complete a Birth Parent Expenses Affidavit in Form 5 of Schedule 3. That affidavit refers to expenses for accommodation, medical services, transportation, counseling, and gifts.

67. *B.C. Regulation 293/96*, section 2 and Schedule. Section 5 of this regulation authorizes a remission of a portion of the fees payable for persons eligible for financial subsidies under the *British Columbia Benefits Act.*

68. *Adoption Act, supra*, note 1, section 84. This section specifically permits a lawyer to receive reasonable fees and expenses for legal services provided in connection with an adoption.

69. *BC Regulation 291/96*, section 26.

70. *Ibid*, section 28.

71. *Adoption Act. supra.* note 1. section 40.

Chapter 6

FAMILY LAW

M. Jerry McHale

INTRODUCTION

The purpose of this chapter is to provide helping professionals with basic information on common family law issues, including the law relating to marriage, divorce, custody, access, maintenance, and division of property. The chapter will attempt to identify the more important elements in each of these areas and explain the rules involved in resolving legal issues arising from marital separation.

There are nearly 100,000 divorces per year in Canada. This means that helping professionals will often come in contact with parents and children from separating or separated families. Information in this chapter will assist helping professionals to understand the legal consequences of marriage breakdown so that they can better understand their clients, and interact in a more informed and effective way with lawyers, judges, and other members of our legal system.

Two major statutes govern these matters in British Columbia: the federal *Divorce Act*,[1] and the provincial *Family Relations Act*.[2] The *Divorce Act* deals with divorce, custody, access, and maintenance. *Divorce Act* proceedings and divorce itself can only be dealt with in the Supreme Court of British Columbia. The *Family Relations Act* deals with property division and can also deal with custody, access, and maintenance. All *Family Relations Act* matters are dealt with in one of two levels of court: the Provincial Court of British Columbia, Family Division (Family Court) and the Supreme Court of British Columbia (Supreme Court). The law is stated as of June 1, 1997.

MARRIAGE

A. Generally

In addition to its personal, romantic, and religious dimensions, a marriage is also a legal relationship that changes the nature of the married person's rights and legal obligations in a number of areas. These areas include: holding property, incurring debt, income tax status, and entitlement to pension and other benefits. A marriage can only be validly entered into on certain conditions, and by following specific legal procedures:

a) one must be over 19 or under 19 with the consent of a guardian or the approval of a judge;

b) consent to marriage must be freely given;

c) one must be marrying a non-relative (the *Marriage (Prohibited Degrees) Act*[3] defines certain degrees of relationship which preclude marriage. For example, a man cannot marry the following relatives: his grandmother, his wife's grandmother, his aunt, his stepmother, or his son's wife);

d) a valid marriage license (or special permit issued by the Department of Vital Statistics) is required;

e) each person must be of marriageable status (i.e. not still married to another);

f) the ceremony of marriage must meet certain procedural requirements and formalities (i.e., performed by a clergyman or an official marriage commissioner); and

g) the marriage must be consummated in order to be valid.

B. Marriage, Common Law, and Same Sex Relationships

With increasing frequency, couples reside together as man and wife without becoming legally married. Historically, the general rule has been that some legal rights between married persons are more clearly defined and more readily enforceable than rights and obligations arising out of common law relationships. For example, a women's right to a share of family assets not held in her name is easier to establish and easier to enforce if she has been legally married to her husband than if she has not. Similarly, entitlement to child and spousal maintenance is often easier to establish for a married partner. This is not to say that property division and maintenance have been unavailable to people leaving a non-marital relationship. Nevertheless, common law spouses are not entitled to claim maintenance until they have resided with their spouses for two years, and the *Family Relations Act* does not, absent a written agreement to the contrary, give spouses any right or entitlement to their partner's assets.[4] This creates problems when joint money has gone into a common family pot but major assets have been purchased in the name of one partner alone. In such cases a non-owning unmarried spouse has not been able to rely upon any statute and must try to assert the common law principle of "trust." Trust claims can be costly and are less certain than the statutory rights given to married persons.

Amendments made in 1997 to the *Family Relations Act* and the *Family Maintenance Enforcement Act*[5] gave same sex couples the same privileges and responsibilities for child support, access, and custody as heterosexual couples. Same sex couples are now included in the definition of "spouse" under the *Family Relations Act* and have the rights and responsibilities relating to custody, maintenance, and access extended to them.[6] As well, common law and same sex couples are able to enter into agreements and be bound by the property division provisions of the *Family Relations Act*.[7]

It has always been the case that common law spouses can go some distance to protect themselves by entering into written agreements clearly defining their mutual rights andobligations in the event of a relationship breakdown. During the relationship they can purchase major assets in joint names. Also, common law spouses do have some rights established by other statutes.[8]

C. Marriage Contracts

Before or even after couples begin living together, they can enter into written marriage agreements defining their mutual rights and obligations for the duration of their relationship and in the event of separation. Typically, these agreements will define roles and responsibilities to be adopted and certain duties and financial responsibilities to be allocated during the marriage, and define how property will be divided and spousal maintenance paid in the event of separation. There are certain formal requirements that must be met in drafting such agreements and it is often difficult to determine when such agreements will be binding. It is best to have a lawyer draft the agreement and to have each party obtain independent legal advice before signing.

Figure 1 illustrates the avenues available for seeking remedy following a breakdown in a relationship. Although each avenue is discussed separately, they can interconnect as illustrated.

SEPARATION

A. The Mechanics of Separation

Couples who decide that their marriage is at an end often feel the need to formalize this decision in some way. Frequently couples speak of wishing to secure a "legal separation." In fact a separation is "legal" when spouses reside separately and apart from each other with the intention of terminating their relationship. It is even possible to be "separate and apart" within the meaning of the law while residing under the same roof.

There are a number of other ways people can formalize the fact and the terms of their separation. They can enter into a written separation agreement or apply for either a Family Court or Supreme Court order.

B. Separation Agreements

A separation agreement is simply a private written contract made between two spouses spelling out terms of agreement on such matters as custody, access, division of property and payment of child and spousal maintenance.

Such agreements are very common among separating couples and are the product of successful negotiations either between the spouses directly or through their lawyers, or with the assistance of a mediator. Sometimes the parties take no further steps to formalize the terms of their separation. The agreement usually takes effect on the date of its signature.

Written agreements dealing with custody and access, or with maintenance, can be filed in either Provincial or Supreme Court under the *Family Relations Act*.[9] Filed separation agreements have the effect of a court order and can later be enforced or varied by the court as if they actually were court orders.

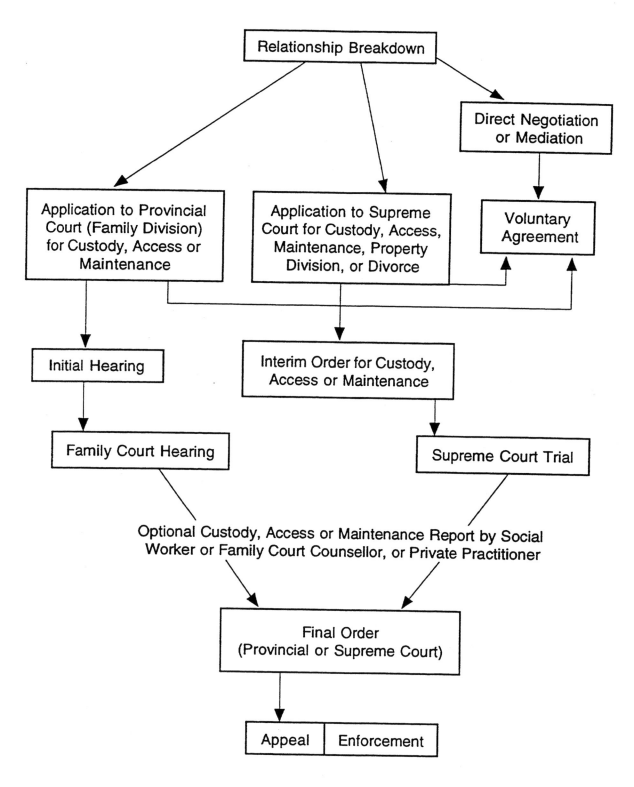

Figure 1. Family Law Legal Process Chart

In other cases the parties can incorporate the terms of a separation agreement directly into a Supreme Court order. For example, they may enter into a written separation agreement shortly after separation, then later decide to divorce. At the time of divorce they may choose to incorporate into the Supreme Court order the separation agreement terms covering, for example, custody, access, and maintenance.

Separation agreements typically address any and every legal issue that could possibly arise upon separation. These matters range from such issues as use, occupation, and disposition of the family home, to custody and parenting arrangements, division of pensions, responsibility for debts, payment of maintenance and so forth. A properly drafted separation agreement followed by independent legal advice for each party helps prevent subsequent legal disputes and court battles over matters such as division of property and payment or receipt of spousal maintenance. A separating spouse should always seek independent legal advice before signing any form of separation agreement. Without such independent legal advice, there is less chance that the agreement will be enforced by the court.

C. Reconciliation

The law encourages reconciliation. The *Divorce Act*[10] imposes upon every lawyer the duty to be satisfied that there is no reasonable prospect of reconciliation before proceeding to file a Petition for Divorce on behalf of a client. Separation for a period of one year constitutes evidence of marriage breakdown and grounds for divorce. The *Act* allows parties to cohabit for the purpose of attempting reconciliation for a period of up to 90 days within that year without losing their grounds for divorce.

D. Name Change

A spouse may apply for a change of name at the time of the granting of a divorce, or at any time thereafter. At that time a wife may revert to her maiden name, or the surname of a previous husband, or to another name. At the same time a parent may apply to change the names of any minor children in his or her custody. However, the consent of the other parent is required before a child's name can be formally changed. Alternatively, a custodial parent may informally create and use an alias for children without the consent of the other parent.

DIVORCE

A. Grounds for Divorce

Under the *Divorce Act*[11] the only ground for divorce is marriage breakdown, but marriage breakdown can be evidenced in three ways:

a) the husband and wife live separate and apart for a period in excess of one year; or

b) either the husband or the wife commits adultery; or

c) either the husband or the wife treats the other with physical or mental cruelty so as to make continued cohabitation intolerable.

Proof of the marriage breakdown must be provided to the court before a divorce will be granted.

B. Living Separate and Apart

Most divorces proceed on the basis of separation for one year. At least one of the spouses must choose and intend to live apart from the other because of marital problems. A separation for some other reason, such as proximity to employment, does not constitute a separation for the purposes of the *Divorce Act*.

Either spouse alone or both spouses jointly may apply for a divorce based on their separation. It is not necessary, or even possible, to designate blame for the failure of the marriage. The court must be satisfied that the marriage has broken down, but it has no interest in attributing fault. The petition asking the court to grant a divorce may be filed any time after the separation, but the divorce itself will not be granted until the separation has lasted for twelve months.

It is possible to be separate and apart within the meaning of the *Divorce Act* while residing under the same roof. If a couple is sufficiently estranged and their lives are sufficiently separate the court will conclude that they were separated even if they had the same address. Typical evidence of such estrangement might be: separate bedrooms, no sexual relationship, no social relationship inside or outside of the home, no performance of domestic services for one another and little or no communication. If there is some reason compelling cohabitation (i.e., economics or inability to sell the matrimonial home) then the court is more likely to accept that the parties were separated while under the same roof.

A couple seeking a divorce based on one year of separation can still cohabit to attempt reconciliation one or more times, as long as the total period of cohabitation is not more than ninety days within that one year period.[12]

C. Adultery

If one spouse has committed adultery, then the other spouse may seek a divorce immediately, without a waiting period. If the adultery is admitted or if there is sufficient evidence to prove the adultery, the court will find that marriage breakdown has occurred and grant a divorce. If, however, the evidence shows that the spouse applying for the divorce had previously forgiven the adultery (in the sense that he or she was prepared to take the adulterous spouse back to live together as man and wife) then the court will not grant a divorce.

Because adultery is defined as sexual intercourse by a husband or a wife with a person of the opposite sex who is not his or her spouse, a homosexual relationship does not constitute adultery.

D. Physical or Mental Cruelty

Physical or mental cruelty that renders continued cohabitation intolerable may serve as evidence of marriage breakdown sufficient for divorce. The victim of the cruelty may apply for divorce whenever the situation becomes unbearable. Again, the order will be made as soon as a judge can hear the matter and rule that the physical or mental cruelty exists. Judges can dismiss such applications and refuse a divorce if they conclude that the victim forgave the cruelty, or that the spouses conspired together to fabricate the evidence of cruelty, simply to get a divorce.

THE MECHANICS OF DIVORCE AND THE DIVORCE PROCESS

A. Jurisdiction and Procedure

In addition to giving the Supreme Court the power to make divorces (section 8(1)), the *Divorce Act* gives the court authority to make orders for access to and custody of children (section 16), as well as child and spousal maintenance (section 15). To initiate a divorce, a Petition must be drafted by one or both of the parties (or by a lawyer acting for one of the parties) and filed with the Supreme Court Registry. The Supreme Court registry issues the petition for Divorce. This petition may be filed jointly by the spouses when the sole ground for divorce is separation of one or more years and they both request and consent to any other orders to be made with respect to children or property division. Alternatively, one of the parties alone (the Petitioner), may file the divorce petition, seeking divorce and other related court orders. In this case, the Petitioner's spouse is known as the Respondent. No petition will be issued unless either the Petitioner or the Respondent has been "ordinarily resident" in the province where the petition is filed for at least one year immediately prior to the filing.

B. Contested and Uncontested Divorces

An "uncontested" or unopposed divorce may proceed when the parties agree on all possible issues including whether or not a divorce should occur, all parenting arrangements, and child and spousal maintenance provisions. If they disagree on one or more of these matters, and possibly if they disagree on how property should be divided, then the divorce becomes "contested."

The Divorce Petition must set out exactly what orders the Petitioner wants the Supreme Court to make. The petition may simply say that the Petitioner wants only a divorce, or that the Petitioner wants a divorce as well as orders for custody, access, maintenance, or property division, or a combination of these orders.

Once the petition is filed (and a fee paid), it must be served upon the Respondent. An Affidavit proving service must then be filed with the court. If the Respondent resides within British Columbia she/he has 20 days within which to file an "Answer." If the Respondent opposes the Petition, then she/he must file an Answer specifying any objections to the Petition. No Answer is filed if all possible issues have been previously settled, and if the settlement agreement has been formalized in an acceptable way. The divorce then proceeds as an "uncontested" divorce. The filing of an Answer makes the divorce "contested."

In an uncontested divorce it is not necessary for either party to actually attend court to obtain a divorce. The Petitioner simply waits until the filing deadline for the Answer has expired and then submits certain documentation to the court, including an Affidavit verifying the particulars of the marriage and evidence of the grounds for divorce. The court, if it is satisfied that adequate arrangements have been made for the care and maintenance of the children, then makes the order for divorce without actually seeing the parties.

If the Respondent opposes any of the relief sought in the petition then he/she must file an Answer. It is also possible to file a "Counter-Petition" with this Answer. In the Counter-Petition the Respondent is free to seek any relief or orders not raised in the petition.

Even when the Petitioner seeks a court order on matters already settled (for example, a separation agreement may already be signed setting out the terms of custody and maintenance) the Respondent may still wish to file an Answer to ensure that she/he has some control over the form of the final order. In these circumstances legal advice is always a good idea.

If there are issues that cannot readily be resolved, then the matter can be set down for trial. It can take anywhere from six to twenty-four months, or longer, before a Supreme Court trial is held, depending upon where it is to be held, and upon the anticipated length of the trial. Obviously, matters such as custody and maintenance will not usually be able to wait this long for a resolution. Accordingly, it is possible for the parties to appear, usually through counsel, before a judge to seek orders covering the period between commencement of the action and the trial. These "interim orders," available on relatively short notice, are usually based on affidavit evidence (sworn statements) submitted by the parties. Such interim orders will prevail until trial unless there is a significant change in circumstances, in which event they can sometimes be modified. Typically the parties will continue to negotiate, through their lawyers or with the assistance of a mediator, prior to the trial. Most cases are settled before trial.

The Divorce Order will state that the divorce does not become final until 31 days after the order is made.[13] Within that thirty-one day period either the husband or wife can appeal the decision. If there is no appeal the divorce will automatically become effective on the thirty-first day following the judge's order and no further steps need be taken by either party. In some circumstances, when both parties agree that they will not file an appeal and there is some pressing need (such as a desire to remarry so a child will be born in wedlock) the 30-day waiting period can be shortened or abrogated altogether.

C. Appeals

A husband or wife who believes the judge made a mistake in granting a divorce order or any related order (regarding maintenance, living and financial arrangements for the children, or division of property) may appeal the decision to the British Columbia Court of Appeal within 30 days of the decision. Outside this 30-day period, a judgment cannot be appealed except in very limited circumstances.

MAINTENANCE AND SUPPORT

A. Jurisdiction: The Authority to Order Maintenance

The federal *Divorce Act*[14] gives the Supreme Court the jurisdiction to order child and spousal maintenance when it has the jurisdiction to grant a divorce. Both the Supreme Court and the Family Court have jurisdiction to award child and spousal maintenance under the provincial *Family Relations Act*.

Under the *Divorce Act*, maintenance may be ordered for a "spouse." A "spouse" is defined as either a man or a woman who are or were married to each other. But under the *Family Relations Act*,[15] a "spouse" applying for maintenance is defined to include a person who is married to another person, or as a person who has lived with another person in a "marriage-like relationship" for a period of at least two years. This definition captures both common law and same gender partners, but requires that applications for maintenance be made within one year after the unmarried partners cease living together. A married spouse must apply for an order within two years of divorce.[16]

Merely starting an action for maintenance within one year may not be enough. It is important that the court actually hear the claim within one year. It is always strongly recommended that parties move with reasonable speed to assert such legal rights.

The Supreme Court can order child maintenance under either the *Divorce Act* or the *Family Relations Act*. The Family Court can order maintenance only under the *Family Relations Act*. The *Divorce Act* says that the court can make a maintenance order for "a child of the marriage," who is defined to be the biological or adopted offspring of the two parents involved, who is either under the age of majority (19 years in British Columbia) and still dependent on the parents, or over the age of majority but still dependent on the parents due to illness, disability, or other causes. A person who stands in the place of the child's parent (for example, a step-parent) may be liable for child support.

"Child" under the *Family Relations Act* is defined in a similar manner. Maintenance can extend beyond 19 years of age and, in fact, often does. The courts may extend maintenance beyond 19 years when considering, for example, the need to fund legitimate and realistic post-secondary educational programs.

The *Family Relations Act* obligates parents to support their children (section 88), spouses to support their spouse (section 89), and adult children to support parents who are dependent because of age, illness, infirmity, or other economic circumstances (section 90).

B. Child Support: Objectives

As previously stated, the *Divorce Act* imposes a duty on the court to ensure that reasonable arrangements for child support have been made before granting a divorce. This means that even in an uncontested divorce situation both parties must make financial disclosure sufficient to enable the court to evaluate the proposed financial arrangements. Both spouses are jointly responsible for the maintenance of a child. The duty to support children is a duty owed to the children and not to the custodial parent, even though the maintenance is paid to the custodial parent. The fact that a custodial parent is receiving welfare payments does not relieve the other parent of child maintenance obligations. The court may override or ignore the provisions of a separation agreement dealing with child support when it is appropriate, having regard to the needs of the children. This means, for example, that a written agreement by a custodial parent fixing a set amount or agreeing to forego child maintenance could well be varied or set aside by the court if the child's best interests require it. The courts take the view that support is the right of the child and cannot be bartered away by the parents. Helping professionals sometimes apply on a child's behalf to obtain maintenance for the child from parents when a child is living away from home.

C. Child Support Guidelines

Significant changes to child support legislation came into effect on May 1, 1997 in the form of Child Support Guidelines (hereafter referred to as the Guidelines).[17] The theory behind the Guidelines is that they will help parents, lawyers, and judges set fair and consistent child support awards in divorce cases. The object of the Guidelines is to make maintenance calculations more predictable, provide a simpler means to update awards, eliminate some maintenance disputes, and lower legal costs. Significant changes to the law include:

a) historically, child support payments made under orders or agreements have been tax deductible in the hands of the payor and taxed as income in the hands of the recipient. There will be no such tax consequences to child support payments made pursuant to an order or an agreement on or after May 1, 1997;

b) child support payment schedules or tables will show the basic amount that the support-paying parent should pay according to his/her income and the number of children. The schedule amounts are fixed by a formula that calculates the appropriate amount of support in light of economic data on average expenditures for children across different income levels in different provinces. The formula reserves a basic amount of income for the payor's self-support and defines exactly how much maintenance he/she must pay. By reference to a table in the schedule one can, with knowledge of the payor's gross annual income, often determine immediately how much child maintenance that person will pay;

c) the legislation will incorporate rules to allow adjustment of the maintenance award to compensate for special child-related expenses, or in cases of undue hardship. Special expenses could include medical and health related expenses over $100 per year, or certain educational or extra-curricular expenses. Matters relating to undue hardship could include an unusually high level of debt, unusually high expenses relating to exercising access, obligations to support other children, or being under a legal duty to support another person.

It is important to note that these new tax rules do not apply to spousal support. Nor do the tax rules apply to orders or agreements for child support made before May 1, 1997, unless:

a) an agreement or court order made on or after May 1, 1997 varies the amount of child support under an existing agreement or order;

b) the person paying the maintenance and the person receiving the maintenance jointly sign a tax form agreeing that the new tax rules will apply to an existing order;

c) an agreement or court order specifically provides that the new tax rules will apply to payments made after a specified date (which cannot be earlier than April 30, 1997).

The Guidelines (now part of the *Divorce Act*) will apply when a child support order is made in a divorce proceeding. The provincial *Family Relations Act* also makes use of Child Support Guidelines. The Guidelines are not mandatory for support awards that are negotiated out of court.

As stated, the child support payment schedules show the basic amount of the maintenance payment required based on the payor's income and the number of children. For example, a parent with an annual gross income of $44,000 would pay $376 a month for one child, $618 a month for two and $811 a month for three.[18] The scheduled payment amount is based only on the income of the paying parent and does not, except in limited circumstances, take into account the income of the custodial parent. Any person may apply on behalf of a child. Children do not apply on their own, someone does it for them.

D. Spousal Support: Basis and Objectives

The law on spousal maintenance is more complicated than the law on child maintenance. There are few black and white answers to questions about when a spouse is entitled to maintenance, how much maintenance should be paid, and how long it should continue. Because much depends on the circumstances and the facts of each case, court orders vary dramatically.

The rules for establishing entitlement to, and quantum of, spousal maintenance differ somewhat between the *Divorce Act* and the *Family Relations Act*. When making an order for spousal maintenance under the *Divorce Act*, the court takes into consideration the condition, means, needs, and other circumstances of each spouse, including the length of cohabitation and their respective functions while they lived together. The objectives of a spousal maintenance order include the following:[19]

a) recognizing any economic advantages or disadvantages to the spouses arising from the marriage or its breakdown;

b) apportioning between the spouses any financial consequences arising from the care of any child of the marriage;

c) relieving any economic hardship of the spouses arising from the breakdown of the marriage; and

d) promoting the economic self-sufficiency of each spouse within a reasonable period of time.

After the enactment of the *Divorce Act* in 1985 the courts were reasonably active in promoting the immediate or eventual economic independence of the spouse receiving maintenance in order to eliminate the need for the payment of indefinite, periodic maintenance. Over time, however, the courts made it clear that there are circumstances (especially relating to longer term and more "traditional" marriages and disadvantaged spouses) when indefinite periodic maintenance is appropriate. The Supreme Court of Canada has said that the objective of the *Divorce Act* is to promote equitable sharing of the economic consequences of marriage or marriage breakdown. While both the *Divorce Act* and the *Family Relations Act* encourage the self-sufficiency of spousal maintenance recipients within a reasonable period of time, the goal of self-sufficiency does not take priority over the other statutory objectives for maintenance payment. Self-sufficiency may or may not be a realistic objective, depending upon the circumstances of the individual case.

The Courts have said that marriage should be regarded as a joint endeavour; the longer the marriage, the greater will be the presumptive claim to equal standards of living upon its dissolution. Increasingly, the cases suggest that marriage must be viewed as an economic partnership. Some cases say that a presumptive economic disadvantage exists after the breakdown of a long term marriage where the claimant spouse has been absent from the work force for a long time. In such cases the appropriate standard of living to be considered, if the means are available, is a reasonable one, having in mind the marital standard of living.

There is no simple rule for determining spousal maintenance rights and obligations, nor is there a formula for determining the amount of maintenance. Spouses should consult a lawyer about their specific situation.

E. Kinds of Maintenance Orders

Typically, maintenance orders are periodic (payable monthly or bi-weekly). Usually a separation agreement provides, or a court orders, that maintenance will be paid commencing on the first day of a given month and continuing on the first day of each month thereafter. As stated, the payments may be ordered for a definite or an indefinite period, or until the happening of a specified event. Maintenance may also be ordered on such terms as the court thinks fit and just.

Maintenance can also be ordered payable as a lump sum. This is much less common and usually reserved for cases involving short marriages, or where a lump sum is combined with a periodic payment to accomplish a particular purpose. It may also be ordered when there is a lump sum of cash available and the court believes that the obligated spouse will not make reliable periodic maintenance payments because, for example, there is an unusual degree of animosity between the parties.

In recent years, the courts have occasionally spoken in terms of "compensatory maintenance." This concept, which is not widely used in British Columbia, is premised on the argument that the value of economic opportunity lost by a spouse as a consequence of a joint decision for that spouse to remain at home and raise the children should be shared equally by the spouses when the marriage breaks down. That is, the cost associated with not being established in a career, not contributing to a pension, not establishing seniority or securing promotions etc., should be calculated and shared. It is often difficult, in practice, to actually calculate these costs and the British Columbia courts seem disinclined to utilize the model.

F. Enforcement of Maintenance Orders

Statutes exist to enforce maintenance orders that have fallen into arrears. For example, the *Family Maintenance Enforcement Act*[20] can be used to enforce maintenance orders made under the *Divorce Act* or British Columbia's *Family Relations Act*, or valid maintenance orders from other provinces. The legislation provides two options.

a) Spouses may file a maintenance order with the Director of Maintenance Enforcement who will take enforcement proceedings for them. The Director has very broad powers and can use numerous enforcement methods. There is no charge for this service.

151

b) It is also possible to enforce payments under a maintenance order without the assistance of the Director of Maintenance Enforcement. Spouses entitled to maintenance and acting on their own have a number of options. For example, they may:

i) apply for a garnishment order (for example, claiming wages from an employer or funds from a bank account);

ii) apply for the appointment of a Receiver of any property of the person owing maintenance;

iii) apply for an order restraining the person owing maintenance from disposing of or "wasting" (destroying or using up) property;

iv) register the order against property held in the name of the payor.

Numerous other legal devices exist to collect and enforce maintenance payments and arrears:

a) spouses in arrears may be subpoenaed to appear for an examination under oath concerning their financial circumstances;

b) the Supreme Court can issue a Writ of Execution (i.e., permitting seizure of property) for the total amount of arrears owing under an order for periodic maintenance;

c) an application can be brought to find a non-paying spouse in contempt of court, resulting in a possible fine and/or imprisonment;

d) other enforcement tools, such as access to federal data banks, withholding entitlement to a federal licence or passport, and garnishment of federal employees are now available under various federal statutes.[21]

For spouses who are unable to pay, the legislation also provides some protection, permitting them to apply to the court for a temporary order reducing the required payments. Under some circumstances, the *Divorce Act* and the *Family Relations Act* also give the court the power to cancel arrears of maintenance.

G. Variation of Maintenance Orders

Both the *Divorce Act* and the *Family Relations Act* allow the court to vary or rescind some maintenance orders. The fundamental principle is that the spouse seeking the variation must be able to show that, since the original order was made, there has been a change in the circumstances of either spouse that is sufficient to justify the variation. The court will generally presume that the amount of maintenance provided for at the time of the original order was correct. There must be shown a change in circumstances with a financial consequence in order to vary the amount of maintenance. This is a relatively common court application, which is typically made on affidavit evidence and almost never requires a trial. Parents with existing orders under the *Divorce Act* may seek variations under the "change of circumstances" provision simply on the basis that the law has been changed with the coming into force of Child Support Guidelines.

CUSTODY AND ACCESS

I. Definitions

The terms custody, access, guardianship, joint-custody, and joint-guardianship are frequently used but, perhaps surprisingly, are not always clearly defined at law.

A. Custody

Neither the *Divorce Act* nor the *Family Relations Act* defines this term with any particular precision. The courts have generally stated that unless an order specifically says otherwise, the parent who is given "custody" is given physical care and control over the child, which includes control over all matters falling within the scope of guardianship of the "person" of the child.[22]

B. Guardianship

Guardianship encompasses all of the rights, duties, and responsibilities of a parent. Rights incidental to guardianship of the person of the child include such matters as the right to determine a child's education, medical treatment, health care, activities, religion, and any significant changes in the child's social environment.

C. Access

Access involves the non-custodial parent's right to visit with the child. Historically, a right of access has included little right to influence the upbringing of the child or to have input into, or make decisions about, the custody and guardianship matters referred to above. However, an order under the *Divorce Act* can give a parent with access the right to information about the child's health, welfare, and education. The Supreme Court of Canada held that a custodial parent has no right to limit or restrict access unless it is in the best interests of the child to do so. The *Divorce Act* supports the principle that the child should have as much contact with each spouse as is consistent with the best interests of the child, but it is also possible for access to be denied entirely or provided on conditions where the child's best interests require it.

D. Joint Custody and Joint Guardianship

Parties can agree to, or the court can order, joint custody or joint guardianship, if satisfied that there is a good prospect of cooperation between the parents. This is possible even where there is some animosity as long as the parties are able to communicate maturely. These orders are most commonly made at the request of, and with the consent of, both parties. The court will often take the view that joint custody should be reserved for parents who are able to communicate and work well together. Disagreement about whether or not a joint custody order should be made will often, but not always, be taken by the court as evidence that parents lack the necessary working relationship. Under joint-custody agreements or orders, the parents share jointly and equally in all custody rights, although the child may or may not live equal periods of time with each parent. In some circumstances, joint custody has been imposed on a parent who is, at least superficially, opposed to it. If there is some ability to communicate and cooperate to achieve parental goals a court might order joint custody notwithstanding conflict between the parties. In other cases, the courts have been less enthusiastic about joint custody and describe it as "a triumph of optimism over prudence."

Joint guardianship typically gives substantially fewer rights to one parent than the other. Often the child will reside primarily with one parent, and the non-custodial joint-guardian will be confined to acting as custodial guardian in the event of the death or incapacity of the other parent.

II. Who May Apply for Custody and Access?

Custody, access, and maintenance can be established by agreement between the parties or by court order. In the absence of an agreement or court order, the person with whom the child usually resides is deemed, by the terms of the *Family Relations Act*, to be the person entitled to exercise custody.

When a relationship breaks down either a husband or wife may apply for custody or access. But the *Divorce Act* also allows any other person who may wish to maintain contact with the child of divorcing parents, such as a grandparent, foster parent, or another relative, to apply for custody or access. Similarly, under the *Family Relations Act* any person can be granted custody of, or access to, a child.

Historically, the courts have been prepared to award custody to third parties (such as grandparents and other extended family members) rather than the parents, when the best interests of the child require it. This might happen when the child's natural parents cannot provide a stable, nurturing environment, or where they have otherwise conducted themselves in a manner contrary to the child's best interests. A third-party custody order is more likely when the child has developed a strong emotional bond and has some historical relationship with the non-parent.

III. Custody and Access Orders: Their Basis and Objectives

The single test determining custody and access rights is: "what custody or access disposition will serve the best interests of the child?" The issue of custody is not a question of what rights the parents or other claimants may have. It is always framed in terms of the rights, needs, and best interests of the child.

In applying the "best interests" test the courts will look at many factors. The more common and important factors include the following:[23]

a) the health and emotional well-being of the child including any special needs for care and treatment;

b) love, affection, and similar ties that exist being the child and the claimant;

154

c) the training and education available for the child;

d) the separate capacities of the people seeking child custody or access; and

e) whenever appropriate, the views of the child. As a general rule, the older the child the greater weight given to his or her wishes. Typically, by 11 or 12 years of age the unprompted views of a child will be given considerable weight by the court.

Many other factors influence a court's determination of what lies in the child's best interest. Financial resources of the parents will be considered by the court but will not, typically, be given disproportionate weight. The court tends to be much more concerned with which parent provides the more stable, nurturing, and positive environment for the child than with which parent can provide the most material comfort. In contentious situations, the court may request that the child's interests be legally represented by a family advocate.[24]

The idea once prevailed that children of "tender years" should, as a starting proposition, always be given to the custody of their mother. This doctrine has essentially fallen out of use, although it still has some limited practical application in the obvious sense that, for example, a very young infant should remain with a breast-feeding mother. The courts will be influenced by which parent has historically been the primary care giver and by the degree of bonding between the child and each parent. The court may seek information on these issues through a custody and access report prepared by helping a professional, such as a social worker or psychologist in public or private practice.

Other factors that the court will consider are the child's need for stability and security and the desire to have as little disruption or change as possible. The court will generally attempt to keep siblings together. The court will only take into account the behaviour, character and conduct of the parents, to the extent that these characteristics reflect ability to care for the child.[25]

Spouses who are separating should be aware of the emphasis the courts place on the stability of the child's environment and maintenance of the *status quo* in making a custody order. Custody, access, and parenting arrangements made by the parties at the time of separation can be of great consequence further down the road. For example, spouses attempting a "trial separation" may establish a *status quo* that could permanently affect their individual custody and access rights if the separation becomes permanent.

IV. Enforcement of Custody and Access Rights

A number of statutes provide mechanisms for the enforcement of custody and access orders. Both the Supreme Court and the Family Court have the power to enforce orders.

When a child has been wrongfully removed from the parent with custody, the law provides certain remedies. Under the *Family Relations Act*[26] the legal custodian may apply to the court for various orders:

a) requiring a peace officer to apprehend and return the child;

b) giving peace officers the authority to enter and search likely locations for the child; or

c) requiring third parties to release information about the address of someone who has actual custody of a child.

This order is also available to parents or other people entitled to enforce access rights.

Under the *Criminal Code* [27] certain acts of interference with court ordered custody rights are punishable offenses. Additionally, the Supreme Court has the power to punish any party for contempt (willful breach of its orders). This power is sometimes invoked by a parent who has experienced ongoing difficulty enforcing custody or access rights against the other parent.

Under the *Hague Convention on the Civil Aspects of International Child Abduction* [28] mechanisms are available, in some cases, to invoke international co-operation for the purposes of returning an abducted child to Canada.

V. Variation

Custody and access arrangements are never carved in stone. They may always be varied as required by changing circumstances and the best interests of the child.

DIVISION OF PROPERTY

A. The Law

The *Family Relations Act* [29] outlines the law on division of property when a marriage breaks down. Each spouse becomes entitled to an undivided one-half interest in any family asset when certain "triggering events" occur: the making of a separation agreement, for example, or a judge's declaration that the spouses have no reasonable prospect of reconciliation. Until such a "triggering event" occurs, the spouses have separate property rights and are free to deal in or dispose of their separate property. Only "family assets" are owned equally.

The statute generally defines a "family asset" as any asset which has been used for a "family purpose" during the marriage. The *Family Relations Act* [30] also broadly defines a family asset as any "venture" to which a spouse has contributed directly or indirectly in money or its equivalent. An "indirect contribution" may include savings made through effective household management, or child-rearing responsibilities assumed by the spouse who holds no actual interest in the property. Other assets, such as pension plans and R.R.S.P.s, are specifically included in the definition of family assets. Business assets owned by one spouse and not the other are specifically excluded from the definition of family asset unless the non-owning spouse has made a direct or indirect contribution as defined above.

There has been much litigation about which assets are included or excluded from the family asset category. That said, it is quite easy to identify the family assets in most marriages. The family home, furniture, family cars, savings, and the pensions earned by the spouses are almost invariably family assets.

Equal entitlement to family assets is the rule, but it is not absolute. When it would be "unfair" to order an equal division, the court can order that assets be divided in some other proportion. The court starts from the assumption of equal division but then assesses if equal division would be unfair based upon:

a) the duration of the marriage;

b) the duration of the separation;

c) the date the property was acquired or disposed of;

d) whether the property was acquired by one spouse through inheritance or a gift;

e) the needs of each spouse to become or remain economically independent; and

f) any other circumstance relating to the acquisition, preservation, maintenance, improvement or use of the property, or capacities or liabilities of the spouses.

A very short marriage, for example, to which one spouse brought substantially all of the assets could well result in a variation in favour of that spouse. A court might also consider an unequal division of assets when one spouse has a substantial income and the other has, by reason of age or illness, no present or future prospect of such an income. Generally speaking, real unfairness is required before the courts will make any order other than for an equal division of family assets.

Historically, these rules have not applied to common-law spouses. In the case of unmarried partners and same gender partners, applications for division of property have been based on the more complicated common-law rules of trust. Such partners can opt into the applications of the property division parts of the *Act* by making the equivalent of a marriage or separation agreement.

While the *Family Relations Act* deals expressly with family assets, it does not refer specifically to the allocation of family debts. While the court cannot make one spouse jointly liable to a creditor for the debt of the other spouse, even if the debt was incurred for a family purpose, family debts can be taken into account in making a property division and it is not uncommon for the court to equalize both debts and assets.

RESTRAINING ORDERS

The court can order exclusive occupation of the family residence in favour of one spouse. When there is a real risk of physical harm, the court may order one spouse not to enter the family home or other premises occupied by the endangered spouse and children.[31]

The court also has the authority to make an order restraining any person from molesting, annoying, harassing, or communicating with an individual and any children in that individual's lawful custody. Restraining orders can be obtained on reasonably short notice, especially in emergency situations. The court can also order a person not to contact or otherwise interfere with a child or the person with custody of the child. Violating one of these orders is a punishable offense.[32]

Also, under the *Criminal Code*,[33] people who fear injury to themselves or children in their custody may ask the court for a "peace bond." If the court concludes there are reasonable grounds for fear, it may order the offending person to "keep the peace and to be of good behaviour" or serve a prison term in default. The court has wide discretion to set conditions ensuring compliance. In practice, however, peace bonds are rarely used.

Under other provisions of the *Criminal Code* a person may be charged with criminal harassment for repeatedly following or communicating with a person, for watching or besetting a person's home, or for engaging in threatening conduct directed at the person or any member of his/her family.

As well as making orders to protect the person, the court can make orders to protect or preserve or prevent the disposal of property.

REACHING AGREEMENT

A. Procedural Alternatives

When a couple decides to separate, a number of issues typically arise. Decisions must be made about a possible divorce, parenting arrangements, maintenance payments, and property division. In deciding how to resolve these issues, spouses have a number of procedural options, ranging from co-operative through to the adversarial. The most co-operative approach is for the spouses to negotiate directly with each another. As long as they are fully informed of their separate rights and obligations, and a fair agreement is made and properly recorded, then this is a desirable approach.

If spouses are unable to resolve all issues without assistance, they must involve a third party. Each spouse could, at this point, choose to retain a separate lawyer who will offer advice and take instructions about how to proceed. This lawyer might be instructed to negotiate directly with the other spouse's lawyer, which means that responsibility for negotiation is, to an extent, removed from the hands of the parties and conducted, in effect, by agents. In the absence of a negotiated settlement, one or both of the lawyers might be instructed to commence litigation, which has the effect of giving the authority to resolve the dispute to a judge. If the dispute gets to this level it will be framed in adversarial terms; that is, in terms of the assertion of one spouse's rights over the rights of the other.

Mediation is another alternative to be considered when spouses cannot fully agree on all issues arising from their separation. A mediator is a trained professional who acts as an informed and impartial facilitator assisting the spouses to directly negotiate their own terms of settlement. The goal of mediation is to reach a consensual resolution of all issues in a fair and workable manner, while accommodating as many of the needs and interests of the parties as possible. Mediation is not about reconciliation, nor the working out of personal relationships. Nevertheless, a mediator will be alert to, and will identify, any relationship dynamics that may be preventing the spouses from reaching a settlement.

Mediators should also be alert to and address any imbalance in power between the parties. Mediation is only intended for circumstances where fair negotiation is possible. Situations involving an unreconcilable disparity in power between the parties or domestic violence are not appropriate for mediation. That said, a spouse may elect to attend mediation in such circumstances with a lawyer.

A mediator has no decision-making authority. The mediator's role is to provide a framework and process for the spouses to address unresolved issues. A mediator will gather the relevant facts, isolate the issues and define an agenda while overseeing a safe and fair discussion of options for settlement. Mediation is voluntary. The participants are free to enter or terminate mediation as they see fit. Research discloses that the settlement rates in mediation are very high and that parties participating in mediation usually feel positive about the process.

The *Divorce Act*[34] specifically recognizes the value of alternate methods of dispute resolution such as mediation. The *Act* requires a lawyer consulted by someone seeking divorce to first recommend a negotiated resolution to issues such as custody, access, and maintenance, and, moreover, to inform the client of any known and appropriate mediation services. Helping professionals should be alert to the distinction between a negotiated settlement, a litigated settlement and a mediated settlement, and the circumstances when each would be appropriate or advisable for their clients. They should also be aware of the mediation resources in their community.

B. Types of Mediators

Mediators come from many professions including law, psychology, social work, medicine, and theology. There are no formal licensing requirements or uniform training standards that apply to all mediators. This means that mediation procedures may vary, and that one mediator may not bring the same level of skill or competence to the task as the next. Various professional bodies and mediation organizations are now working toward uniform training, licensing, and practice standards. Until such standards exist, however, potential mediation clients should carefully investigate the proposed mediator's professional background, training, and qualifications.

Regardless of who the mediator is, terms of agreement reached in mediation should always be reviewed by an independent lawyer before an agreement is signed. This acts as a check on the process and ensures that the parties do not enter into an agreement that is substantially unfair or unworkable from a legal point of view. Spouses sometimes resist the idea of having the agreement reviewed by a lawyer on the basis that a lawyer might bring an adversarial perspective to bear, and draw the parties into the very conflict that they have been seeking to avoid. In answer to this, it should be noted that many lawyers in British Columbia are trained in mediation, and are sensitive to the motives and wishes of clients who choose mediation. Remember also that lawyers simply give advice and make recommendations. It is ultimately up to the parties to decide what they will do. Legal review and advice simply ensures that decisions made by the parties are fully informed by an understanding of the law and of each party's respective rights and obligations. It should also be noted that in the event of a subsequent dispute, an agreement is more likely to be enforced by the courts if the parties have had independent legal advice before signing it.

C. Formalizing Settlement

If mediation is unsuccessful then the parties may continue to negotiate through lawyers or proceed to litigation. If mediation is successful then the terms of the agreement should be incorporated into either a written separation agreement or a court order. If mediation begins after litigation has commenced, it might be convenient and workable simply to roll the terms of the mediated settlement into a consent order in the court. If there has been no litigation, then typically a separation agreement is drafted and signed. Again, the terms of agreement should always be reviewed independently by each spouse's lawyer.

COMMON QUESTIONS

1. <u>How long does it take to get a divorce?</u>

If grounds exist, securing a divorce order in itself is relatively straight-forward. It is the resolution of collateral issues (maintenance, custody, access, and property division) that will most often cause delay. If there are no collateral issues to resolve and if grounds for divorce exist, then divorce orders can usually be obtained in a matter of weeks or months. Sometimes a divorce order can be obtained when there are still unresolved collateral issues, but usually these issues are resolved first. Obviously, spouses who are at odds with one another will take longer to negotiate and resolve these issues and obtain a final divorce order. If the dispute proceeds to litigation, the process may take up to one or more years to conclude. Spouses typically continue to negotiate while waiting six to twenty-four months for a trial date. Any unresolved matters are then determined by the trial judge.

2. <u>What steps should helping professionals advise spouses to take in anticipation of separation?</u>

The first step is an obvious one: encourage the spouse to secure legal advice. The law relating to separation and divorce is increasingly complex and every spouse should have as much legal information about his or her particular case as possible before actually separating. A one-hour meeting with a family lawyer is often long enough to at least get oriented to the legal issues flowing from separation. Understanding legal rights and obligations may have a significant effect upon a separating spouse's choice of action. It may, for example, be crucial to know approximately how much maintenance to anticipate or whether a claim for custody will likely be successful. A spouse may need to know whether assets or chattels would be available for use after separation. Temporary arrangements respecting who occupies the matrimonial home and who cares for the children can have profound significance in the event of subsequent litigation.

The second step is to get the spouse to explore her/his procedural alternatives. Does the spouse need to go to court right away? Can he/she negotiate directly with her/his spouse? Should he/she retain a lawyer? Is it appropriate to consider mediation? This paper provides limited information only on these issues. Ensure the spouse gets the advice needed in order to make these decisions.

3. Is there any danger in spouses making parenting and maintenance arrangements without legal advice after separation?

Yes. The spouses may establish a *status quo* or set a precedent that will have substantial influence on a court at a later date. For example, one spouse may leave the home and the children assuming that she/he will move back if the parties decide to reconcile, and that custody and access will be sorted out later if they do not reconcile. The spouse who leaves may, however, discover that the spouse remaining in the home has a significant advantage in any subsequent court application for child custody.

4. Can a stepparent become responsible after separation for maintenance of his/her spouse's children?

A stepparent can be made liable to pay maintenance for children even if she/he is not the biological father or mother of the child, and even if he/she has not adopted the child. Under the *Divorce Act* one can be compelled to pay maintenance for the benefit of a child for whom one "stands in the place of a parent." That is, if one has stood in the shoes of a parent, and assumed the role and status and responsibilities of a parent toward a child, then one can be responsible to maintain the child. Under the *Family Relations Act*, one becomes liable to support a child where one has contributed as a stepparent to the support of a child for one year or longer. Under the *Family Relations Act* it is necessary for the legal proceeding against the stepparent for maintenance to be commenced within one year after the date the stepparent last contributed to the support of the child. It follows that it is possible under these *Acts* for both a biological parent and a stepparent to pay maintenance for one child at the same time.

5. What can be done to enforce the terms of a written separation agreement or a court order against a reluctant spouse?

Numerous mechanisms exist to enforce the performance of obligations respecting custody, access, maintenance, and property division. The method of enforcement and the ease of enforcement will depend firstly on whether the term to be enforced is in a court order or in a separation agreement. As a rule, court orders are easier to enforce although separation agreements respecting custody, access, and maintenance can, if properly filed with the court, be enforced like court orders. The *Family Maintenance Enforcement Act* creates an agency to assist spouses in the collection of maintenance, and a number of mechanisms exist (such as garnishment) to enforce collection. Registration of separation agreements or court orders against real property can be effected in order to secure payment of maintenance or payment for an interest in property. A spouse who willfully breaches the terms of a court order can be brought before the court and may be found in contempt of court and punished appropriately. There are many ways in which separation agreements and orders can be enforced. Typically, it is best to obtain specific advice from a lawyer or from some other legal resource in the community. It should be noted, however, that a breach of a term by one spouse in no way justifies a breach of term by the other. For example, the spouse who is not paid child maintenance has no legal right to deny child access in return.

6. Are helping professionals who are making an investigation for a custody and access or maintenance report obliged to testify about information obtained during the investigation if requested to do so by the court?

Yes. According to the *Family Relations Act*,[35] a person directed to carry out such investigations "must report the results in the manner the court directs." This is different from the situation of protection of confidentiality in limited circumstances under the *Family Relations Act* and the *Divorce Act*.

Under the *Family Relations Act*[36] when a family court counsellor is offering advice and guidance to assist in resolving a family dispute, a communication from any party must be held in confidence unless the party consents to disclosure. This situation may include counseling or mediation as distinct from an investigation for the court.

Likewise, under the *Divorce Act*[37] a person nominated to assist spouses to achieve a reconciliation is not a compellable witness (does not have to testify), and the evidence from assisting in the reconciliation is not admissible.

CONCLUSION

The dramatic increase in the incidence of family breakdown over the last few decades has carried in its wake an increase in the complexity of the law as it applies to separating families. It is, therefore, increasingly important to ensure that members of separating families have information about their legal rights and obligations, and that they secure this information in a timely fashion. There are many ways in which the law will directly impinge on the well-being of these individuals and, as such, it is incumbent upon all helping professionals to have some understanding of the applicable rules and procedures, and a specific knowledge of the legal resources available in their community.

RESOURCES

Canadian Bar Association "Dial a Law Tapes." Consult your local yellow pages for telephone numbers for pre-recorded messages describing various aspects of family law.

Divorce Law for Counselors, (Ottawa: Communications and Public Affairs, Department of Justice Canada).

M.A. McCarthy, *Family Law for Every Canadian*, (Scarborough, Ont.: Prentice Hall Canada 1997).

Internet: Access to Justice Network Acunet, http:// www.acjnet.org/resource/res_def.html#dispute.

The Public Legal Education Society, 3446 West Broadway, Vancouver, B.C. V6R 2B3.

Family Mediation Canada, 2nd Floor, 123 Woolwich Street, Guelph, Ontario N1H 3V1.

Legal Services Society, 3rd Floor, 1140 West Pender Street, Vancouver, B.C. V6E 4G1.

Mediation Development Association of British Columbia, New Westminister Office, 10256 Sixth Street, New Westminister, V3L 2Z5.

END NOTES

1. *Divorce Act,* 1985, R.S.C. 1986, c.4.
2. *Family Relations Act*, R.S.B.C. 1996, c. 128.
3. *Marriage (Prohibited Degrees) Act*, S.C., 1990, c.46.
4. 1997 amendments to the *Family Relations Act* allow unmarried, same gender spouses to opt into the property division provisions of the *Act* by making the equivalent of a marriage or separation agreement.
5. *Family Maintenance Enforcement Act*, [R.S.B.C. 1996], c. 127, section 1. These provisions passed third reading as of November 10, 1997, but have not yet been proclaimed into force.
6. Previously, British Columbia passed a law allowing same sex couples to adopt.
7. In 1997 the Attorney General stated that he was considering a review of all British Columbia legislation to eliminate inequalities for gays and lesbians. The courts, as well as the legislators, have been reviewing this area of the law. In 1997 an arbitrator ruled that the British Columbia government should not have denied leave to a woman who wanted time off because her lesbian partner had a baby. In so doing the arbitrator rejected as discriminatory arguments that the woman was not entitled to leave because she was not an adoptive or biological parent.
8. For example, a common law spouse may have a claim under the *Workers Compensation Act*, R.S.B.C. 1996, c.492, if his or her spouse is killed at work.
9. *Family Relations Act*, sections 121 and 122.
10. *Divorce Act*, section 9.
11. *Ibid*, section 8.
12. *Ibid*, section 8(3).
13. *Ibid*, section 12(1).
14. *Ibid*, section 15.
15. *Family Relations Act*, section 1.
16. The definition of "parent" in the *Family Relations Act* has also been amended to include some persons in same gender marriage-like relationships.
17. 1997 amendment to the *Divorce Act*.
18. These are the figures applicable in 1997 and are subject to change at a later date.
19. *Divorce Act*, section 15(7).
20. *Family Maintenance Enforcement Act*, R.S.B.C. 1996, c. 127.
21. See for example the federal *Orders and Agreements Enforcement Assistance Act*; the *Garnishment, Attachment and Pension Diversion Act*; and the *Canada Shipping Act*.
22. See for example *Young v. Young*, (1993), 84. B.C.L.R. (2d) 1 (S.C.C.).
23. *Family Relations Act*, section 24. *Gordon v. Goertz* (1996), INRFL (4th) S.C.C. *Divorce Act*, s.16.
24. *Ibid, Family Relations Act*, section 2.
25. *Ibid, Family Relations Act*, section 24(3), and *Divorce Act*, section 16(9).
26. *Ibid, Family Relations Act*, sections 36 and 39.
27. *Criminal Code*, section 282, R.S.C., c.C-34.
28. *Family Relations Act*, section 55.
29. *Ibid*, Part 5.
30. *Ibid*, section 58.
31. *Ibid*, sections 38 and 126.
32. *Ibid*, sections 37 and 38.
33. *Criminal Code*, section 810.
34. *Divorce Act*, section 9(2).
35. *Family Relations Act*, section 15(2).
36. *Ibid*, section 3(3).
37. *Divorce Act*, sections 10(4 and 5).

Chapter 7

FAMILY VIOLENCE AND THE CRIMINAL COURT SYSTEM

Nicholas Lang

INTRODUCTION

We live in a violent society. Sometimes the scope of the problem, particularly on the family level, seems overwhelming. Federal studies show that spousal assault is a serious and widespread reality suffered by one out of ten Canadian women.[1] In 1982 the *Badgley Report*, a Federal Committee on Sexual Offences Against Children and Youth, estimated that at some time during their lives one in two females and one in three males have been the victims of one or more unwanted sexual acts.[2] Eighty percent of those acts were first committed against persons 18 or under.[3]

The family has always been viewed as a basic feature of any stable social structure. Traditionally, violence within the family was seen as a private affair and family members were encouraged to resolve their own differences. Recently, attitudes have changed, and the helping professions have been struggling to find ways to successfully detect dysfunctional families and to intervene in abusive situations. Despite the lack of adequate training, resources, and facilities, front line workers such as police, social workers, and legal and medical personnel have made considerable progress in recognizing and dealing with the problem of family violence.

The purpose of this chapter is to outline the criminal law and related procedures available for identifying and intervening in situations of family violence, especially physical and sexual assault upon family members. In this chapter the term "family" covers both legally recognized and "common-law" units. This chapter does not deal with the procedures and remedies available as part of *Divorce Act*[4] proceedings or civil actions, which are discussed in other chapters. The law in this chapter is stated as of September 1, 1997.

This chapter begins with an overview of criminal behaviour in the family, explores the criminal process and evidence issues including information about child and spousal witnesses, and concludes with some questions commonly asked by helping professionals.

Most family violence can be categorized into three groups of criminal offences. These groups are the following:

a) physical assaults on children, spouses, the elderly, or the disabled;

b) sexual assaults on spouses and other adults; and

c) special sexual offences against children.

The first chapter of this book described some general principles of the criminal law process. This chapter will discuss various procedures and elements of violent offences as they occur in the criminal process, both before and in court. The key steps of the criminal process are:

a) complaint and the investigation by police;

b) decision to prosecute;

c) nature of the charge;

d) arrest of the suspect and first court appearance;

e) issues of detention or release;

f) evidence in court;

g) conviction or acquittal; and

h) sentence by the court.

COMPLAINT AND INVESTIGATION

Many complaints of violence in families come to police attention from the victim, or from witnesses, such as other family members, bystanders, or neighbours. In other cases, helping professionals may observe symptoms or signs consistent with physical assault, sexual assault, or other offences.

As mentioned in Chapter 3, all provinces have created, for all persons, a legal duty to report to the appropriate ministry circumstances where there is reason to believe a child is in need of protection. Protocols oblige the ministry to involve the police in any potentially criminal investigations. Most provinces and the federal government have toll free numbers for children and adults to call to make a complaint.

DECISION TO PROSECUTE

During the 1980s and 1990s, police and Crown Counsel (prosecutors) were directed to apply policies that encourage criminal prosecutions for offences of violence and abuse within families.

A. Policies for Active Prosecution (Spousal)

Attorney General's departments in most provinces, including British Columbia, have developed policies to encourage the prosecution of spousal assaults.

In February, 1993, the Ministry of the Attorney General in British Columbia approved a comprehensive policy on victims in relationships for female victims in any intimate relationships, and for male victims in same sex relationships and heterosexual relationships with a power/control abuse dynamic.[5] Similar comprehensive policies are in preparation for child sexual abuse cases and sexual abuse cases.

Police officers must arrest offenders in all appropriate cases. Officers obtain written statements whenever possible from victims, and will also look for independent evidence to support any assault charges at trial. Many are being trained, individually and in special units, to develop the necessary skills and sensitivity to handle spousal assault situations. Referral to counselling services and support networks is encouraged. Many communities, including Victoria, British Columbia, have hired full-time support workers for victims. Crown Counsel have been encouraged to lay charges, subpoena witnesses to assure attendance, and vigorously pursue the effective presentation of spousal and child assault cases, seeking deterrent sentences in appropriate cases.

B. Policies for Active Prosecution (Child Sexual)

In 1978, the Ministry of Social Services received a total of 708 complaints for both physical abuse of children and sexual abuse of children. In 1993, the same Ministry received 5,565 complaints of child sexual abuse alone (physical abuse complaints are now separately recorded).[6] This dramatic increase arose from a number of factors that include:

a) wider public knowledge and extensive publicity about child sexual abuse;

b) changes in the law that facilitate effective reporting and prosecution of child abuse offences;

c) better training for police and helping professionals, which assists in identifying child sexual abuse;

d) new law, which has made reporting by professionals mandatory;

e) the social climate, which has made reporting by private persons much more acceptable; and

f) that complainants in child sexual abuse cases are no longer the subject of intense doubt, scepticism, and even ridicule that were present in social and legal thinking even in the recent past.

Since the release of the federal *Badgley Report,* the Attorney General's department in several provinces, including British Columbia, Manitoba, and Ontario, have developed policies to encourage prosecution of child sexual assault cases. In many places specially trained police personnel and prosecutors have been designated to investigate and deal with these cases. Government ministries have also trained and designated special workers in this area. Dramatic legal changes in evidence and procedure have been enacted to allow prosecution of these difficult cases.

C. Basis For Deciding to Prosecute

The decision to prosecute remains the discretion (prerogative) of the prosecutor (Crown Counsel). Prosecutions normally proceed if it is in the public interest and there is sufficient evidence to prove that an offence happened. (In British Columbia, the Crown Counsel will ask whether there is "a substantial probability of conviction"). As noted, policies exist to actively encourage such prosecutions.

In many spousal assault cases the spouse is a reluctant witness who will often seek to have the charges withdrawn before the matter comes to trial. While Crown Counsel resists this process, it is difficult to prove a case beyond a reasonable doubt with a reluctant and forgetful witness. This is especially true in areas where there are no victim support systems such as spousal assault workers and Transition Houses in existence. Often the offender, promising that violence will never happen again, will be very successful in persuading a spouse to reconcile before the trial. The dynamics of the "battered woman" syndrome can trap many families in an ongoing and escalating cycle of violence that prevents many prosecutions from proceeding.

Canadian law requires proof from only one witness,[7] although additional proof of any fact is always potentially useful. Prompt reporting to the police usually results in effectively obtaining and preserving evidence, and police are frequently able to obtain statements from the accused that may be admissible as evidence. In addition, the following sources of evidence are important in all cases, including spousal assault:

a) written statements of eye witnesses;

b) written statements of witnesses who heard noises, shouts, cries;

c) written statements of witnesses who can testify about the upset condition of the victim immediately after, or as soon as possible after, the assault occurred;

d) photos of the injury;

e) medical reports of the injury; and

f) torn clothing, damaged items, or any photos of those.

It should be noted that despite the policies outlined above, not all cases proceed to trial. In British Columbia an accused person who acknowledges guilt may enter "Diversion," by contracting with an agency approved by the Attorney General's ministry. This contract permits an accused to avoid the formal court process by making reparation, apologizing to the victim, performing Community Work Service, or taking appropriate counseling such as family violence prevention or "anger control" counselling. Crown Counsel must approve the details of this arrangement which, in assault cases, is usually only recommended when the offence is relatively minor and has caused no bodily harm.

CRIMINAL CHARGE

A charge will only be laid and a prosecution commenced when the violence or abuse fits the definition of an offence created by legislation. Less serious offences are handled by summary conviction procedures in Provincial Court, and generally involve a less complicated court process and a maximum sentence of six months for the accused.

In February, 1995, a second category of summary conviction offences were created with a maximum sentence of 18 months.[8]

More serious offences proceed by Indictment. In most charges by Indictment the accused can decide whether to be tried by Provincial Court, Supreme Court Judge alone, or Supreme Court Judge and jury. The maximum sentence, depending on the offence, can be two years, five years, ten years, fourteen years, or life.

A discussion of the major offences related to physical and sexual assaults follows.

A. Assault

A person commits an assault when he/she:

a) without the consent of another person applies force intentionally to that other person directly or indirectly; or

b) attempts or threatens, by act or gesture, to apply force if she/he has, or the other person reasonably believes he/she has, present ability to do so. (These situations are rarely prosecuted).[9]

Ninety-eight percent of "common assault" charges under the federal *Criminal Code* are handled by summary conviction (maximum penalty of six months imprisonment). Common assault would be the charge laid when one spouse hits another without causing "bodily harm." Bodily harm is defined as hurt or injury that is more than trifling or transient, and interferes with health or comfort.[10]

Since February, 1995, the offences of assault causing bodily harm, assault with a weapon, unlawfully causing bodily harm, and threatening to cause death, can proceed by summary conviction with a maximum imprisonment of 18 months, or by Indictment. Crown Counsel chooses which method is appropriate, with the summary conviction method used in the majority of those cases.[11]

The more serious categories of assault proceed by Indictment and include, for example, a more serious "assault with a weapon" or an "assault causing bodily harm." A simple stick could be regarded as a weapon for the purposes of an assault with a weapon charge. Assault causing bodily harm could be the charge laid when one person hits another, causing bruising or swelling that lasts a week. "Aggravated assault" is an assault that wounds, maims, disfigures, or endangers the life of the complainant. For example, an aggravated assault charge might be laid if someone stabs another person in the chest, or disfigures someone by repeated blows to the face.[12] Aggravated assault proceeds by Indictment.

The *Criminal Code* creates various exceptions to the general prohibition against assaulting another person. Reasonable force can be used in self defence, in defence of a person under one's protection, and in defence of property.[13] In addition, certain people such as parents or school teachers may discipline or correct a child by using reasonable force. However, a recent Supreme Court of Canada case narrowly defined the terms "child" and "school teacher," and denied justification (and legal defence) under this section of the *Criminal Code* to a counsellor at a residential centre for mentally retarded adults. The court also noted that the reasonable force must be "correction" for the benefit and education of the child, and did not apply to a mentally retarded child (or presumably an infant) who was incapable of appreciating correction.[14] Other cases have held that the standards of contemporary Canadian society must define whether or not such force was reasonable.[15] Clearly, there will be very few instances when "correction" ever justifies force that causes bodily harm.

B. Fear of Injury

A peace officer acting on behalf of a person who fears injury, or a person who fears injury from another person may "lay an Information" (one method of making a complaint or laying a charge) before a Justice of the Peace or judge.[16] A person may also lay a "fear of injury" Information if she/he fears that injury will be inflicted against their spouse or child or that their property will be damaged. These provisions are preventive, and are often used to intercept violence before it happens, for example, by keeping the peace between warring spouses or neighbours. Often the prosecution will choose to proceed with a "fear of injury" application instead of a common assault charge.

Usually the person accused of this behaviour appears in Provincial Court where a summary conviction hearing is held. If the grounds for fear are admitted or substantiated beyond a reasonable doubt, then the court may order the accused to enter a recognizance (a promise to the court) to keep the peace for up to 12 months and to comply with other reasonable conditions. These conditions may include non-contact with the complainant, spouse, or child, and a prohibition from a place where the complainant, spouse, or child is regularly found. Failure to enter into or comply with the terms of the recognizance may result in imprisonment or further charges being laid.

Uttering threats to cause death or serious bodily harm to any person is a summary conviction offence with a maximum sentence of 18 months or an indictable offence at the option of Crown Counsel.[17]

The offence of criminal harassment occurs where a person engages in specified conduct that causes another person to fear for his/her safety or the safety of someone known to them. "Repeated following, repeated communication, watching or besetting a dwelling, house, a residence or place of employment or threatening the person or any member of their family is specified conduct," prohibited by the section defining the offence.[18] The specified conduct must be done knowingly or recklessly. Recklessness means the attitude of one who is aware that her/his conduct could bring about the fear specified but nevertheless persists despite the risks of fear created by the specified conduct.[19]

This offence of criminal harassment recognizes that a person infatuated with another may sometimes so ignore reality that the object of their unwanted affections is devastated by the "stalking" behaviour of the infatuated person. Criminal harassment may be summary or indictable. The choice in the method of procedure is made by Crown Counsel (prosecutor).

C. Sexual Assault

Sexual assault is defined as an assault of a sexual nature where the sexual integrity of a victim is violated. In determining whether or not a sexual assault has taken place, a court may consider various factors: the part of the body touched, words and gestures accompanying the act, and all other circumstances, including the intent, purpose, or motive.[20]

Sexual assault may be prosecuted by summary conviction or by Indictment. Examples range from a person placing hands on private sexual parts without consent to a forced act of sexual intercourse, whether vaginal, oral, or anal.

Using a weapon, threatening a third party, or causing bodily harm makes the sexual assault even more serious, and will result in a prosecution by Indictment. For example, a person may be forced at knife point to endure sexual activity. As another example, an offender may force sexual activity on a complainant by threatening to harm a child of the family. "Bodily harm" is defined in the same way as in the offence of assault; for example, non-consensual sexual activity that causes bruising that lasts several days may result in a charge of sexual assault causing bodily harm.[21]

D. Key Offences Related to Child Sexual Abuse

The *Criminal Code* contains several sexual offences that apply specifically to cases in which the complainants are children. These are:

a) sexual interference (touching for a sexual purpose, directly or indirectly with a part of the body or an object any part of the body of a child under 14);

b) invitation to sexual touching;

c) sexual exploitation of a young person 14-18 by a person in a position of authority or trust;

d) anal intercourse with children under 18;

e) bestiality (sexual intercourse or sexual activity with animals) in the presence of a person under 14 or causing such a person to commit bestiality;

f) incest (sexual intercourse with blood relations);

g) procuring the sexual activity of a child by a parent or permitting the sexual activity of a child under 18 by the owner, occupier or manager of premises; and

h) exposing genitals to a child under 14.[22]

Section 810.1 of the *Criminal Code* allows any person who fears that another person will commit a sexual offence involving a child under 14 to lay an Information (see the description of this process under "Fear of Injury"). A judge may order a recognizance for up to 12 months, with conditions prohibiting the defendant from being at or within a specified distance from the place where the child is regularly found, or prohibit contact. Conditions may also prohibit the defendant from engaging in activity that involves contact with children under 14 and prohibiting the defendant from attending a public park, swimming area, day care centre, school ground, playground, or community centre for up to 12 months.[23]

ARREST AND FIRST APPEARANCE IN COURT

Once a charge has been laid, steps are taken for the accused to appear in court. If not arrested initially, an accused may receive a summons commanding his or her appearance. Sometimes, in order to protect the public interest, a warrant for arrest will be issued for an accused. The police may use the powers of arrest discussed below to ensure the safety of family victims.

A. Powers of Arrest (Peace Officers)

A peace officer may arrest:

a) a person who has committed an indictable offence or who, on reasonable grounds, she/he believes has committed or is about to commit an indictable offence;

b) a person he/she finds committing <u>any</u> criminal offence; or

c) a person for whom a warrant exists.[24]

Peace officers also have a carefully restricted power to arrest for a breach of the peace, to arrest under provincial liquor statutes, and to arrest for offences involving intoxicated persons in public places. They also are given specific powers of arrest under certain provincial statutes (i.e., *Motor Vehicle Act*).[25]

B. Restrictions on Arrests by Peace Officers

For all but serious indictable offences, an arrest should only be made in the public interest on reasonable grounds that include the need to establish identity, to preserve evidence, to prevent continuation or repetition of the offence or another offence, or to ensure the offender will attend court based on a reasonable belief that she/he would not otherwise attend.

It is not the purpose of this section to discuss the procedures or details of the law of arrest. It is enough to say that police officers can arrest in all assault cases causing bodily harm. They can also arrest for any assault where the public interest and the specific issues mentioned above provide reasonable grounds.

C. Powers of Arrest (Private Citizens)

In certain circumstances, private citizens may arrest a person they find escaping from or committing an offence.[26] Thus, a person who saw another severely beating a spouse or child could arrest that person and hold him/her for the police. However, "citizen's arrests" should be carried out only in emergencies and as a last resort.

ISSUES OF DETENTION OR JUDICIAL INTERIM RELEASE (BAIL)

In many cases peace officers are required to release the accused on an "appearance notice" (a written promise to come to court). Increasingly, however, people accused of spousal assaults appear in court when the *Judicial Interim Release* provisions of the *Criminal Code* apply.

A person who is arrested has the right to reasonable bail.[27] A bail hearing is normally held at the first court appearance, which must be as soon as practicable and within 24 hours unless a Justice is unavailable. However, sometimes the prosecutor will be able to justify the need for a delay (up to three days) to obtain background material for the bail hearing.

The prosecutor may ask the court to place restrictions on the liberty of the accused or to detain her/him in custody. Such a request is based on the grounds that detention is necessary:

a) to ensure court attendance (the primary ground to be satisfied); and/or

b) in the public interest or for the protection of the public having regard to all the circumstances, including likelihood of further offences or interference with the administration of justice (the secondary ground); or

c) on any other just cause being shown including where the detention is necessary in order to maintain public confidence in the administration of justice. The court can look at facts including the apparent strength of the prosecution's case, the gravity of the offence, the circumstances surrounding its commission, and the potential for a lengthy term of imprisonment.[28]

The bail process has been accurately compared with a ladder the prosecutor must climb to secure increasing limitations on the liberty of the accused. At the bottom of the ladder the prosecutor may ask the court to release the accused on a simple "undertaking" to appear with no conditions attached. As the prosecutor ascends, he/she may ask that additional conditions be imposed, or a more strict "recognizance" be entered into, or cash or other property be pledged as security for good behaviour and attendance at trial. Sometimes another person must post property as a surety to ensure good behaviour and attendance. Any detention order that is made is regularly reviewed.

Some of the possible conditions for release are specified in the *Criminal Code* and include the following:

a) reporting at stated times to a bail supervisor, police station, or courthouse;

b) remaining within a territorial jurisdiction specified (usually a judicial county or a province);

c) notifying bail supervisor any change of address or employment; or

d) abstaining from communicating with persons named, including complainants, witnesses, and their families.[29]

Other "reasonable conditions" may also be imposed, which often include the following:

a) remaining a certain distance away from the complainant's residence and place(s) of employment;

b) refraining from entering specified high crime areas ("red zone" clauses);

c) maintaining a curfew; and

d) abstaining from alcohol or non-prescribed drugs; and

e) alcohol or drug tests on demand.

f) no contact with children under 18 years and not to attend any public park, public swimming area, school ground, play ground, or recreation centre.[30]

The following are examples of how the judicial interim release provisions might apply. A man arrested for "mischief" for letting the air out of his wife's car tires would likely be released on an undertaking if he had no previous criminal record. A person arrested for aggravated assault, with a serious record of convictions, would probably only be released on a recognizance with a surety, and might well be detained until trial.

Since a breach of bail conditions means an accused person can be arrested again and the release terms cancelled, it may be important for complainants to know the actual terms of release and to obtain a copy of the release document from the court registry, police, Crown Counsel, or designated spousal support worker. Conditions of release apply until the trial is completed and, if guilt is determined, until sentence has been passed. Release conditions are often amended, and so complainants and police should make sure the condition at issue is still applicable.

EVIDENCE IN COURT

In spousal assault and child abuse cases, the evidence heard at trial is governed by some special rules. These rules are discussed in the following sections.

I. Spousal Competence and Compellability

Historically, offences in which the victims were legal spouses or children of the offender were rarely prosecuted. In addition, certain restrictions on the kind of evidence that could be presented actually barred many cases from ever reaching court. Today, witnesses in a trial must be "competent" to testify under oath or on a promise to tell the truth. In other words, they must be mentally capable of understanding the nature of an oath or the gravity of testifying. "Competency" refers to whether or not a witness has the legal status to testify. In the past, legal spouses were only competent prosecution witnesses in certain limited circumstances.

While a witness may be found "competent," she/he may still not be "compellable" or required to testify. In the past, a spouse was not compelled to disclose "marital communications" or matters the couple may have discussed between them. However, after a series of cases and amendments to the *Canada Evidence Act* in 1983, spouses are now competent and compellable witnesses for violent offences to children under 14. A series of cases clarified that an unwilling but competent spouse was compellable to answer in a case involving violence to herself.[31] However, the question of when a spouse may be compelled to disclose marital communications is still unclear.

These developments, both statutory and judicial, mean that a wider range of spousal assaults may be prosecuted. Whether they <u>will</u> be still depends on many factors, including social attitudes, the effectiveness of investigation, the willingness of parties to testify, and the availability of important family support facilities.

The "battered woman" syndrome describes how many women react after repeated abusive beatings by their spouse or partner. They become trapped in a cycle of hope, which typically suppresses the memory of the latest attack and relies on the abuser's "honeymoon" behaviour, remorse, and promise that it will never happen again. In a recent case of spousal murder,[32] the Supreme Court of Canada admitted expert evidence of the "battered woman" syndrome to explain why the abused female would remain with the abusing male she eventually stabbed. Counsel for the woman accused of murder successfully argued that the principle of self-defence did not apply to the present alone but could be extended to include a subjective belief in future serious injury. Her Ladyship Madam Justice Wilson commented for the court that "far from protecting women from [domestic violence] the law has historically sanctioned the abuse of women within marriage as an aspect of the husband's ownership of his wife and his right to chastise her" and that "spousal violence was rarely reported."[33]

Judicial recognition of the historical failure of the law to deal effectively with spousal violence is a hopeful sign. Comments such as those just stated from our highest court reflect an approach to spousal assault consistent with contemporary attitudes and beliefs.

Expert evidence of the "battered woman" syndrome can be used to assist a judge or jury to understand why a battered woman's evidence may be evasive, less than forthright and hesitant.

In a recent case, the Supreme Court of Canada held that a witness' video-taped statement out of court which was shown by other evidence to be reliable, was proof of guilt even when the witness at trial denied the truth of that statement.[34] This case has been applied to allow proof of guilt in a spousal sexual assault by a reliable written statement of a witness[35] and <u>may</u> allow successful prosecution when the victim witness recants.

II. Children as Witnesses

Historically, children under the age of 14 could rarely qualify to testify under oath. Moreover their evidence, whether under oath or not, was considered "unsafe" and given little importance or weight.[36] Unsworn evidence could not convict an accused without corroborative evidence that proved that the offence was both committed and that it connected the accused to the offence.

An increasingly flexible and tolerant approach to children's evidence has been recently demonstrated by the courts. Decisions of appeal courts in the early 1980s made it clear a child under 14 need only understand that an oath involves a moral obligation to tell the truth and need not believe in a Supreme Being or religious consequence before an oath could be administered.[37] As more child witnesses were heard, judges became more flexible in qualifying child witnesses to be sworn, and by certain upper court decisions, corroborative evidence rules became less strict.[38]

On January 1, 1988, Parliament abolished the sections of the *Criminal Code* and *Evidence Act* preventing conviction on unsworn evidence unless corroborated. On the same date young children (children "of tender years") were authorized to "affirm" as an alternative to a solemn affirmation before testifying. A solemn affirmation is a secular alternative to a sacred oath.[39] An inquiry is still required before a child under 14 is permitted to affirm or take an oath.[40] A child under 14 who understands the nature of an oath or affirmation and is able to communicate the evidence may testify under one of these procedures.[41] A child under 14 who does not understand the nature of an oath or of an affirmation but is able to communicate may testify on promising to tell the truth.[42]

In a recent Supreme Court of Canada case[43] the court confirmed that a child of four-and-a-half years might well give evidence on the basis of a promise to tell the truth. The only conditions for such a child's evidence would be the intelligence to communicate and an understanding of the duty to tell the truth. The court expressly indicated that in determining whether children's evidence should be admitted, little weight should be given to the fact the child was very young. In another case the Supreme Court of Canada noted courts should take a common sense approach when dealing with the testimony of young children and not impose the same exacting standard on them as they do on adults. The court noted that while children may not be able to recount precise details, times, and locations, this does not mean they do not know what has happened to them and who did it.

In one case, the Supreme Court of Canada held that there is no longer any rule of law that the evidence of children is inherently unreliable and must be treated with special caution.[44] The court again noted that it is hardly surprising that details important to adults such as time and place may be missing from a child's recollection.[45]

III. Witnesses with Disabilities

Lately, the courts are showing increasing flexibility in allowing interpreters, computers, and other mechanical aids and devices to assist witnesses with physical and mental disabilities. More courthouses are now designed or equipped to allow the physically disabled to enter and participate. The law, too, provides certain procedures for the disabled. Section 6 of the *Canada Evidence Act* provides that a witness unable to speak may give his/her evidence in any other manner that is intelligible.

Witnesses of 14 years or older are assumed to be competent unless their competency (capacity to understand the nature of oaths, affirmations, and testimony) is challenged. A lawyer acting for the prosecution or the defence would first have to satisfy the court that the competency of a mentally disabled witness was an issue. Even if she/he does not understand the nature of an oath or solemn affirmation, a witness who can communicate may still give evidence by promising to tell the truth. In most cases, then, witnesses will be allowed to testify and their evidence admitted despite any disability. However, the weight or importance that the court will attribute to that evidence will clearly depend on the witness' level of understanding.[46]

IV. Evidence and Procedure in Sexual Offences

Normally, sexual offence proceedings are held in open court. A limited discretion exists, however, to exclude the public in the interest of public morals, the maintenance of order, or the proper administration of justice. Embarrassment by a complainant or witness will not alone suffice to justify such an order. However, such an order might be appropriate if the public's presence in the courtroom prevented the complainant or witness from testifying.

The court may make an order prohibiting the publication or broadcast of the identity of the complainant or a witness, or of any identifying evidence. In British Columbia such orders are routine for all sexual complainants. Where the complainant or witness is under 18, the complainant or witness must be informed of the right of non-publication and non-broadcasting, and the court, on application of that person or the prosecutor, must make such an order.[47]

No evidence of the complainant's sexual activity is admissible to support an inference of greater likelihood of consent or an inference negative to credibility. No evidence of the complainant's sexual activity is admissible unless the judge determines the evidence is of specific instances of sexual activity, relevant to the trial and of significant probative value that is not outweighed by the danger of prejudice. An application as to evidence of the complainant's sexual activity must be made by advance notice in writing, with details of the evidence sought to be allowed, and a statement of the relevance of the evidence to an issue at trial. Such an application is made at a hearing with the public and jury excluded where the complainant is not a compellable witness. The judge, provincial court judge, or justices must take into account a number of enumerated factors before deciding whether to admit such evidence. The judge must give reasons at the conclusion of the hearing, and the evidence at such a hearing and the reasons for decision cannot be published unless the judge orders they be published. Since this procedure has been in effect, very few applications to introduce evidence of the complainant's sexual activity have been made.[48]

V. The Preservation and Production of
Confidential Records in Sexual Offence Proceedings[49]

In criminal proceedings for a sexual offence, an accused person may seek the disclosure of confidential records relating to the complainant or a witness. Until recently, the disclosure of such records was governed by the common law, and in particular by *R. v. O'Connor*,[50] a widely publicized decision of the Supreme Court of Canada. Unfortunately, *O'Connor* reflected a divided court, and its five separate judgments failed to provide clear guidance on such controversial questions as to when and how these confidential records should be disclosed, if at all.

Bill C-46, *An Act to amend the Criminal Code (production of records in sexual offence proceedings)*, was proclaimed on May 12, 1997 to address this lack of clarity. By adding sections

278.1 - 278.91 to the *Criminal Code*, Parliament established various principles to be adhered to and procedures to be followed when a person accused of a sexual offence is seeking access to any record containing "personal information for which there is a reasonable expectation of privacy."[51] Such records include, but are not limited to, "medical, psychiatric, therapeutic, counselling, education, employment, child welfare, adoption and social service records, personal journals and diaries, and records containing personal information the production or disclosure of which is protected by any other Act of Parliament or a provincial legislature . . . ."[52]

Frequently, Crown Counsel may be in possession of such records, having received them from the police, a complainant, or a witness during the course of an investigation. If so, section 278.2(3) requires Crown Counsel to notify the accused of the existence, but not the content, of the records. Section 278.2(2) makes it clear that unless the complainant or witness has expressly waived the protections contained in sections 278.3 - 278.91, the accused must follow the same procedures to obtain disclosure of these records from Crown Counsel as from any other source.

A complainant or witness may wish to consider placing restrictions on the waiver similar to those presented in section 278.7(3).

The Preamble to Bill C-46 establishes a number of principles, including the following, to guide the courts in making decisions concerning the production of such records:

a) sexual violence is a grave concern in Canadian society and places its victims, primarily women and children, at a disadvantage;

b) the reporting of sexual violence and the treatment of complainants should be encouraged;

c) in sexual offence proceedings, both complainants and accused persons are entitled to the full protection of the law; and

d) applications by accused persons for the production of confidential records in sexual offence proceedings should be carefully considered by the courts in order to ensure the least possible impairment of the privacy and equality rights of complainants and witnesses while still facilitating the right of the accused to make full answer and defence.

Bill C-46 also establishes the following procedures, all of which must be followed when such an application is made:

a) only the trial judge may hear the application;[53]

b) the application must be submitted in writing, and must include "the grounds on which the accused relies to establish that the record is likely relevant to an issue at trial or to the competence of a witness to testify . . ."[54] (several grounds are specifically identified as being insufficient, separately or in a combination, to support a successful application, even though some of these may have been favourably regarded by the courts in the past. These insufficient grounds include an assertion that the record relates to treatment, counselling, or therapy; that the record may disclose a prior inconsistent statement; and that the record may relate to the credibility, sexual history, or sexual reputation of the complainant);[55]

c) the application must be served on Crown Counsel, the relevant complainant or witness, any other person to whom the accused knows the record relates, and the custodian of the record (e.g., an employee of a health region or of the Ministry for Children and Families, or a therapist in private practice);[56]

d) the application must be made seven days before the hearing unless a shorter interval is ordered by the trial judge;[57]

e) at the same time as the application is served, the custodian of the record must also be served with a subpoena in the form prescribed in the *Criminal Code*;[58] and

f) the custodian of the record, the complainant, or witness, and any other person to whom the record relates are entitled to make submissions to the court concerning the application for production, but cannot be compelled to testify at the hearing if they do not choose to do so.[59]

If all these procedural requirements are met, the court may review the record to determine whether to order its production, in whole or in part, to the accused. In making this determination, the court is required to consider the positive and negative implications of any decision for the accused, the complainant, witness, and any other person to whom the record relates.[60]

In ordering production of all or part of a confidential record, the court may impose a variety of conditions, including the following:

a) that only a copy of the record, not the original, may be disclosed;

b) that the record may not be further duplicated;

c) that the accused may not be given a copy of the record and may not discuss it with anyone other than defence counsel or an expert retained for that purpose; and

d) that after the conclusion of the proceeding and any appeal period, the record must be returned to the complainant, witness, or custodian, as appropriate.[61]

At a hearing pursuant to sections 278.1 - 278.91 of the *Criminal Code*, Crown Counsel may speak to questions of relevance, privilege, materiality, and procedure, but may not represent the interests of the complainant, the witness, any other person to whom the record relates, or the custodian. Helping professionals whose records are the subject of such an application may have access to legal counsel through their employers, a professional association, or privately. If unrepresented, those who wish to address the court themselves should review the relevant sections of the *Criminal Code*, which are drafted in relatively plain language, and prepare their submissions accordingly.

Helping professionals should be aware that clients who are the victims of a sexual offence, and whose confidential records are the subject of an application for production, may be referred to the Legal Services Society for assistance. The Attorney General of British Columbia has recently determined that counsel will be appointed to represent such persons, whether or not they meet the financial eligibility criteria for legal aid.

Finally, a cautionary note: helping professionals must resist any temptation to destroy records to prevent their disclosure in sexual offence proceedings. In *R. v. Carosella*,[62] which involved accusations of gross indecency against a teacher by a complainant who, as a child, had been his student, the Supreme Court of Canada stayed proceedings against the accused because the executive director of a sexual assault crisis centre had destroyed a social worker's notes of her interview with the complainant. The majority held that the accused's constitutional right to the production of the records in question had been breached, that the accused did not have to demonstrate that the conduct of his defence had been prejudiced by this breach, and that a stay of proceedings was the appropriate remedy. In the interests of their clients, the complainants, and justice, therefore, helping professionals must create and preserve adequate records consistent with the standards of their professional association, if any, or with those of normal professional practice.

VI. Special Evidence Rules for Child Sexual Abuse Cases

A recent provision allows a trial judge to order that a witness under 14 may have a support person present and close when testifying.[63] Another provision allows a trial judge to order that an accused shall not personally cross examine a child witness but must appoint counsel for that purpose.[64]

A. Testimony Behind a Screen or Outside the Court

In certain child sexual abuse cases, where a complainant (the child victim) is under 18 years of age, the court may order that the complainant testify outside the courtroom or behind a screen or other device if separation is necessary to obtain a full and candid account. Testimony outside the courtroom is only permitted when the accused and the court may watch the complainant testify (i.e. through closed circuit television) and when the accused may communicate with defence counsel during testimony. Since few courtrooms have appropriate television equipment, a one-way screen is usually employed. Such screens are available in most courts in British Columbia and increasingly in other provinces. This special provision applies to the complainant only and not to other child witnesses.[65]

B. Videotaped Evidence

After an alleged sexual offence, a child victim's statements may be recorded on videotape.[66] Many justice facilities have created specialized settings for this purpose with children's furniture and unobtrusive equipment. Teams of police and social workers have developed special skills and techniques for such interviews.[67] In the Province of Manitoba the use of videotaped evidence is more widely used and more officially encouraged than in any other province.

Videotaped evidence will only be admitted as evidence during a subsequent trial under certain circumstances. The complainant must have been under 18 at the time the offence is alleged and the videotape must have been made within a reasonable time. The complainant must, while testifying, confirm the acts complained of in the videotape and thereby adopt it as true. The child will then be subject to cross-examination. A witness who can testify adequately in the witness box probably will not need to be supported by videotaped evidence.

Interviewing techniques will have a bearing on the weight or importance that the court will attribute to videotaped evidence. Accordingly, leading questions (those which suggest an answer) should be avoided, although the answers to them may generally be admitted. A videotape will not be excluded just because it contains leading questions.

One useful purpose for videotaped evidence is to refresh the memory of the child before trial. Also, some courts have approved the procedure of showing the videotape to the accused as part of the process of obtaining a statement.[68] Finally, videotaped evidence has been frequently presented at the sentencing stage, often in conjunction with Victim Impact Statements.

A Supreme Court of Canada case has held that testimony behind a screen or outside the courtroom by a complainant under 18 is constitutional and does not offend the *Charter*.[69] A second Supreme Court of Canada case held that videotaped evidence of a complainant under 18 at the time of the offence, made in a reasonable time, is constitutional and does not offend the *Charter*.[70]

VII. Source of Supporting Evidence

In most sexual offence cases, particularly those involving children, the alleged acts occur in private and the only direct witnesses are the complainant and the accused. Evidence that "strengthens the belief the witness is telling the truth" is of prime importance. Helping professionals may assist in making this evidence known and available to the court.

A. Confessions

A confession of guilt by an accused is the most direct and traditional source of such evidence. An accused may be more likely to confess to a neighbour, friend, relative, or counsellor than to a police officer. A confession may simply amount to the accused agreeing to another person's statement about what happened.[71] A single sentence may be enough to assist conviction. If an accused person confesses to his/her lawyer, her/his statement is "privileged," and the lawyer cannot be compelled to provide such evidence of guilt to the court. However, confessions made to anyone else, including the clergy, doctors, or other professionals, are not privileged, and witnesses to such confessions may be subpoenaed and compelled to give evidence in court.

B. Denial of Opportunity

Other kinds of evidence may support a finding of guilt. The accused may deny that he/she had an opportunity to commit the alleged act, although the opportunity is proven. For example, the accused may deny the child complainant was ever in her/his house, even though a neighbour testifies that the child was there.

C. Suspicious Circumstances

Suspicious circumstances may provide supportive evidence. In one recent case a child's mother testified she saw the accused and the child come from the bedroom area; the child had messy hair and was buttoning up her pants, and the accused had messy hair and was tucking in and buttoning his shirt.[72] Evidence of guilt may be found if the accused flees from the scene during or after investigation[73] or attempts suicide in a manner closely connected to the events.[74] A court's conclusion that the accused deliberately fabricated his/her evidence may support a finding of guilt and may justify it even when guilt might otherwise not be proved beyond a reasonable doubt.[75] Evidence that the accused was upset immediately or shortly after the event is also a strong source of supporting evidence.

D. Physical Evidence

In cases where the accused denies opportunity or argues mistaken identity, traces of the accused found at the scene such as fingerprints, footprints, items of identification or clothing, semen samples, or blood samples are strong supporting evidence. Sometimes the helping professional is one of the first people contacted by the complainant and therefore one of the first to arrive. Since the police are usually in the best position to obtain and secure this kind of physical evidence, professionals should call in the police as soon as possible and prevent anyone from disturbing the scene of the offence. The scientific use of D.N.A. evidence has also greatly increased in recent years.

E. Hearsay Evidence

In a recent case,[76] the Supreme Court of Canada held as admissible evidence the statement of a three-and-a-half-year-old child made to her mother fifteen minutes after a visit to a doctor. The statement indicated oral sexual activity by that doctor. Because the statement showed knowledge of sexual acts clearly beyond the child's normal knowledge, it had "its own peculiar stamp of reliability." It was also important for the prosecution to succeed in getting this "hearsay" statement accepted as evidence because it appeared the child was too young to testify in court. Hearsay (secondhand) evidence is not normally acceptable proof. But the court noted, "In Canada ... the courts have been moving to more flexibility in the reception of the hearsay evidence of children."[77] In a number of provinces the courts have admitted such statements in child protection cases.[78] In a recent British Columbia case hearsay statements of a complainant with a disability were admitted to confirm the identity of his assailant.[79]

F. Corroborative and Similar Fact Evidence

One complainant's evidence may clearly support the testimony of a second. This kind of evidence is especially convincing when the complainants are strangers and have had no opportunity to fabricate a story together. In dealing with cases of suspected child sexual abuse, the investigator and helping professional should attempt to interview other children to whom the alleged offender had access. Their evidence could be critical. Child sexual abuse casts a wide net and the parameters of such activity should not be assumed to be limited to one child. Evidence of other sexual acts by the accused, which are not the subject of the charge, may be admissible. The court will have to decide whether the evidence is important enough to outweigh the prejudice caused to the accused (since no charges have stemmed from these incidents).[80]

G. Medical Evidence

In any case of suspected sexual abuse a medical examination may provide important evidence. Bruising or injury may be consistent with non-consent in adult cases. Traces of the accused from semen and blood type or hair and skin samples may assist in establishing identity. The presence of anal or vaginal injuries and signs of communicable sexual disease are consistent with sexual activity. Police frequently enlist the services of Crime Detection Laboratory experts. Most hospital emergency rooms are well equipped to deal with adult sexual abuse complaints. The police, social workers, Child Sexual Assault Centres, and other professional agencies can refer child sexual abuse victims to pediatricians, gynaecologists, or physicians with experience and expertise in this area.

In this regard, there are three important points to note. First, in some cases where the potential accused is a family member, it may be appropriate to utilize a "neutral" physician and not the familiar family doctor, who may find it difficult to objectively attribute such an abhorrent crime to the family member she/he knows. Secondly, a physician making such an examination need not possess great experience or expertise. Carefully recorded observations from examination can later be examined and commented upon by a recognized expert. Thirdly, the prospect of possibly having to testify in court may seem overwhelming, but it must be remembered that every expert witness once had a first time in court.

VIII. Expert Testimony in Child Sexual Abuse Cases

An expert witness is one who by experience, training, and knowledge can offer an opinion to assist the fact finder on a matter at issue beyond the scope of ordinary human experience.[81] Medical and scientific experts have given testimony for generations. In recent years the courts have increasingly recognized how helpful expert witnesses can be in child sexual abuse cases.[82] Documents such as the British Columbia *Interministry Child Abuse Handbook* list the behavioural and physical symptoms of sexual abuse that need to be observed and recorded by any helping professional who will be testifying.

The following examples demonstrate the kind of evidence an expert might be expected to provide:

a) evidence that explains why the victim failed to disclose the alleged act until long after the event, failed to tell his/her mother, showed an improved memory of the event over the passage of time, and continued to associate with the complainant;[83]

b) evidence of the consistency of the child's complaints to her/his mother, counsellors, the police, and the court;[84]

c) evidence of change in behaviour during the period of time following the sexual assault;[85]

d) evidence of the child's fear of being left alone with an accused and protection of his/her private parts while in the presence of the accused;[86] or

e) evidence that recantation is frequent in child sexual abuse cases.[87]

IX. Court Preparation of Witnesses

Helping professionals will often be involved in preparing witnesses. In many communities Victim Services offices (operated by the Ministry of Attorney General) or personnel from Child Sexual Assault and Women's Sexual Assault Centres assist in this function. It should be noted that court preparation for criminal court should be done under the supervision and with the knowledge of the prosecutor. In most cases an actual visit to the courthouse and the courtroom is a good way of dispelling fear. Complainants should be aware that their identity may be protected by the non-publication provisions, and that in most cases they will be asked to point out the accused in court. Complainants should be encouraged to bring a friend or other support persons with them to pre-court interviews, if any, and to court on the date they are to testify. This kind of emotional support is often invaluable.

Professionals may be able to provide the following sorts of helpful information about a child witness to the lawyer conducting the case:

a) the age of the child and significant dates for the child (birthday, family festivities, anniversaries);

b) names the child uses for family members, the accused, and other significant persons including teachers and caregivers;

c) the best time of day for the child for communicating or interacting with others;

d) special interests of the child;

e) the general language level of the child; and

f) special terms the child uses for body parts.

A helping professional should never be involved in "coaching" or suggesting answers to a witness or complainant. Although the media have exaggerated the dramatic aspects of trial proceedings, there still can be no doubt that testifying, particularly in sexual offence cases and against a family member, can be very stressful. Police and social workers are aware of local resources that will help people through the court process and provide support afterwards. These include Shelters or Transition Houses, Women's Sexual Assault Victims groups, Children's Sexual Assault Centres, Crisis Lines, Victim Assistance counsellors, and psychiatrists and psychologists.

It is beyond the scope of this chapter to discuss the trial process. It is sufficient to note that the police and investigating agencies (often ably assisted by helping professionals) will gather the evidence. The prosecutor (Crown Counsel), who presents the Crown's case, selects the appropriate evidence and decides who will be a witness and in what order witnesses will be called. The accused need not testify at all or call any witnesses, but if this is done it will be at the end of the Crown's case.

CONVICTION OR ACQUITTAL

The accused is always presumed innocent until proven guilty beyond a reasonable doubt. A verdict of "not guilty" frequently means "not proven," and often does not reflect adversely on the honesty or credibility of the complainant or Crown witnesses. A criminal trial is like a jigsaw puzzle and unless every piece of evidence fits, the accused will not be proven guilty. A complainant in a family violence case needs to be emotionally prepared for a possible acquittal.

SENTENCE

All *Criminal Code* offences have a specified maximum sentence. For a summary conviction offence the maximum sentence is six months imprisonment and/or a fine of up to $2,000 and/or up to three years probation for each count or charge of which the accused is convicted.

It has already been mentioned that for the offences of threatening, assault causing bodily harm, assault with a weapon, unlawfully causing bodily harm, and sexual assault there is a maximum sentence of 18 months if proceeded by summary conviction. If proceeded by Indictment the maximum is greater and defined by each individual offence.

Indictable offences have a specified maximum imprisonment of two years, five years, ten years, fourteen years, or life, depending on the offence. The maximum is reserved for the worst offences and offenders with the most serious criminal records.

Pre-sentence reports and psychiatric reports are often prepared to assist a judge with sentencing. Victim Impact Statements may be considered in sentencing proceedings. Jail sentences have become the rule in child sexual abuse cases and are typical in cases of serious physical assaults on children. A jail term is also becoming a more frequent sentence in spousal assaults, particularly those causing bodily harm. Either the Crown prosecutor or defence counsel can appeal a sentence. The Crown will rarely do so, unless the sentence is grossly inadequate or there is some important error in principle that will effect future cases.

The *Criminal Code* provides that in determining sentence the court may consider a written statement of the victim of the offence describing the harm done to or loss suffered by the victim of the offence. The spouse or relative of a dead, ill, or otherwise incapable victim may prepare such a statement. Such a written statement does not prevent the court from considering other evidence concerning any victim for purposes of determining sentence.[88]

In British Columbia, the *Victims of Crime Act*[89] applies to both federal statutes (i.e., *Criminal Code*) and provincial statutes (i.e., *Motor Vehicle Act*). The definition of victim does not include corporations (i.e. The Hudson's Bay Company) or justice system personnel who are acting in their duty (i.e. on duty police officers). A victim is defined as a person who, in relation to an offence, has suffered economic loss, physical or mental injury, or significant emotional trauma. Also included in the definition of victim is the spouse, sibling, child, and parent of those who have suffered significant emotional trauma. Crown Counsel must offer the victims a reasonable opportunity to give admissible evidence (usually in written form of a victim impact statement) of the impact of the offence on them. If victims request, Criminal Justice personnel must arrange to inform a victim of the specific charges, the reasons "why a decision was made respecting charges," the date, location, and reasons for significant court appearances, the length and commencement date of sentences, and information regarding Corrections. A standard Victim Impact form, instructions, and covering letter have been developed. These provisions have proved an effective method of "putting a human face and human personality to the victims of crime."

Counselling may be available for offenders prior to or in conjunction with court proceedings, and appropriate candidates may be required to attend counselling as part of a sentence. Facilities for men, who have historically been pictured as offenders and not victims, are beginning to develop. For example, in Victoria, British Columbia, there is a community-based program for abusive men and a Men's Sexual Assault Survivor's Society staffed by some excellent male counsellors. Attorney General Departments in several provinces have Victim Assistance Counsellors who can provide information about counselling services. Professional associations of psychologists and physicians can also assist in providing names of qualified persons. Family violence counselling, especially for sexual abuse victims, is a relatively new field, and care is necessary in selecting counsellors with knowledge and expertise.

Most provinces now provide compensation for victims of crime or their dependents. Although a criminal conviction is helpful in establishing entitlement, it is not a prerequisite under any scheme presently in force in Canada. In British Columbia funds are provided under the *Criminal Injuries Compensation Act*,[90] which is administered by the Workers' Compensation Board.

Where a person 18 or over is convicted of a sexual offence involving a person under 14, the sentencing judge may make a prohibition order banning the accused for life or any lesser period from attending a public park or swimming pool that are frequented by children under 14, or from frequenting day-care centres, school grounds, playgrounds, or community centres and from seeking, obtaining or continuing employment or volunteer work involving a position of trust or authority toward children under the age of 14 years. This prohibition may be reviewed and varied if there is a change of circumstances.[91]

COMMON QUESTIONS

1. <u>I have a neighbour who is always injured and bruised. I hear loud voices, noises, and the sound of blows from their house from time to time. What can I do?</u>

If you can discuss the injuries with your neighbour, do so. Make your neighbour aware of resources that will provide support if a decision is made to call police. If the neighbour is prepared to call police, provide a statement with details of your observations. Encourage your neighbour to have a medical examination. If you hear a further violent dispute, consider calling the police yourself. You may save your neighbour's life. If the offender is arrested, make sure you and your neighbour are aware of the conditions of release, if any. If a prosecution goes ahead, keep in touch with the police and the Crown to assist in the court process.

2. <u>I am a teacher. A child in my class frequently shows up with unexplained serious injuries. What can I do?</u>

Record your observations of injury. Discuss the injuries with the child in a factual, non-judgmental manner. Record any behaviourial indicators of child abuse. If you have a reason to believe the child is in need of protection, you <u>must</u> report to the appropriate Ministry office (in British Columbia this is the Ministry for Children and Families). Thereafter supply necessary support and be aware of other resources.

3. <u>How can I as a helping professional, find out more about physical and sexual abuse of adults and children?</u>

A reading list is included in this chapter. Professional associations of teachers, psychologists, psychiatrists, and counsellors have many seminars and publications on these topics. The Federal Ministry of Supply and Services is one useful source of such materials. Women's Centres, Child Sexual Assault Centres, and Crisis Lines can put you in contact with local seminars, groups, and publications.

4. <u>How can I prepare if I am a witness in a criminal trial?</u>

Stay in contact with police and the Crown and be certain about the court date. If you have notes of events or gave a written statement to police, get a copy and review them to refresh your memory before court. Attend a court proceeding in advance if possible. Try to attend witness seminars or (in British Columbia) you can view an information video on being a witness. Be fair, objective, and courteous in your answers to all questions asked in court.

5. <u>My child is a complainant in a sexual abuse case. What can I do?</u>

If a videotape was made of your child's evidence, you might arrange for your child to review it with the police or prosecutor before court. See if there is a local Victim Services Office to assist. Have some objective person read "*So You Have To Go To Court*"[92] to your child or, if he/she is capable, have the child read it. If possible, participate in a courthouse tour. Be supportive of your child without creating unnecessary anxiety.

6. <u>I am aware of other witnesses to an abuse case who have not been interviewed by police. What can I do?</u>

This information could be vital to the success of charges already laid or pending. Encourage those witnesses to contact police or contact the investigating police officer yourself with this information.

7. <u>What can the helping professional do to prepare children for the stress of testifying in Court?</u>

See the answers to questions four and five. The facts of the case should <u>not</u> be discussed with the child as part of court preparation. A good first step in the preparation process is to contact the police and/or Crown Counsel offices and determine if a Victim Services Office is available. A tour of the courthouse will familiarize the child with the physical setting. Viewing an information video on being a witness is useful. A few days before court, have the child read or read to the child, without comment, "*So You Have to go to Court.*" Have the child read her/his statement, if any, to the police, or if the child is unable to read have a neutral person, not a witness, read the statement to the child. Avoid commenting on the statement. If a videotape of the child's evidence was made, have the child watch it in the presence of the Victim Service Worker or Crown Counsel, or if neither is available, a neutral person who is not a witness. The helping professional may wish to meet with Crown Counsel before Crown Counsel meets the child witness to explain any special concerns as to the child's use of terminology and level of understanding. Special vocabulary used by the child, including names of body parts and names used by the child for the accused and other persons involved in the case (including family members' names or nicknames) should be explained to Crown Counsel. A discussion should occur between the helping professional and Crown Counsel as to any fears the child has expressed, and the potential use in court of screens or closed circuit TV. A meeting a few days before court between Crown Counsel and the child, with a support person present to assist the child, is highly desirable, and several such meetings may be desirable (be aware however of the extreme workload of many Crown Counsel and be flexible). Training in deep breathing exercises and other relaxation techniques may assist the child to cope with stress in the courtroom. Discuss with Crown Counsel who should accompany the child to court and who will be the support person or persons present in the courtroom. Have the child wear comfortable clothes and bring a favourite toy. See if Crown Counsel can estimate when and how long the child will be required to testify. Once the child has completed his/her evidence, a treat for the child is appropriate. As noted in the paragraph on conviction or acquittal, any complainant needs to be prepared for a possible acquittal. Crown Counsel may be able to assist you with suggestions such as using the jigsaw puzzle analogy to help the child with any disappointment created by the court process.

CONCLUSION

The frequency of family violence, the increasing reporting of such violence to social workers and police, the policies to encourage active prosecution, the increasing flexibility of the laws of evidence, and the increasing use of expert witnesses and counsellors in the criminal system make it certain that more helping professionals will be involved with family violence in the criminal court system. Helping professionals have an increasing need to understand the basic assumptions of the criminal court system and the mechanics of its daily operation. Only with that knowledge and understanding can they adequately serve their clients' needs.

RESOURCES

Badgley Report, *Sexual Offences Against Children* (Ottawa: Minister of Supply and Services Canada, 1984).

Canada, Department of Justice, *What To Do If a Child Tells You of Sexual Abuse: Understanding the Law* (Ottawa: Minister of Supply and Services, 1989).

W. Harvey, *So You Have To Go To Court!* (Toronto: Butterworths, 1986).

W. Harvey, *So There Are Laws About Sex!* (Toronto: Butterworths, 1988).

L. MacLeod, *Battered But Not Beaten: Preventing Wife Battering in Canada*, June 1987, Canadian Advisory Council on the Status of Women.

R. Rogers, *Reaching For Solutions*, Summary Report of the Special Advisor to the Minister of National Health and Welfare on Child Sexual Abuse in Canada, Ottawa, 1990.

Victoria Women's Sexual Assault Centre, *Child Sexual Abuse, Information for Parents*, 1987.

Victoria Women's Sexual Assault Centre, *Sexual Assault: Information for Adult Survivors*, 1987.

Victoria Women's Sexual Assault Centre, *Sexual Assault Information for Partners and Friends*, 1987.

M. Wells, *Canada's Law on Child Sexual Abuse: A Handbook* (Ottawa: Minister of Supply and Services, 1990).

END NOTES

1. Canada: House of Commons, Standing Committee on Health Welfare and Social Affairs: *Wife Battering: Report on Violence in the Family* (Ottawa: Queen's Printer, May, 1982).
2. Badgley, R. (Editor) *Sexual Offences Against Children* (Ottawa: Minister of Supply and Services Canada, 1984). Summary Volume I.
3. *Ibid.*
4. *Divorce Act*, 1985, R.S.C. 1986, C.4.
5. *Policy: Violence Against Women and Children Part I*, Ministry of Attorney General, Victoria, British Columbia, February, 1993.
6. Evidence under oath given by Alan Markwart, Statistician, Ministry of Solicitor General for British Columbia, December 20, 1989. Updated November 1, 1994.
7. *R. v. Vetrovec* (1982), 67 C.C.C. (2d) 1 at p. 8 (S.C.C.) [hereinafter *Vetrovec*].
8. R.S.C. 1994 BILL c-42. Sections 16 to 18 amending *Criminal Code* section 264.1(2); 267; 269 and 271 (1) (G). Offences with eighteen month summary conviction maximums are threatening death or serious bodily harm; assault causing bodily harm; assault with a weapon and sexual assault when proceeded summarily. If proceeded by Indictment the maximum sentence is defined by the particular offence.
9. *Criminal Code*, section 265.
10. *Ibid.*, sections 266 and 267.
11. See endnote 8.
12. *Criminal Code*, section 268.

13. *Criminal Code*, sections 34, 35 and 37.

14. *Ogg - Moss v. The Queen* (1984), 14 C.C.C. (3d) 116 (S.C.C.).

15. *R. v. Dupperon* (1984) 16 C.C.C. (3d) 353 (Sask C.A.).

16. *Criminal Code*, section 810.

17. See endnote 8. *Criminal Code*, section 264.1.

18. *Criminal Code*, section 264 (1). See *R. v. Ryback*, February 16, 1996 CA020245 (B.C.C.A.). *R. v. Gowing* (1994). O.J. 2743 (Ont C.J. General Division).

19. *R. v. Sansregret* (1985), 18 C.C.C. (3d) 223 (S.C.C.).

20. *R. v. Chase* (1987), 37 C.C.C. (3d) 97; 59 C.R. (3d) 193 (S.C.C.).

21. *Criminal Code*, sections 271-273.

22. *Criminal Code*, sections 151-160; sections 170-173.

23. *Criminal Code*, section 810.1, R.S.C. 1993, c-45, c.11.

24. *Criminal Code*, section 495.

25. *Motor Vehicle Act*, R.S.B.C. (1996) C.318.

26. *Criminal Code*, section 495.

27. *Canadian Charter of Rights and Freedoms*, s. 11(e), Part I of the *Constitution Act, 1982*, being Schedule B of the *Canada Act, 1982* (U.K.), 1982, c. 11.

28. *Criminal Code*, section 515(10)

29. *Criminal Code*, section 515(4).

30. *Ibid.*

31. *R. v. McGinty* (1986), 27 C.C.C. (3d) 36 (Y.T.C.A.).

32. *Lavallee v. R.* (1990), 55 C.C.C. (3d) 97 (S.C.C.).

33. *Lavallee* (Ibid) p.112. For a feminist critique of the Battered Woman Syndrome, see E. Comack, *Feminist Engagement with the Law; the legal recognition of the Battered Woman Syndrome* (Ottawa: Canadian Institute of Research for the Advancement of Women, 1993)..

34. *R. v. K.G.B.* 79 C.C.C. (3d) 257 (S.C.C.).

35. *R. v. Merrit* BCSC 68201 Victoria, British Columbia, October 25th, 1993.

36. *Kendall v. The Queen*, [1962] S.C.R. 469; 132 C.C.C. 216 (S.C.C.).

37. *R. v. Fletcher* (1982), 1 C.C.C. (3d) 370 (Ont. C.A.). This was foreshadowed by *R. v. Bannerman* (1966), 48 C.R. 110 (Man. C.A.), affirmed [1966] S.C.R. 50 (S.C.C.).

38. *Vetrovec*, See endnote 7.

39. *Criminal Code Amendment Act* R.S.C. 1985, c. 10-19 section 18.

40. *Canada Evidence Act*, R.S.C. 1985, c. C-5, section 16(1)(a).

41. *Canada Evidence Act*, section 16(2).

42. *Canada Evidence Act*, section 16(3).

43. *R. v. Khan* (1990), 59 C.C.C. (3d) 92 (S.C.C.).

44. *R. v. G.B.* (1990), 56 C.C.C. (3d) 92 (S.C.C.).

45. *R. v. R.W.* (1992), 74 C.C.C. (3d) 134 (S.C.C.).

46. For a useful recent decision see *R. v. Robinson Arthur Pearson*, (1994) CA 018373 (B.C.C.A.)

47. *Criminal Code*, section 486(3); *Canadian Newspapers Co. v. Canada (Attorney General)* (1988), 43 C.C.C. (3d) 24 (S.C.C.).

48. *Criminal Code*, section 276 and 276.1 to 4. See also *R. v. Seaboyer* (1991), 66 C.C.C. (3d), 321 (S.C.C.).

49. The subsection on the Preservation and Presentation of Confidential Records in Sexual Offence Proceedings was written by Laurie J. Soloway, M.Ed., LL.B., Legal Services Branch, Ministry of the Attorney General (British Columbia).

50. *R. v. O'Connor* (1996), 103 C.C.C. (3d) 1 (S.C.C.).

51. *Criminal Code*, section 278.1.

52. *Ibid.*

53. *Criminal Code*, section 278.3(1) and (2).

54. *Criminal Code*, section 278.3(3)(b).

55. *Criminal Code*, section 278.3(4).

56. *Criminal Code*, section 278.3(5).

57. *Ibid.*

58. *Ibid.*

59. *Ibid.*

60. *Criminal Code*, sections 278.4(2) and 278.5(3).

61. *Criminal Code*, section 278.7(3).

62. *Carosella v. The Queen* (1997), 112 C.C.C. (3d) 289 (S.C.C.). See also *R. v. D.D.W.* March 26th, 1997 (B.C.C.A.).

63. *Criminal Code*, section 486 (1.2) to (1.4).

64. *Criminal Code* as above. See endnote 47.

65. *Criminal Code*, section 486(2).

66. *Criminal Code*, section 715.1, *R. v. Levogiannis* (1993), S.C.J. 70, June 15, 1993 (S.C.C.).

67. For a useful discussion see Cpl. H. McDonald, "Child Sexual Abuse" (1988) 50 Royal Canadian Mounted Police Gazette, No. 3.

68. *R. v. Massina*, (3 June 1987), Victoria 41457, (B.C. Co. Ct.) [Unreported].

69. *R. v. Levogiannis* (1993), S.C.J. 70, June 15, 1993 (S.C.C.).

70. *R. v. D.O.L.* (1993), S.C.J. 70, June 15, 1993 (S.C.C.)

71. *R. v. Cowpersmith* (1946), 2 D.L.R. 725 (B.C.C.A.) "Forgive me for what happened in the car." *R. v. Richmond* (1954), 84 C.C.C. 289 (B.C.C.A.) "I guess it may be right ... I don't think I hurt the little girl." *Fargnoli v. The Queen*, 177 C.C.C. 359 (S.C.C.) "You've got it all there. There's nothing more to say."

72. *R. v. Chayko* (1984), 12 C.C.C. (3d) 157 (Alta. C.A.) *R. v. Miller* (1966), 1 C.C.C. 60 (N.B.C.A.) where a man of 34, who had been drinking, took the complainant, a school girl of 13, to a secluded wooded area at dusk. *R. v. Parrish* (1968), 64 W.W.R. 310 (S.C.C.) where "necking" in a state of partial undress under a blanket in a motel room was observed by others and held to confirm an allegation of intercourse.

73. *R. v. Unrow* (1970), 74 W.W.R. 440 (B.C.C.A.).

74. *R. v. Williams* (1973), 12 C.C.C. (2d) 453 (Ont. C.A.).

75. *R. v. Mattessa and Morin*, (16 March 1990), (B.C.C.A.) [Unreported]; *R. v. Webster*, (29 January 1986), (B.C.C.A.) [Unreported].

76. *R. v. Khan* (1990), 59 C.C.C. (3d) 93 (S.C.C.).

77. *Ibid.*, at 103.

78. *D.H.R. v. Superintendent of Family and Child Services* (1984), 58 B.C.L.R. 103 (B.C.C.A.); *M.(W.) v. Director of Child Welfare for Prince Edward Island* (1986), 3 R.F.L. (3d) 181 (P.E.I.C.A.); *Foote v. Foote* (1988), B.C.J. No. 278 (B.C.C.A.) [Unreported].

79. *R. v. Robinson Arthur Pearson*, (1994) CA018373 (B.C.C.A.).

80. *R. v. B.(C.R.)* (1990), 55 C.C.C. (3d) 1 (S.C.C.); *R. v. Green* (1988), 40 C.C.C. (3d) 333 (S.C.C.); *R. v. Robertson* (1987), 33 C.C.C. (3d) 481 (S.C.C.); *Sweitzer v. The Queen* (1982), 68 C.C.C. (2d) 193 (S.C.C.).

81. *R. v. Marquard* (1993), 85 C.C.C. (3d) 193 (S.C.C.).

82. *R. v. B.(G.)* (1990), 56 C.C.C. (3d) 200 at 220 (S.C.C.); *R. v. Belliveau* (1986), 30 C.C.C. (B.C.C.A.). For a useful article see W. Ehrcke, "The Admissibility of Expert Psychological Evidence in Sexual Assault Cases" (Seminar paper, Western Canada Crown Counsel, Banff, 1988) [Unreported].

83. *R. v. C. (R.A.)* 57 C.C.C. (3d) 522 (B.C.C.A.); *R. v. Jmieff* (1994), 94 C.C.C. (3d) 157 (B.C.C.A.).

84. *R. v. C.N.S.*, (14 September 1990), CA009849, (B.C.C.A.) [Unreported].

85. *R. v. Deley*, (25 March 1988), CA343/87, (Ont. C.A.) [Unreported].

86. *Ibid.*

87. *R. v. F.E.J.* (1990), 74 C.R. (3d) 269 (Ont. C.A.).

88. *Criminal Code*, section 735; *R. v. Curtis* 69 C.C.C. (3d) 385, (N.B.C.A.).

89. R.S.B.C. (1996) c. 478 proclaimed July 1, 1996.

90. R.S.B.C. 1996 c. 85.

91. *Criminal Code*, section 161 R.S.C. 1993, C-45, s.I.

92. W. Harvey, *So You Have To Go To Court!* (Toronto: Butterworths, 1986).

Chapter 8

YOUTH JUSTICE AND THE LEGAL PROCESS

Lesley Giles and Alan Markwart

INTRODUCTION

The public profile that youth crime has received in recent decades makes it essential for all helping professionals to have a working knowledge in this area. Professionals may be directly involved with the system as youth workers, social workers, or psychiatrists, or they may be required to advise young persons and their families in their workload about the youth justice system. This chapter has been written to provide helping professionals in general practice with a functional knowledge of the youth justice system in British Columbia. It gives an overview of the federal *Young Offenders Act,*[1] and identifies the various participants in the legal process. Facilities and resources for young offenders are also outlined. Since each geographical area of Canada has its own resources that focus on the needs of a particular community, this cannot be an exhaustive survey of all the resources available to young persons. But this chapter should provide enough information about the youth justice system in British Columbia, including where to seek resources and what to do when the professional is required to assist a young person within the that system. The law is stated as of April 31, 1997.

DEFINITIONS OF LEGAL TERMS

In each profession, one finds "jargon." The legal profession is no exception and often creates, through its own terminology and processes, a complicated maze of unintelligible procedures. Some of the common legal terms and expressions used in this chapter are defined before more details of the law and process are given. The youth justice process is outlined later in the chapter and set out in the form of a chart. A general description of the criminal process can be found in Chapters 1 and 7.

A. Age

The *Young Offenders Act* (hereafter referred to as the *Act*) defines a young person as being 12 or more years old and under the age of 18 at the commission of the alleged offence. Therefore, when a young person first appears in Youth Court, the court must be satisfied that he/she was between the ages of 12 years and 17 years inclusive at the time of the alleged offence. Children under 12 cannot be convicted of crime. Those 18 and over are dealt with as adults in the criminal justice system.

B. Summary Conviction Offence

A summary conviction offence is a less serious offence and is identified as such in the *Criminal Code*.[2] For example, theft of property under $5,000 in value is normally summary. Section 787 states that an adult usually faces a maximum penalty for this type of offence of six months imprisonment and/or a $2,000 fine. With the exception of the offence of breach of probation, a young person charged with a summary conviction offence cannot be given a disposition of secure custody (see F below), but can be committed to open custody for a maximum of six months.

C. Summary Conviction Procedure

Almost all youth court matters, whether the offence proceeds by summary conviction or by indictment (see D below), are dealt with by way of summary conviction procedure, and consequently proceedings remain at the Provincial Court (Youth Court) level. The charged young person, therefore, is not entitled to a trial by Supreme Court Judge (with or without a jury) except in rare instances where the offence is murder, and the young person has elected to be tried by a judge alone or judge and jury, or the young person has been transferred to adult court.

D. Indictable Offence

An indictable offence is a more serious offence, such as theft of property over $5,000 in value, or aggravated assault, or assault with a weapon. (The *Criminal Code* identifies certain offences, such as assault causing bodily harm, as proceeding by indictment or summary conviction at the discretion of Crown Counsel). A young person charged with an indictable offence may be sentenced to secure custody for longer periods than for summary offences in the following circumstances:[3]

a) if the indictable offence is one for which an adult would be liable for a maximum of less than life imprisonment, then up to two years custody;

b) if the indictable offence is one for which an adult would be liable to life imprisonment, up to three years custody;

c) up to four years custody for second degree murder; and

d) up to six years custody for first degree murder.

E. Disposition

Disposition means the same as a sentence for an adult, and details of dispositions are contained in section 20 of the *Act*. Terms different from the adult system have long been used in youth justice, perhaps to try to decriminalize the system. But as the reader will see, the *Act* clearly establishes a criminal justice system for youth. Dispositions range from absolute discharge as the least serious sentence to secure custody (see F below) as the most serious, other than transfer to adult court for sentencing.

F. Custody

Custody is the youth equivalent to "imprisonment" for an adult. There are two kinds of custody for youth, both referring to a youth being sentenced to a particular type of facility:

a) Open Custody - generally a less secure setting than secure custody; the young person is allowed more freedom and often the location is a camp environment where supervision by staff and geographic isolation may be the major security features.

b) Secure Custody - this type of custody is the maximum security for young offenders and offers little freedom. Building structure such as cells, locked doors, enclosed recreation areas and fences provide the security together with close supervision by staff.

Further details of these custody centres are discussed later.

G. Undertaking

An undertaking is a promise by the young person, given in writing to the Youth Court, which states that the young person will obey certain conditions of release. This document is signed by the young person and on occasion by a responsible adult (section 7.1). The court releases the young person on the strength of these promises and can revoke the release if the young person or the adult fails to comply with the conditions, or if the adult is no longer willing or able to exercise control over the young person.

BACKGROUND OF THE LEGISLATION

In order to fully understand the *Act*, the helping professional needs to know about its source, scope, and jurisdiction. These three aspects are now discussed briefly.

A. Federal-Provincial Division Of Powers

Chapter 1 described how the *Constitution* divides legislative powers between federal and provincial jurisdictions.[4] Criminal laws and procedures come within the exclusive legislative authority of the Parliament of Canada. The *Criminal Code* and *Young Offenders Act* are thus federal legislation, and apply across Canada. Provincial legislatures are responsible for the establishment, maintenance, and management of reformatories and provincial prisons, the implementation and administration of the criminal law, and the imposition of punishment for breaches of any provincial law. The *Young Offenders (British Columbia) Act*[5] provides a similar process to the federal *Young Offenders Act*, but deals only with youth who violate provincial statutes, such as the *Motor Vehicles Act*[6] (driving without a licence for example), or municipal by-laws as opposed to violations of the *Criminal Code*. Provincial Young Offenders Acts also provide more lenient penalties for young persons violating provincial statutes than the federal *Act*. This chapter will focus on the federal *Act*.

To the non-lawyer, the federal *Act* appears to have its funding base within the federal budget. However, that is not entirely the case. It is important to understand the source of funds for resources within the youth justice system, why resources vary from province to province, and why certain projects are better funded than others. Section 70 of the *Act* provides a cost-sharing mechanism between Canada and the provinces covering costs incurred by the province or a municipality for care of and services provided to young persons dealt with under the *Act*. Since 1989, the federal government has frozen and then reduced financial contributions to young offenders services. These reductions, along with provincial restraint measures resulting from concerns about budget deficits and debt, help to explain why the available resources often do not meet the need.

B. Scope of the *Young Offenders Act*

The *Act* applies to offences created by Acts of the Federal Parliament (with the exception of ordinances of the Yukon Territory or the Northwest Territories). Usually young persons are charged with offences under the *Criminal Code* (the majority of charges), or under the *Controlled Drugs and Substances Act*[7] (formally the *Narcotic Control Act* and the *Food and Drugs Act)*. The young person will be charged with a substantive offence, such as theft under $5,000 or sexual assault, but dispositions (sentences) are limited to those created by section 20 of the *Young Offenders Act*.

C. Definition of Young Person

The *Act* defines a "young person" as a person who is between the ages of 12 and 17 years of age inclusive. The court of jurisdiction for young persons is the Youth Court, which is a provincial court that deals only with persons who were between these ages when they committed the alleged offence. Note that the offender's age at the date of the offence determines the forum (court of jurisdiction). For example, if a young person commits an offence when she/he is 16, but is not arrested until he/she is 18, the forum is still the Youth Court and the dispositions are still made under the *Act*. However, if a person who has attained her/his eighteenth birthday commits the offence of breaching a Youth Court probation order, the breach will be processed in the adult court system because it was an offence committed while he/she was an adult. Those young people who are 18 years of age and older are, by definition, "adults," and are processed through the ordinary adult courts. Those who are younger than 12 years of age are, by definition, "children," and are not able to be charged under any federal or provincial legislation, although in some circumstances they may be dealt with under provincial child welfare or mental health legislation.

PHILOSOPHY OF THE *YOUNG OFFENDERS ACT*

The philosophy of the *Young Offenders Act* is set out in the <u>Declaration of Principle</u>, section 3 of the *Act*. This philosophy differs a great deal from the previous *Juvenile Delinquents Act*[8] in that Parliament has adopted a "justice" model, rather than the "welfare" model embodied in the *Juvenile Delinquents Act*. The focus of the *Act* is on the protection of society and on the responsibility to be borne by young offenders for their offences, balanced by their special needs.

The *Act* is legislation separate and distinct from the *Child, Family and Community Service Act*,[9] which sets out the only means by which the State may remove guardianship of a child from her/his parents (see Chapter 3). The *Act* contains no mechanism for removing guardianship. Indeed, the *Act* specifically states that "parents have responsibility for the care and supervision of their children, and, for that reason, young persons should be removed from parental supervision either partly or entirely only when measures that provide for continuing parental supervision are inappropriate."[10] The only way a young person can be removed from his/her parents is in the context of punishment such as placement in open or secure custody, or placement in a residential program as a condition of a probation order. Although these measures may temporarily remove the young person from the custody of her/his parents, they do not transfer legal guardianship to the State.

The key theme in the *Act* is to require young persons to take responsibility for their criminal conduct and to punish them in a manner that resembles, though to a lesser degree, the adult equivalent. Some would argue that, considering how many serious offences are committed by young persons, the procedural safeguards built into the *Act* may actually help some young persons avoid responsibility for their criminal acts rather than bear responsibility for them. However, if "responsibility" means "punishment," as popular opinion might suggest, then the *Act* has stressed responsibility because the use of custodial sentences substantially increased after the *Act* came into effect in 1984. Concerns have been raised about the appropriateness of custodial sentences and the impact of this increase in labelling and institutionalizing young persons.[11] It is also worth noting that in many jurisdictions where there has been an increase in custodial sentences, there has been a reduction in community resources available to young persons, especially in terms of access to resources available in the child welfare system.

Under the <u>Declaration of Principle</u>, the principle of public protection has also to be balanced against the principles of the special needs of young persons and of the right to the least interference with their freedom. Section 3(1)(c) states they "require supervision, discipline and control, but, because of their state of dependency and level of development and maturity, they also have special needs and require guidance and assistance." Section 3(1)(f) states that their rights and freedoms include "a right to the least possible interference with freedom that is consistent with the protection of society, having regard to the needs of young persons and the interests of their families." In finding an appropriate balance, the court system will need input from the helping professional to develop effective and minimally detrimental alternatives. For instance, if responsibility can mean facing up to the consequences of the crime and healing the hurt caused, then working for or compensating the victim might be the appropriate sanction as long as public protection is not the paramount issue.

The <u>Declaration of Principle</u> is somewhat confusing because it sets out sometimes conflicting principles without prioritizing them. These conflicting principles include protection of the public, responsibility and accountability, special needs (rehabilitation), legal rights, and minimal interference with freedom. In recent years, however, the principle of rehabilitation appears to have assumed greater importance than the other concepts. In its first decision about sentencing principles under the *Act* in 1993, the Supreme Court of Canada stated that the reformation and rehabilitation of young offenders is the ultimate aim of all dispositions.[12] As well, an amendment to the <u>Declaration of Principle</u> in 1996 provides that: "the protection of society . . . is best served by rehabilitation, whenever possible, . . . and rehabilitation is best achieved by addressing the needs and circumstances of a young person that are relevant to the young person's offending behaviour."[13]

RIGHTS OF THE YOUNG PERSON

A. Rights Contained in the *Charter Of Rights And Freedoms*[14]

A young person has the same legal rights as every citizen of Canada, in particular the following: the right to life, liberty, and security of the person (section 7 of the *Charter*); the right to be secure against unreasonable search or seizure (section 8); the right not to be arbitrarily detained or imprisoned (section 9); the right on arrest or detention to be informed promptly of the reasons; the right to retain and instruct counsel without delay, and to be informed of that right (sections 10(a), (b)); and the rights of a charged person to be tried within a reasonable time, not to be compelled to be a witness in proceedings against themselves, to be presumed innocent until proven guilty, and not to be denied reasonable bail without just cause (section 11).

Of those rights enumerated above, the most commonly invoked are the rights contained in sections 10(a) and 10(b), and the right to silence.[15] The right contained in section 10(a) is the right to know why the young person has been arrested or detained by a police officer. Any person, for that matter, must be told immediately why he/she is being arrested. The right contained in section 10(b) is commonly known as the right to counsel. Not only must young persons be told of their right to counsel, they must be given the opportunity to exercise that right, and the police must cease questioning them until they have had the opportunity to exercise their right to counsel.[16] However, after the opportunity to consult counsel, the police are free to continue questioning young persons.

The right to silence has been held to be the right to choose whether or not to make a statement to the police. The suspect, although placed in the superior power of the state upon detention, retains the right to choose whether or not she/he will make a statement to the police. To this end, the *Charter* requires that the suspect be informed of his/her right to counsel and be permitted to consult counsel without delay. If the suspect chooses to make a statement, the suspect may do so. But if the suspect chooses not to, the state is not entitled to use its superior power to override the suspect's will and negate her/his choice.[17]

B. Rights Contained in the *Young Offenders Act*

In addition to those rights contained in the *Charter of Rights and Freedoms*, a young person is guaranteed certain other rights. The most important is the "right to be heard in the course of, and to participate in, the processes that lead to decisions that affect [him/her]."[18] This right was not available to a young person under the *Juvenile Delinquents Act* and reflects the principle that young persons are responsible members of society who, if they truly are to be held responsible for their criminal acts, should also be responsible enough to make choices and to be heard during the legal process. The *Act* also provides an absolute right for the young person to be represented by counsel (section 11). This right to counsel (a lawyer) goes well beyond the simple right to retain and instruct counsel that is available to adults. For example, once a charge proceeds to court, the judge is obliged to ask the young person whether she/he wishes to retain counsel. If the young person is ineligible for legal aid and indicates he/she wants counsel, then the court must order that counsel be provided at public expense, regardless of whether the young person or parents have the ability to pay and even if the offence is minor and very unlikely to result in custody. A young person is also entitled to counsel independent of her/his parents. This provides a means for the young person to obtain and pay for a lawyer without relying on his/her parents' ability to pay. This removes a potential conflict between the instructions given to a lawyer by a young person and instructions given by her/his parents.

As mentioned, the young person has a right to the "least possible interference with freedom that is consistent with the protection of society, having regard to the needs of young persons and the interests of their families" (section 3(1)(f)). Families, particularly parents, are a vital part of all proceedings taken against young persons. For example, before making a decision about whether or not to make a statement to the police, the young person has a right not only to consult with a lawyer but also to consult with his/her parents, an adult relative, or an appropriate adult chosen by the young person and to make the statement in the presence of such a person (section 56). In addition, section 9 provides notice requirements to parents, encouraging them to participate at every stage of the proceedings. Parents are encouraged to make representations in any application to transfer the young person to ordinary (adult) court and whenever dispositions are made. In preparing a pre-disposition report, the Youth Worker should discuss the relationship between the young person and her/his parents (and, where appropriate, extended family) and their ability to control him/her. In fact, the strength of a family unit is often a critical feature in making a disposition. A young person from a strong and capable family will often be less likely to receive a custodial sentence than a young person from a dysfunctional family.

INTERRELATED PROFESSIONALS AND AGENCIES WORKING WITH YOUNG PERSONS

Many helping professionals play a valuable role within the youth justice system. Unless each of these professionals recognizes her/his role as a member of a team, young offenders cannot be dealt with effectively in Youth Court. The following describes the key players in the systems across the provinces, with a particular focus on the resources available in British Columbia.

I. Professionals

A. Police

Police officers, the most visible members of the law enforcement team, are on the front line, preventing breaches of the peace, investigating offences under the *Criminal Code* and provincial statutes, and making recommendations to Crown Counsel for charges to be initiated. Unlike most other provinces, the police in British Columbia do not directly lay charges. A police officer will often be the person most aware of a young person's profile in the community and will see the young person's behaviour at its most basic level. The fact that a police officer has apprehended a young person does not necessarily mean that the officer must report the matter or proceed further. At common law (meaning according to case law), the police have the discretion to informally divert in minor cases (e.g. shoplifting, non-serious assault) by contacting the parents and warning the youth. This is fairly common practice in British Columbia, comprising almost one-half of the cases that come to the attention of the police.

If the police believe the offence (or offender) requires further action, they prepare a Report to Crown Counsel and may recommend either alternative measures (a formal diversion process) or to proceed with the charges. If the offence is relatively serious, the police must decide whether to arrest and detain the young person, pending appearance before a judge or justice, or to release him/her with or without conditions.

B. Crown Counsel

Crown Counsel (also known as the prosecutor), acts on behalf of Her Majesty the Queen and serves several functions. The Crown receives the recommendations from the police and determines whether to proceed by way of alternative measures or to charge the young person and proceed to court. Before doing so, Crown Counsel must examine the evidence to determine whether it is sufficient to proceed. If the matter proceeds to court, then she/he will process the police "Report to Crown Counsel" and begin the charging process. Crown Counsel is responsible for the conduct of the entire case, from the moment the Report is received until the last appeal is completed.

In each region of British Columbia, there is a ladder of responsibility under the Attorney General and Deputy Attorney General, consisting of the Regional Crown Counsel, Deputy Regional Crown Counsel and Administrative Crown Counsel above the regular local Crown Counsel. The latter has responsibility for the conduct of the case, while the Administrative Crown Counsel makes administrative decisions, may review the decisions of Crown Counsel, and may assist Crown Counsel in making difficult decisions. Deputy Regional Crown Counsel and Regional Crown Counsel oversee the entire operation, control the quality of the prosecutors and prosecutions, and make decisions concerning high profile cases and those being considered for transfer to ordinary (adult) court.

The federal Department of Justice also has Crown Counsel who are the federal counterparts of the provincial Crown Counsel. However, their duties are limited to the prosecution of federal statute offences, such as the *Controlled Drugs and Substances Act*. Criminal Code offences are prosecuted by provincial Crown Counsel.

C. Defence Counsel

Most young people are represented by defence counsel once they are in court or, at least, receive legal advice and assistance from duty counsel. Defence Counsel have a duty to take instructions from their clients - young persons, rather than parents. Their role is to advocate for the legal interests of their clients and to ensure that the prosecution conducts its case fairly and in accordance with the law. At the dispositional (sentencing) stage, they normally try to avoid custody altogether or to minimize its length by suggesting alternatives to the court.

D. Youth Worker

Youth Worker means the same to a young offender as does the Probation Officer to an adult offender. In fact, Youth Workers are commonly known as Probation Officers. The duties and functions (section 37) of a Youth Worker include the following:

a) supervising the young person in complying with the conditions of a probation order, or a conditional supervision order, or in carrying out any other disposition;

b) assisting a young person found guilty of an offence until discharge or the disposition (sentence);

c) attending court when advisable or required (usually to address the court on the young person's situation); and

d) preparing a pre-disposition report or a progress report for the court.

Crown Counsel may also request the Youth Worker to conduct a pre-court enquiry, which includes an assessment of a young person's circumstances and recommendations about whether alternative measures would be suitable in a particular case. Youth Workers also carry out pre-bail reports in cases where a young person has been detained in custody in order to assess whether alternatives to custody, such as bail or house arrest pending trial and disposition, are suitable.

E. Social Worker

A social worker may become involved with a young person before the court in one of several ways. A young person may have previously been removed (apprehended) under child protection legislation and thus be a temporary or permanent "ward" of the director of Family and Children's Services, or be in child welfare care by way of a voluntary care agreement with the parents. Alternatively, the commission of an offence may bring the young person's child welfare needs to light. Therefore, she/he may be removed into care, or taken into care by agreement, after the offences were committed by a separate action in Family Court (see Chapter 3). In either event, the child's immediate supervisor will be a social worker who will provide for his/her housing and care and assume responsibility for all other needs. The relationship between the young person and child welfare authorities can only be terminated by the court or when a care order expires or a voluntary care agreement is ended.

A social worker's mandate is only to house a young person and care for her/his needs. This mandate is sometimes incompatible with the mandate of the youth justice system, which must also seek to protect the public by controlling the young person's freedom. In many cases, the social worker works hand in hand with the Youth Worker to provide a placement that can achieve both ends.

F. Judges

Judges are independent of the legislative and administrative arms of government. Their primary role is quite simple - to interpret and apply the law in accordance with the *Charter of Rights and Freedoms*, applicable statutes, and case law, and to govern the process. Almost all young offender cases are heard by provincially appointed (Provincial Court) judges, who in trials become finders of fact as well as legal arbiters. Cases of murder can be heard by a Supreme Court judge (sitting as a Youth Court judge), if the young person chooses to be tried by a judge and jury.

II. Programs and Services

Before 1997, the responsibility for services and programs for children and youth was divided among several government ministries in British Columbia. The Ministry of Attorney General was responsible for youth workers, youth custody centres, residential attendance programs and a variety of youth community programs. The Ministry of Health was responsible for youth forensic, children's mental health, and alcohol and drug programs. The Ministry of Social Services was responsible for an array of child protection and child welfare services to both wards and non-wards under voluntary care and family service agreements. Finally, the Ministry of Education and local School Boards were responsible for the educational needs of children and youth.

With a reorganization during 1997, all these services (apart from education) will be administered under one umbrella Ministry - the Ministry for Children and Families. It is expected that services will be organized and administered through multi-disciplinary, community-based teams of professionals. These teams will, for example, be comprised of youth workers, social workers, alcohol and drug counsellors, public health nurses, and mental health workers.

While the amalgamation of services under one Ministry will not, by itself, resolve the problem of inadequate resources to meet service demands, it is expected that a more integrated multi-disciplinary approach will result in greater cooperation amongst different professionals, and in greater efficiency. Hopefully, therefore, more children will receive appropriate services as a result of this change and not fall between the gaps in services. School programs will continue to be the responsibility of the Ministry of Education and school districts.

This range of services should become more comprehensive and integrated. While the administration and organization of services will change, the types of programs available (described below) will remain the same.

A. Youth Custody Centres

As noted earlier, there are two types of custody centres, secure and open. The Youth Court (not administrators) decides at disposition whether a youth will be placed in secure or open custody. In British Columbia, there are secure custody facilities in four communities - Victoria, Burnaby, Prince George, and Maple Ridge. The first three centres are co-educational facilities, which receive youth who are remanded in custody pending trial or disposition, who have been sentenced to secure custody by the court, or who have been temporarily transferred (up to fifteen days) from open to secure custody. The fourth centre, Boulder Bay in Maple Ridge, receives male sentenced youth only. It is designated a secure custody facility by virtue of its greater isolation from the community.

Several open custody facilities exist in British Columbia. Some are camps for males only, located near Campbell River and Chilliwack. The centre at Kamloops is co-educational, and the centre in Burnaby has separate male and female open custody residential facilities. There are also some contracted community residential programs where young persons in custody are placed (by way of temporary release) as a pre-release transition to the community. Youth custody centres are reasonably well staffed and have special education, substance abuse, and mental health counseling, and a range of other activities and social programs. They are not, however, treatment programs. The facilities in Victoria and Burnaby are antiquated and are typically over-crowded, with several young persons to a cell as commonplace.

B. Residential Attendance Programs

Residential attendance programs with varying types of services are found in many communities in British Columbia. Length of stay for young persons varies according to their needs and performance and the components of the program. The programs may be completely self-contained or may provide schooling in the community. Attending and completing programs are made terms of probation or conditional supervision orders. All are contracted programs aimed at behaviour modification in a residential setting. They include wilderness challenge camps, sex offender and substance abuse treatment programs, group homes, and family based care homes. These programs do not have physical security in the buildings and, because contracted staff are not peace officers, they are not able to physically restrain or arrest young persons in residence. These programs are offered as an alternative to custody.

C. Special Non-Residential Attendance Programs

There are several specialized, non-residential youth correctional programs available throughout the province (but which are more available in urban areas) for youth on bail or disposition orders. Weekend attendance programs usually offer wilderness challenge programs for ten to twelve weekends, thus allowing the young person to remain in the community during the week. Intensive supervision programs involve a contracted worker being assigned to a small number (six to ten) of youth for monitoring court-ordered conditions, such as curfews and school attendance, and for offering support to the young person and family.

There are also specialized day programs, mostly school-based, which offer specialized educational programs exclusively to youth on probation. Some day programs are not school-based but rather focus on life and work skills training.

D. Forensic Psychiatric Services and Mental Health Resources

Youth Services to the Courts provides forensic psychiatric services to young persons in British Columbia. In larger population centres such as Vancouver (Burnaby) and Victoria, full service psychiatric clinics are available. These offer full assessment services, either in-custody (as in the Inpatient Assessment Unit in Burnaby) or on an outpatient basis. They also provide counseling and treatment services by court order to young persons on probation. These services are also available to more seriously disturbed youth in custody. Smaller centres are often served by traveling clinics, which provide more basic forensic services.

The major advantage of an in-custody assessment is that the young person's behaviour can be observed over a period of time. The disadvantage is that the young person is often removed from his/her own community, and the residential clinic is often unaware of resources in the smaller home community.

A psychiatric assessment is ordered by the court under section 13 of the *Young Offenders Act* for three distinct reasons. These are the following:

a) before plea, to determine fitness to stand trial (here the circumstances of the offence are not considered);

b) after a finding of guilt, to make or review a disposition (here the young person is questioned about the circumstances of the offence); or

201

c) to consider an application to transfer the young person to ordinary court (adult court). Here the young person is questioned about the offence but the psychiatrist or psychologist is called as a witness for the purpose of determining whether the young person should be transferred to adult court.[19]

Many helping professionals working with young persons believe that psychiatric assessments should be ordered, but they do not realize the importance of taking into consideration the circumstances of the offence in order to have a full assessment. For example, a routine breaking and entering is one thing, but the same charge where the offender urinates and defecates in the victim's house and gratuitously destroys personal mementos suggests a level of anger and disturbance in the offender that should be examined.

An assessment may be ordered either with the consent of both the young person and Crown Counsel, or where:[20]

a) there are reasonable grounds to believe the young person may be suffering from a physical or mental illness or disorder, a psychological disorder, an emotional disturbance, a learning disability, or mental disability;

b) the young person's history indicates a pattern of repeated findings of guilt; or

c) the young person is alleged to have committed an offence involving serious personal injury (such as aggravated sexual assault).

Few mental health facilities are available in British Columbia that offer residential treatment to seriously disturbed adolescents. The primary facility is the Maples Adolescent Treatment Centre in Burnaby. This facility may be accessed in four different ways:

a) through involuntary committal under the *Mental Health Act*;[21]

b) through voluntary admission under the *Mental Health Act*;

c) through a Youth Court finding of unfit to stand trial or not guilty by reason of mental disorder; and

d) through a condition of probation requiring the young person to reside and undertake treatment. This rarely employed option is only available when the young person and the treatment facility consent to the order being made and when the order is made in conjunction with a voluntary admission under the *Mental Health Act*, program space permitting.

The only other facilities in the province providing residential service to seriously disturbed adolescents are the Jack Ledger House program in Victoria, which offers a six-week residential program to children and youth, the Vancouver Hospital adolescent program, and placement in psychiatric wards of general hospitals. Other than the very limited availability of the Maples program, there are no mid- to long-term residential psychiatric treatment programs for adolescents in the province. There are, however, specialized residential treatment programs for young sex offenders available in several locations in the province, i.e., Campbell River, Langley, Merritt, Prince George, and Terrace.

E. Schools

Schools play important roles in the lives of young persons. School staff will often see problems long before a child's behaviour accelerates to the status of criminal behaviour. Often an alert teacher may help determine that a child is at risk and, as a result, may assist the parents in addressing problems and involving other professionals before the problems become insurmountable. For example, a teacher may observe that a child is not reading at an age-appropriate level, has other apparent learning, visual, or hearing disabilities, or is having inter-personal relationship problems.

Various school districts have programs to educate children who do not fit into the regular school system. These programs offer such alternatives as work experience, life-skills education, and pregnant teen/new mother education with day care. They also may assist to re-integrate those who, for any reason, may have left school for a lengthy period of time.

F. Drug And Alcohol Programs

There are few residential treatment programs for adolescents with problems of substance abuse. Two key residential resources are the Exodus and Peak House programs in the Lower Mainland. Otherwise, older adolescents are often placed in adult residential treatment programs. However, many areas have community programs, such as the Dallas Society drug and alcohol program in Victoria, which focus on education, abstinence, and personal counselling.

THE LEGAL PROCESS

In Figure 1, the reader will find a chart that illustrates the legal process as it applies to young persons, from the commission of the crime, to disposition by the Youth Court and to review of the disposition. This figure illustrates the various stages in the process, highlighting key legal issues and decisions. It clarifies the different ways the young person may be processed through the youth justice system.

If a young person is charged with an offence, she/he may be processed in one of several ways. These include the following:

a) taking no action based on the decision of Crown Counsel;

b) transfer to the ordinary (adult) court after a Youth Court hearing;

c) diversion from the formal Youth Court system through Alternative Measures; or

d) appearance in Youth Court following arrest or by way of a summons, notice, or promise to appear.

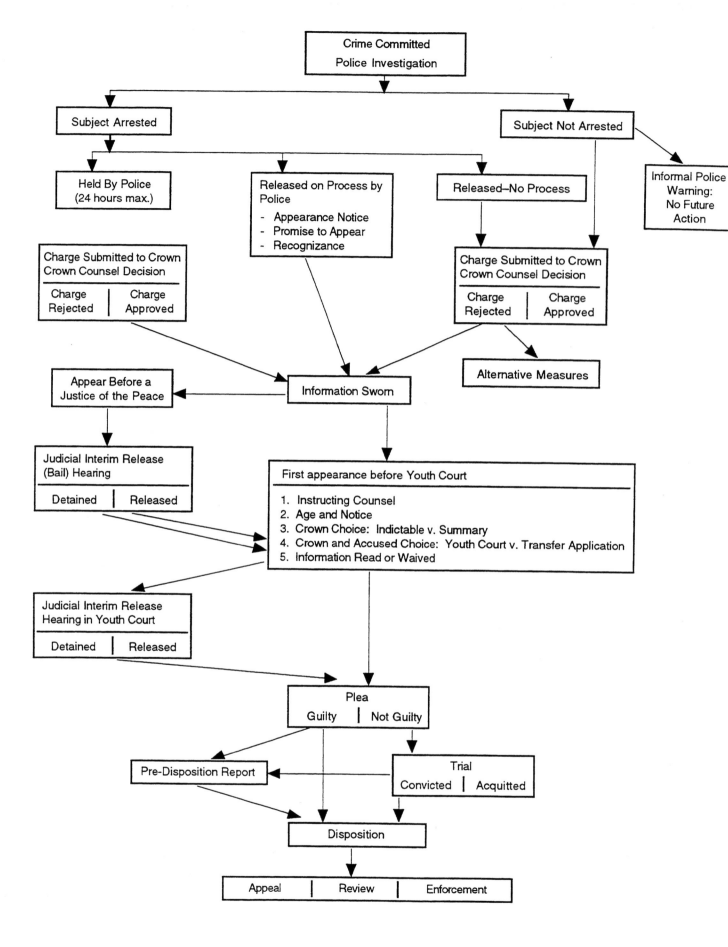

Figure 1. Legal Process in Youth Justice System

Each of these mechanisms is discussed below.

I. No Action

Upon receipt of a suggested charge from the police, Crown Counsel will review the evidence to ensure there is a strong likelihood of conviction. Where the evidence is insufficient or the offence minor, the Crown may decide to take no action or may suggest that the police warn the youth (see Figure 1).

II. Transfers to Ordinary Court

If a young person is transferred to ordinary court, it means the case is dealt with in the adult court system and the young person is, for the most part, subject to the same procedures and sanctions as an adult. This means that the procedures of trial (including jury) are the same as for adults and that the penalties have wider limits than in Youth Court, such as life imprisonment.

There are two processes for transfer of a young person to ordinary court. If a young person was 16 or 17 years of age at the time of the offence and charged with murder, manslaughter, attempted murder, or aggravated sexual assault, the case will automatically proceed to adult court[22] unless the young person applies to have the matter heard in Youth Court. In practice, young persons will invariably make an application, so a transfer hearing will be held. In these cases, the onus is on the young person to satisfy the court that the matter should be retained in the Youth Court, based upon the factors discussed below.

For other serious indictable offences (such as robbery or arson, for example) committed by young persons 14 to 17 years old, Crown Counsel must make application to transfer the case to adult court, and the onus is on Crown to satisfy the court that the matter should be transferred. A young person under the age of 14 years at the time of the offence cannot be transferred to adult court.

In considering transfers to adult court, the Youth Court must consider such factors as the seriousness of the offence and the circumstances surrounding its commission; age, maturity, character, and background of the young person; adequacy of the various correctional systems to deal with the young person; and the availability of resources (section 16). The court must consider the objectives of the protection of society and the rehabilitation of the young person. If these objectives cannot be reconciled by a Youth Court disposition, then the protection of the public is paramount, and the young person will be transferred to ordinary court.

The transfer procedure, somewhat paradoxically, occurs before a finding of guilt. It is a very long and complex process, often requiring as much as two years before appeals to higher courts are complete. Transfers to ordinary court are not very common in British Columbia. Even if a young person is transferred to adult court, he/she is not necessarily dealt with in exactly the same way as an adult. For example, both an adult and a transferred young person must be sentenced to life imprisonment for first degree murder, but the young person is eligible for parole at a much earlier time than an adult. Importantly, the *Act* also allows the court to place transferred young persons in youth custody centres until they are sufficiently mature to be placed in adult facilities.[23]

III. Alternative Measures

Alternative measures, commonly known as "diversion," is a process for dealing with young offenders outside of the formal Youth Court system (see Figure 1). This is different than the police discretion to divert, since in this instance the police have submitted a suggested charge to Crown Counsel. The Crown decides whether use of alternative measures is appropriate, having regard to the needs of the young person and the interests of society (section 4 (1)(b)). Alternative measures programs, usually provided by contracted private agencies, by-pass the court system and impose informal consequences that match the specific criminal offenses. Diversion candidates avoid criminal sanctions and records by agreeing to perform community service work, apologize and/or provide compensation to the victim, or follow other diversion options. Some communities have developed specialized alternative measures programs, such as community accountability panels, family group counselling, and victim-offender reconciliation. Although the *Act* allows for enforcement of non-compliance with an alternative measures agreement (section 4(4)), British Columbia has a policy against re-instituting proceedings against a young person who fails to honour her/his diversion contract. This lack of enforcement is because alternative measures are supposed to be voluntary, but it can hardly be voluntary if the threat of prosecution is hanging over the young person's head. However, diversion usually only happens once, which ensures that a second-time offender will be taken before the Youth Court.

Alternative measures may be an effective way of both meeting the needs of young offenders and preserving the interests of society. Before alternative measures can be considered for a young person, the following conditions must be met:

a) There must be a prosecutable offence. If there is not sufficient evidence to take the matter before a judge, then the young person will be neither prosecuted nor diverted.

b) Crown Counsel who is approving the charge must be satisfied that alternative measures would be appropriate, having regard to the needs of the young person and the interests of society. Certain offences are rarely, if ever, diverted. They include sexual offences, serious assaults, serious property offences, and offences where the victim has lost a considerable amount of property. Young persons with prior criminal records or diversions are rarely treated with alternative measures.

c) The young person must fully and freely consent to participate in the program.

d) The young person must accept responsibility for the offence.[24]

It is important for the helping professional to be reminded that the decision to prosecute in court or divert is entirely the prerogative of Crown Counsel. Crown has the discretion whether to request information to assist in that decision from a social assessment report (known as a pre-trial enquiry) prepared by a Youth Worker.

IV. Appearance in Youth Court

Figure 1 illustrates the routes by which a young offender may proceed to a Youth Court appearance. These include arrest, being held in detention to appear before a justice of the peace, or to make a first appearance in Youth Court. A justice of the peace is used on weekends and holidays to review detention when waiting for the next Youth Court date would violate time limits on detention by police (see below). The justice or the Youth Court Judge may consider bail pending further appearance or trial. This is legally known as "judicial interim release".

Judicial interim release or "bail" is the process that occurs after a young person has been arrested and kept in custody by the police. After an arrest, a young person must be brought before a justice (or judge in Youth Court) within twenty-four hours. As long as the charge is not serious (such as murder), the justice (or judge) must release the young person unless the Crown Counsel shows cause why the young person should be detained in custody. The detention of a young person, as well as an adult, is only justified on either of two grounds:[25]

a) The primary ground - detention is necessary to ensure attendance in court. This factor is relevant for a young person who has a history of failing to appear in court, is a chronic runaway, or has no roots in the community.

b) The secondary ground - for the protection and safety of the public.[26] This ground is only addressed after the court has dealt with the primary ground. An offence such as a series of assaults or arson might fit into this category.

Bail may be granted by consent of the Crown or after submissions from Crown Counsel and the defence. The usual release order will require the young person to give his/her written undertaking that she/he will comply with certain conditions imposed by the justice (or judge). At this stage it is important that the conditions be thought out carefully, as onerous conditions may prove a hardship to the young person or his/her parents. The statutory condition of release requires the young person to appear in court on a future certain date and thereafter as required. Common conditions are the following: to keep the peace and be of good behaviour; to obey conditions pertaining to residence; to attend school or employment; and to obey conditions of non-association with co-accused persons, abstinence from non-prescription drugs and alcohol, and staying away from banned areas of the community ("red zones"). In specific cases such as certain drug offences and breach of release conditions, a young person must show cause why bail should be granted.

Under section 7.1 of the *Act*, when detention would otherwise be ordered, a justice (or judge) may release the young person to a responsible person who is willing to exercise control over her/him. In such cases, release will depend on the undertaking of that person to be responsible for the young person and to comply with any other conditions imposed by the justice (or judge).

An analysis of the application of bail provisions to young offenders reflects the difference between the adult justice system and the youth system. For young offenders, the court will often order detention based on the primary ground, extending it to cover a situation in which a young person has no satisfactory place to reside. The Youth Court is often faced with the dilemma of a youthful accused who is living on the street and who has been charged with a minor offence for which he/she would otherwise have been released. Even though there may have been nothing in the young person's previous history to indicate the young person would fail to attend court, the court may fear that releasing her/him without a satisfactory place to stay would result in his/her failure to attend, or having to commit further offences to financially support herself/himself. This situation has blurred the focus of bail in the youth justice system by introducing problems that are the responsibility of the child welfare system.

A. First Appearance

The Youth Court is concerned about several issues at this stage. First, the court needs to determine whether the young person is between the ages of 12 and 18 as mentioned earlier, in order to establish jurisdiction. Second, the court must determine whether the young person has acquired and consulted with legal counsel. This is necessary before the young person enters a plea. Third, the court must determine whether parents have received notice of their daughter/son's appearance. The Youth Court can order the parents to attend if it decides that doing so is necessary or is in the best interests of the young person (section 10(1)), but in practice rarely does so. Finally, the court will set a date for the next appearance, which may be to determine bail, to obtain counsel, for plea, for trial, or for further information such as medical or psychiatric assessment. The Youth Court will determine whether the young person will be detained in custody or released in this intervening period as discussed above. If detained, the young person must be held separate and apart from adults unless justified because of his/her own or other's safety reasons, or because no place of detention for young persons is available within a reasonable distance (section 7(2)).

B. Trial

A trial takes place after the young person enters a "not guilty" plea. The plea of not guilty essentially means "Crown, prove your case." The onus is on the Crown to prove a criminal offence beyond a reasonable doubt. Only after the Crown has successfully proven its case beyond a reasonable doubt does the young person have to call evidence in his/her own defence. If the Crown is not able to prove its case beyond a reasonable doubt, then the charges will be dismissed. If the Crown proves its case beyond a reasonable doubt, then the court will convict (find guilty) the young person. If the young person is able to call evidence that raises a reasonable doubt in the judge's mind, then the court is obliged to acquit (find not guilty) her/him.

C. Dispositions under the *Young Offenders Act*

When a young person has pleaded guilty or has been found guilty of an offence, the court makes a disposition (sentence). All the alternatives available in creative sentencing are contained in section 20 of the *Act*. The court may utilize one or more of the dispositions, as long as they are not inconsistent with each other. If a young person is found guilty of more than one offence, the court may make the dispositions consecutive (one immediately following the other) providing that the total sentence is no longer than three years (except in cases involving murder). The following are the key dispositions, beginning at the least serious end of the continuum of severity.

1. Absolute Discharge

An absolute discharge amounts to a warning with no actual sanction being imposed. Sometimes it is given for a minor offence. The offender is deemed not to have been found guilty of the offence, and the Youth Court record becomes non-disclosable after one year (section 45(1)(d.1)).

2. Fine

A fine of not more than one thousand dollars may be imposed on young offenders. However, the court must consider how the young person will pay before imposing the fine (section 21(1)), and may allow time to pay the fine and set terms for its payment (section 20(1)(b)). The fine can also be discharged by earning credits in a specified work program, especially for youth who do not have the financial means to pay fines.

3. Compensation Order

A compensation order directs a young offender to compensate a victim for loss of or damage to his/her property (section 20(1)(c)). Again, the court must consider how the young person will pay before imposing the compensation order and may allow time to pay and set payment terms.

4. Restitution Order

A restitution order (section 20(1)(d)) requires a young person in possession of a victim's property to return it. Restitution orders are often confused with compensation orders, which are financial compensation for property lost that cannot be returned.

5. Compensation to Innocent Third Party

If the young person has sold a victim's property to an innocent person and a restitution order has been made, the young person may be required to compensate the third party for her/his loss (section 20(1)(e)). Again, the court must consider the method, timing, and terms of payment.

6. Community or Personal Service

The performance of community service (section 20(1)(g)) may be required at such time and on such terms as the court may direct. The court may not order more than 240 hours of community service and may not extend completion time to more than 12 months (section 21(8)). The order cannot interfere with the normal hours of work or education of the young person (section 21(7)(b)). This is a common disposition when there are no means of compensating an individual or the community for a loss by imposing a fine or a compensation order. The court can also make an order requiring the young person to perform community service for the victim, but only if the victim agrees to that condition (section 21(6)).

7. Prohibition, Seizure, or Forfeiture Order

A prohibition, seizure, or forfeiture order (section 20(1)(h)) allows the Youth Court to prohibit possession of firearms and order seizure and forfeiture of firearms or other prohibited weapons (*Criminal Code*, sections 109 and 110). The court may also make orders prohibiting young persons from driving after a finding of guilt of impaired driving or failing to provide a breathalyzer sample (*Criminal Code*, sections 253 and 254).

8. Probation Order

A probation order is a series of conditions imposed on a young offender for a period not exceeding two years (section 20(1)(j)). The maximum period is three years for a criminal offence punishable in ordinary court by life imprisonment. The two statutory (mandatory) conditions are that the young person must keep the peace and be of good behaviour and appear before the Youth Court when required by the court (section 23(1)(a)(b)). Other conditions may include reporting to a Youth Worker, residing at specified places or where directed by the Youth Worker, attending school, working, attending counselling, abstaining from the use of illicit drugs and alcohol, and attending special programs. The goals of probation are to monitor the young person within the community under the supervision of a Youth Worker, to secure the good conduct of the young person, and to prevent the young person from re-offending. A probation order comes into effect on the day it is made or following the expiration of a period of custody (section 23(7)). Breach of probation means violating its conditions without reasonable excuse and constitutes a new criminal offence.[27]

9. Custody

Custody was described near the beginning of this chapter. It can be either open or secure, and may be required for a period of up to two years unless the offence is one for which an adult faces a maximum penalty of life imprisonment, when the maximum penalty for a young person increases to three years.

For first-degree murder, the maximum sentence is six years custody, and is to be followed by a maximum of four years conditional supervision. For second-degree murder, the maximum sentence is four years custody and three years conditional supervision. Conditional supervision is akin to parole (release from prison under supervised conditions in the adult justice system), but it is court-ordered and more readily enforceable than a probation order. In cases where a young person is reaching the end of his/her disposition for murder, Crown Counsel may apply to have the custody period extended. If the court is satisfied that the young person is likely to commit an offence causing death or serious harm to another person, the custody period may be extended into the conditional supervision period. Unlike the adult system, there is no remission (reduction in time for good behaviour) or parole that applies to young offender custody dispositions, although the young person may be released early by way of review by the Youth Court.

The court may not sentence a young person to custody "unless the court considers a committal to custody to be necessary for the protection of society having regard to the seriousness of the offence and the circumstances in which it was committed and having regard to the needs and circumstances of the young person" (section 24(1)). The *Act*[28] also states that the Youth Court must take the following principles into account:

a) an order for custody shall not be used as a substitute for appropriate child protection, health or other social measures;

b) a young person who commits an offence that does not involve serious personal injury should be held accountable to the victim and to society through non-custodial dispositions whenever appropriate; and

c) that custody shall only be imposed when all available alternatives to custody that are reasonable in the circumstances have been considered.

Before making an order for custody, the court must consider the recommendations contained in a Youth Worker's pre-disposition report. The report includes the results of interviews with the young person, the parents and extended family, and (if applicable) the victim. It also includes information about the age, character, and maturity of the young person, plans to change her/his conduct, court history including alternative measures, availability of community resources, relationship between the young person and his/her parents, and his/her performance at school or work (section 14(2)).

A young person who turns 18 while in custody may serve the remainder of her/his sentence in a provincial adult institution, if upon application by youth custody authorities the Youth Court considers it to be in the public interest or in the best interests of the young person (section 24.5). Custody orders for more than one offence may specify that the periods of custody be served one after the other. However, the continuous combined duration of those dispositions must not exceed three years (section 20(4)), except in the case of murder.

As mentioned earlier, dispositions under the *Young Offenders (British Columbia) Act* are similar in nature to those imposed by the federal *Act*. The only difference lies in the fact that custody cannot be imposed under the provincial legislation unless the young person is charged with a breach of disposition. The maximum custodial disposition is 30 days. Dispositions under the provincial legislation are usually made in respect of provincial statute driving and liquor infractions.

D. Review of Disposition and Appeal

The review provisions of the *Act* take into consideration the progress made by young persons while under the terms of a Youth Court disposition. For those young persons who have been committed to custody for a period exceeding one year, there is a mandatory review of disposition after one year (section 28(1)). There are also review provisions for custody periods of less than one year (section 28(3)). The disposition may only be reviewed on the grounds that the young person has made sufficient progress to justify a change of disposition, or on the grounds that there has been a material change in circumstances, or that new services or programs are now available, or that there are greater opportunities for rehabilitation in the community, or other grounds the court considers appropriate (section 28(4)). After reviewing the disposition, the court may decide not to change the original disposition, may vary the disposition from secure to open custody, or may release the young person from custody to the terms of either a probation order or conditional supervision.

Because the procedures for reviews by the Youth Court are (like most legal procedures) complex and time consuming, there is little opportunity for most youth serving custodial dispositions to have their cases reviewed (section 28(17)). Most custodial dispositions are relatively short.

A young person may also obtain a review of a non-custodial disposition either in his /her own right after six months have expired or, with leave (permission) of the court, before six months have elapsed (section 32(1)). The grounds for review include material change in circumstances, inability to comply with the terms, hardship, or other grounds the court considers appropriate (section 32(2)). After reviewing the disposition, the court may make no changes, terminate the disposition, vary the disposition, or make a new disposition for the remainder of the term (section 32(7)) as long as the new term is no more onerous than the remaining portion of the disposition reviewed (section 32(8)).

The appeal process is used less frequently with young offenders than with adult offenders but the procedure is the same. Indictable offences are appealed to the Court of Appeal of the province and may involve an appeal of conviction or disposition. Appeals against conviction are of three types: an appeal on a question of law; an appeal with leave of the court on a question of mixed fact and law; or on any other ground with leave from the Court of Appeal (*Criminal Code*, section 675). Summary conviction offences are appealed to the Supreme Court of the province and may involve an appeal of conviction or sentence as a matter of right (*Criminal Code*, section 813).

E. Enforcement

A young person who fails to comply with the terms of a non-custodial disposition order (e.g., community service) or probation order may be charged with an offence under section 26 of the *Act*. This is the offence of breach of disposition and is a separate offence punishable by dispositions under section 20 of the *Act*. A young person who is convicted of an offence under section 26 faces the possibility of an open or secure custody disposition for a maximum of six months. A young person who escapes from custody or is unlawfully at large can be charged with that offence.

A breach of a disposition under section 26 (like any other offence) requires proof beyond a reasonable doubt. In contrast, a conditional supervision order may be suspended by youth correctional authorities and then cancelled (revoked) by the Youth Court, only if the court is satisfied on reasonable grounds that the young person has or "was about to breach" a condition (section 26.6). While this does not result in a new offence, the young person may be ordered to spend the remainder of the conditional supervision period in custody.

YOUTH COURT RECORDS AND INFORMATION SHARING

A central theme of the *Act* is the protection of the privacy of young persons accused of offences. This protection of privacy is based on the view that young people should be allowed to mature and integrate into society without being labelled as an offender for youthful indiscretions. Section 38 (1) prohibits the publication of any report by anyone that would serve to identify young persons as accused or convicted offenders. Thus, a well intentioned social worker, notifying parents of a young pedophile associating with children or putting an announcement in a school newsletter, would be committing an offence by contravening this section.

Special exemptions regarding publication and notification are contained in this provision, allowing limited forms of notification in cases where:

a) the young person has committed a serious personal injury offence and poses a risk of serious harm to others; and

b) disclosure of the information is relevant to avoiding that risk.

An application to a judge is necessary, so a helping professional wishing to release the name of a young offender in these circumstances should contact the police, Crown, or the Youth Worker.

Information sharing between helping professionals in the youth justice system is permitted only if necessary to:

a) ensure compliance by the young person with a court order (section 38(1.3)); or

b) for the safety of other persons.

Sharing of names of students who are young offenders at a school staff meeting is thus prohibited unless, for example, it is required to ensure school attendance under a condition of probation, and then only the particular teachers of the students should be informed. Thus, in school-based social service team meetings, any reticence by a Youth Worker to share information may not be a lack of interdisciplinary cooperation but more likely legal compliance. However, information received may be passed on if necessary for the purposes mentioned above.

Youth Workers are often instrumental in deciding when information sharing is necessary. For example, a Youth Worker might inform a school principal that a young person, who is a child sex offender, has a probation condition not to be on school grounds, and the school principal in turn might inform teachers of concerns about the youth's sexually inappropriate behaviour and the condition of probation in order to protect students. Information received by helping professionals from a person in the youth justice system must be kept securely and separately from other records, its recording minimized, and any recording destroyed when no longer required (section 38(1.15)).

A variety of persons may request records information. These include the young person, her/his counsel, the police, an administrator of alternative measures, the young person's parent or social worker who is the young person's guardian and acting as the parent, along with other persons engaged in the supervision or care of the young person (section 44.1). Thus, a Youth Worker preparing a pre-disposition report is entitled to access the young offender's records. Police can disclose information from these records to anyone (such as to witnesses of a crime) that is necessary "in the conduct of the investigation of an offence" (section 44.2).

After a period of time has elapsed, police and Youth Court records become "non-disclosable" to anyone and should be destroyed (shredded, burned, or electronically deleted). The time periods for destruction are as follows:

a) for offences dealt with by alternative measures - two years after the agreement;

b) for dispositions - one year after the finding of guilt for an absolute discharge and two years for a conditional discharge;

c) for offences that are summary conviction and have not been followed by further convictions - two years after the expiration of the disposition; and

d) for offences that are indictable - five years after the expiration of the disposition if there have been no further offences (section 45(1)).

The exception to this destruction requirement concerns records for serious offences (listed in the Schedule at the end of the *Act*) where the records can be kept by the police for longer periods in a special repository and used for criminal justice purposes only. Persons listed in the previous paragraph also have access to these records in repository where the young person has been subsequently charged with a serious offence (section 45.02).

These provisions of the *Act* are technically complex, so if a helping professional is in doubt about a course of action relating to records, he/she should consult a Youth Worker or a Crown Counsel. It is also important to remember that these are federal provisions and they therefore supercede provincial legislation, such as the British Columbia *Freedom of Information and Protection of Privacy Act*[29] (see Chapter 12).

COMMON QUESTIONS

1. <u>What happens to children under 12 who commit crimes?</u>

Children under 12 years of age may not be prosecuted for a criminal offence. However, if there appears to be concern that the child is not being properly supervised or is otherwise in need of protection, the police may refer the matter to child protection authorities. Under the *Child, Family and Community Service Act*,[30] the police are required to report offences by children under 12 that involve death or personal injury to child protection authorities.

2. <u>What is meant by a breach of probation?</u>

A breach of probation, an offence under section 26 of the *Young Offenders Act*, is a wilful failure or refusal to comply with the terms of a disposition order. The Youth Worker is normally responsible for reporting the circumstances to the police and is usually a key witness for the Crown in any prosecution.

3. <u>How is it different from a breach of undertaking?</u>

An undertaking (sometimes known as a "recognizance") is a procedure under section 145(3) of the *Criminal Code*, which is a promise to keep certain conditions while on bail. A failure to comply with an undertaking without lawful excuse is a serious matter. Usually an undertaking is imposed on a young person who is at risk of re-offending, and a breach of the undertaking means that the risk has increased. The young person will likely be arrested, held in youth detention, and will face in addition to the original offence a charge of breach of undertaking.

4. <u>What is the implication of hearings being held in public?</u>

Because the Youth Court is an open court, there is the possibility that the young person may become known. However, section 11 of the *Charter of Rights* guarantees a fair and public trial, and this right is balanced against the desire for anonymity, which is achieved by there being a ban on the publication of identity.

5. <u>What are the limits on media reporting?</u>

Under section 38 of the *Act*, it is a criminal offence to publish the name of a young person or in any other manner reveal her/his identity, except where the young person seeks the permission of the court to publish (often as a way to find witnesses for the defence), or where the young person is at large, considered dangerous to others, and publication is necessary to assist in his/her apprehension. In both cases, the Youth Court must decide whether publication is appropriate. Media publication of identity is also allowed when a young person is transferred to adult court.

6. <u>What should a helping professional do if a youth's parents are not available and the youth wants to make a statement to the police in the professional's presence?</u>

One of the reasons young persons are given the right to consult with an adult is to make them aware of their legal rights. The helping professional should therefore tell the young person that before making a statement she/he has the right to consult with a lawyer in order to have their legal rights explained. Urging the young person to confess should be avoided. It is best to advise the young person to remain silent until he/she has an opportunity to consult with a lawyer.

7. <u>If a helping professional is concerned about the welfare of a youth in a correctional facility, where does the professional go to complain?</u>

First, speak to the director of the youth custody centre and ask her/him to investigate the complaint. There is a ladder of protocol for complaints, which can be made available to the professional through any probation officer or youth custody centre. If the concern is urgent, the Ombudsman may investigate the complaint. The young person's lawyer may also be a good contact. Abuse complaints must also be reported to the Ministry for Children and Families.

8. <u>How does the youth justice system differ from the adult system?</u>

The public generally believes that young persons receive lighter dispositions than adults. In truth, young persons receive heavier sentences for less serious crimes than do adults for the same crime. Young persons, however, do receive lighter sentences for the more serious offences. It should be remembered that the adult justice system is punishment oriented, and the primary concern is the protection of the public. The youth justice system still has vestiges of the rehabilitation-based system, which existed under the *Juvenile Delinquents Act*.

Because of the built-in safeguards in the *Act*, a young person's rights are better protected than his/her adult counterpart. For example, a young person has the right to court-appointed counsel (section 11), and some protection against intimidation when she/he gives a statement to the police (section 56).

CONCLUSION

The non-legal professional can maintain a consistent profile within the youth justice system and greatly assist the Youth Court in making the best decisions for a young person. One apparent difficulty is to penetrate what appears to be a foreign, self-contained system. Therefore, the components of the adversarial system (see Chapter 1) need to be remembered. These include acknowledging that the role of the legal professional is to represent his/her client fully. The Crown Counsel's "client" is the State (or the interests of society) and the Crown must fully protect those interests, as well as protect the integrity of the criminal justice system. A defence counsel vigorously defends the interests of the young person. Even though our legal system is "adversarial," however, the Crown and defence counsel need not be at odds in every case. What is good for society may also be good for the young person. It is important to handle critical issues sensitively, particularly matters connected with bail and disposition.

The Youth Court must have access to all relevant information about available resources before it can make meaningful decisions concerning young persons. It may be the role of the helping professional to provide this information and assistance, which can make a difference in the youth justice process. However, the professional must be willing and able to spend time and energy appearing in Youth Court or making contact with the relevant legal professionals in the court process. Only then can the system have the information necessary to function properly.

RESOURCES

J. Hudson, J. Hornick & B. Burrows, eds., *Justice and the Young Offender in Canada* (Toronto: Thompson Educational Publishing, 1988).

R. R. Corrado, N. Bala, R. Linden & M. LeBlanc, eds., *Juvenile Justice in Canada: A Theoretical and Analytical Assessment* (Toronto: Butterworths, 1992).

A. Leschied, P. Jaffe & W. Willis, eds., *The Young Offenders Act: A Revolution in Canadian Juvenile Justice* (Toronto: University of Toronto Press, 1991).

N. Bala, *Young Offenders Law* (Concord, Ont.: Irwin Law, 1997).

END NOTES

1. *Young Offenders Act*, R.S.C. 1985, c. Y-1.
2. *Criminal Code of Canada*, R.S.C. 1985 c. C-46, Part XXV11 with subsequent amendments.
3. *Young Offenders Act*, note 1, section 20 (1) (k) and (k.1), (i) and (ii).
4. *Constitution Act*, 1867 (U.K.), 30 & 31 Vict., c. 3, section 91 (formerly *British North America Act*, 1867).

5. *Young Offenders(British Columbia) Act,* R.S.B.C. 1996 c. 494.

6. *Motor Vehicle Act,* R.S.B.C. 1996, c. 318.

7. *Controlled Drugs and Substances Act ,* S.C. 1996 c. 19.

8. *Juvenile Delinquents Act,* R.S.C. 1970, c.J-3.

9. *Child, Family and Community Service Act,* R.S.B.C. 1996, c. 47.

10. *Young Offenders Act,* section 3 (1) (h).

11. R. Corrado and A. Markwart, "The Prices of Rights and Responsibilities: An Examination of the Impacts of the *Young Offenders Act* in British Columbia" (1988) 7 Can. J. Fam. L. 94.

12. *R. v. M. (J.J.)* (1993) 2 S.C.R. 421.

13. *Young Offenders Act,* section (3)(1)(c.1).

14. *Canadian Charter of Rights and Freedoms,* Part I of the *Constitution Act, 1982,* being Schedule B of the *Canada Act 1982* (U.K.), 1982, c. 11 [hereinafter *Charter*].

15. The right to silence has been held by *R. v. Hebert* (1990), 57 C.C.C. (3d) 1 (S.C.C.) to be contained within section 7 of the *Charter*.

16. *R. v. Manninen* (1987), 34 C.C.C. (3d) 385 (S.C.C.).

17. *R. v. Hebert, supra,* note 15 at 38.

18. *Young Offenders Act, supra,* note 1 section 3(1)(e).

19. A report may also be ordered for the purposes of considering a continuation of custody (section 26.1 (1)), setting conditions of conditional supervision (section 26.2(1); cancelling or continuing suspension of conditional supervision (section 26.2(2); or authorizing disclosure of identity to specified persons (section 38(1.5).

20. *Young Offenders Act ,* section 13(1)(b).

21. *Mental Health Act,* R.S.B.C. 1996, c. 288.

22. *Idem,* section 16 (1) (1.01).

23. *Idem,* section 16.2.

24. *Idem,* section 4 (1) and (2).

25. *Criminal Code of Canada,* R.S.C. 1985, c. C-46, section 515(10).

26. The specific wording is: "that his detention is necessary in the public interest or for the protection or safety of the public, having regard to all the circumstances including any substantial likelihood that the accused will, if he is released from custody, commit a criminal offence or interfere with the administration of justice." *Criminal Code,* R.S.C. 1985, c. C-46, section 515 (10)(b).

27. *Criminal Code,* section 733.1.

28. *Young Offenders Act,* section 24 (1.1).

29. *Freedom of Information and Protection of Privacy Act,* R.S.B.C. 1996, c. 165.

30. *Child, Family and Community Service Act,* R.S.B.C. 1996, c. 46 section 15.

Chapter 9

MENTAL HEALTH: DISORDER AND INCAPABILITY

Gerrit W. Clements

INTRODUCTION

Knowledge of key aspects of mental health law and process is crucially important for professionals in the mental health field and in related professions like family counselling. The following material will outline the procedures used to admit mentally disordered individuals to psychiatric facilities and the rights guaranteed these individuals before and after admission. Similarly, procedures for having individuals declared mentally incapable will be described.

The chapter will focus on three British Columbia statutes. It will describe the law of civil commitment of mentally disordered persons currently found in the *Mental Health Act*.[1] It will also discuss the *Power of Attorney Act*,[2] which allows individuals to appoint "attorneys" or agents to care for their property in anticipation of future mental incapability. Finally, it will discuss the *Patients Property Act*,[3] which provides mechanisms to declare people mentally incapable of caring for themselves or their property.

Throughout this chapter, the word "patient" will be used instead of "client" because "patient" is the word used in the legislation. The law is stated as of June 1, 1997. See Addendum, 1998 at the end of the Conclusion section of this chapter.

MENTAL HEALTH ACT: AN OVERVIEW

The *Mental Health Act of British Columbia* sets out terms under which patients may be treated in a psychiatric facility. The *Act* identifies how patients may be admitted and released, what treatment facilities are available, and who has the authority to consent to treatment provided.

I. Definition of "Mentally Disordered"

No one can be admitted as a patient to a psychiatric facility under the *Act* unless "mentally disordered." Section 1 of the *Mental Health Act* states that this "means a mentally retarded or mentally ill person." There is a further definition of "mentally retarded person" but the *Mental Health Act* is not normally used in such cases unless the individual suffers from mental illness as well. The definition of a "mentally ill person" reads as follows:

a) a person who is suffering from a disorder of the mind that seriously impairs the person's ability to react appropriately to his/her environment or to associate with others; and

b) that requires medical treatment or makes care, supervision, and control of the person necessary for the person's protection or for the protection of others.

The requirement for the finding of "a disorder of the mind" usually means, in this province, that the physician diagnoses the person as mentally disordered (by referring to a diagnostic category in the *Diagnostic and Statistical Manual of Mental Disorders,*[4] a publication of the American Psychiatric Association). Increasingly, however, a shift in emphasis is being advocated from primary reliance on such diagnostic labels to a conclusion by the physician that the person has difficulty functioning in her/his situation in life as a result of the mental disorder.

II. The Admission and Detention Process

There are two basic forms of admission into an authorized psychiatric facility: voluntary and involuntary. Initially, however a summary of the kinds of facilities that provide treatment for the mentally disordered patient will be helpful:

A. Psychiatric Facilities

There are two types of psychiatric facilities in British Columbia as defined in the *Mental Health Act*: "provincial mental health facilities" and "psychiatric units." There are some 30 hospitals in the province which have been designated as psychiatric units where initial admissions take place. The head of a psychiatric unit who is usually, but not always, a physician is referred to as "officer in charge."

The Minister has also designated certain provincial mental health facilities, which are headed by "directors." Some of these are specialized facilities. The Forensic Psychiatric Institute cares primarily for individuals found unfit to stand trial for a criminal offence or not criminally responsible, on account of mental disorder, of a criminal offence. The Maples in Burnaby provides mental health services for minors, often those on probation for criminal offences. The Queen Alexandra Centre for Children in Victoria also provides, among other things, psychiatric treatment and care to minors. Finally, Riverview Hospital in Vancouver is undoubtedly the best known provincial mental health facility. It functions mainly as a referral facility for patients who require long-term psychiatric care.

For almost all purposes, the *Mental Health Act* treats provincial mental health facilities and psychiatric units the same. Whenever, in the following pages, "psychiatric facility" is used, this should be taken to mean a reference to both provincial mental health facilities and psychiatric units. Similarly, references to "directors" of facilities are meant to include "officers in charge."

B. Voluntary Admission

There are two categories of voluntary admission: the purely "voluntary" psychiatric patient (who is not referred to in any statute) and the "informal" patient (section 20).

1. Purely Voluntary Admission

For various reasons many hospitals do not use the "informal" patient category of admission, and many voluntary patients are, therefore, admitted at their own request and sign the usual hospital admission and consent forms. They can obviously leave again when they want to, unless the hospital feels that their status should be changed to "involuntary." Before admitting a person voluntarily, the admitting physician would, of course, have to be satisfied, for professional and ethical reasons, that the person needed psychiatric treatment.

2. Informal Admission

There are still many psychiatric facilites that use the "informal" patient admission criteria. The procedure is found in section 20 and requires that the director of the facility is satisfied "that the person has been examined by a physician who is of the opinion that the person is a mentally disordered person" (the definition discussed earlier). If an informal patient wishes to leave, the administration is advised of this so that arrangements can be made for discharge unless, again, the patient should be detained involuntarily. Anyone aged 16 or over can apply for admission and give consent to be treated, but children under the age of 16 require a parent, guardian, or nearest relative to request admission and to consent to treatment. The *Act* ensures that young patients are not left in a psychiatric facility simply because parents want to keep them there or do not want them back at home.[5] Patients under 16 have the right to periodic medical examinations, a review panel hearing, and appropriate discharge if found to be no longer mentally disordered (see sections 20 and 21).

C. Involuntary Admission

Involuntary patients are those admitted to a psychiatric facility without their consent. There are basically two forms of involuntary admission: "regular" and emergency.

1. "Regular" Involuntary Admission

Under section 22 of the *Act*, involuntary admission requires two medical certificates. Each physician who completes a medical certificate must have examined the patient no more than 14 days before admission. The certificates should be signed before the patient is detained and treated. In practice, the certificates are often filled out later, even though the legislation does not allow any "grace period" for completion. It is common for a relative or friend to take a person to hospital, where the first certificate is made out by a casualty officer in the Emergency Department fairly soon after arrival. However, the second certificate is often not completed until the next day or even later. Although people are being detained illegally until the second certificate is signed, hospital staff frequently conclude that the potential harm to the patient or to others outweighs this slight legal risk. All reasonable efforts should, of course, be made to obtain a second certificate as soon as possible.

The basic requirement for a valid certificate is that each physician must have examined the person and come to the conclusion that the person is mentally disordered, and "requires medical treatment in a provincial mental health facility [psychiatric unit] and requires care, supervision and control in a provincial mental health facility [psychiatric unit] for the person's own protection or for the protection of others." (Underline added for emphasis.)

Note that before a person can be involuntarily admitted, detained, and treated, she/he must require both "medical treatment" and "care, supervision, and control," unlike the voluntary patient who may be admitted for either purpose. Strictly speaking, then, involuntary patients can only be admitted if they have a treatable mental disorder. This is an important distinction for patients who may need to be detained for "protection" reasons but whose mental problems such as the personality disorder commonly known as psychopathy or sociopathy may not be treatable. British Columbia's criteria in this area differ from those of most other provinces. It is also of note, in this respect, that the British Columbia Supreme Court has decided that an organic brain disorder (brain damage) may satisy the definition of "mental disorder" and the committal criteria in the *Mental Health Act*.[6]

In 1993, the British Columbia Supreme Court in *McCorkell v. Riverview Hospital*[7] clarified the meaning of the word "protection," which had previously been the subject of much controversy. Influenced by recent trends in other provinces and academic opinion with respect to the impact the *Canadian Charter of Rights and Freedoms* would have in this respect, it had been forcefully argued that "protection" means protection from physical harm only. The culmination of the debate as to whether this was the only correct interpretation came in a *Charter* challenge to British Columbia's civil committal criteria. The argument was made in court that these criteria violate, in particular, section 7 of the *Charter*, which protects the "right to life, liberty and security of the person." However, rather than concluding that the British Columbia criteria are too vague and that the *Charter* demands "'dangerousness' as the only permissible criteria" for involuntary committal, the court found "that they strike a reasonable balance." This balance is "between the rights of the individual to be free from restraint by the state and society's obligation to help and protect the mentally ill."[8] In the end, the court decided that "protection" means protection from "serious harm" which, like in the Manitoba legislation, "can include harms that relate to the social, family, vocational, or financial life of the patient as well as to the patient's physical condition."[9]

Although hospital personnel are often frustrated with seemingly petty demands for accuracy in *Mental Health Act* forms, the sober truth is that damages have had to be paid (although usually nominal) when a person was clearly certifiable but admitted on the basis of two certificates, one of which was invalid.[10]

This can happen, for example, under section 22, where certain physicians are disqualified from signing valid certificates, primarily those who work as partners or employees of physicians completing the other certificate. The other point to note is that medical certificates become invalid for the purpose of involuntary admission "on the 15th clear day after the date on which the physician <u>examined</u> the person . . ." (underline added for emphasis). "Clear" means[11] that the first and last days must be excluded. A very common misunderstanding is that the certificate becomes invalid on the 15th day after the date of the certificate. The Act, however, refers to the <u>date of examination</u>, which may or may not be the date of the certificate.

2. Emergency Involuntary Admission

There are two sections in the *Mental Health Act* that provide for "emergency" situations. Section 27 allows a physician who is in a community where no other qualified (see the discussion in the paragraph above) physician is available to complete one certificate. On this basis the patient can be transferred to the closest psychiatric facility. That institution then has the right to examine and treat the person for no longer than 72 hours. In the meantime, a second medical certificate must have been completed.

Section 28 covers situations where immediate intervention is necessary or it is not possible to have the person examined by a physician without taking special measures. The section allows a police officer or constable to take a person "into custody" if, based on "personal observation or information received from others," the person is "acting in a manner likely to endanger his/her own safety or that of others <u>and</u> is apparently suffering from mental disorder." The person may then be taken to a physician, which, in practice, means the Emergency Department of a hospital. A physician who is satisfied that the criteria for involuntary admission apply (criteria for the police officer are stricter than those for the physician), may certify and admit the person as an involuntary patient for up to 72 hours.

Similar provisions also permit an application to British Columbia provincial court for a warrant to apprehend and admit a patient who is mentally disordered and "dangerous to be at large" when normal procedures "cannot be utilized without dangerous delay."

In both situations where the police or court have used their powers, a patient may be admitted, detained, examined, and treated for 72 hours. Before the 72 hours have expired, the normal certification procedures must have been followed or else the person is discharged. It is clear that in both "emergency" situations, the criteria are more restrictive than those found in section 22.

One final, significant point of difference between the admission categories should be mentioned. Only "informal" patients admitted to provincial mental health facilities must pay[12] charges for long-term care, treatment, and maintenance, although a committee may reduce or cancel those charges. This is an obvious disincentive for people to be admitted as "informal" patients.

D. Detention

Under section 23 of the *Act*, involuntarily admitted patients may only be detained for up to one month and must then be discharged unless authority for the patient's detention has been renewed. The reasons for renewal are detailed in a report written by the director or an authorized physician. Initial detention may be renewed for another month, and after that for three months and then six months at a time (see section 24). Although the *Act* does not provide any criteria to be applied at renewal time, in the McCorkell case, (see section C1 above), the British Columbia Supreme Court came to the conclusion that the criteria that should be applied by the review panel are the same as the initial admission criteria.[13] It seems logical that this should also be the case with examinations for renewal of detention.

III. Consent To Treatment

Ordinarily, medical treatment cannot be administered without the informed consent of the patient. In other words, the patient is entitled to know and understand what kind of treatment will be administered as well as the risks and benefits of the treatment, and to agree to this treatment. Obviously, voluntary patients are entitled, and required, to consent before any treatment can be provided. But in the case of involuntary patients, the *Mental Health Act* deals with the issue of consent in an extremely cursory way. The *Act* seems to indicate that involuntary patients have no say in the treatment they will receive. Section 8 states that a director may sign consent forms for the treatment of involuntary patients, while section 31 states that "treatment authorized by the director is deemed to be given with the consent of the person."

The practice is somewhat different, however. Form 5, prescribed under the *Mental Health Act Regulation* and entitled "Consent for Treatment, Involuntary Patient" allows an involuntary patient to sign, as an indication of consent, and all the attending physician has to do is certify that the patient was capable of understanding the nature of the authorization at the time it was signed. If the patient does not sign, the director signs instead. The physician then certifies that the involuntary patient was incapable of appreciating the nature of treatment and/or his/her need for it and was therefore incapable of giving consent. However, the question arises regarding the patient who is capable, but who refuses to consent. The form does not provide for this situation, but in all likelihood the patient's refusal would be taken to indicate an incapability of "appreciating the nature of treatment and [the] need for it." The director would then go ahead and provide consent. It should be remembered that the consent at issue here is to authorize psychiatric treatment as opposed to other medical treatment. This is clear from Section 8:

> A director shall ensure that each patient in a [psychiatric] facility is provided with professional services, care and treatment appropriate to the patient's condition and appropriate to the function of the [psychiatric] facility and, for those purposes, may sign consent to treatment forms . . .

Needless to say, the law of consent to psychiatric treatment must balance the individual's freedom of choice against society's need to care for its members effectively, which creates extremely controversial issues. The mental health acts in other provincial jurisdictions have come up with various legislative solutions to this problem. The debate in British Columbia as to whether the consent provisions of the British Columbia *Mental Health Act* should be amended and, if so, how, particularly in view of the *Canadian Charter of Rights and Freedoms*, is ongoing.

IV. Discharge Procedures for Involuntary Patients

An involuntary patient may be discharged at the end of each of the renewal periods outlined in section II D above, or in any other case, when the attending physician or the director concludes that the patient's condition no longer satisfies the committal criteria. However, a patient is also entitled to have the detention reviewed by a review panel or a court and, in certain circumstances, may be eligible for an extended (or conditional) leave.

A. Review Panel Hearing (sections 24 and 25)

Involuntary patients, or someone on their behalf, can apply to a review panel to determine whether continued detention is justified. Applications may be made at any time during the initial detention period or any subsequent renewal, and a hearing must be held within either 14 or 28 days of the application, depending on how long the patient has already been detained. The chair can convene an earlier hearing if it appears to be in the best interest of the patient or if new information becomes available.

The panel consists of three people: a chairperson appointed by the Minister of Health; a physician appointed by the facility; and a person appointed by the patient. Patients may appoint anyone except themselves or family members. No criteria are given to guide the review panel in making its decision but, because of the McCorkell decision (see section II C1 above), the initial admission criteria apply. The composition of review panels in British Columbia is unique in Canada.

B. Application to the Court

Under section 33 of the *Act*, patients may apply to the Supreme Court of British Columbia for an order prohibiting their admission or requiring their discharge from a psychiatric facility. The application, which may be made by patients themselves or someone acting on their behalf, must be based on the argument that there is not sufficient reason under the Act for their admission or detention. Involuntary patients also have the right to apply to court for a writ of *habeas corpus* (a rarely used procedure asking the court to look at the documents authorizing a patient's detention in hospital under the *Mental Health Act*, to determine if the detention is lawful) and other possible prerogative writ remedies to secure their release.

C. Extended or Conditional Leave

Another controversial provision of the *Act* allows a psychiatric facility to release involuntary patients "on leave for designated purposes for stipulated periods of time on the conditions the director may specify to the care of relatives of the patient or others capable of assuming responsibility for the patient's care" (section 37). Section 39 clarifies that while patients are on leave, the authority to detain continues and patients may be recalled to the psychiatric facility and apprehended by a warrant if necessary. These provisions are frequently used to "try patients out" in the community, reserving the right to recall patients who violate their conditions. Examples of conditions include requirements that patients stay in a designated mental health boarding home or care facility or continue to take prescribed medication.

Many patient advocates consider these provisions unfair, arguing that if patients need protection or society needs protection from them, patients should remain within the facility. The position advanced by patients' families is usually that patients are often well enough to be discharged, but only to another environment where some protection is available. They argue that unless, for example, a patient's compliance with medication necessary for her/him to be able to live in an environment other than a psychiatric facility is monitored and enforced, many patients will be re-admitted as involuntary patients over and over again.

D. Patient Leaving Without Authorization

If involuntary patients leave a psychiatric facility without an authorized discharge, there are procedures in place for returning them. If the police can apprehend patients within 48 hours of escape, there is no warrant necessary, although the police often still require one. Under section 41 the director of the facility may issue a warrant for the patient's apprehension and return but the warrant must be issued and enforced within 60 days or the patient is deemed discharged. Nevertheless, a warrant can be issued in serious cases where the patient is "charged with an offence or liable to imprisonment or considered by the director to be dangerous to himself/herself or others."

This concludes our discussion of the most important provisions of the *Mental Health Act*.

When patients enter a psychiatric facility they often lose touch with the outside world and need help managing their personal affairs. Others are not as mentally ill as to require hospitalization or may have conditions that are not treatable, but they may still require protection. The scope of this book does not permit an introduction to the relationship between mental disability and the law of contracts, property, wills and estates, marriage and divorce, and the like.[14] Nonetheless, this section will provide a brief overview of the legal procedures for:

a) declaring individuals mentally incapable of making personal decisions or looking after their property; and

b) transferring responsibility for their affairs.

I. When Mental Disability is Anticipated: *Power of Attorney Act*

There are some circumstances (a degenerative mental illness, for example) when patients may anticipate a time when they will be incapable of looking after personal business such as banking or paying bills.

Under the *Power of Attorney Act* a document can be drawn up appointing an agent or "attorney" (not to be confused with "lawyer") to act on behalf of the donor (i.e., the person who appoints the attorney). The act of the attorney then legally becomes the act of the donor. The power of attorney can be very broad, or can be very narrow and give the attorney banking powers only, for example. Incidentally, it is useful to know that certain banks refuse to honour powers of attorney unless they are signed on the bank's own power of attorney form.

At the time the donor appoints the attorney, the donor must have the mental capacity to understand the effect of the power of attorney. Section 8 of the *Act* allows this authority to continue even if the donor becomes mentally incapable as long as the document states that this power of attorney may be exercised during any subsequent mental infirmity (known as an "enduring power of attorney").

Although the *Act* does not refer to it, most lawyers believe that any power of attorney can be a so-called "springing" power that can be called into effect upon a certain specified event, such as the donor becoming mentally incapable. The best strategy is to leave the power of attorney with the lawyer or notary who prepared it with specific instructions not to release it unless, for example, the family physician has declared in writing that the person has become mentally incapable of doing the acts contemplated in the document. At the present time, these powers of attorney can only be used to authorize attorneys to care for property, as opposed to personal decisions such as medical treatment. Although enduring powers of attorney for personal and health care purposes may be very useful, there is currently no law in British Columbia, unlike many other Canadian jurisdictions, that can be relied on to make them legally enforceable.

II. Procedures for Managing the Affairs of Mentally Incapable Patients

The *Patients Property Act* sets out the procedures for declaring people incapable of managing themselves and/or their affairs. It is difficult to find anyone who is satisfied with the provisions of this *Act* (see Chapter 10). The *Act* provides two separate procedures for declaring or certifying an individual mentally incapable.

A. Certificate Resulting in The Public Trustee Taking Over Management of Affairs

This procedure is commonly misunderstood and possibly due to the plain words of the legislation, poses problems from a human rights point of view. For example, section 1 of the *Act* suffers from a lack of detail. Under it, the director of a psychiatric facility may sign a certificate declaring a person ". . . because of mental infirmity arising from disease, age or otherwise, incapable of managing his or her affairs." Under section 6 the Public Trustee automatically becomes the "committee of the patient." The word "committee" (emphasis on the last syllable) is archaic, meaning trustee or guardian. The extremely terse language disguises the fact that, as a result of one certificate, people can lose control over all their property, although this procedure cannot be used to declare them incapable of making personal decisions.

In practice, this procedure has some advantages. There is no cost involved and the procedure can be done quickly, which may be very important when mentally incapable people are squandering their property or are being taken advantage of by others. It is the policy of the Office of the Public Trustee not to accept any certificate of incapability unless there have been two assessments of incapability to make financial decisions. One of these is initially done by a physician (preferably the person's own physician) and the other by the director or staff person of a psychiatric facility (including a community mental health centre).

In addition, the patient is informed of the purpose of the examinations. Previously, it had not been uncommon for people not even to realize that they had been certified as incapable until the Public Trustee or the bank notified them.

Also, under the policy, there is a requirement to determine whether informal arrangements such as a special agreement with the person's financial institution as opposed to a certificate may be sufficient. As well, there are much greater efforts to obtain relevant information from care providers, families, and friends than was previously the case.

It is important to understand that, to be certified as mentally incapable under this section, an individual does not have to reside in a psychiatric facility. Certification in the community occurs frequently.

B. Application to the Court

Although the other available procedure, application to the court, appears to be much fairer, it too has its drawbacks.[15] Section 2 of the *Act* allows anyone (usually a near relative or the Office of the Public Trustee) to apply for a court order declaring that the subject of the application is "because of mental infirmity arising from disease, age or otherwise, or disorder or disability of mind arising from the use of drugs, incapable of managing his or her affairs or incapable of managing himself or herself or his or her affairs."

The applicant must present two affidavits from medical practitioners stating that for these reasons the person is incapable of looking after her/his property, person, or both. The court may not be satisfied with affidavits only and may order a trial of the issue and further medical examinations, but this rarely happens.

Of course, the subject of the application, the patient, is entitled to oppose it and to receive notice of the time and place of the hearing. Often, however, the courts use their power to dispense with notice because they decide that this ". . . would be injurious to that person's health" or ". . . for any other reason . . . inadvisable in the interests of that person."

Usually, the applicant is appointed "committee of the estate" or "committee of the person" or both. If no one is appointed by the court, the Public Trustee automatically becomes the committee. The subject of the application becomes known as a "patient," but for the purposes of the *Patients Property Act* only.

It is extremely important to understand that certification as an involuntary patient under the *Mental Health Act*, by itself, will not result in that person being declared mentally incapable and a "patient" under the *Patients Property Act*, although a declaration may happen at the same time or later. When involuntary patients are discharged under the *Mental Health Act*, their status as "patient" under any *Patients Property Act* declaration ceases. However, as if this were not complicated enough, under those circumstances the Public Trustee, under section 11, "may retain the control and administration of the person's estate, so long as it is in the Public Trustee's opinion necessary or desirable in the interests of that person or of the person's estate." As one would expect, the director of the psychiatric facility can also declare people capable again and the court may give such an order.

Two other provisions of the *Patients Property Act* should be mentioned. Section 15 gives the committee of the patient's estate all the rights, privileges, and powers the patient would have if of "full age and of sound and disposing mind." The committee of the person of a patient has custody of the patient which, in practice, is interpreted to include making personal decisions and consenting to health care on behalf of the patient. Section 18 requires the committee to exercise his or her powers for the benefit of the patient and family, in light of their circumstances and needs and the nature and value of the property.

As mentioned in the chapter on Physical and Mental Disabilities, the *Representation Agreement Act* and *Adult Guardianship Act*, which were enacted by the British Columbia legislature in 1993, have not yet been implemented. While this chapter was being written (June 1, 1997), the government had not yet announced a firm implementation date.

COMMON QUESTIONS

1. <u>Both the *Mental Health Act* and the *Patients Property Act* seem to contemplate action by physicians only. What can a nurse, psychologist, or social worker do?</u>

Clients who are apparently mentally disordered can always be referred to physicians for examination. If a physician's cooperation cannot be secured, the police can be asked to apprehend a person under the emergency provisions of section 28 of the *Mental Health Act*, or make an application to the court for a warrant. Sometimes, the police will mistakenly take the position that they must observe the person "acting out" before an apprehension can be made. But section 28 clearly states they can act on the basis of information received from others. Similarly, individuals who appear to be mentally incapable of looking after their property should be referred to a community mental health centre.

2. <u>Why are directors of psychiatric facilities unwilling to give consent to needed medical treatment as opposed to psychiatric treatment for an involuntary patient?</u>

These officials should always refuse to give consent for non-psychiatric treatment since they cannot be substitute decision makers. Sections 8 and 31 of the *Mental Health Act* allow the director to authorize psychiatric treatment only. Admission as an involuntary patient does not take away the person's right to refuse or consent to other medical treatment. If upon assessment the patient is found to be capable to consent but refuses, the medical treatment simply cannot be administered. If the person is found to be incapable, the only procedure currently available under legislation is to apply to the court for the appointment of a "committee of person" (a person appointed under the *Patients Property Act*). However, this is both time consuming and expensive. Since it would be unethical not to treat just because no informed consent can be obtained, health care providers frequently satisfy themselves that the patient is not capable of giving consent. In addition, it must be clear that, without the health care, the patient's life or health is going to be in jeopardy. It is essential in non-emergency cases to canvass the views of near relatives and others close to the patient. If all this is documented, the health care can be provided without undue concern for liability. This process is, generally speaking, also consistent with the provisions of the *Health Care (Consent) and Care Facility (Admission) Act*,[16] which at this point does not yet have the force of law.

One main advantage of this *Act* would be to provide a mechanism in the form of a Health Care Review Board that could be called upon to settle disputes. Since that is not yet available, it may sometimes be necessary to disregard the opinion of a relative, particularly if that individual does not seem to have recent knowledge of what the patient, if capable, would have wanted or of what is in the best interests of the patient. Clear clinical and ethical support for a treatment decision is essential. Above all, the law is clear that emergency treatment must be provided except where it is shown beyond a doubt that the patient had taken all possible steps to ensure that the particular health care <u>not</u> be provided, regardless of the consequences. See also question and answer 12.

3. <u>What, if anything, must people be told upon admission as involuntary patients to a psychiatric facility?</u>

Section 6 of the *Mental Health Act Regulation* reads that the director (practically speaking, a nurse or another staff person):

shall, immediately on admission or transfer or as soon as the person is capable of comprehension, inform the person of

a) the reasons for detention,

b) the person's right to retain and instruct counsel without delay,

c) the person's right to have the validity of the detention determined by way of *habeas corpus*, and

d) [the right to a review panel hearing and to apply to the court].

These provisions largely parallel those found in section 10 of the *Charter*. If on admission the patient was not or may not have been "capable of comprehension" it is imperative that the information be given or repeated at the time the patient is likely to understand.

4. <u>Is there any specific reference to electroshock or electroconvulsive treatment (ECT) in British Columbia law?</u>

No. The general consent provisions in sections 8 and 31 of the *Mental Health Act* therefore apply. Because there is still some controversy surrounding ECT, it is important to keep the patient and family well informed and to involve at least one psychiatric consultant in addition to the attending physician.

5. <u>Since the *Mental Health Act* does not mention confidentiality and access to information, what basic rules apply to psychiatric patients?</u>

Those rules should be the same as the ones that apply to non-psychiatric patients. The *Freedom of Information and Protection of Privacy Act* [17] (see Chapter 12), applies to health care provided in all settings to which the *Mental Health Act* applies. This excludes physicians' offices. However, the basic rules regarding confidentiality and access to information apply here as well. This means that physicians must not normally disclose information unless their patients have given consent or unless disclosure is necessary so that other health care professionals can provide further care and treatment.

Regarding access to information about their treatment, as discussed in Chapter 12, the Supreme Court of Canada in *McInerney v. MacDonald* [18] confirmed that, with certain important exceptions related to the likelihood of disclosure causing harm to the patient or to others, all patients are entitled to have access to their own health care records. In the United States the courts have decided that confidentiality must be breached in cases where a patient informs the therapist of an intention to kill or physically harm someone. [19] Since it is likely that other Canadian courts would follow the reasoning of the Alberta courts in *Tanner v. Norys*[20] and *Wenden v. Trikha*[21] it is almost certain that a therapist practicing here should breach confidentially in order to warn, or otherwise protect, a potential victim.

6. <u>Can transactions be set aside when someone has taken advantage of another person because of a mental condition?</u>

There are specific laws covering fraud and unconscionable transactions, but section 20 of the *Patients Property Act* provides further protections for mentally incapable individuals. Fundamentally, it allows reversal of any transaction (ie. a sale, a gift, a contract) by someone who is later certified or ordered mentally incapable in situations where the deal was unfair ("not made for full and valuable consideration") or the person receiving the property "had notice at the time ... of the mental condition of the person." In those circumstances, the committee could have the transaction set aside.

7. <u>What must patients, whether voluntary or involuntary, be told about proposed psychiatric treatment for their mental disorder?</u>

The standard of disclosure of information is the same as for any other patients. They must be told, objectively speaking, what any individual facing the same situation would want to be told. Patients are entitled to know the nature of their condition, what the course of the illness will be with and without the treatment, and what the anticipated nature and consequences of the treatment are.

8. <u>Can involuntary patients refuse psychiatric treatment?</u>

No. If they refuse to sign the Consent to Treatment form, it will in practice be assumed that they are incapable of "appreciating the nature of treatment and [the] need for it" and the director of the facility will sign the form instead.

9. <u>What are the rules for admission of minor patients to a psychiatric facility?</u>

Persons of any age can be admitted "involuntarily." Anyone of the age of 16 or over can be admitted "informally" and give consent to treatment. However, such a person cannot be "voluntarily" admitted unless it has been determined that the person "understands the nature and consequences and reasonably foreseeable benefits and risks of the health care" and it has been determined that the treatment is in the person's "best interests," in accordance with section 17 of the *Infants Act*.[22]

The rules regarding "informal" admission of patients under 16 (who must be admitted by their parents) are that they have the same rights as involuntary patients. This means that they or someone on their behalf may apply for a review panel hearing to determine whether they are "mentally disordered." This sometimes leads to conflict with parents who would like psychiatric facilities to admit and detain "conduct-disordered" young persons.

10. <u>Can "mentally retarded" individuals be committed under the *Mental Health Act*?</u>

Although the possibility exists under the *Act*, in practice such persons must be mentally ill as well before they are committed to psychiatric facilities.

11. <u>What can be done if "voluntary" or "informal" patients leave a psychiatric facility before they can be certified as "involuntary" patients because they require continued detention and treatment?</u>

If two physicians had examined such a patient within the last 14 days and concluded that certification as an involuntary patient was possible, they can sign certificates allowing return of the patient to the facility. If that is not the case, examination should take place, which may only be possible by having the police or the courts use their "emergency" powers.

12. <u>Are "living wills" legal?</u>

Since there is no law against preparing and signing a living will, the better question to ask is whether they are legally enforceable, i.e., whether health care professionals must comply with them. A living will is an advance health care directive. Such a directive can be an "instruction" directive, like a living will, which attempts to give instructions as to what health care should or should not happen if the individual is not capable of doing this himself/herself at the time. Alternatively, it can be a "proxy" directive that appoints someone to make decisions on behalf of the person. Most Canadian jurisdictions have legislation that legally validates either "instruction" directives or "proxy" directives, or both. In British Columbia, the legislation that would make advance directives legally enforcable is found in the *Representation Agreement Act* and the *Health Care (Consent) and Care Facility (Admission) Act* (see Chapter 10). While this legislation is not yet in effect, it is a reasonable practice to follow advance directives unless it is clear that the individual has subsequently changed her/his mind, or could not possibly have foreseen the particular situation or likely outcome. However, these *Acts* make it clear that certification as an involuntary patient under the *Mental Health Act* supersedes any advance directives or decision making by family members.

This reasonable practice is partly based on the strong likelihood that British Columbia courts would follow the reasoning of the Ontario Court of Appeal in *Malette v. Shulman*[23] and *Fleming v. Reid and Gallagher*,[24] which recognized advance directives in situations where Jehovah's Witnesses refuse blood transfusions in advance and where involuntary psychiatric patients refuse treatment, both in present and for the future.

CONCLUSION

This chapter has discussed the current British Columbia law on civil commitment of the mentally disordered and procedures for appointing someone to care for the property and the person of a mentally incapacitated individual.

Addendum of September, 1998. The provincial government made substantial amendments to the *Mental Health Act* by means of the *Mental Health Amendment Act* 1998 (Bill 22). These amendments include changes in the following areas: admitting procedures; committal and renewal of committal criteria; review panel jurisdiction; criteria for extended or conditional leave; patient's rights notification; and entitlement to a second medical opinion with respect to appropriateness of treatment. These amendments have not yet taken effect. Before this can happen new Regulations need to be drafted and circulated for consultation purposes. At the end of this process the Lieutenant Governor in Council (cabinet) will adopt the Regulations and set a date for both the amendments to the *Act* and the new Regulations to come into force. This process is expected to take until at least the end of 1998.

RESOURCES

G. W. Clements, Ethical and Legal Issues: "A Legal Perspective." In E. Sawyer & M. Stephenson, eds., *The Issues and Challenges for Long-Term Care* (Ottawa: CHA Press, 1995).

R. M. Gordon & S. N. Verdun-Jones, *Adult Guardianship Law in Canada* (Toronto: Carswell, 1992).

G. B. Robertson, *Mental Disability and the Law in Canada*, 2nd ed. (Toronto: Carswell, 1994).

H. Savage & C. McKague, *Mental Health Law in Canada* (Toronto: Butterworths, 1987).

Guide to the Mental Health Act, (Victoria, British Columbia Ministry of Health, 1997).

END NOTES

1. *Mental Health Act*, R.S.B.C. 1996, c. 288.
2. *Power of Attorney Act*, R.S.B.C. 1996, c. 370.
3. *Patients Property Act*, R.S.B.C. 1996, c. 349.
4. American Psychiatric Association. *Diagnostic and Statistical Manual of Mental Disorders* (4th ed., revised). Washington, D.C. 1994.
5. See question and answer 9.
6. *Greggor v. Director of Riverview Hospital* (March 31, 1992, B.C.S.C. Newbury, J.) (unreported).
7. *McCorkell v. Director of Riverview Hospital* (1993), 81 B.C.L.R. (2d) 273 (S.C.) at 300.
8. *Ibid.*
9. *Ibid.* at p. 299.
10. See, for example, *Ketchum v. Hislop* (1984), 54 B.C.L.R. 327 (S.C.).
11. In accordance with the *Interpretation Act*, R.S.B.C. 1996, c. 230, section 25.
12. See *Mental Health Act*, supra, note 1, ss 9 and 10 and *Mental Health Regulation*, R.B.C. Reg 155/97, section 6.
13. *Supra*, note 7 at p. 302.
14. For a discussion of these and other areas, see G.B. Robertson, *Mental Disability and the Law in Canada*, 2nd ed. (Toronto: Carswell, 1994).
15. See, for example, G. Davies & L. Taylor, "Private Committeeship in British Columbia: A Study of Due Process" (1989) 8 Can. J. Fam. L. 185.
16. R.S.B.C. 1996, c. 101, section 223.
17. R.S.B.C. 1996, c. 165.
18. (1992) 93 D.L.R. (4th) 415.
19. *Tarasoff v. Regents of University of California* (1976), 551 P. 2nd 334, 131 Cal. Rptr. 14 (Cal. S.C.).
20. (1980) 4 W.W.R. 33 (Alta. C.A.).
21. (1993), 14 C.C.L.T. (2d) 225 (Alta. C.A.).
22. R.S.B.C., 1996, c. 223, section 17.
23. (1990), 2 C.C.L.T. (2d) 1.
24. (1991). 82 D.L.R. (4th) 298.

Chapter 10

RIGHTS OF PERSONS WITH PHYSICAL
AND MENTAL DISABILITIES

Dulcie McCallum and Peter Carver

INTRODUCTION

Historically, the lives of many people who have been labelled "disabled" have been controlled and ultimately compromised by well-meaning members of the helping professions. In former times, this followed from a social response to disability that emphasized charity and pity. More recently, it resulted from placing too great a reliance on a medical model of dealing with disability. Many people were required to live in institutional settings for treatment purposes, or were placed in sheltered settings for training and rehabilitation suited to what was viewed as their limited potential. The resulting exclusion and segregation have had a devastating impact. From childhood on, many disabled persons have known only paid caregivers and service providers. Their quality of life has depended on a diagnosis, a plan put in place, funding allocated, and services available. The catch-22 is that the natural allies and advocates who might have objected to this distinct or differential treatment have often been unavailable because segregation itself removed the opportunity to develop contact and relationships with others, including family members.

Today, however, more people with disabilities and families with disabled children are becoming their own advocates. Independent and interdependent living within the community is increasingly the norm sought by persons with disabilities and supportive service agencies. Many service providers are in fact finding themselves assuming the dual role of professional and advocate. The charitable and medical approaches to disability have in many ways been replaced or superseded by a rights and advocacy-based approach.

This change has coincided with the arrival of extensive constitutional and legislative guarantees for the rights of people with disabilities. The *Canadian Charter of Rights and Freedoms*,[1] introduced when the *Constitution*[2] was patriated in 1982, contains specific provisions protecting people with physical and mental disabilities. Moreover, in all Canadian jurisdictions-- provincial, territorial, and federal-- people with disabilities are protected under human rights legislation.[3] These reforms recognize the principle that persons with disabilities are entitled to enjoy the same rights, freedoms, protections, and opportunities as all other members of Canadian society.

Unfortunately, the majority of Canadians who have a disability continue to be poor, and the path to equality is a slow and arduous one.[4] Enforcement of rights remains expensive both in terms of money and personal energy. It is, therefore, critical that people working in related professions understand and appreciate what it means to respect the rights of disabled persons.

This chapter highlights several areas where legal issues affecting people with disabilities may be of particular interest to helping professionals, especially educators, health care professionals, social workers, and staff in service providing agencies. The law is stated as of December 1, 1997. The chapter is divided into the following nine major areas:

a) *Canadian Charter of Rights and Freedoms;*

b) consent to medical treatment;

c) adult guardianship law;

d) housing;

e) employment opportunities;

f) access to education;

g) the right to vote;

h) legal rights; and

i) Office of the Ombudsman.

It seems appropriate before beginning to define "person with a disability." One helpful definition is as follows:

A person who has a physical or mental impairment which substantially limits one or more of the person's major life activities, including caring for oneself, performing manual tasks, walking, seeing, hearing, speaking, breathing, learning and working has a record of such impairment, or is regarded as having such an impairment.[5]

CANADIAN CHARTER OF RIGHTS AND FREEDOMS

Canada is the first and only jurisdiction in the world to include disability specifically within a constitutional guarantee of equal rights.[6] The *Charter of Rights and Freedoms*, which contains the guarantee, is part of the *Constitution*, by definition the supreme law of Canada, and is binding on the actions of all Canadian governments.[7]

Section 15 of the *Charter* guarantees equal benefit and equal protection before and under federal and provincial laws to all individuals without discrimination. The equality rights provision enumerates explicit grounds, including physical and mental disability, on which discrimination is prohibited. The stated grounds are not exhaustive, and future analogous grounds may be included as cases arise. However, for analogous grounds to be recognized, it appears they must refer to a matter of historic social disadvantage.[8]

Other sections of the *Charter* also provide rights and freedoms that affect people with disabilities. Section 7 of the *Charter* states that everyone has the right to "life, liberty and security of the person" and the right not to be deprived thereof unless done in accordance with the principles of fundamental justice. It may, in fact, be important to read sections 15 and 7 together. Discrimination under section 15 may constitute a breach of the fundamental justice requirement under section 7.[9] In other words, if government action diminishes a person's right to life, liberty, or security on the basis of his/her disability, the test of fundamental justice cannot be met.

Under the *Charter*, everyone also has the following fundamental freedoms: conscience and religion (section 2(a)); thought, belief, opinion and expression, including freedom of the press and other media of communication (section 2(b)); peaceful assembly (section 2(c)); and association (section 2(d)). All citizens of Canada have the right to vote and to participate in an elected assembly (section 3). The mobility rights guarantee gives citizens the right to move and take up residence in any region of the country and to pursue a livelihood in any province (section 6).

Section 1 of the *Charter* sets out the only conditions under which limits placed by government on equality rights, or other *Charter* rights and freedoms, are permissible: such limits must be prescribed by law, and be reasonable in a free and democratic society. An early Supreme Court of Canada ruling on section 1 decided that it requires limits on rights to be the least intrusive on, or restrictive of, a right as is necessary to meet a legitimate governmental objective.[10] There is also a specific "opting out" or "notwithstanding" clause that allows a government to expressly exempt a law from *Charter* standards (section 33).

A. *Eldridge and Warren v. Attorney General of British Columbia et al*[11]

As this Chapter was being prepared for publication, Supreme Court of Canada handed down the most significant decision to date with respect to the scope of equality rights under the *Charter* for persons with disabilities. In *Eldridge and Warren v. Attorney General of B.C. et al*, a deaf couple whose child was born prematurely and a deaf individual with various illnesses that required frequent medical attention challenged the failure of both Medical Services Plan and the Hospital Insurance Plan to expressly cover the costs of sign language interpreters as part of health insurance in British Columbia. The trial and appeal courts had dismissed the case, concluding that section 15 did not impose a positive obligation on government to pay for what was viewed as a service "ancillary" to medical care.

The Supreme Court of Canada disagreed. In a sweeping (and unanimous) decision, the Court ruled that section 15 is broad enough to impose just such an obligation on government, if that is necessary to ensure that persons with disabilities receive the same quality of benefits that all other citizens are entitled to under legislated schemes such as public health insurance. Mr. Justice LaForest, writing for the Court, found that communication between physician and patient is integral to health care. For deaf persons, therefore, interpretation is not ancillary to medical service but a necessary component of it. To exclude costs of interpretation from health insurance coverage is a form of discrimination, which violates section 15(1).

The Court identified the two main objectives of equality rights to be:

a) to prohibit the attribution of <u>untrue</u> characteristics based on stereotyping attitudes (e.g., racist or sexist attitudes); and

b) to take into account <u>true</u> characteristics (e.g., mobility or communication impairments) that act as "headwinds" to the equal enjoyment of rights and benefits available to mainstream society.

The latter objective is particularly important for persons with disabilities. It gives rise to a duty of "reasonable accommodation." That is, where governments design schemes providing general benefits, they are under a duty to accommodate persons with disabilities so that they have equal enjoyment of those benefits. This duty is subject to a limit of reasonableness, or "undue hardship." This would allow a government to argue as a section 1 defence that the accommodation in question is, in all the circumstances, too costly to undertake.

In the case of sign language interpretation in medical services, the Court found that the cost would amount to a tiny fraction of the province's overall health insurance budget. The Court, therefore, ordered the government of British Columbia to administer its health insurance plans in "a manner consistent with the requirements of section 15(1)" (paragraph 95) - i.e., to pay for interpretation service as part of health insurance.

This breakthrough decision would appear to have important implications for all publicly provided services and programs, including public transit and employment programs, to name only two. It is, in short, the kind of decision that proponents of disability rights have hoped and worked for over the 15 years of the *Charter's* existence.

CONSENT TO MEDICAL TREATMENT

"Over-medicalization" of disability has been an unfortunate tendency in the professional fields of people working and caring for people with disabilities. The term denotes focusing on "deficits" to the exclusion of abilities, making decisions in individuals' medical best interests rather than in accord with their wishes in the context of their life as a whole, and equating disability with incapacity to make decisions. To avoid this tendency, professionals need to strike a balance between four, sometimes competing, imperatives:

a) understanding the medical aspects of a particular disabling condition;

b) distinguishing the medical from the non-medical aspects associated with living with a disability;

c) respecting the right of all persons to quality medical treatment, irrespective of disability; and

d) respecting the individual's rights not to be interfered with unnecessarily, to self-determination, and to privacy.

The latter two points provide guidance in avoiding the most vexing problems affecting health care of persons with disabilities, and what often appear to be two sides of the coin of paternalism: withholding needed medical treatment on "quality of life" grounds; and providing unwanted or unnecessary treatment on the basis of what is viewed as being in the person's best interests.

I. Withholding of Medical Treatment

Parents have sometimes been counselled to withhold consent for necessary medical treatment for an infant born with a disability, on the basis that discontinuing the life of the child is in her/his best interests. A decision to withhold consent in the case of Baby Dan in Montreal resulted in the death of an infant with Down's Syndrome who was left to starve, suffering from an unrepaired duodenal atresia.[12] In cases like this, physicians provide advice based on medical assumptions about quality of life and the possible extent of disability. Other health professionals might also be complicit in the decision to administer only "palliative care." Often this recommendation is made regardless of the nature of the treatment required.[13] It is essential that medical professionals recognize that all infants and children have a right to life-giving or life-sustaining medical treatment regardless of disability.[14]

Re S.D. in British Columbia is a landmark case in which the principal question was "whether S. has the right to receive appropriate medical and surgical care of a relatively simple kind which will assure to him the continuation of his life, such as it is."[15] The court held that custody of a 12- year-old child ought to be removed from the parents and placed in the hands of the Superintendent (now director) of Family and Child Service. The Superintendent was then charged with giving the requisite consent for the needed surgical intervention to be completed during the period of the interim custody order. The court refused to permit a third party, even a parent, from making a judgment about another person's quality of life that would result in that person's death.

The right to life and security of the person in the *Charter* likely includes access to life-giving and life-sustaining medical treatment. Withholding such treatment may also in some circumstances contravene the right to be free from cruel and unusual treatment (section 12). While the *Charter* does not apply to the actions of private individuals, such as physicians and parents, it may apply to hospitals as publicly funded institutions.[16] It is clear, however, that as public facilities, hospitals are subject to human rights legislation and cannot refuse access to treatment in a discriminatory fashion.[17]

A British Columbia case raises the important question of whether the *Charter* requires that medical services provided generally to the public be designed in such a way as to provide full and equal benefit to persons with disabilities. As in *Eldridge and Warren*,[18] mentioned earlier, the British Columbia government was ordered to pay costs of sign language interpretation at a delivery, to accord with section 15 of the *Charter*.

Criminal prosecution for assault, manslaughter, or even murder are possible outcomes for any professional person who is responsible for the injury or death of infants, children, or adults who have disabilities. Children and adults confined to institutional settings are vulnerable to different forms of abuse. A physician was charged and convicted of assault because she instructed her medical students to perform repeated rectal examinations on adults with mental disabilities.[19] Some professionals in such settings continue to use punishing and aversive techniques as a means of behaviour modification. These techniques may be part of a treatment program for the individual, but can be degrading and dehumanizing, and may constitute assault where not based on informed consent.[20] The Supreme Court of Canada has held that physical "discipline" of an adult with a mental handicap by an institutional caregiver constitutes assault, and rejected an argument that a caregiver stands in an analogous position to a parent using reasonable force to correct a child.[21] Even parents may be subject to criminal prosecution if they consent to or themselves use aversive techniques.[22]

In the much-publicized Latimer case, the father of a 12- year-old girl with cerebral palsy was convicted of second degree murder in her death, and given the mandatory minimum sentence of imprisonment for life with no eligibility for parole for 10 years. The trial judge refused to put the defence of necessity to the jury, through which the accused sought to justify the purported act of mercy killing as necessary to end his daughter's pain and suffering. The Court of Appeal upheld the conviction and sentence, deciding in part that the law does not allow for considerations about the quality of life of murder victims in order to assess the accused's sentence.[23] The Supreme Court of Canada subsequently over turned the conviction and ordered a new trial on unrelated grounds concerning misconduct by the Crown Counsel.[24] Latimer was subsequently reconvicted by a jury (November, 1997), sentenced to two years less a day in prison, with the judge making an exception to the minimum 10 year term for second degree murder.

The Sue Rodriguez case[25] involved a constitutional challenge to section 241 of the *Criminal Code*, which prohibits a physician or other person from assisting in a suicide. One of the arguments advanced was that section 241 violates the *Charter* equality rights of persons with physical disabilities by denying an individual who is incapacitated from receiving the assistance needed to end his/her life, an act which is otherwise not illegal. A 5-4 majority of the Supreme Court of Canada decided section 241 of the Code did not infringe the *Charter*, stating in part that the sanctity of life and protection of the vulnerable were important values in Canadian society, and that it should be up to Parliament to balance those values with the interests of individual choice and dignity. The division in society on this question was reflected in the fact that one group of persons with disabilities intervened to support Ms. Rodriguez' position, while another intervened to warn the Court of the risk to vulnerable persons in permitting assisted suicide without strict guidelines.

II. Treatment Without Consent

All adults are presumed to be competent and able to provide consent to treatment on their own behalf.[26] Canadian law provides two principal mechanisms by which a person's inability or refusal to consent to treatment can be bypassed: mental health statutes, and laws dealing with guardianship of persons deemed incapable. Both mechanisms provide for a form of substitute decision-making for and on behalf of the individual.

The British Columbia *Mental Health Act* authorizes a person's involuntary detention in a psychiatric facility where two physicians certify that he/she has a mental disorder and needs hospitalization for their own or others' protection.[27] A section 7 *Charter* challenge to these grounds for committal, arguing that they should be narrowed to dangerousness from protection of self, was rejected.[28] Under the statute, the director of a psychiatric facility can authorize treatment of an involuntarily detained person without a formal process of assessing their competence to consent to treatment. This situation, almost unique in Canada, is believed by many to be vulnerable to future *Charter* challenge. In *Fleming v. Reid*,[29] the Ontario Court of Appeal, dealing with that province's very different statutory scheme in which a hearing had to be held before substituted consent could be given for a competent (though detained) patient, ruled it was an infringement of section 7 to order treatment against the previously expressed competent wishes of an individual who had since become ill and incompetent.

The Fleming decision relied on an earlier Ontario case, which upheld the right of a Jehovah's Witness member to refuse a blood transfusion that would have saved her life.[30] In *Nancy B v. Hotel-Dieu de Quebec*,[31] a Quebec Court refused to intervene to prevent a woman with disabilities from directing her physicians to disconnect her from life-supporting equipment even though she did not have a terminal illness. Many persons with disabilities were concerned that the woman's decision might reflect the lack of social services and support she needed in order to live a fulfilling life outside hospital. Nevertheless, both cases show the degree to which Canadian courts respect individual autonomy in the absence of mental disorder or incompetence.

Most jurisdictions have guardianship legislation that provides for the appointment of a substitute decision-maker when a person has been found to be legally incompetent. Such laws grew out of the common law tradition in which the monarch was being ultimately responsible to care for those who could not care for themselves. This original inherent jurisdiction of the court is referred to as *parens patriae*. The Supreme Court of Canada unanimously decided in the case of *Re Eve* that in the absence of specific legislation, a court does not have the authority under its *parens patriae* jurisdiction to consent to a non-therapeutic sterilization of a woman with a mental handicap intended to prevent a future pregnancy.[32] In addition, even when a third party, including a parent, is authorized by a court, either under guardianship legislation or a mental health statute to give substituted consent, this consent is restricted to medical procedures that are deemed therapeutic. The Court rejected a "best interests" test in deciding whether an invasive procedure that involves the fundamental rights to procreate and to be free from touching without consent ought to be permitted. The Court was also critical of the British Columbia Court of Appeal case of *Re K*, which authorized the sterilization of a female child because the parents alleged she had a phobia about blood and would be distressed during menstruation. The Supreme Court stated that this factual basis was only tenuously "therapeutic."[33]

Recently, the Alberta Court of Queen's Bench awarded over $700,000 in damages to a woman who had been sterilized under a statute of that province, repealed only in the 1960s, that had authorized sterilization for institutionalized mentally handicapped persons.[34] The statute was a holdover from the long-discredited eugenics movement.

Statutes designed many years ago codified the authority of a court to make an order, based on medical criteria, declaring a person incompetent for legal purposes. In British Columbia, the *Patients Property Act*[35] presently governs this process, including the appointing of a guardian or "committee" to make decisions on behalf of the adult declared incompetent. The committee may be authorized to manage the adult's financial affairs, and/or to manage her/his person. The latter includes providing substituted consent for medical procedures. If a committee of the person has not been appointed for an adult who is incapable of giving informed consent to medical treatment, then no one is authorized by law to consent to or provide non-emergency treatment. Because present British Columbia law requires incurring the expense of a court application to have a committee appointed, and further because the associated declaration of incompetence is indefinite and global in effect, many incapable adults do not have committees of person and fall into this decision-making vacuum. Fortunately, in most respects, physicians and hospitals have been willing to provide treatment on the basis of informal consent given by next-of-kin or close caregivers. Still, the gap in legal authority and absence of criteria for acting are worrisome.

In response, and as part of a package of statutory reforms in the guardianship area (discussed below), the British Columbia legislature passed the *Health Care (Consent) and Care Facility (Admission) Act*[36] in 1993. Not yet proclaimed, the statute creates a time-limited form of substitute decision-making for routine medical care, using a list of persons closely related to the adult who are authorized to give consent without court order.[37] The *Act* also sets out the criteria which are to be used by a substitute decision maker (SDM), giving priority to previously expressed wishes of the adult when capable, and known values and beliefs of the adult, over the SDM's own view of what is in the adult's best interests.[38] This may help to deal with a long-standing concern of many about the dangers of paternalistic decision-making in this area.

ADULT GUARDIANSHIP LAW

Vulnerable members of society often need protection from abuse or neglect, or simply from a legal or factual inability to make decisions about their lives. At the same time, formal means for intervening to protect vulnerable adults pose significant risks of diminishing their autonomy and opportunity to be self-determining. Striking a balance between these interests is the great challenge facing adult guardianship law.

The failure of guardianship legislation drafted in the 19th and early 20th centuries to adequately respect interests of individual autonomy has been the subject of complaint in many jurisdictions. In British Columbia, such concerns led to "The Project to Review Adult Guardianship", undertaken between 1990 and 1993. This unprecedented collaboration between grassroots community participants and provincial government officials resulted in a package of reform legislation being passed by the British Columbia Legislature in 1993, comprising four statutes: the *Health Care (Consent) and Care Facility (Admission) Act*, the *Adult Guardianship Act*,[39] the *Representation Agreement Act*,[40] and the *Public Guardian and Trustee Act*.[41] This legislation tries to strike a new balance in guardianship matters by creating extensive procedural protections around the appointment and actions of substitute decision-makers, while enhancing the ability of public authorities to intervene in situations of abuse or neglect. The legislation also enhances the ability of adults to plan for times when they may need assistance in making decisions.

Although passed in 1993, the statutes have not been proclaimed and so are not yet in effect. It is presently anticipated they will be proclaimed in stages, commencing in early 1998. One of the reasons for the delay is the extent and complexity of the changes involved, which are likely to have a profound impact on the professional activity of all those who work with adults whose mental competence is or becomes an issue, as well as on the lives of clients and their families. Only a few of the more important changes intended by this new legislation will be mentioned here.

The *Adult Guardianship Act* will essentially replace the *Patients Property Act* for all purposes except the medical treatment issues covered by the *Health Care (Consent) and Care Facility (Admission) Act*. Major weaknesses of the *Patients Property Act* are seen to include: that a declaration of incompetence is global, effectively removing the adult's decision-making authority in all financial and/or personal matters, even though competence in fact is often task or context-specific; a lack of due process, particularly with certificates of incapability, through which a person can be declared incompetent by a physician's signature; and, the absence of any criteria governing medical

240

assessments of incompetence. The new legislation addresses each of these problems. It mandates that guardianship can only occur by court order, eliminating the certificate route, and requires that detailed assessments of the adult's capability and need for guardianship be provided to the court in support of an application. It also calls on the court to limit substitute decision-making to only those areas of life where the individual needs it. Guardianship orders will be subject to periodic reviews to see whether they remain appropriate and necessary.

In a few jurisdictions in Canada, adult protection statutes designate a Minister of the Crown responsible for investigating and intervening when an adult person is being abused or neglected. The definition of being "in need of protection" most often refers to situations in which a person is disabled or elderly, and in danger of physical, sexual, or mental abuse. The statute will often give the Minister the power to provide the requisite care and treatment without consent. These provisions, however, have been stringently interpreted by the courts.[42] British Columbia has had no comparable legislation, but the *Adult Guardianship Act* will change that situation. It provides for intervention by agencies designated for this purpose where abuse or neglect is suspected, under court supervision.

The *Representation Agreement Act* creates a new means for adults to pre-plan for periods of incompetence, as well as to empower trusted family or friends to assist in their decision-making. Whereas Powers of Attorney are available only with respect to financial matters, Representation Agreements will extend to personal and health care as well. In this way, an individual can decide in advance whether to direct his/her representative to consent to, or refuse, certain kinds of medical treatment. Due to the previously mentioned controversy about the right to refuse treatment in the mental health setting, persons involuntarily detained under the *Mental Health Act* are specifically excluded from the benefits of Representation Agreements in the psychiatric setting.[43] This exclusion may be open to challenge under section 15 of the *Charter of Rights and Freedoms*.

One of the interesting features of the new legislation is its attempt to move much of the responsibility for adult guardianship away from government and the Public Trustee, which has traditionally had that role, and toward individuals, family members, and community-based services. For instance, formally recognized advocates will be funded to support vulnerable adults as they move through the guardianship process. This will be a particular challenge for professionals and service providers who are called on to work with the new framework. Success in ensuring that individual autonomy is respected at the same time vulnerable persons receive needed assistance and protection will depend not so much on the specific terms of the legislation, as on respect for several of the rights and principles that guided the reform process itself:

a) the right of individuals to self-determination;

b) the right to be presumed competent;

c) the right to be empowered or enabled to make decisions;

d) the principle that the law is to be used as a last resort;

e) the principle that formal intervention is to be the least restrictive and least intrusive necessary; and

f) the principle that interdependent decision-making with the support of family and friends is a preferred alternative for adults whose capacity is limited.[44]

For more discussion of this area see Chapter 9.

HOUSING ISSUES

Often people with disabilities do not make their own decisions about where they are going to live. Instead, this decision is made for them by another person, agency, or authority. Most frequently, a disabled person's lack of choice in housing is a consequence of program funding arrangements. On occasion, it may result from a guardian's exercise of authority.[45] In an Ontario case, a young adult with cerebral palsy, Justin Clark, successfully challenged his father's application for a guardianship order, arguing that he wanted to decide for himself where to live.[46] The court held that the extent of Justin's physical disability was irrelevant in determining his competence to make decisions on his own behalf. The court found that he was entitled to decide where and with whom to live, regardless of whether it posed risks to his health.

Mental health and adult protection legislation provides legal authority for institutionalization of persons considered in need of supervisory care. However, the majority of individuals labeled mentally handicapped, who are institutionalized in Canada (approximately 20,000), are considered to be "voluntarily" admitted. Most were placed in institutions as children, as were many persons with physical disabilities. Admission past the age of majority continued on the basis of a guardianship order or an administrator's certificate, or simply because no one questioned it. The government of British Columbia has actively pursued a deinstitutionalization policy since the mid-1980s. The last institutional facility for the mentally handicapped in the province, Woodlands, closed at the end of 1996.

Funding that supports people who have disabilities has, historically, required people to be congregated in agency-operated facilities. Group homes often house people labeled as having the same disability (ie., mental handicap, mental illness, mobility impairment, etc). The Canada Mortgage and Housing Corporation funded social housing projects in the 1970s and 1980s with unit allocations for persons with physical disabilities, but the federal government has now vacated this field. The British Columbia Housing Management Corporation (BCHMC) operates a subsidized housing program, including units for persons with physical and mental disabilities. The waiting lists for accessible BCHMC housing are long.

The British Columbia *Human Rights Code* provides protection from discrimination in tenancy (section 5(1)) and in the purchase of property (section 4) for individuals who have physical or mental disabilities. This prohibition against discriminatory conduct in the provision of housing, however, does little for those forced to live in settings such as segregated group homes designated for a particular category of disabled person. One court aptly described some group homes in these terms:

A group home in many cases is a semi-institutional home. It is an arrangement whereby a number of individuals, usually limited to six or eight persons, agree to live together as a single household unit in order to enjoy the benefits and assume the responsibilities of living in a residential neighbourhood. In the case of convalescent, disabled persons or rehabilitated prisoner, the choice of the individual is rather limited since he or she is sent there by another body or agency. The premises or homes are organized by an association or organization, staffed, maintained and operated by it. An individual either qualifies or does not; is either welcomed or not in the group home. If qualified and welcomed, he or she enjoys the benefits of living in a residential neighbourhood under full-time or part-time staff supervision.[47]

One human rights complaint involved a man who had been labelled by his doctor as being "permanently mentally disabled, in need of extensive assistance" and on that basis was refused the opportunity to apply for tenancy in a boarding home. His complaint was dismissed because the landlord could offer no assistance to his tenants and was therefore justified in refusing the tenancy.[48] In another complaint, a landlord was found to have discriminated because she harassed the complainant for having a mental handicap.[49]

Individuals who bear the label of disabled are often poor, unemployed, and in receipt of social welfare or disability benefits. This state of dependency severely curtails their available residential options.[50] A statutorily approved agency or government department will assume authority for making a placement, depending on the label attached and the community resources available. Group homes do not provide the optimum living situation, but are often accepted as the only option available. Some communities have resisted their presence by enacting bylaws prohibiting living configurations and situations for people who are disabled. The Manitoba Court of Appeal permitted a *Charter* challenge to one such city bylaw that prohibited group homes for people with a mental handicap, finding it discriminatory.[51]

EMPLOYMENT OPPORTUNITIES

People with disabilities experience widespread unemployment and under-employment. Efforts to rectify this situation through employment equity legislation have been sporadic.[52] Systemic impediments continue to prevent people with disabilities from becoming gainfully employed. Federal-provincial cost-shared arrangements fund training and rehabilitation programs that, in theory, are intended to assist individuals to become employable. This funding primarily supports opportunities restricted to day programs, which are designed on a training and rehabilitation model and do not provide adequate income. Provincial legislation permits exemption of these programs from the usual employment standards, including payment of a minimum wage. In British Columbia, a successful section 15 challenge to such an exemption under the *Employment Standards Act* was overturned by the British Columbia Court of Appeal.[53]

All provincial/territorial and federal human rights statutes provide protection from discrimination on the basis of disability in the areas of hiring, firing, and determining conditions of work. Most cases involving disability concern allegations of discrimination on the basis of physical disability: a person who was hired and later discovered to have a disability that affected his work;[54]

a person whose disability was found during a preliminary medical examination;[55] or a person who, once employed, was found to have a pre-existing condition.[56]

A few cases deal with discrimination based on mental disability. In the Boehm case, the complainant alleged a foreman verbally harassed him by calling him "stupid" and "dummy", and unjustifiably criticizing his work.[57] The tribunal ruled this type of harassment amounted to discrimination based on mental disability, and held the employer responsible for the actions of its agent, the foreman. The Supreme Court of Canada has held that a benefits plan that terminated long term disability benefits after two years for employees with a mental disorder unless they were hospitalized (whereas benefits continued indefinitely for all other employees disabled from work), constituted discrimination in terms of employment on the basis of mental disability.[58]

Most human rights statutes provide a defence to a complaint where an otherwise discriminatory consideration constitutes a *bona fide* occupational requirement (BFOR). It is important to realize, however, that what is argued to be a good faith job requirement may be unfounded, or rest on stereotypical assumptions. For example, an apparently neutral requirement that prospective employees have a grade twelve education may be irrelevant to the job in question, yet effectively bar applicants who have had limited educational opportunities.

The Supreme Court of Canada has stated that, in cases of direct discrimination where no statutory defence exists, the employer's hiring requirement or rule will be struck down.[59] If, however, a BFOR defence exists in the applicable human rights statute, it will be a question of objective fact whether the employer's rule is justified as necessary for the work in question. An employment rule that is neutral on its face but has an unintended adverse impact on persons with disabilities can also constitute discrimination. Employers have a duty in human rights law to accommodate disabilities, unless to do so would impose undue hardship on the employer.[60]

ACCESS TO EDUCATION

The *Universal Declaration of Human Rights*, to which Canada and the provinces are signatory, proclaimed the right to a free education at the fundamental, primary levels.[61] This right has been repeatedly cited in international documents.[62] The right has been articulated in the *Convention on the Rights of the Child.*[63]

Beyond this starting point, a debate continues in many Canadian jurisdictions about whether all children have the right to attend a regular classroom at their neighbourhood school. In the past, segregation was the norm for children with a disability. Many school boards continue to provide special education services in a segregated setting. Conflicts arise when parents, faced with a segregated placement decision, believe that their child should be included in a regular classroom with the support services necessary to provide an optimal educational opportunity.

The first case in British Columbia to challenge segregated education claimed that a school board was negligent when it exercised its statutory power to place a child with a mental handicap in a segregated, self-contained, special school.[64] This case pre-dated the equality rights provision of the Charter and was unsuccessful. However, the trial judge did hold that the *School Act* imposed a duty on school boards to provide sufficient school accommodation and tuition, free of charge, to all children of school age.

The first *Charter* challenge arose in Nova Scotia where parents sought an injunction to prohibit the school board from removing their son from his neighbourhood school where he had been registered and placing him in a segregated class for children with disabilities.[65] While the segregated classroom was located in a regular school, it was self-contained and many miles from the child's neighbourhood. The parents claimed on their son's behalf a constitutional right to the equal benefit of education and not to be discriminated against on the basis of a mental disability. One year after the injunction was granted, the case was settled in favour of the parent's position.

The issue of whether section 15 of the *Charter* creates any presumption in favour of integrated placements for children with disabilities was recently considered by the Supreme Court of Canada. The outcome left many advocates disappointed. The Eaton case[66] in Ontario concerned a ten-year-old girl with cerebral palsy. Over the objections of her parents, the local school board decided to place her in a segregated class for disabled students. It said that such a placement fulfilled its statutory obligation to meet the learning needs of "exceptional children,"[67] because evidence showed the girl had encountered difficulties in an integrated classroom. The Ontario Special Education Tribunal and the Divisional Court agreed with this placement, the latter stating that the *Charter* did not create a presumption in favour of "one pedagogical theory over another." The Ontario Court of Appeal rejected this analysis. It ruled that the *Charter* creates a legal context within which educational programs must be assessed. A pedagogical theory that favours segregation is not on the same legal footing as one that favours integration, because the former is discriminatory.

By being neutral on its face between these two approaches, the *Education Act* failed to meet the test of section 1 of the *Charter* or restricting a *Charter* right in no more than a minimal fashion. The Court said the remedy was to read the statute as incorporating a presumption in favour of integrated placements:

> [When parents do not agree with a segregated placement] the school board must select a segregated class as a last resort, having made all reasonable efforts to integrate the disabled child.[68]

The Supreme Court overturned the Court of Appeal's decision in late 1996.[69] In a unanimous ruling, the Court concluded that the equality rights principle of accommodation of disability provides a theoretical underpinning for segregated placements. One of the two main purposes of section 15(1), Sopinka J. wrote for the Court, is:

> to take into account the true characteristics of this group [persons with disabilities] which act as headwinds to the enjoyment of society's benefits and to accommodate them. Exclusion from the mainstream of society results from the construction of a society based solely on 'mainstream' attributes to which disabled persons will never be able to gain access.

The regular classroom can, for some children with disabilities, be a "mainstream" environment that excludes them from the benefits of education. In the Court's view, a segregated placement may be the appropriate accommodation for the unique needs. The choice between an integrated or segregated placement must be assessed on the basis of the best interests of the individual child, without any presumption in favour of one or the other. Such a presumption would risk interfering with the assessment of the child's best interests.

The Supreme Court's analysis in the Eaton case seems unfortunate. The purpose of a presumption in favour of integration is to ensure that segregated placements are used as a last resort, not to rule them out altogether. A substantive reading of section 15 of the *Charter* that placed a hurdle in the way of administrators' decision in favour of segregation would better recognize what has been learned about the harmful effects of segregation in and of itself. Without such a hurdle, segregation too easily comes to look like a neutral solution to the difficult problems of individual children, a particular risk in a period of educational budget cutbacks. The Court missed an opportunity to say that separate is not equal for children with disabilities.

Most educational statutes in Canada use language which, on its face, appears neutral. In British Columbia, section 94(1) of the *School Act* imposes on school boards the duty to "make available an education program to all persons of school age resident in its district." A Ministerial Order then creates a form of presumption in favour of integrated schooling for "students with special needs:"

A board must provide a student with special needs with an educational program in a classroom where that student is integrated with other students who do not have special needs, unless the educational needs of the student with special needs or other students indicate that the educational program for the student with special needs should be provided otherwise.

In addition to *Charter* challenges, complaints of discrimination can also be brought under human rights legislation. Schools have been held to be public facilities under human rights legislation.[70] The Quebec Court of Appeal has, for instance, ruled on two cases brought under the provincial *Code des droits de la personne*. The results were similar to Eaton. The Court found the *Code* required that education provided to students with disabilities meet their individual needs, but did not require this be done only through integrated placements.[71]

In some jurisdictions, including British Columbia, statutory appeal mechanisms enable parents to question placement decisions.[72] Appeal processes in many jurisdictions have, however, been found wanting by parents and advocates, who claim they are biased in part because they assume segregation is a viable outcome.[73] In some jurisdictions the education legislation provides for a final appeal to the Minister of Education.[74] In one such case Alberta's Minister of Education ordered that a child with a disability be enrolled in grade one at her neighbourhood school.[75]

Adult education opportunities continue to be even more problematic. While several institutions have established access for people who have a mental handicap, these institutions are the exception. In part, the tendency to consider that people with disabilities need training and rehabilitation has severely restricted the development of integrated, post-secondary opportunities at community-based colleges and universities. There has been little momentum for people with disabilities to be included in post-secondary planning because of their absence in regular elementary and secondary settings. Human rights legislation has been found to apply to universities because they are public facilities.[76] The difficulty for adults who have an intellectual impairment is that a particular academic background may constitute a *bona fide* requirement for entrance into a university or community college. The solution may rest more with a change of attitude and social policies that will promote the inclusion of all individuals regardless of disability.[77] At present some post-secondary education funding is available through the Vocational Rehabilitation of Disabled Persons program for students who have disabilities.

THE RIGHT TO VOTE

Section 3 of the *Charter* guarantees all citizens the right to vote in federal and provincial elections. The Canadian Disability Rights Council brought an application in the Federal Court of Canada to challenge a provision of the *Canada Elections Act* [78] that disqualified individuals from voting whose liberty was restricted because of mental incapacity. The Court struck the provision down on the basis of it being too broad to be a reasonable limitation on the right to vote, ruling that detention for mental disorder does not necessarily imply incompetence for voting purposes. After that decision, a Royal Commission on Electoral Reform was appointed, with a mandate that included an examination of the appropriate means to ensure that all individuals, regardless of disability, are enumerated and enabled to exercise their franchise. This includes making polling stations physically accessible, and accommodating all disabilities in the enumerating and voting process.[79]

In some provincial/territorial jurisdictions, disqualification provisions remain. The British Columbia *Municipal Act* disqualifies from voting in local government elections those individuals who are detained in a psychiatric facility after being found "not criminally responsible by reason of mental disorder" under the *Criminal Code of Canada*.

LEGAL RIGHTS

Individuals with a variety of disabilities, whether accused persons, victims, or witnesses, have often received differential treatment that prevents their full participation in the judicial process.[80] One important cause of the exclusion of people who are mentally handicapped is the fact that courts have sometimes equated the label of "mental handicap" with legal incompetence. This has impacted on courts' willingness to accept uncorroborated testimony of a person with a disability as proof of an offence. A second cause is the rule that individuals who are the subject of a court order appointing a guardian/committee, or whose competence is questioned, are required to bring civil proceedings by an appointed third person or "next friend."[81]

Prior to 1992, the laws dealing with the insanity defence in criminal proceedings created a number of unfairnesses. First, the Crown was allowed to adduce evidence of an accused's insanity at the time of the offence against her/his objections. Second, accused persons acquitted on the basis of insanity were automatically detained for treatment for an indefinite period at the discretion of the Lieutenant Governor (effectively, the provincial Cabinet). This meant that persons who had recovered from mental illness by the time of trial were nevertheless detained. As well, many individuals spent years in detention following recovery, waiting for a political decision to release them. In *Swain v. Her Majesty the Queen*, the Supreme Court of Canada struck these provisions down as being contrary to sections 7 and 15 of the *Charter*.[82] The Court said they were based in large part on attitudes reflecting the historic abuse, neglect, and marginalization of people with mental illness in Canada. As a result of this decision, extensive amendments to the *Criminal Code* were introduced in 1992, creating among other things independent Review Boards in each province with the power to release persons found "not criminally responsible by reason of mental disorder" (the latter phrase replacing "insanity") once they cease posing a risk to society.

Several Canadian jurisdictions have developed protocols governing the special communication needs of persons with disabilities caught up in the justice system. The need to develop these types of protocols was accentuated by the case of *Evans v. Her Majesty the Queen*,[83] in which the Supreme Court of Canada threw out a self-incriminating statement taken from an accused in violation of his right to retain and instruct counsel. The confession, the only evidence at trial linking the accused to the crimes, was extracted from a man with a mental handicap. The police failed to fully explain to the accused his right to remain silent and his right to counsel even though he indicated his lack of comprehension and they were aware of his disability.

In the past, people with a mental disability were specifically prohibited from entering into a marriage. Many jurisdictions amended their marriage legislation as a result of the *Charter*, but several provinces still prohibit a marriage when one party is under a disability. The British Columbia *Marriage Act* makes it an offence for any person to officiate at (solemnize) a marriage "knowing or having reason to believe that either of the parties to the intended marriage or to the marriage is a mentally disordered person or is impaired by drugs or alcohol."[84] However, a marriage can only be annulled on this basis if it is proved that one party was under a disability at the time of the marriage such that he/she did not appreciate the responsibilities attached to marriage.[85]

OFFICE OF THE OMBUDSMAN

Recourse to the provincial Ombudsman provides a valuable remedy for many persons with disabilities and those advocating on their behalf.[86] As part of the historical disadvantage they have experienced, and as a result of the need to depend on services and supports, the lives of persons with disabilities have been bound up with a wide variety of government services and programs. This makes them more likely to be the recipient of the kind of administrative decision making that generally falls within the Ombudsman's jurisdiction. In addition, the poverty of many disabled individuals puts recourses to courts, even to enforce many of the rights discussed above, out of reach. The informal and cost-free processes offered by Ombudsman offices across Canada are well-suited to pursuing solutions in some areas.

In British Columbia, the position of Ombudsman was created in 1979 with the passing of the *Ombudsman Act*.[87] The statute provides that the Ombudsman is an Officer of the Legislature, appointed for a renewable six-year term by unanimous vote of the Legislature, and ultimately reporting to it (sections 2, 3, 6, 24, and 30). From her/his position independent of the executive arm of government, the Ombudsman has broad authority to investigate any complaint about a "matter of administration" (section 10). This phrase has been interpreted by the Supreme Court of Canada to encompass all decisions and acts of government except those of the courts and the Legislative Assembly itself.[88] The Ombudsman has investigative powers that give him/her extensive access to government files and officials (section 15). On finding that government has acted unfairly toward an individual or group of persons, the Ombudsman may seek to remedy the situation through settlement or making recommendations for that purpose (sections 14(2) and 23). If recommendations are not accepted by government, the Ombudsman can report publicly and to the Legislative Assembly.

In 1993, the jurisdiction of the Ombudsman was extended to cover all hospitals in the province and all self-governing professional and occupational bodies, such as the College of Physicians and Surgeons. Jurisdiction over the new regional health governing bodies (Regional Health Boards and Community Health Councils) was confirmed in 1994. This means that, in addition to the original jurisdiction over government ministries, the Ombudsman now has the authority to investigate complaints in almost all areas where persons with disabilities are affected by public and quasi-public decision-makers. Importantly the jurisdiction also extends to all forms of local governments including cities, villages, towns, and municipalities.

The Ombudsman does not restrict her/his activities to issues raised by individual complainants. Where it is deemed appropriate, he/she may initiate an independent investigation and report to the public on systemic issues of unfairness. Examples include Public Report No. 25 dealing with abuse of persons with mental handicaps in group homes, and Public Report No. 33, "Listening: A Review of Riverview Hospital," which provided a systemic review of British Columbia's major psychiatric hospital and made 93 recommendations to improve the fairness in its services and programs. The Report adopted 15 principles of fairness, which guided its findings. These include the following:

a) Every person is entitled to be treated with dignity and respect.

b) Every person has the right to be heard and listened to regardless of disability or method of communication. Where individuals live in a protected environment that restricts their right to make decisions, every effort must be made to enable individuals to disagree (i.e., to say no, except where it can be demonstrated that respecting an individual's choice will jeopardize the safety of the individual or others).

The easily accessed and non-adversarial means of investigating decision-making by public bodies used by the Ombudsman affords a unique opportunity for many persons with disabilities, their advocates, and families.[89] A recent amendment to the statute deems any form of retribution against a person for being a part of an Ombudsman investigation an offence.

COMMON QUESTIONS

1. <u>What remedies are available to someone with a physical or mental disability who is denied access to a public facility or service?</u>

The *British Columbia Human Rights Code*[90] protects all people with disabilities from discrimination in housing and employment. It also prohibits everyone from denying access on the basis of disability to services and facilities customarily available to the public, including private businesses such as restaurants, hotels, and theatres, and public facilities such as schools, libraries, hospitals, and homemaker services. Although there is no statutory definition of disability in British Columbia, case law suggests that because human rights legislation is intended to have a remedial effect, disability will be broadly defined. An individual can file a complaint of discrimination with the British Columbia Human Rights Commission, which will investigate and attempt to settle or mediate the matter. If the Commission believes after investigation that discrimination may have occurred, and that the matter cannot be settled, it forwards the complaint for a hearing before the British Columbia Human Rights Tribunal. The hearing is a formal process that must respect rules of natural justice, i.e., permitting the parties to present their cases, to cross-examine each other's witnesses, and to be represented by counsel. Complainants may obtain counsel through the Legal Services Society. Where the Tribunal makes a finding that discrimination occurred, it can order various remedies for the complainant, including a formal apology, reimbursement of lost wages or other expenses, reinstatement of the opportunity denied, and damages for hurt feelings and humiliation. The Human Rights Commission also has a responsibility for educating the public about the principles of human rights law.

2. Are there income assistance programs in British Columbia for disabled persons?

The short answer is yes. British Columbia's income assistance legislation was substantially rewritten in 1996. Benefits to the general population, formerly known by the acronym "GAIN," are now provided under the *British Columbia Benefits (Income Assistance) Act*.[91] However, income assistance benefits for persons with disabilities are governed by a separate statute, the *Disability Benefits Program Act*.[92] Formerly, an applicant for "handicapped" status had to be assessed as permanently unemployable. This created a disincentive for seeking even temporary employment as well as harming self-esteem. The new definition requires medical confirmation of a "severe mental or physical impairment . . . [that] is likely to continue for at least two years, or . . . for at least one year and is likely to reoccur." One of the purposes of the new legislation is to move income support for persons with a disability away from a welfare model, toward a pension model. It may also permit better targeting of support programs. Disability benefits are higher than regular income assistance. Applicants cannot have liquid assets in excess of $3,000 if single, or $5,500 if living with a dependent. In addition to the monthly base amount of benefits, a person can qualify for health-related services including prescription drugs, special equipment, and dental care. An individual can earn up to $200 monthly without losing benefits.

3. Can individuals who have been labelled as having a mental handicap make decisions for themselves?

All adults are presumed to be competent to make decisions. Parents cease to have the legal authority to make decisions for their children when they reach the age of majority. When a decision needs to be made involving an adult with a disability who is considered incompetent to make that decision, the only route to obtain lawful authority to make the decision on the adult's behalf is by application under the *Patients Property Act*. This statute, long considered inadequate by many people in the community, is slated to be replaced by the *Adult Guardianship Act* when proclaimed. See discussion above, and Chapter 9. The latter statute provides for a category of "associate decision-maker," whose role will be to assist the adult in making decisions, rather than to act in the adult's place. It also requires all formal substitute decision-makers to consult with the adult, and act on their wishes where possible.

4. <u>Do children who have a disability have a right to integrated placements in their neighbourhood schools?</u>

There has been an ongoing debate about whether or not children who have a disability ought to be entitled to go to their neighbourhood school with their non-disabled peers. While the education legislation and policy in British Columbia supports inclusion of all students in a regular classroom, some school boards continue to assert the right to treat particular students as "special." The so-called "special needs" of some students invariably involves the labelling of children with disabilities. These special classes are often treated as if they were part of the range of program choices. For example, classes for disabled children are placed alongside French immersion classes or classes for gifted students. The critical difference is that French immersion classes and the like enhance the student's education and are selected with the pupil's and parents' consent. When distinctions are based solely on disability, the pedagogical basis for excluding certain children from the mainstream relies at best on out-dated and misconceived notions of what it means to have a disability. Unfortunately, the Supreme Court of Canada in a recent decision failed to see this as an equality of rights issue.

CONCLUSION

Despite the specific rights guaranteed in the Charter to people who have a mental or physical disability and the protections included in human rights legislation, people who have a disability continue to be excluded, segregated, and discriminated against. All professionals working with and for people with disabilities must recognize and respect their rights and avoid professional conduct that may, in any way, compromise those rights. The world has been designed for the able-bodied and, until such time as the resulting inequities can be rectified, helping professionals can play an important role by listening to those they are intended to serve and by setting a standard for others in the community.

RESOURCES

R. L. Burgdorf, *The Legal Rights of Handicapped Persons* (Baltimore: Paul H. Brookes, 1980).

R. M. Gordon & S. N. Verdun-Jones, *Adult Guardianship Law in Canada* (Toronto: Carswell, 1992).

Language of Pain (Downsview, Ontario: G. Allan Roeher Institute, 1988).

W. MacKay, *Education Law in Canada* (Toronto: Emond-Montgomery Publications, 1984).

D. Poirier, L. Goguen & P. Leslie, *Education Rights of Exceptional Children In Canada* (Toronto: Carswell, 1988).

G. Robertson, *Mental Disability and the Law*, 2d ed. (Calgary: Carswell, 1993).

Take Action, Stand Up for Your Rights: Self-Advocates and the British Columbia Human Rights Act (Downsview, Ontario: G. Allan Roeher Institute, 1990) (available from the British Columbia Human Rights Council).

D. Vickers & O. Endicott, Mental Disability and Equality Rights. In A. Bayefsky & M. Eberts, eds., *Equality Rights and the Canadian Charter of Rights and Freedoms* (Toronto: Carswell 1985).

Vulnerable: Sexual Abuse and People with an Intellectual Handicap (Downsview, Ontario: G. Allan Roeher Institute, 1988).

W. Wolfensberger, *Normalization: The Principle of Normalization in Human Services* (Downsview, Ontario: National Institute of Mental Retardation (now the G. Allan Roeher Institute), 1972).

For information on people with mental disabilities contact the British Columbia Association for Community Living (B.C.A.C.L.), the Canadian Association for Community Living (C.A.C.L.), and the G. Allan Roeher Institute at York University, in Downsview, Ontario. The latter has produced many publications dealing with disability and Canadian social policy.

For information on people with physical disabilities contact the Council of Canadians with Disabilities (C.C.D.) in Winnipeg, Manitoba, the British Columbia Coalition of Persons with Disabilities, or the British Columbia Paraplegic Association.

END NOTES

1. *Charter of Rights and Freedoms*, Part I of the *Constitution Act*, 1982, being Schedule B of the *Canada Act, 1982* (UK), 1982, c. 11.
2. *Constitution Act,* 1867 (UK) 30 & 31 Vict., c. 3. (Formerly the *BNA Act*).
3. Human rights legislation prohibits any person, whether an individual or a corporate entity, whether public or private, from discriminating against an individual or group on the basis of specified characteristics, in certain specified activities. In British Columbia, the *Human Rights Code*, R.S.B.C. 1996, c. 210, bars discrimination on the basis of "physical or mental disability" in purchase of property, rental premises, employment advertising, employment practices including hiring, firing or any term or condition of work, membership in unions and associations, and in "a service or facility customarily available to the public."
4. Special Committee on the Disabled and the Handicapped, "Report: Obstacles" (Ottawa: Minister of Supply and Services, February 1981); "Report: Obstacles Progress Report," (Ottawa: Minister of Supply and Services, June 1982).
5. Attorney General of California, "Commission on Disability Report" (California, 1990) at 4. In the *Canadian Human Rights Act*, R.S.C. 1985, c. H-6, s.3(1), "disability" is defined for all purposes of the *Act* as one of the proscribed grounds of discrimination. Section 25 defines disability to mean: "any previous or existing disability and includes disfigurement and previous or existing dependence on alcohol or a drug." The protection under the *Canadian Human Rights Act* is restricted to those matters that come within federal jurisdiction; e.g. employment with banks, access to commercial airlines, rental of federally subsidized housing. The British Columbia *Human Rights Code* does not define "physical or mental disability."
6. It was not until the final draft of section 15 of the *Charter* that mental and physical disability were included. See P. Hogg, *Canada Act 1982 Annotated*, (Toronto: Carswell, 1982) at 50-52.
7. *Canadian Charter of Rights and Freedoms*, Part I of the *Constitution Act* 1982, being Schedule B of the *Canada Act* 1982 (U.K.), 1982, c. 11.
8. *Andrews v. Law Society of B.C.*, (1989), 1 S.C.R. 143.
9. *R. v. Morgentaler*, (1988), 1 S.C.R. 30 at 175.

10. *R. v. Oakes*, (1986), 1 S.C.R. 103.

11. (1995) 7 BCLR (3d) 156 (BCCA).

12. Human Rights complaint filed against hospital by the Canadian Association for Community Living; Quebec Human Rights Commission (1989), No. 8806005301-0001-0.

13. *Re B*, (1981), 1 W.L.R. 1421 at 1422-1424 (C.A.).

14. A troubling ethical issue has arisen with respect to new reproductive technologies that make diagnoses of disabling conditions in the foetus increasingly available. The purpose of some testing is not treatment of the condition *in utero*, but providing parents with information on which to base a decision whether to terminate a pregnancy. In this circumstance, issues of reproductive choice conflict with disabled persons' long-standing abhorrence of anything resembling the eugenics movement of the early 20th century. See Royal Commission on New Reproductive Technologies, *Proceed with Care: The Final Report of the Royal Commission on New Reproductive Technologies*, (Ottawa, 1993), and J. Mosoff, "Reproductive Technology and Disability: Searching for the "Rights" and Wrongs in Explanation," (1993) 16 *Dalhousie Law Journal* 98.

15. *S.D. v. Superintendent of Family and Child Service*, (1983), 42 B.C.L.R. 173 at 183 (S.C.).

16. Although this position is in doubt following a series of Supreme Court of Canada decisions which appear to reject application of the *Charter* to publicly funded institutions, unless they are subject to a significant degree of statutory control. See *McKinney v. Board of Governors of the University of Guelph*, (1990), 3 S.C.R. 229; *Stoffman v. Vancouver General Hospital*, (1991), W.W.R. 576 (S.C.C.); *Harrison v. University of B.C.*, [1990], [1991] W.W.R. 681 (S.C.C.).

17. For example, *Peters v. University Hospital of Saskatoon*, (1980), 2 CHRR D/358 (Sask. Board of Inquiry). The Baby Dan case referred to above is another example. While the coroner's report indicated the cause of death to be Down's Syndrome, a human rights complaint against the hospital was accepted for investigation by the Quebec Human Rights Commission. The Commission limited its inquiry to the issue of how to prevent such occurrences in the future. Of some concern, professional disciplinary proceedings were brought against the nurse who reported the incident for allegedly breaching a duty of confidentiality owed, not to the infant, but to the parents.

18. Supra, note 11.

19. *R. v. Wiens*, (Guilty plea entered June 22, 1984, Ont. Prov. Ct. Crim. Div.) [unreported].

20. D. McCallum, "Aversives: Differential `Treatment' for People with a Mental Handicap" in *Language of Pain*, (Downsview, Ont.: G. Allan Roeher Institute, 1988) c.10.

21. *Ogg-Moss v. R.*, (1984), 2 S.C.R. 171.

22. E.g., *R. v. Atikian*, (7 July 1990), (Ont. S.C.) [unreported], where a child died from the effects of a naturopathic diet and lack of medical treatment. The parents of the child were convicted of causing death by failing to provide the necessities of life.

23. *Latimer v. Her Majesty the Queen*, [1995] S.J. No.402 (Sask. C.A.).

24. *R. v. Latimer*, (1997) 1 S.C.R. 217.

25. *Rodriguez v. Attorney-General of B.C.*, [1993] 3 SCR 519.

26. *Barnes v. Kirk*, [1968] 2 O.R. 213 (C.A.).

27. R.S.B.C. 1996, c. 288, section 22.

28. *McCorkell v. Director of Riverview Hospital et al*, (1993) 81 BCLR (2d) 273 (BCSC).

29. (1991) 82 D.L.R. (4th)298 (O.C.A.).

30. *Malette v. Shulman* (1990), 67 D.L.R. (4th) 321 (O.C.A.).

31. (1992) 86 DLR (4th) 385 (C.S.).

32. *Re Eve*, [1986] 2 S.C.R. 388, 31 D.L.R. (4th) 1. But also see *Re B*, [1987] W.L.R. 1213 (H.L.) for the opposite position on this issue taken by the United Kingdom's highest court.

33. *Re K* (1985), 60 B.C.L.R. 209, revised, (1985) 63 B.C.L.R. 145 (C.A.) leave to appeal to S.C.C. dismissed on jurisdictional grounds, (1985) 62 B.C.L.R. xii (S.C.C.).

34. *Muir v. Alberta*, (unreported, January 25, 1996). See Law Reform Commission of Canada, *Protection of Life: Sterilization*, (Working Paper No. 24) (Ottawa: Law Reform Commission of Canada, 1979) for a discussion of the eugenics movement and its impact on Canadian law.

35. R.S.B.C. 1996, c. 349.

36. R.S.B.C. 1996, c. 181.

37. *Ibid*, sections 15,16 and 17.

38. *Ibid*, section 19.

39. R.S.B.C. 1996, c. 6.

40. R.S.B.C. 1996, c. 405.

41. R.S.B.C. 1996, c. 383.

42. *Nova Scotia (Minister of Community Services) v. Burke*, (1989), 91 N.S.R. (2d) 413 (Fam. Ct.). See also *Minister of Health and Community Services v. Cormier*, (19 September 1990), FDM 282-90 (N.B.Q.B.) [unreported].

43. *Representation Agreement Act*, R.S.B.C. 1996, c. 405, section 10.

44. The British Columbia Association for Community Living has established a Project to Review Adult Guardianship which at the time of publication was ongoing.

45. Guardianship of the person has generally been understood as encompassing all important decisions affecting a person's life, including where they reside. The *Dependent Adults Act*, R.S.A. 1980, C. D-32 is an example of reform legislation that requires the court granting a guardianship order to specify the guardian's particular powers in each case, limiting them only to those decisions which it appears necessary for the guardian to make. The legislation gives an inclusive list of such powers, including the power to determine residence. The *Adult Guardianship Act* in British Columbia, not yet proclaimed, contains similar provisions.

46. *Clark v. Clark* (1982), 40 O.R. (2d) 383, 4 C.H.R.R. D/1187 (Co. Ct).

47. *Alcoholism Foundation of Manitoba v. Winnipeg*, (City) [1990] 6 W.W.R.232 (Man. C.A.)], rev'g. [1988] 6 W.W.R. 440 (Man. Q.B.).

48. *Timms v. Port Moody Senior Housing Society*, (1986) 7 C.H.R.R. D/3491 (B.C.H.R.C.).

49. *Aquilina v. Pokoj*, (1991) 14 C.H.R.R. D/230 (Ontario Board of Inquiry).

50. G. Allan Roeher Institute, *Poor Places: Disability-Related Residential Support Services* (Downsview, Ontario: G. Allan Roeher Institute, 1990).

51. *Alcoholism Foundation of Manitoba v. Winnipeg (City)*, *supra*, note 47.

52. Federal employment equity legislation requires that major employers under federal jurisdiction develop plans for hiring members of historically underrepresented groups, but leaves enforcement to the general provisions of human rights law. For a discussion, see Standing Committee on Human Rights and Status of Disabled Persons, *A Consensus for Action: The Economic Integration of Disabled Persons*, (Ottawa: Standing Committee on Human Rights and Status of Disabled Persons, June 1990). Ontario legislation introduced in 1993 that contained enforcement provisions for large employers that failed to meet employment equity targets was repealed by the new provincial government shortly after its election in 1995. The British Columbia government has adopted an employment equity policy for its own personnel operations, but the province has no legislation in this area.

53. *Fenton v. Attorney-General of B.C.*, [1991] 5 W.W.R. 600 (BCCA), reversing 56 B.C.L.R. (2d) (BCSC). A new *Employment Standards Act* was enacted in 1995. It does not contain the exempting clause referring to "handicapped persons" in the former statute (section 105(3)), but instead exempts "time-limited government incentive program[s]" providing training to income assistance recipients (B.C. Reg. 396/95, section 32(d)).

54. *Villeneuve v. Bell Canada* (1985), 6 C.H.R.R. D/2988 (Canadian Human Rights Tribunal).

55. *Funk v. Stowe-Woodward Inc.*, (1987), 8 C.H.R.R. D/4024 (B.C.H.R.C.).

56. *Swanson v. Steveshire Restaurant* (1985), 6 C.H.R.R. D/2662 (B.C.H.R.C.).

57. *Boehm v. National System of Baking Ltd.*, (1987), 8 C.H.R.R. D/4110 (Ont. Human Rights Bd. of Inquiry).

58. *Battlefords and District Co-operative Ltd. v. Gibbs*, [1996] 3 S.C.R. 566.

59. *Central Alberta Dairy Pool v. Alberta*, (Human Rights Commission) (1990), 6 W.W.R. 193 (S.C.C.). See more recent discussion in *Large v. Stratford* (1995), 24 C.H.R.R. D/1 (S.C.C.)

60. See D. Lepofsky, "The Duty to Accommodate: A Purposive Approach," (1992) 1 Canadian Labour Law Journal 14.

61. *Universal Declaration of Human Rights*, 1948, U.N. Doc. A/811.

62. *International Covenant on Economic, Social and Cultural Rights*, (1966), the *International Declaration of the Rights of the Child*, (1959), and the *Declaration of the Rights of the Mentally Retarded*, (1971).

63. *Convention on the Rights of the Child*, U.N. General Assembly, adopted on November 10, 1989.

64. *Bales v. Board of School Trustees*, (1985), 54 B.C.L.R. 203 (S.C.).

65. *Elwood v. Halifax County - Bedford District School Board*, (February 16, 1987), (N.S.S.C.), (unreported).

66. *Re Eaton et al. and Brant Country Board of Education: Canadian Disability Rights Council, Intervenors* (1995), 22 OR (3d) 1.

67. *Education Act*, R.S.O. 1990, c. E.2., section 8(3).

68. *Eaton et al.*, at 21.

69. *Eaton v. Brant Country Board of Education and Attorney General for Ontario*, (1997), 1 S.C.R. 241.

70. *Attis v. Board of School Trustees District No. 15* (1989), 100 N.B.R. (2d) 181 (N.B.C.A.).

254

71. *Commission Scolaire Saint-Jean-sur-Richelieu v. Commission des droits de la personne du Quebec & Lanoue & Marcil*, (1994), 21 C.H.R.R. D/173, and *Commission Scolaire Chauveau & C.S. Ancienne-Lorette-Montclam v. Commission des droits de la personne du Quebec & Gervais & Rouette*, (1994) 21 C.H.R.R. D/189.

72. *School Act*, R.S.B.C. 1996, c.412, section 11.

73. *Rowett v. York Region Board of Education*, (1989), 69 O.R. (2d) 543, (C.A.), reversing (1988), 63 O.R. (2d) 767 (H.C.).

74. *School Act*, S.A. 1988, c. S-31, section 104.

75. *Eggert v. County of Strathcona No. 20* (December 21, 1990), (Minister of Education), (unreported).

76. *Berg v. U.B.C.*, (1993), 2 S.C.R. 353 (S.C.C.) In this case, a graduate student in a diet and nutrition program complained that once members of faculty became aware of her history of mental illness, they denied her various privileges available to other students, including a ratings sheet needed by prospective employers, and a key to a common area. The university's argument that services provided in a graduate program were not "customarily available to the public" was rejected by the Supreme Court.

77. A national commission of Inquiry on Canadian University Education established under the auspices of the Association of Universities and Colleges of Canada, received advice that the more opportunities for adults with a mental handicap should be created in post-secondary institutions.

78. Report of the Chief Electoral Officer, (Ottawa: Minister of Supply and Services, 1989) at 31-32.

79. *Municipal Act*, R.S.B.C. 1996, c. 323.

80. See D. Lepofsky, "Equal access to Canada's judicial system for persons with disabilities--a time for reform," (1995) 5 National Journal of Constitutional Law, 183.

81. British Columbia Supreme Court Rule 6 provides in paragraph (3) that anything that is required or authorized by the rules of court to be done by or invoked against a person under a disability shall be done by the guardian.

82. *Swain v. Her Majesty the Queen*, [1991] 1 S.C.R. 933.

83. *Evans v. Her Majesty the Queen*, [1991] 1 S.C.R. 869.

84. *Marriage Act*, R.S.B.C. 1996, c. 282, section 35.

85. *Webb v. Webb*, (1968), 3 D.L.R. (3d) 100 (N.S.S.C.).

86. Every province except Newfoundland has an Ombudsman, statutorily authorized to investigate in an independent way the administrative decision-making of government, and make recommendations to correct instances of maladministration. There is no federal Ombudsman to perform a similar role for that jurisdiction.

87. R.S.B.C. 1996, c. 340.

88. *B.C. Development Corporation v. Friedmann*, [1984] 2 S.C.R. 447.

89. For general discussion of the role of a legislative Ombudsman, see articles in L. Reif, M. Marshall, C. Ferris, eds., *The Ombudsman: Diversity and Development* (Edmonton: International Ombudsman Institute, 1993). For a particular discussion related to disability, see *Righting Wrongs: Disability, Your Ombudsman and You*, (Downsview, Ontario: G. Allan Roeher Institute, 1989).

90. R.S.B.C. 1996, c. 210.

91. R.S.B.C. 1996, c. 27.

92. R.S.B.C. 1996, c. 97, (proclaimed in force March 31, 1997).

Chapter 11

EDUCATION AND THE LAW

Yvonne M. Martin

INTRODUCTION

Most of the important decisions that school teachers make daily are guided by their professional knowledge, professional judgment, and even by common sense; but there is a constellation of predetermined legal rules that also must apply to some of these decisions. These rules most often deal with situations in which conflict of values arise -- a frequent occurrence since school teaching takes place in an increasingly more complex social setting with conflicting values. These conflicts may occur between teachers and parents, teachers and students, teachers and school administration, and even among teachers themselves. Whichever is the case, teachers face increasingly difficult decisions that call for the exercise not only of professional knowledge and professional judgment, but also for the application of legal rules; that is, laws.

These laws are important because, although they are subject to change, they contain at any point in time prevailing provincial values, which as such are enforceable by the courts. (See Table 1 for a summary of the major laws which form the legal basis of public school education in British Columbia). When conflicts arise these laws become an important point of reference and are applied in the resolution of conflict. They spell out, among other things, important aspects of the relationships among students, parents, and teachers. They also specify the legal functions, duties, rights, responsibilities, and liabilities of teachers and other school officials.

Teachers and other school officials are sometimes unsure of what these laws are and of the implications they hold for their professional lives. This uncertainty or lack of knowledge about the law sometimes renders teachers less effective as professionals, because it prevents them from taking necessary and appropriate actions in their students' interests, and even in their own interests.

For example, a teacher-counsellor who is unclear of the laws relating to student records may in good faith and on sound professional basis attempt to deny a parent or principal access to counselling notes made about a student. This denial of access may be on either or both of two grounds that are clearly reasonable, but which may be unsupported by law at this time. Such a teacher may argue first, that the notes are the counsellor-teacher's personal and therefore private record of information made to jog the memory. Second, the disclosure of information that was gained in confidence would violate the counsellor-client relationship. This could breed distrust and put students at jeopardy. They may thenceforth withhold trust and refuse to seek help. There is a need to protect the student's privacy at all cost. This example will be dealt with more fully later in this chapter, but it highlights here the need for professional values and legal rules to be considered jointly when such decisions are to be made. It is by no means clear that the law would support the teacher-counsellor's position in most cases.

Table 1. A summary of the legislation (with corresponding major feature) governing public education in British Columbia.

LEGISLATION	MAJOR FEATURE
Child, Family and Community Service Act, 1996	Obliges any person who knows that a child is in need of protection to report to the director of Family and Child Service.
Constitution Act, 1867	Gives the Provincial Government exclusive authority to make laws related to education.
Constitution Act, 1982 (*Charter of Rights and Freedoms*)	Guarantees fundamental rights and freedoms to individuals.
Criminal Code of Canada, 1985	Decriminalises reasonable use of force by school authorities for purposes of correction.
Criminal Record Review Act, (1995)	Makes criminal record checks mandatory for all current and prospective employees who work with children in agencies which are operated or licensed by or receive funding from the Government.
Infants Act, 1996	Gives a child under 18 the right of access to health care without parental consent.
Freedom of Information and Protection of Privacy Act, 1996	Gives right of access to public information while protecting the privacy of personal information held by public bodies (schools and boards).
Human Rights Code, 1996	Provides protection for human rights of all British Columbians.
Labour Relations Code, 1996	Governs employer-employee labour relations.
Ombudsman Act, 1996. (The Ombudsman's jurisdiction over education was proclaimed in 1992.)	Provides for investigation of complaints against public schools and school boards.
Public Education Labour Relations Act, 1996	Provides for a two-tiered system of collective bargaining between boards and teacher unions.
School Act, 1996	Governs the provision and delivery of public school education.
Teaching Profession Act, 1996	Provides for the regulation of the teaching profession by the College of Teachers.
Young Offenders Act, 1985. (Amended by the S.C. c. 19, 1995. Assented to June 22nd, 1995. Proclaimed Dec. 1995).	Provides for young persons (12 to 18 years old) who commit crimes within federal and provincial jurisdiction.

Teachers and other school officials may sometimes be unclear of the content of the laws relating to schools and schooling, and of the implications these laws hold for their professional lives. This ignorance of the law exacerbates problems that occur naturally when individuals with differing roles, duties, responsibilities, and powers under an *Act*, and with differing personal interests and values, are required to collaborate. The primary purpose of this chapter is to provide all helping professionals, and especially public school teachers, with basic information about the law as it relates to the full and proper role of teachers.[1] First, the chapter presents in summary form legislation and policy defining the roles assigned to teachers, parents, the principal, the school board, and the Minister. Second, the chapter highlights for discussion some of the major areas of conflict, tensions, and uncertainty when teachers interact with others, and attempts to clarify the law related to the education of children. Lastly, the chapter concludes with an attempt to answer several common questions asked by teachers and other educators.

In pursuit of these ends, the following section will describe the law regarding the rights/entitlements, responsibilities, duties, and powers, where applicable, of parents and students, teachers, principal, Minister, and school boards in British Columbia. Professionals who read this chapter will find information designed to improve their understanding of the law and to help them function in a more legally defensible and professionally responsible manner. The law is stated as of December 31, 1997.

RIGHTS, RESPONSIBILITIES, DUTIES, AND POWERS

A. Parents and Students

Although the *School Act, 1996*[2] (hereafter referred to as the *Act*) technically provides for <u>entitlements</u> rather than <u>rights</u> of parents and students, functionally rights and entitlements are the same. Some of these are given exclusively to parents, others exclusively to students, and yet others to both parents and students. In practical terms, however, it is not always possible to separate exclusive student entitlements from those of their parents, as most often a parent acts as a child's advocate before the law when issues related to his/her rights or entitlements arise.

A student is entitled in the *Act*:

a) to enroll in an educational program provided by a board;[3]

b) to consult with a teacher or administrative officer regarding her/his educational program;[4]

c) to receive an educational program in English;[5] and

d) to receive an educational program in French where parents have a right to have their children receive instruction in French under the *Charter of Rights and Freedoms*.[6]

With these entitlements to students come two primary responsibilities, namely:

a) to comply with the rules authorised by the principal and with the code of conduct and other rules and policies of the board; and

b) to participate in the educational program.[7]

Failure to comply with either of these are the only grounds upon which a board may refuse to offer an educational program[8] to a student over 16 years of age. There are no provisions for refusal to offer an educational program to a student under 16 years of age.

Parents are entitled in the *Act*:

a) to information on a student's attendance, behaviour, and progress. Reporting by teachers to parents must occur <u>at least</u> five times during the school year-- three written reports and at least two informal reports (emphasis added).[9]

b) upon request, to annual reports respecting the general effectiveness of educational programs in the school district;[10]

c) to membership on a parent advisory council (PAC). A PAC may advise the board and the principal and staff respecting any matter relating to the school;[11] and

d) to consultation regarding the placement of a special needs student in an educational program.[12]

Ministry of Education, Skills and Training policy toward a special needs student and his/her parent is clear. Parents are to play a vital partnership role with educators and other service personnel in the education of their children. A parent is to be an active partner in the decision-making process related to special needs students, because this process works best when there is collaboration and ongoing consultation among teachers, administrative and support personnel, parents, and students. The current policy, as contained in Ministry of Education, Skills and Training policy and procedures manual, requires that the parent is to:

a) be involved in all phases of the identification/assessment process;

b) be involved on a case-by-case basis as a member of the school-based team set up to plan and provide support for the development of the individual education program (IEP) and for classroom strategies; and

c) be involved in all the planning phases for the special needs student.[13]

With respect to the working relationship between teachers and parents of special needs students, the onus is on teachers:

to maintain the ability to manage their classrooms while respecting the advice and role of parents. When disagreements occur, they may be resolved through a review of the IEPs to determine how classroom activities can best relate to the goals established in the IEPs. Every attempt should be made to resolve differences at the level of the school or district level.[14]

On her/his part, a parent has a duty to go to the school and consult about a student's educational program if a teacher or administrative officer makes that request.[15] It does not seem, however, that, on the face of the law, the intention in the *Act* is to force parents to comply with this duty. Parents who do not comply with a teacher or principal's request to come in and consult appear to be able to do so without any legal consequences. It should be noted, however, that technically, failure to comply might be considered punishable under the *Offence Act*.[16] By contrast, parents who refuse to register a child who is being schooled at home face serious consequences under ministerial orders.

Ministry of Education, Skills and Training policy, announced as an order in council,[17] gives the parents with a child in a school the following rights, option, and responsibilities:

a) the right to participate in the process of determining the educational goals, policies, and services provided for their children. Correspondingly, they have the <u>responsibility</u> to ensure that children are provided with the healthy and supportive environment necessary for learning. Also, they have the <u>responsibility</u> to help shape and support the goals of the school system and to share in the tasks of educating their young.

b) the right to enroll their children in a registered independent school of their choice, and the corresponding <u>responsibility</u> to ensure the curriculum and programs offered are of suitable quality.

c) the option to school at home with the corresponding <u>responsibility</u> to register their children in a public school or independent school, or a correspondence or regional school.[18]

It is not yet clear what is the status of these rights, which appear to offer substantially more than parents are entitled to under the provisions of the *Act*.

With respect to rights jointly held, parents and students each have all the rights and freedoms guaranteed by the *Charter*. In addition, under the *Act* they are entitled equally to do the following:

a) to examine all student records pertaining to that student; and

b) to receive a copy without charge.[19]

Also, either parent or student may separately (and reasonably jointly) appeal a decision or indecision of an employee of a board, which they perceive as significantly affecting the education, health, or safety of the student.[20]

These expressly given entitlements, options, and responsibilities, particularly those to parents, are of historic significance. They mark the first time in post-Confederation British Columbia that parents have gained legal recognition in the education of their children. The fact that these entitlements are so recent in origin seems to go a long way in explaining why several of the current areas of conflict for teachers centre on parental exercise of these newly gained entitlements.

B. Teachers

At the constitutional level teachers, as all Canadians, have all the rights and freedoms guaranteed by the *Charter*. In addition, they have all the employment rights, responsibilities, and entitlements negotiated in the collective agreement under the *Labour Relations Code*.[21] The *Act* and *Regulation* to the *Act* lay out clearly the duties and responsibilities of teachers; however, it is the collective agreement that specifies precisely how teachers carry out their legal duties. In addition, it specifies the consequences that will follow a board's exercise of its legal powers over a teacher.

A teacher's responsibilities include designing, supervising, and assessing the educational program, and providing instruction to individual students and groups of students. A teacher's duty includes:

a) the provision of instruction;

b) assistance with the supervision of students;

c) ensuring that students understand and comply with the rules of the school and with the code of conduct of the Board;

d) maintaining school records; and

e) providing parents regularly with progress reports on students.[22]

Note too, that the *Child, Family and Community Service Act* provides that a person "who has reason to believe that a child needs protection must promptly report the matter to a director (of the Ministry for Children and Families) or a person designated by a director."[23] This provision relates specifically to protecting children from physical and emotional harm, sexual abuse and exploitation, and abandonment.[24]

The *Teaching Profession Act*[25] (*TPA*) and the professional *Code of Ethics* established by the British Columbia Teachers' Federation[26] both deal with some aspects of inter-teacher relationships. The *TPA* establishes the College of Teachers which is charged (among others) with the responsibility of establishing standards for the education, professional responsibility, and competence of teachers, and with the discipline of its members. The College may initiate disciplinary action against a member under all or any of the following three circumstances:

a) upon the receipt of a report from a board of a public school or an authority of an independent school that it has dismissed, suspended, or otherwise disciplined a member, or that the member has resigned and the board/authority considers that it is in the public interest to report the resignation;[27]

b) upon a receipt of a complaint made against a member in writing and signed by five members; or

c) upon the receipt by the Registrar of the College of a report relating to the conduct of a member.[28]

A relevant tenet of the *Code of Ethics* is that a teacher be "willing to review with colleagues, students and their parents/guardians the quality of service rendered by the teacher and the practices employed in discharging professional duties" (*Code of Ethics*, item 4). Also relevant to later discussion in this chapter is item 5, namely:

A teacher directs any criticism of the teaching performance and related work of a colleague to that colleague in private and only then, after informing the colleague in writing of the intent to do so, may direct in confidence the criticism to appropriate individuals who are in a position to offer advice and assistance.

A footnote points out that the reporting of suspected child abuse to the proper authorities according to legal requirements under the *Child, Family and Community Act*[29] does not constitute a breach of this item of the *Code*.

C. The Principal

A principal is responsible for the administration and supervision of a school. This responsibility includes:

a) implementing the educational program;

b) the placement and programming of students;

c) timetabling of teachers;

d) the maintenance of school records;

e) the general conduct of students; and

f) student evaluation and assessment, and reporting to parents.[30]

Furthermore, it is the principal's duty to evaluate a teacher and to report to the board, and to make recommendation to the superintendent respecting dismissal or discipline. With regard to student discipline, the principal has paramount authority and may suspend a student in accordance with the rules of the school and rules and policies of the board, if the board does not expressly forbid such action on a principal's part.[31]

D. The Minister

The Minister, by law, has complete and final powers over the educational programs, or the curriculum. Specifically, the Minister:

a) determines the general provision for the educational programs;

b) specifies educational program guides;

c) governs educational resource materials used in support of the programs;

d) determines requirements for graduation from an educational program; and

e) assesses and reports on the effectiveness of educational programs.[32]

These powers are viewed by the BCTF as excessive and it has called for their repeal.[33]

E. The School Board

Responsibility for the provision of schooling lies at the local or district level. In accordance with the *Act*, a school board has responsibility for determining the local policies and rules in each school district. In addition, the board is responsible for providing educational programs, for establishing a code of conduct for students and for rules related to suspension, for the hiring and the grounds for discipline of teachers, and for assignment and reassignment of students to programs and specific schools.

AREAS OF CONFLICT

This section of the chapter highlights conflicts that currently stem from the intermeshing of the roles, responsibilities, and powers of the various roles described above. These conflicts seem to fall generally into two categories: those stemming from confusion or uncertainty about parental entitlements and powers; and those stemming from confusion or uncertainty about teacher duties, responsibilities, and professional relationships among themselves.

I. Conflicts Respecting Parental Entitlements

In the wake of the current provisions of rights and entitlements for parents, conflicts surrounding the parental role have become more frequent than they have been formerly. Such conflict often centres on:

a) the involvement of parents in the preparation of individual educational programs (IEPs) for special needs students;

b) their demand for accurate, reliable progress reports on their children;

c) their request to have their children excused from certain subjects or classes;

d) their attempts to gain access to information about their children's teacher; and

e) their efforts to appeal decisions they consider not in their or their children's best interest.

These will be dealt with in order below:

A. Teacher-Parent Tensions and the Preparation of an Individual Education Plan (IEP)

The development and implementation of an IEP is a significant potential source of tensions between a parent and the teacher. Current requirements seem to put teachers on the frontier of a change in policy that is a significant departure from tradition. This change puts a strain on the exercise of professional autonomy as parents assume decision-making powers not formerly held.

At the heart of the *Act* is the educational program -- an organised set of learning activities, which, "in the opinion of the board, is designed to enable learners to develop their individual potential...."[34] As noted in the summary of the relevant provisions presented in the section above, all students are entitled to receive an educational program. The Minister has power to determine all aspects of the educational program,[35] a school board is obliged to provide a program for a student, a principal is responsible for implementing the program at the school level, and it is a teacher's duty to deliver the program.

There are special provisions for the educational program of <u>special needs students</u>. Special needs students are those with either a disability of an intellectual, physical, sensory, emotional, or behavioural nature, or who have a learning disability, or who have exceptional gifts or talents. These students are entitled to an <u>individual</u> educational program (IEP). This program differs from the regular program in three ways: first, it is tailor-made for the student; second, expectations and outcomes generally established for students in the regular program may be modified or adapted, or both, to meet the needs of the student; and third, a parent has a legal right to participate actively in all phases of its development and delivery.[36]

This recently acquired right (1988) exceeds those of parents of students without disability or exceptional gifts, and teachers have not been traditionally accustomed to having parents participate at this level. Furthermore, although this policy is laudable and necessary, it results in a restriction of a teacher's freedom as a practitioner, and in some cases difficulties with its implementation might be anticipated. It clearly gives extra duties and responsibilities to teachers and presents them with further challenges. As professionals with autonomy in their classrooms, teachers have been unaccustomed, before now, to sharing with parents (their clients) the business of "diagnosis" and "prescription": that is, the act of identification and assessment of problems and of determining the policies, goals, and services to be provided a student, and the strategies to be used in the provision of the services.

Some teachers are likely to feel fear, either because of the lack of a tradition of such a relationship or of the lack of relevant training. Others may feel resentment because of the extra burdens the new requirement might entail. Yet others may feel a loss of face in those instances in which they may be dealing with parents who might have garnered over the years more knowledge of a child's disability or area of exceptionality than the teacher, or may, in the teacher's view, be overly zealous or unrealistic about a student's future. These will likely be major sources of conflict.

In summary, two things seem clear: first, a parent has the right to participate actively in all important decisions regarding special needs students; second, the Ministry perceives that the onus is on teachers to find the point of balance between their role and that of parents. Such a point of balance might become clearer over time with more specialised training and carefully worded contract language.

B. Teacher-Parent Conflicts Respecting Reports

Parent-teacher conflicts respecting reports on the progress, behaviour, and attendance of a student seem to be largely a matter of particular interpretation by each of statutory provisions for these reports. There seems to be scope for error on both sides.

In law a teacher has a duty to provide reports on a student, and a parent is entitled to these reports. There are to be three mandatory written reports, and <u>at least two informal</u> reports. Further, the professional *Code of Ethics* requires that a teacher be willing to "review with parents/guardians the quality of service rendered by the teacher and the practices employed in discharging professional duties" (*Code of Ethics*, item 4).

The mandatory written reports appear to be less of a source of conflict than the informal reports. The law is clear about the number of formal reports and about what they should contain. This form of reporting has also had a long-standing tradition and legal history. By contrast, although there have traditionally been informal reporting to parents, <u>informal reports</u> have only recently been legislated, and the law is less specific about what they should contain and about how many of them should there be. Areas of conflict, therefore, are more likely to arise around them.

There are several examples of instances in which this might be the case. Conflict might arise:

a) when a parent insists on a right to talk to a teacher whenever or as many times as he/she wishes to do so;

b) when a parent who does not have legal custody of a student attempts to get information about a student;

c) when a parent of a truant high school student seeks almost daily reports in the attempt to gain greater control over attendance; or

d) when a teacher chooses to interpret the statutory provisions more narrowly than more broadly by attempting to set limits on the number of informal contacts a parent may have.

It seems clear that it is only a legitimate parent under the *Act* -- that is, a guardian, a person legally entitled to custody, a person who usually has the care and control of the student -- who has the right to reports on a student. Hence, it seems that a teacher may legally, and perhaps rightly ought to, refuse to give information to a biological parent who has neither legal custody, nor guardianship, nor usual control of a student.

A parent who insists on greater than average contacts with a teacher (especially if these contacts are confrontative) may, in fact, be harassing a teacher. There may be need for school boards to develop policy and guidelines to help provide guidance both to parents and teachers. The professional position on the matter seems clear. A teacher who either refuses to talk with parents, or, without good reason, is too legalistic in interpretation of the provisions for information to parents, may be in violation of the law or may be breaking the professional *Code of Ethics*, or both.

C. Parental Right to Have A Child Excused From Certain Classes or Courses

Parents do not have a statutory role in curriculum matters nor are there statutory provisions in the *Act* or the *Charter* which, *per se*, give a parent a right to withdraw a child from a class or a course. Furthermore, although it seems that there may be scope for the board to develop policy on the basis of which a parent may receive permission to have a student excused from portions of some classes, there may be limits to exemption from whole courses of study.

Under the *Act* the Minister, by order, sets the programs for study (for example, Fine Arts, Language Arts, Social Studies, and Mathematics), and provides the guides to these programs (for instance, Drama 10 Curriculum Guide, Composition 11 and 12 Curriculum Guide, Economics 12 Curriculum Guide, and Mathematics Grade 7-12 Curriculum Guide).

Program Guides set out the expected learning outcomes for each program of study and for each subject at each level of the school system. These guides also set out the requirements for graduation from each program. The specific content of a course, however, is first, a matter of board policy, and second, a choice by the teacher in the classroom. A student must participate in the educational program provided by the Board, and participation clearly includes working towards graduation.

The courts have long confirmed a province's powers under the *Constitution* to make decisions like these about education. By way of balance, however, the Supreme Court of Canada has endorsed a parent's right under the *Charter* to educate according to her/his own conscience and religion,[37] and to choose from among alternatives that meet reasonable standards set by a province.

Accordingly, under the *Act*, parents may choose to educate their children within the public system or outside the system at home or in independent schools. When they choose to opt out of the public system, they have power under the *Act* to decide upon the curriculum the child follows.

On the contrary, as noted earlier, parents who have opted for the public system forfeit the power to make unilateral decisions about students' curriculum. It seems clear that their children must follow the program of studies developed by the Minister and provided by a board. In these cases it seems that students may not be exempt from a course determined to be a requirement for graduation.

When all these points are taken into consideration, it seems that there may be scope for local boards to develop policy and rules to accommodate parents who wish, for reasons of religion and conscience, to have their children exempted from portions of classes as long as they are later able to satisfy the expected learning outcomes required for graduation from each level.

D. Teacher-Parent Conflicts Respecting Right of Access to a Teacher's Record

Sometimes a parent may attempt to gain access to a teacher's personnel file for derogatory purposes. Such a parent may have a case against a teacher and may suspect that the teacher's file contains information that would be supportive of the parent's position. Because the policy of government is toward openness and easy access to information held by public authorities, some parents mistakenly believe that they have a right of access to a teacher's personnel file. The law that grants freedom of access to information equally protects privacy and specifically personal information in the keeping of public bodies.

The *Freedom of Information and Protection of Privacy Act* (*FIPPA*) generally gives a person "the right of access to any record in the custody or under the control of a public body, including a record containing personal information."[38] It empowers the head of a public body (in this case a school board)[39] to disclose such a record to a third party (in this case the parent) only under the following conditions:

a) with the consent of the individual (teacher in this case),

b) if it is subpoenaed or ordered by a court,

c) to an officer/employee if the information is necessary for performance of duties (section 33(b)(e)(f)).

Since the parent is neither an officer nor an employee who needs the information for the performance of a duty, nor has the consent of the teacher, there seems to be no legal basis for gaining access to a teacher's file. Such access would be an unreasonable invasion of privacy. The Privacy Commissioner has ruled on such a case.

II. Conflicts/Issues Respecting Teachers

A. Teacher Right to Have a Violent Offender in Classroom Identified

Although the *Young Offenders Act* (*YOA*) provides generally for the protection of the privacy of young offenders, as of December 1995 it also provides for disclosure of information about young offenders to professionals including teachers and other school officials. However, this provision for disclosure is limited, and it does not seem to guarantee that teachers with young offenders in their classroom will necessarily have easy or automatic access to information about these students.

The *YOA* forbids all publication of any report that identifies a young person who may have or is alleged to have committed an offence. It also forbids the publication of any hearing or decision or appeal concerning a young offender in which the identity of the young person is made known.

There are some exceptions to this general rule, however. Information about a young offender may be disclosed to "a professional...engaged in supervision...of a young person, including the representative of any school board, school..."[40] where that disclosure is deemed necessary for either or all the following reasons:

a) to ensure compliance of the young offender with a court order; or

b) to ensure the safety of staff, students... (section 38(1.13)).

Further limits on disclosure are set in the requirement that a person to whom information is disclosed for the reasons stated above:

a) keep that information separately from the student's school records;

b) ensure that no other person has access to it; and

c) destroy the information when it is no longer required for the purpose for which it was disclosed (section 38(1.15)).

Youth workers are required by law to make reports that would normally include school attendance and performance records of a young offender for whom the court ordered school attendance. Therefore, a principal and a superintendent as representatives of a school board may be required to report to a youth worker on a young offender's attendance and performance in school. Note that this reporting does not seem necessarily to require the disclosure of all information about the young offender.

In the interest of ensuring the safety of staff and students, a principal as well as a teacher may sense a need to have the identity of a young offender in the school or classroom disclosed. While the law presented above provides for disclosure where safety of staff and students is at stake, there seems to be a strong argument that disclosure may only be legally justified when the risk is demonstrably clear, and when it can be established that disclosure is not merely a precautionary measure. Even where risk to safety can be demonstrated, disclosure of important details of the student's case may not be necessary. For instance, where a student has been convicted of a violent offence and has been ordered by the court to attend school it seems in keeping with the spirit of the law that a teacher be made generally aware of the fact that there are legal issues in the student's life but not of the specific details.

The rules that will govern the implementation of the disclosure to school officials will need to be clarified in Regulation and school board guidelines.

COMMON QUESTIONS

1. Does a student have a right to be in school despite her/his behaviour?

A school board has legal grounds to refuse to offer an educational program to a student, 16 years and over, who does not obey school rules, or comply with the code of conduct or policies of the board, or does not participate in the educational program. To be legally enforceable, however, the process by which a board refuses to offer a program to a student must be fair and just.

On the contrary, students under 16 years of age (that is, still within compulsory school age), who misbehave in these ways, may not be similarly refused an educational program. A board has no statutory grounds upon which to refuse to offer them an educational program. In both cases, that is more than and less than 16 years of age, the law provides for disciplinary action which could include suspension.

Note that technically, children in British Columbia of school age (5 to 19 years) have no right to be in a school, but rather, they have the right to enroll in an educational program. For most, this educational program is offered in a school. For others, it may be offered in a hospital, a detention centre, or, if home-bound, at home. A board has the power to assign and reassign students to specific schools.

While the board has final powers over suspension and over whether or not a school continues to offer a student an educational program, a principal may also suspend a student according to the rules of the school if board policy does not forbid such suspension.[41] The principal has paramount authority over discipline in school. In all cases of suspension, the student must continue to receive an educational program. In the case of the less than 16 year-old student, a board has some options. It may design an individual program to help deal with the student,[42] or assign the student to a special school. It must, however, continue to provide him/her with an educational program.

2. What are the rights of a student who has been suspended from school?

A student may legally be suspended from school by a board, a superintendent, or a principal. Although the *Act* provides for an appeal from suspension initiated by a principal or a superintendent (section 11), it does not provide for an appeal from a school board's decision to suspend a student. The principles of natural justice, however, require that a board provide a process for appeal from its decision to suspend a student. The Office of the Ombudsman also encourages school boards to develop an appeal process. Most if not all school boards, then, are likely to have a by-law that details the process for the appeal of a suspension.

Under common law a student has a right not to be suspended unfairly and a right to have an opportunity to a hearing before the suspension takes place. Furthermore, a student has a right to full notice of the reasons for the suspension, a right to defend himself/herself, and to have a legal advocate.

3. Do students with severe disabilities have a right to be integrated into regular classrooms?

The current law in British Columbia provides that unless the educational needs of a special needs student (which includes a student with severe disabilities) dictate otherwise, she/he must be integrated into classrooms with other students as long as the needs of the other students are not affected negatively.[43] It also empowers a board to assign and reassign students to specific schools or to educational programs (section 94). Special classes and schools that in the past used to be run for students with severe disabilities by some school jurisdictions now currently have no legal basis in British Columbia. The current law also requires that a principal consult with a parent of a student with disabilities regarding the placement of that student.

Sometimes a principal and a parent may disagree on the educational needs and, therefore, on the placement of a student with disabilities. Conflict may arise, therefore, and there may be need for a court of law to decide whose position should prevail. The Supreme Court of Canada has ruled (October, 1996) in favour of integration, while upholding a school board's right to put a child in a special class after reasonable efforts to accommodate that student in an integrated classroom have failed. The decision is in keeping with policy in British Columbia. It is not clear if it will in any way affect practice.

4. Do students have a right to an individualised or special program?

All students are entitled to an educational program, but only special needs students -- students with a disability or with exceptional gifts -- have a right to an individual educational program (IEP). An IEP is a program that has been modified and adapted to suit the specific needs of a special needs student. It appears that unless students are classified as having special needs, they may have no right to an individual program. This, though, is the legal position. Personal and professional ethics may sometimes leave a teacher with no option but to give extra assistance to a student who fails to qualify technically as having special needs, but who evidently needs individualised help.

5. Do students whose native language is not English have minority language protection in British Columbia?

All students in British Columbia whose first language is not English do not have equal protection for their native language. The *Act* guarantees every child of school age in British Columbia the right to an educational program in English (section 5(1)). The *Charter* provides for English and French minority language educational rights. In brief, the *Charter* guarantees native speakers of French who live in Anglophone provinces (and *vice versa*) a right to have their children instructed in their language when they live in a province in which their language is a minority language. Consistent with the *Charter*, the *Act* extends to French language minority students in British Columbia a right to instruction in French (section 5(2)).

This constitutional right is not extended to other language groups, and it seems that they do not have such minority language educational rights. The teaching of other minority languages (for example, Punjabi and Mandarin) occurs in schools in British Columbia largely as a result of provincial and local school board policy rather than protection of a legitimate right.

6. Do students have a right to English as a Second Language?

Although English as a second language (ESL) is offered by several school districts in British Columbia and is supported by the Ministry of Education, Skills and Training, there seems to be no legislation or specific provincial policy that provides a right to ESL or guarantees its provision. The strongest legal basis for ESL seems to be the general provincial policy towards greater diversity and choice in education.[44]

7. Do students have a right to race relations protection?

There are no provisions in the *Act* that offer race relations protection to students in British Columbia. In addition, provincial policy does not deal specifically with protection for racial groups. Furthermore, although the *Charter* offers protection against racial discrimination (section 15), it is not clear that even this provision can be said to offer race relations protection. The strongest legal provincial basis for race relations protection seems to be the general policy towards equity.[45] Equity as defined in the policy relates to the fair allocation of resources.

In the absence of legislation and clear policy that deals specifically with race relations, the Social Equity Branch of the Ministry of Education, Skills and Training and local school boards have developed guidelines for helping to deal with race relations issues in schools. The Special Programs Branch (formerly Social Equity Branch) of the Ministry of Education, Skills and Training works closely with curriculum writers and resource reviewers to promote the concepts of race relations and anti-racism throughout the curricula. Integrated Resource Packages for each subject and grade level have been reviewed by ministry staff and specialist teachers to ensure they are non-discriminatory, and enhance understanding of and respect for cultural diversity.[46]

8. Do teachers have the right to search students if they have good reason to believe that they are in possession of illegal substances or devices?

Although teachers have a duty under the *Act* to ensure that students comply with the rules of the school and the code of conduct of the Board, and although teachers are generally regarded by the courts as having authority to discipline students, in the absence of specific references to searches of students in the *Act,* there seem to be at least three good reasons to suggest that teachers should be cautious about searching students even if they believe that they have good reasons to do so.

First, the *School Act Regulation* (section 5(7)(g)) gives to the principal the responsibility for the general conduct of students and for exercising "paramount authority" over matters of discipline within the school. Reported cases both in Canada and the USA have dealt thus far with the consequences of searching by principals of both the person (for example, searching a pocket) and personal effects (for example, searching a locker or purse) of a student. It does not seem clear that a teacher has equal authority to search a student under the current law. Without such authority it may be illegal for a teacher to carry out such a search.

Second, the *Charter* guarantees everyone the right to be secure against unreasonable search and seizure. The courts have made a distinction between searches for disciplinary purposes and searches with the intent to prosecute, and they have established clear principles and rules that should be followed by a person with the authority to search students and their personal effects. Two primary rules have emerged as very important in carrying out a search that will not violate a student's constitutional rights. First, a person with the authority to search students must have reasonable grounds to believe that he/she will find evidence of an infraction of school rules. Second, the search should not be too invasive and should be reasonably related to the seriousness of the infraction and to the age and gender of the student.

Third, a student may be perceived as having a legitimate expectation of privacy of person and of personal effects. Hence, this legitimate expectation must be balanced with the school's duty to see to it that the school is a safe environment and that rules and codes of conduct are followed. Some schools seem to deal with this conundrum by taking steps to reduce students' expectation of privacy with respect to locker searches. They do this in some or all of the following ways:

a) Enter into a locker rental agreement in which the student agrees that the principal or a designate may search the locker without notice at any time.

b) Have students agree, as a condition of rental, to give to the principal the combination to the lock with the proviso that the student will be told if and when the locker is to be searched.

c) Include in a rental agreement an understanding that the locker remains the property of the school and could be searched at any time.

d) Outline in the School Handbook the circumstances in which the locker will be searched.

e) Set restrictions in school policy on the contents of lockers.

9. <u>Does a teacher have a duty to report to the police students who commit a crime?</u>

It is a crime under the *Criminal Code*[47] (*C.C.C.*) to "assist, comfort, or receive" for the purposes of enabling an escape, someone who has committed a crime (section 23(1)). However, the *C.C.C.* does not seem to place a legal obligation on a teacher or teacher-counsellor to report to the police, for instance, a student who has admitted in a counselling session to committing a crime. Teachers who counsel students in these circumstances must take care to avoid behaviour or action which could help the student escape detection and possible arrest. It should be noted, too, that withholding information from law enforcement authorities could result in a criminal charge. Also, withholding information from school authorities when asked may infringe school board policy and attract disciplinary action.

A related question concerns whether or not a teacher should notify the authorities of a student who threatens to commit a crime. There are no *C.C.C.* provisions which require that the police be notified in such a circumstance. There are, therefore, no hard and fast legal rules. In these instances, however, professional judgement might dictate that if a teacher believes that a student has the intention to carry out a criminal or self-destructive act, and the student cannot be dissuaded, it might be wise and in the student's best interests to inform the parent/guardian, the principal, or the police as the case requires. Factors which should affect this decision should include the following: 1) the seriousness of the threatened behaviour, 2) an assessment of the probability that the student will actually carry it out, and 3) the student's frame of mind. The teacher should also question the reasonableness of not informing the necessary authority/authorities, and also make some assessment of what other teachers would do under those circumstances. It is wise to check school and school board policy for relevant provisions about what things are to be reported to the principal and who should do the reporting to authorities outside the school.

10. <u>If teachers have reason to believe that a student is in need of protection must they tell the principal before telling social services?</u>

The *School Act* has no provisions relevant to this question. Under the *Child, Family and Community Service Act (1996)* (*CFCSA*) a person who has reason to believe that a child is in need of protection has a duty to report promptly to a local director (of Family and Child Services) or a person designated by the director (section 14). A report to the child care worker within the school is not sufficient. Reporting to the local director or person designated by the director is required even if the information upon which the belief was formed is confidential or is prohibited from disclosure under other legislation (for instance, *FIPPA*). It is an offence not to report such belief, and failure to report now carries a potential penalty of a fine of up to $10,000 or to imprisonment of up to 6 months, or both.

Some school boards may develop policy and guidelines pertaining to how such reports should be made by its employees. In the interest of maintaining the principal's administrative and supervisory authority over the school, some boards may likely require either that a principal be informed of the belief that the child is in need of protection and then make the report. Or, alternatively, the teacher may be directed to first inform the principal, who then makes the report.

The requirement in the *CFCSA* is that a teacher report directly to a local director of the Ministry for Children and Families, or a designate. Since local board policy may not supersede legislation, it seems reasonable to argue that boards which direct the principal to make the report or require that the principal be informed first of the suspicion, might be putting teachers who comply with that policy in jeopardy of the law.

11. <u>Does a student have the right to give consent for medical purposes</u>?

As of January 1993, a person less than 19 years of age in British Columbia has the right to give consent for "therapeutic, preventive, palliative, diagnostic, cosmetic or other health related purpose . . ." without reference to a parent or guardian (*Infants Act*, section 17).[48] Such services include:

a) birth control counselling and methods;

b) weight control and fitness regimes;

c) cosmetic surgery, e.g. breast augmentation;

d) sexually transmittable disease testing, counselling, and treatment;

e) alcohol and drug counselling and treatment; and

f) mental health counselling and treatment.

The health care provider must determine that the service is in the best interest of the young person, and must explain the nature and consequences of the service and the benefits and risks.

This provision applies to <u>health care providers</u>, which is defined broadly to include a person who is licensed, certified, or registered in a profession recognized by statute to offer the services listed above. It also includes other practitioners who may offer some of the same services although they are not licensed, registered, or certified in a profession.

Most teacher-counsellors are registered teachers, though they may not be registered in the Province under legislation, as are psychologists. It seems that when they offer students "therapeutic, preventive, diagnostic, of health related services," they may qualify as <u>health care providers</u> and the *Infants Act* would apply to them. In short, if a counsellor-teacher has determined that the counselling or treatment about to be offered is legal and is in the student's best interest, and if the nature and consequences of the service have been explained to the student, and the counsellor-teacher understands that the student does not want a parent to be informed, there seems to be no legal barrier to the provision of such service. The student alone may consent for the procedures listed above.

12. <u>Does a parent have a right to information given in confidence to a teacher-counsellor by a student</u>?

The current policy in British Columbia regards the parent as the primary client of education, and accordingly gives a parent right of access to information about a student. Specifically, the *Act* currently gives parents general entitlements to information about a student's attendance, behaviour, and progress (section 7(1)(a)). It also entitles a student and his/her parents to examine <u>all student records</u> kept by a board pertaining to that student. Furthermore, a parent and the student may receive a copy of the student's record, if so desired (section 9). Students and parents possess these rights either together or individually. Thus, at the present time a parent seems to be able to gain access, without the student's consent, to information given in confidence and contained in a student's record. These provisions give rise to at least three sets of questions. One set has to do with what is a student record. Another relates more generally to the protection of privacy for students. The other deals with the handling of confidential information.

The *Act* defines a <u>student record</u> as "a record of information in written or electronic form pertaining to a student...but does not include a record prepared by a person <u>if that person is the only person who will have access to the record</u>"[49] (emphasis added). Stereotypically, student records are understood to include all academic records and such prescribed documents as <u>report cards</u>, <u>PR cards</u> and, <u>confidential files</u>. On the face of it, the *Act* expressly states that a student record (to which a student and her/his parents are entitled to examine and receive a copy) excludes notes made by a teacher-counsellor for personal use only. However, there is a conflict between the narrow definition of record in the *Act*, and a broader defintion of the same term under the *Freedom of Information and Protection of Privacy Act (FIPPA)*. The latter includes <u>all</u> notes, whether or not they were intended for personal and private use.

The *FIPPA* provides that if there is a conflict between its own provisions and those of another piece of legislation (in this case the *Act*), the *FIPPA* provisions predominate unless the other piece of legislation expressly states that its own provisions will prevail despite the *FIPPA*. The *Act* does not expressly contain such a provision with respect to parental right of access to a student's record. This suggests that, despite the wording of the current *School Act*, parents may not have easy access to a teacher-counsellor's written notes without permission of the student.

Current provisions (*FIPPA* and the *Act*) also give rise to questions about a student's privacy. The record of information to which parents may have access under the *Act* is personal information to which only the student has right of access under the *FIPPA*. Parental right of access without the student's consent seems to run contrary to the general direction of the *FIPPA*, which generally prohibits the disclosure of information to a third party unless there is consent in writing. One, then, might anticipate a problem for a teacher-counsellor in those instances in which there is on record information given in confidence by a student who expressly requests that his/her parents not have access to the information.

With respect to the confidentiality of records, teacher-counsellors need to note the recent revisions to the *Legal and Ethical Guidelines* of the British Columbia School Counsellors Association[50]. While they still stress the confidentiality of information received from students, they now clarify the situations under which this information needs to be shared. These new guidelines permit the breaking of confidentiality into five circumstances. These circumstances read as follows:

a) CONSENT: With the consent of the student, the teacher-counsellor may divulge information received through the counselling relationship.

b) POTENTIAL HARM: If behaviour of the student threatens potential harm to him/herself or another person, the teacher-counsellor shall take appropriate action to protect the student and/or other person.

c) CHILD PROTECTION: A teacher-counsellor who has reason to believe that a child is or might be in need of protection shall forthwith report the information to the appropriate authorities in accordance with legal obligations pursuant to child protection legislation.

d) CONSULTATION AND COLLABORATION: A teacher-counsellor may consult and collaborate with other professionals for purposes of more effectively helping the student. The teacher-counsellor shall share only such information that will serve the best interests of the student.

e) LEGAL REQUIREMENTS: A teacher-counsellor may be required to provide records in compliance with the law.

The *Act* and the *FIPPA* also impose on a counsellor and other school officials a duty to keep information about a student confidential. In a recent ruling (1996), the Supreme Court of Canada limited disclosure of a counsellor's notes to only those portions relating to the incident in question.[51] It seems that teacher-counsellors should inform the students they counsel that they may have to disclose information given to them in confidence.

Since parents and students are rightly viewed by Government as the clients of the education system, there is a need for them to have access to information upon which to make educational choices. It seems likely that the *School Act* will be amended to allow the parents to continue to have legal access to information which might otherwise be considered unreasonable disclosure and invasion of personal privacy. For a fuller discussion of this matter see Martin and Uhlemann.[52]

13. Do teachers have any discretion in the choice of textbooks?

The answer to this question seems to be both yes and no. "Yes," if the book is to be used for instruction in the delivery of the Provincial Curriculum, and if it is recommended by the Minister or approved by the Board in charge of the school. Conversely, "no," if it is to be used to teach the Provincial Curriculum, and is not recommended by the Minister nor approved by the board.

By contrast, if the book is to be used in a teaching area that falls outside the Provincial Curriculum, but within the local curriculum adopted by the Board, then the book would have to be approved for use in the school by the Board alone.

The *Act* gives the Minister of Education powers to determine the educational program or curriculum. This includes the power to make orders about resource materials. In keeping with this power the Minister of Education publishes from time to time the "Catalogue of Learning Resources, Primary to Graduation," which contains materials recommended for use in public schools.

A board, which has the legal responsibility at the school level for providing an educational program, may ordinarily only use resource materials from two sources in its provision of the program: namely, the Catalogue published by the Ministry, and a list evaluated and approved by the Board.

A teacher who wishes to "select a set of books" must first consider the following questions:

a) Will this book replace material that has been authorised for use in my grade level? If it will, its use may be questionable.

b) Is the book on the recommended list found in the Catalogue? If "yes," then there seems to be no problem with its use as long as it is not expressly prohibited by school board policy. If "no," then:

c) Has the book been approved by the Board for use? If "yes" then there seems to be no problem with its use. If "no," then:

d) Does the Board have evaluation and selection criteria and procedures for the approval of books for use in the classroom? If "yes," then the teacher would have to seek board approval for use. If "no," then the teacher may choose to encourage the Board to establish these criteria and procedures.

14. A colleague of mine was suspended by the board for hitting a student but was acquitted by the court on a charge of assault for the same incident. How can this be?

When a teacher hits a student in British Columbia two different laws may come into play. First, the *Act* provides that discipline of a student should not include corporal punishment.[53] A teacher, therefore, who hits a student, contravenes this provision and may be guilty of an offence under the *Act*. Consequently, such a teacher is likely to be disciplined by the board, and perhaps, depending on the facts and the circumstances, by the College of Teachers and by the BCTF under the *Code of Ethics*.

Second, hitting a student may also bring a charge of assault under the *Criminal Code*.[54] Assault occurs when a person applies force intentionally on another without the other's direct or indirect consent (section 244(1)). A teacher, then, may be charged not only under the *Act* with an offence, but also under the *Criminal Code* with a crime. The latter is punishable by fine or imprisonment, or both.

The *Criminal Code* also provides for the exemption of teachers, who use reasonable force to correct a student. In one such case in British Columbia, the court agreed that the teacher had reasonable grounds to believe that a student was undermining his authority and that the slap on the head was reasonable force in the circumstances as a means of correction. The teacher was absolved of the criminal charge of assault by the courts under section 43 of the *Criminal Code*, but was, nevertheless, punished under the *Act* for using force as a means of disciplining a student. There have been calls from several quarters for the repeal of section 43 as it represents a double standard in our laws.

15. Do students have a right to wear whatever they feel like to classes?

The answer to this question is very likely yes. Traditionally, it would very likely have been no, but the proclamation of the *Charter* in 1982 has made a major change. The *Charter* gives to all Canadians the fundamental freedom of expression, which includes expression in the clothes one chooses to wear. It does not mean that every kind of dress is acceptable. What seems clear from court decisions in the US is that a student's dress would have to be shown to be unsafe, unhealthy, or to create disorder and indiscipline in the school before it could legally infringe that right. Clothes that are merely considered in poor taste may not legally be prohibited.

16. May school rules be enforced outside the school?

School rules may be enforced off school premises only during activities organised and sponsored by the school (*School Act Regulation* section 5(7)(g)). Outside of these instances, there does not seem to be a legal basis for enforcing school rules for misbehaviour that occurs, for example, in a shopping mall in the evening after school or on the weekend. It used to be the case that students were subject to the school's code of conduct "while travelling to and from school" (*School Act Regulation*, 1979, section 36). This is no longer the case and should be noted by all school personnel.

17. How are school officials held accountable?

School officials, including the Minister of Education, principals, and teachers, are all subject to the rule of law. That is, like all citizens, they must abide by the laws of the Province, and furthermore, they can be held accountable for the manner in which they exercise their duties and responsibilities. This means that they are accountable to those who supervise their work as well as to those agencies who are given control over them. For example, in the organizational setting: the Minister is answerable to the Premier; a school board is answerable to the Minister; a principal is answerable to the Superintendent and the Board; and a teacher is answerable to the principal, the Superintendent, and the Board. The courts are the final arbiter when disputes arise.

However, school officials are also answerable to officials and other persons external to their organizations, and it has been argued that this accountability has increased in recent times.[55] School boards and the Minister are answerable to the electorate for the decisions they make. In addition, the Ombudsman may now hear complaints against decisions of school and school district officials. (This includes some decisions made by teachers.) They may also be accountable to the Privacy Commissioner, under the *FIPPA*, for decisions related to the privacy of students and their parents. As professionals they may also be answerable to the British Columbia College of Teachers (principals and superintendents must be members of the College) and the British Columbia Counsellors' Association (if members). They must also comply with the British Columbia Teachers Federation *Code of Ethics*.

CONCLUSION

Teachers need to carry out their profession in a manner that is both professionally sound and legally defensible. This requires that they develop a knowledge of the law, and of how it relates to their professional practice. Despite the fact that the law sometimes is not clear and sometimes fails to provide comprehensive guidance, knowledge of it constitutes the best possible preparation for coping with areas of uncertainty and conflicts.

RESOURCES

British Columbia Teachers Federation, Code of Ethics, Members Guide to the BCTF Member's Guide.

Constitution Act, 1867 (UK) 30 & 31 Vict., c. 3. (Formerly the *BNA Act*).

Charter of Right and Freedoms, Part 1 of the *Constitution Act, 1982*, being Schedule B of the *Canada Act, 1982* (U.K.), 1982, c. 11.

Criminal Code, R.S.C. 1985, c. C-46.

Infant's Act, R.S.B.C. 1996, c. 223 as am. by Miscellaneous Statutes Amendment Act, c. 77, 1992, section 2.

Child, Family and Community Service Act, R.S.B.C. 1996, c. 46.

Labour Relations Code, R.S.B.C. 1996, c. 244.

Y. M. Martin & M. R. Uhlemann, Ethical and Legal Issues in the Administration of Education (January, 1995) *BC Counsellor*.

Ombudsman Act, R.S.B.C. 1996 c. 340.

Public Education Labour Relations Act, R.S.B.C. 1996 c. 382.

Province of British Columbia, Ministry of Education, Skills and Training (Special Education Branch). *Special Education Services: A Manual of Policies, Procedures and Guidelines.* (Victoria: Crown Publication, 1995).

School Act, R.S.B.C. 1996 c. 412.

Teaching Profession Act, R.S.B.C. 1996 c. 449.

Young Offenders Act, S.C. c. Y-1, 1984.

An Act to Amend the Young Offenders Act and the Criminal Code, S.C. 1995, c. 19.

END NOTES

1. Teachers in independent schools in British Columbia are not governed by the *School Act*. Their rights, duties, and responsibilities are determined by their contract of employment. Nevertheless, common law, that is the legal principles developed by the courts would likely apply in cases dealing with independent school teachers. While the standards set in the *School Act* may be a good guide to them, there is no obligation that they be followed.
2. *School Act*, R.S.B.C. 1996 c. 412.

3. While a student is entitled to enroll and education between the ages of 5 to 16 years of age is compulsory, there is no expressed duty on the part of a parent to enroll a child. By contrast, parents who chose to home school is duty bound to register the child and failure to do so is an Offence under the *Act*. *School Act*, sections 2, 4, 5.

4. *School Act*, note 2, section 4.

5. *School Act*, section 5(1).

6. *Charter of Rights and Freedoms*, Part 1 of the *Constitution Act*, 1982, being Schedule B of the *Canada Act*, 1982 (U.K.), 1982, c. 11.

7. *School Act*, section 6.

8. "Refusal to offer an educational" program is the language which replaces "exclusion," or more commonly understood, "expulsion." The current language is consistent with a student's entitlement to "enroll in an educational program". In the old Act the student's entitlement was "to school accommodation" from which there might more reasonably be exclusion.

9. *School Act*, section 7(1)(a) and *School Regulation* (B.C. Reg. 265/89), section 7(1)(a).

10. *School Act*, section 7(1)(b).

11. *Ibid*, section 8.

12. Special Needs Students Order Ministerial Order M397/95.

13. Ministry of Education, Skills and Training, 1995. *Special Education Services: A Manual of Policies, Procedures and Guidelines*. (Victoria: Special Education Branch, Crown Publications, 1995).

14. *Ibid*, p. A9.

15. *School Act*, section 7(2).

16. *Offence Act*, R.S.B.C. 1996 c. 338.

17. Policy statements are not usually enforceable until they assume the form of a legislative instrument. This policy statement, unlike other statements of policy, was introduced as an Order in Council which is considered subordinate legislation, and hence, enforceable. This raises the question of the substantive difference, implied or intended, between an *entitlement*, as used in the *Act*, and a *right*, as used in the Policy Order. Neither is defined in the *School Act* or in the *Interpretation Act* of BC. The *Interpretation Act* of Canada, however, includes an order in council within the scope of an enactment. To date, there appears to have been no judicial clarification of the implications of this Order in Council for parents.

18. Statement of Policy Order (Mandate for the School System). OIC 1280/89.

19. *Ibid*, section 9.

20. *Ibid*, section 11.

21. *Labour Relations Code*, R.S.B.C. 1996, c.46.

22. *School Regulation* section 4.

23. *Child, Family and Community Service Act*, R.S.B.C. 1996 c. 46, section 14.

24. *Ibid*, section 13.

25. *Teaching Profession Act*, R.S.B.C. 1996 c. 449.

26. Code of Ethics, Members Guide to the BCTF (1995).

27. In the case of an independent school, a report from the school authority, *Independent School Act*, S.B.C. c. 51, 1989, section 6.1.

28. *Teaching Profession Act*, R.S.B.C. 1996 c. 449.

29. *Child, Family and Community Service Act*, R.S.B.C. 1996, c. 46.

30. *School Regulation*, section 5.

31. *School Act*, section 25.1.

32. *School Act*, section 182.

33. Member's Guide to the BCTF, 1993-94, 9.B01,p. 40.

34. *School Act*, R.S.B.C. 1996 c.412, section 1.

35. The Minister, under the authority of section 182, determines a) the general nature of the educational program, b) the general requirements for graduation from an educational program, c) the process for the assessment of its effectiveness, and d) educational resource materials.

36. Special Needs Students Order, M397/95.

37. *T. Larry Jones* v. *Regina* [1986], 2 S.C.R. 284.

38. *Freedom of Information and Protection of Privacy Act*, R.S.B.C. (1996), c. 165, section 4.

39. Although in the *Act* it is a board which has statutory responsibility for the schooling and is the head of a school within its jurisdiction, it seems likely that a board may choose to designate a principal as head of a school for the purposes of giving access to records kept in his/her school at the time when access to them is sought under the FIPPA.

40. *Young Offenders Act*, S.C. 1980-81-83, c. 110, section 38; R.S 1985, c. 27 (1st Supp.), section 203; c. 24 (2d Supp.), section 29; 1995, c. 19, section 27.

41. *School Act*, section 25.1.

42. An educational program is defined as a set of learning activities which in the opinion of the board is designed to enable the learner to develop individual potential. *School Act*, section 1.

43. Ministerial Order 150/89 as am by M397/95.

44. Statement of Policy Order (Mandate for the School System). OIC 1280/89.

45. *Ibid.*

46. Thanks to Shirley Avril of the Social Equity Branch, Ministry of Education, Training and Skills, British Columbia Government, for discussing this section.

47. *Criminal Code*, R.S.C. 1985, c. C-46.

48. *Infant's Act*, R.S.B.C. 1996 c. 223, section 2.

49. *School Act*, section 1.

50. *Legal and Ethical Guidelines* (1995), British Columbia School Counsellors' Association, page 5.

51. *R. v. O'Connor* [1995] 4 S.C.R. 411.

52. Y.M. Martin and M.R. Uhlemann, *Legal and Ethical Issues in the Management of Counselling.* (January, 1995) B.C. Counsellor. 5.

53. *School Act*, section 95.

54. *Criminal Code*, section 43.

55. See Martin, Y.M. (1995) "Controls on Administrative Discretion in Decision-making:" 1872-1994. Education and Law Journal. 232.

Chapter 12

FREEDOM OF INFORMATION AND
PROTECTION OF PRIVACY

Bill Trott, Lorrainne Dixon, Max R. Uhlemann, and Jo-Anne Sargent

INTRODUCTION

Information is power. In the age of information, access to information is essential in order for citizens to hold public officials accountable. As public institutions continue to gather and hold increasing amounts of personal information, the public expects those institutions to protect information it holds in trust for its citizens. At the same time, government has increasing ability to monitor citizens in a wide range of ways.

Within this context, almost all helping professionals keep records of some type. These records may include case files on clients, statistical information on workload, reports on policy and procedures, or information about programs. Whether it be case records of child protection workers, medical files of physicians, client files of psychologists or counsellors, or student records accessed by teachers, information in the hands of helping professionals can have a direct impact on their decisions. In the hands of clients or the person about whom the helping professional is making decisions, such information can be used to hold professionals and their agencies accountable and to ensure the accuracy of the information in the records. At the same time it is important that information in records be appropriately controlled so that privacy is maintained. In addition, agencies and public institutions are kept accountable by public access to their decisions and policy.

Rules regarding the access of the public or clients to information are found in several sources. These sources include the following:

a) Helping professionals in private practice or working for voluntary agencies may find standards of practice within their own profession in each province. For instance, the *Code of Ethics for the British Columbia Association of Social Workers*,[1] *Standards of Professional Conduct*[2] for psychologists in Ontario, and *the Ethical Standards of Psychologists*[3] in British Columbia comment on standards of confidentiality and client access to case files.

b) Helping professionals working for public bodies in the federal sector, such as employment counsellors for Human Resources Development Canada or parole officers with Correctional Service Canada, are governed by the federal *Access to Information Act*[4] and the federal *Privacy Act*[5] in dealing with information access and privacy issues.

c) Helping professionals working for public bodies at the provincial or local government level are covered by provincial access and privacy legislation. This chapter will focus on this aspect only as it applies to British Columbia. The law is stated as of November 1, 1997.

The *Freedom of Information and Protection of Privacy Act*[6] (hereafter referred to as the *Act*) is a law that came into effect in British Columbia in 1993, which describes access and privacy rights with regard to recorded information that is collected or controlled by public bodies in British Columbia. The purpose of the *Act* (section 2(1)) is to make public bodies more accountable to the public by:

a) giving the public a right of access to records, with limited exceptions;

b) giving individuals a right of access to, and a right to request the correction of, personal information about themselves;

c) specifying limited exceptions to the right of access;

d) preventing the unauthorized collection, use, or disclosure of personal information by public bodies; and

e) providing for an independent review of decisions made under the *Act*.

In this chapter an overview of the *Act* is first provided. This description is followed by an explanation of the duties of the Information and Privacy Commissioner's Office. A number of issues are presented that deal with access to information and privacy. The process for making requests for information is described. Finally, a series of commonly asked questions are addressed.

SCOPE OF THE ACT

The *Act* balances the two principles of access to information and the protection of privacy. The *Act* is not meant to replace other procedures for access to information, nor is it meant to limit access to non-personal information that is normally available to the public. This means that most records and information that were previously available to the public continue to be available without requiring a freedom of information request.

The *Act* applies to public bodies in the Province of British Columbia (section 3). The term "public body" means provincial government ministries, agencies, boards, commissions, Crown Corporations, municipalities, universities, school boards, municipal police forces, hospitals, and self-governing professional bodies such as the College of Physicians and Surgeons, the College of Psychologists, and the Law Society. A complete list of the agencies, boards, commissions, and corporations covered by the *Act* can be found in Schedule 2 of the *Act*. A list of the self-governing professional bodies that are covered can be found in Schedule 3. The term "public body" does not include the office of a person who is a member or officer of the Legislative Assembly nor does it include the Court of Appeal, Supreme Court, or Provincial Court.

The *Act* does not apply to private groups, such as corporations, banks, and insurance companies, or to individuals, such as landlords, psychologists, social workers, nurses, child care workers, and doctors. Nor does the *Act* apply to federal departments or organizations, such as the RCMP. These groups are under federal jurisdiction and are covered by the federal *Privacy Act* and the federal *Access to Information Act.* More information about these two *Acts* can be obtained by contacting the Information Commissioner of Canada or the Privacy Commissioner of Canada.

If it is unclear whether a public body falls within provincial or federal jurisdiction, the public body should be contacted. This information can also be obtained by contacting the federal Privacy Commissioner, the federal Information Commissioner, or the Information, Science and Technology Agency of British Columbia.

Under the *Act*, people have the right to request access to records in the custody or under the control of a public body (section 4(1)). A "record," as defined by the *Act*, includes books, documents, maps, drawings, photographs, letters, vouchers, papers, and any other thing on which information is recorded or stored by graphic, electronic, mechanical or other means, but does not include a computer program or any other mechanism that produces records.

The *Act* applies to all records in the custody or under the control of a public body (section 3(1)). The *Act* does not, however, apply to some types of records, including the following:

a) records in court files, including the records of judges, masters, justices of the peace, judicial administration records or records relating to support services provided to judges (section 3(1)(a));

b) a personal note, communication, or draft decision of a person who is acting in a judicial or quasi-judicial capacity such as coroner or arbitrator (section 3(1)(b));

c) a record created by or in the custody or control of an Officer of the Legislature, such as the Ombudsman and the Child and Youth Advocate, that is related to the exercise of that Officer's function under an *Act* (section 3(1)(c)); and

d) a record of a question that is to be used on an examination or test (section 3(1)(d)).

The *Act* does not restrict the information that is available to a person involved in a court case or other type of proceeding. A proceeding includes quasi-judicial processes, such as labour relations tribunals.

The terms "custody" and "control" are key starting points in determining the scope of the *Act*. Records in the custody or under the control of the public body are covered by the *Act*. The term custody means physical possession, and the term control means that the public body has the authority or ability to control the creation, use, or disclosure of the record.

Because the current legislation in British Columbia covers provincial and local government bodies only and does not extend to the private sector, it is important to clarify how the concepts of custody and control of records differ according to the helping professional's employment setting. For helping professionals who are employed by a public institution (e.g., hospitals, mental health agencies, schools, and provincially funded community agencies), the employer is ultimately responsible for, and decides issues of, access and disclosure of client records.

For helping professionals who contract their services to public bodies covered under the *Act*, the general guideline is that a record is covered by the *Act* if the public body may require custody of the records (may need to physically keep them) during or after the term of the contract; or the public body may have control of the records if specified by the contract or a statute that gives the public body the right to control access and disclosure. In some cases, individual client files may be under the control of the public body.

This discussion may be illustrated by some cases decided by the Information and Privacy Commissioner. The Commissioner first considered the issue of control of records by public bodies in Order 11-94, June 16, 1994. In that case, the applicant requested policy manuals prepared by an intermediate care facility that was partially funded by the Ministry of Health and that had a contract with the Ministry to operate a continuing care facility. The contract was silent on the issue of custody and control of records although the Ministry had a right of access to, and inspection of, the manuals. The Commissioner found that the manuals were highly individualized to each facility operated by the contractor and were significantly different from standard government-issue policy manuals. On the issue of control, the Commissioner found that if a public body does not have the right to have custody of the record, control means "the right to have a say in the contents, use or disposition of the document." Further, control must "derive from a contractual or specific statutory right to review records of a contractor which relate to the services being provided, as well as a right to have a say in the content, use, or disposition of the document" (Order 11-94, June 16, 1994, p.12).

In this case, the Commissioner found that the Ministry had a statutory right to require the contractor to prepare and create the manuals and to access and inspect the manuals to ensure the appropriate standards were maintained. However, this did not give the Ministry custody or control of the records within the meaning of the *Act*. Thus, the applicant was not granted access to the policy manuals.

The issue of custody or control also arose in Order 115-96, August 23, 1996. In this case, a school counsellor refused a School District access to her interview notes with two students (siblings). The School District required access to the notes to process an information request from one of the students' parents. The counsellor submitted that the records were not in the School District's custody or control because they were her own raw notes prepared during an interview. The notebooks were her own and were kept in her own home, not the school. The British Columbia Teachers' Federation and the British Columbia School Counsellors' Association supported the counsellor's position, submitting that the records were not in the school district's custody and control because it "does not provide access to them, manage them, maintain them, preserve them or dispose of them."

The School District, the Ministries of Education and Health, the British Columbia Confederation of Parent Advisory Councils, the British Columbia School Trustees' Association and the College of Psychologists took the opposite position to the school counsellor. In their opinion, because the school counsellor was an employee of the school district, her notes were in the custody and control of the district because they were created by the counsellor in the course of her employment.

The Commissioner agreed with the School District that the notes were within its custody and control and agreed that the notes were records created by an employee in the course of her employment. He disagreed with the position of the counsellor that the notes were not in the district's custody or control, because it did not access, manage, maintain or dispose of the notes. In addition, the Commissioner stated that it would not be an unwarranted invasion of a confidential relationship between counsellor and student for the School District to have custody and control of the notes, because they were created within an employer-employee or contractual relationship. Thus, the Commissioner ruled that the counsellor turn over these records to the School District so that the Commissioner could now conduct the inquiry to determine the parent's right of access to the information.

Order 144-97, January 17, 1997 also considered the issue of control of records. A former patient of the Greater Vancouver Mental Health Services Society (GVMHSS) applied for access to a report written by her psychiatrist about his management of her treatment. The report was created as a result of a complaint made by the former patient about her psychiatrist. This report was provided by the psychiatrist's lawyer to GVMHSS for its review during an investigation into the complaint. By agreement with the psychiatrist's lawyer, the GVMHSS returned the report after the investigation. Therefore, the report was not in the custody of GVMHSS at the time the access request was made. The issue in this case was whether the record was under the control of GVMHSS.

The Commissioner found that the report was under control of the GVMHSS. It used the report as part of its decision making concerning the applicant's complaint, therefore it had a duty under section 31 of the *Act* to retain a copy of this information for possible access by the applicant. In addition, the Commissioner found that the GVMHSS was the psychiatrist's employer. The GVMHSS submitted that it used the report to consider whether there should be an alteration or termination of the contract between the psychiatrist and the GVMHSS. It was this contractual relationship and ability to discipline the psychiatrist that led the Commissioner to find that the GVMHSS had control of the record. Although the public body did not have custody of the report, it did have control within the meaning of section 3(1) of the *Act* because it was able to make an agreement with the psychiatrist about return of the report.

It is important to state that Orders 115-96 and 144-97 are under judicial review and will be heard in 1998. This situation makes it apparent that the meaning of "custody" and "control" under the *Act* is not certain, although, in the opinion of the Commissioner, if a record is created by an employee in the course of employment (such as in Order 115-96), that record is under the control of the employer. Further, the public body may exercise control over a record, not only in direct employment relationships, but also in contractual situations (such as in Order 144-97).

It is recommended that a reference to "control of records" or specifications about access should be included in the contracts of helping professionals who contract their services to public bodies. If the contract is unclear, requests should be made for written clarification. Possible implications are that the public body could exercise its right of access to the record, including, for example, case notes and raw test scores.

Finally, records created by a helping professional in private practice are not covered by the *Act*. However, helping professionals in this situation would be wise to practice according to legislated information standards, both as a matter of sound professionalism and because the legislation may one day be extended to include the private sector, as is currently the case in Quebec.

THE COMMISSIONER'S OFFICE

Part 4 of the *Act* (sections 37-51) specifies the duties of the Commissioner's Office. The Information and Privacy Commissioner is appointed for a 6-year term by the Legislative Assembly in a manner similar to the Ombudsman (section 37(3)). It is the responsibility of the Commissioner's staff to assist individuals upon request with access, advise public bodies on issues of compliance, and mediate disputes regarding information (section 55). The Commissioner may:

a) review a public body's decision about a request for records under the *Act*;

b) order a public body to release or to withhold records;

c) investigate a complaint about a public body's protection of the privacy of personal information;

d) require a public body to take steps to better protect the privacy of individuals;

e) conduct audits or investigations of public bodies to ensure they comply with the information and privacy requirements of the *Act*;

f) comment on proposed laws affecting information and privacy rights; and

g) inform individuals about their information and privacy rights.

The remainder of the information in this chapter regarding the duties of the Commissioner's Office will be restricted to a discussion of the first item above, the review process.

BALANCING ACCESS AND PRIVACY

The *Act* provides a statutory balancing of two concepts that may on the surface appear to compete. The *Act* requires a decision maker to balance the right of access with the protection of personal information. The Supreme Court of Canada has recently commented on this balance in the context of the federal privacy legislation. In *Dagg v. Canada (Minister of Finance)*,[7] the court stated "[t]here is no doubt that they are complementary and must be construed harmoniously." The court recognized the need to balance "competing values." The court further stated, "Such a balancing process, where mandated by legislation, cannot be avoided simply because it might be easier to apply a clear, bright line that favours one interest over another." The court recognized that the two values must co-exist and the balance must be decided on a case by case basis.

Perhaps the best way to understand this balancing is to examine a case decided by the British Columbia Information and Privacy Commissioner (Order No. 27-94, October 24, 1994). A newspaper reporter requested the audit reports of two investigations about the events leading to the suicide of a teenager in a mental health facility in Vancouver. In addition, the reporter asked for the teenager's personal diaries. The Commissioner found that in order to expose the institution to public scrutiny, some parts of the audit reports should be released. He stated "the public had a right to know, in more detail than previously disclosed, about the treatment and handling of her case and the quality and level of care provided to her." However, he added, "the need for public scrutiny in this matter does not completely override [the patient's] privacy rights but encroached on them to a certain extent in order to meet the requirements of public scrutiny." He described a core of privacy that protected the details of the teenager's behaviour, diagnosis, and her innermost thoughts, as well as details of her family.

This case illustrates the need to balance the public's right to know through access to information and the need to protect the privacy of the individual. This balance is not an easy one to find. It requires a careful examination of the record in dispute, an understanding of the context in which the record is created, and an opportunity for all the parties to comment on the right balance to be achieved.

EXCEPTIONS TO ACCESS TO INFORMATION

The *Act* gives the public a right of access to records in the custody or under the control of public bodies. The *Act* specifies limited exceptions to that right of access where disclosure would result in harm to government or to a third party. Even if a reasonable expectation of harm is identified, information can be withheld only if the *Act* provides an exception for that type of harm. A record must be released unless the *Act* expressly provides for some or all of the information in that record to be exempted from disclosure. There are two types of exemptions under the *Act*, mandatory exemptions and discretionary exemptions.

A. Mandatory Exceptions

If information falls under a mandatory exception, the head of the public body has a duty to refuse the right of access <u>unless</u> it is in the public interest to disclose the information. Three mandatory exceptions are found in the *Act*:

a) cabinet confidences (section 12);

b) disclosure harmful to the business interests of a third party (section 21); and

c) disclosure harmful to personal privacy (section 22).

The last exception may be the most relevant to helping professionals. Under this exception, a public body must refuse the disclosure of personal information held by the public body if disclosure would constitute an unreasonable invasion of a third party's personal privacy. Helping professionals should be aware of references to third parties in records being accessed by applicants (that is, references to parties other than the applicant). In most cases third party references must be severed or blacked out on the copy provided to the client. Included in this exception are, among others, requests for access to medical records, access to the files of helping professionals, such as psychologists, social workers, and counsellors, criminal investigation records, income assistance files, employment histories, financial status/activities, racial or ethnic background, and information to be used for mail lists or solicitation.

In an earlier section on balancing privacy and access, Order 27-94, October 24, 1994 was

287

discussed. The balancing of the protection of personal information and the right to access information is structured by the provisions of section 22 of the *Act*. The purpose of the balancing is to determine whether the disclosure of personal information would constitute an unreasonable invasion of privacy.

The starting point is whether the information in dispute is personal information (see the discussion on page 294). If it is personal information, then it is important to determine whether the personal information is about the person applying for the information. If it is about the applicant, in most cases, the information will be disclosed (see discussion on section 19 below).

If the personal information is about someone other than the applicant, section 22 sets out the process for determining whether the release would be an unreasonable invasion of privacy. If the information falls within the categories in section 22(4), the *Act* states the release of the information would not be an unreasonable invasion of privacy. The categories include information about the position, functions, or remuneration of an employee of a public body, information about a contract to supply goods or services to a public body, and travel expense information of an employee of a public body.

If the information does not fall within these categories, then section 22(3) of the *Act* outlines the categories of information in which disclosure is presumed to be an unreasonable invasion of privacy. These categories include the following:

a) medical, psychiatric or psychological history, diagnosis, condition, treatment or evaluation;

b) the personal information was compiled and is identifiable as part of an investigation into a possible violation of law, except to the extent that disclosure is necessary to prosecute the violation or to continue the investigation;

c) the personal information relates to eligibility for income assistance or social service benefits or to the determination of benefit levels;

d) the personal information relates to employment, occupational, or educational history;

e) the personal information describes the third party's finances, income, assets, liabilities, net worth, bank balances, financial history or activities, or creditworthiness;

f) the personal information consists of personal recommendations, or evaluations, character references or personnel evaluations about the third party;

g) the disclosure could reasonably be expected to reveal that the third party supplied, in confidence, a personal recommendation or evaluation, character reference or personnel evaluation; or

h) the personal information indicates the third party's racial or ethnic origin, sexual orientation or religious or political beliefs or associations.

If the information falls within any of these categories, there is a presumption that it should not be released. However, under section 22(2) of the *Act* there are a number of circumstances that may in certain cases cause the information to be released. These include the following:

a) the disclosure is desirable for the purpose of subjecting the activities of the government of British Columbia or a public body to public scrutiny;

b) the disclosure is likely to promote public health and safety or to promote the protection of the environment; or

c) the personal information is relevant to a fair determination of the applicant's rights.

On the other hand, there are circumstances that would support the presumption not to release the information. These circumstances include the following:

a) the third party will be exposed unfairly to financial or other harm;

b) the personal information has been supplied in confidence;

c) the personal information is likely to be inaccurate or unreliable;

d) the disclosure may unfairly damage the reputation of any person referred to in the record requested by the applicant.

If the information does not fit into the categories in section 22(3), the above circumstances must be weighed in order to determine if the release of the personal information would constitute an unreasonable invasion of privacy.

The following case is an example of disclosure harmful to personal privacy (Order No. 62-95, November 2, 1995). A parent's teenage son had been involved in a physical altercation with a teacher at a school, and after an investigation of the teacher's actions, the parent was informed that disciplinary action had been taken against the teacher. The parent requested a record of the disciplinary action that was recommended by the Delta School Board, but the School Board refused to release it based on sections 12(3) (local public body confidences) and 22 (disclosure harmful to personal privacy) of the *Act*. The Commissioner upheld the decision of the School Board not to release the records, as disclosure of the withheld information would reveal the substance of deliberations of an *in camera* meeting of the School Board. As the records already released to the applicant were sufficient for the purpose of subjecting the School Board to public scrutiny, it was decided that the School board had met its obligations under section 22(2)(a) (subjecting a public body to public scrutiny).

The Commissioner also considered the need to protect the privacy of the teacher. The privacy rights of the teacher were found to be paramount with respect to the specifics of the disciplinary decision. As the record in dispute falls within the meaning of section 22(3)(d) (the personal information relates to employment, occupational, or educational history), its disclosure was presumed to be an unreasonable invasion of privacy. Further, the personal information contained in the record was supplied with an expectation that it would be kept confidential.

This case is important for helping professionals. The fact that the incident was a "public" event that took place on the grounds and facilities of a school does not automatically mandate or legitimate further disclosures to the public. Where there are complaints against public body employees the public is entitled to know whether any action was taken, but does not necessarily have a right to know the details of the decision made by the public body. However, in the case of complaints to a professional body, the body may under its rules disclose the details of the decision.

B. Discretionary Exceptions

Discretionary exceptions allow the public body to determine whether to disclose records despite the existence of an exemption. The public body first must determine if the information under consideration is subject to an exception, and secondly must decide whether to use that exception to either refuse disclosure or to release the information despite the exemption.

Nine discretionary exceptions exist under the *Act*. They are the following:

a) local public body confidences (section 12(3)), such as an *in camera* meeting of a municipal council;

b) policy advice or recommendations (section 13), such as recommendations to a provincial government minister by an employee of the ministry about a controversial public policy matter;

c) legal advice (section 14), such as a confidential written communication from a lawyer to his/her client (a government ministry);

d) disclosure harmful to law enforcement (section 15), such as a police investigation report while the investigation is still open;

e) disclosure harmful to intergovernmental relations or negotiations (section 16), such as a letter from the federal government to the provincial government on a matter the governments are currently negotiating;

f) disclosure harmful to the financial or economic interests of a public body (section 17), such as the provincial estimates of the costs of settling outstanding First Nations land claims prior to the negotiations being concluded;

g) disclosure harmful to individual or public safety (section 19) (see discussion below); and

h) information that will be published or released within 60 days (section 20), such as a report of a public inquiry into the death of a child in care.

The exception from this group most relevant to helping professionals is disclosure harmful to individual or public safety. A public body has the discretion not to disclose information, including an individual's own personal information, when the disclosure could threaten another person's safety, mental or physical health, or interfere with public safety. In addition, section 19(2) of the *Act* states:

"The head of a public body may refuse to disclose to an applicant personal information about the applicant if the disclosure could reasonably be expected to result in immediate and grave harm to the applicant's safety or mental or physical health."

Section 5(1) of the Regulations to the *Act* (B.C. Reg. 323/93) states that "The head of a public body may disclose information relating to the mental or physical health of an individual to a health professional for an opinion on whether disclosure of the information could reasonably be expected to result in grave and immediate harm to the individual's safety or mental or physical health." Accordingly, helping professionals may consult by sharing information in a client's record with a medical doctor or mental health professional before deciding whether the client would be harmed by the information in the record.

Some helping professionals may have other concerns about releasing records to clients besides the potential harm to the client or a third party. For example, psychologists may be concerned about releasing the raw test protocols of psychometric test instruments. As pointed out elsewhere, the issues include "possible copyright infringement, ethical issues concerning requirements for test security and the possible release of answers to the general public."[8] It may be acceptable to clients in most cases if helping professionals provide clients with summaries of test results rather than raw test protocols, along with an explanation of the concerns involved.

PROCESS OF MAKING REQUESTS FOR INFORMATION

A. Requesting Records From a Public Body

Section 5 of the *Act* specifies that in order to access records in the custody or under the control of a public body, an applicant must submit a written request to the public body stating what records are being requested. In order to ensure that a request is processed as quickly as possible, the request should be addressed to the person or branch responsible for handling Freedom of Information Requests for the public body. Larger public bodies, such as government ministries and Crown Corporations, generally have an entire branch dedicated to information and privacy. Smaller public bodies, such as municipalities, school boards, and hospitals, will generally have one or two people who are responsible, on a full-time or part-time basis, for processing freedom of information requests.

The Information and Privacy Office within each of the British Columbia Ministries can be contacted by using the toll-free Enquiry British Columbia Phone Service (Victoria - 1-250-387-6121; Greater Vancouver - 1-604-660-2421; elsewhere in British Columbia - 1-800-663-7867). The Enquiry British Columbia operator then connects the caller to the Information and Privacy Office of the Ministry that has custody or control of the records to be requested.

The information and privacy coordinator for other public bodies can be contacted by calling the general reception area for the public body and asking to be put through to the person responsible for freedom of information and privacy issues. A complete list of the addresses and phone numbers of all the public bodies covered by the *Act* can be obtained from the Information, Science and Technology Agency of British Columbia.

Initially, the public body has 30 days to respond to an applicant's request for records (section 7). However, the public body may extend the time for responding by another 30 days under the following circumstances:

a) the applicant has not provided the public body with enough detail to identify a requested record;

b) there is a large number of records and meeting the request within the time limit would unreasonably interfere with the operations of the public body;

c) more time is needed to consult with a third party or another public body; or

d) a third party has requested a review of a public body's decision to release information to the applicant.

An extension beyond 60 days requires the Commissioner's permission (section 10(1)).

B. Fees for Record Requests

Fees for record requests are covered under section 75 of the *Act*. There is no fee charged to an applicant for the request for her/his own personal information. However, fees may be charged for other types of records. Applicants requesting records other than their own personal information may be charged a fee for the following reasons:

a) locating, retrieving, and producing the records (after the first 3 hours);

b) preparing the records for release;

c) shipping and handling of the records; and

d) making a copy of the records.

A public body cannot charge fees for the time spent reviewing the records.

The maximum rates that government Ministries and certain other public bodies can charge are listed in section 7 of the Regulations to the *Act* (B.C. Reg. 323/93). However, local public bodies, such as municipalities, regional districts, municipal police, school boards, hospitals, regional health boards, and self-governing professional bodies may set fees that are different from those found in the Regulation.

Fees may be reduced by narrowing the request for records or by asking to view the records rather than requesting copies. If an applicant is unable to pay the fee charged for requesting records, he/she may ask the public body for a fee waiver, which will excuse the applicant from paying all or some of the fees (section 75(5)). To request a fee waiver, the applicant must write to the public body and provide the public body with reasons why the fee cannot be paid. Under this same section, a fee waiver may also be requested if an applicant believes that a fee should not be charged because a request is being made for records that are in the public's interest.

C. Requests for Review

Under sections 52 and 53 of the *Act*, if an individual wishes to request a review of a public body's decision regarding the records that she/he requested, an application must be made to the Office of the Information and Privacy Commissioner within 30 days of receiving the public body's decision. Requests for review should include the following:

a) a copy of the initial request to the public body;

b) a copy of the public body's response to the request; and

c) a request, in writing, that the Office of the Information and Privacy Commissioner review the public body's decision.

It is helpful if applicants can be as specific as possible in telling the Commissioner's Office what they want reviewed.

Under the *Act*, the Office of the Information and Privacy Commissioner has 90 days to resolve a request for review (section 56(6)). If an individual's request has not been resolved within the 90-day period, the Commissioner will hold an inquiry and will make a binding decision regarding the request.

Once a review has been requested and it is determined that the request falls within the Commissioner's jurisdiction under the *Act*, the Office staff will open a review file and assign the case to a Portfolio Officer. The Portfolio Officer will attempt to mediate a settlement between the individual and the public body (section 55). The mediation portion of the review generally takes the first two-thirds of the 90-day time limit allowed under the *Act* to resolve requests for review.

If mediation is unsuccessful, the issue will then proceed to a formal inquiry before the Information and Privacy Commissioner. The inquiry process generally takes up the last third of the review period. To maintain impartiality, the Commissioner is isolated from the review and mediation process in case a matter comes to him/her as an inquiry (section 56).

An inquiry is similar to a court proceeding. The Commissioner will receive statements and arguments from both the applicant and representatives of the public body, and will ask questions of each. The Commissioner will also review the records that have been withheld from disclosure. The person who asked for a review, representatives of the public body concerned, and any person or organization that was given a copy of the request for review are entitled to make presentations to the Commissioner during an inquiry. The applicant may also be represented by a counsel or an agent.

Not every inquiry will be the same. The Commissioner may receive written or oral submissions. Oral submissions may be made without the other party present. Some inquiries will be open to the public; others will be private. The Commissioner has broad discretion to determine how an inquiry will be conducted. Following an inquiry the Commissioner must make an order (section 58). He/she may, for example, order the public body either to withhold or disclose requested information, to reconsider its decision, or to correct personal information.

Finally, the *Act* is remedial rather than punitive. It does not provide a means to assess monetary damages to compensate a person who is aggrieved because information was not released or because personal information was handled in a manner that violated the fair information practices under the *Act* (section 74). The Commissioner cannot award monetary settlements due to a breach of the *Act*. If an individual is seeking financial compensation for a breach of privacy, she/he must do so through the normal civil court process.

PROTECTION OF PRIVACY

A. Confidentiality, Privacy, and Privilege

In the helping professions the concept of confidentiality is well know. However, there exists some confusion about the concepts of privacy, confidentiality and privilege. "Privacy" is the right to be left alone, to remain anonymous and free from intrusion. This is a fundamental value in Canada. This general notion of privacy includes the limits on visual surveillance. "Information privacy" is the ability to control the flow of one's own personal information. This is achieved through "fair information practices." These practices, outlined in sections 26 to 35 of the *Act* and set out in detail below, establish the conditions under which personal information can be collected, used, and disclosed. While the concept of confidentiality is an element of fair information practices, it does not encompass the full spectrum of these practices. "Confidentiality" is the ethical or legal requirement not to disclose personal information, unless the client consents to the disclosure or unless the professional is required by law to disclose. "Privilege" is the legal obligation not to disclose personal information in any circumstances, including a court process, without client consent. The issues surrounding privilege and the court process have become particularly complicated in the past few years and are discussed in another section (see Chapters 1 and 7).

B. Collection and Disclosure of Personal Information

Personal information is any recorded information that uniquely identifies a person, such as his/her names, address, telephone number, age, sex, race, religion, sexual orientation, disability, fingerprints, or blood type (Schedule 1 of the *Act*, definition of "personal information"). Also included are health care, educational, and financial information, criminal or employment history, and anyone else's opinions about the person or his/her own views or opinions.

Under the *Act* (section 26), a public body can collect personal information in the following situations:

a) the collection of that information is expressly authorized by or under government legislation;

b) the information is collected for law enforcement purposes; or

c) the information relates directly to and is necessary for the operation of a program or activity of the public body.

Section 33 of the *Act* describes when a public body can disclose an individual's personal information. According to this section, personal information can be disclosed only in certain defined situations. These include the following:

a) if the person to whom the information belongs has consented in writing to the disclosure of that information;

b) if the disclosure is part of the purpose for which the public body collected the information in the first place;

c) if the disclosure has a reasonable and direct connection to the purpose for which the information was collected and is necessary for the duties or obligations of the public body;

d) for the purpose of complying with an enactment, or a treaty, or arrangement made under an enactment;

e) for the purpose of complying with a subpoena, warrant, or court order;

f) to an officer of a public body or a Minister, if the disclosure is necessary for the performance of a duty or is necessary for the protection of the health and safety of that office or Minister;

g) to a representative of the bargaining agent who has been authorized in writing to make an inquiry by the employee to whom the information pertains;

h) to a public body or law enforcement agency in Canada to assist in an investigation undertaken with a view to law enforcement proceeding or from which a law enforcement proceeding is likely to result;

i) if the head of the public body determines that there are compelling circumstances that exist that affect health and safety, and if notice of the disclosure is mailed to the last known address of the individual the information is about; or

j) so that the next of kin or a friend of the injured, ill, or deceased may be contacted.

Helping professionals should be particularly aware of the first point above, which states that personal information can be disclosed only if the person to whom it belongs has consented *in writing*. Accordingly, many helping professionals now use *release of information* forms, which ideally should include the following elements[9]:

a) the name of the party to whom the records will be released;

b) the records to be released;

c) the purpose or intended use of the information;

d) the date the form was signed;

e) an expiry date;

f) any limitations on the information to be provided (e.g., limiting further disclosure of the record to other third parties without prior consent);

g) signature of the client or signature of the person authorizing the release, as well as that person's relationship to the client (e.g., parent or guardian); and

h) signature of the helping professional.

The reason for including an expiry date is to discourage the use of blanket release of information forms, whereby portions of the record are released on multiple occasions without explicit consent for each release.

C. Security of Records

Under the *Act* it is expected that public bodies, and thus the helping professionals they employ, will undertake reasonable measures to ensure that personal information is properly stored and secured (section 30). The definition of "reasonable security" depends on the function of the office. In general, reasonable security arrangements for personal information in the custody or under the control of the public body are arrangements that fair, rational people would think were appropriate to the sensitivity of the information and to the medium in which it is stored, transmitted, handled, or transferred.

"Reasonable security" encompasses a range of practices. "Stringent security" measures (i.e., locked filing cabinets, computer access codes, and a physically secure room to which access is controlled by a guard, receptionist, locked door, or electronic access device) are appropriate for particularly sensitive information such as medical records, personnel files, and the client notes from psychologists, counsellors, and social workers. In addition, in the case of electronic storage of information, security measures such as individual passwords that are changed on a regular basis, computer screens located away from public access, and audit trails are recommended. Less severe methods (i.e., locked office doors and unlocked filing cabinets) may be adequate for less sensitive information such as names and addresses.

Practitioners in private practice are guided by their Codes of Ethics to take all reasonable steps to safeguard the confidentiality of their records. Following the "reasonable security" guidelines described above will ensure good practice.

Public bodies should analyze the types and level of sensitivity of the personal information under their control. Necessary precautions, taking into consideration available time and resources, should be implemented to guarantee appropriate physical and procedural safeguards. Staff training on privacy issues and concerns should be considered as a means to ensure that individuals are aware of the need to safeguard sensitive information.

D. Record Retention

If a public body uses an individual's personal information to make a decision that directly affects her/him, the public body must keep that information for at least one year after last using it (section 31). The information is kept for one year so that individuals have a reasonable opportunity to obtain access to it. The *Act* says nothing about how long public bodies must keep non-personal information.

The length of time that a provincial public body must keep records containing personal and non-personal information is set out in the schedule to the *Document Disposal Act*,[10] which applies only to provincial government Ministries. This *Act* specifies a general retention period of seven years for public records and states that no government document should be destroyed without the written recommendation of the Public Documents Committee. The length of time that a Ministry keeps records will depend on the type of record and its purpose.

The general records retention periods or schedules of other public bodies are governed by separate legislation. For example, the length of time for which hospitals should keep records is set out in the *Hospital Act*.[11] Hospital records should be kept for seven years or longer, depending on whether they are needed for legal or patient care reasons. The *Limitation Act*,[12] provides for a limitation period of six years for civil actions against hospitals, employees of hospitals, and medical practitioners. In addition, the Supreme Court Rules allow one year to file a statement of claim in a civil action. For many other public bodies, the period for which they must keep records is set by a bylaw or an internal policy. Information about how long a specific public body keeps records can be obtained by contacting the Information and Privacy Manager or Coordinator for that public body.

While it is recognized that there is no specific statutory requirements for the retention of records created and kept in the offices of a helping professional in private practice or in a community-based agency, prudent practice suggests a retention period of a minimum of seven years for client records. This covers the maximum period for the launching of a civil action. At the end of seven years the practitioner may wish to transfer the critical information from the original record to a file summary or database. In the case of clients who were children at the time of the creation of the record, the record should be kept for seven years after the client turns 19 years of age.

E. Corrections to Personal Information

Individuals have the right, under the *Act*, to request that the public body that has their personal information in its custody or control correct that information if they believe errors exist in their files (section 29). However, this does not mean that all files must be re-written whenever an individual suggests a mistake has been made with regards to his/her personal information. In the case of factual errors (i.e., birth date or address), the public body can simply make a correction to the files provided sufficient proof of error is provided. If an individual wants a correction made to an opinion, not a fact, the public body has the option of correcting or annotating the file with the applicant's version of the information. In either case, correction requests should be made in writing to the public body, and should specify the information that is believed to be incorrect or omitted. Persons making correction requests should also specify what they believe to be the correct information, and should provide copies of any documents that support their request.

The Workers' Compensation Board has developed a set of guidelines, which the Commissioner adopted (Order 124-96, September 12, 1996), that may be of assistance to others when faced with a request for correction of information:

c) Whatever the decision (correction or annotation), it is a decision that should be exercised in good faith by the public body, without prejudging the issue and without bias against the applicant.

d) It is appropriate to correct rather than annotate where the information in dispute is objective fact, and where it is within the reasonable administrative resources of the public body to make the decision that the information on record is in fact incorrect and that the applicant's version is the correct one.

c) Given that it is the public body's discretion whether to correct or annotate the personal information at issue, and provided that the public body should not be required to meet a standard that involves expending a significant amount of time, financial, or other resources in assessing the situation to decide where the 'truth' lies, and provided that the applicant's version of the events is documented in the public body records where personal information is contained, then the provisions of the *Act* dealing with the correction of personal information have been met.

A helping professional in private practice should correct a record at the request of a client only when the record is clearly factually wrong (as opposed to opinion). Otherwise, the client should be invited to supply her/his own written version of the disputed entry, so that it can be appended to the record and both can be preserved together.

The Privacy Code for Physicians' Offices in British Columbia[13] (see Appendix A) may serve as a guide for other helping professionals in setting privacy standards for private offices. This Code was developed as a result of consultation amongst the College of Physicians and Surgeons, the British Columbia Medical Association, and the Office of the Information and Privacy Commissioner of British Columbia.

COMMON QUESTIONS

1. <u>How does the helping professional make a decision if asked for access to files in her/his custody?</u>

First, the helping professional needs to decide if the requested information is covered under the *Act*. If the information is not covered by the *Act*, the professional should consult his/her professional Code of Ethics or Conduct for the correct procedure for release of information. If the information is covered by the *Act*, the professional is required to assist the applicant in obtaining the information. The professional's first step is to identify possible sources of the information. The duty to assist the applicant includes the responsibility to conduct a reasonable search for the records. In large organizations, there may be records managers who can assist in the search.

Once the professional has located the records being requested, she/he should review the records to determine whether any of the exemptions apply. In the case of client's files, the most common exemption may be third party information (personal information about another person such as another family member). Another possible exemption is that of solicitor-client privilege, if the professional has been involved in litigation. Where a professional is involved in law enforcement activities, another exemption covering law enforcement activities may apply.

The professional should keep in mind that some exemptions (such as the protection of personal information) are mandatory, which means that if the information falls within the exemption, it must be withheld. Other exemptions are discretionary, meaning that the professional has a choice of whether or not to apply the exemption. In the case of information falling within a discretionary exemption, the professional may consider the following:

a) the age of the record;

b) the harm in releasing the information;

c) the public interest;

d) the historical practice of the public body;

e) the nature of the record and the significance and sensitivity to the public body; and

f) the compelling need to release the information.

2. <u>What if the ethical obligations of the helping professional conflict with the *Act*?</u>

There may be circumstances where the *Act* requires disclosure of information that the professional believes conflicts with his/her professional obligations. In these cases, the professional should contact the professional organization to seek guidance. In most cases, practical solutions can be found depending on the nature of the record and the professional environment.

3. <u>Do children have privacy rights under the *Act*?</u>

Under section 3 of the Regulations to the *Act* (B.C. Reg. 323/97), in cases where children do not have the capacity to understand the concept of release of the information, the custodial parent may act on behalf of the child to access information about the child. In other words, parents may act on behalf of a child to access the child's personal information if the child is too young or is otherwise incapable of requesting access. However, this issue becomes complex in cases where the child does not want the parents to have access to his/her personal information. Although the Information and Privacy Commissioner has not issued an order specifically addressing this issue, he has alluded to the stance he would take in a previous order involving a dispute between a custodial and non-custodial parent. In that particular case, the Commissioner stated that, "I am persuaded that an older child should be able to exercise more control over access to his or her personal records... I fully agree with the Ombudsman's contention that a minor has privacy rights" (Order 2-94, February 7, 1994).

The best approach in resolving this issue is to check who gave initial consent to the involvement of the professional. Was it the child alone, the child with the involvement of the parents, or the parents alone? If a child under the age of majority (19 years of age in British Columbia) has consented alone, then access should only be given with the child's consent. If both the child and parents were involved or only the parents, the parents should be given access unless the child has in the meanwhile attained the age of majority. In rare circumstances, the helping professional may assess the capacity of the child and the expectation of risk to the child if the information was released. In these circumstances the professional should document the capacity and the risk.

As illustrated in the following case, the issue is different once the child is no longer a minor. A mother requested a copy of her personal file containing information about her daughter's apprehension by the Ministry of Social Services some time earlier. The mother believed she had a right to the record because the child was a minor and in her custody at the time of the apprehension. While the ministry disclosed copies of the records to the applicant, it withheld most of the personal information about her daughter on the basis of section 22(1) (disclosure harmful to personal privacy), as the daughter was now an adult and her consent would be required before the ministry could release her personal information.

The Commissioner confirmed the decision of the Ministry to withhold most of the information in dispute, but ordered it to release basic information, obviously known to the mother, that had been improperly removed because disclosure would not constitute an unreasonable invasion of privacy. The Commissioner stated that the mother must have the consent of her adult daughter to obtain access to her daughter's information. Under section 3(a) of the Regulations to the *Act*, as a custodial parent, a mother has the right to exercise a child's right of access to personal information while the subject of the record is a minor, but such rights of access terminate completely once the subject becomes an adult. The Commissioner found that it would be an unreasonable invasion of the daughter's personal privacy for the mother to have access to the daughter's personal records, even for the period when she was a minor. (Order 49- 95, July 7, 1995)

4. Can the parent of a child under the age of 19 be denied access to information on the child's record?

According to the *Infants Act*, a minor can give lawful consent to health care under the following conditions:

a) The health care provider has explained the nature, consequences, reasonably foreseeable benefits and risks of the proposed treatment, and the minor appears to understand.

b) The health care provider is satisfied that the proposed treatment is in the minor's best interests.

Therefore the practical approach is to determine who gave initial consent to the involvement of the professional with the minor client. If the client consented alone, access to his or her records should be given only with the client's consent. If the parents gave consent, alone or with the minor client, then the parents should have access to the client's records unless, in the interim, the client has attained the age of majority.

5. Can police demand copies of records covered by the *Act*?

Section 33 of the *Act* (disclosure of personal information) sets out the only circumstances under which a public body can disclose personal information. In order to obtain information under section 33, it will be necessary for police departments to provide evidence that at least one of the criteria under section 33 has been met. This evidence may take the form of a written description of the information required, the authority for gathering it, the purpose of the collection, and the name, title, and address of the person from a police force needing the information. The *Act* will not prevent public bodies from disclosing information to police departments in cases where a legitimate need for the information exists. However, "fishing expeditions" or unwarranted and undefined searches for information are not authorized under the *Act*.

6. <u>What if the police walk into the office of a helping professional and demand information or access to a client's record?</u>

The police should not be given access to client information without a search warrant, or, if the *Freedom of Information and Protection of Privacy Act* applies, in compliance with section 33(n), which reads as follows:

A public body may disclose personal information. . .to a public body or a law enforcement agency in Canada to assist in an investigation

(i) undertaken with a view to a law enforcement proceeding, or

(ii) from which a law enforcement proceeding is likely to result.

7. <u>Are school counsellor's notes covered by the *Act*?</u>

According to the *Act*, all records created by an employee of a public body in the performance of her/his professional duty are deemed to be subject to the *Act*. As an employee of a school district, notes and records taken by a counsellor are the product of an employer-employee (contractual) relationship, and are therefore covered by the *Act*. It should be noted, however, that while a school counsellor's notes are subject to the *Act*, any decisions as to who can have access to them, whether school officials or parents, and under what circumstances are completely separate issues to be decided. A recent Commissioner's decision about school counsellor's notes is discussed in the section on the Scope of the *Act* (above). Counsellors in post-secondary educational institutions should follow these guidelines as well.

Counsellors in private schools are not covered by the *Act*.

8. <u>Are student records subject to the *Act*?</u>

Whether or not student records are included in the *Act* depends on the precise definition of "student records." Based on the broad definitions of "record" and "personal information" presented under the *Act*, it can be assumed that any recorded information about a student that is in the custody or under the control of a school board will be subject to the *Act*. This includes not only "official records" such as progress reports, health services information, disciplinary statements, and permanent student record cards, but can also include private notes of a conversation with a student prepared by teachers or counsellors and notes or materials prepared for the exclusive use of a teacher, administrator, or other school staff member.

School records created by students, such as notes taken during class, are deemed to be the private property of the student, and therefore are not subject to the *Act*. Likewise, classroom files including assignments, papers, or examinations submitted to teachers for the purposes of evaluation are considered temporary and are thus beyond the scope of the *Act*. However, Student Learning Plans created under the Career and Personal Planning (CAPP) Curriculum are subject to the *Act*, as these records are maintained at the school by the teacher in charge of administering the program.

9. Are adoption records released under the *Act*?

A freedom of information request is not required to obtain adoption records. Changes to provincial *Adoption Act*[14] in November, 1996 permit adoptees access to their adoption records. The Vital Statistics Agency, Ministry of Health, can provide original birth registrations and adoption orders to adult adoptees. The address is the following: Vital Statistics Agency, Ministry of Health, 818 Fort Street, Vital Statistics Agency, Victoria, British Colubmia, V8W 1H8 (Victoria - 1-250-952-1829; toll free for those outside of Victoria - 1-888-212-1188).

An individual can request access to his/her adoption records from the Information and Privacy Division of the Ministry for Children and Families. The Ministry will only provide access to non-identifying information in the adoption records unless a copy of the adoption order or original birth registration (obtained from the Vital Statistics Agency, Ministry of Health) is enclosed with the request. The Information and Privacy Division can be contacted at the following address: Information and Privacy Division, Ministry of Children and Families, 110-333 Quebec Street, Victoria, British Columbia, V8V 1X4 (telephone - 1-250-387-0820; fax 1-250-387-0817).

The Commissioner has considered the interaction between the *Adoption Act* and the *Freedom of Information and Protection of Privacy Act*. Although the *Adoption Act* has since been changed, the principles developed in Order No. 35-95, March 27, 1995 still apply. In that case the applicant, an adult adoptee, claimed to know his birth last name and his birth mother's full name. The adoptee wanted to have copies of the records on his adoption file, with all the information which would identify the birth parents removed. In addition, he requested a copy of a hand-written letter by the birth mother that was included in the adoption file.

The Commissioner decided to preserve the birth mother's right to privacy by not disclosing the applicant's surname at birth, even though he and others claimed to already know it. In addition, the Commissioner did not release the hand-written letter from the birth mother, but released a typed version of the letter. The Commissioner was concerned that the handwriting may identify the birth mother. In this way, the Commissioner was able to maintain the birth mother's "right of informational self-determination by deciding that she does not want contact with her natural child." In this case, the Commissioner did establish the principle that the *Act* could be used to obtain non-identifiable information in adoption files.

The Adoption Services Branch of the Ministry for Children and Families will provide information concerning the medical or genetic background of an adoptee, if a physician submits a written request indicating that it is necessary for the care of the individual adoptee. Individuals may contact this branch at the following telephone number: 1-888-237-8888.

The Adoption Reunion Registry assists individuals to locate family members. The Registry can be contacted at the following telephone numbers: Victoria - 1-387-3660; Vancouver - 1-736-7917; elsewhere in British Columbia - 1-800-665-1899.

10. Can patients get access to their medical files?

If the medical records are in the custody or control of a public body under the *Act*, such as a hospital or health unit, a patient can request access to them. However, the *Act* does not apply to medical records in the private offices of private physicians or other health care professionals. The Information and Privacy Commissioner, therefore, has no jurisdiction to review a private health care professional's decision not to disclose medical records to a patient.

However, a patient can still request records directly from a doctor. In a 1992 court decision, *McInerney v. MacDonald*,[15] the Supreme Court of Canada stated that a person should generally be able to request and gain access to his/her medical records. If a doctor refuses a patient access to her/his records, a complaint can be made to the College of Physicians and Surgeons and/or the patient can go to court to compel the doctor to produce the records. The College of Physicians and Surgeons and the British Columbia Medical Association have produced a Privacy Code for Private Physicians Offices (see Appendix A), which includes a discussion of the patient's access rights.

The general rules of patient access discussed above would also apply to files of psychologists or social workers in the employment of a public body.

11. What information in a police file is accessible?

Police complaint investigation files held by the British Columbia Police Commission and local police departments are covered by the *Act*, and may be the subject of a freedom of information request. Relatively few factors limit the disclosure of the subject matter of a complaint, and in most cases the information will be releasable. However, there are circumstances where disclosure of the information could harm a law enforcement matter, and it could then be withheld.

Police cases that are currently under investigation may be protected from disclosure under section 15 of the *Act* (disclosure harmful to law enforcement). It is necessary to evaluate each situation on a case-by-case basis to determine if the harm to law enforcement outweighs the public's right to information. The degree of harm in each situation will vary with the sensitivity of the information. The police can withhold information only if disclosure could reasonably be expected to be detrimental to or damage a law enforcement matter.

The determination of whether disclosure of the name and other personal identifiers of victims and witnesses would be an unreasonable invasion of their personal privacy is also made on a case-by-case basis. To protect the identity of a victim or witness, it is necessary to withhold all personal information that would reveal the identity of the individual. While an individual's name is the most obvious identifier, other personal information may, by itself or in combination with other information, reveal the identity of a victim or witness. The circumstances of each case must be individually assessed to determine what information can be released without invading the privacy of the individual(s) involved.

12. Can telephone conversations be recorded?

The only prohibition to recording telephone calls is found in the *Criminal Code*.[16] As long as one party to the conversation consents to having the telephone conversation recorded, it is not considered an invasion of privacy, nor is it a breach of the *Criminal Code*. This means, however, that a person talking to you on the telephone can legally tape your conversation without having to tell you.

13. When can someone ask for an individual's Social Insurance Number?

Under federal law, an individual is required to give his/her social insurance number (SIN) under the following circumstances:

a) for Old Age Security, Unemployment (now Employment) Insurance, and Canada Pension Plan contributions or claims;

b) for income tax identification;

c) to your employer for the purpose of sending your contributions to federal Employment Insurance, Canada Pension Plan, and income tax authorities;

d) to banks, trust companies, and stock brokers when they sell financial products or services that generate interest (Guaranteed Income Certificates, Cananda Saving Bonds, or bank accounts);

e) for various Veterans Affairs benefit programs;

f) for Canada Student Loans;

g) for Native people's programs; and

h) for Gasoline and Aviation Excise Tax applications under the Gasoline and Aviation excise Tax regulations;[17] *Canadian Wheat Board Act*;[18] *Labour Adjustment Benefits Act*;[19] and *Tax Rebate Discounting Regulations*.[20]

Other organizations may ask for the individual's SIN, but the individual does not have to give it to them. However, if an individual refuses to give an organization or person her/his SIN, he/she may be denied access to the service it is providing. It is not illegal for an organization to deny access to its service because of refusal to give it one's SIN.

Provincially, the SIN can be collected for use in verifying income for some government programs where entitlement or participation is based on income. These programs include premium-assisted Medical Services Plan, various British Columbia benefits, provincial student loans, and seniors' bus passes.

If the reader has any further questions about the collection of the SIN by a provincial body, she/he may contact the Office of the Information and Privacy Commissioner or the Information,

Science and Technology Agency of British Columbia. If the reader wants more information about the use of the SIN by federal bodies she/he may contact the Privacy Commissioner of Canada.

CONCLUSION

The *Freedom of Information and Protection of Privacy Act* is relevant to all helping professionals, given that their work involves information about individuals that is recorded in any way, shape, or form. At least three factors have combined over the last decade to justify the necessity for helping professionals to increase their awareness of privacy protection issues:

a)   the move in the helping service industry toward a collaborative, team approach;

b)   the advances in communication technology, which have outraced the development of appropriate security measures; and

c)   the lack of specific guidance regarding privacy issues from traditional codes of ethics.

Although the *Act* applies specifically to records in the custody or control of provincial and local government public bodies, it would be to the advantage of all helping professionals and their clients to follow the guidelines the legislation offers, both when faced with difficult information issues and in their day-to-day standards of practice.

RESOURCES

Canadian Standards Association, *Model Code for the Protection of Personal Information and Making the CSA Privacy Code Work for You* (Ontario: Canadian Standards Association, 1996).

Canadian Association for the Advancement of Computers in Health, *Security and Privacy Guidelines for Health Information Systems* (Edmonton: Healthcare Computing & Communications Canada Inc., 1995).

A. Cavoukian & D. Tapscott, *Who knows: Safeguarding Your Privacy in a Networked World* (Toronto: Random House, 1995).

G. Goldman & D. Mulligan, *Privacy and Health Information Systems: A Guide to Protecting Patient Confidentiality* (Washington, G.C.: Centre for Democracy and Technology, 1996).

M. McEvoy & G. Reid, *Balancing Conflicting Interests: A Counsellor's Guide to the Legal Process* (Vancouver, British Columbia: Justice Institute of British Columbia, September, 1996).

Ministry of Government Services, Information and Privacy Branch, *Policy and Procedures Manual: The Freedom of Information and Protection of Privacy Act*, Volumes I & II (Victoria, British Columbia: Ministry of Government Services, 1994).

Office of the Information and Privacy Commissioner for British Columbia, *Guidelines for the Secure Transmission of Personal Information by Fax* (Victoria, B.C.: OIPC, 1996).

Office of the Privacy Commissioner, *Health Information Privacy Code 1994* (New Zealand, 1994). Available at http://www.knowledge-basket.co.nz/privacy.

S. Peck, *Review of the Storage and Disposal of Health Care Records in British Columbia* (Victoria, B.C.: British Columbia Ministry of Health and Ministry Responsible for Seniors, 1995).

G. Ruebsaat & T. Portous, *Records Management Guidelines: Draft for Field Testing* (Victoria, British Columbia: British Columbia Association of Specialized Victim Assistance Programs, 1995).

G. Ruebsaat, S. White & G. Smith, *Records Management Guidelines: Addendum for CWWA Programs* (Vancouver, British Columbia: British Columbia and Yukon Society of Transition Houses, October, 1996).

END NOTES

1. *Code of Ethics*, British Columbia Association of Social Workers, (Vancouver, British Columbia Association of Social Workers, 1984).
2. *Standards of Professional Conduct*, The College of Psychologists of Ontario, (Ottawa, The College of Psychologists of Ontario, 1995).
3. *Ethical Standards of Psychologists*, College of Psychologists of British Columbia, (Vancouver, B.C., The College of Psychologists of British Columbia, 1985).
4. *Access to Information Act*, R.S.C., 1985, c. A-1.
5. *Privacy Act*, R.S.C., 1985, c. P-21.
6. *Freedom of Information and Protection of Privacy Act*, R.S.B.C. 1996, c. 165.
7. *Dagg v. Canada (Minister of Finance)* (1997), 148 D.L.R. (4th) 385 (S.C.C.).
8. M. Joschko, "Requests To Provide a Photocopy of Your Client's Clinical Record May Become Increasingly Common and You Will Probably Have To Oblige," (1992/1993) 2 Canadian Practitioner, 11.
9. P.C. Keith-Spiegel & G.P. Koocher, *Ethics in Psychology: Professional Standards and Cases,* (New York: Random House, 1985) c. 3 at 67.
10. *Document Disposal Act*, R.S.B.C. 1996, c. 99.
11. *Hospital Act*, R.S.B.C. 1996, c. 200.
12. *Limitations Act*, R.S.B.C., c. 266, s. 8(1).
13. Privacy Code for Private Physicians' Offices in British Columbia, (1997), *British Columbia Medical Journal*, 39(12), 646-649. (See Appendix A).
14. *Adoption Act*, R.S.B.C. 1996, C.5.
15. *McInerney v. MacDonald*, (1992) 2 S.C.R. 138.
16. *Criminal Code of Canada*, R.S.C., 1985, c. C-46.
17. *Gasoline and Aviation Excise Tax*, SOR/83-107.
18. *Canadian Wheat Board Act*, R.S.C. 1985, c. c-24.
19. *Labour Adjustment Benefits Act*, R.S.C. 1985, c. L-1.
20. *Tax Rebate Discounting Regulations*, SOR/86-108.

Chapter 13

LEGAL LIABILITY

Terry J. Wuester and Terry Wuester Milne

INTRODUCTION

Legal liability will be an important issue for many helping professionals who must be acutely aware of the duties implicit in their professional relationship with clients or patients. Often professionals will carry malpractice insurance as a matter of course and will, through professional training and upgrading, appreciate some of the obvious danger areas.

This chapter will focus on three areas of civil liability: actions arising from intentional interference with another person; actions arising from accidental interference with the person or property of another; and, actions arising from negligent statements made to a client or patient or to others. The law is stated as of April, 1997.

INTENTIONAL TORTS

A "tort" is a civil wrong inflicted on one person by another for which damages may be awarded. Tort law developed as a way to resolve private disputes between individuals when some form of injury, financial loss, or property damage occurred. Claims may arise from either intentional or accidental injuries or losses and, today, even an emotional injury might entitle a plaintiff to a successful court claim. The civil standard of proof is "on a balance of probabilities."

Historically, the "intentional" torts were the first to develop. For three hundred years under English law an individual could seek damages for intentional or deliberate interference with his/ her person by initiating actions for assault, battery, or false imprisonment. Actions for "intentional infliction of mental suffering" developed more recently.

A distinguishing feature of intentional torts (except intentional infliction of mental suffering) is that, once the intentional nature of the defendant's act has been established, it is not necessary for the victim to prove any loss or injury in order to recover at least nominal damages. Defendants who commit intentional torts are liable for any resulting damages, regardless of whether the damages could have been anticipated. (By contrast, damages in negligence actions will only be awarded if the loss or injury was foreseeable, that is, anticipated.) The following sections briefly discuss each of the intentional torts.

A. Battery

Battery, for purposes of civil liability, is the intentional touching of another person, in an offensive or harmful nature, without the other person's consent. Any touching, however trivial, may constitute battery, and a battery may be committed even though no harm or insult is intended. Battery may even include touching another person's clothing, or touching something another person is holding, or touching something on which another person is sitting. Indeed, any intentional interference with another person that would offend a sense of personal dignity and honour may be a battery. Thus, for example, tapping someone on the shoulder to attract attention or accidentally jostling someone in a crowd would probably not be battery. However, if the contact is unwelcome to the person touched, it may be a battery even though the contact was intended as a compliment (such as a hug or kiss) or was intended to be beneficial to the other person (such as helping a person with a physical disability down stairs).

B. Assault

An assault may be established even though no physical contact actually occurs. Assault is the intentional arousal in another person of an apprehension of imminent harmful or offensive physical contact. The actor must desire to create this apprehension, but the focus is upon the effect of the actor's conduct on the victim's mind, not upon whether the actor actually intended to carry through with the threatened act.

The victim, who will be referred to as the plaintiff, must establish two things:

a)   that the actor, who will be referred to as the defendant, created an apprehension of imminent harmful or offensive contact in the plaintiff; and

b)   that the plaintiff's apprehension was reasonable in the circumstances.

Even if one were in no real danger of contact, one could still recover damages for assault if one's apprehension was reasonable under the circumstances. For example, it would likely be an assault if one man standing near another shook his fist in the other's face even though no actual contact was made. The assault victim does not actually have to have been frightened. A brave person receives the same protection from unwanted threats of physical contact as a more timorous person.

In recent years victims of incest and other sexual assaults have brought civil actions in assault and battery for damages against those who have perpetrated such abuse. An interesting issue which was recently considered by the Supreme Court of Canada is whether these civil claims are time-barred where the actions occurred when the victim was a child or teen, but the suit is not commenced until the victim is an adult. In *K.M. v. H.M.*[1] the plaintiff was a victim of incest for some six or seven years beginning at the age of eight. The evidence did not clearly establish that she thought having sex with her father was wrong, however, she knew that she wanted it to stop. While in therapy at the age of 27, the plaintiff realized that the incest was not her fault. She then attempted to sue her father for assault and battery and for breach of fiduciary duty to care for and minister to his child. Before trial, the father's lawyer moved to dismiss the action, arguing that it was time-barred. The case eventually went to the Supreme Court of Canada on this issue, and Mr. Justice LaForest summarized the court's holding in the following language:

    . . . I am of the view that this appeal should be allowed. Incest is both a tortious assault and a breach of fiduciary duty. The tort claim, although subject to limitations legislation, does not accrue until the plaintiff is reasonably capable of discovering the wrongful nature of the defendant's acts and the nexus between those acts and her injuries. In this case, that discovery took place only when the appellant entered therapy, and the lawsuit was commenced promptly thereafter. The time for bringing a claim for breach of a fiduciary duty is not limited by statute in Ontario, and therefore stands along with the tort claim as a basis for recovery by the appellant.[2]

Later in the judgment, Mr. Justice LaForest said that a reasonable person in position of the plaintiff could not, and in this case she did not, discover the wrongful nature of her father's acts and her own injuries until she was in therapy.

Following the 1993 decision of *K.M. v. H.M.*, the *Limitation Act* of British Columbia, section 3(3)(k)(1) was amended to read:

Section 3 (3)   A person is not governed by a limitation period and may at any time bring an action . . .

(k)   for a cause of action based on misconduct of a sexual nature, including, without limitation, sexual assault,

   (i) where the misconduct occurred while the person was a minor, and

   (ii) whether or not the person's right to bring the action was at any time governed by a limitation period;

(1)   for a cause of action based on sexual assault, whether or not the person's right to bring the action was at any time governed by a limitation period.[3]

This change in the *Limitation Act* should prevent the problem that arose in *K.M. v. H.M.* from arising in British Columbia. In a recent British Columbia Supreme Court case,[4] the province was found liable for compensatory and aggravated damages for breaching its legal duty to children in care. Four men who as teenagers were sentenced to a Youth Ranch for children in trouble were awarded almost one million dollars in damages from the Ministry for sexual and physical abuse committed by the foster parent between 1960 and 1990. This principle of vicarious liability for the employer is discussed later.

In other provinces that may not have changed their legislation, however, it may be necessary to rely upon *K.M. v. H.M.* where the victim of sexual abuse does not bring the action until after the normal limitation period has expired.

C. False Imprisonment

While an action for false imprisonment may include incarceration in a prison, the most common cases arise when someone, intentionally and without lawful excuse, confines another within certain boundaries. An action for false imprisonment protects one's freedom from being unlawfully restrained or coerced.

Restraint or coercion may be accomplished by actual force or by mere threats of force. (A person who reasonably believes that force may be employed and who submits rather than risk the application of force is nonetheless imprisoned.) The force may be physical or psychological. Failure to release a person from confinement or restraint may also constitute false imprisonment. For example, if in a dispute over a payment, a shopkeeper holds or detains a customer at the till, this may well provide the basis for an action for false imprisonment.

D. Intentional Infliction of Mental Suffering

As noted above, an action for assault merely protects one from threats of physical contact that are imminent. Thus, the threat of physical injury in the future cannot constitute an assault even though it might well cause severe mental distress.

Only at the end of the 19th century did courts begin to recognize an action for the intentional infliction of mental suffering. In a landmark 1897 case, the defendant, as a practical joke, told the plaintiff that her husband had been seriously injured in an accident and that her immediate help was needed. The plaintiff suffered shock which led to long illness, and the court awarded damages for her mental suffering. In such actions, the courts weigh the plaintiff's interest in being free from emotional distress against society's concern that mental suffering is difficult to prove and that false claims may easily go undetected.

As with the other intentional torts, a defendant need not have intended to harm the plaintiff, nor is it necessary that a defendant have anticipated the kind or extent of the plaintiff's injuries in order to be held liable. The law at present requires the plaintiff to establish three things:

a) that the defendant's conduct was intended to cause emotional distress;

b) that the defendant's conduct was of a kind reasonably capable of causing severe emotional distress to a normal person (or to a person with the plaintiff's particular susceptibility if the defendant was aware of the plaintiff's special susceptibility to emotional shock); and

c) that the emotional distress of the plaintiff resulted in substantial and objectively verifiable physical or psychological injury. Liability will not be found for mere ruffled dignity or hurt feelings.

Actions for battery, assault, false imprisonment, or even the intentional infliction of mental suffering, can and do arise in most of the helping professions. For example, health care professionals cannot treat a person against that person's will, no matter how beneficial or necessary the treatment may be. However, conduct that would ordinarily give rise to liability may, in certain circumstances, be excused by the consent of the person involved. The person who consents to intentional interference with her/his person will be precluded from recovering damages for injury caused by intentional interference. (See the discussion later regarding negligence claims.)

DEFENCES TO INTENTIONAL TORTS

A. Consent

In establishing the defence of consent, the defendant must prove facts from which consent may be found. The consent must be genuine - it cannot be obtained by force, threat, or abuse of authority, and it should not be given by a person under the influence of drugs or alcohol. The person giving consent must be aware of the true nature and quality of the act for which the consent is given. This is illustrated in a recent Supreme Court of Canada decision[5], in which a 22 year old teacher engaged in oral sex initiated by a 14-year old student during the summer holidays. The teacher had taught the student during the previous academic year and was likely to teach the student again during the following year. The majority of the Court found that teachers are in fact in a position of trust and authority in most cases, given the importance of the duty entrusted to them by society. This duty imposes a burden of evidence on teachers to show they are not in such a position of trust in the particular circumstances. In this case, it was determined that the teacher's behaviour violated section 153 of the *Criminal Code*, which makes it an offence for a person who is in a position of trust or authority toward a young person between the ages of 14 -18 years old to touch him/her for a sexual purpose. A civil action could also arise from these circumstances.

Consent to an intentional interference may be express, such as when a patient signs a written consent to a particular operation. However, a "written consent" is not the consent itself - it is only evidence of consent and it may be undermined by other evidence of duress, fraud, or misunderstanding of the nature of the consent.

Consent may also be implied from the circumstances. For example, a person may imply consent by standing in a line and then holding out an arm to a nurse who is giving vaccinations. When a psychologist outlines a plan of therapy to a client and makes an initial appointment, the client's attendance at the appointment would likely constitute implied consent to what otherwise might be battery. When an emergency patient with a life-threatening condition is unconscious and no family member is present to give consent, the courts have found that the emergency situation implies consent to be treated. If, however, the patient is able to give or withhold consent, the patient's wishes must be respected or legal liability may follow.

A health care professional must carefully consider how much information should be shared with the patient about the proposed treatment in order to obtain a valid consent. A physician, for example, may not wish to frighten her/his patient by dwelling on the remote risks associated with a proposed medical procedure. However, failure to obtain the fully "informed consent" of the patient may expose the health care professional to potential liability for battery. Also, if the treatment goes beyond what was consented to, a court may find that there was no valid consent to that portion of the treatment.

Young children cannot give valid consent; consent in such cases should be obtained from a parent or guardian. In many provinces there is legislation that allows older adolescents to give valid consent under certain circumstances even though they have not reached the age of majority. In 1992 and 1996, section 17 (previously section 16) of the British Columbia *Infants Act*[6] was amended to allow an infant (a person under 19 years of age)[7] to consent to health care where the health care provider meets the following two requirements:

a) the health care provider must explain to the infant and be satisfied that the infant understands the nature and consequences and the reasonably foreseeable benefits and risks of the proposed health care; and

b) the health care provider has made reasonable efforts to determine that the health care is in the best interests of the infant.

Where the health care provider has met the above requirements, the infant's consent to the proposed health care will be effective and should preclude an action for battery against the health care provider.

A recent case that sought to have section 17 declared unconstitutional under the *Charter* was dismissed.[8] However, in the course of her judgment Madam Justice Huddart made several points concerning this area of the law and section 17 in particular:

a) no one is required to accept health care even if the result is death - a person can refuse treatment if competent to make the decision;

b) a health care provider is not required to treat an infant merely because the infant has the capacity to give consent;

c) it is the health care provider, rather than the parent or guardian, who determines whether an infant is capable of consenting to health care under section 17;

d) where an infant is too young to meet the requirements of section 17, the consent of the parent (or guardian) would be required (unless there are special circumstances that change the basic rule - e.g., a medical emergency where no parent or guardian is available to give consent; where the parent refuses to consent to treatment and the court overrides the parent's decision under provincial legislation[9] or under the court's *parens patriae* jurisdiction);

e) where the infant is old enough for the health care provider to comply with section 17 and the infant does consent to the proposed health care, that consent overrides the wishes of the parent(s).

Section 17 raises an issue which is, as yet, unresolved. Where the infant is old enough for the health care provider to comply with section 17, but following the explanation of the benefits and risks, the infant decides against the proposed health care, does this end the matter or could the parent give consent to the proposed health care? Section 17 itself does not address this problem.

B. Other Defences

Other less frequently invoked defences to actions for intentional torts include: self-defence, defence of another person, legal authority, and necessity. For example, a school teacher may well be allowed to detain a student after school on the basis of "legal authority" given under school legislation or regulations.

UNINTENTIONAL TORTS: NEGLIGENCE

Negligence is probably the most important area of tort law for helping professionals. Negligence law is the law of unintentional or accidental injury, and can be used to encourage a standard of conduct or competency. In a negligence action, the courts have to determine whether to compensate an injured party for a particular loss by shifting the loss to the person who caused it. In making this decision, courts are guided by certain elements that must be found in negligence actions.

The necessary elements for a successful action in negligence are:

a) the plaintiff must suffer an actual loss and that loss must be caused in whole or in part by an act or omission of the defendant;

b) the defendant must owe a "duty" to take care not to injure the plaintiff's interests;

c) the defendant must breach that duty by failing to meet the relevant standard of care; and

d) the plaintiff's loss must be a consequence that is not too remote from the defendant's act or omission.

If the plaintiff fails to prove any one of these elements, the plaintiff will lose.

A. Actual Loss Caused by the Defendant's Act or Omission

As discussed above, the intentional torts based upon intentional interference with another person are so offensive to our society that they are penalized by at least nominal damages even when no actual loss or injury results. However, in a negligence case -- when the defendant's conduct is not intentional -- the plaintiff must prove an actual loss or injury that was caused by the defendant. It is not enough to show merely that the plaintiff suffered a loss, or that the defendant was negligent (careless, etc.) -- there must be a link between these two facts.

There is more than one test to determine straightforward causation. The most common is the "but for" test: if the loss or injury would not have occurred but for the conduct of the defendant, then the defendant's conduct is considered to be a cause of the plaintiff's loss or damage.

However, sometimes the "but for" test is not helpful. Suppose two different parties - A and B - have each negligently lighted separate fires which then converge and burn down the plaintiff's house. In the plaintiff's action against A, the plaintiff likely could not satisfy the "but for" test because the house would have been destroyed anyway, by B's fire. In such situations, courts often apply a "substantial factor test." Under this test, as long as the defendant's conduct was a substantial factor in causing the plaintiff's loss, then the defendant may be found liable in negligence. The "substantial factor" test is used along with the "but for" test where there are multiple defendants whose actions or omissions have together caused loss or damage.

B. Duty of Care Owed to the Plaintiff

Duty of care is a legal concept to limit liability and is based on public policy. Even if the defendant caused the plaintiff's loss or damage, he /she is not liable in negligence if the court determines, under the circumstances, that the defendant did not owe to the plaintiff a "duty of care."

Courts usually find "duty" where, before the injury occurs, there was a relationship between the parties that created a reasonable expectation that carelessness by one may cause loss or damage to the other. Many kinds of relationships give rise to a duty of care. A driver of a car, for example, owes a duty of care to other users of the road to operate the vehicle without injuring them.

Helping professionals, such as physicians or counsellors, have a distinct relationship with patients or clients based on their special knowledge and expertise. As a result, the courts almost invariably find that this relationship imposes a duty of care on the professional. In fact, the trend seems to be toward expanding, rather than limiting, the scope of the duty of care owed by helping professionals.

A rather extreme example of this expansion of duty is found in *Tarasoff v. The Regents of the University of California*.[10] In that case a psychotherapist had been told by a patient that the patient was planning to murder a particular individual. The psychotherapist believed the patient, and took some initial steps to confine the patient for further assessment and treatment. However, the psychotherapist's superiors ordered that no further attempts be made to confine the patient. Later, the patient did kill the person that the patient had identified to the psychotherapist. The court held that the psychotherapist had a duty of care to warn the potential victim or her family. Consequently, the psychologist could be found liable in negligence for failing to warn. In this case the court extended the usual duty of care beyond the patient to include the potential victim.

C. Standard of Care

While a defendant may have owed a duty of care and caused the plaintiff's loss, liability will not be found unless the defendant has failed to exercise the relevant standard of care. The heart of most negligence cases is whether or not the defendant has met this standard.

In setting the standard of care in negligence cases the courts use an objective, not subjective, standard. In a negligence case that does not involve professionals or others who hold themselves out as having superior knowledge or skill, the "reasonable person" standard is the benchmark for measuring the conduct of a defendant. Thus, in most negligence cases, the question is whether the defendant acted in the same manner as a "reasonable person." Did the defendant do or fail to do anything that a reasonable person would have done or failed to do in similar circumstances? If the defendant's conduct meets this standard, then the plaintiff will not succeed.

Helping professionals, performing within their areas of expertise, cannot escape liability merely by meeting the "reasonable person" standard. The standard (also objective) required of a professional is the standard of the "professional reasonable person" -- the standard of the reasonably prudent professional of average competence -- in the professional's field. Perfection is not expected. A higher degree of expertise will be expected of a specialist, but no allowance is made for the inexperienced professional. The novice is measured by the same standard as the experienced professional when he/she performs services of the same kind.

Evidence of customary procedure in the profession is relevant (but not necessarily determinative). Where custom lags behind advances, custom no longer provides an appropriate standard. The professional will be expected to follow new procedures, involving fewer risks, if she/he is aware or should have been aware of them.

A helping professional is not, however, expected to achieve uniform results regardless of the circumstances. For example, when a physician is performing emergency first aid at an accident site, the physician is not judged by the same standard as a physician performing in a fully equipped hospital. The question would be whether the physician's conduct met the standard of a reasonable physician acting at an accident site. Probably the social worker who is required to handle a double caseload would not be held to the same level of care and supervision as a caseworker with a normal caseload.

As discussed above, the intentional tort of battery will be the legal remedy for patients who have not consented to the "touching" or treatment provided by a medical practitioner. A patient's consent to a certain operation will waive any right of action against the physician for the intentional tort of battery. However, if the physician failed in his/her duty of care to disclose the material risks of the operation, the patient who suffered the consequences of one of these risks may have a negligence action against the physician. Although the case law to date in regard to disclosure and consent has focused primarily on physicians and their patients, it is likely that other helping professionals should be disclosing to their clients any material risks that may be involved. The client may then decide whether or not to undergo the treatment, the counselling, or other services offered.

The leading Canadian case involving a physician's obligation to disclose information about a proposed medical treatment is *Reibl v. Hughes*.[11] In that case, the defendant physician failed to inform the plaintiff of the risk of stroke attending the proposed elective surgery. Although the surgery was competently performed, the plaintiff suffered a stroke that paralyzed part of his body. The plaintiff sued the physician both in negligence and for battery. Because the patient had actually consented to the surgery, the claim for battery was rejected. However, the court gave judgment in favour of the plaintiff on his negligence claim. At the time of the surgery, the plaintiff had only a year and a half left to work before earning a retirement pension. The plaintiff's medical problem did not present any immediate danger to his life, and the surgery could have been postponed for a few years. Had he been informed of the actual risks of the surgery, the plaintiff testified he would have delayed the surgery and continued to work until his pension vested. Instead, because he consented to the surgery and was paralyzed, he lost his pension. The Supreme Court of Canada held that the physician had a duty to inform the plaintiff of any "material risk" attending the surgery. The Court also held that it would have been reasonable for a person in the plaintiff's circumstances to have refused to consent to the surgery. The physician's failure to adequately inform the plaintiff of the risks of the surgery was found to be the cause of the plaintiff's consent to the surgery. Had the plaintiff known of the risks he would not have consented to the surgery. The physician was found liable for the plaintiff's loss of his pension.

The general conclusion, then, is that helping professionals should inform the client or patient about any material risks associated with the care or service provided, whenever these risks would be otherwise unknown to the client or patient. Only after such information has been revealed will consent be effective.

In *Ciarlariello v. Keller*[12] the Supreme Court of Canada recently dealt with the duty owed by a physician to a patient when, during a medical procedure, the patient withdraws consent. In *Keller*, the plaintiff consented to a procedure to determine the site of a suspected aneurysm, and the patient was conscious during the procedure. During the procedure, the patient began yelling and flexing her legs, and the patient said, "Enough, no more, stop the test." After talking with the patient in an attempt to calm her, the physicians asked if she wished to go ahead with the test. The patient said "Please go ahead." The final injection of dye was then administered, and the patient suffered a reaction to it which rendered her a quadriplegic.

Two major issues were addressed by the court. First, did the final injection of the dye constitute a battery? The court said "no" because the patient was capable of giving her consent and she had consented to the continuation of the test. Second, in regard to negligence, did the physicians meet their duty of disclosure (under *Reibl v. Hughes*) in obtaining the patient's consent to the continuation of the test? Once the original consent had been revoked, did the doctors have a duty to explain to the patient any new information or risks that might be present in the continuation of the test? The court indicated that in many situations where a medical procedure is stopped by the patient having revoked consent, the physicians must share with the patient any risks and other information that may have changed since the original consent. However, on the facts in this case, the court found that there were no additional factors or information which had arisen that needed to be brought to the attention of the patient. This case does point to the need for the helping professional to be alert to not only obtaining initial consent, but also to "updating" consent by explaining new information and risks where withdrawal of consent is present or threatened.

The *Health Care (Consent) and Care Facility (Admission) Act* was passed in British Columbia in 1993;[13] however, as of the date of this writing (Spring 1997) the *Act* has not yet been brought into force. Nonetheless, a brief summary of selected portions of this *Act* may be useful in the event this *Act* comes into force. Part 2 (sections 4-19) deals with consent to health care by adults. Under this Part, every adult is presumed to be capable of giving, refusing, or revoking consent to health care until the contrary is demonstrated (see sections 3-4). Subject to the exceptions discussed below, the health care provider must obtain the consent of the patient before providing health care. Where the patient has consented to health care by a named health care provider, no one else may provide that health care without further consent unless the health care is in progress or where any delay may endanger the life or health of the patient.

The *Act* contains exceptions. First, the health care provider may provide health care without the adult's consent if the adult's formally appointed "substitute decision maker, guardian or representative" has given consent (see section 11). Second, health care may be given without consent if it is necessary to preserve the adult's life, to prevent serious physical or mental harm, or to alleviate severe pain, and the adult is incapable of giving or refusing consent and no substitute decision maker who is authorized to consent is available (see section 12(1)). Third, a health care provider may undertake triage or a kind of preliminary examination or diagnosis without complying with the requirement of consent if the adult indicates that he/she wants health care or if, in the absence of any indication from the adult, her/his spouse, relative, or friend indicates that he/she wants the adult to be provided with health care (see section 13). Finally, the *Act* provides that a temporary substitute decision maker may give or refuse consent in certain circumstances (see sections 14 and 16).

It should be noted that this legislation may be amended or changed before it comes into force.

D. Remoteness of Damage

The concept of "remoteness of damage" is used by courts to limit liability. Thus, even when the plaintiff establishes all of the other elements of a negligence action, the court may deny recovery of any damages if those damages were not reasonably foreseeable -- i.e., if the damages were too remote, there is no liability. The more unusual or bizarre the chain of events leading to the plaintiff's loss, the more likely that a court will consider the loss or damage "too remote." For example, if at the time of the incident a reasonable person would not have anticipated that the defendant's act or omission would have caused the plaintiff's loss or damage, the court will likely find no liability in negligence on the basis that the damages were "too remote." Nevertheless, if the *kind* of damage was reasonably foreseeable, the defendant will be held liable even though the actual *extent* of the damage could not have been reasonably anticipated.

NEGLIGENT STATEMENTS

Until 1963, there was no legal liability for negligent statements unless fraud was established, or unless there was a contractual or a financial relationship of trust (a "fiduciary relationship") between the parties. A British case decided by the House of Lords changed the law -- *Hedley, Byrne & Co. Ltd. v. Heller & Partners Ltd.*[14]

Although this case involved a bank's opinion about the credit-worthiness of a customer, the general principle is applicable. The bank was protected by a disclaimer clause, but the court made it clear that in the absence of such a disclaimer, liability could be recognized for negligent statements where the statements are relied upon to the detriment of the party to whom they are made. The basis for such liability was articulated at page 486 of the report:

A reasonable man, knowing that he was being trusted or that his skill and judgment were being relied on, would, I think, have three courses open to him. He could keep silent or decline to give the information or advice sought: or he could give an answer with a clear qualification that he accepted no responsibility for it or that it was given without reflection or inquiry which a careful answer would require: or he could simply answer without any such qualification. If he chooses to adopt the last course he must, I think, be held to have accepted a relationship with the inquirer which requires him to exercise such care as the circumstances require.

Liability for negligent statements has been imposed upon physicians, lawyers, architects, bankers, accountants, car salespersons, municipal officials, and others. This area of law is still developing and its exact reaches are uncertain. However, helping professionals should be aware that if they do make negligent statements to people who would reasonably rely upon their knowledge, skill, or expertise, then they may be exposed to liability for resulting losses or injuries.

VICARIOUS LIABILITY

Generally, an employer may be held liable for the negligent acts or omissions of any employee if the employee was acting within the scope of employment at the time. This is referred to as vicarious liability. Often, the injured plaintiff will bring an action in negligence against both the employee and the employer. A claim of vicarious liability improves the plaintiff's chances of collecting any judgment obtained because the employer usually has "deeper pockets" (or insurance) which may cover the damage. However, note that if the employer or the employer's insurance company pays damages, either may then be able to sue the negligent employee for "reimbursement" of the amount paid out. The individual employee's liability in such a situation may be modified by statute (see below), or affected by the wording of the employer's liability insurance policy.

STATUTORY IMMUNITY PROVISIONS

Certain legislation provides "statutory immunity provisions" which protect the professional or others from claims of negligence or malpractice in certain situations.

A. Statutory Immunity for Self-Governing Professions

One type of statutory immunity provides limited protection to those involved in many of the self-governing professions. In particular, immunity is extended to people conducting discipline proceedings or other activities within the professional association or group. Almost invariably, the protection afforded is conditioned upon the exercise of good faith on the part of the individual. An illustration of this type of statutory immunity provision is found in section 36 of the *Nurses (Registered) Act*[15] of British Columbia, which reads:

> No liability is incurred by the association, the board of directors or the professional conduct committee or by a committee or member of those bodies or by an officer, employee, agent or appointee of the association, for an act done or omitted in good faith in the performance or intended performance of a duty or in the exercise or intended exercise of a power under this *Act*, a rule, the constitution or a bylaw or for neglect or default in the performance or exercise in good faith of that duty or power.

Another illustration is found in section 101 of the *Child, Family and Community Service Act*,[16] which applies to social workers and others and reads:

> No person is personally liable for anything done or omitted in good faith in the exercise or performance or the intended exercise or performance of
>
> a) a power, duty or function conferred by or under this *Act*, or

b) a power, duty or function on behalf of or under the direction of a person on whom the power, duty or function is conferred by or under this *Act*.

Although there are a few reported decisions about statutory immunities of this type, these provisions seem to apply only to activities under the relevant legislation and in disciplinary proceedings. These provisions would not, therefore, apply when a client or patient sues a professional in negligence for acts or omissions concerning professional activities.

B. Policy-Based Statutory Immunity

A second type of statutory immunity provides wide protection in certain specific negligence actions. For example, to encourage people to render assistance at the scene of accidents, sections 1 and 2 of the *Good Samaritan Act*[17] of British Columbia read:

1. A person who renders emergency medical services or aid to an ill, injured or unconscious person at the immediate scene of an accident or emergency that has caused the illness, injury or unconsciousness is not liable for damages for injury to or death of that person caused by his act or omission in rendering the medical services or aid unless he is grossly negligent.

2. Section 1 does not apply where the person rendering the medical services or aid

   a) is employed expressly for that purpose, or

   b) does so with a view to gain.

In *Fraser v. Kelowna Motorcycle Club and St. John Ambulance et al.* (Vancouver Reg. No. C826791 - judgment Feb. 26, 1988, Supreme Court of British Columbia) a ten-year-old boy suffered brain damage as a result of an accident during a motorcycle race. The organizers of the race had arranged for St. John Ambulance to have a first aid station on site, staffed by volunteers. When the accident happened, two St. John's volunteers immediately placed an oxygen mask under the boy's goggles and called the paramedics. The paramedics did not arrive for nine minutes, and in the interim, the St. John volunteers cut the chinstrap and removed the boy's helmet. The boy suffered serious brain damage. In his allegations against St. John Ambulance and its two attendants, the plaintiff argued that under the *Good Samaritan Act* the two attendants were "employees" and as such the ordinary standard of care rules for negligence (and not the rules for 'gross negligence') should apply and that when measured by that standard they had fallen short of that standard of care. The judge dismissed the plaintiff's case on the basis that the brain damage was caused by the contact with the ground and not by oxygen deprivation. Because the attendants from St. John Ambulance were not being paid, the judge held that section 1 of the *Act* was applicable and that there could be no liability except for "gross negligence." The judgment does not define "gross negligence." From cases in other areas of the law where "gross negligence" is the test for liability, it has been defined as "very great negligence."[18]

A similar policy-based statutory immunity is found in the *School Act*[19] of British Columbia. Section 112 of the *School Act* reads:

1. No action for damages lies or shall be instituted against a trustee, an officer or an employee of a board for anything said or done or omitted to be said or done by him or her in the

performance or intended performance of his or her duty or the exercise of his or her power or for any alleged neglect or default in the performance or intended performance of the duty or the exercise of the power.

2. Subsection (1) does not provide a defence where

   a) the trustee, officer or employee has, in relation to the conduct that is the subject matter of the action, been guilty of dishonesty, gross negligence or malicious or willful misconduct, or

   b) the cause of action is libel or slander.

3. No action shall be brought against a trustee, an officer or an employee of a board or a student or volunteer in respect of personal or other injuries sustained by a person arising out of the operation by the board of traffic patrols.

4. Subsections (1) and (3) do not absolve a board from vicarious liability arising out of a tort committed by the trustee, officer or employee of the board, student or volunteer for which the board would have been liable had subsections (1) and (3) not been in force.

The public policy is to grant protection to persons who carry out educational functions in our society. However, these sections do not provide protection against allegations of "gross negligence" or dishonest conduct, or malicious or willful misconduct. Nor do these provisions give protection in libel or slander situations. Further, it is important to note that the injured party may sue the school board even though he/she cannot sue the individual trustee, officer or employee of the board.

C. Statutory Immunity in Higher Education

Although it is not directed toward those usually identified as the helping professions, a possible third type of statutory immunity exists which may give an even greater measure of protection than those already mentioned. Section 84 of the *University Act*[20] of British Columbia provides substantial protection to those covered by its provisions. Section 84 reads:

1) No action or proceeding shall be brought against a member of a board, senate or faculties, or against an officer or employee of a university, in respect of an act or omission of a member of a board, senate or faculties, or officer or employee, of the university done or omitted in good faith in the course of the execution of his duties on behalf of the university.

2) In an action against a university, if it appears that the university acted under the authority of this *Act* or any other *Act*, the court shall dismiss the action against the university.

As long as a university employee is acting in good faith and in the course of university duties, this section should protect the employee from liability for negligence. Although the section says "no action shall be brought. . ." it is still possible that the employee could be a defendant in a case where the court had to decide whether the employee was acting in good faith and within the course of his employment. Thus, even a fairly broad statutory immunity section such as section 84 of the *University Act* may not ensure that a university employee will never be involved in litigation.

320

A discussion of all of the possible statutory immunity provisions applicable to each of the helping professions is beyond the scope of this chapter.

COMMON QUESTIONS

1. Could a professional "contract for services" expressly exclude liability for negligence?

One possible way of excluding liability for negligence might be a contract with a client or patient which contains a clearly worded waiver of liability or disclaimer clause. However, for various reasons, it is unlikely that such a disclaimer clause would be effective in excluding liability for "helping professional" services. The law on disclaimers, generally, is far from clear, and the circumstances surrounding the contract generally determine whether or not such a disclaimer is effective. The following analysis describes how the courts have approached this subject in the past.

In a contract between two large corporations, the courts would likely enforce a disclaimer clause. On the other hand, such clauses would probably not be enforced in circumstances where one party has unilaterally required the other party to waive liability as a condition of entering into a business or a professional relationship. Still, two Canadian sports accident cases[21] seem to allow a wider scope for such clauses, permitting parties to rely on such disclaimer issues under certain circumstances. However, both of these cases involved non-essential and high-risk sporting events and it may well be argued that the courts would not take the same approach to therapeutic or essential services.

In deciding whether to give effect to a disclaimer, the courts might consider the "reasonableness" of the contract and the relative bargaining strengths of the parties in situations where a professional is contracting with a "consumer" for services. Some American courts have asked whether such clauses violate public policy and have revealed a reluctance to allow those charged with a public duty to rid themselves of liability by contract.

2. How can helping professionals be sanctioned under professional codes of ethics?

Codes of ethics are guidelines for professional conduct which set standards of behaviour and which operate to protect the consumer. Violation of those standards may lead to sanctions by the profession, including possible removal of registration and dismissal from the profession. The violation itself may not provide grounds for any other legal action. For example, consensual sexual relations with an adult is explicitly stated as a violation of ethics for many professions (e.g., Canadian Association of Social Work Code of Ethics, Canadian Guidance and Counselling Association, and College of Psychologists of British Columbia). Such behaviour, however, because of its consensual nature, would not constitute grounds for a criminal prosecution. It would, of course, lead to possible disciplinary action under the code of ethics. If the professional is employed, the employer may also attempt to terminate the employment.

Sanctions for breach of codes of ethics may only occur for those professionals who are bound by a particular code. This includes those who are registered under provincial legislation, such as psychologists, teachers, and nurses who have to be registered to practice, or those voluntarily registered with the profession, such as social workers in most provinces. (Only Prince Edward Island and New Brunswick have compulsory social worker registration.) These professional bodies all have governing statutes that provide for disciplinary procedures following a complaint. The ultimate forum is usually a hearing before a disciplinary board or committee where natural justice (due process) must be followed (see Chapter 1).

Some developing professions such as child and youth care enjoy no supportive legislation. Hence, their commitment to a code is purely optional and unenforceable. Some other professions, such as public school teachers, stand at the other end of this continuum, and operate under legislation which allows their employer (the school board) to investigate allegations of ethical violations in addition to the professional association or body (see generally the *Teaching Profession Act*, S.B.C. 1987, c. 19 and the *School Act*, S.B.C. 1989, c. 61).

Helping professionals may reduce their vulnerability in regard to breaches of ethics by being aware of the requirements of their particular profession and by focusing on these ethical requirements in making decisions in their daily practice. Peer and outside consultation and various forms of continuing education can provide support in this area. Clients may not wish to register complaints and frequently will need support to pursue complaints. Most helping professionals will work diligently to hold themselves and their colleagues accountable to the code of ethics of their particular profession.

3. Can the same conduct by a helping professional result in more than one kind of legal action or proceeding?

The answer is "yes." There are situations where conduct may have violated the *Criminal Code* and lead to criminal charges. The same conduct may also result in a civil action for damages -- for example, a negligence action. In addition, the professional organization may seek to impose sanctions upon the helping professional.

For example, if a lawyer steals money from a client, several results may follow:

a) the Crown will prosecute the lawyer under the *Criminal Code*;

b) the client will likely sue the lawyer in a civil action for the loss of the client's money; and

c) the Law Society will almost certainly bring disciplinary action against the lawyer seeking to disbar the lawyer.

4. Will a professional's liability insurance policy provide coverage for all possible legal actions for damages?

Not always. Professional liability insurance will usually cover the professional's defence costs and any judgment within the monetary limits of the policy. Such coverage, however, only covers negligent acts or omissions by the insured party.

On the other hand, liability insurance policies expressly exclude liability for "intentional injury" such as assault or battery. For example, if the insured person intentionally 'beat up on' another person, the injured party could successfully sue for damages which would not be covered by the insured person's liability insurance policy.[22]

In the last few years several well publicized criminal cases have been brought against professionals and others for sexual misconduct with children. Many convictions have been obtained. As discussed previously, what has now attracted so much attention are the civil actions for damages brought by the children (now often adults) against the person who sexually abused them.[23] Although the sexually abused child may sue the abuser for damages in a civil action, there appears to be no reported Canadian case which has considered whether or not the liability insurance policy of the abuser will cover such a claim. The vast majority of recent U.S. cases have held that liability insurance does not cover such claims. Liability insurance policies always exclude liability for "intentional injuries" and these U.S. cases have held that such sexual misconduct is intentional behaviour.[24]

Slightly different considerations likely apply when the child's civil action for damages arises out of conduct by a teacher or other helping professional, and is maintained against the employer of the person who sexually molested the child. In such cases the child may allege negligence on the part of the employer -- e.g., that the employer was negligent in the screening and in the hiring of the employee, did not properly supervise the employee, or did not respond adequately to complaints about the employee's prior improper conduct in regard to small children.

CONCLUSION

Although it is impossible to avoid being sued, a suggestion or two may reduce the chances of being sued successfully. In regard to the intentional torts -- particularly battery -- if the helping professional has explained to the client or patient the nature of the proposed treatment and if the client or patient has consented to the proposed treatment, then the helping professional may be able to rely on the defence of consent.

In regard to negligence or malpractice actions that may be brought against a helping professional, perhaps the best way to reduce the chance of being sued successfully is for the helping professional to be aware of the objective standard of care against which her/his conduct will be measured and to attempt to meet that standard at all times. Thus, even in those quick decisions that must be made from time to time, the helping professional should still take a moment to consider whether the proposed decision will likely meet that objective standard of care for his/her profession. Although the helping professional needs to be aware of the other elements of a cause of action in negligence, generally the helping professional will have less control over those other elements.

RESOURCES

R. W. M. Dias, ed., *Clerk and Lindsell on Torts*, 16th ed. (London: Sweet & Maxwell, 1989).

J. G. Fleming, *The Law of Torts*, 7th ed. (Sydney: Law Book Company, 1987).

W. P. Keeton, ed., *Prosser and Keeton on the Law of Torts*, 5th ed. (St. Paul, Minn.: West Pub. Co., 1984).

A. M. Linden, *Canadian Tort Law*, 5th ed. (Markham, Ont.: Butterworths, 1993).

END NOTES

1. (1993), 96 D.L.R. (4th) 289 (S.C.C.).
2. *Ibid*, at p. 298.
3. Stats. B.C. 1994, c. 8., section 1.
4. Canadian Press, Vancouver, reported in Victoria Times Colonist, May 1st, 1997.
5. *R v. Audet* (1996) 2 S.C.R. 171.
6. *Infants Act*, R.S.B.C. 1996, c. 223, section 17.
7. *Age of Majority Act*, R.S.B.C. 1996, c. 7, section 1.
8. *Ney v. Attorney General of Canada* (1993), 102 D.L.R. (4th) 136 (B.C.S.C.).
9. See e.g., *B(R.) v. Children's Aid Society of Metropolitan Toronto* (1995), 122 D.L.R. (4th) 1 (S.C.C.). Under the *Child Welfare Act*, R.S.O. 1980, c. 66, section 19, a month old infant was made a ward of the court for a short time as a "child in need of protection" when the parents had refused permission for a blood transfusion which might be necessary during surgery. The parents argued that the court in making such an order under the *Act* was in violation of two *Charter* provisions: section 2(a) ("freedom of conscience and religion") and section 7 ("Everyone has the right to life, liberty and security of the person and the right not to be deprived thereof except in accordance with the principles of fundamental justice."). Five justices took the view that freedom of religion included choosing medical treatment for children; however, they upheld the state's infringement on such rights under section 1 of the *Charter* where the infringement is based on the health and well being of the child. The other four justices did not think that the parents' freedom of religion included the imposition of their religious practices on the child where the child's safety, health or life might be affected. Thus all of the judges rejected the section 2(a) argument. The judges rejected the section 7 argument as well, but for various reasons. The Chief Justice took the view that "liberty" under section 7 only related to the loss of physical liberty through the legal system, thus in this case, there was no section 7 problem. Four of the judges indicated that the *Child Welfare Act* did infringe upon the liberty interests of the parents in their decision as to what medical treatment they wished for their child. However, the process leading up to the court order was in accordance with the principles of fundamental justice. The other judges held that nothing in section 7 allows the parents to override the child's right to life and security of the person.
10. (1976), 551 P. 2d 334 (Supreme Court of California).
11. (1981), 114 D.L.R. (3d) 1 (S.C.C.).
12. (1993), 100 D.L.R. (4th) 609 (S.C.C.).
13. Stats. B.C. 1993, c. 48.
14. [1964] A.C. 465 (H.L.) (1963).
15. *Nurses (Registered) Act*, R.S.B.C. 1996, c. 335.
16. *Child, Family and Community Service Act*, R.S.B.C. 1996, c. 46.
17. *Good Samaritan Act*, R.S.B.C. 1996, c. 172.
18. See e.g., *The City of Kingston v. Drennan* (1897), 27 S.C.R. 46, at 60 (by-law made city liable for accidents resulting from ice and snow on sidewalks where city was grossly negligent).
19. *School Act*, R.S.B.C. 1996, c. 412.
20. *University Act*, R.S.B.C. 1996, c. 468.
21. *Dyck v. Manitoba Snowmobile Association Inc.* (1985), 18 D.L.R. (4th) 635 (S.C.C.); *Delaney v. Cascade River Holding Ltd.* (1983), 44 B.C.L.R. 24 (C.A.).
22. See generally, *Co-operative Fire & Casualty Co. v. Saindon* (1975), 56 D.L.R. (3d) 556 (S.C.C.).
23. See *M. v. K.* (1989), 61 D.L.R. (4th) 392 (B.C.C.A.) where the court allowed the civil action against the defendant foster parent. In that case the civil action against the then Superintendent of Family and Child Service was dismissed because the court did not find negligence on the part of those who supervised the foster parent.

24. See generally an annotation "Construction and Application of Provision of Liability Insurance Policy Expressly Excluding Injuries Intended or Expected by Insurance," 31 A.L.R. (4th) 957-1184, together with the 1995 pocket part; see also N. McKibbin, "Defending Sexual Molestation Clauses Under a Comprehensive General Liability Policy," (1989-90), 39 Drake L.J. 477.

PART II

Skills for Action

Chapter 14

ADVOCACY AND EMPOWERMENT: USES, STRENGTHS, AND LIMITATIONS

David Turner and Max R. Uhlemann

INTRODUCTION

Many helping professionals are mandated to work for positive change at an individual, family, or community level. Some helping professionals, like social workers, counsellors, and psychologists have an ethical obligation to promote social justice for both individuals and society. For instance, the *Canadian Social Work Code of Ethics* states: A social worker shall advocate change

a) in the best interest of the client, and

b) for the overall benefit of society, the environment and the global community.[1]

The *Canadian Code of Ethics for Psychologists* states: " . . . if structures or policies seriously ignore or oppose the principles of respect for the dignity of the person, responsible caring, integrity in relationships, or responsibility to society, psychologists have a responsibility to be critical and advocate for change to occur as quickly as possible."[2]

The kind of strategies needed to bring about change depend on professionals' perspectives, ideological values, the parameters of their function, and their agency. For instance, a child welfare worker for a neo-conservative government or agency may feel obliged to advocate for traditional family values, making decisions and using strategies that involve strong social control. Likewise, a human rights advocate for a more liberal agency might become involved in coalition-building to empower minorities such as race, class, youth, and seniors groups to deal with the establishment. The skills described in this chapter, which are individual and class advocacy, empowerment, political action, and legal advocacy, may be used to promote the interests of a variety of individuals, groups, or causes, both progressive and conservative.

THE NEED FOR ADVOCACY AND EMPOWERMENT

The perception of need in this section inevitably reflects the authors' political and ideological perspective as to why these skills are required and how they might be exercised. In discussing the nature of law and society in Chapter 1, the authors indicated three views on how societal values are incorporated into laws and policies. This merits a quick review. The <u>consensual</u> view suggests law reflects majority values, the <u>conflictual</u> view suggests that the interests and values of the powerful minority elite are incorporated into law and policy, and the <u>competitive</u> view suggests that the values are of those who can exert the most influence and can capitalize on the political opportunity.

The authors' opinion clearly favours a combination of the conflictual and competitive models. Certain groups seem both excluded from and oppressed by the mainstream structures of society, including the legal system. For example, the criminal justice system is heavily weighted against women in its sexist process, its lack of resources for women as offenders or victims of violence, and in its male oriented staffing. First Nations people seem victimized by the criminal justice system because of its cultural inappropriateness and, as a minority, are grossly over represented in its incarcerated population. The poor and working classes feel discriminated by their predominance as both victims of violent crime and in the disproportionate severity of punishment. Family law still fails to recognize and protect minority lifestyles such as gay and lesbian or communal. Tax law continues to mainly benefit already wealthy individuals and corporations. Welfare (income assistance and employment benefits) laws and policies come under more excessive public and legal scrutiny compared with income taxes, import duties, and the underground economy. Certain groups such as children, racial minorities, and the mentally ill rarely have a voice in the legal and political worlds. Likewise, many women feel silenced by the court processes and patriarchal personnel. Judges, lawyers, and politicians hail primarily from the privileged classes, so it is not surprising that the protection of their interests seems paramount in the judicial and political system at the expense of economically and socially disempowered minorities. Minority groups do not usually have the financial and political clout or media connections to influence these systems to be sensitive to their needs. Competition, therefore, is often a lopsided battle between unequals and does not greatly offset the conflict that may develop between parties. Equal opportunity of access to the legal system for redress is often a cruel illusion; "it's open to all", as a perceptive English judge once quipped, "just like a famous luxury hotel".

Given the huge differential in power, privilege, influence, and distribution of resources among the general public, helping professionals need skills that will facilitate the empowerment of underprivileged individuals and groups to be heard, and to protect their rights and interests. As will be seen, advocacy, empowerment, and political lobbying are essential tools in creating a fairer, more just, and egalitarian society.

DEFINITIONS OF ADVOCACY

Advocacy literally means <u>speaking</u> to an authority (such as a court, tribunal, committee, or an official), usually on behalf of another person or group representing a cause. Lawyers are the most formal category of advocate. With the plethora of agencies, tribunals, inquiries, appeal processes, and bureaucracies today, there are a variety of forums where the general public, particularly disempowered minority individuals and groups, has a voice. The helping professional may be in a key position to advocate, especially where issues of public and social services (such as income, employment, health, education, justice, housing and child welfare) are concerned, or where rights violations have occurred. Many individuals and groups are unable to access lawyers because of financial limitations. For instance, the Legal Services Society of British Columbia, which funds Law Centres, has recently restricted legal aid with respect to people having complaints under the *Human Rights Code*,[3] (see Chapters 2 and 10). Now, potential complainants can receive legal assistance only when the Human Rights Commission has decided, based on an investigator's report, that a tribunal is warranted and one has been setup. But victims of rights violations, especially those seriously disempowered, usually need assistance and advocacy to justify their case with the investigator. Many often feel helpless or overwhelmed by this task, sometimes even blaming themselves for their injury.

Included in the notion of advocacy are the following components, which are decided in collaboration with the client or client group:

a) supportive emotional and technical assistance;

b) validation of concerns;

c) research and collation of evidence for the case;

d) exploring the possible consequences of their choice of action;

e) presentation of the case; and

f) implementation of results or appeal.

The focus may be to bolster the confidence and skills of the aggrieved person or group so that they can effectively advocate on their own behalf. This approach is part of a strategy known as *empowerment*. Guterrez[4] states that empowerment is a "process of increasing personal, interpersonal and political power so individuals can take action to improve their life-situation." Mondros and Wilson[5] define empowerment as "a psychological state - a sense of competence, control and entitlement - that allows one to pursue concrete activities aimed at becoming powerful." It is a process that develops a feeling of power as one actually becomes more powerful.

ASSUMPTIONS OF ADVOCACY

Advocacy is a useful skill for dealing with disempowered client situations and, through powerful and effective representation, may compensate for some of the power differential that frequently exists between individuals and groups in our society. The advocacy model also has generic applicability to diverse types of dispute, but is especially valuable when one party feels ignored, aggrieved, or victimized, and where no compromise seems possible. It is often the only option other than expensive court litigation when the other party refuses to mediate or negotiate. Advocacy is based on the following assumptions:

A. A response in favour of one party restores the damage from the conflict or equalizes the power imbalance.

Successful advocacy may result in change; either a return to the status quo (or condition prior to the conflict) or a transformation through a shift in power. Power shifts and structural change rarely happen if the advocacy is done on an individual case by case basis, unless it has the force of legal precedent. In the political sphere where advocacy inevitably challenges the power structure, there can be no guarantee of freedom from repercussions from the losing, yet more powerful party. Retaliatory law suits (known as slapsuits) to break individual complainants who have limited financial and other resources, are becoming more common, and some governments are considering prohibiting such actions. An example is legal threats made against environmentalists after they have challenged resource companies. Therefore, advocacy may actually aggravate the conflict and worsen the oppression. Helping professionals need to think through the consequences of advocacy actions and prepare their client accordingly.

B. The client or group is able to give instructions and the advocate has the authority (legal and ethical) to represent.

Client-centred advocacy involves the client as much as possible. The assumption is that the client has given instructions to the advocate regarding the objective and means of the advocacy. It is also assumed that there is a choice for the client in the advocate's use of timing and sequence of steps in the action plan. Munro[6] indicates that a deliberate decision or a contingency contract must be made with the client concerning escalating from assertiveness to aggressiveness, in the advocacy strategy used. As well, some groups such as children may find it difficult or impossible to articulate their interests. In these cases, advocates must ensure that they have the authority to represent and to use their professional judgment in interpreting those interests.

C. The advocacy model is effective in that reasonable arguments or escalating pressure may ultimately sway the more powerful other party.

This assumes people will willingly and openly admit their mistakes or wrongdoing in the face of reason and surrender their privilege and power. Obviously, to expect this to happen consistently is naive. Advocates may be forced to turn to legal mechanisms, such as civil actions or binding arbitration, to get results, or to organize political and social challenges. These strategies can be combined with specific advocacy actions.

D. Advocacy is likely to be more effective when the outcome meets the interests of both sides of the dispute.

If the advocate presents the request for change in such a way that the other party is also seen as winning, then resistance to the request is more likely to be reduced. Therefore, the advocate needs to know the values and interests of the other side or of the arbitrating tribunal. Preferably, when politicians are involved, their ideology needs to be known in order that the impact of the advocacy can be maximized by shaping the presentation to their interests. This can also reduce resistance. Some politicians respond to legal or human rights arguments. Others are sensitive only to publicity and public opinion, which can be used to the advantage of the advocate. It is perhaps harder, however, to determine the values of the senior civil servant who makes policy and tries to remain employed throughout changes in a political administration.

TYPES OF ADVOCACY

Four types of advocacy can be identified. The purpose, focus, and distinctions for each type will be described below.

Client (individual or case) advocacy is action on behalf of an individual. It focuses on the rights and interests of a particular person or family, assisting to obtain their entitlement and/or redress for any violation of rights.

Class or systemic advocacy has the purpose of advancing the interests of a group or sector of society "in order to establish a right or entitlement to a resource or opportunity."[7] A strategy to achieve this may involve group empowerment through consciousness raising and coalition-building,[8] as well as possible social and political action and legal recourse.

Political advocacy, also known as lobbying, is both a type of advocacy and a strategy. It includes an important set of skills, whether used internally within an agency or bureaucracy, or externally in public democratic processes. It involves advocating for a cause or policy changes and usually includes a planned strategy to influence politicians, decision makers, or the public at large to support particular issues. Class and political advocacy overlap in both intent and strategies used. For example, a coalition to fight welfare cuts is often advocating on behalf of a class (people in poverty, such as recipients of income assistance) and will use the public and political arena to challenge welfare policies.

Legal and social service advocacy is a set of skills appropriate to judicial and quasi-judicial forums. These skills are practiced by lawyers or helping professionals acting as para-legals. It is important not only for lawyers but all helping professionals to be familiar with formal procedures, case presentation, rules of evidence (see Chapter 16), and assisting the client to testify, as many quasi-judicial bodies such as welfare appeal tribunals, parole boards, or disciplinary committees are adopting similarly structured formats for reasons of due process. Both advocates and their clients need to know what to expect.

CLIENT ADVOCACY

Advocacy is the partisan representation of the interests of a client. Like lawyers, advocates have the role and ethical obligation to represent, to the best of their ability, those interests. The advocate is clearly in her/his client's camp and not neutral, as a mediator should be. This positional approach can clearly be confrontational, so skills of dealing with resistance, using principled negotiation, and an awareness of the advocate's own conflict style (see Chapter 15) become important.

There are four distinct stages in this generic model of client advocacy. Each stage emphasizes particular skills. (The following comments are taken from the first author's recent experience as an advocate for the Vancouver Island Human Rights Coalition, a volunteer organization of support and advocacy for complainants.)

A. Taking Instructions from the Client

The advocate must receive clear directions and a mandate, both referred to as instructions, from the client. This means that in order to work on behalf of a client, the advocate acts only with the client's knowledge and consent. Some complainants may not wish to proceed any further than an acknowledgment of their concern. Others want to know the implications of taking action, such as possible repercussions, unfavourable publicity, or lawsuits. Still others want to charge into action, or hand over complete responsibility to the advocate. Preferably, all decisions to act, including how and where, should be developed in partnership with the client.

Taking instructions means listening to a client's wishes and identifying the interests behind the positions. The focus has to remain on the protection of the client's interests, both current and future. This allows more choices to be considered. For instance, a young person may categorically state to the advocate that he/she wants to live anywhere but at home because of an argument with parents. Sensitive questioning may reveal her/his need (interest) to deal with the sense of rejection. This opens the possibility that the client may require a sanctuary to work on her/his feelings, and from which to negotiate a reconciliation. However, the client may require assistance in prioritizing her/his interests. For example, is the client's need for safety currently more important than reconnecting with her/his parents?

Joint planning with the client includes working together in the following areas:

a) identifying the client's issues and interests;

b) choosing an advocacy strategy;

c) clarifying the client's objection(s), presenting options, and identifying the appropriate forum;

d) formulating a plan for achieving the objective(s) and determining the parameters of potential solutions, perhaps with fall-back options;

e) deciding upon the tactics and timing;

f) evaluating the plan with a reality check and determining whether it meets the client's interests; and

g) determining the advocate's authority and terms of mandate.

In order to facilitate empowerment, clients should be encouraged to be involved in decisions and action as much as possible. Sometimes the feeling of rage, humiliation, or blame stemming from personal violation of their rights is initially paralyzing. It is often necessary to validate the client's concern through the skills of empowerment (see below) and empathic listening.[9] Empathy means communicating an understanding of both the content of a client's statements and of the feelings underlying them. An example might illustrate this.

Omar (not real name, circumstances altered to protect confidentiality), a recent black immigrant from a middle eastern country, came to see the first author for human rights advocacy. He claimed a police officer had used racist stereotypes and epithets in singling him out for questioning, wrongfully accusing him of being "a pimp and drug-peddler." He could not believe police in Canada could be as racist as was his experience of police in his country of origin. He felt humiliated and somewhat powerless. Acknowledgment was required that indeed the police officer's comments and actions as described did appear racially biased, and that these comments and actions had caused him tremendous pain and embarrassment. This process of using empathy released considerable energy for Omar to pursue a complaint (with the advocate's support in the background) to a very successful conclusion. The advocate supplied information about the police grievance process and acted as a sounding board for discussing possible choice outcomes. This included weighing the advantages and disadvantages of going directly to the media before approaching the police chief. The client realized that going public immediately might be counter productive. It would only increase the resistance and defensiveness of the police department when what he was seeking was an apology and an assurance that the offending party would be reprimanded. He chose to complain first to the Chief of Police, who acted swiftly to investigate the complaint, discipline the officer concerned, and facilitate an apology. Omar declined to take any further public action fearing identification and repercussions. Although the advocate would have liked to use his example to educate the public through the media, Omar's refusal to consent had to be respected.

A collaborative partnership between the advocate and the client means the advocate must respect the client's wishes and judgments, and keep the client consulted and fully informed at all stages of the process. It includes conveying concern and realistic hope, and identifying potential challenges from opponents, while strengthening the client's resolve through coaching and support.

It is important to avoid unwittingly escalating a negative response by premature use of confrontational tactics. Sometimes a conflictual approach can be chosen by both client and advocate if it will ultimately serve the client's interests. But normally, less risky and less heavy-handed alternatives should be considered first. Munro[10] has developed a useful Step Approach model of advocacy that uses a sequenced strategy. It ranges from the least escalating response, such as private intervention with bureaucrats, to lobbying influential leaders including politicians, and on to non-violent civil disobedience. The next step is taken to increase pressure only when less drastic measures do not obtain the desired results. The advocate should help the client to realistically assess where a difference can be made. Outcomes are not always easy to predict. In the political arena, speaking out for the record on the issue may be the only achievement currently available, but this may build allies for the future.

This stage concludes when an agreement has been reached on the issues and choices of strategy, and steps for implementation have been made. Contracting with the client on these matters is an essential skill. If the advocate is acting on behalf of the client outside of her/his presence, the advocate will usually contract to consult with the client before arriving at agreements or commitments on his/her behalf. Sometimes the client may give the advocate full authority to determine the path of the negotiations.

B. Preparation and Research

The advocate needs to identify with the client the information that is required, and develop a plan of research, such as accessing the client file or finding caselaw. Understanding the complete facts of the matter is preferable to relying simply on hearsay or one-sided accounts. Some processes allow for prior disclosure of the other side's case. If at all possible, the advocate should know or find out about the background and values of the opponents, the composition of the forum, and its procedures. Knowing the forum members, especially their values, allows the advocate to more appropriately shape her/his arguments.

Next, a presentation/negotiation plan must be developed, again involving the client as much as possible. Complaint letters drafted by the advocate should be approved by the client. Roles and expectations of the presentation should be discussed, such as what function the client should take during the hearing. For example, will the client be expected to testify orally? Rehearsal of the hearing and clarification of expectations should take place accordingly.

C. Presentation and Negotiation

As indicated in the chapter on evidence giving, credibility is the hallmark of an effective presentation. The advocate should appear to be prepared, competent, sincere, informed, clear, and focussed on the issues. Both the advocate's demeanour and content of the presentation are important. The style of presentation needs to be predetermined, taking into account the nature of the issue and the perspectives of the tribunal members. An appropriate combination of passion and reason is required.

The type of forum will determine the nature of this process. Statutory tribunals such as Human Rights and Welfare Appeals are quasi-judicial, and follow a structured process similar to, though not always as formal as, courts. Political forums, such as City Councils, School Boards, and Parliamentary Committees have their own procedural bylaws, which the advocate should understand. A formal presentation of the client's case is normally required during these kinds of hearings but little opportunity exists to negotiate over the decision in these forums. Other types of forums, such as informal meetings with politicians, decision-making committees in governmental agencies, or mediation sessions with the opponent, sometimes allow for negotiations between the parties. As well, inter-ministry social service committees may need encouragement to collaborate rather than unilaterally determine responsibility for problems. Therefore, it is important that advocates are competent in principled negotiation.

The presentation should follow the expected process, taking direction from the Chair unless a more direct intervention is needed by the advocate to protect client interests. Most structured tribunals follow a quasi-judicial format, including the following procedural steps:

a) an opening statement by each party outlining their case;

b) presentation of legal arguments, evidence, witnesses, and supporting documents (see Chapter 16);

c) cross-examination by the other party;

d) clarification from tribunal members;

e) closing statements; and

f) retirement of the tribunal to consider its decision.

Whereas in judicial proceedings the appellant (or complainant) normally presents first, in some less formal situations, such as welfare tribunals where the appellant has been refused service by a government, the practice is to allow the appellant to hear the reasons for refusal in detail before proceeding with his/her case. This procedure recognizes the power differential in challenging State resources and provides more opportunity for informed response.

When the forum is yet more informal, such as a committee meeting, some negotiation may be appropriate depending on the committee's mandate, policy, and the discretion of the Chair. The advocate should diplomatically capitalize on this opportunity. For instance, the reader should notice the advocate's possible role in the process described below of a placement meeting, which is allowed in some British Columbia Child and Youth Committees. The purpose of the Committee is to implement cooperative planning across government ministries for hard-to-place children and youth. The advocate is seeking a special child care resource, which is not currently available, for placing a particular child at risk. One format used by some child and youth committees is as follows:

a) The Chair introduces the committee members (who are usually middle managers of social service ministries) and describes the process to be followed in the meeting.

b) The advocate introduces self and thanks the committee.

c) The advocate makes an opening statement, and outlines the child's needs.

d) The advocate then invites members to respond (through the Chair) to questions, such as the following.

    i) What do the committee members believe the child needs?

    ii) What other interests may influence the committee members' decision (e.g., public interest, costs)?

    iii) What resources or components of a plan are available for the child?

e) The Chair facilitates responses from committee members, which often clarifies their interests.

f) The advocate summarizes and reinforces positive parts of the committee members' responses.

    i) Identifying shared interests.

    ii) Noting key differences.

    iii) Encouraging creative collaboration between ministries (perhaps no one ministry has the resources the child needs but together they can build an effective individualized program). Sometimes the advocate can tactfully point out opportunities for collaboration.

    iv) Dealing with resistance of individuals or committee (see below).

v) Providing evidence in a non-confrontational way.

vi) Facilitating a problem-solving dialogue.

g) The advocate closes by highlighting how a special resource or a cooperative plan can meet shared interests.

h) The committee retires to consider its recommendation.

Whether the interaction is informal and private or formal and public, the advocate's approach should be to remain as cordial as possible to avoid raising unnecessary resistance. Demonstrating that the advocate understands the position of the other side without necessarily accepting it can be disarming. Clear, non-abrasive communication that conveys the strength of the client's conviction is preferred. Face-to-face confrontation should be used as a last resort only when a collaborative approach fails, or when the advocate sees that client interests will not be met; however, its escalating effects should be recognized. As Munro[11] states in his rules for effective advocacy: "Never use a cannon when a pea shooter will do."

The advocate should try to point out that where interests are shared, efforts should be made to capitalize on the ideas of the opposing side or the tribunal. Tuning into the values and interests of the other side can often result in fruitful directions for negotiation. When dealing with defensiveness, a useful tactic can be to pose a question to the opponent or tribunal: "What would it take to allow for you to feel okay about acceding to my client's request?" The answer can sometimes give valuable clues for a potential solution. As well, many decision makers can be reluctant to make a firm decision to which they are permanently committed. Conditional agreements that are reviewable and subject to progress may be more palatable and provide a shift in positions. In informal settings, commending useful ideas from opponents and tribunals without sounding patronizing can sometimes pay dividends. Humanizing the concern is important especially if a bureaucratic response is anticipated. These strategies can promote more constructive and sensitive problem solving. Identifying commonalities and differences and presenting alternatives can improve chances of a successful negotiation.

Forums that are more formal, however, such as those in the judicial system, may not allow for this dialogue to take place, so an understanding of the appropriate protocols is essential to retaining credibility. The advocate should share justification for her/his client's position in an organized, non-threatening fashion. Clients can be involved in this process through testifying directly or briefing the advocate on pertinent questions for examination of witnesses. Where possible, advocates should follow the old legal maxim for lawyers - never ask a question unless you know the answer. The advocate and client should discuss whether or not it is in the best interests of the client to testify, and subsequently to be open to cross-examination.

D. Contracting and Follow-Up

Many clients are nervous throughout the proceedings, and may not grasp the outcome. As a result, the advocate should review the decision with the client as soon as possible. Together, they should explore the implications of the decision and ways to implement and enforce it. If the outcome was unsuccessful, appeal mechanisms should be considered. The client may wish to debrief the experience as a way of learning how to effectively self-advocate in the future. All actions and decisions should be documented for clarification and future reference.

CLASS OR SYSTEMIC ADVOCACY

Class or systemic advocacy seeks to change law, policy, or practice for the betterment of a group or sector in society. Such advocacy often involves skills for bringing about effective community change, as well as the skills of presentation and negotiation. Social and political action and a public education strategy are usually required to influence law and policy makers and to impact the decisions and practices of governments and agencies that affect large segments of the population. Class advocacy often begins by empowering individuals, politicizing their concerns, and organizing coalitions as a basis of power, solidarity, and support before taking action in the public arena.

Circumstances sometimes require legal action. It is notable that class actions have recently become possible in British Columbia. An example is the civil suit by women who received faulty breast implants. However, rules of standing (acknowledgment by the court that the complainant has the legal status to be a party in the dispute) can be complicated.[12]

Class or systematic advocacy has several advantages. Groups have more power than individuals do because they are (or can act as) a collective, and so are often more credible to power brokers such as politicians, as long as the group is viewed as truly representative. Sharing similar experiences of oppression can be empowering for individual members. Also, coalitions allow for the pooling of energy and resources. People with media skills can act as spokespersons while others engage in fund raising or developing strategies. For example, in a local coalition of anti-poverty groups, some more courageous members chose civil disobedience, while others took a less confrontational approach of public education in the media. Others lobby the organisations they represent on issues of poverty or provide emotional support to their activist allies. This shared, multi-level, collaborative approach is more effective than dependency upon one set of individuals and upon one strategy.

Mullally[13] describes some skills for advocating from within the system while still maintaining credibility. Coaching in self-advocacy, as Munro[14] suggests, may be a key empowerment strategy for helping professionals and their associations. The stages are similar to client advocacy mentioned above with some important differences. It is more difficult to obtain a mandate, clear instructions, and common interests from a larger number of people or groups. Causes may compete for priority. Sensitive, collaborative leadership and skills of conflict resolution and consensus-building are invaluable to the advocate working with large groups or coalitions. For example, in a local anti-poverty coalition, conflict was heightened between the confrontational activists who wished to defy authority through civil disobedience and others who wanted to avoid police intervention. A focus workshop for the coalition helped to define the common interests and shared goals, allowing for greater tolerance of the diverse means with which to achieve them. This increased solidarity allowed the group to crystallize its shared priorities. Likewise, ongoing consultation with a group and determination of its interests may be more complicated and take more time than with a single client. The advocate must develop mechanisms for effective relating to the group or coalition. Frequent reporting-back sessions by the advocate may be required.

POLITICAL ADVOCACY/LOBBYING

A planned public campaign of lobbying may be necessary to influence decision makers. Penney Kome[15] suggests that advocacy groups should develop action lists identifying targets such as politicians, key civil servants, media outlets, supporters' names, and other organizations that are allies in the cause. Using official channels, such as presentations to elected bodies during public question periods or submissions to legislative committees, needs to be complemented by personal lobbying through letters and phone calls, and by a diverse media campaign of news releases, conferences, talkshows, and demonstrations. A planned public strategy should elicit support from beyond the advocacy group itself. The cause might need to be made an election issue through media exposure and persistent questioning at all-candidate meetings. The campaign needs to be monitored, fine tuned, and evaluated. This set of activities however, may not be enough to get the attention of the people in power, and legal action may be required.

In face-to-face discussions with politicians, the lobbyist should be as factual as possible, and should be prepared to answer questions pertaining to the costs or social impacts of implementing changes or failure to do so. Straightforward presentations backed by data need some research capabilities within the lobbying group. As mentioned earlier, an awareness of the values and interests of the person being lobbied can be useful in framing the approach to impact at both a rational and emotional level. Pressure from constituents may need to be applied as well. However, helping professionals should not forget the importance of relationship building and friendly communication in their lobbying efforts. Making useful contacts and building friendships can sometimes influence the decisions of legislators and policy-makers.

To bring about substantial change, an integrated strategy of advocacy and lobbying may be required. This will be illustrated later in this chapter with an example of lobbying the School Board.

LEGAL AND SOCIAL SERVICE ADVOCACY

While helping professionals are most likely to become involved in advocating for individuals or groups within their various disciplines, such as social services, health, and education, many marginalized sectors in society are organizing to form advocacy organizations to respond to the needs of individuals, classes, and causes. Whether it is human rights coalitions, women's support networks, lesbian/gay/bi-sexual alliances, anti-racist groups, student action committees, or poverty and tenants action agencies, all require staff or volunteers skilled in a variety of advocacy techniques. Some key skills used in various areas of society are identified here.

A. Legal and Human Rights Advocacy

Many people, especially the disempowered, do not understand their legal and human rights. They require support to become empowered, and need connecting to legal resources. Knowing legal avenues such as accessing lawyers for civil suits, or knowing complaint processes such as the steps required to lay a complaint under the Provincial or Federal *Human Rights Act*, is important information for the helping professional to have. For example, assisting a client to fully document his/her complaint of sexual harassment can reduce the stress of convincing a busy human rights investigator of the details of the harassment. In a situation in which an advocate in a human rights coalition was able to help a complainant to clearly identify her own sexual harassment and the repeated harassment of several previous employees by her employer, the case was given urgent priority by the investigator, resulting in a speedy and substantial remedy.

B. Child and Youth Advocacy[16]

Burnett[17] identifies six principles or constructs that comprise a framework for child and youth advocacy practice. The first principle provides a definition of child and youth advocacy which Burnett states is any activity that promotes or ensures respect for the needs or human rights of children and youth. The first priority for doing this should always be to support children and youth to speak for themselves. He emphasizes the right to speak because many human services systems, such as government ministries, are frequently criticized for ignoring the views of their youthful clients.

The second principle states that advocates need to be clear about the rights of children or youth and to inform them of those rights. This is discussed later, but includes legal and extra-legal rights such as social rights, needs, and interests. Incorporating both rights and needs spans the male-oriented ethic of justice and the feminist ethic of care.

Third, advocates need to determine the role of children's and youth's voice in their practice. Advocates differ in the extent to which they are willing to listen to the wishes of children. As all adults do, they filter these voices through their own perceptions and values. But delivery of services to children and youth becomes more relevant to them if their participation in those decisions can be maximized. Burnett's last three principles are common to all advocates.

His fourth principle points out the need for advocates to have knowledge and skills of how society and its systems construct problems to be dealt with. Structural analysis of what is defined as "deviant," and why, is required. In the examples below, mainstream society sees panhandling as a problem to be socially controlled. Advocates need to redefine it as creative responses to poverty and limited income earning opportunities.

Fifth, advocates need to have knowledge and skills for promoting structural change, including individual empowerment and social/political intervention. Advocating for child rights will not have a lasting impact if powerful social structures, such as parental value systems, churches, or school hierarchies, do not acknowledge that such rights are legitimate.

Burnett's final principle states that advocates need to have knowledge of the implications for working within and without bureaucratic systems. Where children and youth are concerned, trust rather than power or status may be the determining factor for whether or not they feel supported by the advocate. If parents or other service delivery personnel are viewed as intrusive and intimidating, then advocates need to consider their own role and its impact on the children's and youth's perceptions.

The patriarchal and paternalistic nature of Canadian society tends to render children and youth vulnerable and exploited, and to ignore their views. Jurisdictions have established some formal mechanisms, such as the Children's Ombudsman and the Child, Youth and Family Advocate in British Columbia, but there are limitations. The Ombudsman has in the past shied away from partisan

339

advocacy, preferring a more impartial investigative and mediating role focused more on the fairness of the process, while the Advocate Office at present is confined to dealing with children in care or in the protection process. However, in a recent public report,[18] the Ombudsman has proposed greater child and youth advocacy through natural advocates, such as young people, parents, and friends, and through formal (professional) advocates. School systems and health and welfare services often require external advocates to protect children's rights. Many helping professionals and private agencies have long assumed such an advocacy function at the community level.

Special skills and sensitivities are required for working with children. Not only may they be unable to express their wishes appropriately, but the adults in authority who purport to speak for them, though well intentioned, may not always accurately represent the child's interests. Furthermore, a child's rights, wishes, and interests (needs) may clash. For example, a child's wishes for total freedom from restrictions may not be in her/his best interest. Care must be taken in receiving appropriate instructions and acting on a child's behalf.

C. Welfare Advocacy

The economically disadvantaged are another group in Canada often requiring advocacy. It can feel scary to challenge the government or agency who is supplying one's only souce of income, especially when the income is at a subsistence level. An advocate can help reduce that stress. Most jurisdictions have appeal processes when income assistance recipients believe the financial assistance worker's decision is wrong or unfair. This process consists of an administrative review, followed where necessary by an appeal tribunal or board (see process described below). Because the advocacy takes place before an arbitrating panel, more formal processes of presentation are often expected, though not to the degree of a court. Advocates must become familiar with these processes, as well as with the law, regulations, and policies that govern income assistance. Non-governmental agencies in many provinces have published welfare rights and appeal processes in handbooks for the lay person. A serious shortage of trained welfare advocates exists in many provinces usually because governments are reluctant to fund this service. Structural deficiencies in the provision of adequate welfare incomes often means these appeal systems and advocate services are seriously overloaded.

D. Patient and Mental Health Advocacy

Persons who through sickness and disability are confined to institutions often require advocacy to access their rights and appropriate services. Social workers affiliated with these locations can usually perform this function, though an external advocate may be required when the worker becomes too closely identified with the institution. Most hospitals have internal complaint procedures. Mental health patients confined against their wishes have review processes that include a panel hearing. Advocates need to understand the mental health and human rights law as well as rules of due process and appeal mechanisms. It may be difficult to obtain coherent instructions because of drugs administered to the patient or because of his/her condition. This calls for skill in exercising professional judgment and approximating as far as possible the patient's wishes.

E. Prisoner Advocacy

Lawyers can often play a key role in advocating prior to sentence or upon appeal. In some jurisdictions, lawyers are provided through legal aid to advocate on disciplinary or parole hearings for inmates of penal institutions, but often voluntary agencies take on this function. Again, knowledge of the law and processes is crucial for the advocate.

CRITIQUE OF ADVOCACY

As mentioned, the outcome of advocacy may not always be successful, especially when taking on more powerful parties. Reducing resistance is not always possible. People do not easily give up or share their power. If forced to concede, the powerful party may deem the concession temporarily expedient, seek ways to minimize their loss, and perhaps engage in future oppressive behaviour. When entrenched power is threatened, a _pressured_ outcome may not be honoured, or repercussions can harm future relationships. Advocacy is _positional_, with win-lose outcomes: it can result in continued resistance, bad feelings, and soured relationships.

When publicity surrounds advocacy, it can often lead to the entrenchment of the positions on both sides in order to avoid losing face, and to the escalation of resistance. Arguments that appeal to reason may not be accepted if ideological or emotional forces are present. Increasing pressure may cement positions or lead to repercussions. Helping professionals advocating for marginalized groups or unpopular causes should be prepared for resistance and backlash. Media intervention is difficult to avoid or control. Sometimes negotiations in private followed by an outcome report to the media, may be preferable to advocacy in the public spotlight, and could be attempted first. In other situations only a strong showing of support, such as a large public demonstration or sit-in, will shift positions. But this risks an escalated response by the State, such as police intervention, which may or may not elicit public sympathy for the cause. Education through informed exposure in the media may heighten public sensitivity and prevent backlash. While a carefully planned strategy can reduce the potential for unwarranted escalation, the step approach may not be entirely within the advocate's control. Presentation of complaints in the public eye is not always welcomed, and "troublemakers" are often further marginalized, which can be scary for the disempowered party. Persuading reluctant clients to agree to confronting the powerful, even with or through an advocate, can be difficult. The client should be warned of these possible consequences .

In some instances, advocacy by others may actually reduce the client's self-reliance and feeling of empowerment. Skilled advocates try to avoid this by maximizing the partnership with the client as much as possible at every step.

Advocacy is often seen as a high risk, low paying (unless hired as a lawyer), or volunteer activity with high burnout potential. Although it is increasing as part of the helping professional's skill repertoire, government bureaucracies and publicly-funded private agencies often forbid them to engage in advocacy. Sometimes advocacy has to be done discreetly, and on the professional's own time.

EMPOWERMENT

Victims of oppression are blamed by the public and often blame themselves (or others in their group) for their plight. When this blame is internalized it can paralyze persons into acquiescence to injustices. They can feel totally helpless, self-defeated, and fatalistic. Much has been written about consciousness-raising and self-healing to overcome this disempowering condition.[19] As noted earlier, validation of these feelings is very important. In addition, teaching, coaching, gradual desensitization, getting in touch with grief and anger, and group support can all be empowering. The facilitator should operate as a partner to or enabler for the client or group, helping refocus their energy on previously ignored sources of power, such as survival skills, knowledge, and life experience. Guterrez[20] suggests that the facilitator assist in building a positive network and group consciousness as support that will allow clients to experience individual effectiveness in influencing others. This may require the skill of *reframing* so that negative feelings are channelled into productive strengths. An important component to reframing is to help clients understand how they came to view themselves as helpless, understand the social forces that shaped them, and express their rage so they can move beyond it.

I. Empowerment with "Involuntary" Clients

A crucial test of empowerment skills occurs when the helping professional is exercising a statutory function, such as supervising a client under a court order or performing an investigation under legal authority. The roles of many helping professionals, especially those working for governmental authorities, can involve functions where their power is derived from statute. For instance, all provinces have statutes which allow for the provision of income assistance by financial assistance workers or social workers. The criteria for eligibility to receive assistance are found in regulations pursuant to that statute. The *Young Offenders Act*[21] describes the duties of a youth worker (a probation officer dealing with young offenders aged 12 to 17) as supervising young persons bound by probation, assisting them prior to sentence, enforcing conditions of orders, attending court as required, preparing a pre-disposition (sentence) or progress report and performing such other duties and functions as the provincial director requires.[22] Even the components of a pre-disposition report are delineated in statute, including results in writing of interviews with the young person and the victim, and including the kind of information required such as the young person's "age, maturity, character, behaviour and attitude . . . and willingness to make amends."[23]

Other examples of statutory roles include child welfare workers (see Chapter 3), family court counsellors (see Chapter 6), and parole officers. Recipients of these functions usually have little choice in accepting the service. Issues of dealing with power and authority together with the client's resistance that is aroused through involuntariness can severely compromise the notion of client empowerment. Certain roles such as probation officer, youth worker, or family court counsellor have an additional duty as court officer which means they must follow the judge's directions in carrying out their functions. This can sometimes result in conflicts between the court, the client, and the helping professional's employing ministry or agency.

A brief exploration of the skills involved in these statutory functions might indicate some opportunities to maximize empowerment for clients, taking into account the above mentioned limitations.

II. Skills of Investigation and Reporting to Court

The stages involved with the process of statutory investigations and reporting to court include the following.

A. The Triggering Event

This may be a complaint such as a citizen informing the child welfare worker of the suspected abuse of a child. The social worker should be very careful in documenting the nature of the allegation, such as including specifics about the child, the kind of abuse or neglect, and information on the alleged perpetrator, recognizing that this information may form part of the evidence that may be presented later in court. Commending the complainant for following their legal obligation to report the concern may lead to a more willing witness if required. Another kind of initiating event is the court ordering an investigation such as requiring a social worker to report on the evaluation of the parties in a dispute over the custody of their child.

In order to empower the interviewee as much as possible, the helping professional's understanding of the alleged event should be shared as fully as possible. The helping professional should acknowledge that her/his information is only one perception of the event

B. Preparation

The social worker needs to be familiar with his/her legal mandate and the authority both actual and perceived that is involved. Interviewing for an investigation is similar to a police function and is often intrusive and unwelcomed. A strategy for intervention to reduce this natural resistance and maximize cooperation needs careful planning. Legislation as mentioned will often determine some of the parameters of such an investigation and court report. Helping professionals need to be familiar with the purpose and focus of the investigation and in particular the specifics of the legal rights of the interviewee throughout the process.

C. The Interview Process

Apprehension towards authority figures is a natural response that can be exacerbated by the setting such as a detention cell and by the importance of the outcome (incarceration or liberty). Beyond the normal social skills of empathic communication, several components are usually needed. For example, extra care must be taken with explaining the role and its powers in a non-confrontative way. Clients require a sensitive approach and a careful explanation of the purpose of the investigation, the details of the allegation and possible outcomes, the helping professional's powers, authority, and obligations including how that function will be exercised. For example, with young offenders, the first author as youth worker involved the youth in preparing a presentation to the court in their own words as part of the pre-disposition report. This often helped the youth to feel more empowered because, while all young offenders have lawyers speaking for them in court, many feel personally uninvolved in this experience.

An investigation plan is necessary, identifying the key informants who will need to be consulted. This should be shared with the clients, inviting their input into how the investigation might be conducted and what sources of information might be approached. It should be made clear what information is legally required. The rights of the client (to counsel, to read the report, and to raise objections in court) and the limits to such issues as client confidentiality require thorough explanation and discussion.

The advocate should make clear to the client that her/his role is to make recommendations only, and that the client's input in making recommendations to the judge is important as well. However, the client should fully understand the implications of the information to be included in any report. A skilled interviewer will ask appropriate questions, often presenting contradictions, confusions, or recommendations for client response. Sometimes inviting clients to assist in clarifying the helping professional's own dilemmas in their observations can be empowering. For example, a helping professional may share with the client the wish to accept the client's sincerity in wanting to change behaviour yet comment on the history of failure to do so. Clients may be asked for their recommendations as part of problem solving, such as asking young offenders how they can try to heal the hurt caused by their crime. This upfront approach can maximize collaboration and "voluntariness."

D. Recording Key Information and Court Report Writing

Documenting statements from the client and informants is crucial as evidence for the report, especially because it may eventually be examined in court as part of the helping professional's testimony (see Chapter 16). Facts, tentative interpretations, and conclusions should be explored for areas of corroboration, and where possible a draft or tentative report should be shared with the client for reaction. A credible report for court is based on a competent investigation, is focused on information required by the court, is well-written (lucid, succinct, articulate, free of jargon), and presented well in terms of layout and visuality. In content the report should be sufficiently comprehensive, clearly distinguishing opinion and fact with conclusions being supported, and appear to be as fair and objective as possible.

III. Supervision and Enforcement of Court Orders

The social control functions of supervision and enforcement of court orders are common to the helping professionals with distinct statutory authority, as above. Probation officers are often directed by courts to have clients under supervision report to them at intervals. Child protection workers may visit a child in order to monitor her/his health and welfare. Both probation and supervision orders can be unique opportunities for the provision of services in a less restrictive environment yet involving some monitoring. The skills necessary for dealing with authority situations, namely reducing resistance and maximizing collaboration, come into play again. Helping professionals often have considerable discretion in how they exercise their powers of social control. "Reporting" can take many forms, from no contact at all, to sporadic phone contact initiated by the probationer, to home visits or office appointments at intervals scheduled by the probation officer. The initial pattern is usually established by a process of risk assessment and can be modified depending on progress and the development of greater mutuality and trust. The nature of the contact and the reasons for it should be clearly justified with the client, and documented for the agency supervisor and the court. Effective assessment, negotiation, and contracting with the client are important skills here. Clear explanation of what may constitute violation of conditions resulting in a legal response should be identified, especially at the outset.

ASSUMPTIONS AND CRITIQUE OF EMPOWERMENT

The concept of empowerment is based on several assumptions. First, it is assumed that the client has the capacity or potential to break the cycle of oppression and through reframing to learn the necessary skills for action. Not everyone, however, can benefit from empowerment through the individual or group approach. Some people are overwhelmed by oppression or incapacitated through their experience or current limited ability. They may be totally reliant on others, such as advocates, to act on their behalf.

Second, it is assumed that empowered groups have the capacity to tolerate diverse problems and personalities and to develop consensus and mutual support. Any group may develop factions, internal tension, or competitiveness. Some individuals operate on the principle of "power over" rather than "power with," which can be destructive in collaborative groups. Others may resist structure and process in groups because they are reminded of oppressive and hierarchical experiences from the past. Shields[24] describes this as the "tyranny of structurelessness," which can be extraordinarily disempowering. "In the vacuum, power struggles, hidden agendas or plain confusion may reign; also the inherent oppressive structure will take over." She discusses useful ways to maximize the empowering potential of a group.

Third, it is assumed that individuals in the group require greater power in order to access resources to fulfil their needs. Not all disempowered individuals perceive themselves as belonging to an oppressed or disadvantaged group. However, many do share the experience of self-blame through the process of "internalized inferiorization". Empowerment involves acknowledging this, and also includes the identification of private troubles as public issues arising from the unequal and unfair distribution of power and resources. The resulting dynamic of reducing paralyzing guilt can often release energy to begin a power shift.

Fourth, the empowerment approach is considered to be client-driven and client-centred, and the process should lead toward greater self-determination. While helping professionals might wish to empower certain groups or pursue certain causes, the helping professional's motive must be based on client needs and desires. This motive should take into account the mission of a shift to greater equality and fulfilment for all those involved in the issue. Self-determination is therefore a key feature in the process. The process must allow the clients to maximize their choices. This means that the skills used in educating adults and coaching people to take part in decision-making processes could be very useful. Helping professionals use their political role to act as catalysts in encouraging the notions of self-help and self-determination whenever possible.

Finally, the process involves a partnership between the client group and the professional. This avoids professional control resulting in paternalism, elitism, classism, or racism. As Moreau[25] emphasizes, the working relationship must itself be empowering, supporting, and defending the client's initiative. Many disempowered people defer to a helping professional as they would to any powerful person of authority, reflecting classist, paternalistic, or racist divisions. Awareness and explicit discussion of this dynamic is often required. The implementation of partnership strategies is an essential skill for the facilitator or advocate.

EXAMPLES OF ADVOCACY AND EMPOWERMENT

Oppressed and marginalized individuals and groups are most often in need of empowerment and advocacy. The following examples illustrate some of the issues described above when working with such persons.

A. Case Advocacy

Two examples of case advocacy are presented here. The first involves Anita (not her real name, circumstances changed to protect confidentiality), a domestic worker at a local hotel who recently emigrated to Canada from Central America and who speaks heavily accented English. As an intelligent, conscientious worker, she could not understand why she was being berated constantly by her supervisor. Through friends she approached the local Human Rights Coalition where the advocate encouraged her to talk about the chronology of her oppression at work. This process released energy to explore her condition. She soon linked the start of the harassment to an incident in which she defended an East Indian female employee against the racist harangue of a white male employee, and realized her maltreatment was rooted in covert racism. Feeling stronger after this discussion, she wanted to try to handle the situation herself before any advocacy. However, the labelling of her experience as "racial harassment", or as being caught up in a racially intolerant work environment, empowered Anita to write down in detail all her grievances. This document would be very useful in the event that she could not resolve the situation by confronting the supervisor, and had to resort to a human rights complaint.

The second example involves Joan (not her real name, circumstances changed to protect confidentiality) who, as a disabled woman unable to work, is dependent on social assistance from government. Bureaucracies such as social welfare systems are often intimidating for the individual to confront, particularly if the individual is dependent on the benefits the system provides. Before discussing her case, it is important for the reader as a potential advocate to understand the income assistance (welfare) appeal process. It is a daunting system for many recipients to endure for several reasons, and advocates therefore become an essential resource.

In British Columbia, appellants (persons who are appealing an income assistance decision in which their request was denied) first need to obtain appeal information (available in an appeal kit) from their financial assistance worker, a delicate situation at times if the recipient wants to remain on good terms with their worker. The next stage is an administrative review by the area manager. Assistance from an advocate is usually very important in framing reasons for appeal. If the rejection of the appellant's request is upheld, then an appeal to a tribunal is the only recourse. Under regulations, requests for a tribunal are time limited, so advice and advocacy support are required urgently. The appellant chooses a nominee (a friend or sympathetic colleague but not a relative), the Ministry of Human Resources selects its nominee (often former but not current employees), and together they choose a chair. These three persons constitute a welfare appeal tribunal, which is established to hear both sides in the dispute and arbitrate a decision. A majority decision is sufficient. Its focus is whether the Ministry interpreted the *British Columbia Benefits (Income Assistance) Act*[26] (formerly the *Guaranteed Available Income for Need Act* or *GAIN Act*) and its regulations correctly or not in rejecting the appellant's request. Tribunals can be creative in their decisions as long as they stay within their jurisdiction and make a reasonable interpretation of the law and its intent. The

Ministry or appellant can have the tribunal's decision further reviewed through a provincial British Columbia Benefits Income Assistance Appeal Board panel, then can make application to the Supreme Court for Judicial Review for errors of law or fact.

As mentioned, Joan is a middle aged single woman, who has a serious respiratory problem. She was receiving disability allowance under income assistance, but required special treatment, drugs, and above all, a safe air-conditioned environment. She had found an apartment that met her needs, which was rented below the average amount for Victoria but still over $100 a month more than her shelter allowance provided. Her financial assistance worker felt unable to provide more money, though crisis grants were available on an *ad hoc* basis at her discretion. She insisted Joan move to cheaper premises, though she could not identify any place that had the safe environment Joan required. Joan found it humiliating to keep requesting monthly crisis grants to meet her financial shortfall, and so fell into debt, jeopardizing her special diet and thereby her health. She sought out an advocate from a local anti-poverty group who assisted her with an appeal. At the tribunal, the advocate argued that the intent of the *GAIN Act* was to eliminate poverty, neglect, and suffering, and that the worker's demands were unreasonable in the circumstances given the medical evidence of Joan's condition presented by the advocate. With coaching from the advocate, Joan was able to testify about her physical condition and needs. Her testimony had a great impact on the tribunal, who agreed with her position. While the tribunal had no power to order more payment than the regulations allowed, it directed the Ministry to pay automatically a monthly crisis grant to cover the rental shortfall until other appropriate and cheaper accommodation could be found.

B. Class Advocacy

Class empowerment usually focuses on marginalized groups to improve their share of and access to power and resources. Neo-conservative politicians frequently play on people's fears of change by promoting the *status quo* under the banner of law and order. For example, claims such as "the more police we have, the safer we are" and "let's crack down on loitering youth, drunks, and panhandlers," serve to fuel alarmist public sentiments and to marginalize those who could challenge the unequal distribution of wealth and resources. Presented below are three examples of class advocacy at the municipal level of government.

In 1991, City Council in Victoria, British Columbia, with its conservative majority, responded to business and tourist pressure by passing a bylaw banning skateboarding on streets and sidewalks downtown. This was framed as a general safety measure, but it was directed against a particular group of unruly youth who were perceived as a nuisance for merchants and shoppers. David Turner, who was Mayor at the time, and progressive councillors supported the City's social planner in establishing a Youth Council. This Council lobbied effectively for alternative recreation facilities identified by the young people themselves, such as a skateboard park and a downtown youth centre. Skateboarding youth formed a loose coalition led by teenagers called Victoria Street Surfing Association. With the help of the planner and interested adults in partnership, they made powerful presentations at City Hall and to the media. Coaching on the content and style of their presentation was used, along with two useful techniques mentioned by Munro:[27] cognitive restructuring used to channel emotions of frustration more constructively to build self-esteem; and behaviourial rehearsal used to role play the lobbying presentation. The youth argued effectively, using the concept of equality and discrimination, that any prohibition must provide an alternative outlet for this growing youth sport (adults had tennis courts and bowling greens provided by the City). The Association demanded and was eventually given a legitimate voice in the design of the new skateboard park, an authentic way to maximize choice. Mayor Turner used consensus building among the nine councillors to have them all agree that money had to be set aside for an alternative outlet for youth energies. Council formally confirmed this decision, ostensibly to respond to youth recreation needs, but also to avoid escalating the oppression of youth, which in turn could have alienated political support from many constituents who are parents of teens. The final agreement closely met the interests of the disputing parties, in that the prohibition of skateboards downtown remained, yet teen-supported alternatives had been created. This strategy of change, called "playing both ends against the middle," created both internal and external pressure to shift and is invaluable in the political arena.

The second example of class advocacy involves the homeless and street people in Victoria. According to the Region's Housing Report,[28] few people in Victoria can afford to buy homes, and 30% of renters are unable to afford the rents for decent housing. In 1992, the Victoria City Council was lobbied by its own Housing Advisory Committee (expanded to include various interest and consumer groups) to take action at a local level to improve conditions. One strategy was to obtain provincial funds to hire a social-work planner who could report on the situation and recommend solutions. The planner found that there was no emergency or long-term housing for the poor. All that existed was short-stay hostels for singles, which were overloaded, and subsidized family housing with lengthy waiting lists. Because the poor, homeless, and unemployed suffered discrimination in finding housing, many were forced to survive on the streets, which led to increases in panhandling and drinking. This resulted in increased public attention and selective police enforcement. Street people were feeling harassed, disillusioned, and angry.

Mayor Turner spearheaded a non-blaming, public campaign to reduce hostility, while the planner took an empowering community development approach, using the principle that individual problems need to be dealt with collectively. This approach means that private troubles are generalized to public issues in order to identify their causation and to overcome the paralyzing feeling of total personal responsibility. As Moreau[29] states, "Work with service users should be carried out in collaborative fashion rather than from an expert, top down position. Problems need to be reframed in their social context to reduce self-blame and learned inferiorization."

It is often a challenge to persuade people to meet together to work on issues beyond immediate survival. The planner, in talking with the street people, determined that food was a real incentive, and so the strategy of "power lunches" (to borrow a term from the business community) was used as a focus for empowerment meetings. The group planned Street Meet, a conference for street people moderated by street folks themselves. Politicians were invited to listen only as guest participants. As a result, the group decided to lobby the Provincial Government to provide funds to acquire their own housing units. With City planning help, a motel was purchased and converted into decent apartment housing for the homeless, and was subsequently managed by a former street person. This was a small but crucial step in closing the poverty gap.

The Victoria Street Community Association was formed out of this process. It is run by former street people who now advocate for the homeless. The Association worked in partnership with the professional social service community to extend the hours of the emergency detoxification centre and has hired its own professional social worker, while still providing employment to former street people.

The Association continues advocacy to combat discrimination in housing and public services, such as policing. It has recently combined with other social justice groups to successfully postpone a proposed anti-panhandling City bylaw which, in its view, would have legitimized further police harassment of the poor.

However, the limitations of the political arena with its ever-changing ideologies, means that advocacy groups can never rest on their laurels. A more conservative regional council has terminated the position of a housing planner, which was hard fought for during an earlier period. Advocacy requires continual exploration of ways to reduce resistance, as well as monitoring practices of governments and agencies, and creating pressure as necessary.

A third example of class advocacy involves efforts to improve race relations. As oppressed groups, racial minorities are reluctant to speak out, especially in the public arena. Many fear a continuing backlash, or that taking action will not make a difference. Political leaders are in unique positions to influence public attitudes. They need to capitalize on opportunities to make a positive structural shift. An example happened in Victoria, British Columbia when, after several individual allegations of racial discrimination against the Police Department, an anti-Semitic group came to town to hold potentially racist public meetings. The incident upset the progressive minority on Council including Mayor Turner, but the majority denied there was a problem. The Mayor gave a moderate Liberal councillor, known for championing individual human rights, the task to investigate and make recommendations to Council. Lobbied by race relations advocates, she promoted a research project that included several public forums where some visible minorities, empowered by the Inter-Cultural Association, felt comfortable in speaking. As a catalyst for promoting tolerance, the councillor's report suggested the creation of a regional Race Relations Council. This council, along with a now more racially diverse Police Board, called for greater cultural sensitivity training for police officers. The Race Relations Council is now doing research to monitor progress in police-minority interactions.

C. Political Advocacy

Politics in a democracy deals with the distribution of power between competing interests. In this first example of political advocacy, Mayor Turner of Victoria, British Columbia, wanted to facilitate the democratic empowerment of the general public of the city in issues of local governance. The challenge was to create a political climate for collaboration, including an open and responsive government, with wide cross-sector representation at City Hall and access to decision-making by as many groups as possible. In our present politically competitive system, it is often hard for minority groups and disempowered sectors to be heard. Yet the hallmark of an effective government is the degree to which it can respond to the diversity of competing voices in its community. To do this, governments must promote the kind of climate that allows for a multitude of voices to express themselves and be heard. This maximizes the important component of self-determination. Mayor Turner's administration, therefore, established a Task Force on Public Participation. The Task Force was comprised of many members of the public, including such traditionally disempowered groups as the poor and working class. Consensus building was used by a facilitator to identify shared interests. The report of the Task Force made many constructive recommendations, including that councillors must act as facilitators of decision making by actively seeking input from and promoting consensus building among all interested parties. It promoted the notion of facilitated public forums as a key medium for involving the public in existing and new initiatives. It suggested mechanisms to equalize power and influence at City Hall. Finally, the Task Force effectively lobbied the Council, who accepted the report and devised a system whereby all advisory committees (such as the Parks and Recreation Commission, the Social Planning Committee, and Advisory Planning Commission) were to be made up of representatives from across the sectors of the public.

Another example that involved both case and class advocacy as well as lobbying, occurred during drastic funding cutbacks at the local School Board of Greater Victoria, British Columbia. The first author, in advocating successfully to retain elementary school counsellors, invited children seeing counsellors and their parents to lobby the School Board Trustees publicly and privately. The author also presented a research report of case studies to demonstrate the valuable function school counsellors played in the prevention of behaviour problems in the school system. It was argued that it was in the best interests of the Board to reduce these problems and their accompanying costs. The researcher collected quotes from children who had been positively impacted by their counsellor's assistance, and with their permission, passed them on to the media. Newspaper and television showed considerable interest in the story and quoted the views of the students, who were fearful of losing their trusted counsellors. This strategy elicited public sympathy for retaining the counsellors, and the School Board agreed. This example introduces the following discussion of the rights of children and the need for advocacy.

ADVOCACY AND CHILDREN'S RIGHTS

The concept of children's rights is that children enjoy all the rights in law that adults do, provided those laws are not limited by age, plus special rights in law based on the assumption that children are vulnerable and require special protection.[30] Advocacy is a key strategy used to ensure this protection, which is not always recognized by parents, care-givers, and service deliverers such as schools. The major rights of children can be classified[31] as follows.

A. Legal and Administrative Rights

Theoretically, children and youth enjoy many of the same rights as adults. These include those in the *Charter of Rights and Freedoms*,[32] legal rights to representation by counsel, to equality and anti-discrimination, and to fairness in court processes and bureaucratic decision-making. However, in reality few statutes are explicit about child and youth rights. At the federal level, the *Young Offenders Act*[33] is one of the exceptions that clearly delineate legal rights for youth. Provincially, children are not parties to child welfare actions and their rights are limited to aspects of the planning process and standards (see below) only if they are in care. Also, many provincial human rights codes, including British Columbia's *Human Rights Code*[34] are limited to adults over 19. As a result, no protection exists for children under this age against discrimination in public facilities, tenancy, and employment. For example, an adult could take action if denied accommodation on the grounds of family status, but a person under 19 could not. This gap may be seen as violating the *Charter* provision on age equality in section 15 and could be open for future legal challenges.

It will be remembered that in many provinces the Ombudsman has jurisdiction to review the administrative fairness of decisions by government ministries dealing with children. In British Columbia, the Ombudsman's jurisdiction has recently been extended to cover two other authorities:

school boards governing public schools; and municipalities offering public services such as recreation. The creation provincially of external accountability mechanisms for children's rights and services, such as the Official Guardian in Ontario, the Child Advocate in Alberta, or the Child, Youth and Family Advocate in British Columbia, means that decisions by adults (including teachers, social workers, and foster parents) that affect children are now more open to public scrutiny and review.

B. Rights to Social Services

Distinct statutes[35] covering child welfare and income assistance services allow for the provision of services for children and their families, such as social services, health care, child care, family support, and education. However, it is questionable whether children have rights to demand services other than the basic provision of education or protection from abuse or neglect. Preventative services, such as counselling, homemakers, and child care workers, are all dispensed at the discretion of bureaucrats,[36] and are subject to funding as politicians in government choose. Advocates need to assist children, youth, and families to persuade these decision-makers to ensure such services are provided to these groups. Sometimes arranging for politicians and policy makers to meet young people or their parents face-to-face can be influential in overcoming the gap of impersonal bureaucracy, especially at the senior management levels.

C. Rights to Standards of Care

In an ideal society, children and youth should have the legal right to a particular standard of care quality in their own or relatives' homes, and in State facilities such as foster homes, child care and treatment centres, schools, and correctional institutions. Minimal community standards of parental care are enforced through the child protection legislation of each province. Certain state facilities, such as daycare centres and hospitals, are licensed, and some schools are accredited regularly. Foster homes can be monitored by social workers. Following complaints, remand homes, correctional centres, and care facilities can be inspected by Offices of Government, such as the Deputy Ombudsman for Children and Correctional Inspectorate in British Columbia, and the Office of Child and Family Service Advocacy in Ontario.

The incorporation of principles of rights to services and standards for children who are in the care of the State is becoming more usual in recent child welfare legislation. Ontario's *Child and Family Services Act*[37] includes a section on rights, including the right to reasonable privacy and possession of personal goods, to meals that are well-balanced and of good quality, and to age-appropriate clothing. Also included is "the right to be consulted and heard whenever significant decisions are made respecting education, religion, medical treatment, and discharge, placement and transfer plans." British Columbia's new *Child, Family and Community Service Act*[38] reflects the above rights (see Chapter 3), but adds an additional right "to receive guidance and encouragement to maintain their cultural heritage." Children not in the care of the State also may require similar protection, but no province has yet enacted a general Bill of Rights for all children.

Children require appropriate nurturing, care, and supervision in our society to ensure healthy development. Ideally, in the spirit of the *United Nations Convention on the Rights of the Child*,[39] the basic rights should be explicitly enshrined in Canadian law for all children. In reality, this is only approximated through the three classifications of rights listed above. Protection of children through

351

the child welfare system ensures that violations of minimal community standards of parenting are monitored, services are provided, and where necessary children are cared for by the State. The British Columbia Child and Family Review Board ensures the Ministry for Children and Families adheres to reasonable standards of care by reviewing the rights of children in care. Section 70(1) of British Columbia's *Child, Family and Community Service Act* contains rights in all three classifications but is primarily focused on standards of care and rights to be consulted about plans.

Since children are often especially vulnerable and powerless, helping professionals need to understand children's legal rights and mechanisms for their special protection. Advocacy and empowerment skills are crucial here and may involve supporting disempowered parents in seeking services for their family and children, or advocating for children who are being abused by their care givers.

OBSTACLES TO THE IMPLEMENTATION OF CHILD RIGHTS

There are several obstacles to the extension and implementation of child rights that advocates need to be aware of and understand. Some of the key obstacles are presented here for consideration.

A. Concepts of Child Rights Compete with Parental Rights and Authority, Values of State Social Control, and Law and Order

Before the current era of State intervention, parents, especially fathers, had total control over the welfare, discipline, and religious education of their children. The prohibitions in the criminal law for killing or maiming a child, or depriving him/her of the necessities of life, were often ignored so that children were at their parents' mercy. Even today this parental power, though tempered, is reflected in Canadian law. Section 43 of the *Criminal Code*[40] allows a defence to what might otherwise be a charge of assault for a parent, guardian, or teacher (in *loco parentis*) to exercise reasonable force in correcting or disciplining a child. It is important to note that in most provinces and territories teachers are now prohibited from using corporal punishment in public schools. Also, in family law children in custody disputes are still <u>awarded</u> to either parent as if they are owned as "property." The concept of parent rights and authority still has priority in the minds of many.

The *Young Offenders Act*[41] currently seems to promote the interests of society over the needs of young people in conflict with the law, despite their right to the least interference with freedom. Holding young offenders "responsible" by substantial imprisonment in youth and adult correctional facilities may not be in their "best interests" as the *United Nations Convention*[42] directs. But youth are seen as threatening the values of law and order prevalent among many members of the public, so the call for even tougher sentences is receiving attention.

Likewise, the fact that most family income assistance levels paid by law or regulation are well below the poverty line across Canada seems to violate Article 27.1 of the *United Nations Convention*, which reads: "States Parties recognize the right of every child to a standard of living adequate for the child's physical, mental, spiritual, moral, and social development." The United Nations has recently condemned Canada's rates of child poverty. But many Canadians see this as strictly a parental responsibility in which government has no justification for interfering. Advocates should be aware of this resistance when developing political strategies for change.

B. Child Rights may Conflict with Child Needs

Legal rights may interfere with child needs and interests. For example, the *Young Offenders Act*[43] is one of the few laws where children and youth have an automatic right to counsel. Their legal rights are protected, but some argue that it is at the expense of their interests. For instance, the right to due process may interfere with the needs of young people for swift and meaningful consequences for their illegal behaviour. Legal defences and technicalities may widen the gap between the "legal" and "moral" guilt of youngsters who are still developing a social value system. Others see these rights as a protection from the abuses of the earlier *Juvenile Delinquents Act*,[44] where children and youth were imprisoned as criminals (delinquents) for such nebulous status offenses as being beyond the control of their parents or running away from foster homes. Where conflicts between rights and interests occur, advocates should discuss this with the child or youth as appropriate.

C. What Appears to be a Right May Not be, Because it is Unenforceable

Rights should impose duties on others. In most cases, governments have great discretion in the provision of services to children. For example, do children have a right to protection in British Columbia and across Canada? They probably do but in a limited fashion; a government or private child welfare agency may have the obligation to investigate child abuse allegations, but the removal (apprehension) of children or the provision of preventive services to those children and their families is purely discretionary and rarely enforceable by the courts. There is no obligation on the part of the government ministry in British Columbia to provide preventive services (see Chapter 3).

Do children have a right to an education? Most provincial laws compel parents to have their children attend school at certain ages, but children do not necessarily have the right to an individualized education. It is often at the discretion of the province, school board, or particular school as to what happens there. Advocates need to understand this, and be aware of appeal or political mechanisms to bring about change.

D. Children Often Cannot Access Their Rights to Ensure Their Voice is Heard

Cutbacks to public services directly affect children, yet as non-voters it is a challenge to have their voices heard in the legislative chambers of Canada. There is a great need for advocacy when new laws or changes to existing laws are being considered. Legal advocates are sometimes available for help with individual family matters affecting children, such as custody battles, but in British Columbia the appointment of an advocate is at the discretion of judges or the Attorney-General.[45] Now many jurisdictions are developing permanent advocacy and review mechanisms such as an Ombudsman for Children. This Office monitors the ministries dealing with children. Also, the recent establishment of the Office of Child, Youth and Family Advocate[46] in British Columbia deals with complaints on behalf of children in the child welfare system. Ontario has an Official Guardian employing social workers to investigate custody and access issues or education complaints. In Quebec, Youth Protection Committees monitor child welfare and corrections complaints, especially rights violations.

Both formal and natural advocates need to work together to protect child rights and interests from within and outside the child welfare system.

COMMON QUESTIONS

1. <u>How does a helping professional advocate for persons who are unable to give instructions?</u>

This issue is crucial to consider for very young children or incapacitated clients. The advocate needs to understand as much as possible the interests and needs of those persons. This may mean considering special measures for communication through interpreters, play therapists, or consulting with allies, such as family or professionals, who are trusted by the clients. The advocate should remember that sometimes the family member or professional can only report their perception of the client's interests and wishes. The advocate may need to exercise his/her own professional judgment in determining the client's interests.

2. <u>What pitfalls should an advocate be aware of?</u>

Because advocates often act on behalf of others, the interests of the client must always be kept in mind, even when it might conflict with the policy of the advocate's agency. Conflicts of interest or role should be clearly identified and discussed at the instructions stage. The parameters of those instructions need to be determined. Advocates should be acutely aware of their legal and ethical obligations to avoid violations and potential liability (discussed in Chapter 13).

3. <u>How can clients find advocates?</u>

Most formal advocates are affiliated with government ministries or independent Offices of the Legislature (such as British Columbia's Deputy Ombudsman, and the Child, Youth and Family Advocate). Phone numbers can be found in the Government pages of the directory. Other advocates are employed by or volunteer with not-for-profit agencies such as human rights coalitions, youth-serving agencies, anti-racism and poverty action groups. Local directories may be available, or phone numbers can be accessed through the Social Service Organizations section in the Yellow Pages of the phone book. In British Columbia, the community offices of provincial MLA's often have staff who will advocate on issues within provincial jurisdictions, or who will refer to appropriate assistance.

CONCLUSION

As can be seen from the above examples, the skills utilized by advocates and facilitators of empowerment can apply to case, class, and political situations. Skilful advocacy is needed to deal with oppression in our society and to ensure that individuals and groups have their rights respected and that they receive a fair share of resources. Where possible, individuals and groups need support in empowering themselves to exercise their own rights and potentials. Helping professionals have an ethical responsibility to be involved in this effort, to acquire skills to assist the disempowered to obtain social justice, and to work for a fairer society.

RESOURCES

A. Bishop, *Becoming an Ally: Breaking the Cycle of Oppression* (Halifax: Fernwood, 1994).

Fair Schools, Public Report No. 35/May 1995, Office of the Ombudsman, British Columbia, Victoria.

M. Moreau, S. Frost, G. Frayne, M. Hlywa, L. Leonard & M. Rowell, *Empowerment II, Snapshots of the Structural Approach in Action* (Ottawa: Carleton University Press, 1993).

R. Mullaly, *Structural Social Work: Ideology, Theory and Practice* (Toronto: McLelland & Stewart, 1993).

J. B. Mondros & S. M. Wilson, *Organizing for Power and Empowerment* (New York: Columbia University Press, 1994).

K. Shields, *In the Tiger's Mouth: An Empowerment Guide for Social Action* (Gabriola Island, Canada: New Society Publishers, 1994).

END NOTES

1. *Social Work Code of Ethics*, (Ottawa, 1994, Canadian Association of Social Workers), Ethical Responsibilities no. 10.
2. *Canadian Code of Ethics for Psychologists*, (Old Chelsea, PQ, Canadian Psychological Association, 1991).
3. *Human Rights Code*, R.S.B.C. 1996, c.210.
4. L. Guterrez, "Working with Women of Color: An Empowerment Perspective," Social Work 35 (2) (1990), 149-153. Also, see Empowerment in B. Sheafor, C.R. Horejsi, and G.A. Horejsi, *Techniques and Guidelines for Social Work Practice*, (4th ed.) (Boston: Allyn and Bacon, 1997), p. 503-506.
5. J.B. Mondros and S.M. Wilson, *Organizing for Power and Empowerment*, (New York, Columbia University Press, 1994), p.5.
6. J.D. Munro, "Training Families in the Step Approach Model for Effective Advocacy," (Ottawa, Canada's Mental Health, 1991).
7. B. Sheafor, supra, note 4, p.552-554.
8. See Anne Bishop, *Becoming an Ally: Breaking the Cycle of Oppression*, (Halifax: Fernwood Publishing, 1994).
9. For information on such skills, see J. Lishman, *Communication in Social Work*, British Association of Social Work, (London: McMillan UK, 1994) Chapters 5 and 8.
10. *Supra*, note 6.
11. *Ibid*, rule no.1.
12. J. Swaigen, *How to Fight for What's Right: The Citizen's Guide to Public Interest Law*, (Toronto: Lorimer Press, 1981).
13. R. Mullaly, *Structural Social Work: Ideology, Theory and Practice*, (Toronto: McLelland and Stewart, 1993) pp.153-181.
14. *Supra*, note 9.
15. P. Kome, *Every Voice Counts: A Guide to Personal and Political Action*, (Ottawa, Canadian Council on Status of Women, 1989) p.40.
16. The author is grateful for the assistance of M. Burnett, Victoria's former regional child and youth advocate, with this particular section.
17. M. Burnett, "Child and Youth Advocacy Practice," unpublished paper, Victoria 1996.
18. *Fair Schools*, Public Report No. 35/May 1995, Office of the Ombudsman, British Columbia, Victoria.

19. For example, see A. Bishop, *Becoming an Ally: Breaking the Cycle of Oppression*, (Halifax: Fernwood Publishing, 1994); J.B. Mondros and S.M. Wilson, *Organizing for Power and Empowerment*, (New York: Columbia University Press ,1994).

20. *Supra*, note 4.

21. *Young Offenders Act*, R.S.C. 1985, c. Y-1, section 37.

22. For information on predisposition reports, see A. D. W. Leschied and J. S. Wormith, "Assessment of Young Offenders and Treatment of Correctional Clients," in D. Evans, (ed.) *The Law Standards of Practice and Ethics in the Practice of Psychology* (Toronto: Edmond Montgomery Publications, 1997), c.9.

23. *Supra*, note 21, section 14 (2).

24. K. Shields, *In the Tiger's Mouth: An Empowerment Guide for Social Action*, (Gabriola Island, Canada: New Society Publishers, 1994) p.82.

25. M. Moreau et al, *Empowerment II, Snapshots of the Structural Approach in Action*, (Ottawa, Carleton University Press, 1993).

26. R.S.B.C. proclaimed October 1996, c. 27.

27. *Supra*, note 6.

28. *Capital Region Housing Report* (1993) Capital Regional District, Victoria.

29. M. Moreau, *supra*, note 25, p.4.

30. For more details on the notion of special protection and on a summary of rights that apply to children in various areas of law, see D. Turner, "Children, Youth and the Law," in R. Carson and L. Olivo (eds), *Introduction to Law in Canada*, (North York, Canada: Captus Press, 1996), pp.457-476.

31. See D. Turner: *Holding Governments Accountable for Children's Rights: The Canadian Experience*, (monograph, Sedgewick Society for Consumer and Public Education, University of Victoria School of Social Work, 1990).

32. Part 1 of the *Constitution Act*, 1982 c.11. See Chapter 2.

33. *Young Offenders Act*, R.S.C.1985, c.Y-1.

34. *Human Rights Code of British Columbia*, R.S.B.C., 1996 c.210.

35. For example Ontario's *Child and Family Services Act*, S.O 1984, c.55; *British Columbia's Benefits Act*, S.B.C, 1996; Manitoba's *Public Schools Act*, S.M. 1980 ,c.33.

36. See note 31.

37. S.O. 1984, c.55, section 46.

38. R.S.B.C. 1996 c. 46.

39. *Convention on the Rights of the Child*, Resolution of the United Nations Assembly, December 1989.

40. *Criminal Code of Canada*, R.S.C. 1985, c. C-46.

41. *Supra*, note 33, section 3.

42. *Convention on the Rights of the Child, Supra*, note 39

43. *Supra*, note 33, section 11.

44. *Juvenile Delinquents Act*, R.S.C. 1970. c. J-3, replaced by *Young Offenders Act*, 1984, supra, note 33, (proclaimed 1985).

45. *Family Relations Act*, R.S.B.C. 1996 c.128 section 2.

46. Appointed under the *Child, Youth and Family Advocacy Act*, R.S.B.C. 1996 c.47.

Chapter 15

CONFLICT RESOLUTION:
A FIVE STAGE GENERIC MODEL OF MEDIATION

David Turner and Max R. Uhlemann

INTRODUCTION

All helping professionals, regardless of their discipline, have to confront conflict in their daily practice. This may be interpersonal conflict between individuals, families, and groups, conflict between an individual and the social system, or conflict between systems. Relationship disputes, such as custody battles between parents over their children (see Chapter 6) fall into the first category. The second category may include an individual's dispute with an employer over wages, a parent's clash with a child protection authority over an allegation of abuse (see Chapter 3), or an ethnic group's upset at racial discrimination by a school (see Chapters 2 and 10). The third category of conflict, between systems, often occurs in the political arena. An example is the current resource dispute among logging companies, First Nations bands, environmentalists, unions, and provincial and local governments in British Columbia.

Several structured methods are available to resolve disputes between parties. They are listed here in ascending order of formal intervention and adversarial quality:

a) negotiation - individual bargaining between the disputants;

b) advocacy - partisan negotiation assisted by advocates representing either party;

c) mediation - negotiation/problem-solving facilitated by a neutral third party;

d) arbitration - a formal or informal process of decision making by an impartial third party or tribunal /panel; and

e) litigation - legal /court action using formal mechanisms.

This chapter will focus on a generic model of mediation, which can be modified to deal with a wide range of disputes. A brief coverage of the nature of conflict is presented first, followed by the assumptions, structure, stages, and skills of mediation, then the strengths and limitations of the mediation model. The chapter concludes with answers to some questions commonly asked by helping professionals.

THE NATURE OF CONFLICT

Conflict can be defined as a struggle between at least two interdependent parties who have real or perceived incompatible goals or activities, or are in competition for scarce rewards or resources, or experience interference in achieving their goals or activities.[1] Conflict is normal and inevitable in a pluralistic, ever-changing society. Conflict can bring about constructive or destructive change. A positive outcome of conflict can be that it prevents stagnation and provides impetus for new information and appropriate solutions. If handled properly, conflict can result in a more equitable distribution of power and resources, building individual esteem and group cohesion. Resolving conflict can "tap off" destructive energy that might otherwise result in more harmful, escalated disputes. For example, settling a business dispute can avoid a lockout by the employer or walkout by workers, or dealing with racial tension may avoid ethnic violence.

A negative outcome of conflict can be that it results in oppression and exploitation of the less powerful. It may entrench animosity and resentment, often leading to explosive outcomes if not dealt with satisfactorily. For instance, bitter unresolved feelings following marital breakdown can lead to the use of children as pawns in a power struggle, and to escalating family violence. Reactions to negative conflict can include stress, unhealthy resistance, and entrenchment. Factionalism and heightened competitiveness may interfere with smooth functioning or productivity. Huge amounts of energy can be consumed in defensiveness, leading to damaged self-esteem and feelings of disempowerment and victimization. Above all, unresolved conflict fuels the notion of the other as the "untrustworthy enemy," a depersonalizing process that can escalate to the point at which each side is willing to inflict serious harm on the other.

So it is important that the participants involved in conflict and the facilitating professional discover ways to reach a positive resolution of conflict that will result in the de-escalation of tension and in beneficial outcomes for all involved. Mediation is one of the processes that can maximize the "wins" for all parties.

SOURCES AND TYPES OF CONFLICT

Conflicts are caused by a variety of factors that interact with each other to escalate a problematic situation. These factors include characteristics of the parties, such as their perceptions, emotions, values, demands, and expectations, and components of the situation, including the dynamics of power, stress, time pressures, and communication patterns. These characteristics can combine in ways that result in inequality, tension, and excessive competition. For instance, the stress of a relationship breakdown combined with competition for affection, the expectations of parenting, and damaged communication between parents can result in an entrenched custody battle over the children. A power imbalance coupled with the values or differing expectations of equality can lead to feelings of oppression, and result in aggressive behaviour used to counteract these feelings. The conflict between merchants and the homeless street people in many cities today is an example that confronts politicians, police, and social service workers alike. Several types of conflict have been identified:[2]

A. Data Conflicts

Data conflicts may result from different information being available to the parties or different perceptions of that information. For example, feuding parents see themselves as best able to care for the children and often do not consult either the children or each other.

B. Resource Conflicts

Resource conflicts involve actual or perceived threats to or competition for power and resources. These may be substantive, such as money or time, or intangibles, such as status or friendship. Social service bureaucracies or private agencies in a particular service field competing for scarce dollars can fall into this type of conflict.

C. Relationship Conflicts

Relationship conflicts involve differing communication styles, expectations, psychological needs, values, and motivations. Colleagues in an agency may have different working styles or goals and develop an adversarial relationship.

D. Value Conflicts

Value conflicts may be caused by differences in beliefs or ways of behaving, as exemplified by religious and ethnic disputes. For example, the values of conservative religious groups about abortion conflict with other more liberal groups.

E. Structural Conflicts

Structural conflicts may arise through systemic inequalities of power, resources, and control, or procedural constraints such as time limits, accountability, or different routines. Systemic inequalities based on class, race, gender, abilities and sexual orientation are examples of conflicts of this kind.

DYNAMICS OF CONFLICT

Many disputes have components from several types of conflict. A parental dispute may involve differences in values and power as well as differing styles and expectations of parenting. Various components can interact to influence the nature of the conflict and the responses of the people in the dispute. Powerful persons may try to control the process and the options available. One party may behave autocratically, pressuring the other party to make a quick decision based on limited information or choices. A confrontational context, coupled with the expectation or demand to make a decision within a limited time, increases stress, which in turn can distort perception, impair communication, and heighten emotions. Given the preceding dynamics, an escalation of the conflict is likely.

The emotional arousal cycle and its physiological components in the stress response[3] are well known. An event such as an argument, physical attack, perceived threat, or painful memory can trigger the cycle. This leads the body's alarm system to prepare for a crisis by a response of fight, flight, or capitulation. Increased heart rate, respiration, and release of adrenaline shift blood from the large organs of the body to the large muscles in preparation for action. As a result of less blood/oxygen supply to the brain, the quality of judgment and decision making at this point is usually significantly reduced. A person's volatility and stress level can rapidly increase, emotions start flowing, and escalation of the conflict is likely. This is not usually the time to productively resolve the dispute. Only when some action is taken to reduce stress does the body begin to recover. Reasoning then gradually replaces this survival reaction. As we shall see, mediation provides a context and safe process to manage and reduce such tension, thereby enhancing the quality of decision making.

The participants may also have differing conflict styles. One model for understanding conflict[4] looks at one continuum of the concern for relationships and another continuum of concern for personal goals. These two factors may be important in determining outcomes. Some people are more accommodating than others, having a higher investment in relationships than in personal goal achievement. In contrast, a highly competitive person who values personal success over the relationship may employ a strongly adversarial style. Some may withdraw from conflict, while others may soften it by compromise. Still others with a high commitment to both relationships and goals may be more collaborative. All these styles have their worth, although the collaborator style may be easier to work with in mediation because it stresses the partnership, "win-win" approach.

Helping professionals should become aware of their own styles of dealing with conflict. These styles can affect their perception of the intensity of conflict in a dispute and their own approach to mediation. Such awareness can counter a preference for the approach of one participant over the other, which would influence neutrality and impartiality.

WHAT IS MEDIATION ?

Mediation is a structured process of dispute resolution that assists the parties in conflict to come to their own agreement. The process is facilitated by a neutral third party, the mediator.[5] Mediation relies on promoting collaborative, interest-based negotiation and problem solving rather than competitive, positional bargaining.

Key concepts used in the mediation model include the following. A "position" is a unilateral focus on one's own choice, "the way it must be," and it is usually attained at the expense of the other party. Positional bargaining focuses on competition, "me versus you," promoting conflicting positions and "win-lose" options. "Interests" include the needs, wants, fears, hopes, priorities, and concerns that each party wants to have met by the final agreement. Interest-based or principled negotiation[6] focuses on collaboration, "us versus the problem," dealing with underlying interests and needs, and promoting mutually satisfying outcomes and win-win options.

There are some fundamental differences between positional and interest-based bargaining. Positional bargaining tends to focus on differences or tends to ignore them, depending on whether it suits the position sought. In its extreme form, positional bargaining can lead to the ruthless attitude of doing what it takes to win, raising competition, threat, suspicion, and the dynamic of a power struggle, "my way or the highway!" This can result in the parties using subversive, unfair tactics to "outwit their opponent," such as lying, coercion, bluffing, withholding key information, power plays, blaming, and intimidation. The relationship is subverted to the winning outcome, with the loser often feeling resentful and cheated. Commitment to honour the final agreement is often suspect.

In interest-based bargaining, the focus is on common ground and shared interests, and the goal

360

of producing an outcome that will meet as many of both parties' needs as possible. The climate is viewed as fairer, more open, and respectful, with differences being tolerated. One hallmark of this form of negotiation is encouragement of the parties to work together to find a resolution to their common problem. A second hallmark is separating the problem from the persons involved; energy is focused on working on the problem, not attacking or blaming each other. Safety, trust, and honesty are promoted in the interests of the relationship. Open disclosure of information, needs, and ideas is encouraged. The collaborative approach combined with the goal that the outcome must be mutually satisfying fosters a commitment to honour the result.

ASSUMPTIONS OF INTEREST-BASED MEDIATION

This model of mediation is anchored on the following five assumptions. Each assumption is discussed below.

First, it is assumed that it is possible to restore or approximate harmony. In the ideal world all human conflicts are resolvable. Balance and harmony in human relationships can be restored. In practice, of course, some disputes seem and may be in reality irreconcilable. When disputes result in intense hatred or serious damage to the parties involved, it is hard to imagine how resolution or compensation can come about. This model is consensual in that the parties choose to engage in the process, and they eventually decide what constitutes a satisfactory outcome. However, their participation does not prevent the mediator from commenting on the fairness or appropriateness of the parties' actions at the point when they are considering options for resolution, although the parties do have the ultimate decision.

Second, it is assumed that the mediator is a neutral facilitator. It is essential that the mediator is not perceived as being allied to either party but as having equal allegiance to both, and as being fair and impartial. The mediator's behaviour, language, and posture should reflect this. However, no person can be truly neutral on any issue, nor value-free. Mediators need to be aware of their values, biases, and presumptions in order to reduce their impact on the mediating role. They need to avoid the decision-making role by facilitating a process that empowers the parties to develop and choose solutions. Note that, with the parties' consent, the mediator in some models may use an arbitration function on some particularly intractable aspects of the resolution, but this practice is discouraged here as contaminating the empowering process.

Third, it is assumed that honouring the process is as important as the outcome. It is important that the parties are committed to following the process and especially the ground rules used in this model of mediation. The process and ground rules are pre-established to maximize equality of participation, to reduce the power differential as much as possible, and to generate the greatest potential for consensus in the outcome. Failure to follow the key components may jeopardize these principles. The process itself and the opportunity for more effective communication can often improve the working relationship of the parties.

A fourth assumption is that, with assistance, the parties have the capacity to focus on interests, not positions, and to find a joint resolution of the dispute. Interest-based or principled negotiation is the hallmark of this mediation model. It seems that it is a combination of the personality of the individuals and the context of the dispute that promotes the ability to separate the person from the problem, to keep distracting emotions in check, and to collaborate. However, a person's investment in the issue, the competitiveness of his/her personality, her/his experience of the dispute, and the degree of entrenchment and the purpose it serves, all have an impact. Moreover, the parties must want to settle the dispute in order to overcome any resistance to their face-to-face negotiation. The mediator may have to assist (teach) them to manage their own emotional reactions, and to work together to find their own resolution.

Finally, it is assumed that the parties are operating from a position of equal power and are willing to share power in decision making, and if not, that the process can compensate for that inequity. This is perhaps the most difficult assumption to actualize. Power imbalance is a reality in every day life and explains the unequal distribution of wealth and resources in society, structural inequality, and violations of rights in most countries. Disputes most frequently arise between unequals, often over an abuse of power. The process of mediation assumes a willingness to share power, but if the parties are not able to do that, the model can only go so far in compensating for that inequity. This limit invites the criticism that mediation does little to change the status quo and existing power structure, unless the parties are willing to share their power both in the decision-making process and the ultimate outcome.

STAGES OF MEDIATION

The key stages and their components of mediation are presented below. Refer to Table 1 by Stanley and Turner[7] on the next page for a summary of this discussion. Each stage identifies key objectives and the activities required to achieve those objectives. The skills required of the mediator to facilitate each stage are also mentioned.

This structured process is generic in that it is applicable to a whole range of disputes including private and public conflicts. Key skills and components are described, although the unique characteristics of individual disputes may require additional skills. For example, dealing with resistance may be necessary in a long-standing dispute, managing intense emotions may be required in a relationship conflict such as a custody battle, handling media exposure may feature in a public dispute, or compensating for a power imbalance might be essential in a situation where one party feels intimidated.

The stages are sequential, but while each stage may be dependent on the satisfactory completion of the preceding one, the process need not be viewed as entirely linear. The mediator, who controls the process, may loop back to earlier stages to reconfirm commitment or rework objectives. Failure to complete a stage properly may lead to derailment of the process at a later stage and an unsuccessful outcome to the entire process. There are five stages in all, with an important preliminary stage that prepares the parties for the mediation process.

GENERIC MEDIATION MODEL	Preliminary Stage	Stage 1 Introduction	Stage 2 Opening Statement & Issue Identification	Stage 3 Determining Interests and Needs	Stage 4 Problem Solving	Stage 5 Formalizing an Agreement
Objectives	A. To obtain consent of parties to participate in mediation. B. To assess readiness of the parties and appropriateness of issues.	A. To establish climate of trust and safety. B. To ensure understanding of process and commitment to rules. C. To reaffirm readiness and obtain commitment to proceed.	A. To allow an opportunity for the parties to tell their story. B. To allow an opportunity to express feelings (ventilate) and hear the other side. C. Further clarification of issues in dispute.	A. To identify the interests and needs that must be met in the final agreement.	A. To generate and evaluate options. B. To facilitate choice of appropriate options.	A. To convert options into a clear agreement. B. To obtain commitment to the agreement and its implementation, and/or to further mediation.
Activities	Explain role, purpose and process. Joint meeting and/or individual caucus. Address fear and misconceptions (resistance). Determine issues for mediation. Arrange logistics (who will participate, support persons, location, etc.).	Give welcoming and commending statements. Introductions. Explain process and mediator's role. Explain ground rules. Assess level of understanding by inviting questions. Obtain commitment to rules and commitment to proceed.	Have each party tell their story. Ask for summaries and reflections confirming that the story has been heard. Summarize issues in dispute. Identify common ground.	Review concept of interests and needs. Probe to identify underlying issues and interests. Continue to develop climate of empathy. Allow sharing of perceptions of the problems and issues. Further identification of common ground. Obtain commitment to proceed.	Explain problem-solving process. Facilitate choice of issues to work on. Work through problem-solving process (brainstorming). Facilitate evaluation and choice of appropriate options.	Develop an agreement (preferably in writing). Evaluate the agreement in terms of interests, its fairness and practicality (reality testing). Develop implementation/ monitoring plan. Obtain commitment. Closing remarks.
Skills	Clear communication. Assessment. Empathic listening and responding. Contracting re: logistics.	Greeting. Communication. Empathy: attending and observing. Inviting feedback. Attention to resistance. Contracting re: commitment.	Facilitation of story telling. Active listening. Encouragement of collaboration. Enforcement of rules. Summarizing and clarifying. Inviting feedback.	Communication of concepts. Use of probing and confrontation. Reframing. Summarizing. Reinforcement of rules. Teaching. Facilitation of empowerment.	Facilitation of problem-solving. Brainstorming. Clarifying. Evaluating.	Drafting agreement. Evaluating. Contracting. Closure.

Table 1. Stages of Mediation

I. Preliminary Stage: Preparing the Parties

The importance of this stage is that it prepares the parties to be willingly, knowingly, and effectively engaged in the process. The general public has little idea of what is involved and may fear manipulation by the mediator or by the other party. This stage has two main objectives: (1) to obtain the parties' willingness to engage in mediation; and (2) to assess the suitability of both parties and their issues for the mediation process.

A. Obtaining Consent of the Parties

The parties' preconceptions of mediation and understanding of the process may determine their willingness to be involved. Research by Turner and Jobson[8] exploring why people choose to mediate rather than fight in court, indicates some of the factors that the parties to small civil disputes consider in their decision to accept or reject the opportunity for mediation. For instance, there may be gender differences based on a perception (or reality) of power differentials. Women may be more likely to refuse to face the opposing party except in the controlled and separated environment of a courtroom, perhaps fearing mediation as an overpowering confrontation. Examples like this reinforce the need to convince participants that the mediator's role is to serve as an umpire, and that the process can provide sufficient protection during mediation. Turner and Jobson's[9] research into private disputes indicates people are more likely to consider mediation when:

a) they want control of the setting, a strong voice in the dispute, and to deal with underlying value issues;

b) they understand the mediation process and the role of the mediator through adequate information or previous successful experience; and

c) they are assured that their interests will be protected, and that the process is safe.

The mediator has a number of activities to complete at this stage in the process. Using empathy, the mediator needs to explain his/her role and the mediation process clearly to both parties. The mediator should address the fears and misconceptions of both parties. In addition to an initial discussion over the phone, many mediators use a preparatory caucus (individual meeting with each party) to reassure the parties and to establish an aura of neutrality, fairness, and safety. Issues such as who should attend (an individual may wish to bring an advocate or support person), identifying a neutral location, assessing willingness and readiness to engage in mediation (a party may need to consult her/his legal counsel or need parallel emotional support from a social worker or psychiatrist), and payment of fees should be considered in the initial caucus. In the case of a group or multi-party dispute, such as a neighbourhood feud, it may be necessary to identify credible representatives who have the authority to make decisions on behalf of their group. The representatives may need to obtain a mandate from their respective groups before proceeding in the mediation process. The mediator may also have to employ strategies to reduce resistance, such as a conditional (without obligation) acceptance to the mediation process, in order that the parties attend the first meeting.

B. Assessing Readiness of the Parties and Appropriateness of Issues

The mediator must assess whether the parties are ready for mediation and whether the issues in dispute are appropriate for mediation. Highly charged situations, such as personal rights violations, may be inappropriate. Because of damage done to one of the parties, the parties may be unable to put aside the intense emotional impact of the conflict. For example, Whittington[10] argues that mediation in sexual harassment cases is inappropriate not only because of the power differential but also because it gives the implicit message that the resolution is a joint responsibility, implying that the victim has been at fault in some way. Nevertheless, success has been noted in some serious victim-offender conflicts using a controlling style of mediation.[11] Other limitations to appropriate use of mediation might include when the parties hold entrenched ideological positions, regarding abortion for instance, or when one party feels he/she has too much to lose, such as the threat of losing one's job or the permanent destruction of pristine wilderness.

Sometimes appropriate representation is very difficult to define in a multi-party dispute. For example, how can it be determined which group or person represents the "public at large" in an environmental conflict? Approximations may have to be made in consultation with the stakeholders of the opposing views.

Discussion with the parties prior to starting the mediation process should provide information about the appropriateness of mediation as the vehicle for potential conflict resolution. In complex problems only certain aspects of the dispute may be amenable to mediation. Different resolution methods such as arbitration or litigation may have to be employed for other issues. The parties may have too much personal investment in the conflict, and remain adversarial, as can happen in bitter custody disputes. Counselling may be needed to deal with the parties' anger issues before they are ready to do business with each other. Or, they may be afraid to face each other, and need encouragement and assurances of safety from the mediator to reduce their resistance. Once these problems are dealt with, the mediator must contract with each party over the logistics (timing, location) and the issues for focus.

II. Stage 1: Introduction

This is the first face-to-face encounter in mediation, and it is crucial to the whole process. Without the appropriate climate, agreement, or commitment, the mediation process is likely to become derailed. Maximizing a collaborative interaction now can lead to payoffs later. An overview of the three objectives and corresponding activities for this stage are presented below.

A. Establishing a Climate of Trust and Safety

A healthy climate can be achieved by a warm and encouraging welcome and a sensitive response to the parties' anxiety, confusion, or apprehension. The modelling by the mediator and the explanation of the protection involved in both her/his "refereeing" role and in the process should convey a feeling of comfort and safety. A comfortable climate is fostered by the setting and the demeanour of the mediator. A neutral meeting place mutually agreed upon by the parties is best. Ideally, a small round table is appropriate for mediation involving two parties plus the mediator, where all three sit equidistant from each other at the points of a triangle. For a small group a larger table, preferably round, can nurture a cooperative, team-like spirit. For even larger meetings the setting should attempt to reduce the cross-table confrontation. The positioning of the mediator and the location of both parties around the table should convey a sense of safety.

The mediator should warmly introduce him/herself to both parties, determine how they wish to be addressed, and have them both come into the room at the same time to avoid any misconception that one party has had the ear of the mediator prior to the session. The mediator should invite the parties to choose their seating from pre-established positions, and once comfortably settled, commend the participants for attending and considering mediation. This is often a good opportunity to empathically acknowledge how difficult the dispute might be for them. The mediator should explain the time commitment required for the meeting, and check for any constraints.

Trust is also conveyed with a clear explanation of the mediator's role. It is crucial to reaffirm that the role is neutral, that the mediator is a referee and will not be a decision maker nor takes sides (as an arbitrator or advocate might), but that she/he will assist the parties to come to their own decision. The mediator should also point out that ground rules will be enforced to ensure a sense of fairness and security. The parties are invited to ask questions to clarify their understanding of the mediator's role before proceeding. The mediator should seek feedback to expose any confusion.

B. Ensuring Understanding of Process and Commitment to Ground Rules

The second objective is to provide a clear explanation of the purpose of mediation, the stages in the process, and the rationale for the ground rules (discussed below). This must be done in language easily understandable by all parties.

A further objective is to obtain agreement that the parties will adhere to the process and ground rules. The mediator should remind the parties that the process is voluntary, that it focuses on interests not positions, and that it is based on a structured, fair procedure. Further, the parties should be informed that the structure is intended to provide each party with a sense of safety through ground rules, an equal opportunity to speak, a chance to work together for a mutually satisfying outcome, and confidentiality within legal limits (e.g., such as an investigation for court or an obligation to report child abuse).

For clarity, the purpose and intended outcomes of the process should also be explained. The subsequent stages will clarify the issues in dispute, the needs and interests that must be dealt with, and will generate alternative solutions. The structure is intended to provide a sense of empowerment and equality as well as safety.

C. Assessing Readiness and Commitment to Proceed

The mediator at this stage must assess whether the parties are ready to proceed and are prepared to make a commitment to the ground rules. Activities may include inviting comments and questions for clarification and seeking statements from the parties that indicate their understanding and acceptance of the established structure and the intended process.

An important objective of this stage is to assess again, now that the parties are face-to-face, whether mediation is appropriate, and their readiness to proceed. It may only now become clear that the nature of the conflict (involving violence, rights violations or harassment, or an intense emotional attachment to the issue) may make it inappropriate or very difficult to mediate. Likewise, a severe power imbalance may only now become apparent and prove tough to counteract. The presence of a support person of the disempowered party's choosing, preparatory assertiveness training, or a mediator of similar racial or gender background (this is where co-mediation can be useful) might assist in balancing power.

Some conflicts are not specific enough (too multi-faceted, complex, and entangled) to offer much hope of a mediated settlement. However, getting the parties to focus first on more manageable pieces of the first is the task of the mediator and may cultivate an initial climate of collaboration and success, which can then lead to tackling more challenging aspects.

The parties must have an investment in the resolution of the dispute. Some parties may prefer to live with the conflict rather than appear to compromise. Others are not prepared to put in the necessary time, energy, and courage to deal with their antagonist. However, coming to the first meeting can indicate a willingness to try.

1. Ground Rules

A minimum of eight basic ground rules are commonly used in establishing a working relationship between the parties. These rules may be modified to meet the needs of each mediation. The rules and their alternative options are presented below:

a) all information relevant to the dispute will be shared;

b) all shared information will be kept confidential (subject to limits). Parties are free to share their information with counsel (or support persons such as their executives and association members if community groups). The parties will decide after the first meeting whether meetings will remain *in camera*;

c) each party will be allowed an equal opportunity to speak. The contributions of each party will be respected;

d) there will be no interruptions, blaming, name-calling, put-downs, threats, or repercussions;

e) parties will keep their emotions in check, (time-outs can be called for a chance to cool-off, to talk to the mediator separately but equally, or to consult with colleagues);

f) parties will focus on the interests and needs of each other or of third parties affected, such as children, and not on positions, and will engage in collaborative problem-solving;

g) either party can terminate mediation at any time, but shall give notice and reasons for terminating before leaving;

h) parties will abide by the final agreement(s), subject to ratification by their members. In the event of dispute over or breakdown of the agreement, parties agree to attempt further mediation prior to independent action or litigation; and

i) other rules as agreed to by the parties may be established to meet the circumstances as required.

The mediator must obtain an understanding and commitment from both parties to abide by the rules before proceeding. Absolute adherence may be impossible if the parties have a history of argumentative interactions. In that case, the mediator may accept a commitment that the parties will try to follow the rules, and use opportunities for enforcement as teachable moments so that the parties can learn what is expected. Explaining that the stages of the process will eventually allow each party to have an equal opportunity to tell their story will often allay the parties' natural impatience to get started and "let off steam" prematurely.

The mediator needs to explain three concepts to the parties: interests as opposed to positions; separating the person from the problem; and holding back questions or denials when the other party is misleading. After explaining them, the mediator should discuss each of these concepts in relation to the current mediation issues. A pad and pen should be provided for the parties to record their questions and objections without interrupting the party who is speaking.

These objectives of Stage 1 need to be followed properly to foster a climate that encourages the parties to proceed further. But they must understand, accept, and commit themselves to the rules, process, and roles before the next stage begins. A clear contract of understanding, acceptance, and commitment is essential. Some mediators obtain a contract in writing. The skills of immediacy and gentle confrontation may be required when apparent confusion or a token commitment needs identifying.

III. Stage 2: Opening Statement and Issue Identification.

This stage (often known as "story telling") involves three objectives: to provide an opportunity for each party to share their story with the other in a controlled setting; to allow for ventilation of key emotions connected with the story and to ensure the other side hears both the content and the emotion; and to clarify the issues in dispute. Presented below is an elaboration of each of these objectives.

A. Allowing an Opportunity for the Parties to Tell Their Story

For each party to make an opening statement without emotive outbursts of how she/he sees the dispute can be difficult, yet therapeutic. The mediator should instruct the parties in how to own their statements and how to frame their comments so as to avoid blaming the other. Gentle enforcement of the no-blaming rule might be required. The speaker should be encouraged to address comments directly to the other party, usually with eye contact. These comments must be presented in a culturally sensitive manner. Sometimes the mediator can modify such direct discussion between the parties, especially for those parties exceptionally nervous about face-to-face contact or confrontation. The mediator becomes the conduit for the stories but, where possible, direct involvement and mutual discussion are more empowering. The listener is encouraged to not interrupt but to write questions down. After the statement is given, it is important that the other party demonstrates that they both heard and understood the other's perception of the concerns and feelings. It is a very useful exercise to have the listener repeat a summary of the concerns presented to them, with the speaker or mediator clarifying any mistakes. This communicated understanding can begin a process of bridge building between the parties.

B. Allowing an Opportunity to Ventilate and Hear the Other Side

The parties usually have considerable emotion attached to their perceptions, which often contributes to the development of the conflict. The opportunity for ventilation should not prevent the presentation of the narrative information from conforming to the ground rules. It is often at this point that mediators can determine how much business the parties can do with each other without professional counselling assistance. This initial presentation by each party may be the first time that information has been heard without an argument breaking out. To ensure this the mediator will need to enforce the rules effectively. The mediator needs to use empathic active listening to acknowledge the parties' feelings, yet must refrain from engaging in counselling, which can be perceived as alliance-building and violating neutrality.

C. Clarifying Which Issues Are in Dispute

At the finish of both narratives, the mediator should identify the issues that appear in contention. The mediator should have noted each story, in order to check whether it is complete and accurately understood. Once both parties have had the opportunity to speak, the mediator should summarize the issues from both sides, identifying which aspects are shared by both parties and which are unique to each. The mediator should check with both parties regarding agreement on the issues and any omissions. Shared aspects of the issues are also fertile ground for collaborative problem-solving. The aspects common to both parties might reveal some of their shared interests and needs, such as a desire to maintain a working relationship, or a concern for the welfare of a child. Any demonstrated willingness to try to resolve the problem should be commended. These shared interests are reinforced in the next stage.

IV. Stage 3: Determining Interests and Needs

The key objective here is to identify the interests and needs that must be met in the final agreement. At the beginning of this stage it is useful to review with the parties the concept of interests, needs, and positions. For an agreement to be feasible and receive commitment, it must satisfy a sufficient number of the needs and interests of both parties. This may require probing by the mediator for underlying interests following the sharing of stories, issues, and positions in Stage 2. Communicated understanding, reframing, and summarizing are crucial skills here. The mediator must demonstrate that he/she has heard both parties' concerns, and can help to reframe their positions as interests and needs. This phase can be tough, especially if the parties are wanting the mediator to take sides or to suggest/impose solutions. The mediator should resist the temptation to rush toward premature solutions that fail to take both interests and needs fully into account. Resorting to positions is often the parties' natural response to impatience and frustration, or to having lost sight of the purpose or rules. The mediator may need to remind the parties of these and confront the fact that commitments obtained in the first stage of the mediation may be wavering. Confrontation must be non-judgmental, with the mediator pointing out the seeming contradictions in statements and behaviour without blaming. The mediator should take advantage of this opportunity to model effective adherence to the ground rules and to teach the parties how to deal with tensions and manage the emotional climate.

The following communication, in which the mediator tries to facilitate a shift from positions to interests, might be helpful:

First Party A: "I think it sucks the way you (Second Party B) always dominate our self-help group meetings! I don't want to go any more."

Mediator: (empathy) "Seems like you're feeling overwhelmed by what B says and does at those meetings, and so you want to quit going."

First Party A: "You're right! B is such a tyrant! He always interrupts me and takes over. No one listens to what I have to say!"

Mediator: (ground rule reminder and reframe) "Must be a frustrating experience for you, but it's essential we don't attack each other right now. So A, it sounds important for you to get a fair chance to say your piece without interruption and to be heard and respected." (Pause for confirmation). "Is that just by B or everyone in the group?" (Pause for clarifying answer). "Could you tell B this directly?"

An empathic response reflects both the feeling and the content of the speaker's message and indicates hearing and understanding. Reframing combines reflection and probing to identify the underlying interest, transforming the negative into a positive value. Notice in the example how the mediator used empathy, reinforcement of the rules, reframing, probing for clarification, and re-empowering with A to make the shift. The mediator might also pick up on the possibility that A is feeling intimidated by B during this session, check it out, and seek A's ideas on what is needed to reduce this feeling. It may be as simple as a reminder of the no-interruption and no-repercussion rules. Sometimes the response itself can give clues to the need for support in the interview or for outside help with assertiveness training. A caucus (individual meeting) with each party might clarify this. In the situation described above, it might be helpful to have an adjournment for A to access resources. At the same time, it might be useful to inform B that such domineering powerplays (if true) are counterproductive.

Once the parties have had an opportunity to express feelings, to be heard, and to share their perception of the problem and issues, the mediator should work with the parties to identify both differences and similarities that have emerged, and to summarize the interests and needs each have presented. Focusing on shared or common interests can restore a more collaborative climate. Recording the issues (points of conflict) and the common ground on a flip chart can be helpful, especially as a template for evaluating solutions. It can also clarify any confusion. Concurrence on the points of conflict and common ground by the parties must be sought before moving to the next stage of collaborative problem solving.

V. Stage 4: Problem Solving

The two objectives of problem solving are to provide a process for the parties to generate and evaluate options (alternative solutions) and to facilitate the parties in choosing appropriate options.

A. Generating and Evaluating Options

Having focused on identifying the interests and needs that must be met by the final agreement, the mediator should discuss with the parties the actual process of problem solving. There are several models that may be used. A modified form of brain storming is the most common, and is the one presented here. Working together to break down the problem into major and minor issues is a useful place to start. The parties then select an issue to work on. They may require help in choosing one that is manageable especially in the early stage of collaboration, as even a small success can be a valuable building block.

For each issue, as many options as possible should be generated. The mediator may need to encourage creative thinking and may wish to add some ideas once each of the parties have had their initial turn. This can often stimulate further productive notions.

Each option must be clarified to determine what it involves, and then evaluated objectively in terms of the extent to which it meets the mutual interests and needs of the parties (or of a third party, such as a child in a custody dispute.) The parties should mutually agree to the minimal criteria or principles the options must meet. For instance, fairness and equality may be two principles agreed upon, but their application to the options must be defined. As well, identifying the most important interests for each party may help to prioritize options. And finally, the advantages and disadvantages of each option should be compared.

B. Facilitating Choice of Appropriate Options

Several preferred choices should to be identified, and the parties may need time to think about the options and possible variations. Sometimes a single choice can be threatening and subsequently raise resistance. The mediator might wish to discuss the next best alternatives to a negotiated agreement (see the concept of BATNA in "Getting to Yes"[12]), which are the alternative outcomes each party would walk away with should an agreement not be reached. This might persuade the parties that, while not every single need can be met by agreement, the alternative might be much more dissatisfying.

Time and energy spent here may also make the difference between a meaningful and a token agreement. The parties need to feel that their choice is crucial. This feeling can help to cement commitment to the agreement. This stage ends by the parties deciding upon appropriate solutions.

VI. Stage 5: Formalizing an Agreement

The objectives of the last stage are to formulate the chosen options into an agreement and to obtain a commitment from both parties to the agreement and to further mediation should it be disputed or break down. A clear, unequivocal agreement is necessary to reduce further conflict or confusion.

A. Converting Options into a Clear Agreement

So far, the parties have verbally agreed on the preferred solutions. The task here is to convert the verbal commitments into a clear, comprehensive, accurate and enforceable agreement. An agreement in writing is the best guarantee of clarity, and offers the parties an opportunity to consult with their lawyer or support person. Any agreement will need to be evaluated as to whether it truly addresses mutual interests, is fundamentally fair, and is realistically achievable (reality testing). The skill of formal contracting and drafting a clear document is essential.

B. Obtaining Commitment to the Agreement and its Implementation

Reality testing can be used to assess the commitment of both parties to the agreement, and sometimes a trial period followed by a review is useful. The parties need to decide how their agreement will be implemented and monitored (if necessary). It should also include a fail-safe mechanism as mentioned in ground rule "h" (see page 390). Before committing themselves to a final agreement, the parties may want to consult a lawyer about legal implications, or try it out gradually by a process of implementation in instalments. Manageable pieces can be given trials and the parties allocated homework to test implementation. Then the mediator might invite the parties back to deal with other issues, returning to the appropriate stage as needed. Once agreements have been reached, commitment to them must be monitored. Follow-up sessions with the mediator may be required to keep the process of implementation on track.

Closure involves clarifying the parties' commitment to the agreement and contracting for future eventualities. The parties can also be invited to evaluate the process, which can often lead to a shift to a more productive working relationship.

Here ends the specific details of the mediation process. While each stage is distinct, transition between stages should be smooth and timing discussed with the parties as appropriate. The next part of the chapter deals with a critique of the model and answers some common questions posed by the helping professional and potential consumers of mediation.

CRITIQUE OF THE MODEL

An important positive characteristic of this model is its wide applicability to all kinds of disputes, public and private. Once the parties have agreed to mediation, success varies with the issue and the capacity of the parties, but successful completion rates of 60% to over 80% are not uncommon, often with much higher rates of compliance to mediated agreements than court orders.[13] Vidmar suggests this rate of successful completion is found because the parties develop a psychological commitment to self-developed agreements.[14] Unlike court, this model of mediation can lead to educating people about a self-applied process that can improve feelings and the relationship between the parties. The "win-win" outcome and the parties' choice to keep the dispute private are advantages over the court or public tribunal approaches. It is well known how media can sensationalize conflicts, leading to further entrenchment of positions.

A major weakness of mediation is that it may only superficially restore the relationship of the parties to what it was prior to the dispute. Rarely does mediation transform that relationship or deal with the underlying issues of power, oppression, and possible abuse. In other words, mediation usually serves to maintain the status quo power structure, though it can involve greater power sharing if the parties are willing. Mediation may bring reconciliation between disputants, but it cannot guarantee better equality. Critics argue that it not only gives insufficient protection to the disempowered, but it can be a manipulative device by the powerful to seduce the powerless into a false sense of equality. The power differential can be used to the advantage of the powerful party.

Another criticism levelled at mediation concerns the style of the process. Its structure and emphasis on verbal discussion and intellectual concepts such as personal or organizational interests, can give advantage to white, middle-class, articulate males who most often are already privileged in society. Benoit concludes that mediation participants are more inclined than those who don't choose this form of conflict resolution to have a strong belief in their own ability to control their lives, and are less likely to exhibit feelings of alienation, normlessness, or powerlessness.[15] The process is seen as failing to respond sufficiently to diversity and power, especially in aspects of race, gender, and class. For example, certain versions of events have more legitimacy than others in our society. Gunning links this to the competing narratives in the story-telling process at the second stage of mediation, pointing out that mainstream cultural myths have greater legitimacy than minority cultural myths.[16] This effect may reduce the power and impact of the minority person's concerns, especially if the mediator is not sensitive to these issues. Some argue that the protection of legal rights, which only the court process can guarantee, is necessary for these groups.[17] Other criticisms include the failure of mediation to deal with oppressive tactics of the powerful. Such critics argue that only the court system, as part of a strategy of partisan advocacy, or political and social action (see Chapter 14), can effectively deal with eliminating oppression.

Finally, the limitations of mediation in dealing with disputes involving personal violations such as human rights or sexual harassment have been mentioned earlier. Whittington argues that mediation privatizes and depoliticizes sexual discrimination, and reduces a matter that should be a public issue to a merely private concern.[18]

There is some validity to all of these criticisms. Within limits, however, a perceptive and skilful mediator can use the process to offset some of these deficiencies.[19] Modifications can be employed to make the process more responsive to most of these criticisms, but limitations may still remain. Two examples of mediation, each with differing success, may illustrate this.

The first example involved two neighbouring families, who because of a long-standing personal disagreement over a fence dividing their properties and repeated complaints of mutual harassment, had come to be known at the local City Hall as the "Hatfields and McCoys," after the notorious feuding families of Wild West fame. The position, style, and height of the fence so aggravated both families that a vendetta of insult and injury was exchanged over many years between all family members. As well, other neighbours and City officials were frequently dragged into the dispute.

The head of each family agreed to a temporary truce while they attended mediation with a local municipal councillor. Both parties seemed to respect the councillor's authority and consented to a joint meeting as long as she was there to referee. The ground rule of mediation that each party must be allowed an equal opportunity to speak without interruption was difficult for them to follow after a decade of shouting at each other. It took considerable empathy and directive communication from the councillor to calm them down. After fifteen minutes of coaching and learning how to not interrupt, both parties listened intently and were near to tears after hearing each other's comments of why the fence was so important and how repercussions of the dispute were so destructive and exhausting to the lifestyle of each family. It quickly became evident that the vendetta was contrary to their mutual interests. The mediator's empathic responses allowed them to express their suffering without blaming each other and to shift away from the positioning power play. Within a short while they were absorbed in the process of designing a new fence together. They left with a shared plan and later sent the councillor a Polaroid photo of the new fence collaboratively built as proof that they had followed through on their agreement and ceased hostilities. This example is a general illustration of successful mediation.[20]

In the second example, a lawyer contacted the author about a middle-aged woman who wanted to have a separation agreement mediated so as to avoid fighting her husband in court. In preparatory caucus the woman felt nervous about facing her husband, so the mediators arranged for an adult daughter to be present to support her mother. At stage two, it became very clear that not only was the woman at a serious power disadvantage, but that she was prepared to make unreasonable concessions to her husband. She seemed unable to accept that her husband wanted to leave the long-standing marriage for a younger woman, and was disempowering herself by a willingness to give all away to buy back his affection. Despite her insistence on continuing to mediate, the mediators halted the process, called a caucus (a separate consultation with each party), and directed the husband to level with his wife about his true feelings that he no longer loved her. The daughter agreed with this and supported the suggestion that her mother see a counsellor if necessary, to help her accept the new information from her husband. Upon hearing the painful truth from her husband, the mother became extremely angry and rushed out, followed by her daughter. Although the mediators had mixed feelings about the inappropriateness of mediation for dealing with the situation, the lawyer later congratulated them on empowering his client to give clear instructions to fight for a fair share of assets. This example shows how important it is to assess each situation for the appropriateness of mediation and modify the mediation process when needed.

COMMON QUESTIONS

1. <u>What are the legal implications for the mediator and the parties?</u>

Since mediation is normally voluntary, the parties usually decide how binding the agreement will be. In family law, courts will often convert a consensual agreement into a court order. Some jurisdictions use mandatory mediation sessions of limited duration in an effort to reduce court time in family law. Even if an agreement is not forthcoming, these sessions can often focus the issues for speedier court arbitration.

Mediators in private practice should carry liability insurance (see Chapter 13) and should be sure that all agreements are checked independently for legal implications (see Chapter 6). Information from a mediation is normally confidential and respected by the courts unless both parties agree to release the information. Mediators governed by the *Family Relations Act*[21] and the *Divorce Act*[22] are not compellable witnesses (do not have to testify as to the content of the mediation). Courts have so far extended this limited protection (privilege is the legal term) to mediators who are not family court counsellors or court-appointed divorce mediators under those statutes. However, this restriction on having to testify does not apply to criminal proceedings.

Statutes are beginning to acknowledge the importance of mediation. *The Divorce Act*[23] obliges lawyers to inform spouses disputing custody or support of mediation facilities that might assist in negotiating those matters. *The Child, Family and Community Service Act*[24] of British Columbia gives a director or social worker the power to use "mediation or other alternative dispute resolution" to resolve an issue relating to the child or a plan of care.

2. What ways are there to deal with power imbalances?

Davis and Salem[25] make some useful comments about relative power. Assumptions about power should always be checked out. "Outward appearances notwithstanding, everyone has some power. An indigent tenant with few apparent resources may have the ability to organize an entire building." What matters is that person's own perceptions, their access to power, and the level of willingness to exercise that power.

Obviously, not everyone has equal power or access to powerful resources. The mediation process described can itself be empowering through such mechanisms as information sharing and equal opportunity to speak, and the authors make suggestions on how to optimize the process. But additional support, such as an empowerment group or individual coaching, might also assist. Some parties may wish to be accompanied to mediation by their lawyer or advocate, but these representatives should be encouraged to take a back seat in the proceedings to maximize the participation of the disputants. The representatives need to be informed of the process beforehand to ensure their contribution is appropriate. Male-female partnerships as joint mediators, or mixed race pairs may offset some power imbalances.

As in the second example at the end of the critique, if an imbalance cannot be dealt with adequately, the only ethical action may be to terminate the mediation process, especially if the potential outcome will apparently be grossly inequitable to one of the parties. Remember that a mediator's opinion is normally secondary to the parties' decision, but fairness is a basic criterion for evaluation of the outcome.

3. How are mediation services delivered?

Several social service mandates, especially those with statutory or court-based roles, now incorporate mediation. These include human rights investigators, residential tenancy dispute investigators, probation and family court counsellors, and social workers in British Columbia under the new child protection legislation.[26] Government Ministries are listed in the blue pages of the telephone directory. Many lawyers, social workers, and psychologists are in private practice as mediators on a fee for service basis. The consumer needs to be aware of the mediator's qualifications, mediation style, expertise, and ethical and legal liability. Professional associations of mediators are emerging, but they do not yet enjoy licensing responsibilities. Phone numbers of private mediators can be found in the Yellow Pages of the phone book. Not-for-profit groups, such as Victoria's

Mediation Place, often provide a service for the community on a sliding scale of modest fees. Usually the mediator will contact the other party to assess willingness to participate in mediation. A directory of governmental and non-governmental agencies offering various types of dispute resolution services in British Columbia is available.[27]

Most mediation training in British Columbia is done through the Justice Institute, which offers courses in many major centres. The Mediation Development Association of British Columbia is a voluntary professional organization that has published guidelines for mediators. Social Work and Law Schools usually have courses in conflict-resolution, though they are often optional for students.

4. Is mediation time-consuming and inefficient?

Participants can usually enter mediation faster than waiting for a court date. The length of time for mediation depends on the complexity of the issue and the skills of the mediator and participants. Sessions are normally up to 1 1/2 hours in length and anywhere from one to six in number. Costs are considerably less than when each party hires legal counsel and pays for expensive court time. The initial sessions may take longer than a court hearing, but time and expense is saved through the commitment to the outcome, reduced challenges, and faster implementation. The long-term costs of recurring problems and hostile, deteriorating relationships are usually avoided. People who choose court do not usually consider efficiency the main criteria. Most parties think they will win, but only one of the parties actually does. Some court decisions appear to penalize both parties. In court decisions the outcome is often uncertain and outside the control of the participants, whereas it is the participants who have the final say in mediation.

CONCLUSION

In today's world of increasing local and global interaction, conflicts are an inevitable product of social turmoil and change. Helping professionals often work at the vanguard of such conflict. They must understand the nature of conflict and the advantages and disadvantages of the various dispute resolution models. Mediation is a distinct set of skills that is an essential component in the arsenal of intervention options for the effective helping professional. The authors trust that the model presented will be a useful guide to dealing with situations of conflict. We suggest this chapter should be read together with Chapter 14 for more alternative strategies.

RESOURCES

R. F. Fisher, W. Ury & B. Patton, *Getting to Yes: Negotiating Agreement without Giving In*, 2d ed. (New York: Penguin Books, 1993).

J. Folberg & A. Taylor, *Mediation: A Comprehensive Guide to Resolving Conflicts Without Litigation* (San Francisco: Jossey Bass, 1984).M. Duryea & J. B. Grundison, *Conflict and Culture: Research in Five Communities in Vancouver, B.C.* (Victoria, Canada: University of Victoria Institute for Dispute Resolution, 1993.)

H. J. Irving & M. Benjamin, *Family Mediation: Theory and Practice of Dispute Resolution* (Toronto, Canada: Carswell, 1987).

C. W. Moore, *The Mediation Process: Practical Strategies for Resolving Conflicts* (San Francisco: Jossey Boss, 1986).

C. Morris, ed., *Resolving Community Disputes: An Annotated Bibliography About Community Justice Centres* (Victoria, Canada: University of Victoria Institute for Dispute Resolution, 1994).

A. Pirie & D. Stanley, *Dispute Resolution and You: What You Need to Know* (Victoria, Canada: University of Victoria Institute for Dispute Resolution and Law Foundation of B.C.) Undated. This book contains a useful list of resources and agencies in British Columbia.

L. Susskind & J. Cruikshank, *Breaking the Impasse: Consensual Approaches to Resolving Public Disputes* (New York: Basic Books, 1987).

E. A. Stewart & D. Turner, *When Differences Escalate: Managing and Resolving Conflict* (Victoria, British Columbia: School of Social Work, 1995).

B. Whittington, *Mediation Power and Gender: A Critical Review of Selected Readings* (Victoria, Canada: University of Victoria Institute for Dispute Resolution, 1992).

W. Ury, *Getting Past No: Negotiating your Way from Confrontation to Cooperation*, 2d ed. (New York: Bantam Books, 1993).

END NOTES

1. This definition is used by D. Stanley, a mediator in Victoria, in her training programs offered through the Justice Institute of British Columbia.
2. See C.W. Moore, *The Mediation Process: Practical Strategies for Resolving Conflicts*, (San Francisco: Jossey Boss, 1986) who identifies explanatory causes of conflict. This taxonomy has been adapted here by Elizabeth Azmier Stewart and David Turner.
3. L. Miller, and A. Smith, *The Stress Solution: An Action Plan to Manage Stress in Your Life*, (New York: Simon and Schuster, 1993).
4. For example, R. Blake and J. Moulton in *Corporate Excellence Through GRID Organizational Development*, (1970) present this two dimensional model.
5. This is the authors' definition, combining the essential components of their mediation model.
6. See R. Fisher and W. Ury, *Getting to Yes: Negotiating Agreement Without Giving In*, (New York: Penguin Books, 1981, revised 1993).
7. Dinah Stanley, a mediator in Victoria, developed the basis of this chart in conjunction with the Justice Institute of British Columbia. It has since been modified by David Turner.
8. D. Turner and K. Jobson, *The Decision to Mediate Not Litigate*, (Victoria, Canada, University of Victoria Institute for Dispute Resolution, 1990)
9. *Idem.*
10. B. Whittington, "Mediation in Cases of Sexual Harassment: Issues of Power and Gender," in L. P. Spratlan, ed., *Sexual Harassment, Workplace Abuse and Abuse Management* (University of Washington Conference Proceedings, Seattle, USA, 1990).
11. M. Umbreit, *Mediation of Victim Offender Conflict*, Journal of Dispute Resolution, (Minneapolis, USA, 1988).

12. *Supra*, note 6, pp.97-106, 183-187.

13. Success rates vary with the type of dispute and mediation project. For instance, a variety of business disputes in Matsqui/Maple Ridge, BC yielded a 60% success rate, in a Victoria project an 86% success rate of small claims cases set down for mediation, a Winnipeg criminal diversion project (possibly involving a coercive atmosphere) an 87% rate. The factors in studies from Canada and United States are summaraized in Turner and Jobson, (note 8) pp. 2-23.

14. N. Vidmar, "The Small Claims Court: A Reconceptualization of Disputes and an Empirical Investigation," Small Claims Court, London, Ontario, Law and Society Review, (1984), 18(4), 515-550.

15. J.H. Benoit, J.P. Kopachevsky, W.S. MacDonald, and E.G. McDonald, *Evaluating the Effects and Methods of Delivery of Mediation: Summary Report on the evaluation of the Halifax Community Mediation Network and Other North American Mediation Services*,(Ottawa, Ministry of Solicitor General, 1986) p.6.

16. I.R. Gunning, "Diversity Issues in Mediation: Controlling Negative Cultural Myths," Journal of Dispute Resolution, Vol. 1995, No. 1 University of Missouri-Columbia Law School, pp.55-93.

17. R. Delgado et al. "Fairness and Formality: Minimizing the Risks of Prejudice in Alternate Dispute Resolution," 1985 Wisconsin Law Review, USA 1359-1362.

18. B. Whittington, *supra*, note 10. She has also reviewed mediation readings for power and gender issues in *Mediation Power and Gender: A Critical Review of Selected Readings*, UVic Institute for Dispute Resolution, Vol. 1995, No. 1, University of Missouri-Columbia Law School, pp. 55093.

19. See A. Davis and R. Salem: "Dealing with Power Imbalances in the Mediation of Interpersonal Disputes," Mediation Quarterly, no. 6 Procedures for Guiding the Divorce Process, (San Francisco, Jossey-Bass, 1984) 17-26.

20. For more community examples for conflict-resolution, empowerment and advocacy, see D. Turner, "Social Work Skills in the Political Sphere: A Case Study of Community Empowerment, Advocacy and Conflict Resolution," (Unpublished paper presented to the Social Workers World Conference, Colombo, Sri Lanka, 1994).

21. *Family Relations Act*, R.S.B.C. 1996, c.128, section 3.

22. *Divorce Act*, R.S.C. 1985, c.3, section 10.

23. *Idem*, section 9(2).

24. *Child, Family and Community Service Act*, R.S.B.C. 1996, c.46, section 22 (to be proclaimed).

25. *Supra*, see note 19.

26. *Supra*, see note 24.

27. A.J. Pirie and D.J. Stanley, *Dispute Resolution and You: What You Need to Know!* (no date) UVic Institute for Dispute Resolution, Victoria, Canada.

Chapter 16

LEGAL EVIDENCE AND EXPERT TESTIMONY

James R. P. Ogloff and Natalie H. Polvi

INTRODUCTION

As any non-lawyer -- and lawyer -- knows, the law is complex and threatening. Perhaps this is why helping professionals typically become anxious when asked to provide information for legal purposes or when notified that they will be required to appear in court. Their reasons for becoming anxious vary, but generally fall into one of the following categories. First, the law is a very insular profession and few people in the helping professions have much knowledge of the law. Therefore, when called into the legal system, people tend to be anxious because of their lack of knowledge about, and familiarity with, the system. Second, for most helping professionals, their work will never be subjected to the high level of scrutiny that the adversarial legal system may demand of them. Indeed, horror stories abound about helping professionals who have been humiliated and humbled on the witness stand. Third, helping professionals are trained to help people and, unfortunately, their involvement in the legal system is demanded by those with very different (i.e., legal) goals.[1] Finally, one of the cornerstones of helping practice is client-therapist confidentiality. To the extent that the law requires them to breach their patients' confidentiality, then, helping professionals become concerned and anxious about how best to protect their clients. The law is stated as of July 1, 1997.

Over the years, the extent to which helping professionals have become involved in the legal system has grown. It was not so long ago that one could enter helping practice confident that it would be very unlikely to become enmeshed in the legal system. This is just not the case any longer. For example, McWilliams[2] comments that the increase in prosecutions for cases of sexual abuse has caused the courts to acknowledge that expert opinions may be helpful to the court in understanding those effects of abuse which may not be part of common knowledge. Furthermore, issues concerning child and domestic violence, mental disability, child and family services, and the like, have entangled mental health professionals -- often unwittingly -- in the legal system. As the scope of work in which helping professionals is involved expands and becomes enmeshed in the legal system, the chances become greater that a helping professional will be required to provide information for legal purposes or even to give evidence in court. The goal of this chapter, therefore, is to provide readers with basic information about legal evidence and expert testimony that will allay their anxiety, and provide them with basic information should their work be required or scrutinized by the legal system.

The chapter begins with a discussion of the nature and type of requests for information from lawyers and courts. We then review the law concerning direct witness testimony and expert witness testimony. Finally, we discuss witness preparation and examination, providing readers with helpful suggestions for making their experience less threatening.

REQUESTS FOR INFORMATION

As we suggest in the introduction to this chapter, there are any number of reasons that someone in the legal system will want access to records -- or to the helping professional's personal knowledge -- of a client. In Canada, there is no therapist-client privilege, and helping professionals are often put in the difficult position of revealing information about clients or patients in legal settings. For example, in a recent case, *R. v. O'Connor*,[3] the Supreme Court of Canada held that under some circumstances even information that a sexual abuse victim relays in confidence to her/his therapist may be subpoenaed and used in court during the trial of the accused abuser. As this case demonstrates, even very sensitive information revealed in therapy may be subpoenaed for use in a case.

Besides having the helping professional's records subpoenaed, the legal system may wish to have the benefit of the professional's testimony, as an expert or otherwise, in deciding a case. Regardless of the reason, the helping professional's initial contact with the legal system will likely come in the form of a request for information from a lawyer. In this section, we discuss briefly the nature of such requests.

A. Informal Requests for Information

Although mental health professionals usually are cautious about releasing confidential information -- especially on an informal basis -- it is surprising how many practitioners have turned over confidential patient records or information about patients following "informal" requests from lawyers.[4] Perhaps it is the perceived authority of the lawyer's request, either confidently made by telephone or professionally presented on quality letterhead, that has on occasion caused mental health professionals to release information -- often against their better judgment. By informal requests here, we are referring to telephone calls or letters written by lawyers requesting information about clients or patients. All informal requests by lawyers should be treated the same as any other informal request. Statements such as "I am not at liberty to provide any information about that person or even to discuss whether that person is now or ever was a patient of mine" are perfectly appropriate for handling such requests.[5] The helping professional also would not be acting inappropriately if he/she simply ignored the request.[6]

In the case where the request for information comes from a lawyer who claims to represent the person whose records are being requested, the helping professional should still be extremely cautious. Regardless of whether the request for information comes from the lawyer of the helping professional's clients, or from an opposing party's lawyer, the helping professional must have a <u>valid</u> signed release of information form before any information can be provided to the lawyer. As Stromberg and his colleagues[7] point out, the helping professional should not presume that any consent for the release of information is valid. The helping professional should review the document carefully. Obvious things to check include the date of the consent, the client's signature, and the nature and scope of the information for which the release is intended. If <u>any</u> doubts about its validity exist -- or any related questions -- a lawyer should be consulted.

Upon receiving an informal request for information, including one that includes a valid consent for the release of information, contact the patient or client whose records are being requested and ask whether she/he consents to such release of information. This will enable the client the opportunity to consider whether to consent to having the information released. If the client did not know about the request, it will provide him/her with an opportunity to take any steps necessary to protect her/his interests. Of course, if the lawyer does not send a valid consent for the release of the information, be sure to obtain one from the client or patient before releasing the information. The more specific the release is, the less likely it will be that the client will return at some later point complaining about any potential harm that could come from the release of the information.[8] At the very least, the consent should be made in writing, should specify clearly with whom the information should be shared, and what information should be released.

Some exceptions exist where one would, of course, choose to release information without the consent of the client or patient. Such exceptions include emergency situations where the client or another person is at risk of harm and the information is needed to protect them.[9] Because these exceptions vary from situation to situation and among jurisdictions, it is still a good idea to consult with a lawyer if unsure about how to proceed. Such foresight may provide the helping professional - and the client or patient - with protection for future proceedings.

B. Subpoenas and Court Orders

The technical term for a subpoena may vary across jurisdictions or even vary with the intended purpose for the release of the information. Therefore, the helping professional is always encouraged to consult with a lawyer prior to releasing records or other information that has been "subpoenaed." Simply stated, a subpoena is a formal legal demand for information.[10] Depending on the nature of the demand, the helping professional may be summoned to testify at a hearing or trial, subpoenaed to release records or documents, or required to both release records and attend a hearing or trial (what is called a *subpoena duces tecum*).[11]

To obtain a subpoena, a lawyer has to make application to the court. In the application, the lawyer has to state the reasons for requiring the subpoena, and must indicate that the material or persons sought are relevant to the case. Generally speaking, subpoenas are not that difficult to obtain. However, as they are a formal legal demand for information, they must never be ignored. To do so may result in being penalized by the court. Upon receiving a subpoena the helping professional has several options:

a) Comply with the subpoena and release the documents as required. Because subpoenas are legal demands for information, the helping professional will not be considered in violation of ethical or legal confidentiality obligations if he/she chooses to comply with the subpoena. When deciding to comply with the subpoena at the outset, be sure that the only material disclosed is that which was demanded in the subpoena. Providing information beyond that specified in the subpoena may be considered a breach of confidentiality.

b) File a motion to quash (or cancel) the subpoena. To file a motion to quash the subpoena, it will be necessary to retain counsel. A subpoena could successfully be quashed if the helping professional has no information that is relevant to the case, or if the court decides that there is some important reason for maintaining the confidences in the information (quite unlikely).

Finally, even if the court is not willing to quash the subpoena, the judge may agree to narrowing the scope of material requested in the subpoena.

c) Consult with the client so that she/he may contest the subpoena. Generally speaking, since the client "owns" the confidentiality of the material being requested, courts may be more sympathetic to arguments from clients' counsel that their privacy right in the material should not be infringed.

d) There may be some benefit in writing a letter to both parties in the dispute, with a copy to the judge, expressing a willingness to comply with the order but stating that professional obligations do not permit the release of information without consent of the patient or a court order. In this case, if the client does not consent, or chooses to challenge the subpoena, the court will decide whether to issue a disclosure order. In this option, again, courts may concede to restricting the scope of the material to be released.

e) Finally, it may be possible to negotiate with both parties and with the court a partial disclosure of information that is relevant to the case. As is quite often true, subpoenas are unnecessarily broad because the lawyer who seeks them may not know the scope and nature of information possessed by the helping professional. Therefore, there may be some flexibility in attempting, almost informally, to narrow the scope of material released.

If, after trying to quash or narrow the scope of the subpoenas, the court orders the disclosure of confidential information, it is necessary for the helping professional to disclose that information in accordance with the order of the court. Not to do so can result in serious penalties by the court. Similarly, never engage in any form of destroying or changing the information being requested because this, again, will result in penalties. Because subpoenas and court orders are legal demands for information, it always is a good idea to consult with a lawyer about how to proceed. Finally, not consulting with a lawyer could put the helping professional in the difficult situation of trying to advise the client about how to proceed with respect to the subpoena.

The Committee on Legal Issues of the American Psychological Association recently developed strategies for private practitioners coping with subpoenas or compelled testimony.[12] The committee's report provides useful information for dealing with the ethical and legal concerns that arise when client records or test data are compelled by a court.

LEGAL PARAMETERS OF TESTIMONY

Beyond providing records, reports, and other types of information to be used in the legal system, there will be occasions when a helping professional will be required to testify in court. The helping professional may be called to provide testimony as a witness in a case to provide either direct evidence or expert evidence. In this section, we begin with a brief overview of some basic facts about evidence law, provide a discussion of direct witness testimony and expert witness testimony, and outline the procedures for examining witnesses in court.

A. Some Basic Facts about Evidence Law

The purpose of a trial in our adversarial system of law is to enable both sides -- whether they are the Crown and an accused in a criminal trial, or two private parties or corporations in a civil trial -- to present information in open court that supports their side of the dispute. The information that will be presented in court is called evidence. Evidence can consist of a variety of types of information, including oral testimony of witnesses, the presentation of documents, and a range of exhibits including drawings or photographs, weapons, and the like. Because trials are adversarial, a strict and complex set of rules have developed to help judges determine what evidence will be admissible in court. These rules are called evidentiary rules. It is beyond the scope of this chapter to provide a detailed discussion of these rules, but two of the basic rules are outlined below.

1. Admissibility and Relevance

Generally speaking, relevance is a threshold issue for the admission of evidence at a trial.[13] In *R. v. Morris,* Justice Lamer, writing on behalf of the Supreme Court of Canada, referred to this quotation as reflecting the law of relevance in Canada:

> The two leading principles should be brought into conspicuous relief, (1) that nothing is to be received which is not logically probative of some matter requiring to be proved; and (2) that everything which is probative should come in, unless a clear ground of policy or law excludes it.[14]

In the first part of the quotation, the term "logically probative" simply means that the evidence will provide information about some question that is at issue in the trial. For example, an autopsy photograph of a murder victim would be "logically probative" in a murder trial, since it would help establish that the victim was murdered. Thus, evidence that will either help establish or dispose of some fact that is at issue in a trial generally will be considered logically probative and will be admissible in a trial. As the second part of the quotation makes clear, though, evidence that is logically probative may not be admissible if it would be excluded from evidence because of another evidentiary rule.

To some extent, the relevance rule serves as protection for both the helping professional and his/her client, the reason being that only information the helping professional has about the client that is relevant to the matter at issue in the case will be admissible in court. Therefore, helping professionals should be careful not to obtain information from their clients that strays too far from the purpose of the contact -- especially when there is a chance that the client will be involved in a trial. Furthermore, the therapist should be sure to maintain clinical records that are concise and accurate, and do not include extensive speculation or theorizing about the client.[15]

2. Hearsay and Exclusionary Rules

The hearsay rule is one of the most common rules for excluding evidence from a trial. Hearsay occurs when witnesses testify about what another person has told them rather than what they have observed first-hand.[16] Usually, though, if the other person is a party in the case, the evidence will be admissible, because the person would have the right to appear in court. For example, if Mr. Jones confesses to a social worker that he abused a child and this social worker is called as a witness in his trial, the social worker will be permitted to repeat his confession because Mr. Jones has the right to take the stand on his own behalf to challenge the statement. However, if Mr. Jones' neighbour tells the social worker that he/she witnessed the abuse, this social worker will not be permitted to recount in court what the neighbour had said. This would be inadmissible hearsay, because Mr. Jones would not have the opportunity to challenge the truthfulness of the neighbour's statement, since the social worker's only knowledge of the statement comes from what the neighbour stated. In this case, the neighbour could be summoned to testify, under oath, about what she/he saw. Then, Mr. Jones' lawyer could cross-examine the neighbour to challenge the veracity of his/her statement. Although the concept of hearsay is relatively straight-forward, there are many complicated exceptions to the hearsay rule.[17] It is beyond the scope of this chapter to review those exceptions. Now that the reader has a very basic understanding of evidence in law, the next section presents a discussion of direct witness and expert witness testimony.

DIRECT EVIDENCE AND EXPERT EVIDENCE TESTIMONY

As Sopinka et al. note, "the adjudicative process in our adversarial system relies overwhelmingly on *viva voce* (live voice) testimony adduced from witnesses examined before the trier of fact (judge or jury)."[18] The trier of fact simply refers to the person or persons given the responsibility of determining guilt or innocence (i.e., the judge or the jury). Indeed, in most trials the judge and jury must render a verdict based almost solely on hearing testimony by witnesses. In this section, we focus on general or direct evidence testimony, followed by a discussion of expert evidence testimony. As will be discussed, a helping professional may be called either as a witness to give direct evidence or as an expert witness in a trial.

A helping professional's foray into the witness box to provide evidence via testimony will generally fall into one of two categories: (1) as a witness called to give direct evidence testimony, and (2) as an expert witness. A person -- including a helping professional -- called to give direct evidence testimony is summoned to court due to having first-hand knowledge of the situation at hand.[19] That is, the person has directly observed something via her/his senses which is relevant to the case. The direct evidence rests on factually based information and not personal belief, opinion, or inference.[20] By contrast, an expert witness is called to testify in a trial where his/her area of expertise is required by the judge and/or jury to decide the matters at issue on the case. Each of these types of testimony is discussed below.

A. Direct Evidence Testimony

Direct evidence consists of testimony based on a witness' first-hand knowledge of some event (i.e., what she/he saw or heard).[21] If a helping professional is called to testify to give direct evidence, he/she will be asked to provide first-hand knowledge of some matter or person. Consider, for example, the scenario above where Mr. Jones revealed he had abused a child. If all the social worker was asked to do in court was to relay that information, then she/he would have been called to give direct evidence.

It is normally the case that those persons called as witnesses to give direct evidence testimony are not permitted to draw any inferences from their observations. Similarly, they are not permitted to provide their opinion about any matter.[22] Indeed, it is a fundamental premise in law that evidence is presented to the judge and jury, and it is their role to draw inferences from that evidence -- including testimony -- in order to decide upon a verdict. There is a fear that the judge's or jury's role would be jeopardized if a witness was allowed to draw inferences or express opinions about the testimony they provide. Thus, "opinion evidence" generally is excluded from evidence in trials.[23] Therefore, if the social worker was asked to describe how Mr. Jones' personality and mental state influenced his behaviour in abusing the child he admitted abusing, the answer to that question would not be admissible if the social worker had been called to give direct evidence. As we will see next, though, there is an exception to the opinion evidence rule for those witnesses who are qualified as <u>expert witnesses</u> by the court.

B. Expert Witness Testimony

The expert witness generally serves one of two functions (or very possibly both in the same court case). First, the expert may provide the court with information that assists in the understanding of the issue facing the court. Second, the expert witness may provide the court with an opinion.[24] This is the fundamental difference between the general witness and the expert witness. In providing their testimony, witnesses deemed to be experts by the court offer opinions in order to assist the trier of fact in better understanding the issue or question at hand.[25] Recall from the above discussion that witnesses giving direct evidence testimony are only able to testify regarding those facts that they have directly observed. They will not be permitted to draw inferences from those facts or state their opinions about any matter. By contrast, expert witnesses are permitted to provide their opinions pertaining to matters within their domain of expertise (for example, social workers on issues of child safety and parental discipline).[26] Limited qualification is often assumed by courts where professionals have a statutory function. For example, probation officers and youth workers can give evidence about offenders and their situation within the areas of the pre-sentence reports (see Chapter 6) and social workers can give evidence about child welfare (see Chapter 3).

Due to this exception to the opinion evidence rule, courts have grappled with the issue of under what circumstances expert testimony should be held admissible.[27] In some respects, we are very fortunate in the timing of writing this chapter. Indeed, the Supreme Court of Canada decided a case called *R. v. Mohan*[28] in which a central issue was the admissibility of expert evidence. Thus, we have a recent case that clearly lays out the rules for the admissibility of expert evidence in Canada.

In *R. v. Mohan*, a pediatrician was charged with four counts of sexual assault on four female patients who ranged in age from 13 to 16 at the time the abuse was alleged to have occurred. During the trial, the accused's lawyer indicated that he wished to call a psychiatrist to testify on his client's behalf. The nature of the psychiatrist's testimony was that the pediatrician did not fit the profile of individuals who would usually commit the offences for which he was charged (e.g., sexual psychopath, sexual deviant, or the "psychosexual" who suffers from a major mental disorder). The Crown sought a ruling from the judge regarding the admissibility of the evidence. The psychiatrist's testimony was heard by the judge alone during a *voir dire* (a hearing) and the judge ruled that the testimony was inadmissible. The accused was found guilty by the jury and he appealed the conviction. The Court of Appeal for Ontario allowed the appeal, reversing the lower court's decision, and ordered a new trial. The case was then appealed to the Supreme Court of Canada. The Supreme Court overturned the appellate decision and ordered that the psychiatrist's testimony be excluded. The reasons the Court gave in its judgment form the basis of the current rules regarding the admissibility of expert testimony -- or expert opinion evidence.

In *R. v. Mohan*, Justice Sopinka, writing the unanimous judgment of the Supreme Court of Canada, set out the following criteria for the admissibility of expert evidence: (a) relevance; (b) necessity in assisting the trier of fact; (c) the absence of any exclusionary rule; and (d) a properly qualified expert. As with all evidence that will be admitted at a trial, an expert's testimony must be legally relevant to the case. The judge has the power and the responsibility of deciding whether an expert's testimony will be relevant in any particular case. A discussion of the intricacies of legal relevance is unnecessary and is beyond the scope of this chapter. For our purposes here, suffice it to say that the expert's testimony will be deemed relevant if the testimony is closely -- or logically -- related to a matter that is at issue in the case.

Just because a judge decides that an expert's testimony will be relevant does not mean that the testimony necessarily will be admitted into evidence. Courts will balance the <u>costs</u> of having the expert testify (i.e., time and risk of having an expert's opinion carry too much weight) against its <u>benefit</u> (i.e., the extent to which the testimony will assist the judge or jury in making its decision).

With respect to the second criterion, the only reason an expert is permitted to provide an opinion in a case is that the "subject-matter of the inquiry must be such that ordinary people are unlikely to form a correct judgment about it, if unassisted by persons with special knowledge" [citations omitted].[29] Thus, to find the expert's testimony admissible, the court must decide that the expert evidence is required to provide information that is likely outside the knowledge and experience of the judge or jury.

In addition to the general discussion of necessity, the Court addressed the matter of ultimate issue testimony. The ultimate issue in a case is the question the judge or jury is asked to decide. For example, in a case involving a custody dispute the ultimate issue is generally what living arrangements would be in the child's best interests. Therefore, a mental health professional who offered an opinion about which living arrangement would be in the child's best interests would be answering the ultimate issue. If the expert is allowed to answer the ultimate opinion, he/she is basically telling the jury or judge how to decide the case. Formerly, ultimate issue testimony was actually barred in courts. While the current rules of evidence are not as strict, the Court in Mohan noted that when the expert's testimony addresses the ultimate issue, "the criteria of relevance and necessity are applied strictly, on occasion, to exclude expert evidence as to an ultimate issue."[30]

In addition to considering whether the expert's testimony is relevant and whether the testimony is necessary to assist the judge or jury in deciding the case, there are many reasons for the exclusion of evidence in a trial. For example, testimony concerning the credibility or truthfulness of a witness has traditionally not been held admissible. Thus, courts still may exclude expert witness testimony if it meets the exclusionary criteria.

Given that the expert is permitted to provide opinion evidence, the Supreme Court also noted in the final criterion that there must be an evaluation of so-called experts to ensure that they "have acquired special or peculiar knowledge through study or experience in respect of the matters on which he or she undertakes to testify."[31] It does not matter whether this skill is obtained via formal study or experience. The individual's qualifications may be challenged by the opposing lawyer and cross-examination of these qualifications may ensue. The judge determines the admissibility of the witness' qualifications. If the witness' qualifications are not accepted then, of course, the witness would not be deemed an expert and could not engage in that role and offer opinion testimony. If the qualifications are accepted, the witness is deemed an expert and proceeds to testify. In practice, expertise in mental health or other specialty areas can be acquired via formal university education, practical training, supervised experience, and ongoing reading and study.

THE EXAMINATION OF WITNESSES

As we have already seen, a number of rules exist governing witnesses and the admissibility of their testimony in trials. In this section, we will outline the procedure for examining witnesses in a trial. Generally speaking, the procedure does not vary depending on whether the witnesses are called to give direct evidence or expert evidence testimony. Because the plaintiff in a civil case, and the Crown (prosecution) in a criminal trial, has the burden of proving liability or guilt, respectively, they call their witnesses first. Parties in criminal and civil cases have the right to call those witnesses whom they wish. Further, they have the right to determine the order in which they will question witnesses, and what questions to ask those witnesses.

A. Examination-in-Chief

The party who calls the witness to testify in a trial questions the witness first in what is called the examination-in-chief. In the examination-in-chief, open-ended questions are permitted, enabling the witness to tell her/his "story" fully. As Sopinka and his colleagues note, the examination-in-chief can serve a number of purposes in a trial: "(1) build or support the calling party's case; (2) weaken the opponent's case; (3) strengthen the credibility of the witness; (4) strengthen or weaken the credibility of other witnesses."[32] Subject to the rules of evidence, lawyers will be permitted to decide upon what questions to ask the witnesses they call. However, lawyers are usually prohibited from asking the witness "leading questions" (questions that suggest an answer) unless the questions are about facts that are not in dispute in the case (e.g., "we have heard from Ms. Green that she works at X").

Very often when a mental health professional is called as a witness, the lawyer calling him/her will ask detailed questions that may require that the clinician refer to his/her clinical notes. In such a case, the lawyer will have to ask the court's permission for the witness to refer to the notes. In that case, the opposing party's lawyer typically will be allowed to review the material the witness relies upon.

During the examination-in-chief -- or direct examination -- as it is sometimes called, the witness will have the opportunity to clearly lay out the information that supports the side of the case for whom she/he was called. Of course, as a helping professional, one should remain as neutral as possible, which may even include providing the court with information that may not support one's own position. Notwithstanding that, though, if the examination-in-chief does not go well, the effect of the witness' testimony will be greatly weakened. Melton, Petrila, Poythress and Slobogin note that in the examination-in-chief, "it is probably best to structure the body of the testimony like an inverted pyramid -- beginning with evaluation techniques and the data those techniques have produced; then proceeding to inferences; and ending with the "peak," the summary conclusion."[33] While this will require the cooperation of the lawyer leading the examination-in-chief, it is a useful strategy for effectively covering the information one intends to convey. In addition to the organization of the examination-in-chief, it is useful for the expert to avoid using unnecessary jargon, and to attempt to answer the questions asked directly and completely.

Finally, as they relate to forming, supporting, and presenting opinions, the use of "supplementary"[34] or "authoritative"[35] literature is permitted by the court. Essentially, there appears to be recognition by the court that opinions, theories, and ideas do not operate in a vacuum. Indeed, McWilliams[36] stresses that the potential expert witness must stay current with the literature in the field and maintain contact with others in the discipline. Sopinka et al.,[37] referring to previous cases, concluded that "it appears that, if a written work forms the basis of the expert's opinion, then counsel is allowed to read extracts and obtain his/her judgement on them. The written view of the author thereby becomes the opinion of the witness."[38]

B. Cross-Examination

As a result of the adversarial nature of our legal system, once the lawyer who called the witness completes the examination-in-chief, the opposing party's lawyer has an opportunity to cross-examine the witness. As with general witnesses, cross-examination of the expert witness is an avenue open to the opposing counsel. Generally, the strategy to challenge the expert's opinion is to undermine the foundation upon which the opinion rests. Therefore, the expert is likely to be cross-examined regarding the relevance and comprehensiveness of particular facts upon which the opinion rests,[39] and the biases he/she has regarding the issue at hand.[40]

Sopinka and his colleagues specify three purposes of cross-examination: "(1) to weaken, qualify or destroy the opponent's case; (2) to support the party's own case through the testimony of the opponent's witness; (3) to discredit the witness."[41] Because cross-examination is one of the few methods available in a case to challenge the testimony of a witness, lawyers are given considerable flexibility by courts when cross-examining a witness. The scope of the cross-examination is very broad and lawyers may ask questions about any matters raised in the examination-in-chief as well as matters that were not addressed in the examination-in-chief.

Although we will provide some suggestions for dealing with testifying later in this chapter, including being cross-examined, it is important to comment on one important rule regarding cross-examination here. As we have emphasized, cross-examination is a valuable tool in the trial process, and it is highly improper for a witness's lawyer to communicate with the witness either directly or indirectly during the period of cross-examination. This obviously is true while the witness is on the stand, but it is equally important during recesses or adjournments for the lawyer not to communicate with the witness.

C. Re-examination

Once witnesses have been examined by the party who called them, and by opposing counsel, the witness may be re-examined by the lawyer who called her/him. Re-examination is allowed so that the witness may clarify any testimony that may have been distorted or weakened during cross-examination. The subject of re-examination is limited to material already discussed during the examination-in-chief and the cross-examination. As Sopinka et al. point out, though:

> the right to re-examine . . .extends to rehabilitation of the credibility of the witness which may have been impaired in cross-examination. This includes the right to ask the witness to explain or clarify discrepancies between the witness's evidence-in-chief and in cross-examination. In addition, this may entail the introduction of a previous consistent statement to rebut the suggestion that the witness' evidence was a recent contrivance [citations omitted].[42]

WITNESS PREPARATION

By now it is clear that rules of evidence and the procedures of examination during a trial are complex, and that the thought of providing information to the legal system, or -- even worse -- being called as a witness in a case, can be anxiety arousing. In this section of the chapter we begin with a brief discussion of some general strategies that can be employed in routine helping practice to decrease some of the concern that normally arises when one becomes involved in the legal system. We then review some information about the basis of witness examination and the importance of working with counsel to prepare for testifying in a case. Finally, we give some tips that might be useful if one is called to testify.

A. Strategies of Practice to Cope With the Law

Like most things in professional practice, the worst time to try to figure out how to handle a difficult situation is when one arises. In other words, prevention is a far better alternative to developing strategies for handling difficult situations. In this section, we will highlight some useful strategies for practice that may reduce some of the difficulties faced once information about a client or patient is requested for use in the legal system. Readers are also referred to Eberlein[43] and Soisson et al.[44] for a discussion of related matters concerning the maintenance of record keeping and client records.

Helping professionals need to review and consider the extent to which their current record keeping and client record maintenance practices protect their clients' confidentiality. As noted earlier in this chapter, it is important not to write extraneous, tangential, information about a client and place it in the person's file. We have advised psychologists and other helping professionals to prepare their notes, reports, and any other documentation about a client or patient as though they had to justify their decisions of what to write and include in the file to another helping professional -- or even to a lawyer. By being conscious about what is included in clients' files, one is less likely to include material that does not relate directly to the reason for seeing the person. In turn, this extraneous information will not harm the person.

In addition to being conscious about what to include in a client's file, the helping professional should routinely review the file to ensure that information in the file that is inaccurate -- or no longer valid -- is updated. For example, if the helping professional raised some issue in a report, only to find out that his/her suspicions were not later valid, it would be responsible practice to add a note to the file stating that, and providing the reason why. Regularly reviewing records enable the helping professional to ensure that the files are as accurate as possible. Furthermore, since the helping professional will not be permitted to alter individual files once they are subpoenaed, by regularly reviewing current client files, the likelihood that erroneous information may make its way into the legal system will be decreased. Finally, consider the need for establishing a protocol for destroying files at some point following the termination of involvement with the client. In some clinics, only a cover sheet with the most basic information is kept after an appropriate period of time has passed (typically five or seven years).

Carefully informing clients about the nature and limitations of confidentiality can be one of the best strategies for ensuring that clients do not relay information that they would never have revealed, had they known the information could be released to some third party or a court. As an example, let us return to the case, *R. v. O'Connor*,[45] which allows confidential records about mental health intervention with sexual abuse victims to be used at the trial of the accused sexual abuser. Now that the case has been decided and people who work with sexual abuse victims know about the outcome of the case, there may be an ethical obligation to inform clients who have been sexually abused about the ruling. Specifically, if such clients choose to relay any information to the therapist about the abuse, that information may have to be released to the court to be used in proceedings against the person accused of abusing them. In this case, once the abuse victim knows of the limitations of confidentiality, she/he will be able to decide whether to go ahead and disclose information about the abuse -- knowing that it might be subpoenaed for use by the court. Although this is not a good choice from a therapeutic perspective, by informing the person of the limitations of confidentiality the therapist respects the person's right to make autonomous decisions about whether to disclose the information. Thus, helping professionals need to be familiar with the limitations of confidentiality -- and to convey those limitations to their patients or clients.[46]

While the above suggestions cannot account for all of the potential difficulties that will face a mental health professional when her or his records are subpoenaed, they should be helpful for reducing the scope of problems and for providing some protection for the client's privacy.

B. Basics of Witness Examination

Two additional topics relevant to preparation of the expert witness include the witness's use of notes, and strategies for coping with the cross-examination experience. As we discussed above, the use of notes during testimony is generally acceptable as long as the judge agrees to this practice. However, Thompson[47] and Shapiro[48] offer some cautions in deciding whether to use notes during expert testimony. Both warn against excessive reliance on notes, stating that notes should be used primarily to refresh the memory and not serve as a crutch. More importantly, there are legal ramifications to taking notes into the courtroom. As we stated above, any notes taken into the courtroom can usually be inspected by opposing counsel and entered as evidence. As a result, any information in the expert witness' notes can become a target for cross-examination.

The strategies used by opposing attorneys during cross-examination are varied. Descriptions of many such strategies and recommendations on how to respond can be found in a number of sources, including those by Thompson,[49] Brodsky,[50] and Shapiro.[51] We recommend that the reader who anticipates being called as a witness in a trial takes the opportunity to read one or more of these sources, and to fully prepare himself or herself for the experience.

While we cannot review all strategies that have been suggested for testifying in a case here, there are a number worth noting. Thompson outlines the three general purposes of cross-examination as being: "(a) to obtain statements especially admissions of fact, useful to his or her case; (b) to test and discredit the story of the witness by exposing inconsistencies, gaps or errors; and (c) to discredit or impeach the basic credibility of the witness."[52] He states that the overall strategy of the cross-examining lawyer is to control the witness. The primary means of gaining such control is through asking leading questions or making a series of leading, short, pointed statements requiring a yes/no answer. Both methods ultimately leave little room for the witness to manoeuvre.

Shapiro[53] presents a hierarchy of cross-examination strategies stating that, as a rule of thumb, lawyers will first attack an expert witness' opinion. If this is unsuccessful the lawyer will attack the witness' credentials and, if this is unsuccessful, the lawyer will then make attacks on the witness' personal credibility. Thus, he suggests that if a lawyer is making a personal attack, the witness should take this as an indication that his/her opinion and credentials are sound. In terms of cross-examining strategies, Shapiro warns that a lawyer will attempt to draw the witness into taking sides and the witness should hold firm in her/his opinion, while remaining as neutral as possible. He stresses the importance of the expert knowing the field of expertise and relevant literature well, since a lawyer will sometimes introduce irrelevant literature, refer to an obscure article, or attack the field or expert as being unscientific. Shapiro also emphasizes the importance of the use of the hypothetical question, referring to it as "one of the most difficult legal traps to deal with."[54] He outlines the many forms it takes, from seeking a change of opinion by providing hypothetical situations, to overgeneralization, to leading the witness into speculation. A final, general type of cross-examination tactic that Shapiro describes is for the attorney to attempt to portray his/her client as normal by picking out isolated symptoms, equating "within normal limits" with normal, and attempting to demonstrate that the defendant was unimpaired while engaged in a number of behavioural activities on the day of the offence.

Melton and his colleagues [55] provide a very useful and enlightening discussion of cross-examination in their text on *Psychological Evaluations for the Courts* (section 14.04 (d)). While we will not summarize their entire discussion here, they do provide a list of "common cross-examination ploys" used by lawyers in cross-examining helping professionals that is worth quoting here:

a) "Infallibility complex." To overcome any perception the jury may have of the witness as infallible, the attorney asks a question designed to suggest fallibility. The attorney may ask the witness about the relevance of some very new, or very obscure, research with which the witness is not familiar; this, the attorney hopes, will result in an "I don't know" response.

b) "God only knows" gambit. The attorney may ask questions to which there is no sure, easy, or precise answer (e.g., "What really causes schizophrenia?").

c) "Yes-no" questioning. The attorney attempts to box the witness in by phrasing questions in such a way as to force a "yes" or "no" answer.

d) "Bought or biased" testimony. The attorney tries to portray the witness as having been bought (e.g., "Doctor, how much are you being paid for your opinion in this case?") or as biased toward one party (e.g., "Doctor, you quite frequently testify for the plaintiff in these malpractice cases, don't you?").

e) "Unreliable examination" gambit. The attorney will question the witness about the uncertainty of her/his findings (e.g., low reliability/validity of individual tests or diagnosis, low accuracy of predictions, etc.).

f) "Subjective opinion" ploy. The attorney will ask whether the witness has personally been involved in systematic research to investigate the reliability and/or validity of his/her own clinical opinions and judgments.

g) "Loaded question" ploy. The attorney will misstate what the witness has said or agreed to in an earlier response, usually by "loading" the prior statement with additional information. For example, if a witness has previously agreed to assertions X, Y, and Z, a later question by the attorney might be, "Doctor, you earlier testified that W, X, Y, and Z were true. Doesn't that mean that . . .?"

h) "Lawyer as expert" ploy. Here the attorney graciously volunteers to testify for the clinician regarding the clinician's own field (e.g., "Doctor, doesn't a standard psychological evaluation consist of . . . ?"); this sets the clinician up for later questions that depend on the lawyer's definition of what is "standard."

Simply by being made aware of these "ploys," helping professionals can recognize them when the lawyer attempts to use them, and can prepare for the cross-examination. For example, if the mental health professional relied on tests in conducting the evaluation, he/she should be fully knowledgeable about the reliability and validity of the tests, as well as research in which the test was used -- particularly that research which examines the use of the test for the purposes for which it was employed in the assessment.

As the "ploys" suggest, lawyers quite often try to "trap" the expert in a situation that might embarrass her/him. It is always best to give direct, truthful responses. If the helping professional is not aware of a study or fact, he/she should admit it. As Melton et al.[56] point out though, in so doing, one could ensure that one demonstrates expertise in the area. For example, if the witness is asked about a particular study that is unfamiliar, she/he could say, "Well, the work by X and Y is generally considered the best in the field; however, I am not familiar with the study you are referring to." Melton et al. further suggest that the helping professional state his/her willingness to review the paper during a recess -- if the lawyer has it. This strategy will show that the expert witness is open to new information and not trying to "hide" anything.

Finally, if the expert does not know the answer to a God only knows question -- rather than saying I don't know, she/he might say, The field (or the state of science) does not yet enable us to know the exact answer to that question. Again, this strategy will not only show that the expert witness is truthful, but that an expert relies on the field of science -- not just on one's own opinions or experience.

In addition to the material discussed above, the reader is directly referred to books by Brodsky[57] and Ziskin.[58] Brodsky's book describes many cross-examination techniques and explains how to respond to them. It is short, easy to read, and written like a "Bridge Manual," with a number of maxims to help the helping professional who is called to testify. Ziskin's[59] writing is directed primarily towards assisting attorneys with cross-examination of psychiatrists and psychologists and will assist the prospective witness in learning more about many general and specific approaches a lawyer might use. In addition to arming the lawyer with a means of attacking the general principles underlying psychology and psychiatry (e.g., whether psychiatrists and psychologists should even qualify as experts, the scientific method in these disciplines, classification, clinical judgement, clinical examination, and evaluations in general), Ziskin provides the means by which to cross-examine particular areas of expertise and specifically counters Brodsky's advice with a chapter entitled "Dealing with Experts' Tactics."[60]

C. Working with Legal Counsel

The importance of working with legal counsel before and during the hearing is highlighted by Shapiro[61] and Thompson[62], and we strongly recommend the same. Unfortunately, in our experience, the lawyer who calls the helping professional to testify very often spends too little time with the professional to adequately allow for preparation in either the examination-in-chief or the cross-examination. While it would not be proper for the lawyer to "coach" the witness into what to say, it is very helpful to know the nature and range of questions they will be asked, as well as some information regarding the type of questions that can be anticipated on cross-examination. Shapiro stresses the importance of anticipating what the opposing lawyer's challenges will be so that they can be dealt with in the examination-in-chief. By doing this, the impact of cross-examination can be diffused and one can minimize being caught off-guard during cross-examination. Shapiro emphasizes that as a part of examination-in-chief, the lawyer should elicit the basic thrust of the expert's opinion, the basis for the opinion, and the variety of sources contributing to the opinion. The intent is to minimize opposing lawyer's future fragmentation and twisting of the opinion and its underpinnings.

Thompson outlines that at the minimum, the lawyer working with the expert witness should provide "an explanation of what the hearing is about, what the major issues are, what your testimony is needed to prove, and a very rough outline of the topics to be covered."[63] He suggests that the expert witness should be actively involved in preparation when issues surrounding the opinion are discussed so that the witness can provide information about parameters of questioning in relation to the opinion and the use of accurate language.

D. Skills of Evidence Giving

This section is directed at those helping professionals who are new to the experience of giving evidence in court. These may be expert witnesses or professionals with functions, such as probation officers (or youth workers dealing with young offenders) who are giving testimony about a pre-sentence report, child welfare workers who are giving evidence of abuse or neglect, or family court counsellors who are testifying in a contested custody issue. The procedures for qualifying professionals with statutory functions as experts are usually less demanding than for other helping professions for two reasons:

a) Family Courts, where custody, child welfare and young offenders matters are heard, tend to be somewhat more informal and the statutes more liberally construed (as for example section 3(2) *Young Offenders Act* demands).

b) These professions may have statutory duties as officers of the court to investigate and report to the judge. Probation officers and family court counsellors in British Columbia fit this category. They are normally deemed to have expertise in the areas of young offenders/sentencing, and custody/family matters respectively. This does not prevent their qualifications and expertise from being challenged in contested cases. Social workers in child protection matters are the authorized agents of the director of Family and Child Services in British Columbia (or Children's Aid Society in some provinces) and are usually called as the director's or Society's main witness in abuse or neglect issues. Their evidence normally has expert status in these areas of child welfare.

Credibility is the hallmark of an effective evidence-giver. This is conveyed by both the quality of the evidence presented and the way it is delivered. A thorough investigation and assembly of facts, with well thought-out opinions drawn from them enhances quality. This requires sound preparation, including an understanding of the investigator's role, the focus of the investigation, and anticipation of the strengths and weaknesses of the evidence collected. Consideration of which "facts" are open to different interpretation can also assist in anticipating questions. In time-limited enquiries demanded by the court, not every aspect can be covered in equal depth. The helping professional will need to be able to justify the process and priorities of the investigation. The novice testifier may wish to rehearse in advance with colleagues challenging the testimony. Assuming the position of each party and imagining how counsel might be instructed to challenge the testimony and conclusions can be a useful experience. Observing the court in process can be valuable, as judges can vary in their expectations, such as in the degree of specificity required.

In presentation, the content of the testimony needs to:

a) clearly distinguish fact and opinion. Prefaces such as, "I believe that the facts indicate" and "It appears that," are useful here;

b) demonstrate how opinions are supported by facts, which include direct observations and statements to the investigator;

c) be delivered in clear and concise statements whenever possible. Candidness and authority, without appearing defensive in the way testimony is structured, is ideal. For the professional to clearly state when they do not understand questions or do not have answers to them can enhance the trustworthiness of the testimony and the sincerity of the witness. Taking time before launching into a reply suggests the answer is well considered; and

d) demonstrate an awareness of any personal biases in the investigation or conclusions drawn.

Another key component that speaks to credibility is the demeanour of the testifier. Posture on the witness stand, appearance, facial expression, and voice tone all need to suggest appropriate confidence as a professional. For example, well moderated and paced speech, non-verbal expressions that are congruent with the content, appropriate humour, non-jargon language, reasonable eye-contact with the bench, and poise can all reinforce credibility. However, nervous reactions such as inappropriate facial expressions or mid-sentence pauses can be interpreted as uncertainty or evasiveness. Refraining from defensiveness or sarcasm in answers is obviously important. If questions appear to be too personal, asking the judge whether an answer is required can often alert the court to an issue of relevance.

Competence is also demonstrated by thorough understanding of the court roles, rules of evidence, and protocols. For instance, examination-in-chief is a clear opportunity for the helping professional to present all of her/his evidence in a generally unrestricted fashion. This opportunity to present all relevant information needs to be seized prior to cross-examination. Speaking directly to the Judge and showing respect through occasional insertion of Your Honour or Your Lordship (and knowing which to use) can enhance credibility.

Overall, the helping professional needs to come across as conscientious, candid, thorough, honest, thoughtful, competent, and as objective as possible. Warmth, humanity, and concern also need to be displayed without compromising the professional and objective approach.

HELPFUL HINTS FOR WOULD-BE WITNESSES

Thompson provides some general do's and don'ts for potential expert witnesses. His pointers are as follows: tell the truth; listen to the question; take your time in answering questions; say "I don't know" if you don't know; if you don't understand the question being asked, request that the lawyer rephrase it; speak clearly and firmly; be as precise as possible and approximate a date or time if need be; "never say never, never say always; "admit it if you make a mistake; be courteous, polite, and serious; do not argue with the opposing lawyers; do not lose your temper; do not volunteer information; if you are certain about something do not back down; and, look at the judge when making a point.[64] In addition to these pointers, Thompson recommends additional concerns should be addressed to your lawyer during the preparation period.

In our experience, there is no substitution for preparing to be cross-examined. Cross-examination is one situation where the Latin maxim, *experientia docet* (experience is the best teacher) holds true. However, reviewing the literature, being completely familiar with the subject matter, and being able to understand the nature of the proceedings will help the prospective witness prepare for the situation.

COMMON QUESTIONS

1. <u>What procedures should the helping professional follow if a lawyer contacts him/her to obtain information about one of your clients for whom the lawyer is working?</u>

Helping professionals should treat <u>all</u> requests for information, regardless of whether they come from a lawyer or other person, similarly. Generally, helping professionals should not provide any information about the person, including whether or not the person is their client. Instead, the helping professional should insist that any request for information be made in writing and accompanied by a release of information form. Then, it may be prudent to contact the client to ensure that he or she consents to having the information released.

2. <u>Should helping professionals ever simply ignore a subpoena or other formal legal order for the release of confidential information?</u>

No. Although helping professionals may have ethical obligations to maintain client confidentiality, all such obligations are superceded by a valid legal order requiring the release of information. As discussed, there are formal legal procedures available for challenging subpoenas or court orders.

3. <u>What factors may determine whether a helping professional is called to testify in court to give direct evidence testimony or expert witness testimony?</u>

The answer to this question turns on whether the helping professional is being asked to provide testimony about his/her first-hand knowledge of some situation at issue in the case, or whether she/he is being asked to draw inferences from facts at issue in the case, or to provide an expert opinion. Witnesses providing direct evidence testimony typically have first-hand knowledge of some matter at issue in the case and will be required to restrict their testimony to relaying to the court what they saw or heard. Generally, witnesses giving direct evidence testimony are not permitted to draw any inferences from their observations, and they may not testify about their personal belief or opinions about any matters. By contrast, experts are permitted by the court to use their training and experience to draw inferences from the matters at issue in the case to arrive at an expert opinion that will assist the court in deciding the case. To determine whether a helping professional will be allowed to provide expert opinion evidence, courts must determine that the opinion the <u>expert</u> will give is admissible. For such testimony to be held admissible, the judge must determine that the the testimony is relevant to the case, that its benefits outweigh its costs, that it is necessary to provide the judge or jury with information that is beyond their knowledge, that the testimony is not subject to general exclusionary rules of evidence, and, finally, that the person submitted as the expert is properly qualified by virtue of study or experience.

4. <u>The formality of the court situation and the level of scrutiny the expert witness will be subjected to makes it quite difficult for the helping professional, especially when he/she has not had prior experience in this role. What can the helping professional do to help ensure that she/he is perceived by the court as a credible witness?</u>

The helping professional needs to be fully aware of the expectations and operation of the court system. It is most helpful if the lawyer who is calling the professional to testify can devote ample time to help prepare the witness. Overall, the helping professional needs to come across as conscientious, candid (not defensive or sarcastic), thorough, honest, thoughtful, competent, and as objective as possible.

5. Should the helping professional volunteer information and/or elaborate on her/his answers when giving direct testimony?

No, answer the question that is asked as succinctly and simply as possible while trying to avoid being backed into a corner by a series of <u>yes</u> and <u>no</u> questions. The helping professional should remember that he/she is in the legal arena where the rules are different and unfamiliar. The rules that guide the behaviour and practice of helping professionals (e.g., empathy, a desire to help) are not the same as those that guide the process of court cases. Because helping professionals are likely to be empathetic and desirous of being helpful, they may have a tendency to answer questions at greater length than is needed.

6. As a general rule, unless specifically requested via subpoena or court order, should helping professionals bring notes (e.g., clinical notes, interview notes) to the witness stand?

While each court case and expert witness is different, as a <u>very</u> general rule, it would be best to consider doing without notes in the court room and on the witness stand, particularly. It is advisable for the helping professional to review relevant notes and refresh his/her memory prior to attending the courtroom. But generally it is better to leave notes behind, because once brought to the witness stand, it provides ammunition for the opposing counsel in cross examination.

7. Should the helping professional bring to court a written document which highlights or summarizes the area or question about which she/he is about to testify?

If time allows the production of such a document it is recommended. Not only can it be a useful source of information for the trier of fact, submitting a written document increases the probability that the expert's opinion will be accurately outlined and understood.

8 What if the opposing counsel asks the helping professional to hypothesize or speculate by extrapolating from his/her expertise in the area?

The helping professional should be careful when doing so. She/He should specifically communicate the conditions and/or limitations upon which the answer is based. If there is no basis for such extrapolation, then he/she should simply state that is the case.

9. What should the helping professional do if, during cross-examination, the opposing counsel becomes very aggressive or hostile?

The helping professional should not respond in kind. She/He should remain calm, polite, and rational. By doing this the lawyer's approach may appear so outrageous that it may backfire. Even if the tactic does not backfire, by remaining calm and rational, it is more likely the answers will be appropriate and relevant.

CONCLUSION

As this chapter demonstrates, the area of legal evidence is a complicated one that presents a real challenge to the helping professional. However, a review of the information presented here will help the clinician prepare for an encounter with the legal system. As the fields of mental health, social work, child care, nursing, education, and law become more entangled, helping professionals can expect to find their files subpoenaed more frequently. In addition, they may be called as a witness to either give direct evidence or expert evidence testimony.

Generally speaking, the helping professional should <u>never</u> provide information following an informal request by a lawyer -- even if it is the client's lawyer who makes the request. By remaining on guard to such attempts, the helping professional can better ensure that his/her client's rights to confidentiality are not easily infringed. When confronted with a subpoena, the helping professional has a number of options for proceeding. Should the clinician feel strongly about the matter, she/he can consult a lawyer in an attempt to quash or narrow the subpoena. In any case, it is useful and appropriate to notify the client or patient that a request for information has been made. This will enable the client or patient to take steps to protect his/her own interests.

Aside from having their records subpoenaed, helping professionals are often called as witnesses in hearings or trials. If called as a general witness, the helping professional's testimony -- like that of all other witnesses -- will be restricted to his/her first-hand knowledge of the client. However, if for any reason the helping professional's opinion is being sought, he/she may be introduced to the court as an expert. Assuming the testimony will meet the legal prerequisites (i.e., be relevant to the case; is necessary for assisting the judge or jury in deciding the case; does not violate other exclusion rules; and, the mental health professional has specialized knowledge in the area in which she/he is being asked to testify), the expert will be permitted to give opinion evidence in the case.

Regardless of whether the helping professional is called to give direct or expert evidence, it is important that he/she is familiar with the basic legal procedures (the examination-in-chief, cross-examination, and re-examination). There exist a number strategies that may be useful for assisting the helping professional in maintaining files and records in a manner that will decrease the likelihood that material in them will be misused in the legal system (e.g., being sure to keep notes that are relevant to the purpose for the patient contact, being careful not to write extraneous or unsubstantiated information about the client). Furthermore, by informing her/his client of the limits of confidentiality, the helping professional allows the client the choice of whether to disclose personal, sensitive, information that may eventually make its way into the legal system.

Finally, we have relayed considerable advice about both the nature of the cross-examination experience and the strategies that lawyers might employ during the cross-examination. As we point out, it is useful to become familiar with the legal system before testifying, and to review the nature of one's testimony and the cross-examination with the lawyer who will lead one's examination-in-chief. There is little doubt that the best way to prepare for cross-examination is to be thoroughly knowledgeable about the material about which one is to be testifying. By answering the questions asked directly and truthfully, the helping professional reduces the risk of being "trapped" by the lawyer.

In closing, it is important to note that while the helping professional may be reluctant and anxious about becoming involved in the legal system, that system must often rely upon the expertise of a helping professional. By being professional and well-prepared for those experiences, the helping professional can very often assist the courts in arriving at decisions that are better informed and more just than they would have been without that assistance.

RESOURCES

S. L. Brodsky, *Testifying in court: guidelines and maxims for the expert witness* (Washington, D.C.: American Psychological Association, 1991).

Committee on Legal Issues, American Psychological Association, "Strategies for Private Practitioners Coping with Subpoenas or Compelled Testimony for Client Records or Test Data" (1996) 27, *Professional Psychology: Research and Practice* 245.

T. T. Daley, "Guidelines for the expert witness" (1996) 65, *The Social Worker* 1.

D. Faust, & J. Ziskin, "The Expert Witness in Psychology and Psychiatry" (1988) 241, *Science* 31.

G. B. Melton, J. Petrila, N. G. Poythress, & C. Slobogin, *Psychological evaluations for the courts: A handbook for mental health professionals and lawyers* (New York: Guilford, 1987).

R. Rogers, & C. N. Mitchell, *Mental health experts and the criminal courts: A handbook for lawyers and clinicians* (Toronto, Ontario: Carswell, 1991).

D. A. R. Thompson, "Rules of evidence and preparing for court." In N. Bala, J. Hornick, & R. Vogl (Eds.), *Canadian Child Welfare Law* (Toronto: Thompson Educational Publishing, 1990).

W. T. Tsushima, & R. M. Anderson, *Mastering expert testimony: A courtroom handbook for mental health professionals* (Mahwah, New Jersey: Lawrence Erlbaum Associates, 1996).

J. Ziskin, ed., *Coping with psychiatric and psychological testimony,* 5th ed. (Los Angeles, California: Law and Psychology Press, 1995).

END NOTES

1. N. Falconer, *Preparing for practice* (Toronto: Children's Aid Society of Metropolitan Toronto, 1983); C. D. Stromberg, D. J. Haggerty, R. F. Leibenluft, M. H. McMillan, B. Mishkin, B. L. Rubin & H. R. Trilling, *The Psychologist's Legal Handbook,* (Washington, DC: The Council for the National Register of Health Service Providers in Psychology, 1988).
2. P. K. McWilliams, *Canadian Criminal Evidence* (3rd ed.), (Aurora, ON: Canada Law Book Inc., 1994).
3. *R. v. O'Connor*, [1995] 4 S.C.R. 411.
4. D. Birch, J. R. P. Ogloff, & J. Petifor, *Legal and ethical issues of record keeping and access to psychological records.* Paper presented at the Annual Meeting of the Canadian Psychological Association, Charlottetown, PEI, 1995, June.

5. For a general discussion of confidentiality, see J. R. P. Ogloff, "Navigating the quagmire: Legal and ethical guidelines for mental health professionals," In D. Martin & A. Moore (eds.), *First Steps in the Art of Intervention* (Pacific Grove, CA: Brooks/Cole, 1995 at 347-376).

6. Stromberg et al., *supra*, note 1.

7. *Ibid.*

8. *Ibid.*

9. J. R. P. Ogloff, *supra*, note 5.

10. Stromberg et al., *supra* note 1.

11. *R. v. O'Connor*, *supra* note 3.

12. Committee on Legal Issues, American Psychological Association, "Strategies for Private Practitioners Coping with Subpoenas or Compelled Testimony for Client Records or Test Data," (1996) 27 Professional Psychology: Research and Practice 245.

13. J. Sopinka, S.N. Lederman & A.W.Bryant, *The Law of Evidence in Canada*, (Toronto, Ontario: Butterworths, 1992); *R. v. Mohan*, [1994] 2 S.C.R. 9

14. A. B. Thayer, *A Preliminary Treatise on Evidence at the Common Law*, (New York: Augustus M. Kelley, 1969) in *R. v. Morris*, [1983] 2 S.C.R. 190.

15. L. Eberlein "Client records: Ethical and legal considerations," (1990) Canadian Psychology, 31, 155-166, E. L. Soisson, L. VandeCreek & S. Knapp "Thorough record keeping: A Good Defense in a Litigious Era," Professional Psychology: Research and Practice, 18, 498-502. 1987.

16. Sopinka et al., *supra*, note 13.

17. R. J. Delisle, *Evidence: Principles and Problems*, (Toronto, Ont.: Carswell, 1996); Sopinka et al., *supra*, note 13.

18. Sopinka et al., *supra*, note 13 at 821.

19. Delisle, *supra*, note 17.

20. R.E. Salhany, *A Basic Guide to Evidence in Criminal Cases* (2nd ed.), (Toronto, ON: Carswell, 1991).

21. Falconer, *supra*, note 1.

22. *R. v. Mohan*, *supra*, note 13; Sopinka et al., *supra*, note 13.

23. E. W. Cleary, *McCormick on Evidence*, (3rd ed.) (St. Paul, Minn.: West, 1984); *R. v. Mohan*, 1994, *supra*, note 13; Sopinka et al., *supra*, note 13.

24. Sopinka et al., *supra*, note 13.

25. P. K. McWilliams, *supra* note 2.

26. Sopinka et al., *supra*, note 13.

27. *R. v. Abbey*, [1982] 2 S.C.R. 24; *R. v. Beland*, [1987] 2 S.C.R. 398; *R. v. McMillan* (1975), 23 C.C.C. (2d) 160 (Ont. C.A.).

28. *R. v. Mohan*, *supra*, note 13.

29. *Ibid.*, at 23.

30. *Ibid.*

31. *Ibid.*, at 25.

32. Sopinka et al., *supra* note 13.

33. G. B. Melton, J. Petrila, N. G. Poythress & C. Slobogin, *Psychological Evaluations for the Courts: A Handbook for Mental Health Professionals and Lawyers*, (New York: Guilford, 1987) at 357.

34. McWilliams, *supra*, note 2 at 9-11.

35. Sopinka et al., *supra*, note 13 at 560.

36. McWilliams, *supra*, note 2.

37. Sopinka et al., *supra*, note 13.

38. *Ibid.*, at 560.

39. *Ibid.*

40. R. Rogers & C. N. Mitchell, *Mental Health Experts and the Criminal Courts: A Handbook for Lawyers and Clinicians*, (Toronto: Carswell, 1991).

41. *Ibid.*, at 857.

42. Sopinka et al., *supra*, note 13 at 879.

43. L. Eberlein, *supra*, note 15.

44. Soisson et al., *supra*, note 15.

45. *R. v. O'Connor*, *supra*, note 3.

46. Ogloff, *supra*, note 5.
47. D. A. R.Thompson "Rules of evidence and preparing for court." In N. Bala, J. Hornick, & R. Vogl (eds.), *Canadian Child Welfare Law*, (Toronto: Thompson Educational Publishing, 1990).
48. D. Shapiro, *Psychological Evaluation and Expert Testimony: A Practical Guide to Forensic Work*, (New York, NY: Van Nostrand Reinhold Company, 1984).
49. Thompson, *supra*, note 47.
50. S. L. Brodsky, *Testifying in Court: Guidelines and Maxims for the Expert Witness*, (Washington, DC: American Psychological Association, 1991).
51. Shapiro, *supra*, note 48.
52. Thompson, *supra*, note 47, at 275.
53. Shapiro, *supra*, note 48.
54. Shapiro, *supra*, note 48 at 86.
55. Melton et al., *supra*, note 33 at 358.
56. *Ibid.*
57. Brodsky, *supra*, note 50.
58. J. Ziskin (Ed.). *Coping with Psychiatric and Psychological Testimony* (5th Edition), (Los Angeles, CA: Law and Psychology Press, 1995).
59. *Ibid.*
60. Brodsky, *supra*, note 50 at 58.
61. Shapiro, *supra*, note 48.
62. Thompson, *supra*, note 47.
63. *Ibid.*, at 269.
64. *Ibid.*, at 270.

PART III

Conclusion

Chapter 17

IMPLICATIONS FOR THE FUTURE

Max R. Uhlemann and David Turner

INTRODUCTION

This handbook was written in order to provide a wide range of helping professionals with much of the legal information they might need to function effectively in their various roles. This purpose came out of the editors' teaching and practical experience, which indicated that it is often difficult for the average helping professional to gain access to basic legal information without considerable effort. To the degree that the editors and contributors have been successful in compiling such information, we are pleased.

In the chapters of this handbook, the editors and contributors have taken considerable care to present the law as it currently exists and to relate that law to the practice of helping professionals. The goal was to provide a solid overview of basic legal information in each area examined, as well as to give an introductory understanding of some of the intricacies involved.

In concluding the handbook with this chapter, it seems necessary to return to the basic perspective presented by the editors in the Preface. It was pointed out that legal rules are not static, and opinions on the interpretation and application of specific laws can vary greatly. Most importantly, helping professionals need to realize that the law is constantly changing with the social context. Governments are continually creating or revising legislation, and courts are developing interpretations and applications of that law. Thus, in this chapter, the editors present a brief overview of some of the factors in society they believe contribute to changes in the law. This is followed by a summary of the speculation of the contributors to the handbook on changes in the law that may occur in the near future in their areas of writing. Finally, the editors conclude with some thoughts about the possible implications for the practice of helping professionals.

SOURCES OF CHANGE TO THE LAW

As the social context of Canada changes, the law must evolve to reflect an accurate expression of public policy. The editors speculate that some of the following social trends in Canada are affecting, and will continue to affect, the development of our laws. These trends include the increase in and urbanization of the Canadian population linked with limited financial resources, an aging Canadian population, increasing cultural diversity, the widening economic gap between the wealthy and the poor, new lifestyles, advances in medical science and technology, and an increasing public awareness of personal rights regarding the use of the courts to resolve disputes. Each of these will be addressed briefly below.

The continuing increase in[1] and urbanization of[2] the Canadian population coupled with current and projected economic restraints, have a definite impact on the law. With the increase in population, it is difficult to satisfy the interests of the various groups in society with the apparent limited financial resources. This, in turn, leads to more competition for those resources. Legislative law, in particular, is influenced by the struggles among groups to ensure a share in those limited resources. Increasing urbanization may lead governments to enact laws with a stronger emphasis on social control and stabilization.

The impact of increasing cultural diversity[3] raises many social and legal issues including the demand upon social institutions to reflect, in their personnel compositions, the diversity of Canadian society. Governments are being pressured to bring in laws promoting employment equity in their public sector workforces. Increasingly important are the *Charter*[4] and human rights protections for cultural, religious, and aboriginal minorities, plus provisions in the *Criminal Code*[5] prohibiting dissemination of hate information.

An aging Canadian population[6] is another source affecting the development of law. As an example, when pension benefits were under attack, seniors groups lobbied the federal government to drop proposed legislation that would remove pension indexing to the cost of living. It is also likely that seniors will continue to place demands on legislators and the courts to remove the public policy of mandatory retirement. Demands for increased law and order protections in the criminal law may also reflect the wishes of the elderly regarding safety.

The widening economic gap[7] between the wealthy and the poor in Canadian society is not a new phenomenon. Perhaps because the wealthy and powerful may have easier access to the law and lawmakers, this may allow them additional influence on the direction of new laws. Individuals with average incomes find it increasingly difficult to finance expensive law suits against governments or large corporations. Class action suits have only recently become available under the Canadian system, so that collective efforts on the part of individuals or small groups, were limited. Legal aid continues to face financial limitations from governments.

New lifestyles in society result in demands for new and more open legal responses from government and courts. For example, modifications to family law, adoption, and child welfare legislation will reflect the changing nature of the family (e.g. communal, homosexual, blended, single-parent, and common law[8]). Persons of a different family style are also seeking better protections in human rights acts against discrimination, which currently affect family and pension benefits.

Advances in medical science and technology to save foetuses at a younger gestation period, and to prolong life in the elder years, raises some questions of medicolegal ethics in issues such as genetic engineering, euthanasia, and the use of life-sustaining machinery. New communication technology like the Internet[9] and electronic mail have spawned different challenges, such as control of hate communications and child pornography, freedom of information, and privacy in criminal and administrative law areas. Law Reform Commissions have studied some of these dilemmas and their subsequent impact on criminal and civil law.

Law reform is often driven by political considerations. Political highlighting has focused attention on a variety of issues across Canada in this decade, such as the child welfare system, aboriginal treaty negotiations, the legal reparations from trauma in residential schools, labour legislation, environmental codes, free trade, the distinct society status for Quebec, and the blight of sexual abuse of children and youth in sports organizations, fosterhomes, and schools.

Political pressure has mounted for the development of alternatives to the justice system in the form of dispute resolution mechanisms. The expense and emotional costs of the adversarial aspects of the legal system are increasing the popularity of alternative conflict resolution methods, such as mediation. Costs are forcing many individuals and groups to approach other helping professionals rather than lawyers for help with advocacy. For instance, immigration consultants who are not lawyers are giving advice prior to immigration or deportation hearings. Also, recent legislative changes in British Columbia are allowing judges in small claims cases to use the mediation process in their courts. These alternative procedures tend to spur on legal reforms until other political priorities emerge.

Finally, because the general public has become more aware of personal rights in recent years, there is a more frequent use of the court system to settle disputes. Perhaps, the *Charter* has increased this public focus on personal rights. Nevertheless, this trend is creating some overload and time delay in the court system, occasionally resulting in *Charter* defences of unreasonable delay in the criminal justice system.

DIRECTIONS FOR CHANGE

To give the reader some idea of future directions in the law related to the roles of helping professionals, the editors asked the contributors to the handbook to speculate on the changes that might occur in the near future. Their comments confirm the idea that law is always changing in response to societal needs. Presented below is a summary of their thoughts about change in the law that will have an impact on the practice of helping professionals.

David Turner and Max Uhlemann indicated that the content of the *Charter* and human rights legislation create a challenge to the courts to keep their interpretation relevant to the current social scene. In the future, citizens will increase their reliance on the *Charter* and human rights legislation in seeking legal remedies to their problems. This means that helping professionals must grasp the ramifications of these basic laws to assist their clients and practice in an appropriate manner. Laws, policies, programs, and decision-making by those who deliver social and psychological services will be even more closely scrutinized by the direct consumers and the public to ensure that services are fair and non-discriminatory. Pressure to expand the protections in the human rights laws will continue to mount as more individuals and minority groups become empowered. A variety of affirmative action strategies will continue to be developed for minority persons to deal with systemic discrimination in both the public and private sectors. These strategies will possibly be tested in the courts. As the awareness of systemic discrimination against certain groups (i.e., women, racial minorities, First Nations people, persons with disabilities and with differing sexual orientation) in society increases, helping professionals will need to use strategies to bring about legal change in partnership with these groups. Advocacy and political action through coalitions of groups concerned with social justice is required to bring about legal and social changes. The increasing use of civil suits to deal with human rights issues such as sexual assault and harassment illustrates the importance of such remedies.

Turner and Uhlemann speculated that over the next decade new criminal law and human rights responses will be needed to combat potential rights violations arising through technological advances. The Internet, World Wide Web, Electronic Mail, and other computer links are making communication and information sharing easier, faster, and more global, especially for affluent individuals and multinational corporations. Some[10] have suggested that this technology is often used to manipulate the international transfer of capital and wield international power without reference to the laws and policies of sovereign nations. Treaties like the North American Free Trade Agreement (NAFTA) and the proposed Multilateral Agreement on Investment (MAI) do have an impact on Canada's ability to enforce human rights laws such as those related to working conditions, environmental standards, taxation and investment.

This technology also creates new challenges for the protection of human rights. Communication of hate messages, pornography, harassment, and the development of mechanisms that invade personal privacy, such as surveillance and collection of personal information from a variety of data banks, have drastically increased through the use of electronic and other media. The protection of human rights through the *Charter* and other legislation will need to advance rapidly in response to these technological advances.

In 1997 public hearings were held by the Human Rights Council across the province of British Columbia to review amendments to the *Human Rights Code*.[11] In the hearings a variety of limitations of the *Code* were revealed, and there were demands expressed for a wider coverage of human conditions under the *Code*. Pleas were heard from social justice groups and individuals for protection in the *Code* for many groups of persons, including the transgendered, those with lower economic status or who receive assistance and benefits from governments or aboriginal bands, and for specific protection for persons under 19 years of age. Recommendations from the public included the need to clarify the duty of employers and providers of housing[12] to accommodate persons with special needs. The importance of providing paralegal help for those unable to pay for or to access lawyers prior to tribunal hearings was emphasized. Recent recommendations by the Commission[13] to the Attorney General go some way to alleviating these issues, but protections for "under 19" age and political affiliation are still absent, and assistance for complainants is not mentioned. Hopefully, these will be addressed in the near future. Finally, Turner and Uhlemann indicated that, given the political will of the public and government, the *Charter* and human rights legislation should evolve to encompass many of the above-mentioned areas so that a fairer, more egalitarian, and less oppressive society may become a reality.

In the chapter on child protection, David Turner and Max Uhlemann noted how child welfare in British Columbia and other provinces is under intense public, political, and media scrutiny. This means that changes are rapidly being introduced, often in reaction to crises and tragedies. For example, recent deaths of children while in care has resulted in the increased profile and powers of the Office of the Commissioner for Children. In September 1997, a task force on the foster care system[14] made 32 recommendations ranging from increased funding and caseload standards and limits to increased worker training and planning for and monitoring of children and care homes. The degree to which these recommendations will be implemented in the near future is not easy to predict, as much rests on the political will and values of legislators. Helping professionals working in child welfare are directly impacted by these political issues, and often feel besieged. In one instance, they are criticized for failure to act to protect a child and, in the next instance, they are criticized for overzealous interference in a child's or family's private life. Further high profile tragedies, such as the death of a child or a controversial court case alleging an inappropriate apprehension, can shift public opinion either way. Turner and Uhlemann believe increasing court litigation will continue to refine the grounds for intervention and provision of services by governmental agencies, including child care workers, social workers, and other helping professionals. How far community and neighbourhoods will be involved in the protection, caring, and nurturing of their children remains to be seen. Also, with the increasing pressure on helping professionals to exercise a social control function in society, they must endeavour to balance this function with another component of their professional mandate, the caring function.

The greater focus on child and youth rights creates demands that helping professionals become more accountable to protect those rights and to advocate when violations occur. The new child welfare legislation in British Columbia, followed by the amalgamation of the ministries that work with children and youth, is raising challenges for practice. The ministries and the courts are developing new modes of operation at the same time that professionals are having to learn more effective interdisciplinary collaboration. Rapid change and steep learning curves coupled with even greater monitoring of adherence to work standards affect the morale and feelings of competency for the helping professional.

The child welfare law and system is expected to have to deal with several key issues in the near future. The first issue is the debate about the compulsory licensing of child welfare professionals and what that means for training and legal adherence to professional codes of ethics and discipline. Licensing of child welfare workers is on the horizon, perhaps through a College of Child Welfare Social Workers. The second issue is the apparent flaw in the child welfare and income assistance legislation that fails to address the poverty that so many families face who encounter the child welfare system. Systemic poverty must be addressed but as noted in Chapter 3, child welfare for the most part remains residual, not preventative. It should be noted also that the amalgamation of child and youth services in British Columbia excludes the Ministry of Human Resources, which is responsible for income assistance. A third issue concerns the child welfare system's response to the increasing ethnic diversity of Canadian children and families. Helping professionals remain predominantly white and mainstream, and, while the law acknowledges cultural heritage, the child welfare standards continue to represent the views of white and middle class society. Helping professionals will need to focus on truly diversifying the system.

Kathy Absolon and John Macdonald reported in Chapter 4 that many First Nations communities are located on a continuum from no movement to complete movement in regaining control of child welfare. First Nations political organizations are asserting their right to self-governance and self-determination though it cannot be assumed that political movements are always congruent with community based realities. As discussed in the chapter, some communities are in a transitional phase toward autonomy and control and are dealing with internal community based issues. While some communities are in the initial stages of preparing their vision of child welfare takeover, other communities may have their vision but are stalled in actualizing it because of government resistance to releasing power and resources. This resistance may continue to be the central struggle in the next few years as provincial governments enact a more conservative agenda because of deficit reduction plans.

While many communities are in a healing process, some communities cannot look forward because of the degree of internal random chaos and trauma. The communities that are on the threshold of receiving mandated protection authority are moving forward with inspiring clarity, strength, and determination. Communities already in the process of delivering family support services, with potential protection mandates on the horizon, are faced with structural challenges because of financial restraint. The process of developing First Nations child welfare services is then plagued with the forced need to restructure, lay off staff, and change emphasis in programs. When front line workers or support workers are laid off, families who are suffering from trauma do not receive the help they need. Those First Nations agencies that are successfully, yet stressfully, operating under difficult conditions must be applauded and recognized for their vision and strength. And those non-First Nation professionals who act in solidarity to assist where appropriate must be acknowledged and recognized.

Absolon and MacDonald further indicated that First Nations' movement toward regaining complete control over their children, families, communities, and lives is not in question. Regaining this control is a process, and the need for this process has been quite evident for decades. The level of control provincial and federal governments insist on retaining in this area continues to be a question. At a more practical level, First Nations communities need to develop economic power, resources, and training to fully support the process of self-determination. This level of support is not only a Treaty obligation. It is an issue of humanity toward a people and their children who have been grossly abused and disempowered. This history must not be forgotten, not cast aside. The *Royal Proclamation of 1763* reminds the public that the obligation for this level of support exists and must continue with any future agreement. The healing of Indian-White relations and within First Nations means that the past is a part of the future. To imply otherwise is to sever ties from which the present is based on. Giving voice to authentic experiences and accounts of the impact of the colonial government's child welfare policy will continue to be a thrust among First Nations and those allies of the resurgence.

In the area of adoptions, Glenn Gallins noted that the *Adoption Act*[15] and Regulations underwent a major revision in November, 1996. The revision incorporated many new policy initiatives. Therefore, it is unlikely that significant new initiatives will occur in the near future. Rather, as experience is gained in working with the new Act, some fine tuning might take place. Gallins also noted that some of the consequences of the new *Act* and Regulations were already beginning to come to light. For example, the new Regulations imposed significant fees to complete the various steps required to obtain an adoption order. While the Regulations provide the possibility of some relief from those fees for prospective adoptive parents who receive social assistance, the fees have created a substantial impediment to stepparent adoptions by the working poor. The new *Act* also increased the circumstances where the consent of the birth father to an adoption is required. This change has in some cases made it more difficult to complete an adoption because of the difficulty in obtaining the consent of the birth father. No doubt other problems will become apparent over time. Thus we can expect minor changes in the *Act* and Regulations to rectify these problems.

Jerry McHale reported that the area of family law is continually subject to change and refinement as the structure of the family changes and because so many family law cases come before the courts. In the past few years, there have been significant changes to the law with respect to entitlement to spousal maintenance, the use of Child Support Guidelines[16] to determine child maintenance, the division of pensions between spouses, and broadening the definition of "spouse" to include same gender, marriage-like relationships. As the structure of the family changes in society, we can expect the law in matters of parenting, custody, and access to evolve accordingly.

Most jurisdictions are shifting more and more towards post-marriage arrangements structured, in a real way, around the best interests of the children. Some foreign jurisdictions have shifted away from the use of terms like "custody" and "access" on the basis that these terms encourage a sense of exclusive ownership that is not really appropriate for children. Future legislation could focus on avoiding custody contests by encouraging the development of "parenting plans," and having judges make "responsibility orders." In this way, other jurisdictions are already trying to reframe the way parents think about post-marriage child care.

Much of the developing law will relate to protecting the best interests of children. For example, the new *Hague Convention on the Civil Aspects of International Child Abduction*[17] negotiated in 1996 is likely to be ratified by Canada in the foreseeable future. This convention will make it simpler for parties to assert rights and obligations existing with respect to children where their parents reside in different countries.

McHale also reported we can expect more attention to be given to the process of how families separate. British Columbia will likely expand the availability of education programs to separating parents in the near future. These programs will be designed to provide parents with a basic orientation to the law and to their procedural options, and will educate them as to how to best meet the needs of their children on separation. There will almost certainly be a greater emphasis on the collaborative resolution of post-marriage conflict. Some Canadian jurisdictions (Saskatchewan and Quebec, for example) are already moving towards mandating mediation for appropriate family law cases.

Nicholas Lang indicated that increasing public awareness and concern about family violence is likely to lead to continuing change in both statute and case law in this area. He speculates that we will see more flexible laws for the procedure in giving evidence and for the type of evidence to be received by the court. These changes will allow family violence cases to be more effectively presented in court. We can also expect an increase in the use of diversion as an alternative means to the prosecution of minor family violence cases. Further, we can expect an increase in the referral to specific treatment programs in sentencing for family violence offences. This change in sentencing will target groups such as parental physical abusers, spouse abusers, alcohol abusers, and child sexual offenders. Finally, Lang indicated that Criminal Injury Compensation can be expected to provide a wider availability of treatment programs for specific victim groups such as male victims of child sexual assault, spousal assault victims, and physically abused victims. These latter changes will lead to increased involvement of helping professionals in providing service to these various groups.

Lesley Giles and Alan Markwart indicated that the *Young Offenders Act,*[18] which has always been controversial, was the subject of comprehensive reviews by a Parliamentary Committee and a federal/provincial task force in 1997. Although the *Act* was amended in 1986, 1992, and 1995, the newly appointed federal Minister of Justice has promised more change. It is likely that conservative interest groups will again be successful in pushing for tougher sanctions for serious violent young offenders. On the other hand, it is also likely that liberal interest groups will be successful in achieving a greater emphasis, at least for non-violent youth, on community-based alternatives to custody and increased diversion from the formal court system, particularly involving restorative justice measures such as family-group conferencing, victim-offender reconciliation, and mediation.

In effect, Giles and Markwart suggested that a kind of bifurcated youth justice system seems to be emerging, with a line being drawn between violent and non-violent youth. Ironically, these apparently divergent interest groups appear to share one thing in common, a dissatisfaction with the youth justice system as it is presently structured. Yet, legislation is merely a vehicle for legislation - ultimately, the effectiveness of the youth justice system will depend on who drives that vehicle (i.e., personnel) and what fuel (i.e., resources) is available to it. While tight fiscal policy will probably preclude any significant infusion of new resources, the establishment of an integrated Ministry for Children and Families offers hope for the future of young offenders. Ultimately, the community will be better served by a more coordinated and comprehensive system of service delivery.

Gerrit Clements indicated that it remains unclear whether there will be any amendments to the *Mental Health Act*[19] in the near future. If any amendments will take place, they will most likely be minor in nature, since any major changes will be too controversial. For example, family members of people with mental illnesses most commonly want legislation that enables quick admission of patients to hospital with immediate and effective treatment. In addition, they want the option of involuntary treatment, while the patients live in the community. This procedure is desired because many patients require frequent re-admission to hospital as a result of their resistance to treatment and failure to keep taking their medications. On the other hand, organizations who advocate for the further extension and enforcement of legal rights for involuntary patients usually want involuntary hospital admissions restricted to those persons who are, or are likely to be, physically dangerous to themselves or others. Organizations advocating for this approach would, as a rule, like to see those persons with mental disorders who are capable of making decisions about psychiatric treatment, make those decisions for themselves, even if this means that treatment will be refused. At present, these two perspectives seem irreconcilable, and make any amendments a hazardous undertaking for the government.

As far as the "adult guardianship" legislative package is concerned, it is likely that the government will soon decide what parts of the legislation to implement and on what dates. These changes will be most welcome if only to prevent, if that is still possible, British Columbia from becoming the only province without legal recognition of advance health care directives.

Clements indicated that two parts of the current adult guardianship legislation require attention. The first deals with the legal recognition of the role family members play in deciding medical treatment for those who are mentally incapable of making health care decisions. Second, legal intervention is required to make support and assistance available to those who are being abused or neglected and for those who are neglecting themselves and are unable to make decisions to protect or care for themselves because of mental incapability.

According to Dulcie McCallum and Peter Carver, equality is not a reality for people with disabilities. Fundamental changes need to occur so that all people with disabilities can be respected as full and participating citizens. The role of helping professionals is critical to the process of change. The principal issues for both the professionals, and those they serve, will be those that advance the rights of people with disabilities, such as integration in school, and access to transportation, the justice system, the workplace, and community services. It is for the helping professional, states McCallum

410

and Carver, to respond with knowledgeable awareness, respect, and courage in advocating for people with disabilities.

Yvonne Martin reported it is most unlikely that the rights, duties, and responsibilities assigned in legislation to the major players in education -- parents, students, the Minister, school boards, superintendents, principals, and teachers -- will change in the near future. Although some parents are actively pursuing greater influence, if not power, over matters like curriculum and some aspects of school governance, including some control over teachers and teaching, provincial policy does not seem inclined to move in these directions.

With respect to current areas of conflict in education, it is Martin's view that most of these issues would best be resolved through cooperation, collaboration, and accommodation, rather than by legislative changes. Legislative changes often contain seeds of even further conflict. In the absence of legislative changes, school boards could clarify regulation and procedures, for example, relevant to disclosure of information within a school. Teachers and parents may seek agreement on how much informal information is reasonable to give and receive, respectively. The Minister may attempt to achieve greater communication with parents, and so on.

Martin further indicated that the areas most likely to see legislative changes are those related to parental right of access to information about their children, especially adolescent children. The current lack of consistency between the *Freedom of Information and Protection of Privacy Act*[20] and the *School Act*[21] with respect to the rights of parents and children in this area needs early attention.

Bill Trott, Lorrainne Dixon, Max Uhlemann, and Jo-Anne Sargent indicated that access and privacy issues will continue to be concerns for helping professionals. They anticipate that the public will make increasing demands upon public bodies for access to information. At the same time these public bodies will seek more efficient and effective means to provide public access to records, and they will make greater use of Internet access to provide government information to the public. There may also be an increased interest from government in seeking revenue from the sale of information. Technological and scientific developments will bring new challenges to privacy. These challenges will include greater surveillance of the public through such initiatives as drug testing in the workplace, the use of genetic information in employment decisions, use of video surveillance in public areas, and the use of data bases of personal information.

Trott and his colleagues indicate further that technology may also bring tools to enhance privacy, such as biometric identification. This includes the use of personal markers, such as fingerprints, to ensure restricted access to sensitive personal information. This procedure is currently being explored for use in the health field. These developments will challenge our concepts of access and privacy.

In regard to legal liability, Terry Wuester and Terry Wuester Milne indicated that today helping professionals are involved in more litigation than in the past. This trend is likely to continue. Although legislation could be passed to limit such law suits, or to limit the amount of damages which may be awarded, it is unlikely that such legislation will be adopted because the general public usually takes the view that if a professional person has negligently injured a client or patient, then liability for that injury should follow. In the absence of such legislation, how can the helping professional best protect himself/herself? Perhaps, the best answer lies in taking care to conduct all dealings with clients or patients with the care that a "reasonable professional person" would. This will not prevent law suits from being brought against the helping professional, but it should help the court to find no liability on the basis that the standard of care has been met. Also, Wuester and Wuester Milne suggested it must be noted that the helping professional should make sure that she/he has ample professional insurance coverage, just in case an action is brought against him/her.

Regarding skills for action, David Turner and Max Uhlemann indicated that increased sophistication and competency of all helping professionals will be required as their practice engages the legal arena more frequently. At the same time the legal system is looking to helping professionals to find ways to meet shortcomings of the system and/or develop alternatives. Examples include the increased demand for mediation in all its forms for a range of culturally diverse settings. Helping professionals for instance are collaborating with native bands in supporting aboriginal traditions, such as sentencing circles, custom (informal) adoption, and acceptance of the aboriginal notions of community and extended family. In the mainstream system, professionals are continuing to explore the notions of diversion, victim-offender reconciliation, neighbourhood accountability boards, and a variety of conflict-resolution strategies. Individuals and groups, such as victims and witnesses of crime, are being empowered by helping professionals to withstand the often traumatic experience of the adversarial process. As politicians demand more cost-effective ways of delivering criminal and civil justice, helping professionals are required to develop the skills to work with new mechanisms. The slow transformation of the legal system will continue to require challenge through individual, systemic, and political advocacy.

Jim Ogloff and Natalie Polvi believed the timing of the chapter on legal evidence and expert testimony was very fortunate in many ways. Recent cases and legislation have helped clarify several matters for mental health professionals compelled to provide legal evidence or to testify as an expert in a case. However, two matters require further clarification in the future: a) the ultimate issue rule; and b) the release of psychological test scores. While the Supreme Court of Canada's decision in *R. v. Mohan*[22] has helped clarify the criteria for the admission of expert testimony, the case leaves questions about the propriety and permissibility of ultimate issue testimony. As described in Mohan, experts provide ultimate issue testimony when they provide an opinion about the specific matter that is at issue in the case (e.g., whether it is in the child's best interests to live with the father or mother in a matter where the custody of a child is in question). While such testimony has been prohibited by courts in the past, the Supreme Court leaves open the possibility of experts providing ultimate opinions so long as the criteria for admissibility are followed closely. Future court decisions will be necessary to see to what extent courts will permit such testimony. In addition, mental health professionals need to closely consider the ethical propriety of rendering opinions that directly relate to legal questions, questions that often have no direct "translation" in mental health terms (e.g., "fitness to stand trial," "criminal responsibility," "dangerous offender," etc.). As a separate matter, considerable controversy exists concerning whether psychological test data should be released as part of a client's file. With recent cases such as *R. v. O'Connor*,[23] and legislation including *the Freedom of Information and Protection of Privacy Act*, it is clear that mental health professionals are compelled to provide clients access to their entire files. Given the sensitivity of raw test data, though, it would be helpful for mental health professionals, and psychologists in particular, to be given further guidance by courts regarding how best to balance the competing interests of protecting the test security and providing clients with their right of accessing their files.

CONCLUSION: IMPLICATIONS FOR PRACTICE

The practice of helping professionals is shaped by the changing social and psychological needs of individual members and groups, and by the changing demands of the elected authorities in society, as expressed through law or policy. It is expected that helping professionals will convey a close understanding of their clients' needs to administrators of services and to legislators so that new laws and policies are compatible with the needs and best interests of all of their clients.

For example, empowerment through the legal system for victims of family violence has gained prominence in the last decade, in part through the activities of helping professionals and the women's movement. Traditionally, the counselling approach in this case would have been to counsel for a "domestic dispute." Today, police, justice workers, mental health, and social work personnel are being directed by policy to give greater attention to family violence as a crime. The role of helping professionals is to encourage the legal system to provide a more effective response in such situations and to continue assisting victims of family violence through the emotional trauma of the crime and the legal system. Fortunately, courts are becoming increasingly aware of their limitations in dealing with family violence. For instance, data continues to indicate that courts have a gender bias. They are often more sympathetic to men (usually the perpetrator) than to women[24] (usually the victim), perpetuating stereotypes and double standards. This type of documentation has lead to calls from the public and from helping professionals for better gender equity.

Victim support groups in the family violence area, often accompanied by support from helping professionals, have been working to bring about other changes in the legal system. They have promoted the use of victim impact statements, which often empower the victim and contribute information to court proceedings. Helping professionals have also been called upon to testify about the assaulted spouse syndrome, which is a crucial educational function. Similarly, helping professionals are supporting adults and children, who were victimized by family violence, when they decide to take civil action against the perpetrator.

As well, helping professionals are assisting in the development of alternative remedies (such as voluntary or court-ordered treatment programs for spouses who physically abuse) which are supplements to, or substitutes for, the formal criminal process. They may assist in developing new systems, such as sentencing circles for First Nations, or perhaps arranging for First Nations communities to take over their own justice systems, including criminal, child welfare, and civil.

This example serves to illustrate some of the complex demands placed on helping professionals. Given the growing importance of their roles in an increasingly litigious society, helping professionals should prepare themselves in as many areas as possible to serve that society. Most importantly, they should learn about and understand the legal system itself. They need to know its strengths and weaknesses, its ideology and biases, so that they are be able to prepare their clients for participating in that system as well as to challenge legal structures to shift to meet human need. As helping professionals work to alter the legal system and their own and others' attitudes towards it, it will come to be viewed as an empowering mechanism, rather than as a system to fear. They can prepare themselves to work more effectively with the legal system by improving their skills of mediation, advocacy, and evidence-giving. Where it fails to empower or offer justice equitably, helping professionals should assist in the development of alternatives. Finally, helping professionals, both individually and collectively through their professional associations or as allies of oppressed groups, can lobby legislators for the legal reforms that will reflect our evolving society. Social justice for all must be the goal.

We trust this handbook has encouraged helping professionals to become more aware of the role of law in society and its potential for direct impact on their practice, both now and in the future. It is hoped this handbook will serve as an aid and a continuing reference for the helping professional, and to that end, the editors feel they will have achieved their purpose.

END NOTES

1. Statistics Canada, *Canada Year Book 1997* (Ottawa, Ministry of Supply and Services, 1997). According to Statistics Canada, our population was 29.606 million persons in 1995. Although growth is increasing, the rate of growth has been slowing down due possibly to a declining birth rate and lower immigration levels. Growth continued to be higher in British Columbia (Canada Year Book 1997, p.77).

2. M.A. Burke, "Urban Canada, " in *Canadian Social Trends*, C. McKie and K. Thompson, (eds.), (Toronto: Thompson Educational Publishing, 1990) at 68. In 1995, according to the Canada Year Book 1997, Toronto reached 4.33 million, and Vancouver, Ottawa/Hull and Montreal all passed the million population level.

3. P.M. Waite, "Ethnic Origins of the Canadian Population," in *Canadian Social Trends*, note 2 at 3. An increasingly wider ethnic spectrum of persons was admitted into Canada. See Canada Year Book 1997, p.67.

4. *Charter of Rights and Freedoms*, Part 1 of the Constitution Act, 1982, which is Schedule B of the *Canada Act* (U.K.), 1982, c.11.

5. *Criminal Code*, R.S.C. 1985, c.C-46.

6. M.S. Devereaux, "The Aging of the Canadian Population," in *Canadian Social Trends*, note 2 at 68. Increased life expectancy and low fertility rates has tilted the population in the direction of seniors (Canada Year Book 1997, p.61). This is true apart from First Nations where over 50% of the population is under the age of 24.

7. United Nations Development Program, *Human Development Report 1991* Canadian Press, reported in Victoria Times-Colonist, May 23, 1991, A1.

8. M.S. Devereaux, "Marital Status", at 138, O. Adams, "Divorce Rates in Canada," at 147, P. Turcotte, "Common Law Unions," at 148 in *Canadian Social Trends*, note 2.

9. See "Human Rights and the Internet," Human Rights Forum, (Ottawa, Canadian Human Rights Commission, 1997) Vol.7 Issue 1.

10. See T. Clarke, *Silent Coup: Confronting the Big Business Takeover of Canada,* (Ottawa: James Lorimer and Co. 1997).

11. *Human Rights Code*, R.S.B.C. 1996, c.210.

12. For instance see submission of The Capital Region Race Relations Association, "Human Rights in the Next Millenium" (Victoria, British Columbia, October 3rd 1997).

13. *Human Rights for the Next Millenium: Recommended BC Human Rights Code Amendments for British Columbians by British Columbian*, (Victoria: British Columbia Human Rights Commission, January, 1998). See chapter 2, page 51 for more details on these recommendations.

14. Report of the Task Force on Safeguards for Children and Youth in Foster or Group Home Care (1997, Ministry for Children and Families, Victoria).

15. *Adoption Act*, R.S.B.C. 1996, c.5.

16. Child Support Guidelines, amendment to the *Divorce Act*, 1985, R.S.C. 1986, c.4.

17. *Hague Convention on the Civil Aspects of International Child Abduction*, incorporated into *Family Relations Act*, R.S.B.C. c.128, s.55.

18. *Young Offenders Act*, R.S.C. 1985, c. Y-1.

19. *Mental Health Act*, R.S.B.C. 1996, c.288.

20. *Freedom of Information and Protection of Privacy Act*, R.S.B.C. 1996, c.165.

21. *School Act*, R.S.B.C. 1996, c. 412.

22. *R. v. Mohan* (1994) 2 S.C.R. 9.

23. *R. v. O'Connor* (1995) 4 S.C.R. 11.
24. M.G. Brown, ed. *Gender Equality in the Courts: Criminal Law.* A study by the Manitoba Association of Women and the Law. (Ottawa, National Association of Women and the Law, 1991), 2-34.

Appendix A

PRIVACY CODE FOR
PRIVATE PHYSICIANS' OFFICES IN BRITISH COLUMBIA[1]

PREAMBLE

This Code is to guide physicians and their staff members in the collection, use, disclosure, and handling of personal information in their private offices. This document reflects current practice based upon legislation, ethical requirements, and legal precedent.

The *Freedom of Information and Protection of Privacy Act* covers personal information in hospitals, mental health centres, health units, and student/employee health centres located in provincial or local government offices or post secondary institutions. It does not cover personal information in the private offices of physicians.

The Code reflects the ethical principle that information that is compiled about a patient should be held in confidence, unless the patient consents to the disclosure, or the law authorizes its disclosure, or a court orders disclosure. Since confidentiality is the cornerstone of the trust relationship between doctor and patient, a physician should ensure that his/her patients are aware of the limits to confidentiality, under certain circumstances.

This Code recognizes the need for physicians and staff members to collect and record a wide range of health-related personal information for the benefit of the patient.

The Code covers a patient's personal information that is recorded or stored by graphic, photographic, electronic, mechanical, or other means. The Code does not cover the disclosure of unrecorded information (e.g. verbal), which is governed by the ethical principle to respect the patient's right to confidentiality.

I. Collection of Personal Information

1. Purpose for Which Personal Information May Be Collected

In providing health care for a patient, a physician or staff member may collect personal information about a patient:

a) when that information relates directly to and is necessary for providing continuity of health care services to a patient, or for related administrative purposes; or

b) when the collection of that information is expressly authorized by or under an *Act*.

2. Sources of Personal Information

   a) Direct collection;

      i) a physician or staff member should collect personal information about a patient directly from the patient;

   b) Indirect collection;

      i) a physician or staff member may also collect personal information from another individual or organization, if the patient has authorized such collection of personal information from another person (such as a family member, or the patient's previous doctor or a consultant);

      ii) A physician or staff member may also collect personal information from another individual or organization, if the collection is specifically required by law (either by an enactment, subpoena, warrant, or court order);

      iii) A physician or staff member may also collect personal information from another individual or organization, if the physician has reasonable grounds to believe that indirect collection is necessary for the safe and effective treatment of the patient (including urgent and immediate circumstances, or where the patient is incapable of providing the information).

3. Accuracy of Personal Information

   In accordance with Rule 13 of the rules under the *Medical Practitioners Act*, physicians and staff members must make every reasonable effort to ensure that personal information is recorded accurately, completely, and legibly.

II. Use of Identifiable Personal Information

A physician or staff member may use personal information for the purpose of providing health care services to the patient or for related administrative purposes.

Use of identifiable personal information for any other purpose (for example, research or fund raising) requires the written consent of the patient.

III. Disclosure of Personal Information

A physician or staff member may disclose personal information:

1) for the purpose of providing health care services through a referral, consultation, or report to another health care professional who is involved with the patient's care;

2) if the patient has consented, in writing, to its disclosure;

3) to comply with a court order, subpoena, or requirement of an *Act* or regulation of British Columbia or Canada;

4) to the College of Physicians and Surgeons of British Columbia in accordance with the *Medical Practitioners Act*;

5) to an employee or service provider of a physician, if the information is necessary for the performance of the duties of, or for the protection of the health or safety of, the employee or the service provider;

6) if a physician determines that compelling circumstances exist that affect anyone's health or safety, and if the physician takes all reasonable steps to inform the patient that the confidentiality of his or her personal information will be breached; or

7) to communicate with the next of kin, or representative of the patient, or appropriate family members, in accordance with professional ethics.

IV. Patient Access to Personal Information

For the purposes of this section, "access to" means the opportunity to examine or make copies of the original record.

2. If a patient or an authorized representative of the patient makes a request for access to personal information about a patient, a physician must comply as soon as practicable, but not later than 30 working days following the request, by:

   a) providing access to the patient or patient's representative;

   b) providing access to the remainder of the personal information where the information excepted from disclosure under subsection (2) can reasonably be severed; or

   c) providing written reasons for the refusal of access to the personal information or to any portion of the health records.

3. The physician may refuse to disclose personal information to a patient or patient representative:

   a) where there is a significant likelihood of a substantial adverse effect on the physical, mental, or emotional health of the patient;

   b) where there is a significant likelihood of harm to another individual;

   c) if the disclosure of personal information would be an unreasonable invasion of another individual's privacy; or

   d) if the records were created or compiled in contemplation of litigation or other legal privilege.

4. Where a physician provides access and the patient or patient's representative requests a copy of the personal information, a copy may be provided if it can reasonably be reproduced.

5. A physician is entitled to charge a reasonable fee, commensurate with the time, cost, and effort involved and the patient's ability to pay, for the search for the record, preparation of the record for disclosure, and copying and shipping the record.

6. Subject to subsection (2), a patient under 19 years of age may have access to a record where, in the opinion of the physician, the patient is capable of understanding the subject matter of the record.

V. Right to Request Correction of Personal Information

A patient who believes there is an error or omission in his or her personal information may request, in writing, that the physician who has custody or control of the information correct factual and biographical information.

If no correction is made in response to a written request, a physician must add the patient's request for correction to the patient's record.

On correcting a record, where the correction is required for the safe and effective treatment of the patient, a physician must notify any other individual to whom that information has been disclosed during the six-month period before the correction was requested.

VI. Protection of Personal Information

A physician and staff members must protect the personal information of their patients by making reasonable security arrangements against such risks as unauthorized access, collection, use, disclosure, or disposal.

VII. Retention of Personal Information

A physician must retain a patient's personal information in a record for at least 7 years from the date of the last entry. Where the patient is a minor, records should be kept for at least 7 years from the age of majority, which is currently 19 years of age.

VIII. Disposal of Personal Information

A physician or staff member must ensure that he or she disposes of patient records only by the following means:

a) by effectively destroying a physical record through shredding or by complete burning; or

b) by erasing information recorded or stored by electronic or magnetic methods on tapes, disks, cassettes, or other media in a manner that ensures that the information cannot be reconstructed.

IX. Ceasing to Practice

A physician must try to notify patients of his or her intention to leave the practice of medicine and the proposed securing and disposal of their personal information.

A physician should adopt a records management plan to secure or dispose of the personal information of patients to cover the following circumstances:

1) ceasing practice; or

2) in the event that the physician dies or becomes unable to practice.

A physician should provide in his or her will for a responsible person to ensure the security or disposal of patient personal information.

A physician who ceases to practice for any reason must provide the College of Physicians and Surgeons with a copy of his or her records management plan.

X. Contracts for Handling Personal Information

A physician must ensure that, where personal information is transferred to any individual or organization for processing, storage, or disposal, a contract is made with that individual or organization, which includes an undertaking to maintain the confidentiality and physical security of such personal information.

XI. Responsibilities and Dispute Resolution

A physician is accountable for his or her office's compliance with this Code, even though other individuals may be responsible for the day-to-day collection and handling of personal information.

The College of Physicians and Surgeons is responsible for handling complaints that arise from this Code that are not settled by the physician concerned.

GENERAL COMMENTARY

This privacy code is the product of a consultation amongst the College of Physicians and Surgeons of British Columbia, the B.C. Medical Association, and the Office of the Information and Privacy Commissioner for British Columbia. The intent is to reflect best practices of physicians and their staffs in the treatment of patient information. The participants included Dr. Morris Van Andel, Dr. Derryck Smith, Dr. Norm Finlayson, Dr. Mark Schonfeld, Dr. Ray Simkus, Commissioner David Flaherty, and William Trott. We are grateful to others for their critical comments on successive drafts.

The Code follows the basic privacy principles set out in the B.C. *Freedom of Information and Protection of Privacy Act* (1992) and the Canadian Standards Association's *Model Privacy Code* (1996).

The Code will be kept under ongoing revision to reflect the emergent realities of the practice of medicine in British Columbia and the automation of health records. The latter especially requires reasonable security and audit trails to ensure a chain of accountability for controlling access to automated patient information.

This commentary on the meaning and implications of the provisions of this Code will be expanded, particularly in response to queries and comments on the current text.

DETAILED COMMENTARY

Preamble

The Code covers personal information, which means recorded information about an identifiable individual. Personal information includes the health care information in the patient record as well as identifying information such as the name, age, family status, financial history, etc.

Anyone else's opinions about a patient are the personal information of that patient.

Physicians should post this Code and provide copies of this Code in a location in their offices visible to patients in the waiting room.

While this Code covers only recorded information, verbal disclosure based on recorded information is covered by this Code. Therefore the following general discussion from the *Canadian Medical Association Journal*, Vol. 139, Nov. 15, 1988 may assist physicians:

You can ensure that examining rooms are adequately soundproofed, provide piped-in music throughout the office and make sure that telephone [or personal] conversations cannot be overheard.

The Code covers the actions of a "staff member." Staff member includes employees and voluntary staff.

Section 2

In certain cases of research into rare diseases, where the research requires the inclusion of the total research population, special arrangements may be made for access to patient data with approval of an ethics committee.

Section 3

Consent for the use or disclosure of patient personal information may not be possible in certain cases. In the event of the patient's death, surrogate consent should be sought from the person authorized to provide consent.

Confirmation of consent may be sought from the patient in situations where the consent is not specific or is not current.

Examples of disclosing patient information for compelling circumstances include situations where the maintenance of confidentiality would result in a significant risk of substantial harm to others or to the patient, if the patient is incompetent.

Section 4

The section reflects a Supreme Court of Canada decision which held that while medical records are owned by a physician who compiled the record, a patient is entitled to reasonable access to the information. The court provided that a physician may refuse access in certain circumstances. These are reflected in this section.

Physicians are advised not to permit unsupervised examination of the original record in order to maintain the integrity of the record.

4(1)   The requirement to respond within 30 working days may be extended in extraordinary circumstances such as processing requests during a physician's holidays.

4(5)   Under the *Infants Act*, section 17, a capable minor may give consent for medical treatment. In these circumstances, the physician may provide the guardian or parents access to the capable minor's record only with the minor's written authorization.

Section 6

The written policies and procedures for the physician's office should include the office's security arrangements. For guidance for security of information stored electronically, see the COACH guidelines cited below. For fax transmission guidelines, see the British Columbia Office of the Information and Privacy Commissioner's fax guidelines.

Section 7

Limitation Act, section 8(1)(b) establishes the limitation period. No action may be brought against a physician, based on professional negligence or malpractice, after the expiration of 6 years from the date on which the right to bring an action arose. The Supreme Court Rules allow a writ of summons to be in force for 1 year. Therefore, the *College of Physicians and Surgeons of BC, Policy Manual*, M 4-1, June 1995 recommends retention of records for at least 7 years from the date of the last entry.

Where the patient is a minor, records should be kept at least until the patient is 26 years of age.

In cases based on misconduct of a sexual nature, there is no limitation period. The *College of Physicians and Surgeons of BC, Policy Manual*, M 4-1, June 1995 recommends that where the patient is under a disability or where there is an untoward outcome, it may be prudent to keep the records for periods in excess of 7 years.

Section 8

The *College of Physicians and Surgeons of BC, Policy Manual,* M 4-2, June 1995 states that the methods of disposing of records should be supervised.

The physician should be aware that simple deletion of automated records may not ensure that the information cannot be recovered.

The report by Dr. S. Peck (see below) provides details on the destruction of records.

Section 9

Notification may be through a general announcement in the local press, through form letters available in the physician's office or upon request, or similar means. Person to person mailing or communications, while obviously effective, may not be feasible.

Section 10

This section covers individuals on contract with a physician, who are providing services such as installing a computer software program, staff of laboratories, other health professionals providing services, cleaning staff on contract with the physician's office, or companies under contract to dispose of personal information.

RESOURCES

A. Cavoukian and D. Tapscott, *Who Knows: safeguarding your privacy in a networked world.* (Random House, Toronto, 1995).

Canadian Standards Association, *Model Code for the Protection of Personal Information* and *Making the CSA Privacy Code Work for You* (1996). Available at http://www.csa.ca/83000-g.htm

Canadian Association for the Advancement of Computers in Health (COACH), *Security and Privacy Guidelines for Health Information Systems.* Healthcare Computing & Communications Canada Inc., Edmonton, Alberta., 1995.

J. Goldman and D. Mulligan, *Privacy and Health Information Systems: a guide to protecting patient confidentiality.* Centre for Democracy and Technology, Washington, D.C., 1996.

Office of the Privacy Commissioner for British Columbia, *Guidelines for the Secure Transmission of Personal Information by Fax,* Victoria, British Columbia, August 1996. Available at http://www.oipcbc.org

Office of the Privacy Commissioner, *Health Information Privacy Code 1994,* New Zealand. Available at http://www.knowledge-basket.co.nz/privacy.

Shaun Peck, *Review of the storage and disposal of health care records in British Columbia.* British Columbia Ministry of Health and Ministry Responsible for Seniors, July 1995.

END NOTES

1. Privacy Code for Private Physicians in British Columbia, (1997), *British Columbia Medical Journal* , 39(12), 646-649.

REVISED INDEX

435

SUPREME COURT OF CANADA DECISIONS

Brief summary of major decisions mentioned: